H.M.S. SWIFTSURE

ISBN 0-9690551-0-2

Canadian Shared Cataloguing in Publication Data:
Golby, Humphrey
Swiftsure: The First Fifty Years
Includes index.
ISBN
1. Sailing, British Columbia racing
I. Golby, Humphrey II. Title

Lightship Press Limited
1005 Broad Street
Victoria, British Columbia
Canada
V8W 2A1

Printed in Canada by Manning Press Limited,
Sidney, British Columbia.

Designed by Robert G. Wilson

SWIFTSURE

THE FIRST FIFTY YEARS

BY HUMPHREY GOLBY & SHIRLEY HEWETT

EDITED BY ED GOULD

Published 1980 by LIGHTSHIP PRESS LIMITED

Foreword

The theme that we, as authors, have set for this the first history of the Swiftsure Classic, is to tell the very human story of the men and the boats who have played the roles.

We realize all too well that there are hundreds of individual stories of comedy, tragedy, heartbreak and heroism that are omitted. The task of reconstructing sailing events that reach back for fifty years has been exciting and revealing, but we have also come to know that there are many contradictions in existing reports. Many of the early stories were done by reporters off the news beat with little, if any, experience in sailing. As this history goes to press we trust that many a skipper will send us pictures and accounts of their Swiftsure adventures. If families of the really old-timers have tales to tell and classic shots of boats and crews we would welcome the information. It is our sincere hope that we may, as time goes by, reprint this work with as much new information as we can get into a revised version.

With Swiftsure now attracting 400 or more entries annually we can only scratch the surface with the highlights of the story as it has unfolded over the years. However, we have made every effort to give all entries their day in the sun: to record the evolution of design, to give credit where it has been truly earned, and to record the steady tidal stream of change. In the face of the assault upon the boat builders' art by the introduction of exotic new materials, we have ever striven to carry the exhiliration and poetry that is forever in a wind driven ship.

Dedication

THIS BOOK IS DEDICATED TO THE COMMITTEES WHO HAVE SERVED SWIFTSURE SO WELL FOR "THE FIRST FIFTY YEARS"!

Much has been written in this book of famous skippers and wonderful boats, old and new, and now the authors would like to salute the committees who have made it all possible. Year after year, dozens of hard working men and women have slugged it out so that every sailor could be sure of his just rewards.

It would be impossible to name them all. It must suffice that we name the Sailing Committee and General Committee chairmen who have served since 1930, and we ask all members who have done so many jobs so well, to accept our thanks for their efforts. Plotters and spotters, escorts and communication, safety and inspection, starters and finishers, printers, computers and co-ordinators, we thank you all. Without you Swiftsure could never have become the World Classic that it is.

Benjamin B. Temple has to be the first name. Royal Vic's grand old man of sailing fired the first gun for the first Swiftsure. His slight form, jaunty cap and smoking shot gun, were Ben's trademark and he was loved and trusted by all who sailed under PIYA.

As the starts swung back and forth from Port Townsend to Victoria, Seattle sent many to serve. We remember names like Eustace Vynne Sr., Andy Joy, Mid Chism and John Soderberg. From Royal Van came such stalwarts as Art Jefferd, Jack Cribb, Claude Thicke, and the father and son team of Bill and Bud Day (PIYA secretaries). As the reorganization of Swiftsure placed Royal Vic more and more in charge after World War Two, three great chairmen took the helm in those formative years. Frank (Beau) Ohrt, who learned well from Ben Temple, giving many years to PIYA and the establishment of Swiftsure on a permanent basis; E.B. (Monty) Christopher worked for several races with Beau Ohrt and on many PIYA Regattas. When he took over the Race Committee job he did it quietly, diplomatic-ally and with endless patience. To read his files of correspondence to the Navy, the Coast Guard, the handicappers, the contestants, the Civic Officials, is to realize just how hard he worked for Swiftsure.

The race grew by leaps and bounds and the Committee appointed Jack Gann to serve as General Chairman with Monty Christopher to handle all matters to do with the start, the course, the finish and the results. Jack Gann made Swiftsure news a headline item up and down the coast. He was convinced that Swiftsure would grow only if more people knew about it. His prayers were answered in 1957 when Harold Elworthy loaned the committee a tug for the express purpose of taking the press, photographers and radiomen to sea. By the time Jack was laid low by illness, his efforts, and the goodwill of Island Tug, had made Swiftsure a household word.

With Jack on the sidelines, Sid Bryant took over with Frank Piddington as his first lieutenant. Sid's Navy job took him to Ottawa within a year and Frank took charge as General Chairman. Frank's genius for organization was an invaluable asset to the Swiftsure Committee as the entry lists quickly reached 100, 200, 300, and now 400 yachts. He has the persistence and ability to gather and process the mass of information that pours in for weeks prior to a race; to choose and direct a multi-skilled crew of men and women to handle details; and to enjoy the satisfaction of knowing that everything possible to make any Swiftsure the ideal race, has been done and, God willing, will be done even better next time.

CLARIBEL /

WHITE CLOUD / KENNETH OLLAR

Acknowledgements

The authors gratefully acknowledge the limitless help and the infectious enthusiasm of so many of the old-timers in the Pacific Northwest.

Our thanks to the historians, curators and members of the three pioneer PIYA yacht clubs: The Royal Vancouver Yacht Club, the Royal Victoria Yacht Club and the Seattle Yacht Club.

To the Pacific International Yachting Association for allowing us to peruse their records, and to Ken Reid in particular, the present Secretary, for his patience and co-operation.

To the librarians and their assistants in the University of Victoria library, the Victoria Public Library, the Museum of History and Industry, Seattle, Provincial Government Archives and Victoria Maritime Museum.

To the wonderful group of sailors and craftsmen who took time from their busy rounds to talk to us and tell, each in his own way, his part of the Swiftsure Story. We thank Norman Blanchard, Garrett Horder, John Graham, Henry Kotkins, the Buchan family, especially Bill Buchan Jr., Bill Garden, Bonar Davis, John Long, David Skinner, J.C. (Bill) Baillargeon, Ches Rickard, Yvonne and Pat Leslie, Frank Lock, Gerry Palmer, Peter Hatfield, Mrs. Pat Brandlmayr, Lol Killam, Hubie Wallace, Harry Barnes Jr., Lt. Cmdr. James Butterfield, RCN (ret'd.), Lt. Cmdr. Bill Walker, Jorgen Baess, Dr. George Wilkins, Jim Davis, Geoff Coleman, Jeremy Hewett, George and Pat Dufour, Peter Young, Barry Wright, P.R. Sandwell, Mrs. H. Lyne, Peter and Monica Coombs and Ace Lindsay, for their memories, for the boats they built and sailed and loved.

To Ray Cooke and Captain Barney Johnson who inspired this book.

To Ned Ashe who set an unequalled pattern for the dedicated Swiftsure sailors for the years gone by, and for many years to come.

To those men who paved the way, did the work, and kept the faith and have now been called to their final harbour: their names are legion but here are some for all of us to thank and to remember — Rad Pratsch, Bill Hedley, the Hellenthal brothers, Doug and Wavell Urry, Beau Ohrt, Monty Christopher, Ben Temple, Charlie Frisbie, George Askew, Ted Geary, Ben Seaborn and Captain James Griffiths.

To the Rainbow Sea Cadets for Sunset Ceremonies.

To the Island Tug and Barge Company and the late Harold Elworthy for their generosity and public spirit in providing the tugs that gave the press, the radio stations and the photographers the opportunity to cover Swiftsure live from the course where the action was.

To Radio Stations CKDA, CJVI and CFAX for their untiring efforts to bring the hour by hour story of Swiftsure home to listeners everywhere.

To Ken Ollar for his beautiful photographs of the early boats and for his life time dedication to record Swiftsure.

To Jim McVie for his magnificent pictures, both black and white and in colour. This internationally renowned artist is very much a part of the Swiftsure story.

To Sib Dow for his pictures that tell the story of life aboard the press tugs in the 60s and 70s.

To Alison Brown and Denis Mason for their splendid colour shots in recent years.

To Pacific Yachting for its fine preview of this book, and for the support they have given the authors to bring this work to fruition.

To Island Colour Labs for providing the "Island Gypsy" for the CFAX offshore radio coverage and thus giving the 'Voice' a sure and comfortable base for broadcasting.

To the Victoria store of the T. Eaton Company for the many years that they made their corner window available to the club for their use during Swiftsure. The charts displayed and the broadcasts made from the window were a solid factor in popularizing the race with the general public.

To Ed Gould, whose expertise transformed our accumulated information into a readable text.

To Bob Wilson, our designer, whose book speaks for itself.

To Manning Press Ltd., for their critical attention to every detail in the printing of this volume.

NATOOSE

ORTONA

WESTWARD HO / H.A. TOMLIN

LIGHTSHIP "93" / UNITED STATES COAST GUARD

Contents

APHRODITE / JAMES McVIE

1/ *The Voice of SWIFTSURE*

The Seattle yacht *L'Apache* made one of Swiftsure's most significant debuts. In one fell swoop, she started what would become a noteworthy Northwest racing career, and claimed the distinction of being the first radio communications ship. Not only in Swiftsure history, but also in yacht racing anywhere.

Humphrey Golby recalls: "For many years, we who were involved with Swiftsure had dreamed of the day when those on shore would be able to enjoy radio reports of the race progress. Because Royal Victoria Yacht Club had acted as Swiftsure's permanent host since 1949, we felt it was our bounden duty to get news of the yachts as they sailed the course. Accordingly, Jack Gann, Monty Christopher and I enlisted all the available help to make this dream come true. We received some rounding times from the Lightship itself, but these reports were inconsistent and incomplete. As well, since the information had, of necessity, to be relayed through several U.S. Coast Guard procedures, there was a very considerable time lag.

"Discussions with Dr. Ben Nickells brought an offer of help. Ben was a ham operator. He suggested that if we could arrange to send a radio signal from one of the lead yachts, he would monitor the band from his home set.

"Meanwhile, *L'Apache* (later renamed *Diamond Head*) had joined the Seattle fleet. As she had been an active participant in the Trans Pac races from Los Angeles to Honolulu, she was radio-equipped.

"For the 1952 race Max Wyman and Howie Richmond, the new owners, agreed to take Andy Wright and me aboard, and do their best to help us get a message back to Victoria. We co-ordinated our set with Ben's. Because wave lengths just weren't available to yachts, we had to settle for the common band, popularly known as the fisherman's band. Little did we know just how crowded that band was.

"*L'Apache* had the best possible equipment. The main backstay had been set up as an aerial. This was accomplished by separating the antenna section of the backstay from the ship and the mast head by inserting tremendously strong porcelain insulators (the kind used in power cable transmissions) into eye splices in the ends of the stay.

"Time and again I went down into the aftercabin to try to make contact with Ben. The hubbub of fishermen and tugboats made it impossible to get a word in edgewise. In desperation, several of us on board tried our luck at the mike. We had no idea whether or not we were getting through. But we sure as hell got the fishermen on our backs! We were treated to much caustic comment over the air-waves . . 'Dose crazy yotsmen, out here for one day and dey tink dey own de hol blankety-blank ocean.' 'Yeh, it's de true, dey sure got more money than brains!'

"Just as darkness set in, the night watch on deck, and the bulk of the crew fed and in their bunks to get some rest for the dawn call, somewhere off Neah Bay we must have hit some tidal water. *L'Apache* pitched and shuddered, repeatedly burying her long, fine bow, flinging the spray to leeward as she headed for the turn. Then an amazing thing happened. The rhythm of the ship was suddenly broken by a stunning blow.

"The sound and weight of the impact brought all hands on deck. What the hell could we hit out here? 'It must have been a submerged log,' said the skipper. We looked back at our wake, but saw nothing but the oily black swells. We went over all the standing rigging and deck fittings, but found nothing amiss, except that the impact had unexplainedly loosened the whole rig. 'Nothing we can do till daylight. Check the bilges every half hour. And keep her sailing,' said skipper Max.

"Back in my bunk, in the aftercabin, I could feel the great mast and rig groaning in a most unusual way. When we came about, there was much rattling and banging of the turnbuckles in the chain plates. Other than that, the night passed without further trouble. I had made one last try at the radio, but even the tireless fishermen had shut down for the night.

"At first light, someone picked up a fragment of porcelain on the after deck and brought it to the skipper. The mystery was solved. It was a piece of one of the insulators. The repeated pounding had shattered one insulator and automatically the back stay let the whole rig lunge forward at least three inches. The two eye splices miraculously held under the thrust, otherwise the whole rig might well have gone overboard.

"We set up a jury back stay, gradually getting the mast back in position. Once again, *L'Apache* set out for Victoria with rigging tension near normal. Obviously, no more radio, but the interesting item when we returned was the report of our monitor, Ben Nickells. He reported that it was one big jumble of calls on top of calls, so that he could not get a clear signal. His key remark was that when I was on the mike, he always got a few words that he could understand.

"He said to me, 'Humphrey, you have a certain voice quality that makes it good for radio transmissions. One day you will be *The Voice of Swiftsure*, or I'm very much mistaken.'

"Swiftsure was at last on the air. And I had found my voice!"

L'Apache began her colourful career in Los Angeles as the dream of George Craig, then resident architect of Fellowes and Stewart boatyard. The basic design was developed to produce a winning yacht to contest the much sought after laurels of the Trans-Pac Race. *L'Apache* was built to endure. No detail of her construction was left undone. Prior to building, Craig had selected fine woods to set aside for seasoning. With many of the strakes full length, her double mahogany planked hull is a fine example of the boatbuilding art.

When she slid into the water in 1939 and her towering mast was stepped, *L'Apache* stood ready to be admired, to win, to forge an indelible record for the next 35 years in California and Pacific Northwest yacht racing annals.

"George Craig created a long, lean hull with very fine entry and beautiful, easy running lines right to her tucked up stern, taking every advantage of the CCA rule wherein water line length was a key factor. Hence, *L'Apache* had a total overhang of 26 feet. Her powerful bow with its great sloping stem line easily dominated any fleet. Under the rule, she gained many feet of waterline length when she was heeled and sailing. That stabbing prow was to become her signature, as well as the point of focus for some of the world's best marine photography. On one occasion when I was reporting from the Island Tug, *Sudbury II*, we ran beside her as she scorched across the strait from the U.S. side to Race Rocks. The tug was flat out at close to 14 knots, *Diamond Head*, as she was then known, matched us stride for stride for many minutes. Under spinnaker, spinnaker staysail, main, mizzen, and mizzen staysail, *Diamond Head* was flying, embodying all that sailors hold dear, with power, speed, and symmetrical beauty in every line. The great bow split the sea, while her quarter wave would do justice to any ocean liner. Involuntarily, the crew aboard the tug raised their hats to cheer her. The perfect picture of a magnificent yacht.

"I was to share other adventures aboard *L'Apache*. One episode I've dubbed 'Sixteen Men on a Dead Propane Tank'.

"Nineteen yachts stirred themselves in that early morning of Swiftsure 1952. Andy Wright and I were signed on with Howie Richmond on board *L'Apache*. By 7:30 a.m. we tumbled across the assembled fleet to *L'Apache*, where we stowed our sleeping bags and wet weather gear. We were among the last to leave the moorings as other boats were berthed outside us. But this was only one of our problems. The skipper's wife, Polly, had been dispatched to Eaton's to pick up fresh foods, vegetables, fruit and so on, but up to this minute, she had not returned.

"Finally, skipper Howie, who had had a long, hard night, could stand the wait no longer and said, 'The hell with food — let's go. We've got loads of food in the deep freeze. Cast off.' We headed for the fuel dock at the harbour entrance to pick up fuel and fresh water. As we were taking on these supplies, the paid hand, who also doubled as cook, came on deck and asked Howie to put on a new tank of propane. No sooner said than done; the attendant uncoupled the old tank and hitched up the new one.

"On this fine Victoria morning, *L'Apache* was now a bustle of deck activity, as the sails were shaken out and hoisted. From a moderate westerly at the start, we were soon out among the leaders. Before the crew had really settled down, we had left Race Rocks astern and were beating hard up the Canadian side. It must have been close to 1:00 o'clock when the cook shoved his head up to announce that the stove wouldn't work. Much fiddling with valves and jets. Still no fire. Finally, someone unhooked the tank and made the solemn announcement that it was empty! The cook produced a tiny emergency Primus stove, the kind that boy scouts use on the trail, and started to heat some soup. By heating a fairly large pot of water and immersing several cans of soup in the water, he managed, in time, to get some soup and biscuits into the now starving crew. The sight of 16 big, tough sailors glowering at the tiny burner was just too much for it, and with a final pop, it went out forever.

"It was cool for the end of May, and by nightfall, all hands were cold and hungry. The night watch were allowed the last of the ship's biscuits and some cold soup. The rest had a drink and crawled into their sacks to dream of better days.

"We rounded well up in the fleet, but the night watch captain elected to head back to Port Renfrew on the Canadian shore. The breeze died at dawn. As the sun came up over Port San Juan, *L'Apache* rolled listlessly as she lay, without steerage way, and cast crazy distorted reflections of herself on the sea's glassy surface. Finally, the sails slatted so badly that we took down all canvas, except the mizzen.

"At least the sun was shining now as, one by one, the crew appeared on deck, haggard, unshaven, and all with that haunted look of starving men. The ship's doctor, sensing a mutiny that surely would have led to starting the engine and making a run for the nearest restaurant, smiled his most charming bedside smile and said, 'I'll get breakfast.'

"Without a further word, he was gone below. In two

minutes flat, he reappeared with the ship's bucket (a two gallon model) and several commercial size cans of grapefruit juice. With great cool, he proceeded to open one can after another, pouring them into the bucket. We were too far gone to object, and just stood and stared in disbelief when he calmly reached down to the first step of the companionway and brought out two bottles of Gordon's Gin. With equal aplomb, he added the gin and, looking up once again with that lovely smile, announced 'Breakfast's ready boys. Come and get it.'

"To say that we became hilarious would be the understatement of the year. Undernourished as we were, in 20 minutes, we were delirious! The sun shone. The ship rolled. The doctor told endless, inimitable stories of his experiences, real and imagined, of his work in the hospitals of Japan. The unusual breakfast brought laughter. Laughter brought a gentle breeze. Someone found two packages of shredded wheat. Before we realized it, we were well on our way. But those who were on board *L'Apache* that day can smile as they look back on those less competitive times. My guess is that those old timers will always be willing to pass on the old Boy Scout motto to young sailors everywhere — Be Prepared.''

L'APACHE / KENNETH OLLAR

ORIGINAL CUTTER RIG

2/ *In the Beginning*

Swirling eddies sculpted stark rock, mist-shrouded, framed by brooding evergreen forest, a hostile and unforgiving coastline forging a maritime tradition unique in North America.

In this setting, the tiny communities dotting Puget Sound, Juan de Fuca and Georgia Straits share a common heritage: each carved their waterfront settlements from the inhospitable wilderness. Travel, commerce, communications and later, recreation, were waterborne. Settlers continued the pattern set by local Indian bands; water travel linked the villages together like beads on a necklace. Competition for the natural wealth of the land was determined geographically along these established routes, ignoring the superimposed political national boundaries.

In the tight little triangle anchored at its apexes by the cities of Seattle, Vancouver and Victoria, each local regatta attracted boats from the whole Pacific Northwest, so that yacht racing here has always been international. The three senior yacht clubs in these cities nurtured Swiftsure: Royal Vancouver and Seattle nudging it into existence, with Royal Victoria hosting the event.

Victoria guards the eastern entrance to Juan de Fuca Strait, fixing the westernmost point of the triangle bounded by the urban sprawl of Vancouver and Seattle. This strategic gateway location attracted the earliest settlement. Victoria reigned supreme as an Outpost of Empire, and supported the Royal Naval Garrison plus a hardy sealing fleet.

Victoria's earliest recreational activities were influenced by the Royal Navy men stationed there, men who used to amuse themselves with boat races, under sail and oars. Records as far back as 1859 record contests between the military and the colonists. One of the first regattas celebrating Queen Victoria's birthday on May 25, 1870, was organized by the crews from Esquimalt's Royal Naval Squadron. Meanwhile, across the border in the United States, Seattle and Bellingham organized events to celebrate their 4th of July holiday.

In Vancouver, some of the first boats were built by young workmen from the two sawmills which were established on either side of Burrard Inlet in the 1860s. From this group

came the first organized racing, usually in conjunction with Dominion Day or on the Queen's Birthday. R.H. Alexander, manager of Hastings Mill at the foot of Dunlevy Street, was a keen yachtsman. Competitors came from New Westminster, Nanaimo, Bellingham, and Vancouver for annual races, which saw open sailboats tied to a line stretched between the wharves until the start signal was given. Vancouver's first regatta on July 1, 1887, had $325 as prize money. American Yacht Racing Association handicapping was introduced the following year.

In the year 1892, both the Seattle Yacht Club and the Victoria Yacht Club came into being. Keen sailors in Victoria, who had previously gathered only when formal competitions were being arranged for special celebrations, such as the 24th of May, met in the old Burnes House in what is now Bastion Square. Founding fathers at that historic meeting were Capt. J.G. Cox, G.A. Kirke, and J.G. Elliot. This meeting coincided with the first truly international regatta of 23 boats as part of the May 24th Victoria Day celebrations.

At this Queen's Birthday Regatta, the course was set off Royal Roads, close to the Esquimalt naval base. This event also marked the Seattle Yacht Club burgee debut at a Canadian racing event. The American club members returned home fired with enthusiasm, which led to the founding of the club's first official quarters in West Seattle. At the time, their total assets consisted of a float, a boathouse and a Commodore. However, things for the embryo club didn't run smoothly, and a splinter group broke off and formed the Elliot Bay Yacht Club, with mooring at Brighton's Boathouse on Battery Street.

The success of the Queen's Regatta of 1892 was followed by a meeting at Fairhaven on August 26. The Northwestern International Yachting Association (NIYA) was formed by the seven charter clubs which had sent delegates: Victoria, Anacortes, Port Townsend, Seattle, Tacoma, New Whatcom, and Fairhaven (the latter two were both on Bellingham Bay).

The new association scheduled its first regatta for October 3, 1892 at Seattle. Here, the Universal "waterline rule" was adopted. The rating was determined by the length of the load waterline, plus one half of the overhang. This simple formula produced a corrected rating length. There were no restrictions on sail area.

This group was the forerunner of the Pacific International Yachting Association, which succeeded it in the early 1920s, and set the precedent for the annual PIYA Regattas, which scheduled their racing to coincide with the Canadian July 1 Dominion Day holiday and the American 4th of July.

With the NIYA running smoothly, the Vancouver and Seattle Clubs were both having growing pains. Several organized clubs were born, and died, including the first Vancouver Yacht Club in 1897. Five years later, a resurgence of interest in yachting swept both Seattle and Vancouver. A fine trophy, a goat's head snuff moll, was put up by a British firm, and dedicated as the Mackie Trophy for international competition. In the interests of competition, the Seattle-ites reasoned that a strong Vancouver Yacht Club was a necessity. Hence, the *Seattle Times* took upon itself the mission of rekindling the nucleus of a club, starting a vigorous newspaper campaign which even included sending a representative to Vancouver to interview prospective members.

On February 5, 1903, a meeting was called at the office of Gravely & Company's real estate firm on Cambie Street. The new Vancouver Yacht Club was organized, with Walter Gravely as Commodore. In 1904, Barney Johnson began his lengthy affiliation with the club, which by now had a clubhouse at the foot of Bute Street.

In 1905, the group leased a site on the Coal Harbour shore of Stanley Park and towed their floating clubhouse across. Application was made for a Royal Charter, confirmed in early 1906. The present Jericho property was first leased from the government in 1925, eventually being purchased outright.

The fledgling Seattle Yacht Club retained its identity, while the membership drifted back to Battery Street in search of safer moorings.

For sailors under 21, a third group, the Queen City Yacht Club, was formed. Keen inter-club competitions followed for the next decade, but when the QCYC lost its boathouse and moorage, the club amalgamated with the Elliot Bay group. In 1909 the three factions joined forces, forming the Seattle Yacht Club as it exists today. The first clubhouse and moorage was sold to the government during World War I, and a fresh water mooring and clubhouse was established on the present Portage Bay site when the war was over.

Compared to the two mainland clubs, Royal Victoria experienced smooth sailing. Incorporated under the Companies Act in 1895, it is the oldest yacht club in Western Canada. Its first home was a room rented from the Canoe Club (which it later absorbed) and later, in 1893 and 1894, from the James Bay Athletic Association at the foot of Wharf Street in the Inner Harbour.

When the new clubhouse was built on two levels, it included ample storage for dinghies, sails, and gear, and in the smoking room, the ubiquitous piano, a focal point for the relaxations which inevitably followed a hard day on the water.

This new building had a hard time staying afloat, three times succumbing to the Inner Harbour waters. First rammed and sunk by a rampaging steamship, the clubhouse again submerged during the winter of 1895-96. In 1897, its pontoons, which had been constructed without sealed tops, filled with water during a rising tide and southwest winds. On each occasion the stalwart piano was dunked, but always reclaimed and pronounced mellow after each sousing.

From those rather precarious origins, the club moved three times as progress, in the form of harbour development, usurped its territory. Forced from the Inner Harbour by the new post office construction, members temporarily utilized Ben Temple's Erie Street foreshore until 1908 when a new clubhouse was built on Kingston Street near Laurel Point. Eventually, tired of coping with increased marine traffic in the harbour precincts, they started searching for new premises.

The decision to relocate in Cadboro Bay infused interest and attracted new members. The new Uplands Company was anxious to have the club locate within the boundaries of their exclusive development, and they made the club a most attractive offer on the new waterfront site. The Oak Bay Boat Club immediately rallied to cast their lot, while many enthusiastic sailors from such northern points as Cowichan, Maple Bay and Nanaimo, joined because the difficulties of reaching Victoria Harbour through the rough tidal rips off Trial Island had been eliminated.

The expectation of spending approximately $10,000 realized from the sale of the James Bay property excited everyone. Now, at last, they could expand their social functions, and there was even talk of allowing ladies to become members (albeit at a reduced rate, and without voting privileges).

After Royal Victoria Yacht Club acquired its property in 1911, they built a fine new clubhouse at the foot of the Upland's Ripon Road which opened the next year. Coinciding with this move was the granting in 1911 of the coveted Royal Warrant. This achievement was only awarded when a club fleet had sufficient tonnage to meet exacting British Admiralty requirements. And the honour carried with it the right to fly the Blue Ensign under Admiralty warrant.

Thomas Golby joined as a charter member of the new club, and automatically the Golby children had access to the new floatage. To celebrate the move to Cadboro Bay, an order had been placed for 12 clinker built, 14 foot International dinghies.

Humphrey Golby recalls: "Since I almost lived at the club, it was not long before Dad arranged with one of the members to take me as crew. The club dinghies were racing every weekend, and the competition was fierce. My skipper was a retired Naval officer, W.B. Hotham, who hated to lose. When we lost, he gave me hell, but I learned to sail, win or lose.

"The managing committee of the yacht club made a

ruling in 1924 admitting Junior Members. In July of that year, I became the club's first Junior Member. That winter, my Dad bought one of the club boats for $50 and presented it to me for Christmas.

"All the club dinghies were named after sea birds. Mine was *Tern*. I loved every rivet in her. My brother, Tom, and I raced her locally and on the PIYA circuit regattas for 20 years. With every design advance, we modernized *Tern*, doing all the work ourselves as money was very scarce. *Tern* lost her bowsprit, went from dipping lug to gunter, to Marconi rig. But always she repaid us with her unquenchable spirit. When we lost, WE lost. *Tern* never let us down.''

The move to Cadboro Bay in 1912 ensured the continued growth of the Royal Victoria Yacht Club, whose fortunes have always been intermingled with international racing, a hallmark which has been especially evident for the past 30 years, as Royal Vic assumed the host role for Swiftsure. Ironically, Royal Victoria is the only major yacht club in the Northwest never to have its name engraved on the Swiftsure Trophy. In those early years, the club just did not have the big, powerful boats needed to compete. However, Victoria has now served notice for the future: Greg Oliver's the *Distant Drummer* lost out by a scant three minutes in overall time in 1979.

RED JACKET / KENNETH OLLAR

3/ *Labor Pains*

Over the past half-century, the Swiftsure Yacht Classic has evolved from a purely local, casual event to internationally recognized status as one of the world's most demanding ocean races. This evolution parallels the development of yacht design, particularly in California, where design and ocean racing have complemented one another since the end of the Second World War, using the prestigious Trans Pac Race as the proving ground.

Eventually, every top design from California, as well as proven boats from the Eastern United States, Great Britain, and Scandinavia, sifted their way to the Pacific Northwest, where local designers and builders were also turning out yachts capable of holding their own with the best of the imports.

In the late Twenties, that eternally contagious malady, "Sea Fever", increasingly pervasive along the Pacific Coast, gathered momentum in the immediate pre-depression years, perhaps as an antidote to the ominous political and economic storm clouds which were gathering to mar the Thirties. Puget Sound and British Columbia sailors eyed the recently established British Fastnet Race as a contest to be duplicated in their own rugged conditions. In fact, as far back as the First World War, Seattle sailors had raced to Cape Flattery, turning at Waada Island in Neah Bay (from which the race took its name). However, the building of a breakwater terminated that endeavour, as the causeway so created blocked circumnavigation.

John Graham recalls, "I know that races were held prior to the First World War, around 1914. My father at that time owned the *Ortona* and was a participant. *Gwendolyn II* may have been a participant before the war. My father sold *Ortona* in 1918. Although I was actively sailing throughout the Twenties, I do not recall hearing of any Waada Island Races during that time."

The stage was now set for the keenest American and Canadian skippers to organize an ongoing deep sea challenge. The Royal Vancouver Yacht Club delegation, headed by Commodore Barney Johnson, proposed a race around Vancouver Island, patterned after the Fastnet. However, Seattle's pragmatic Ray Cooke responded somewhat cynically that they could all get just as seasick if they sailed around the Swiftsure Lightship in the open ocean. Not to mention that recruiting a crew would be so much simpler.

And so Swiftsure was born, with the intent to "sponsor ocean or offshore racing amongst clubs of PIYA for yachts of wholesome type, 27 feet 0 inches to 40 feet 0 inches waterline length, to comply with NAYRU Rules . . ."

For that inaugural 'Swiftsure Lightship Cup Race' of 1930, the trophy provided by the Royal Vancouver Yacht Club was named the 'Swiftsure Lightship Cup'. It was ordered from London, England, and featured an engraving of Johnson's *Westward Ho*. The deed of gift specified, "The race this year (1930) will be from Victoria to *Swiftsure Lightship* and return."

Almost as if by gentleman's agreement, the race co-founders, Johnson and Cooke, shared the trophy equally during the Thirties. As it turned out, two of the contests were essentially match races between *Westward Ho* (sometimes with alternate skipper Capt. St. Claire Jellett) and Cooke (in *Claribel* and *Circe*). The light winds typical of July caused most of the opposition to retire under power, and ultimately led to the re-scheduling of the race to a more advantageous time, wind-wise.

Until the Second World War, international racing focused on the annual PIYA Regatta, which brought together all the member clubs in Washington State and British Columbia during the first week in July. While the PIYA Regatta location shifted, the race to Swiftsure Bank started and ended at Victoria. With no race in four years, the council of PIYA decided the "competition for this race has now proven inadequate." Council met at Vancouver, and subsequently recommended that "this trophy be raced for during PIYA Regatta each year by yachts rating over 37 under Royal Ocean Racing Club Rules."

The ensuing amendment to the Deed of Gift on June 22, 1938 renamed the cup the "Swiftsure Trophy", to be raced for at sometime during the annual regatta. "The course shall be a gulf or straits race, at least 15 miles in length and, wherever feasible and practical, shall be run simultaneously with other PIYA trophies: namely, the Northwest Perpetual Challenge Trophy, the Lipton Two Sticker Trophy and the Key City Trophy. Confusing the issue for future Swiftsure historians, a Juan de Fuca Trophy was designated in 1936 for an overnight straits race. For the years 1936 and 1937, competition for the Juan de Fuca Trophy was the only overnight event scheduled under PIYA jurisdiction.

The fortunes of the fledgling race paralleled those of the sport of sailing. In a word, rough. For one thing, the stock market crash of the Thirties created an international malaise, and money was in very short supply with many yachts grounded. In some clubs, half the existing fleets tied up.

Added to the financial problems of the early Thirties, sailing declined proportionately to the rising popularity of the internal combustion engine. The novelty of motor car touring occupied those who might otherwise have preferred yachting for recreation. Those who were fond of the water turned to the motor boat, as the gasoline engine had put that form of propulsion within the reach of the average man for the first time. (Steam powered yachts had been the perogative of the very rich, until then.)

Pleasure boating was in limbo during the Second World War as yachtsmen from both countries enlisted in the forces. In Seattle, 60 craft from the Seattle Yacht Club, and over 300 men, formed the centre of a Coast Guard Auxilliary Flotilla. During this period, 1938 to 1940, the *Swiftsure Trophy* was used for the AA Class long distance race at PIYA Regattas.

The first post war race, 1947, started in Victoria and finished off Port Townsend, on the Olympic Peninsula. For the next few years, the start and finish were juggled between Port Townsend and Victoria, partly to keep the race truly international and also to share the organizational chores. There was also a theory that the strong tidal conditions at Race Rocks, eight miles west of Victoria, could be avoided. However, Port Townsend had its own problems with strong tides and light capricious winds, so the PIYA finally settled on Victoria as the permanent host port.

The next amendment to the Deed of Gift, in November, 1951, restored permanently the course to be set for *Swiftsure Trophy* competition: "The course for the race shall start and finish at the easterly end of the Straits of Juan de Fuca, and lead around the Swiftsure Lightship, anchored between Cape Flattery and Cape Beale." Cruising yachts rating 23.5 or over under the CCA rule were eligible. Race management was under the permanent race committee of the PIYA.

The explosive opulence of the era and the extension of bank financing to yacht purchases, coupled with the new building techniques, put a never ending stream of boats into competition. Now Swiftsure was firmly established with a permanent course and a burgeoning entry list. Equally important were the Swiftsure Bank itself and the Lightship stationed there.

The turning mark was established, probably out of convenience, at the Swiftsure Bank, where soundings of 20 fathoms are recorded along a 3½ mile bank lying off the Juan de Fuca Strait entrance, approximately midway between Cape Flattery and Pachena Point (Lat 48° 33'N. Long 25° 55'W.).

The name Swiftsure commemorates the 280 foot Royal Navy vessel *H.M.S. Swiftsure*. She was designed to fight and manoeuvre under steam power, and also to negotiate long Pacific passages under sail, as coaling stations were few and far between.

The *H.M.S. Swiftsure* first visited Victoria in 1883, sparking many lively social gatherings. In the course of her two duty tours on this coast, she recorded the first official soundings at the Bank, in 1889, thus lending her name to the site. Actually, the history of Cape Flattery, Tatoosh Island, and the Swiftsure Bank surfaces in United States Lighthouse Service records when a lighthouse was established on Tatoosh Island in 1857. The first surveys were done by the survey ship *Active* in 1853, which recommended that a light station be set up on Tatoosh.

The local Makah Indian tribe objected strenuously to this intrusion on their traditional whaling, sealing and fishing ground. First attempts to establish a station met with such strong resistance that all U.S. personnel had to carry out their assignments fully armed. The light station went into operation in 1857 with the impressive lens manufactured by Sauter & Co. of Paris which has faithfully guided mariners for almost a century.

The U.S. Coastguard Lightship was set on station in 1909 when the *Lightship Swiftsure* anchored for the first time on the Bank. She was the old yellow painted #93, identified by "Swiftsure" in towering black letters on her side. She was the only yellow vessel in the service, and so painted to distinguish her from the Lightship stationed on the Umatilla Reef, approximately 12 miles south of Flattery almost directly west of Cape Alava on the rugged Washington coast. Old #93 remained on station until the spring of 1930 when she was relieved by the new diesel-electric #113. It was the now red hulled #113 with the same *Swiftsure* in dazzling white letters that became the first turning mark for the Swiftsure race in July of 1930.

From the beginning the Bank has been marked by U.S. Coastguard Lightships, *Swiftsure*. Since 1909, both fog horn and light have warned and welcomed countless deep sea ships, fishing craft, naval vessels and smaller boats, often at the end of a trans-Pacific voyage.

When the ships first went into the service, sperm whale oil burned bright in the lanterns. Later, this was replaced by lard oil and, eventually, kerosene. With the advent of diesel driven power generators, the Lightship was outfitted with all the latest navigational aids: radar, radio beacons, gyro compasses, and hydraulic steering. To avert lapses due to breakdown, every piece of equipment was carried in duplicate. Ponderous mushroom anchors weighing up to 8,000 pounds secured the Lightship on station. Emergency anchors used during high winds and heavy seas kept position constant, as the slightest error could have meant disaster for mariners.

During the Second World War, the Lightship was fitted with anti-aircraft guns and sent north to aid in the defence of Alaska. During this period, the shoal was marked by a lighted whistle buoy.

Early in 1961, the Canadian Department of Transport installed a radio beacon at Carmanah Point, while also increasing the power of the light there. The corresponding American shore station was also given a great boost in power, rendering the Lightship obsolete. So the historic vessel left station on July 1, 1961, to be refitted and re-named before assuming the station at Umatilla on July 10.

In 1972, *Swiftsure* was officially retired, moving to a new home in Tacoma, and a new status: flagship of the Puget Sound Maritime Museum. Since 1961, the Royal Canadian Navy has supplied a mark ship each year, which maintains station for the race weekend on the Swiftsure Bank. This strategically located shoaling bank at the entrance to the Strait of Juan de Fuca has forever lent its name to one of the world's most demanding ocean races, the annual *Swiftsure Classic*.

SWIFTSURE / KENNETH OLLAR

ORIGINALLY SEAWEED

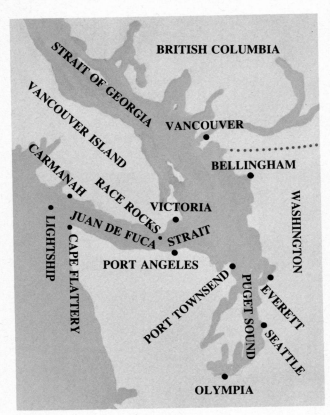

STRAIT OF GEORGIA

BRITISH COLUMBIA

VANCOUVER ISLAND

VANCOUVER

CARMANAH

RACE ROCKS

BELLINGHAM

VICTORIA

WASHINGTON

LIGHTSHIP

CAPE FLATTERY

JUAN DE FUCA

STRAIT

PORT ANGELES

PORT TOWNSEND

PUGET SOUND

EVERETT

SEATTLE

OLYMPIA

18⁹²

The year 1892 saw the formation of the Northwestern International Yachting Association, forerunner to PIYA. Prime movers were the Seattle Yacht Club and the Victoria Yacht Club with support from Anacortes, Port Townsend, Tacoma, New Whatcom and Fairhaven. Five years later, the first Yacht Club in Vancouver flourished briefly before disbanding.

Early growth in all three cities included several location shifts and amalgamations.

Victoria moved from the Inner Harbour to Erie Street to Laurel Point before settling permanently in Cadboro Bay in 1912, only one year after acquiring the ''Royal'' charter.

In 1905, Vancouver leased a site on the Coal Harbour shore of Stanley Park, and became ''Royal'' in 1906. The present Jericho property was leased from the government in 1925 and later bought outright.

West Seattle was the first home of the Seattle Yacht Club, although it wasn't long before a splinter group formed the Elliot Bay Yacht Club, with mooring at Brighton's Battery Street Boathouse. Next, the Queen City Yacht Club opened, and keen inter-club competitions continued for a decade. In 1909, the three groups amalgamated forming the Seattle Yacht Club as we know it. This group established their present Portage Bay site at the end of World War 1.

VICTORIA YACHT CLUB / *CITY OF VICTORIA ARCHIVES*

1900

20

VANCOUVER YACHT CLUB / CITY OF VANCOUVER ARCHIVES

BEFORE 1905

SEATTLE YACHT CLUB / THE MUSEUM OF HISTORY & INDUSTRY, SEATTLE

1909

21

Early Swiftsures were all run within the framework of the annual PIYA summer regatta, with friendly Canadian/American rivalry including crew exchanges between the two countries.

That first race to Swiftsure Bank in 1930 was an anticlimax tacked on to the regatta's end, because the feature event was the ongoing competition among the glamourous R Class yachts: Seattle's *Sir Tom* and Vancouver's *Lady Van* and *Lady Pat*. *Riowna* and *Turenga* were the also-rans in that exalted company.

Courses for racing were set off Victoria's Cordova Bay and Gordon Head. Categories included sloops over 25 foot waterline, such as *Spirit II*, *Cresset*, and *White Cloud*; yawls and schooners over 30 foot waterline: *Minerva*, *Claribel*, *Westward Ho*, *Sinbad*, and *Andi Lailey*; sloops 25 feet and under; yawls 30 feet and under; Stars, and dinghies, all of which were named for sea birds such as Humphrey Golby's *Tern*, except for the *Margaret* and *Helen*, named and sailed by host Royal Victoria Yacht Club Commodore Lindsay's daughters.

The concluding race for that 1930 regatta, the first ocean going event ever sailed in the Pacific Northwest, was open to cruising yachts over 10 tons from 27 to 40 foot waterline.

Since this is the Swiftsure Story, let us take a fond look at the six stalwart yachts assembled at 11 a.m. on Friday, July 5th, the first and only time the race ever began in Cadboro Bay.

First came the *Claribel*, winner of that first race and the first name to be engraved on the *Swiftsure Trophy*. Her name rings like the words in an old song: ''I remember Claribel.''

Claribel came to the line that morning after three days of successful round the buoys racing at the PIYA Regatta, where she had won her class. At the same time, the skipper's wife, the former Mrs. Charles Seaborn, had won the ladies' race. It augered well for Ray Cooke, *Claribel's* owner. That morning, he had a crack crew on board: from Victoria, an original Victoria Yacht Club member for whom the Straits held few secrets, Charlie Malandine. From Seattle, his stepsons, Ben and Jack Seaborn, and young John Graham Jr., from *Sir Tom's* crew.

Ray had bought *Claribel* (the old *Helvetia*) and extensively rebuilt and completely rerigged her as a surprisingly high-aspect staysail schooner. Her spars were tall and slender by the standards of the day. She had a rakish look about her: low freeboard, gentle sheer and a trimness that bespoke her skipper's deep love of sailing ships.

Claribel was considered to be a skimming dish in her day. It is true that she was comparatively light displacement with long, fair lines and fine, wine-glass keel sections. These characteristics gave her speed and an easily-driven hull, but she lacked the power to be competitive when it blew hard. Her real secret for light to moderate conditions was the fact that she carried lots of sail, and could muster a variety of sail choices to match most conditions.

But not to be discounted was the stature of *Claribel's* skipper, Ray Cooke, who was to earn his place in yachting history as a founding father of Swiftsure.

Ray Cooke was born in 1889 and first joined the Seattle Yacht Club in 1918. He actively sailed his schooner *Claribel* in all the club events. Ray was never one to talk of his past, but this much is known: he went to sea in square riggers and learned his trade at a very young age. Rumour has it that he was injured in a fight with a bucko mate, impairing the use of his right arm for the rest of his life.

Most of Cooke's working days were spent in the automobile business. Quietly successful, he was regarded as one of General Motors' top Northwest salesmen. It is not, however, for his business ability that we remember Ray. He was a legend in his own lifetime. His intuitive, instinctive gifts enabled him to get the most out of any boat under his command. His record with *Claribel*, and later *Circe*, placed his name on the major trophies of the day, both in Seattle and on the PIYA circuit.

Cooke's first big victory in *Claribel* came in the 1925 Protection Island Race, followed by wins in yawls and schooners in PIYA 1929 and 1930, climaxed by the *Swiftsure Trophy* in 1930. In 1926, Cooke planned to take *Claribel* to California for the Honolulu Race, now known as the Trans-Pac. However, they ran into gear failure off

Cape Flattery and *Claribel* returned to Seattle. Undaunted, Cooke and Swift Baker drove down to San Francisco and joined the crew of Don Lee's *Invader*, skippered by Ted Geary. This taste of trans-ocean racing brought Cooke back to the Trans-Pac in 1936 and again in 1939 and 1955. In 1936, *Circe* finished second, 13 minutes behind *Dorade*, with Ben and Jack Seaborn among the crew.

With the launching of *Circe* in 1932, Ray's racing career began all over again. She won the *Hat Island Trophy* in 1933 and 1934, followed by the 1934 *Swiftsure Trophy*. As Seattle Yacht Club Vice-Commodore and a member of PIYA Council, Ray Cooke actively promoted the first Swiftsure Race.

Ray Cooke went on to become First Vice-Chairman of PIYA in 1935, becoming a Life Member of Seattle Yacht Club around this time. As a finale, Cooke took his beloved *Circe* to the line in 1963 Swiftsure. He was ill and unable to leave his bunk, but he felt that *Circe* should be there. Many watched at the start to see *Circe*, her rig now much shortened, sadly outclassed by the new greyhounds of the fleet which sailed by, leaving *Circe* to her memories. Later that summer, Ray Cooke sailed again in the Commodore Frisbie Race for his beloved Seattle Yacht Club. He died quietly as he had lived, in the cabin of the *Circe*.

On that Friday morning in July, 1930, observers marked *Claribel* as the boat to beat, although Cooke later admitted that he had expected to be forced out of the race if he encountered strong winds.

Claribel's competition was by no means nondescript. First and foremost, from the Royal Vancouver Yacht Club was Commodore Barney Johnson's 54 feet of rugged sailing capability, *Westward Ho*. Formerly *White Wings*, she was built by George Askew in Vancouver in 1927. Her original owner, Walter Cline, sold her to Captain Johnson in the spring of 1930. Her racing record already well established locally, *Westward Ho* came to the line as the favoured Canadian yacht. Given the right weight of wind, Royal Van supporters looked to *Westward Ho* for top honours.

Swiftsure co-founder Barney Johnson, more than Cooke, was the prime instigator of the race. A man of formidable stature and achievements, Johnson had a lifetime of seagoing experience. Twice Commodore of the Royal Vancouver Yacht Club, Captain Barney Johnson, CBE, DSO, RCN, was a sailor's sailor. He was still sailing at 87 years of age, three years before his death.

His legendary maritime exploits spanned more than half a century as Cape Horner, master mariner, wartime hero, shipping pilot, master, executive, towboatman, and yachtsman.

At age 12, Barney apprenticed to a Liverpool shipowner, serving under a total of five different skippers, three times rounding the Horn in a square rigger. He first arrived in Vancouver in 1894, as an apprentice aboard the iron clipper ship *Borrowdale*, returning in 1898 to take up permanent Canadian residence. In 1900, he signed on as master with the Union Steamships, and his name is synonymous with

the growth of Vancouver's port facilities. He became superintendent of pilotage in 1919, resigning to organize Johnson, Walton Steamships. He also pioneered log barge towing on the coast, founding Hecate Straits Towing Co. From 1924 to 1954, Captain Johnson was Naval Officer in charge of the Port of Vancouver.

Barney Johnson's yacht, *Westward Ho*, was a big, powerful gaff-rigged yawl. She carried a very considerable spread of sail, and was one of the first yachts in the Pacific Northwest to carry a Genoa jib, nicknamed "Little Willie". She also had a formidable ballooner for reaching, and a quite credible spinnaker. Strange cuts by today's standards, but then, a big help to a heavy boat off the wind.

Westward Ho loved wind. The harder it blew, the better she went, and the harder it was to beat her. In the light westerly that first Swiftsure morning, *Westward Ho* was a proud sight. It was a day for full sail, and she flew her biggest topsail, high above her already tremendous gaff main. A jib, jib topsail and Marconi mizzen completed her rig. Every inch of canvas drawing, she heeled easily, and was soon out of sight.

Next, there was the 40 foot *Cresset*, the glamour boat of this group, a fan-tailed cutter owned and designed by Vancouver's Urry brothers. Douglas and Wavell Urry were primarily engineers but, also, artists. They proved to the world that they were supreme naval architects with their plans for the famous Cogge ketches, which have become accepted design classics. In fact, *Cresset* was a basic English pilot cutter, but the artist in these talented men made her the handsomest cutter afloat. Who could ignore the balanced beauty of her rig, with the boom of her great main well out over the counter, her topsail sprit high above the tip of the slender topmast and three sporty jibs? All this, with her dramatically piratical bowsprit made *Cresset* the picture of Victorian magazine elegance.

Cresset was 40 feet on deck plus her nearly 11 foot bowsprit, with a water line length of 31 feet, beam 10 feet and draft 6 feet 6 inches. Under her original rig, she carried 1,045 square feet of sail.

Cresset's design was worked out in minutest detail by the Urry brothers in what spare time they had during 1926-27. George Askew built her in 1928. Using British Columbia yellow cedar on oak frames with teak trim, *Cresset's* framing was unique, being on 4½ inch centres in way of the mast step. Throughout the keel support sections, she carried an extra set of U-shaped frames, from bilge stringer to bilge stringer in a single piece down and across the floors, which were cut out in an arc to receive them. These sister ribs greatly contributed to her longevity and kept her garboards from wringing. Her slightly raised aftercabin was an early forerunner of our present day doghouse. It gave extra head room in the galley and enabled the designers to raise the floor and gain additional width. Not to mention the practicability of the skylight stationed over the sink.

In 1957, *Cresset* was sold to Gerry Palmer, who took her in the 1958 race, where she recorded her best showing, a fourth in BB Class. Still valiant, she entered 1979 Swiftsure, but prudently retired during the early rough going, under new skipper, ocean veteran Jack Hutchinson.

When *White Cloud* came to the line that day, she was another *Cresset*, but not so graceful, yet no one could deny that she made a sturdy picture. The boat and her skipper are certainly a colourful chapter in the history of Pacific Northwest yachting.

White Cloud and Rad Pratsch added life and anecdote to any gathering of sailors. Rad hailed from Tacoma, where he managed a movie theatre. The remarkable aspect of his personality was that, despite one withered arm, he was a keen sailor; his handicap never stopped him from sailing single handed down to Frisco and back — and once even to Hawaii.

Built by Tacoma's Karl Rathfon, *White Cloud* was a typical Atkin's Bristol cutter, very heavily constructed: 35 feet overall with 11 foot 9 inch beam, and 6 foot 4 inch draft. When built, she had a square transom and outboard rudder, but later on, Rad added a canoe stern which placed his helm inboard. The great gaff mainsail, surmounted with a rakish topsail and the defiant bowsprit with three spanking jibs, gave her the indefinable air of a lady who knew just where she was going.

When Swiftsure began, it was expected that Rad and *White Cloud* would be there. He had been a force in the early discussions that worked so hard for that "open sea venture".

It was no fault of *White Cloud* that the almost flat July calm and her heavy displacement forced her to retire early. But this was always Rad's way. Win or lose, he would be there with his amazing vitality, his hearty humour, and his priceless stories. We are not sure just where *White Cloud* is today, but we hope that somewhere she still sails, and that somewhere her sturdy heart makes some sailor proud to own her.

There was always a flutter of excitement when Royal Van's Hubie Wallace brought *Minerva* to the line. Skipper Wallace was at the helm, and among his crew that first Swiftsure were Jack Cribb, Graham King, and Blake Wilson. Frank Lock, now of Tacoma, remembers that Hubie's short notice crew retained only one of his regulars, "a guy called Pete". Also recruited was one fellow from a tug, as well as Jim Billingsley, of Sidney. There was also a boy of 14 or so. "After Friday night, we didn't see him again. He was sicker than a pup," recalls Frank.

On this day, *Minerva* was the ultimate well-dressed yawl, with gaff-rigged main and mizzen; a towering topsail, and two jibs. If there was to be any breeze, all competition knew that *Minerva* would give them a run for their money.

The year was 1906. Designed by C.D. Mower and contracted to Ah King, a well-known builder of yachts in Kowloon, China, *Minerva* was built to the order of James Adamson, Chief Engineer of the trans-Pacific liner, *Empress of India*. Rumour had it that full length British Columbia fir planking was shipped to Hong Kong from Vancouver for her hull. All the interior and trim was finished in teak and choice hardwoods. *Minerva* was shipped out to Vancouver in 1907 and sold to a syndicate consisting of W.E. Gravely, P.N. Thompson, F.M. Chaldecott and Jack Scott in the year 1908.

Royal Vancouver Yacht Club records show that *Minerva* left her name on many club trophies of the time. As soon as racing resumed after World War I, *Minerva* was back to her winning ways, taking more than her share of events around Vancouver, as well as at PIYA Regattas in the Sound. In 1927, P.N. Thompson, the last surviving member of the original group, sold *Minerva* to Hubie Wallace. Under Hubie's drive, *Minerva* took a second lease on life, and he raced her hard wherever and whenever races occurred and competition was offered. In 1933-34, she was converted to Marconi rig. Hubie took a crew into the bush behind North Vancouver, where he cut two sticks for the conversion. Money was scarce in the Thirties, but good spruce sticks were available, and many an owner used the do-it-yourself routine to save hard-to-come-by dollars.

The zephyrs of that long ago July weekend were not to *Minerva's* taste, and she drifted almost without steerage way, making little or no progress during the first day, ultimately powering back to Vancouver. A remarkable yacht for her time, her long record speaks volumes for her prowess, and though she was to enter Swiftsure three times, she only once succeeded in making the full circuit. In 1936, *Minerva* burned to the waterline, ignited by a spark from a plumber's torch making emergency repairs at Ganges on Salt Spring Island. A sad end to a fine vessel, which by her very presence added a touch of class to the 1930 Swiftsure fleet.

Last, but not least, in that first starting line-up was another superb yawl, also with a long string of local successes: Ernest T. Rogers' *Andi Lailey*.

Christened *Dawn* when first launched, *Andi Lailey* was 49 feet overall, 41 feet 7 inches on the waterline, with 12 foot beam and a gross tonnage of 19.13. Built in New York in 1917 by James Lawley and Sons, she was sailed on the East Coast and Great Lakes for several years before heading west through the Panama Canal and up to Victoria for the 1926 PIYA Regatta. Ernest Rogers bought her in Victoria after that regatta. From then on, she made her home port Vancouver. Her new owner renamed her *Andi Lailey*. The word Andi is Fijian for princess, while Lailey was Rogers' nickname for his daughter.

Every detail of this superb yawl was of the finest. She was planked with choice mahogany with bent oak frames, all copper fastened. When launched, she had pine decks, but later on, Skipper Rogers had the pine replaced with teak. The records of the Royal Vancouver Yacht Club are full of the exploits and races between *Minerva*, *Andi Lailey*, and *Westward Ho*, so when all three of these famous yawls came to the line on that Swiftsure morning, all hands knew that this offshore event would be a test of strength between very capable competitors.

The problem for these heavy displacement hulls was lack of wind, which the Juan de Fuca Strait was famous for in mid-summer. As it turned out, *Westward Ho* made the right moves in the late afternoon of the first day, while *Minerva* and *Andi Lailey* sat immobilized by the calm.

Tragedy stalked *Andi Lailey* in 1939. When Ernest Rogers was cruising with his family off Pender Island, the boat running before a gentle summer's breeze, an unexpected jibe by the boom knocked Lailey, taken unawares, overboard. Without giving it a thought, her father threw a life ring and dived in to help her. Mrs. Rogers swung *Andi Lailey* head to wind and, after several minutes, she was able to start the engine. However, the main sheet lying slack over the stern caught in the spinning propellor, stalling the motor. The intensely cold water was too much for *Andi Lailey's* skipper, and he suddenly released his grasp on the life ring, sinking from sight. His body was never found, but it was thought that the sudden exertion and shock of the extreme cold had brought on a heart attack. Lailey, a good swimmer, was not hurt and was rescued minutes later.

This beautiful yacht remained in the Rogers' family until 1941, when she was sold to a Tacoma sailor. All three brothers owned her during her career in local waters. Ernest bought her in 1926 and raced her until 1932. In that year, Philip Rogers bought her and in 1935 she was sold to the youngest brother, Forrest Rogers.

The chapter "At The Starting Line" utilizes references from local press accounts of the event. However, some of the crew members on that race have come forward to give their own versions.

Frank Lock, one of Hubie Wallace's pick-up crew, has these memories: "I came to the PIYA Regatta held in Victoria in 1930 from Bellingham with my skipper Dr. Erb of that city on board his boat, the *Thetis*. The Regatta proper was over, and there was talk in the club bar that evening of the newly organized race to go around the Swiftsure Lightship and return. Barney Johnson, of Royal Van, was promoting the idea, and most of the skippers were not too enthusiastic, but Ray Cooke and Hubie Wallace said that they would go for sure. The paper reports six entries but, to the best of my knowledge, there were only three: *Claribel, Westward Ho,* and *Minerva*.

"Hubie Wallace came up to me in the bar and said, 'Frank, how would you like to sail with me on *Minerva*?' I said that I would sure like to go. 'Fine,' said Hubie. 'Be aboard by 9 a.m. in the morning.'

"We got away to a fair start with a light westerly blowing and made pretty good progress toward Race Rocks. The skipper set the watches at six hours on and six hours off. Jim Billingsley and I were assigned one of the watches. Jim had only sailed dinghies before, but he was all for the adventure. Pete Marshall and Hubie shared the helm on the other shift. One of the interesting things that I remember was that we discussed Barney Johnson's remarks of the night before, when he voiced the opinion that *Claribel* was too light and too small for offshore racing.

"*Claribel* was as pretty a little schooner as you would wish to see, and her sails set beautifully. She soon left us far behind. When I read the account of the race in the 1930

paper, I disagree with it. They mention *Cresset, White Cloud*, and *Andi Lailey* as starters but, in my mind, they never did start.

"By 6 a.m. Saturday morning we were off Tatoosh, and it was almost flat calm, but with big, smooth rollers. I got seasick for the first time in my life and Hubie took over. At 9:30 a.m. we sighted *Claribel's* topsails coming back in. We later learned that Cooke had rounded the Lightship at 8:03 a.m. The point that I would like to make is that we saw no other sail in the vicinity of the turning mark. It was still slow going, but we finally rounded at 2:30 p.m. and set out for home. At 4 p.m. the skipper took a vote to say we'd quit at 6. By 5 p.m. we voted again to quit at 7. At 6 p.m. we said, 'The hell with it,' and we turned on the engine.

"By this time, it was very misty, with visibility down to less than a mile, and *Minerva* was steering a compass course for Race Rocks. At one point, a great passenger liner, lit up like a Christmas tree, passed so close that the yacht had to swing hard to port to avoid her. At midnight, Hubie took over and I turned in. When I woke up, we were off Oak Bay and getting ready to put Billingsley ashore in the dinghy. At no time did we go into Pedder Bay like the paper said."

When Humphrey Golby heard this story, he said, "That is a big piece of water out there and it is not unusual to miss sighting a boat, especially if it is hazy. I spoke to Ace Lindsay (age 15 at the time), who was crew on *Westward Ho* with Barney Johnson, and he assures me that there was no question in his mind that *Westward Ho* rounded and completed the race."

There is no doubt that this, the first experimental race around Swiftsure Lightship, was very sketchily written up, and since there were no radio reports then, it was impossible for any yacht to advise the committee of its intention to withdraw.

However, the most reliable information available would seem to indicate that *Claribel, Westward Ho* and *Cresset* rounded and completed; that *Minerva* rounded and did not complete, and that *White Cloud* and *Andi Lailey* started but dropped out very early in the race.

MINERVA CREW, 1930 / FRANK LOCK

Wind ran true to form for the second *Swiftsure Lightship* Race in 1931. Following the race, the winning skipper, H. St. Claire Jellett, commented that the sailing conditions were "exceeding poor". Nevertheless, taking temporary command of Barney Johnson's *Westward Ho*, Jellett managed to maintain the lead throughout the race, travelling the course in 44 hours to return at 11:09 on Monday, June 29.

Although *Minerva's* crew lodged a complaint, it is not recorded whether the competition officially protested any advantage the yawl might have gained Sunday morning, when the *Swiftsure Lightship* was replaced by a relief boat from Portland, after *Westward Ho* had rounded at 9:30 a.m., as relayed back to Victoria through the courtesy of the Gonzales Wireless Station staff, in the first known communications report.

This alternate vessel assumed station farther out, to the distinct disadvantage of tail end *Minena*, which was approaching as the wind died, inevitably to be swept backward away from the mark by a flooding tide. *Minena* finally powered to the mark at 4 o'clock Sunday and reported his withdrawal before retiring for the night in Port San Juan.

Minena, owned and custom built for Commodore Harry T. Barnes, was the first Royal Victoria Yacht Club boat to enter Swiftsure. She was a wholesome 42 foot yawl, built in 1924 in Hong Kong to the design of Ted Geary. The plans were modified to Commodore Barnes' special requirements by Tom Halliday, of Vancouver. *Minena's* outstanding feature was her raised deck profile, which gave unusual accommodation below and a wide easy platform for sail handling. She was beautifully constructed of the best teak, copper fastened to eastern hardwood frames. The lining was select British Columbia fir and the masts were solid Oregon pine. The original engine was a three cylinder Kelvin, and the original sails were sewed in Hong Kong. When last reported in 1974, *Minena* was in New Zealand and had just been surveyed. The surveyors' report gave her a clean bill of health, sound as a bell, after 50 faithful years.

Otherwise, the second *Swiftsure Lightship* Race followed a fairly typical pattern. A stiff breeze started the four yachts over the line between the head of Rithet Pier #2 and the Imperial Oil Company dock on the opposite harbour shore at 3 p.m. Saturday, June 27. *Westward Ho* assumed the lead early Saturday evening at Race Rocks, and the breeze held most of the evening.

By nightfall, however, light airs, strong tides and extended calm spells prevailed. *Westward Ho* arrived at Race Rocks around 6 a.m. only to inch toward the finish line for the next five hours, crossing at 11:09:40, followed by *Cresset* at 1:18:35 and *Minerva* at 3:44:30.

On corrected time, it was *Westward Ho* over *Cresset* by 29 minutes. The winning crew included Clinton Elliott, Bill Roedde, J.E. Haswell, J.C. Acland (Victoria), Harry Bird, and juniors Jack Lindsay and Derek Wilks.

However, this Swiftsure Race was but a prelude to the PIYA Regatta, and the Victoria yachts and Swiftsure competitors continued on to Bellingham Bay, with a leisurely cruise, overnighting at Suchia Island.

In the American city, *Westward Ho* continued her winning ways. Skippered by owner Barney Johnson, she topped her class for yawls over 30 foot waterline, and also copped the ladies' trophy race with Mrs. R.W. Purvis at the helm.

There were no contests for the *Swiftsure Trophy* in 1932 and 1933. "En fete" for 1934's annual PIYA Regatta, the sedate Royal Vancouver Yacht Club's English Bay backdrop provided an appropriate setting for the debut of Seattle's elegant *Circe*.

Humphrey Golby remembers:

"By the summer of 1934, I had been a member of Royal Vic for 10 years, and was considered to be a fair hand on any of our local craft. But my life suddenly changed the day that Cliff Adams (our club secretary) called me and asked if I would like to crew on *Circe* in Swiftsure. As soon as I hung up the phone, I sensed that sailing for me was about to take on new dimensions.

"Cliff and I tumbled aboard with our gear in the early afternoon. The skipper welcomed us and introductions were made all around. Next, we were taken on a detailed tour of the deck where the skipper made sure that we understood the layout and all the pertinent factors of the rig.

"Ray Cooke was tall but very slight and agile. The way he moved pleased me. As 14 foot International Dinghy sailors, we had been taught to flow from one spot to the next, with no jerks and no sudden changes. Ray was like that. He just seemed to float along the deck, perfectly balanced, completely effortless. His voice was quiet, but you knew immediately that he expected to be obeyed. I had heard many stories about Ray Cooke at the different PIYA regattas that I had attended. 'He was a man of mystery. He was related to our own Captain Cook. He was given to moody spells when at sea.' To me he was considerate, helpful, a soft-spoken, convincing storyteller, and an extremely sensitive man. It was his great appreciation of the world and its wonders, and of the sea in all its power and beauty that made him the outstanding sailor that he was. He truly sensed the wind, and the weather was his handbook.

"Circe was brand new and without question the finest yacht in the Sound. She was the product of Ray Cooke's skill and experience, plus the budding genius of the young naval architect, Ben Seaborn. The record of her winning ways in the Thirties and Forties attests to her remarkable qualities. On this, my first ocean race aboard a true offshore racer, I can remember how amazed I was to feel how light she was on the helm, and how easily she responded to the slightest touch. Canvas sails, wooden spars and few winches by today's standards made for hard work for the crew. But when Circe heeled to the mounting westerly and shouldered her magnificent way through the Strait of Juan de Fuca, you knew that you were aboard a true, sea-going thoroughbred.

"We had a long, tough beat all that night, tucking in a reef in the early going and shortening down to her double headsail rig. Almost continuous tacking and sail changes had kept food preparation to a bare minimum. The breeze held well during the night, and we rounded at 11:30 a.m. and soon settled into a long awaited broad reach. The incoming ocean swell gently lifted Circe time and again, as she gurgled and surged forward on her course for Tatoosh.

"Ray took advantage of the break and went below to cook up our first hot meal. The aromas that floated up through the hatch honed our already ravenous appetites. First call to lunch found most of us below, with Ray presiding at the range. Suddenly, Circe lurched and, quick as a cat, Ray was up the companionway and calling for all hands on deck. A fluke squall had come off the land as we passed into the entrance of the Straits, precipitating a sudden unexpected jibe. In a matter of minutes, we were all straightened away and returned below for our hot grub. What a sight greeted us. A wayward cushion had slid under the counterweight of the gimballed table and every plate lay upside down on the cabin floor. Hunger prevailed. Eager hands scooped up the food. Never was there a better tasting meal, served as it was, from the shining teak floor of Circe's main cabin.

"That squall was the last gasp of the dying wind and we lay becalmed until nearly midnight on Saturday. For me, it was a magic night: the stars, the silence, the indescribable beauty of the yacht as she moved noiselessly across the gently undulating silver black surface of the sea. At first light, we could see Race Rocks, but hours of frustrating calm allowed minimum progress. Even when the breeze filled in, it took us 6½ hours from just outside Race Rocks to the finish line. It was 12:30 Monday when our gun rang out, 52 hours and 45 minutes elapsed time. A long, hard, wonderful race for my first ever Swiftsure."

A 'Depression Baby', Circe was built by Jim Chambers at Lake Union Shipyards. The story goes that Ray Cooke, when assembling materials for her construction, went to a junkyard around Seattle's First Avenue, scratched the lumber with a pocketknife, and enquired the price. For just $100, he got a whole pile: all the Burma teak he could load on a two ton flat deck truck. It had come out of the waterline bulge of the old style battleships where it reinforced the structure against the impact of a torpedo. Circe's decks, floors, and cabin house were all finished with this teak.

That third Swiftsure, after a two year absence, dawned bright and brisk, with every indication of increasing westerlies later in the day. The start had been set for 8 p.m. to take advantage of the evening ebb, and Ben Temple fired the gun on that Friday, July 13 at Rithet Pier in Victoria's Outer Docks.

When the tiny fleet of Circe, Westward Ho, Minena and White Cloud set sail into the July sunset, they were missing four other yachts which had preregistered and failed to appear: Cresset, Minerva, Saturna (A.P. Dawe, Victoria) and Mehero (Roy Corbett, Seattle).

The Lightship operator alerted Gonzales Station when Circe rounded in excellent time at 11:30 a.m. on Saturday, July 14. This good breeze held until she reached Flattery, where she sat, becalmed, until Saturday midnight, when a northerly filled in to take her to Pillar Point. Sunday morning's breeze died again at Race Rocks, where the tide had definite ideas on the direction she should be travelling.

Westward Ho, which had rounded Saturday at 12:30, only one hour after Circe, was becalmed in rain, mist and fog off Neah Bay and again Sunday evening, finally finishing under full sail at 9:30, 61½ hours later.

The other two entries did not fare so well. Minena had a good run to Cape Flattery before hitting the calm at 6 a.m. Saturday, with White Cloud astern and Circe some four miles in the lead. Realizing he probably couldn't get back within the time limit, Skipper Harry Barnes opted to turn on the engine and headed for Port Renfrew to spend the night. White Cloud, the smallest entry, battled for four hours off the Lightship in a choppy sea.

Crew lists included Northwest yachting's elite. Circe carried the skipper's step-sons, Ben and Jack Seaborn, John Graham Jr., and Victoria's Cliff Adams and Humphrey Golby. Captain St. Claire Jellett, again skippering Westward Ho in Barney Johnson's absence, had Victoria's J.B. Acland, Capt. P. Cunningham and Russell Baker, plus Clinton Elliott, J.L. Haswell, Frank Duff-Stewart and James Longley, of Vancouver. Minena took Ian Acland, Major Frank Warner, Ned Ashe, Roy Denny, and Stewart

Mitchell. *White Cloud* carried in her complement an anonymous crew wife, the first known female.

The maverick scheduling of the 'annual' race again skipped a year, with no ocean going contest in 1935. For an equally obscure reason, which would confuse the *Swiftsure* story for future historians, the leading lights of the three senior clubs once again conspired, producing yet another trophy for a race to be held, "in the Strait of Juan de Fuca or adjacent waters . . . the course being not less than 40 nautical miles, and shall lead well out into the exposed waters of said Strait, or adjacent waters."

In the spring of 1936, they designated 'a massive silver punch bowl, appropriately engraved and embellished', as a perpetual trophy. It was named the *Juan de Fuca Trophy*. Donors were the Royal Victoria Yacht Club, together with Messrs. Paul C. Harper, Paul M. Henry, Cully Stinson and Stanley Griffiths of the Seattle Yacht Club. Since the original *Swiftsure Trophy* had been presented at PIYA long distance races for several years, the new trophy was substituted for the overnight jaunt to Swiftsure Bank. Hence there appeared a four year gap in the names engraved on the *Swiftsure Trophy*, from 1934 to 1938.

Race intent was "to encourage ownership and racing of sailing/cruising yachts of wholesome types, capable of an open sea venture," with eligibility "dependent largely on their seaworthiness, as well as compliance with other regulations."

Safety requirements stipulated that all yachts had to carry, either towed or on deck, a non-collapsible, seaworthy dinghy, as well as lifebelts for each person aboard, the usual lights required by law, and at least one regulation life ring on deck or in the cockpit at all times during the races, with a causton light attached after sunset.

Like the preceding three Swiftsures, the first competition for the new trophy was set within the framework of the annual PIYA Regatta, still eagerly anticipated as the highlight of the May through Labour Day racing season.

For the 15th annual PIYA Regatta (1936), which coincided, as usual, with the July 1 holiday weekend, the visiting yachts arrived at Victoria in flotillas: everything from the palatial cruisers of the millionaires to the small sailboats of the younger set, the Flatties and Stars. Vancouver's high powered contingent included the *Westward Ho, Cresset, Spirit II* (Harold Jones), *Blue Wings* (Phil Miller), *Here and There* (George Askew) and the R yachts, *Lady Pat, Riowna,* and *Turenga*.

The *Victoria Times* reported: "The waterfront has seldom been so gay as it was yesterday, with scores of white-winged sailing craft; luxurious yachts, crowded excursion steamers and sundry other boats. Hundreds of people, instead of leaving town for the holiday, chose to sit on beaches and watch the bright panorama which extended as far as Royal Roads, where the chief committee boat, *HMCS Armentiers*, lay."

The only event of the final day, this new feature race, started at 10:10 a.m. on Saturday, July 4, from Victoria Harbour to a buoy off Dungeness Spit, to a mark boat off Ediz Hook, Port Angeles, and return to a finish line across Esquimalt Harbour entrance.

The six competitors included four Victoria entries: Harry Barnes' *Minena*; A.P. Dawe's *Florence May*; Tom Denny's *Westwind*; and F.C. Holden's *Richmond II*. Cully Stinson's *Angelica* and George Parsons' *Red Jacket* represented Seattle, with *Red Jacket* the lead yacht across and round the marker buoy, returning only to retire off Race Rocks. All the other entries gave up at various stages throughout the Saturday night, except *Richmond II*, which finished over two hours beyond the expiry time limit of 24 hours.

The absence of any Vancouver entries suggests that they might have returned to the mainland city in time for work Monday morning.

Port Townsend's Eagle Harbour was the site of PIYA 1937 for the second running of the new Juan de Fuca Handicap course from Point Wilson to Dungeness to Hein Bank returning to Point Wilson, with a 24 hour time limit.

First to cross the line was the Seattle sloop *Tola*, while SYC Flagship *Red Jacket* won on time allowance. Other entries were Victoria's *Buccaneer* (skippered by Dr. J.C. Foote), *Westwind*, and *Richmond II*.

Newspaper coverage devoted equal space to the social activities in the benign elegance on the eve of the Second World War. Royal Vancouver Yacht Club was declared a superb host, and "Courses for all classes could be clearly seen from the Clubhouse lawn and veranda," with afternoon teas and flannel dances almost as important as the yachting events at PIYA 1938.

Only two AA and A Class yachts contested the *Northwest Perpetual Trophy*, with Cully Stinson's *Angelica* defeating the *Circe*. The *Swiftsure Trophy* lists *Westward Ho* first and *Angelica* second, according to the specifications of the new dedication. The Special Sloops class included everything from the Six Metre *Oslo* through yawls and R Boats such as *Tola, We're Here, Turenga, Spirit II, Alexandra,* and *Lady Alice*.

While the war was on, the *Swiftsure Trophy* was again awarded for a short distance race at a Cowichan Bay PIYA Regatta sponsored jointly by Royal Van and Royal Vic, from July 1 through July 4, 1940.

Almost half the fleet, some 40 yachts, accompanied Royal Victoria Yacht Club Commodore Ned Ashe in his sloop *Shangri-La*, to the Bedwell Harbour rendezvous on South Pender Island, where the entire fleet assembled on the Sunday evening prior to the long distance race to Cowichan Bay.

In those colourful days, Harold Jones' *Spirit II* contributed a bright splash. It was her routine to appear with the crew decked out in red matched sweaters with *Spirit II* in big white letters across their chests, replete in immaculate white trousers.

Among them, they mustered two trumpets to accompany their lusty voices in the theme song, "Sweet vi-o-lets. Sweeter than all the roses . . ." in a rendition which became a familiar ritual as *Spirit II* circled her mooring prior to picking it up. The yacht, a familiar fixture on the racing scene, was a 48 foot sloop designed and built by Ted Geary in 1909, which Jones acquired in 1923. He rebuilt and actively raced her until 1947, when she was replaced by the *Spirit*.

Another prominent yacht of this era, George Parsons' 62 foot schooner *Red Jacket*, was a Honolulu Race veteran. Designed by Ted Geary and built by Blanchard's yard in 1921, she was originally dubbed the *Katedna*, and spent some time cruising the South Pacific following the ocean race before returning to a Phoenix-like rebirth in the Northwest.

Back in Seattle, and renamed *Red Jacket*, having been rerigged as a sloop, she caught fire and burned one day on Lake Washington's Medina in 1932. The only way to douse the flames was to sink the boat! Accordingly, the hull was shot full of holes, sending the hapless yacht gurgling to her grave. But not for long. She was resurrected and rebuilt by Frank Protheroe. Later, Paul Henry bought her.

Earlier, Henry had been involved with SYC Commodore Cully Stinson in another rig conversion; this one, in the mid-Thirties, of *Angelica*, from a jib-head ketch to a sloop. Designed by Boston Naval Architect John Alden, *Angelica* was one of several similar hulls built in Maine. Her original rig was excellent for North Atlantic cruising, but inadequate for Puget Sound racing. Accordingly, Seattle Naval architect, Leigh H. Coolidge, was commissioned for the conversion, which included an additional 3,000 pounds of ballast, accomplished by Blanchard Boatyard. A short bowsprit of 5 feet 6 inches complemented the revised rig, which included a gaff-head mainsail, a sprit topsail, a baby jib topsail, a staysail, a Genoa jib, and a spinnaker.

These three elegant yachts vied in the rarified atmosphere of the select group which rated above CCA 34. Two of them challenged in the long distance race starting at 10 a.m. on July 1, which had a time limit of eight hours. The fleet found light, squally winds and strong currents. Commodore Jones outclassed the field, collecting three trophies: the *Keyes*, for the fastest time between Bedwell and Cowichan; the *Swiftsure* for yachts rating over 34, and the *Spicer Trophy*. *Spirit II* finished at 4:18:15, followed by Charlie Frisbie's *Tola* at 4:39:39 and *Red Jacket* at 4:46:59.

This same long distance race also offered a trophy for all those yachts rating between CCA 23.5 and CCA 34. It was the *Pacific Northwest Perpetual Challenge Trophy*, won by *Oslo*, whose skipper Hans Otto Giese later crewed with Henry Kotkins on *Diamond Head*, along with other Six Metre aces like Sunny Vynne.

This was the last year for the venerable R Class, still featured, but already doomed to oblivion, scuttled by the impending world conflict. Lieutenant Governor Hamber's *Lady Van* beat *Sir Tom* in three straight races, while Sid Miller's *Clear Sky* topped the Star Class, winning the *Griffiths Trophy* and contributing to the Vancouver supremacy.

While informal PIYA racing appears to have continued during the war years, formal records are missing. Harbine Monroe claims to have been awarded the *Swiftsure Trophy* at one such event, he thinks 1945, in *Nautilus II*.

PORT TOWNSEND START / KENNETH OLLAR

MINENA LOG

LOG NO. "2"
of the
AUXILLARY YAWL "MINENA" R.V.Y.C.
Aug. 10th, 1931 to Sept. 3rd, 1934

1931, June 27 Saturday. Had been during the week getting ready for the Swiftsure Lightship Race the weather had been so bad all week that two of the Vancouver boat's skippers phoned over to see what I thought about calling the race off on account of the rotten weather; told them I was ready to go any kind of weather, but left it up to them. As it happened it broke and today opens up fine. Had asked Capt. Ward of the junk "AMOY" and "COQUET" fame, Geo Murray, Chas Lovell, Charley Mallandine for crew. Busy all morning getting grub and racing gear aboard and at noon dropped the mooring and started out for Victoria where the starting line was off the Outer Wharf. Blew a heavy squall off Clover Point and could hardly made it round for 15 minutes or so. A yawl went ashore just the other side of the point. After rounding the point set jib and mizzen and soon up to the Breakwater where we spoke to Frank Kelly of the 'Colonist'. The following crossed the line at 3 p.m. WEST-WARD HO, MINERVA, CRESSET from Vancouver, MINENA, Victoria. Soon after crossing went about on the

port tack and stood for Albert Head, wind southerly about 20 miles per hour.

3.50 p.m. Went about on starboard tack off Albert Head.

5.10 Race Rocks Light and point abaft beam and 3 miles distant.

5.40 Went about and laid Beechy Head. Set jib topsail

7.10 Went about off Sentinel Island

9.00 Went about off Otter Point. Breeze had been holding well up to now but showing signs of weakening.

11 p.m. Sherringham Point Light abeam, wind nearly all gone. Bright moonlight lovely night except for lack of wind.

Midnight, June 28 Still off Light heading toward middle of Strait.

1.00 a.m. Sunday. Making practically no headway, stood inshore to see if we could pick up a breeze off the land. Capt. Ward and self on watch, consumed several hot coffees and rum, which went well.

2.30 a.m. Called Geo Murray and Mallandine and made them hot soup and coffee.

3.00 Light easterly air heading course.

4.00 Still light easterly at daylight sighted CRESSET and MINERVA abeam and right across the Strait on the American shore.

5.00 Wind hauled into north and got very light.

5.30 Dead calm no steerage way.

6.00 Light N.E. air making a little time, Port Renfrew abeam.

7.00 Wind dropped, head swell.

8.00 West light air hardly enough to keep sails full, weather dull and overcast. Capt. Ward entertained us by singing shanties for about an hour, and how he could sing them!

9.00 a.m. Still light air, barely steerage way. Fair swell, head on.

10.00 Breeze freshening, set spinnaker, looks as if we may be round the Lightship first. Shortly after the wind dropped for us while the boats on the American shore seemed to be having an air which kept them moving.

10.30 Flat calm. Sighted Lightship flying signals denoting she was bound home, another releiving her that morning which we had not picked up yet.

1.30 p.m. Rolling and slatting in practically flat calm since 10.30 this morning. Lightship about 3 miles off. MINERVA and CRESSET look as if they had rounded, but rolling and slatting in the dead calm and swell. No sign of WESTWARD HO, think he must be under the high land of Cape Flattery. Think she looks like a sure winner as she will have the benefit of the big flood tide all afternoon, which we will miss.

2.30 Still flat calm, rolling and slatting around. CRESSET passed ¼ mile abeam bound home.

3.30 Light air from the west, dead ahead for us, fair for the others.

3.50 Passing through a lot of Portugese Men of War.

4.45 Still calm, heavy swell, tide sweeping us off toward Cape Beale; saw race hopeless for us so turned on motor, went round and spoke to the Capt. of the Lightship and headed for Port Renfrew arriving at 8:30 p.m. when we anchored for the night behind the wharf

June 29 Monday. Under weigh by 6 a.m. bound up the Straits for Victoria.

8.45 a.m. Sighted MINERVA on the American side.

11.00 Sherringham Light abeam, made 8 miles per hour from Port Renfrew under motor. No wind.

12.15 p.m. Passed Race Rocks.

12.30 Wind getting up. Hoisted sail and shut off motor. Sighted CRESSET about a mile ahead. Had a fine sail up to Trial Island. Rain squall came up and wet things up. Picked up mooring at 3.00 p.m. Heard later that WESTWARD HO had crossed the finish line about 11.45 a.m. beating CRESSET by about 10 minutes after allowing for time. MINERVA arrived about 4.00 p.m. reported having broken her boom. And so ended the Swiftsure Light Race, we didn't have much of a race but a fine cruise, we had tough luck without wind but may be better next time.

CIRCE / KENNETH OLLAR

ANGELICA / KENNETH OLLAR

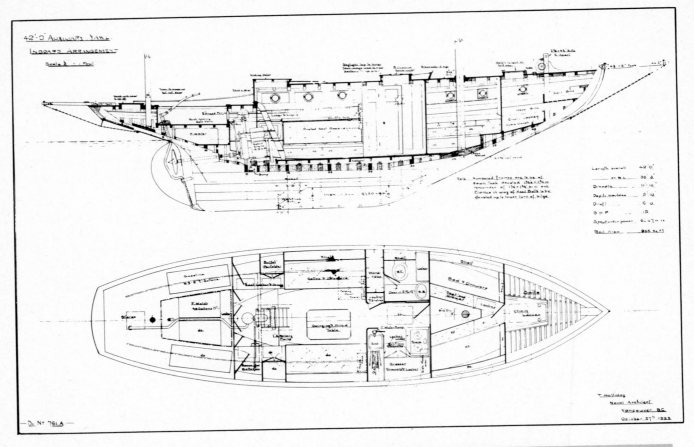

Owned and custom-built for Commodore Harry T. Barnes, MINENA was the first Royal Victoria Yacht Club boat to enter Swiftsure. She was a wholesome 42 ft. yawl built in Hong Kong 1924 to the design of Ted Geary of Seattle, as modified by Tom Halliday in Vancouver. Minena's outstanding feature was her raised deck profile which gave unusual accommodation below and a wide easy platform for sail handling. She was beautifully constructed of the best teak, copper fastened to eastern hardwood frames. The lining was select B.C. fir and the masts were solid Oregon pine. The original engine was a three cylinder Kelvin, and the original sails were sewed in Hong Kong. When last reported in 1974, MINENA was in New Zealand and had just been surveyed and the surveyors report gave her a clean bill of health, sound as a bell, after fifty faithful years!

MINENA & SINBAD, 1930's / TOM DENNY

32

6/ *The Blanchard Seaborn Connection*

Ben Seaborn's natural genius for designing outstanding sailing craft, when combined with Blanchard Shipyard's unquestioned skill and integrity, produced many highly competitive yachts. Coming to Seattle before the turn of the century, the Blanchard family has, for three generations, been a vital part of the wooden shipbuilding industry in the Seattle Puget Sound area. The story of the Blanchards is the story of driven and hard driving men. Men who would rather build boats than anything else in the world. From the very beginning, they built fishing boats, freight carriers, government craft of many types, and always, when the opportunity arose, they built fine yachts, both power and sail.

The original company started in 1912 as Johnson Brothers and Blanchard. The first Blanchard to be involved was Norman Joseph Blanchard, father of Norman C., who has long been associated with the Seattle Yacht Club. The company, over the years, went through many changes of location, ownership, and management, but always there were one or more family members at the helm. The best area craftsmen gravitated toward the firm. One of the finest was Charles Seaborn, Ben Seaborn's father, whose skills in the many arts of wooden construction were unbelievable. He was a leader of men. His method was to set the pace for the whole crew. He was fast, accurate, and capable of any job in the yard. And he was a relentless driver of men. When Charles Seaborn was in charge of a gang of shipwrights, the work output was doubled. He drove the men and himself to superhuman effort: six days a week, 10 hours a day. Boats that today would take months to build were beautifully finished in a matter of weeks.

Of the early days in the business, Norman Blanchard, son of the founder, recalls the simplicity of the transaction. "A client wanted a boat and contacted the firm. Terms were worked out, the delivery date set, and the price fixed. The client then went to the bank and deposited the money. Each Saturday, Blanchard Senior, my dad, went to the bank and drew a $10 gold piece for each man who had worked on the job that week. At 6 o'clock, he paid the men and that was that! No bookwork, no taxes, and no problems.

"When the boat was launched, ran her trials, and was accepted by the owner, the final bills were paid. What remained was the profit. The jobs were finished so fast and the men were so skilled that there was almost always a profit. Not a paper profit, either. It was money in the bank."

Not only were the Blanchards able to attract skilled workers, but the firm became a magnet for the best naval architects. One of the most successful working partnerships grew up between the company and Ted Geary. During his years in Seattle, Geary's skill, together with Blanchard's expertise, produced many of the finest yachts ever built on this coast. Ted had the ability to convey that certain eye-pleasing satisfaction in his power craft. Many are still afloat, holding their heads high in the company of the finest. Even with his great success with power craft, Geary was a sailor at heart. His many winning yacht designs bear testimony to his intuitive skill. From his truest love, the famous R Class *Sir Tom*, through such beauties as the schooner *Red Jacket*, to his simplest success, the Flattie 18 footers, Ted Geary repeatedly proved that he had the feel and eye for a trim, capable ship.

Another architect who worked over many years with the Blanchard firm was Leigh H. Coolidge. His primary interest was in working craft of all types, with some powerful tugs still plying these waters, a tribute to his fine designs. A specialist in larger heavy wooden commercial boats, whether cannery tender or coastal freighter, he also designed many boats for the U.S. Government. Coolidge, while not primarily engaged in the pleasure boat business, did design many yachts. One of his best known was the *Sinbad*, for the legendary Bill Hedley. Coolidge also designed a fine production, raised deck power cruiser, which became a family favourite during the Thirties and early Forties. These 26 footers were simple to build, and Blanchard could turn out a hull in a very few days. The interiors were also completely pre-fabricated for quick installation before the deck went on. Quite an innovation for those times.

Ben Seaborn, son of Charles, became a vital part of the

Blanchard team when he joined the firm in the early Thirties. Ben had lived and breathed boats from childhood. Although his dad had died while he was still in his teens, he inherited his father's natural ability and feeling for the lines of a sailing yacht. Ben also fell heir to his father's shipwright's tools, moving into the yard for practical training. It wasn't too long before his uncanny skill at the drafting table became apparent. Ben worked at all phases of the boat builder's craft to familiarize himself with every facet of construction. During this vital training as a shipwright apprentice, Blanchards gave him every encouragement to produce designs for the firm. Norman Blanchard says of Ben, "He had no real formal training in naval architecture. He was a natural genius."

His innate ability along with the exposure he obtained in Blanchard's yard gave him the confidence and competence to become one of the best known and most successful sailing craft designers in Puget Sound. His *Tola, We're Here* and *Stormy Weather* became household words. He numbered *Nautilus II, Kate II,* and *Mistral* among his Swiftsure winners.

Ben Seaborn's most permanent legacy to Northwest sailors was his brainchild for the Firply Association, a 26 foot family racer/cruiser that could be simply and cheaply built at home. It was called the *Thunderbird*.

The hard chine *Thunderbird* has maintained its popularity for an unprecedented 22 years, largely because of the strong fleet associations and one design racing throughout the Pacific Northwest. It is an indigenous boat, utilizing fir plywood to form the unique hull. An average handyman could build it with a minimum outlay of both cash and time. The design was first called the Firply 26, but the finalized plans accepted by the sailing public transformed it to the *Thunderbird*.

When the Firply Association first approached Ben Seaborn for a suitable design, he patterned it after his round chine, strip planked Sierra 26. (Later the Sierra 26 was produced in fibreglass and renamed the Rawson 26.) The first T-Bird took shape in Ed Hoppen's Gig Harbour Boatyard. The whole boat was built from line drawings without glue. It was just screwed together, and then taken to pieces again, each panel making in effect a master template out of the original pieces. By this method, the builder arrived at the plans for a completely dimensioned Thunderbird, down to the last ⅛ inch. For himself, Hoppen constructed a 50 per cent larger T-Bird, which had the same basic lines and the same proportions. Named *Diosa*, she raced in several Swiftsures, but without much success.

The first set of T-Bird plans came to Canada in 1959 (the year after the prototype was built). Ship chandler, Jeremy Hewett, and Michel de Ridder, of *Magic Dragon* ocean cruising fame, never completed that boat, but in Vancouver, Seattle, and Victoria, fleets grew rapidly, providing keenly contested one design keel boat racing which immediately attracted some of the top local skippers. The continuing success of the T-Bird as a strictly controlled one design with good overall handicap potential has been maintained, with world competitions which have gone as far afield as Australia and California.

The first Thunderbirds appeared in the Juan de Fuca Race to Clallam Bay in 1964. For the first time, Ned Ashe was at the helm of his own yacht, the *May D II*. He placed fourth behind Larry Pardy's *Annalisa*. Alex James' *Blue Moon* was the other T-Bird in that race. In 1965, Ned set a race record which was to stand for 13 years: a triple win — first boat to round; first boat home; and first overall on a corrected time of 23:47:59.

For three quarters of a century, the Blanchard Boat Company played a key role in the production of some of the finest yachts ever built on the west coast. To illustrate the foresight and ingenuity of their designers and craftsmen, they led the vanguard of a breakthrough in wooden boat construction methods in 1932-1933. They pioneered the wedge seam and glue system.

It so happened that one of Blanchard's top men was invited by the Seattle Edison Vocational School to teach boat building. His name was Jimmy Chambers. The school was a great success, eventually going on to become the Seattle Community College. Many of the leaders in the boat building fraternity today attended classes there, along with many of the leading architects who lent their teaching skills to the project.

It was during these years that Jimmy Chambers is credited with developing the wedge and glue seam process. The Blanchard Boat Company saw the great benefits of the system, then set to work developing the skills and special tools to do the job. The method made it possible to plank a hull in half the time. For the first time since boat building began, the yachting world had a dry hull with no caulking above the water line, and an unbelievably smooth contoured skin.

In today's world of mass produced moulded glass hulls, we cannot forget the triumphs of the remarkably resilient Blanchard family who carved their name with a firm hand on the waters of the Pacific Northwest.

DIOSA / JAMES McVIE

7/ *The Post War Years*

Anticipation and excitement pervaded the first formal peacetime Pacific International Yachting Association Regatta in 1947, a week-long competition at Seattle. It was preceded by the first postwar offshore race around the Swiftsure Lightship for the Juan de Fuca Trophy. Again, Swiftsure was set in the larger Regatta context, and served as the launching pad for the return to the northwest of the ordered racing scene interrupted by the Second World War.

When the Swiftsure fleet assembled on the line off Victoria's breakwater that June afternoon, the field included John Graham's *Maruffa* in her Swiftsure debut, Ray Cooke's *Circe*, Cully Stinson's *Angelica*, George Parsons' *Red Jacket*, Ralph James' *Dorade*, Allan Engle's *Neoga*, and Ed Prentice's *Seaweed*, representing the Seattle Yacht Club.

Like *Dorade* before her, *Seaweed* started life on the East Coast: a 72 foot Francis Herreshoff stays'l schooner, launched in 1932 in Long Island Sound. And, like many another substantial yacht of that vintage, she sailed through the Panama Canal to San Francisco, her next port of hailing. At war's end, *Seaweed* arrived in the Pacific Northwest to a new home in Puget Sound. Her outdated rig, 80 foot mainmast and a main boom, which extended 10 feet aft of the transom, fated her to be a racing "also ran". Nevertheless, her next owner, Tacoma's Gus Gratzer, basically a cruising man who acquired her in January, 1949, renamed her *Swiftsure*, in honour of the Lightship and Race.

Corinthian Yacht Club (a new Seattle group devoted entirely to sailing as opposed to the older and more socially slanted SYC), mustered Charlie Frisbie's schooner *Alotola*, the production yacht *Owen's Cutter,* skippered by Charlie Ross, and the self-designed, self-built sloop which heralded the first presence of the hustling Buchan family, Bill Buchan's *Linda*.

Canada was represented by Royal Vancouver Yacht Club's flagship, H.A. Jones' new 66 foot sloop, *Spirit*, and Victoria's *Galatea*, rated one of the pre-race favourites because Ned Ashe, considered one of the area's top helmsmen, would be at the tiller.

Although very active in PIYA affairs, the Royal Victoria Yacht Club had very few Swiftsure entries in those early days. One reason, of course, was that the club had few larger yachts. For this 1947 race however, much interest was focused on the only Victoria entry, Dr. Jack Stewart's classic yawl, *Galatea*. Jack was a keen sportsman who wanted Royal Vic to be represented in Swiftsure. So he invited Ned to join him. Thus, the die was cast. *Galatea* was to be completely rerigged. Arnold Moran undertook to build the new masts and rerig her. Fred Jeune was to make the sails.

Work went ahead at a fast pace. No effort was spared to make *Galatea* a shining example of the new look with gleaming brightwood spars complemented by even brighter stainless steel rigging. Swaged fittings were the newest thing for all rigging ends, and *Galatea* was swaged to a nicety. When all the work was done and the new sails set, she looked the picture of the perfect yacht. The fact that she had an old fashioned, deep displacement, narrow hull, ruling out any real turn of speed, was well concealed by the smart new sails and twinkling rigging. Time was short, and Ned and the Doctor worked her up as best they could before the race. Old *Galatea* really did show new life. There had not been enough time to do sea trials but, ready or not, *Galatea* was on the start line.

It was a bright Victoria day. A brisk 12-15 knot westerly rippled the sea, with here and there a whitecap. The gun sounded shortly after 1 p.m. on Saturday, June 28, 1947, sending 15 yachts outward bound over a 160 mile course which ended at Port Townsend's Protection Island. This course was patrolled by a USCG cutter, carrying PIYA Committee members who were to fire the finish gun.

Very early in the race, heavy weather socked the fleet, as high winds combined with strong tides, created havoc near Race Rocks. *Galatea* heeled with the best of them, proudly showing her shining masts and whitest sails to all who watched. Ned trimmed and retrimmed the sheets. After a few minutes, he remarked to the Doctor that the old girl was doing very nicely. Just off Albert Head, in the first glow of this her finest hour, the main shroud parted at the swaging, and the whole rig went unceremoniously over the side.

Doctor Jack stood in the hatch and viewed the wreckage in stunned silence. Then with the laconic humour that had made the Stewart name famous at Royal Vic, he said, "Well, Ned, that didn't last long." Meanwhile, *Spirit's* roller reefing jammed and *Red Jacket's* reef points pulled out.

Dorade led around the Lightship, followed by *Maruffa* and *Angelica*. Typically, the winds lightened, leaving the boats slatting on the ocean swells after midnight until late morning before they freshened again.

Maruffa chalked up the first of her many first-boat-home performances, crossing the line at 11 p.m. Sunday, followed by *Dorade*, *Seaweed*, *Angelica*, the *Owen's Cutter*, *Circe*, and *Alotola*, with late finishers *Neoga*, *Linda*, and *White Cloud*. Three Seattle yachts, *Thetis*, *Tahuna*, and *Red Jacket*, along with *Galatea* and *Spirit*, failed to finish. These placings corrected out to: first overall: *Owen's Cutter*; second, *Dorade*; third, *Maruffa*; fourth, *Seaweed*; fifth, *Alotola*; sixth, *Circe*.

The winning yacht injected several new dimensions into Swiftsure competition. Her shape was right: broad, high-sided with lots of freeboard. She was the look of things to come for the next 15 years. A design breakthrough which anticipated the Lapworth 36 of the Fifties, *Owen's Cutter* was a power boat company's version of what a sailing yacht should look like, and had been trailed west from her Baltimore builders, rather than arriving under her own steam. Possibly, someone at Owen's had picked up the idea from Laurent Giles' 1946 *Myth of Malham*, the prototype light displacement postwar yacht.

As well, *Owen's Cutter* introduced the first hint of commercialism into what had heretofore been a gentleman's sport. Not only was the boat on display to promote the merits of her builder's wares, but it was also the first time that a racing crew included a company representative along with the local broker. Eugene Hauck, manager of Coast Cruiser Company, Owen's Seattle distributors, accompanied skipper Charlie Ross, the local salesman. Other crew members were Ray Elliott, Barney Eren, Scott Osler, and Larry Norton Jr.

The builders utilized the Owen's Duraform process, with the hull built upside down over steel jigs. Timbers were steam bent; skin ½ inch marine ply, laid on diagonally with ⅞ inch clear cedar planking, laid fore and aft. The two skins were screwed together between, as well as on, the frames. Sitka Spruce spars were hollow. Her dimensions were: loa, 40 feet 6 inches; lwl, 28 feet 6 inches; beam 10 feet 6 inches; and draft 5 feet 10 inches.

Some of the Swiftsure Bank contestants continued on for the Seattle Regatta, where the first day's racing on Puget Sound included competition for the *Swiftsure Trophy*. This first day, the race was held in the open Sound waters. The kick-off on Tuesday, July 1, with six trophies up for grabs, fielded 65 yachts on a course from the Port Madison entrance down to Eagle Harbour, across to Duwamish Light, and up to the finish line off the Ballard Locks, and thence to Lake Washington for three days of fresh water competition.

At five minute intervals, staggered starts using the same line began at 10 a.m. with the *Swiftsure Trophy* gun for yachts rating CCA 37.0 and over, followed by *Key City Trophy* (CCA 30.0 to 36.9); *Northwest Perpetual Trophy* (CCA 23.6 to 29.9); *Lipton Trophy* (CCA 23.5 and under) and the *Corinthian Yacht Club Trophy* for Special Sloops. Also on the agenda was a mayor's race with mayors riding as honourary skippers on boats representing their cities or towns.

Cully Stinson's *Angelica*, sailed by the 'old man's crew', with an average age of 64 years, led the fleet across the finish line to capture the *Swiftsure Trophy*. Andy Joy, Ellis Provine, Dr. Herb Coe, Paul Harper, Swift Baker, and the 'young one', Carl Zecker, outfoxed the competition on the last leg, going inshore from West Point until the lead sounding line indicated two fathoms. Here, *Angelica* picked up a strong rip and carried it to the finish, outmanoeuvring the fleet which chose to steer straight for the finish line. Other winners were: *Key City Trophy*, *Tola* (C. Olmstead); *Reverie* (Dr. Guv Teats); *Oscar IV* (Dr. Carl Jensen). All names destined to appear in Swiftsure statistics. Top boats in the *Northwest Perpetual Trophy* were the *Owen's Cutter* (Charlie Ross); *Lady Alice* (John Soderberg, later to crew on *Maruffa*); and *Manana* (Bud Newell). The *Lipton Trophy* went to *Cirrus II*, the same boat that became *Mistral* in 1961 (John Warren); *Jaunty* (N. Christenson); and *Gypsy* (Pearl Marshall).

The new *City of Seattle Trophy*, awarded to the overall winner on corrected time for the six divisions contesting the Puget Sound races, went to John Locke's *Indian Scout*, which also took the *Corinthian Trophy* for special sloops. All were American yachts.

By 1948, as the popularity of Swiftsure grew, the race was rescheduled to the last weekend of May, for two reasons. First, by PIYA Regatta time in July, the very light airs of summer prevail in the Strait, often with days on end of pervasive calms. Secondly, it gave the skippers a breathing spell, prior to the annual July 4 weekend.

The 168 mile Lightship course for the *Juan de Fuca Trophy* got underway on Memorial Day weekend at 10 a.m. Saturday, May 28, 1948 from Discovery Bay, a point off Protection Island near Port Townsend. The finish was set for Victoria at the harbour entrance. Harbine Monroe's *Nautilus II* was the corrected time overall winner. *Dorade*, using her great ability to windward, was first to round the Lightship, finishing second on corrected time. *Maruffa*, once again was first boat home, but dropped to third overall on corrected time in the 10 boat fleet.

Harbine Munroe joined the Tacoma Yacht Club in 1938 and bought his first *Nautilus*, a 35 footer, from Howie Richmond at about that same time. *Nautilus II*, a Ben Seaborn 45 foot sloop and sistership to *Kate II*, was built by Blanchards for him in 1945. When she was launched, Harbine also joined the Seattle club. Local success around the Sound sent him to Swiftsure in 1948.

Of the race itself, Munroe tells this story: — "It had been a long, frustrating night, and although *Dorade* had rounded ahead of me, we realized that *Maruffa* had passed us in the night and was on her way home. At first light *Dorade* picked up a breeze and was on her way with us in hot pursuit. *Dorade* gradually lengthened her lead, and as she neared Sheringham Point she suddenly disappeared into a fog bank.

"I did some quick thinking and brought my new fangled radio direction finder up on deck. I was great on gadgets and would try anything to win. The thing worked like a damn! We homed in on the beacon at Race Rocks and made a careful note of the compass bearing. We allowed a couple of degrees south to clear the rocks and set our course. We held firm to the set course and plunged into the fog. An hour passed, and another; we couldn't see 100 yards, but we kept sailing. By our dead reckoning we figured we were about a mile clear of the rocks, and suddenly we burst out into bright sunshine. The crew cheered like crazy: Victoria lay right ahead and *Dorade* was nowhere to be seen!"

For the next 16 years there was always a *Nautilus* in Swiftsure. 1949 saw *Nautilus III*, a Blanchard - Seaborn Swiftsure Class, finish sixth. *Nautilus IV* joined the fleet in 1956 and continued to race until 1964. Harbine Munroe, through his appreciation of modern technology, had introduced electronics to Swiftsure and by his constant search for better designs, had brought the development of the ocean racer many steps further along the way.

The charming informality of the day was illustrated by an incident when a USCG cutter, which was one of the escort vessels carrying PIYA race committee officials, dropped out. She had received a call from the Coast Guard station at Port Townsend to search for crew members from the *Swiftsure Lightship*, who had gone fishing in a small boat and got lost in the fog.

Meanwhile, the *Swiftsure Trophy* was still being awarded under the amended deed of gift for a PIYA Regatta Long Distance Race. In 1948, this race got underway on June 29 when over 100 large yachts sailed from Bedwell Harbour to Cadboro Bay. For the second consecutive year, this trophy went to *Angelica*, skippered by John Locke.

The actual race around the Lightship for the *Juan de Fuca Trophy* in 1949 got away to a good start at 10 a.m., on Saturday, May 28 from Port Townsend's Dungeness Light, with the finishing line designated at Victoria's harbour entrance.

Wind patterns included the usual drop during the darkness hours. However, favoured by a fair wind and a flood tide, 10 Seattle yachts crossed the Victoria finish line within an hour, at roughly five minute intervals. Clocked in by RVic Commodore Dr. Reg Wride and H. Gann, *Maruffa* led the parade at 7:55:30 followed by *Alotola* at 8:00:30 and *Circe* at 8:03:50. Then *Cholita, Amorita, Angelica, Red Jacket, Dorade*, and *Avalonte*. However, *Maruffa* was subsequently disqualified for motoring to avoid the reefs off Tatoosh.

Dr. Phil Smith's *Gossip* had first been announced as the overall winner. However, a course remeasurement added 8/10 mile, adjusting the corrected distance total to 154.55

miles, and reassigning the overall trophy by a mere seven seconds to A.G. Woodley's Seaborn designed 42 foot sloop *Avalonte*, the lowest rated boat to finish. (Possibly this influenced the committee to standardize the course in future years.)

The results mirrored the mixture of northwest racing boats; the California imports shared top honours with indigenous designs.

Gossip, Cholita and *Amorita* were imports. *Gossip*, a PCC designed by George Kettenberg, was destined to go on to fame and fortune in Swiftsures yet to come. Dolph Zubick's *Cholita*, a California 32 Class, had been the hottest ocean racing yacht in the San Diego fleet. This was a pre-war design by Nick Potter, and at war's end, such designs immediately started to win races in California waters. Only seven boats were built, five by Fellowes and Stewart, and two by the South Coast company under the guidance of Merle Parke. As offshore racers they made their mark, and *Cholita* went on to some impressive victories on the Seattle circuit, although she never appeared in Swiftsure again. Carl Jensen's *Amorita*, fifth to finish, was another of the 46 foot California 32 Class.

Hottest locals were two Blanchard-built Ben Seaborn-designed yachts from the new 40 foot Swiftsure Class. Named for the race, they were seaworthy craft, examples of the new light displacement thinking, and the first light displacement yachts ever built in the Pacific Northwest.

Harbine Monroe's *Nautilus III* and Norman Blanchard's *Swiftsure I* (not to be confused with the former *Seaweed*, renamed *Swiftsure*, also in the 1949 race) shared the top spots with the California imports. Designed to the CCA Rule rating 33 feet, they were fast, due to the long waterline length of 30 feet with the characteristic ample freeboard. Seaworthy, with fine forward sections, their 16,200 pounds displacement and almost nine foot beam characterized the newest thinking.

GOSSIP / KENNETH OLLAR   RACE PASSAGE KNOCKDOWN

8/ The Two Loves of Charlie Frisbie

The hungry Thirties had been hard on Northwest boat builders, but by 1935 things were definitely on the move again. Blanchard's yard had managed to keep their crew together by mass producing their popular 23 foot Knockabout. It became increasingly obvious that there was a market for a really capable sailing craft; one that not only had a fair turn of speed, but one that could accommodate four or five persons for family cruising.

Young Ben Seaborn was working as an apprentice in the yard at the time and spent all his spare moments and evenings sketching boats. From his father he had inherited a natural gift for the development of sweet lined hulls for sail craft of many types. One day, during the lunch hour when the crew was gathered, Norman Blanchard Sr. asked a straightforward question — ''Why can't we build a good-looking family cruiser that will really sail?''

Ben took up that challenge and went immediately to his drafting board. In a matter of days he came back with the plans for a sleek racer-cruiser. The boat that was to become *Tola* had been born. Without delay the lines were laid down and within a month she began to take shape. Now enter Charlie Frisbie, insurance salesman supreme. Frisbie took one long look at the boat on her cradle in the big shed — and bought her on the spot.

She was christened *Tola*, destined under Frisbie's skilled drive to lead the Pacific Northwest into a new era. For the next five years, Charlie Frisbie and *Tola* were inseparable. If anyone on the PIYA circuit had ideas of winning, he knew that he had to beat *Tola* first. During the Second World War, *Tola* was sold, as her skipper enlisted in the U.S. Navy.

By war's end, Charlie Frisbie was a full fledged Captain. When he mustered out, he bought a 57 foot Alden schooner, sailing her up to Seattle from California. He promptly christened his new love *Alotola*. *Alotola* first appeared at Swiftsure in 1948. The sweet Alden sheer of her gleaming black hull, offset by a truly romantic schooner rig, made her an immediate favourite of the photographers and fans.

By 1950 Frisbie has grown tired of just being picturesque. He wanted to win some races. With this in mind, he converted *Alotola* to a 7/8 rig sloop. With the new rig came new life. *Alotola* was first boat home in Swiftsure 1950. Garry Horder was one of the crew. He recalls this incredible event: ''*Alotola's* crew, with the exception of myself, was made up of Charlie's cronies who had served with him in the Navy. There were Commanders, Captains, and at least one Rear Admiral, and everyone of them tried to run the ship! It was a circus, but one of the happiest trips I ever made.''

Charles Frisbie was very much a part of the yachting scene wherever yachts gathered in Puget Sound. With his infectious accent, irresistable laugh, and great voice, he endeared himself to all he met. Buoyant, fun-loving, a master raconteur, gentleman, and above all, a sailorman's sailor, he was unique. To sit with friends in the spacious cabin of *Alotola* and watch the magic fingers of the skipper as he fashioned an intricately knotted garter for the leg of the prettiest girl aboard was one of life's rare moments. His salty wit, shining eyes and flying fingers always left some happy girl with the souvenir of a lifetime, plus memories of *Alotola* to last forever!

In 1959 Charlie Frisbie and his wife Betsy set out for San Francisco with the ultimate goal of sailing *Alotola* through the Panama, across the Atlantic, for a year cruising the Mediterranean. At the end of this voyage, *Alotola* was sold in Greece. She has been reported many times since by visiting yachtsmen and still in wonderful shape, busy chartering.

When the Frisbies returned to Seattle, they attended several more Swiftsures as spectators in their Newport motor sailer. Through his two loves, *Tola* and *Alotola*, Charlie Frisbie gave much to yachting. His name will ever be deeply engraved in the legend that is forever — Swiftsure.

ALOTOLA / KENNETH OLLAR

9/ Tactics and Handicapping

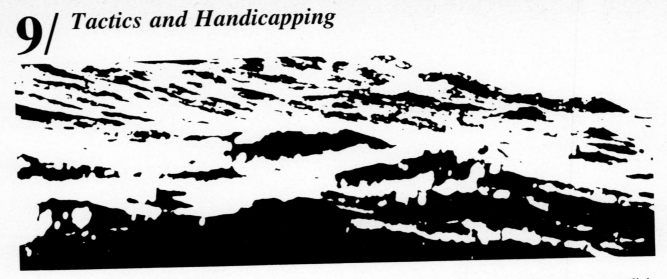

Challenging men and yachts with an unpredictable variety of wind and tide combinations, Swiftsure is one of the most demanding offshore yacht races. It is also one of the most difficult to judge.

Officially, for purposes of corrected time calculations, the Swiftsure course is 136.2 miles (outward, 68.0) from the start line at Brotchie Ledge off Dallas Road to the Swiftsure Bank, leaving the mark boat to port, and back to the finish line at Victoria's Ogden Point Breakwater. Aids to navigation include Race Rocks, which may be left to either side.

The Swiftsure Mark, in the vicinity of the 19 fathom patch (48°33'N, 125°00W) is generally rounded during the dark hours by the faster yachts.

The time limit is 50 hours from the start gun. In the event that no boat finishes within the time limit, the time of rounding the mark is used to determine positions and winners. Any yacht requiring more than 74 hours to complete the course is recorded DNF.

The Juan de Fuca Race is roughly half the distance: 75.6 miles (outward, 37.7 miles) with the rounding mark located in Clallam Bay, west of Port Angeles.

Any yacht which has not rounded Swiftsure by 1600 hours Sunday is recorded DNF. Any yacht which has not rounded the Juan de Fuca mark in Clallam Bay by 1200 noon Sunday is recorded DNF.

Are successful skippers born, or are they made? There are certain ingredients common to all winners. The problems of sailing Juan de Fuca Strait have been known since the advent of the earliest explorers and subsequent traders which brought settlers and carried away cargoes of fish, lumber, furs, and gold. Every skipper was put to the test to bring his craft safely to port in Victoria or Port Townsend. Wind and tide conditions put many a ship ashore in the Graveyard of the Pacific, as the stretch of coast between Pachena Point and Bamfield was known in those days. Those oldtimers lacked the manoeuvrability of today's yachts, and their windward performance was limited. Yet even today, the sleekest racers have their work cut out to accomplish this course without stunning setbacks.

Set in the Juan de Fuca Strait, Swiftsure presents all the challenges and obstacles needed for spirited yacht racing. The long, comparatively narrow channel, one end wide open to the Pacific Ocean and the southern shore fringed with the Olympic Mountains, creates wind and tide variations that make bad guessers out of the best weather prophets. Prevailing winds sweep in from the Pacific, ensuring a long tough beat to windward on the way out. The sou'westerly usually builds all afternoon before dying away at night, with a tendency for the late afternoon wind to follow the sun and shift from a true sou'west to almost due west. Add to these wind shifts the constant tidal swings, whose speed, direction and duration provide an ever moving platform for even the best of navigators. As conditions change hourly, only the most sensitive and experienced stay in the vanguard.

If there could be such a thing as a perfectly sailed Swiftsure, the log of such a race would read much as follows:

First entry: Tactics that produce Swiftsure winners are always well planned variations on the established theme. The skeleton of that theme is detailed tidal information for those two crucial days, and not only for the immediate Victoria area, but for all vital data for the whole length of the course to the *Lightship* and return. Any winner is assumed to have done his homework, completed his preparation, and obtained all the information. The theme on the outward passage goes on: "Play the ebbs to take full advantage of the lifts; work the eddies during periods of flood; and gauge your position in the late afternoon to place your yacht in the most favourable spot to get maximum benefit from the westerly wind shift."

So much for the theme.

Start: On the starting line, wind west-sou-west, six to eight miles and tide ebbing. Studied current at Brotchie Ledge beacon and observed how committee vessel swung at outer end of line. Made close hauled test starts at both ends of line, noting compass headings. Starts are important, even if it is a long distance race. Picked leeward end and had clear air right from the gun. First decision now coming up: to go inside through Race Passage, or hang on to your tack and go outside Race Rocks? Since the ebb has several hours to run, the decision is to go through inside and then head for the American shore. The ebb during the late hours of the tide runs diagonally across the Strait to the American side. The tidal line of demarcation between the established ebb and the potential incoming flood is usually visable to the eye, but if the breeze is fresh and the sea choppy, it is not so easy to follow this split. The crossing has to start just beyond the Race. If you go across too late, in other words, if you hang on to the Canadian side too long, it can mean a difference of several miles.

1 P.M. Wind south west 12 to 15 and sea moderate. Tacked up the American side for the next two to three hours, averaging a mile to a mile and a half offshore. It is four to five o'clock in the afternoon: the critical point in the outward journey. The race can be won or lost right here. The decision has to be made whether or not it is better to continue to short tack the U.S. Shore, or cross to the Canadian side during the relatively slack period of the flood. The experienced skipper makes the choice by weighing the critical factors of wind strength and direction, and the duration and speed of the tide for the next four hours. If the wind pattern is a typical, fresh south-west day, then the general pattern is to head away from the U.S. side and work the middle of the Strait, possibly favouring the Canadian side of centre until such time as you can sense the westerly shift and fetch Neah Bay on starboard tack. Since the winds invariably die away to a drifter during the night, most early leaders make their final hitch for the turning mark from a point close in under the U.S. shore in the vicinity of Tatoosh. The prime reason for this move is to take advantage of the northerly tidal set flowing north at approximately one to two knots.

As the wind dies, the northerly tidal set becomes more and more of a factor. Yachts that choose to leave for the *Lightship* from the centre of the Strait, or from the Canadian side, are most likely to be carried far north of the marker. This distance will then have to be recovered in very light airs, heavy swell, and against the current. Since the whole area surrounding Swiftsure Bank is relatively shallow, the Pacific swells are greatly magnified, making a tough night's work for the fleet just to maintain headway with the sails slatting badly in the rollers. As often as not, many of the slower classes are unable to round until the westerly picks up again late next morning.

Lead boats have a distinct advantage by arriving several hours earlier and can, in fact often do, round well before midnight. With every passing hour, the next group has a tougher and tougher time to make the turn as the breeze dies away altogether. Having rounded, lead yacht skippers have another big decision to make: head back down the middle, or hold to a course as far south as possible, with the object of getting in under the U.S. shore in the vicinity of Neah Bay. If they make it, they have the chance to play any and all shore breezes that will normally occur due to thermal changes as the sun strengthens. From midnight until well after dawn, flat calm usually prevails in the entrance to the Strait, right out to the marker. Late comers, whether they have rounded or not, are trapped by the glassy calm and the endless rolling swell.

As an airborne observer flying over the fleet at first light, I have found literally hundreds of yachts lying in a vast pool stretching all the way from the Neah Bay marker on the American side, as far as Port Renfrew on the Canadian shore. To view this armada from high above, the whole fleet literally motionless, except for the gentle ceaseless rolling in the great Pacific swells, presents a picture that few sailors are ever privileged to see. The lead boats still lead, but if the calm persists far down the Strait, they too must stop. Then, the long wait begins. Will the early morning thermals set up a gentle south west air flow, continuing to carry the leaders on their way home, or will the new day's westerly start to build up outside and bring the tail enders down on the fleet? At this point, from early dawn to around nine in the morning, it's the luck of the draw, and many place changes can and do occur. If the calm conditions persist too long, almost certainly, the smaller, very light displacement boats will close the gap.

The group of early leaders that did make it back in under the Neah Bay shore can usually maintain their advantage by playing the inshore air movement, and will hang close to the beach all the way down the American coast to a point somewhere in the area of Clallam Bay. By noon, the breeze usually steadies, with the beginnings of the regular afternoon westerly in the making. As the wind builds, the leaders head out across the Strait for Race Rocks. They have now set themselves up on a broad reach with every rag flying, driving for home. Minutes, even seconds, count as the big high handicappers strive to save their time. As John Graham has often said, "If you can see them, they're too damn close!" But win or lose the overall, there is always the classic battle of the giants to be first boat home.

Later Afternoon: If the westerly is its usual boisterous self, it is now one glorious sleigh ride through the Race and on to the finish. However, as evening comes, the wind slackens. Should the leaders meet an outflowing ebb in Race Passage or outside Race Rocks, they can be slowed to a crawl. In the first hours of the ebb, they can expect currents of up to six knots swirling against them. If the wind holds, there are no real problems; if the wind is gradually petering out, the experienced skipper has to compute the capability of his boat against the wind and tide conditions of the moment. It is a fact of competitive sailing that the light displacement, easily driven hulls are at a distinct advantage against the tide in light airs. If the time of arrival at the race is in the early afternoon, the chances are good that the wind will hold and most of the yachts will get through. Not so, however, if it is well along toward evening, for almost without fail, the wind will die, eliminating progress until the ebb has run its course.

Finish: The finish line is in sight, but as so often happens, the summer night claims the breeze. Once again, the fleet lies quiet. Great spinnakers hang limp in saddest folds as crews lean forward in desperation to catch even the lightest breath of air. As all this drama plays to the shore crowds, who are usually unaware of the subdued frenzy, the spectre of inexorably closing yachts, far back in the Strait, now looms large on the leaders. These middle of the pack boats are still sailing full bore under the strong winds that still blow in the Sooke, Pedder Bay area. As the minutes tick away, early leads, built with such skill and hard work during the past 20 or more hours, are just as suddenly gone. Many a Swiftsure has begun all over again at Albert Head. At this point, radio commentators are now computing the chances of any of the leaders saving their time. The next group is past Sooke. Is through Race Passage. Is still sailing. And farther behind but well within their time distance, the even smaller boats are hurtling home for their share of glory. Who will win? Who most deserves to win? The Committee is impassive and impartial. Their judgements are of the stop watch variety. To them, there are no "variations on a theme," only cold, hard results.

It has been learned over the years that consistently successful skippers choose and play their choice of variations with greater intuitive finesse. They are scrupulously prepared. They have really done their homework on the tides and barometric pressure patterns of the 24 hours of Swiftsure, which is for them an open book.

You can fluke a Swiftsure, but not more than one in any one lifetime. The prizes go not only to the swift, but to the surely prepared. As the results come in, year after year, the truth becomes more and more apparent: it takes a special kind of sailor to win a Swiftsure.

Now that you have studied and digested the tactics necessary to place a boat among the winners, let us briefly examine the difficult task performed by the Committee to arrive at the correct results which declare who is the overall winner.

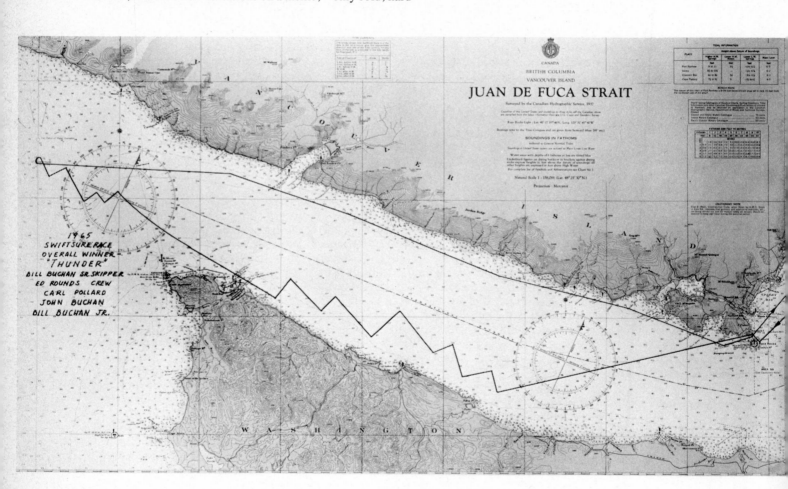

ROYAL OCEAN RACING CLUB
MEASUREMENT RULES.

AS ADOPTED BY THE P.I.Y.A. ON DEC. 10, 1932.

$$\text{Rating} = .15\ \frac{L\sqrt{S}}{\sqrt{BD}} + .2(L+\sqrt{S})$$

as below;

Where L equals length; B beam; D depth and S=sail area as measured by the N.A.Y.R.U.

L₁ to be taken between the points, forward, where the girth taken vertically, from top of covering board to top of covering board, is equal to one half B, and aft, where the girth, taken vertically, from top of covering board to top of covering board, is equal to three-quarters of B. The distance between the girth stations shall be called L₁.

The standard for the sum of freeboards at the forward and after girth stations shall be based on .1 of L₁ plus 2.5'. If ~~short~~ *twice* such deficit shall be added to L₁ and if greater, such excess to be deducted from L₁. This deduction shall not exceed 4% of L₁. *The resultant length to be the L in the formula.*

B to be the greatest beam wherever found, to be taken to the outside of normal planking, but not higher than half the freeboard height at D₂.

D to be taken in two positions, at quarter and half of L₁ from the forward girth station, both measurements to be taken vertically from a straight line joining the upper side of the deck beams at the side.
(1) At the forward position to a point one-tenth of B out from the center line to inside of wood planking.
(2) At the midship position on the center line, to the top of the wood keel, but should this measurement exceed the mid-over all depth at one-quarter B from the same height to inside of wood planking, by more than fifty percent, the depth is to be taken as ~~one~~ and-a-half times the depth at quarter B.

This midship depth will not be taken further aft than .6 of the L.W.L. from its forward end, nor as exceeding the maximum draft limit of .16 W.L. plus 2'.

The mean of the sum of one-and-a-half times the forward measurement plus the midship measurement shall be taken, and to this shall be added one-fifth of the height of the bulwarks to the top of the rail amidships, the sum to be D in the formula.

The propeller allowance shall be a deduction of one per cent on the rating of the yacht.

Scantlings must be of strength equal to that required by Lloyds for cruising yachts.

Jan. 10, 1938

Respectfully submitted,

Ben Seaborn
Ben Seaborn

Additional notations added by
Royal Vancouver Yacht Club Measurer Douglas Urry

Have pencilled notes where I think meaning would be made clearer

RIG ALLOWANCE
Jib Head Sloops & Cutters 100%+R.
Gaff Head Sloops,
Gaff Head " = } 93%+R.
Schooners and Fore
and aft Head Ketch
.15 loos Ketches } 96%+R.
Gaff Schooners & Ketches 93%+R.

Time Allowance per Tables of N.A.Y.R.U.

Girth = ¾ B

Girth = ½ B

Section at Mid-Overall Length.

¼ B

Landerside Covering Board

Top of Wood Keel

L = Length, from a station forward where girth, top covering board to top covering board = ½B, to a station Aft where girth, top covering board to top covering board = ¾B.

B = Extreme Breadth, out to out of Normal Planking.

D = D₁, whichever or is Least .15D₂ + ½H.

S = Sail Area N.A.Y.R.U. Universal Rule

B =   , ½B=   , ¾B=   ;
L =
D₁ =   .15D₂ =
½H =
D =

Anderson S. Fry
ACTING SECRETARY P.I.N.A.

R.O.R.C. RULE (for 30 raters)

$$\text{Rating} = .15\ \frac{L\ \sqrt{S}}{\sqrt{BD}} + .2(L+\sqrt{S})$$
with deduction for propeller allowance

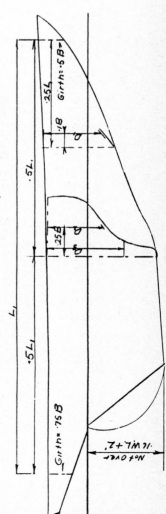

.254   .18   Girth = .5 B

.5L

.25 B

.5L₁

Girth = .75 B

17 L.W.L. + 2' Not over

From the earliest beginnings of yacht racing in England, there has always been the problem of setting up a system of handicapping to make it possible for yachts of different capabilities to compete together with the hope that all entrants would, theoretically, have an equal chance to win. Over the years, many formulas have been tried and have always served well for a few years, but just as soon as the capabilities of the yachts improved with the advent of better design, just as quickly, the formula became obsolete.

Throughout the last 50 years, there has been a running battle between those who would standardize design, and those who would modify the rules to accommodate progress. Always, there have been compromises, and many of the finest minds in sailing have devoted years to the evolution of a system that would provide fair racing for all. When *Dorade* set out to conquer the sailing world in 1930, she was the first of a new breed, and ocean racing was never to be the same again. With one stroke of genius, Olin Stephens had made the then existent ocean racers obsolete. The formula used in those years was the Royal Ocean Racing Club rule. Swiftsure began in 1930 under the auspices of RORC.

The equation to calculate the rating of a given vessel was based on the straight forward physical facts of that vessel — primarily, its length, depth, beam, and sail area. Even then, it is interesting to note that in adopting the formula for PIYA in December, 1932, allowances were made for the various rigs of the day. For example, jib headed sloops and cutters paid 100 per cent of the rating; gaff head sloops and cutters, staysail schooners and jib headed yawls were penalized only 96 per cent of the rating, while gaff head yawls, schooners with gaff fore and jib headed main, and jib headed ketches were let off with 93 per cent. In the final category, gaff rigged schooners and gaff ketches were allowed 90 per cent. From such deviations, it becomes apparent that even in those early days, the rule was far from perfect. The fact was that, for the most part, hulls were heavy displacement and lines of both small and large yachts had more similarities than notable variations. RORC worked well when all the yachts in a given race were of much the same size, but when it was applied to widely different sized boats, it gave the smaller ones no chance against the big fellows. It must be remembered that even the smallest entry permitted in Swiftsure was a deep draft heavy boat, usually with a comparatively small sail area to comply with the ocean going requirements of the day. Hence, if the weather was light, such a small vessel had no real advantage, and when it blew hard, she was hopelessly outclassed.

After World War II, yachtsmen all over the world struggled to bring in a truly international rule. The chief parties to any such new formula were the British and American representatives. On many of the major changes, the parties were deadlocked. So it fell to the small Scandinavian block of delegates to exercise the balance of power. Since the Scandinavians were almost totally committed to the International rules as used in Dragons, Six Metres, Eight Metres, etc., they led the decision-making toward the International regulations. As a result of these meetings, new ocean racing rules were adopted, appearing in the United States and Canada as the Cruising Club of America, or CCA rating.

When PIYA adopted CCA on December, 1939, all competing yachts in the Pacific Northwest were duly measured and assigned a Cruising Club of America rating. For Swiftsure, these ratings were grouped to form four, and eventually five, classes within the race. All yachts competed on a handicap basis for the overall trophy, but they also were eligible for individual trophies put up for each class recognized by the regulations of the day. Careful scrutiny and attention to precise measurements under CCA produced ratings with which the fleets, in general, found no fault. But, as with previous systems, new boats started to appear. Without any question, they were designed to beat the rule. From 1948 on, these so called "Special Sloops", such as Ben Seaborn's *Stormy Weather, Tola*, and *We're Here*, were obviously too fast for their measurement rating. In order to assess higher penalties for these new and obviously faster boats, PIYA set up a committee under the chairmanship of Bob Withington of the Seattle Yacht Club to modify

VICTORIA INNER HARBOUR / KENNETH OLLAR   **CIRCE**   **MARUFFA**

the basic CCA ratings on the data obtained from actual races involving the yachts then competing in the Pacific Northwest. From these tabulated results of the major long distance races, including Swiftsure, Bob produced a curve that modified the time allowance tables of NAYRU by taking into account the capabilities of the various boats as shown in actual racing conditions in this area. This became known as the 'grey scale' from the fact that a parallel curve was drawn above and below the master curve and 1 and 1½ rating points from it. The area between these curves was shaded grey. Boats whose ratings fell within this grey area on the scale were then placed in their proper classification. In applying the grey scale, the result was that faster boats went up into a higher rating group (i.e. from BB to A), while the slower boats dropped in the next lower rating group (i.e. BB to B).

As we look back on it now, what we see is really the beginning of what was to become performance handicapping. During these early attempts to provide a basis for fair competition, Bob Withington's grey scale was widely distributed and hotly debated. From the mid-Fifties to mid-Sixties, CCA, with our special modifications, worked very well, and the PIYA Swiftsure fleet raced with excellent results, producing overal winners in every category. However, the advent of new designs, new materials, and performance capabilities that were unheard of in the 1950s sounded the warning that the time had come to formulate a truly International Rule for offshore racing.

For several years, yachting bodies around the world had been meeting, finally adopting universally the International Offshore Rule in 1968-69. During 1969, 1970, and 1971, the PIYA gradually re-rated its fleets under the new IOR formula. The first Swiftsure sailed under IOR was in 1971. By now, naval architects and sailmakers had access to the computer in yacht design. Yacht performance spurted forward in an unprecedented surge. The radical new boats were scientific masterpieces. Every aspect of their design bespoke their computerized heritage. The older boats which had paved the way were just as suddenly obsolete. Therefore, to fill this gap, PHRF was born.

Performance Handicap Racing Fleet first came to Seattle in 1966, and spread rapidly throughout the Pacific Northwest Clubs. Classifications were opened to PHRF boats in the Juan de Fuca Race in 1967, and Swiftsure in 1969. These were the years when new materials, new, ever lighter designs, fin keels, and spade rudders began pouring out of yards up and down the length of the coast. The fine older boats with their wooden hulls, heavy displacement and large wetted surfaces were instantly obsolete, with winning out of the question. PHRF offered a ready solution: many skippers applied for ratings under the new performance system.

Once again, the age old problem confronted officials. How do you devise a formula or system that is easily administered, simple, and cheap to apply, providing good competition for all who wish to join? The sudden influx of craft representing the gamut of age and type created some

initial certification snarls, but gradually, enough data accumulated on various hull and rig types, and actual racing began under the system. Obviously, there were difficulties, but the non-IOR fleet had found an answer to their sorrows. They were still racing.

The fact that many top boats and top rated skippers joined PHRF shifted the emphasis once again. These newer entries were essentially racers but not family cruisers in the accepted sense, which meant that the formula had to be tightened. The basis for handicapping was gradually shifted from "performance" to "speed potential" for any given yacht participating in one of the major events, namely Swiftsure, Juan de Fuca, the Straits of Georgia Race, the Great Equalizer, and so on. The new speed potential rating arrives at very much the same conclusion that the CCA ratings produced in the late Fifties when they used a weighted tariff against the so-called Special Sloops. They were, by performance, faster than the median set for the class, so they paid a penalty in handicap minutes.

The original strictly performance basis PHRF still has its useful role to play in small groups where the handicaps allotted are really an arbitrary judgment by the local handicapper on the basis of observed past performance. However, the new "Speed Potential" rating is a good yardstick of any standard yacht's actual ability. Identical or very similar boats rate equally because the potential is the same: the differential that produces winners is the ability of the skipper.

AMORITA / KENNETH OLLAR

10/ *More Freeboard — More Speed in the Fifties*

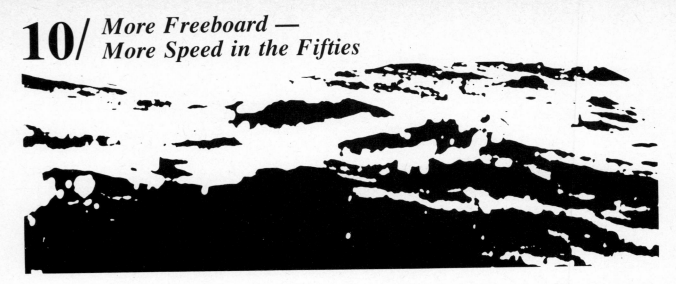

Ono, the first of the new Kettenberg 38's, and smallest entry, led a 12 boat fleet into the teeth of gale force, gear busting winds in the race that started from Port Townsend on May 28, 1950. In spite of her small size, *Ono* was the only yacht to escape some form of damage as winds gusted to over 50 knots and seas crested at 30 feet. Even the doughty *Maruffa* came within an inch of losing a man overboard; he was grabbed at the last second as giant seas swept her from end to end.

Charlie Frisbie's *Alotola*, with her new 7/8 sloop rig, set a new course record of 29 hours, 36 minutes, 17 seconds. Charlie's famous smile just wouldn't come off as he brought his black hulled beauty first across the line 20 minutes ahead of his old rival John Graham in *Maruffa*.

Third across the line, Dr. Phil Smith's *Gossip*, easily saved her time for the overall win. It was a rare sight to watch *Gossip* literally plane down the straits as westerly gusts reached 55 knots. Patrol vessels clocked her at better than 13 knots. In one last burst, as she shot out of Race Passage, an offshore blast knocked her flat in the water as the spinnaker pole snapped. Photographer Ken Ollar was right there. His memorable picture shows crew men up to their waists in water as they struggled to free the spinnaker sheets.

Trouble stuck everywhere. *Maruffa* and *Nautilus III* both split spinnakers and *Circe* ended up in Esquimalt Harbour after she over-ran her spinnaker and the whole mess became entangled in the rudder. The Royal Canadian Navy came to her rescue on that one, and *Circe* gained an extra crew member from the ranks of Her Majesty's finest, in the person of Cdr. Jim Davis. For many years to come, he was to be a valued hand aboard *Circe*. At another point in this wild contest, *Serada* was located by the Canadian Destroyer escort, headed for the Hawaiian Islands, before she was directed back to the Lightship.

The 1950 Swiftsure fleet, which had started in brisk westerlies off Port Townsend and finished in surfing splendor at the Victoria finish line, now took off for the PIYA Regatta in Seattle. An informal send-off race was arranged for the Seattle yachts from the Golden Gardens to Marrowstone Island Light. During this event, *Dorade* cut a corner a little too close and was pulled off by Ken Ollar, the Tacoma photographer who was to follow successive Swiftsure fleets around the Lightship in his 19 foot craft. *Dorade's* owner, Franklin Eddy, was not amused.

Swiftsure finally settled down to a permanent course and a permanent host in the year 1951. PIYA appointed the Royal Victoria Yacht Club to act for the Association in both starting and finishing all races at Victoria. It had taken 21 years, but the race was now established on a firm foundation. The PIYA Regatta Committee appointed Frank M. Ohrt to act as chairman of the new Swiftsure Race Committee, under the jurisdiction of the Royal Victoria Yacht Club.

The new committee was charged with organizing the start and finish lines, and the starting line for this and all future races was established between Brotchie Ledge Beacon and the Race Committee Boat. The course was now clearly designated in these terms.

Regulations under NAYRU rules as amended in 1950, required all yachts to lash a non-collapsible dinghy in place, and carry a radio capable of receiving USCG frequencies 2670 and 2698. (In case of gale force winds in the vicinity of the Lightship, the race may be called off by radio.)

The navy tug *Glendevon* anchored one end of the starting line, when 13 yachts set out at 11 a.m. on Thursday, May 31, 1951. *Circe* and *Maruffa* battled for the lead in the early going but by late afternoon the Seattle based Kettenbergs took over and soon showed their transoms to the fleet. Herb Day's *Ono*, first to arrive in the vicinity of the mark, miscalculated her position in the fog and darkness and overstood the turn by 15 miles. The Canadian Naval escort vessel reported: "It was chillingly cold. Sleeting rain and a dull swirling mist cut visibility to a few hundred yards. As the day dawned, we ran a patrol out into the Pacific and began a wide circle course to check for stragglers or misplaced yachts. While on this action, we sighted a yacht with K38 on the sail, rail down, double reefed with storm jib, headed for Japan. A single numbed figure crouched immovable at the helm as she plunged on and on. We wheeled and came alongside within hail and told the stunned night watch that he was almost 20 miles beyond the mark! Bodies appeared and, in moments, the boat bore off, shook out the reefs, hoisted a jenny, and was on her way home.'' It was *Ono*, and sad to say, she missed the mark on the way in and was disqualified.

Amorita, under the practised hand of Dr. Carl Jensen, was first to round and maintained her lead all the way to the finish line to cover the course in 29 hours and 59 minutes. Harbine Munroe's *Nautilus III* placed second, and *Dorade* took third. *Gossip*, the 1950 winner, was missing from the line-up as she had entered the Trans-Pac to Honolulu. Charles Ross and owner Phil Smith were joined in San Diego by Bill Kettenberg for the race. It was during this race that the crew rigged an outboard trailing oar, attached to a spare spinnaker pole, to help keep *Gossip* from broaching in the rush of tropical rainstorms. With this addition to their rig, *Gossip* was able to carry a heavy weight spinnaker through squalls that registered close to 60 knots.

Ono made up for her hard luck of the previous year by winning Swiftsure overall in 1952. The wind was very light that Friday, May 24 morning when 19 starters crossed the line at 11 a.m. By early afternoon, however, the fleet was moving well under fresh westerlies which prevailed until dusk. There were exceptionally heavy swells that year and, with almost no wind, the fleet made little progress during the night. *Dorade* rounded shortly after midnight, but it was late in the morning before there was enough breeze to fill even the lightest of spinnakers as the yachts slatted and rolled in the great, smooth swell. As the wind strengthened, *Maruffa* pulled into the lead and crossed first at 6:25 p.m., followed by *Dorade* at 7 p.m. *Gossip* finished third, but on corrected time placed second overall, losing out to *Ono*, the smallest Kettenberg in the race, by 21 minutes.

Ono was the first K38 to enter the winner's circle. Owned and sailed by Dr. Herb Day, SYC, she was one of the first really modern, one design class to compete in Swiftsure. Their performance reflected in the race results over the next many years, reinforcing the fact, that the light displacement yacht was here to stay. With their rounded bow and much lower freeboard than the later Lapworth designs, the K38s signalled the beginning of the trend that rendered the older boats forever obsolete for racing.

If the Sixties sparkled with Lapworth's brilliance, the Fifties certainly belonged to Kettenberg.

No sooner was World War II over than the San Diego Kettenberg yard geared up to produce George Kettenberg's 46 foot Pacific Cruising Class on an assembly line basis. The first PCCs came off the line in 1946, with the company advertising that ''the ability to win races is designed into every boat.'' This was no idle threat, because the PCC, with its clean lines, folding propellor, and many innovations for the day, was soon winning major races in California. In 1948, Kettenberg himself sailed *Gossip* up from San Diego to compete in the July, 1948 PIYA Regatta in Victoria. The sleek 46 footer won her class in that regatta, which convinced Dr. Phil Smith of Seattle to buy her. For *Gossip*, the rest is history. She went on to win Swiftsure overall in

1950 and again in 1953, losing out by narrow margins to place second overall in both 1949 and 1952.

During the late Forties, Kettenberg's PC and PCCs were among the most successful California racers. In 1948, George introduced yet another variation on his theme: a yacht modified for proportionately more beam and freeboard. This was the Kettenberg 38, which immediately caught on with Seattle's racing sailors who captured just about every possible trophy during the Fifties with these amazing boats.

Altogether, 39 Kettenberg 38s were built over five years, with the first, *Tomboy*, going to Paul Kettenberg, the San Diego yard's chief engineer and co-owner. The second went to Dr. H.W. Day in Seattle. Christened *Ono*, she won two Swiftsures — the first in 1952 and the second in 1958. Then followed Doug Sherwood's *Rebel*, 1959 winner; Henry Kotkin's *Totem*, overall winner in 1954; and Bob Regan's *Thetis*, which figured prominently in several races, placing third in 1961, third in 1962, and losing out on a protest in 1963, after being initially declared the overall winner. The K 38s posted a string of victories so formidable, that even John Graham's mighty *Maruffa* only once during the decade managed to save her time against them.

As the Kettenberg decade drew to a close, the K40 was introduced, with the same profile as the famous K38, but with additional freeboard. Always a proving ground for successful new designs, the 1961 Trans-Pac had an even split with three K40s and three Lapworth 36s. Lapworth had arrived.

Not all Swiftsure stories are fraught with excitement or glamour. There are also the plodding, consistent, almost-made-it boats, which maintained a high level of performance against the hot designs.

In this category fit the Roedde boats, designed and built in Vancouver, and always at or near the top of B Class. First came *Elusive* in 1952, followed by Len Murrell's *Treveda*, which made the transition to PHRF in the 1970s, after winning B Class in 1957.

The 34 foot Roedde class sloops were a post war improvement on the 30 foot turtle decked Spencer Class, Royal Van's ''depression baby''. During this low ebb in everyone's purchasing power, the Jericho sailors came up with a novel idea to keep sailing alive. A nucleus of Star skippers, including Bill Roedde, saw a place for a low-cost, small, one design racer/cruiser, a little larger than a Star.

Advised by Marine Architect Tom Halliday, five sailors pooled their thoughts, producing the Spencer Class, named for ''angel'' Colonel Victor Spencer, one of four wealthy men who floated the venture financially. Five original boats were auctioned at a club smoker, racing as a class until 1942, when the entire group was sold to Seattle.

After the war, Bill Roedde updated the Spencer design, building in cruising comforts. Bert Tupper, Jack Williamson, along with Bill, and again advised by Halliday, transformed the basic hull, renaming the new design the Roedde Class. The prototype, launched from Taylor's Boat Works in 1949, was Roedde's own *Carita II*.

Best Swiftsure showing by a Roedde Class yacht was Bill Morrow's *Elusive*, second overall in 1954.

11/ Adios and Gometra (the Gold Ship) — 1953

Two long to be remembered names were added to the 21 boat entry list for the 1953 race. They were *Adios* and *Gometra*. But more about them later.

The fleet got off to a good start in a fresh westerly breeze which built steadily as they moved out into the Strait beyond Race Rocks. By early afternoon, the wind had reached 40 knots, with higher gusts and punishing seas, plus the added disadvantage of a roaring full flood tide. The conditions were just too much for almost half the fleet. By mid-afternoon, 13 boats had dropped out. One of the disabled, *Zingara*, an Owen's Cutter, was the subject of a combined search by the RCAF and USCG and RCN ships. Dismasted, she had made her way to Bellingham, unaware of the efforts mounted on her behalf, which had failed to locate her.

By evening the winds had dropped to 25 and the eight survivors rounded without further incident. *Gossip*, who had fought for the lead all day, finally went out ahead and rounded first. She kept her position all the way home to win her second Swiftsure overall, with *Maruffa* and *L'Apache* taking second and third after a thrilling stretch dual.

Two very different yachts arrived in 1953, by two very different routes, to take part in Swiftsure. As *Adios* took her place among the 21 entrants in the soft evening light of the Inner Harbour, Dr. Carl Jensen could be justly proud of his new love.

Adios was a fine example of Sparkman-Stephens at their very best. She carried her towering yawl rig with a certain authority, and the soft sweep of her sheer made the artist's heart rejoice. Her meticulously laid teak decks were clear, providing the crew with all the space needed for sail handling. The clean, uncluttered look of competence, plus the traditional inherent beauty of a truly fine yacht were accorded to *Adios* by all who came to admire her.

Adios was built as *Clemencia* by the City Island Boat Company in New York in 1938. Every component of this beauty was the best available. The detail of her mahogany planking; the traditional pattern of the beautiful teak decks; the minute attention to matters of rigging and fitting out, coupled with a quietly elegant interior, comfortable but workable, made *Adios* the realization of every yachtsman's dream.

During World War II, *Clemencia* was taken over by the U.S. Navy and used as a picket boat in the New York area. In 1946 she was purchased by Charles Langley and brought through the Panama Canal to San Francisco. Langley kept her for two years, and sold her in 1950 to Roy McCullough, who in turn sold her to Dr. Carl Jensen in 1952. Carl rechristened her *Adios*, and a new chapter in her life began.

So it was that *Adios*, showing every inch of her fine heritage, came to the starting line in May, 1953. This was to be the first of many battles among the AA boats to be first boat home. (The categories had by now been broken down into four classes, with AA the largest yachts.)

For the next 25 years, *Adios, Maruffa*, and *L'Apache*, (later *Diamond Head*) were to continue their hard fought battles for the *City of Victoria Trophy* that is annually awarded to the first boat home. Over this period, Carl Jensen switched back and forth from yawl to cutter rig in an effort to achieve the best possible rating under the current amendments to the CCA Rule.

Always a versatile performer, she often surprised us with her uncanny speed off the wind, even in the lightest of airs. Her first big win came in 1956 when Carl brought her across the line to be overall winner. She had saved her time from arch rival *Maruffa* by a scant 11 minutes and 25 seconds, and staved off the efforts of wonder boats *Gossip* and *Ono*. Many times first in her class, several times first boat home, and one overall win. A fine record for a fine yacht, and a tribute to Dr. Carl for his wholesome approach to the art of sailing the family boat in the best amateur way — with the family aboard.

Adios sailed her last Swiftsure in 1972 before she was sold to the Barient Winch Company in California. The doctor reports that the firm maintains her in showcase condition, using her for testing and demonstrating their products. So after 40 faithful years of contributing to the sport, *Adios*, still magnificent after a long and busy life, still makes her indelible mark. She is a living illustration to yet another generation: a tested, proven masterpiece in the finest tradition of the wooden yacht craftsmen who built her almost half a century ago. Adios, *Adios*. But never good bye.

Gometra gave no hint of her bizarre past history as her black, graceful, flush deck hull came to the line that May morning in 1953. Sometimes, truth really is stranger than fiction. Little did the skipper of the handsome *Gometra* guess that his yacht would secure a special niche in Norwegian history when he set sail for a fiord cruise in the summer of 1939.

Designed by Alfred Milne and built on Clydebank in 1924, *Gometra's* chief function was to be a day sailer, primarily to navigate the west coast of Scotland. The locale is reflected in her name: a small islet off the Isle of Arran. Mentioned in several books on yacht design, *Gometra* was a very pretty boat, her flush deck broken only by a couple of skylights. She was in effect, a heavy duty Eight Metre.

When European hostilities broke out in the fall of 1939, two cruising yachts were stranded, and prudently abandoned at Trondheim, ''for the duration''. A 28 foot cutter, *Sinbad,* joined the retired British Admiral's 43 foot sloop in the calculated risk which was to become their joint destiny.

The gallant defence of the Norwegians is recorded in history. When the King and Government retreated from Oslo, they carried the Norwegian gold reserves with them. Later, it was stored at Trondheim. The resourceful Norwegians arrived at an ingenious solution for the trans-shipment of the gold. Canada was selected as the best place to direct the bullion for safekeeping.

They decided to remove the inboard ballast and store the gold in the two sailboats, *Gometra* and *Sinbad*, which were to be deck cargo in specially designed cradles. If the mother ship was torpedoed, they would then float free. With this in mind, the ship's carpenter built special flooring into the cockpits, so that the yachts would right themselves and stay afloat, no matter how they were thrown into the water, if the worst happened.

However, the Viking Gods must have smiled upon the expedition, because the mothership cradling the two yachts and their precious cargo made it safely across the Atlantic, unloading at Halifax. The floating treasuries remained in Nova Scotia for the war's duration.

After the war, Gus Ortengren bought *Gometra* from the Norwegian government and brought her to Vancouver. She was subsequently sold to Ken Glass and Elmer Palmer.

Flying the Royal Van burgee, *Gometra* first entered Swiftsure in 1953. On this occasion, and for the next two races as well, Victoria's Ned Ashe took the helm, initiating owner Elmer Palmer, his young son Gerry and also, Bonar Davis into the challenges of Swiftsure. Both Gerry and Bonar went on to greater fame in Vancouver. Both now have 24 Swiftsures tucked under their wet weather gear.

Ned recalls, of these three races, that two were in very heavy weather, blowing up to 40 knots. ''She was a little wet, but not as wet as she looked. A very good sea boat, she put up a pretty good performance to windward, but she wasn't particularly fast. There seemed to be a little discrepancy in the design of her underwater lines, which appeared to hold her back. A hump in the underbody was put there for some purpose, I guess, but it didn't accomplish anything. But she was a lovely boat to sail.''

Gerry Palmer adds, ''*Gometra* was extremely heavy, with very little reserve buoyancy and a very deep run off. She throws a terrific quarter wave. When they took her in Swiftsure, they had a life raft over the skylights. We had a canvas bag that filled the cockpit right up to the deck, so that if the boat was filled or pooped or anything, it was absolutely watertight. She had lovely sails: Egyptian cotton. Ned was a tower of strength on those races. He was incredibly strong.'' (This comment was to be echoed by his crews of the 1970s, even when approaching his 80th year.)

Gometra reappeared after an absence of 20 years in 1978's PHRF Swiftsure, skippered by RNSA's D.A. Millis.

GOMETRA   **THE GOLD SHIP**

The combination of a brand new K38, and a seasoned skipper spelled success in Swiftsure 1954. Henry Kotkins' *Totem*, with three time winner Charlie Ross at the helm, made the best use of the light conditions to out-ghost the heavier competition. (Nine of the 15 entries were AA Class yachts.)

The race got off to a brisk start in a stiff westerly and *Red Jacket* lost her main with a broken halyard in the early going. However, she was able to make repairs on the run, and was under full sail again before evening. *Maruffa* led at the mark, followed by *Polho III*. There they slatted in the ocean swells with scarcely a breath for most of Sunday. *Totem*, one of the new light displacement K38s, had both small size and a minimum of wetted surface going for her during the doldrum hours. When the breeze finally picked up early Monday morning, it was a straight spinnaker run home. *Dorade* was first to cross, but the BB and B class boats had no difficulty saving their time. The corrected results gave the overall to *Totem*, with *Elusive*, *Reverie*, *Polho III* and *Gometra*, in that order.

An interesting new entry, and the first Twelve Metre to ever appear in Swiftsure, was *Jenetta*. Designed by Alfred Milne and built in 1939 in Ardmaleish, Scotland, the 71 footer was one of the largest yachts brought to the Pacific Northwest as deckload of a Liberty Ship, the *Pacific Nomad*. With a rating of 61.7, *Jenetta* was scratch boat for the 1954 race. She had been acquired by Vancouver's Urry family to replace *Cresset*. And Mrs. Victoria Urry, a keen sailor, was usually numbered among the crew. In 1954, *Jenetta* had difficulties in the early blow and retired.

In 1955 prerace festivities set the precedent for traditions which would please the crowds for years to come. The Swiftsure Committee requested all yachts to dress ship for the occasion. Thousands thronged the Causeway. Hundreds of signal flags chattered in the rigging. And a formal Roll Call of every entered yacht boomed across the harbour over powerful loud speakers, following an official welcome at 8 p.m. by Mayor Claude Harrison, Royal Victoria Yacht Club Commodore Ben W. Nickells, and PIYA Vice Chairman Andrew Wright. Bill Tellier's picturesque schooner,

Black Dog, was a floating stage for the sea chanties concert given by the Meistersingers.

Eaton's Department Store transformed their corner window on Douglas Street into a visual information center where spectators and contestants' families could follow race progress on a large map of the course with pin-up boats, accompanied by up-to-date information supplied by the Yacht Club race committee. These reports came in from the Royal Canadian Naval escort vessels, the U.S. Coast Guard, and the Island Tug press and radio boat.

The 1955 race offers good examples of the many ways a yacht can win or lose in the Swiftsure sweepstakes. Humphrey Golby tells the following two tales:

"It was a soft May morning in 1955, the 28th, with most unusual weather conditions when the boats assembled at the line off Brotchie Ledge. There was a vestige of breeze coming off the land, northerly but obviously very local, for as I looked to the south and west, the Strait shone in undulating calm.

"Nineteen yachts came to the line and drifted aimlessly about in the very light air. *Serada* held close inshore. When the gun went, she was sailing gently, spinnaker set, and as we watched, it soon became obvious that she was really the only boat moving. *Serada* held on to the shore breeze, never faltering, all the way to Race Rocks. By this time, the northerly was spreading out, but the area around the start was still very spotty. *Serada* and *Maruffa* led the fleet through Race Passage. The leaders immediately crossed to the American side and continued to run before light east winds until they reached Neah Bay. We followed *Serada* in the tug, as Skipper Chris Goodhope kept her sailing, spinnaker filled, at the head of the pack. The offshore airs stayed with her all day long, carrying her beyond Neah Bay by early evening. Then for a brief hour there were a few westerly squalls to deal with before she resumed her run for the Lightship. The lead yachts, including *Serada*, made it to the Lightship with spinnakers still flying when, just as suddenly, the westerly filled in. Late arrivals had a tough, reefed down beat from Neah Bay to the mark.

"Flat calms prevailed at night, but with the sun in the

morning came a light southwesterly. Once more, the faithful spinnaker filled, and *Serada* gathered way for the run home. Several spinnakers were blown out as *Maruffa*, *Westward Ho*, *Adios*, and *Red Jacket* fought for the lead. From Race Rocks to the finish, gusts were particularly strong. *Maruffa*, first boat through, elected to carry full main and her biggest spinnaker as she bore down on the line. Within 1,000 yards, the top 18 feet of her mast crumpled as a baby stay parted in one last wicked gust. The mishap cost her the overall, but the sturdy yawl, in spite of the confusion on deck, hung on to cross the line first, followed by *Westward Ho*, *Adios*, *Red Jacket*, and *Serada*. (*Maruffa* placed second overall.)

Meanwhile, *Serada*, after her remarkable performance on the outgoing leg, easily saved her time. *Serada* had truly run the course. She won the start. She won her class. And she won the overall. Some run!

"1955 was the year of *Serada's* great run, better than 24 hours of sailing (except for a brief interlude off Tatoosh), without taking down the spinnaker. But it was also the year that skipper W.B. Holms made his second attempt at Swiftsure. In 1954, *Dragoon* had made a very creditable showing, finishing 11th overall on corrected time. Now, Bill had her in top condition, and the crew had spent many hours tuning up and generally getting to know this big, husky, double-ended ketch.

"Like any lady with real class, *Dragoon* captured the hearts and affections of many men, including British actor, David Niven, who wrote in 1977 to present owners Marge and Fred Schuberg, 'Please don't sell her — she'd hate it!' One of the finest ships ever built for rough water and a 60 knot wind, but she was no good in light airs; a workhorse needing a big, strong crew to sail her to capacity.

"*Dragoon's* performance in the Swiftsures 1952 through 1955 set consistent records at the lower end of the race results; a record matched by her vintage counterpart, HMCS *Oriole*. Her presence enhanced the entry list, but her performance in the generally light conditions gave no hint of her legendary past, or former racing conquests.

"Built of pitch pine planking over oak frames, the 67 foot Bermuda ketch was delivered in December, 1925 to *Yachting Magazine's* R.N. Bavier Sr. of New Rochelle, New York, who had her built especially for the 1926 Bermuda Race. *Dragoon* lived up to expectations in her maiden race, crossing the line first, while placing second on corrected time.

"She came to the west coast in 1930, where she was campaigned very successfully in California by St. Francis Yacht Club Commodore, Stanley Barrows.

"British movie star Ronald Coleman bought her in 1938, loaning her to the U.S. Coast Guard for offshore patrol during the Second World War. Her famous guests during that period included Sir Lawrence Olivier and Vivian Leigh, who honeymooned on board, and David Niven, who mentions *Dragoon* in his books, *The Moon is a Balloon* and *Bring On the Empty Horses*.

"Fourth owner, Californian Henry B. Grandin, raced *Dragoon* from San Francisco to Hawaii, placing third in A class in 1947 and 1951. However, by this time, the Rating Rules measurement changes had turned her previously advantageous short overhangs into a significant handicap.

"During her Swiftsure years, Victoria's Capt. W.B. Holms, RCN (RET'D) owned her, also skippering her in the 1953 Honolulu Race. (*Dragoon* was, to that date, only the second Canadian yacht ever to enter the 2,300 mile San Pedro - Honolulu Race since its beginning in 1906.)

"For this 1955 effort however, *Dragoon* was in her best shape, and ready to show some of her old fire. Alas, the fresh to strong winds she needed failed to appear, and the gentlest of northerlies did nothing for her on the way out to the Lightship.

"When *Dragoon* arrived in the vicinity of the mark vessel, there was a heavy sullen swell, a strong tidal set, and not a breath of wind. *Dragoon* rolled and plunged as she neared the Lightship. For a few moments, it was touch and go as to whether or not she would round. Then it happened. The tide carried her below the ship just as a great surging sea lifted her bodily straight at the mark. There was a great hollow boom, and *Dragoon* fell back and the tide carried her clear. Several minutes passed before we on the escort tug realized that we had been witness to yet another Swiftsure first. *Dragoon* had scored the only recorded contact with the Lightship!

"This sad ending to months of hard work and expense, crew build-up and training, all went for naught as once again the evil Genie of Swiftsure devised a new way to beat a fine yacht, this time, with too much gentleness of a soft summer morning.

"The impeccably maintained *Dragoon* nowadays enjoys Dowager Queen status, thanks to the continuing care lavished on her by the Schubergs, who have made her their home while cruising the coast for the past 17 years. Perhaps some of the glamour of her previous film associations gave her an extra patina, because she has twice been featured (1970 and 1971) on CBC-TV *Klahanie* and *Take 30*.

DRAGOON / JAMES McVIE

13/ *Adios Wins in 1956, and We Remember Dorade*

Pre-race activities orchestrated excitement to new heights the week before Swiftsure 1956. Sea Cadet projects benefitted when Navy League Officials and Sea Cadet parents sold memberships, with the proceeds going toward Cadet activities. Each new membership contained a guess on the finish time of the first boat home in the yachting classic. Closest guess won a small dinghy.

A circus gaiety prevailed in the Inner Harbour where 23 yachts, worth at least $1 million, assembled for the rendezvous festivities. The Elks Clown Band was followed by Sea Chanties, sung with gusto from the deck of *Black Dog*, this year, replete with piano. (Quite an item to manhandle aboard a yacht.)

Communications had improved as, for the first time, continuous progress reports could be relayed, thanks to the Island Tug and Barge company's generosity in loaning their 205 foot salvage tug *Sudbury* and the use of her communications equipment.

The race itself was one of the most exciting on record. *Adios, Dorade*, and *Maruffa* engaged in a windward battle to the mark ship, rounding the Light within 20 minutes of one another at 1 a.m. despite almost non-existent winds. By morning, *Adios* and *Maruffa* picked up the first fingers of the morning westerly, and rode it to a substantial lead. By the time the full westerly had filled in, they had disappeared from view of the fleet.

It was a two boat match down the strait, as *Adios* and *Maruffa* continued their stretch dual. *Maruffa* finally overhauled *Adios* as they came abreast of Jordan River and held her slim lead all the way to the line. *Maruffa* ghosted across in 30 hours to capture the new *City of Victoria Perpetual Trophy*. Donated by the city, it is still given to the first vessel to cross the line without the benefit of handicap.

In spite of the light going around the Lightship early Sunday morning, there had been plenty of action on the outbound leg, Saturday morning. *Oriole* had split her mainsail vertically and was forced out, as were the two *Yankees*. The 40 foot cutter *Yankee Doodle* withdrew with a blown out main, while the 44 foot *Yankee Clipper*, manned by a crew of young Sea Scouts from Seattle, had put in to Port

Angeles with a parted main stay.

Other action saw *Adios* overrun her spinnaker and lose precious seconds cutting it free. *Dorade* sailed into a hole and was passed by *Gossip, Kate II, Ono*, and *Tasco II*. Flagship of San Francisco's St. Francis Yacht Club, this latter yacht had been sailed up the coast by Tom Short, to try his experienced hand at Swiftsure, aided by his most enthusiastic crew member, his wife.

Design progress was apparent in 1956, when the pressure from such new boats as *Kate II, Ono, Zingara*, and *Totem* made it apparent that a new era was dawning. California had produced the high priests of the design revolution and, in a sense, the Fifties decade is the story of their successes. However, the shift was gradual. In the beginning, certainly the stalwarts of yesteryear still dominated on the start lines, little realizing that they were inexorably sliding into oblivion.

Chief among these old timers was the reigning Ocean Queen, *Dorade*, fondly remembered by Humphrey Golby:

"It is only once or twice in a decade that a truly remarkable design captures the imagination of the yachting world. Such a yacht was created in 1930 when Olin Stephens laid down the lines for *Dorade*. Stephens called on all his skill and drew heavily on the success of his Six and Eight Metre designs. He was determined that *Dorade* would be the living embodiment of all that was known to be fast in a deep sea racing yacht.

"*Dorade's* slim, deep hull slid into the water the same year that Swiftsure began, but it was to be 20 years before we saw her here on the West Coast. To say that *Dorade* was a forerunner of things to come, is an understatement. She was the fastest ocean racing yacht of her day, and her design proved to be so advanced that it carried her to victory after victory for the next 20 years. Her mahogany hull was strong and light, and built with the flexibility and care of a racing dinghy. To save the weight of traditional teak, *Dorade* even had cedar decks. The deck layout was simple, with ample space for the crew to work. The split headsail rig, her lifetime trademark, was designed to make fast sailing possible in any kind of weather, day or night. The interior was clean and utilitarian; even the bunks were specially designed, narrow and deep, to give rest to weary crewmen on long passages. The galley was so simply and ingeniously set up that it was possible to prepare hot food and feed the men, no matter what the weather. There was no engine, just the best of proven equipment to ensure that *Dorade*, come hell or high water, would be among the finishers.

"The Trans-Atlantic race of 1931 was her first big test and she cut two full days off the record in her run from New York to Plymouth, beating many boats double her size. *Dorade* made the headlines: her jaunty, powerful profile appeared in yachting journals around the world. While in England, she entered the Fastnet, and with Rod Stephens at the helm, completely dominated the fleet of much bigger boats. Now, there was no stopping her. She won her class in the 1932 Bermuda Race, although she missed the overall by a scant margin. Then, it was back to England in 1933 and another Fastnet win. At this time, she was bought from the Stephen brothers by James Flood, who continued to race her hard, bringing her to the Pacific Coast in 1936. In that year, she took the Trans-Pac in her stride. By now, her list of trophies was long and studded with stars. She had now conquered the oceans of the world. *Dorade* was a household word.

"It was inevitable that sooner or later, *Dorade* would come to the Pacific Northwest. This happened at the end of World War II, when she was bought by Seattle's Franklin Eddy. 1947 marked the first of her many Swiftsures. Although overall honours eluded her in many a gallant battle with the early giants of Swiftsure, she captured AA class honours in 1951, 1952, 1954, and 1964.

"But, win or lose, *Dorade* brought her magic name, her shining international record, and her rugged power to Swiftsure, her very presence making it a more important and more widely recognized open sea yachting event. We all knew that when *Dorade* came to Seattle, the best of her racing years were already behind her. The days when the skill and youth of the Stephens brothers and their marvelous crews, and later the dedication and determination of James Flood, had carried her far beyond her designer's fondest dreams. Now, she was a middle-aged lady, with an engine and many added comforts. Some of the fire and drive was gone, but *Dorade* had only to be there to thrill all who were privileged to see her.

"As I stood in the spring sunshine, in 1978, and looked at *Dorade* as she lay, retired, at her dock in the Seattle Yacht Club, my mind ran back across the years of this historic yacht's many contributions to the sport of competitive sailing and of her indelible imprint on the evolution of the modern racing machine. Looking just as she looked 48 years ago when her keel first tasted the Atlantic, *Dorade* lay at rest in the morning sun. The deck is clean and sparse; the cockpit small by today's standards; the rigging old fashioned, but the feeling of power is still there. In spite of the few small winches, she still has the look of the thoroughbred that she is. The unmistakably raked wooden spars and double headstay rig still say, 'This is *Dorade*.'

"In the first postwar PIYA Regatta, a no-host affair, the clubs met at Orcas Island. *Dorade* was there, and I was loaned to her as an extra hand. This informal regatta, insofar as I can remember, was held in 1946. I was entranced just to be on board *Dorade*. The way she moved and the way she went to windward was uncanny. At one point, I was down below as we came about, tacking back and forth in the narrow channel. The memory of what happened has remained with me over these many years. As *Dorade* came around, the stainless steel strapping that ran from corner to corner of the trunk cabin eased momentarily, and as the strains came on the new tack, one strap hummed taut, while the opposite number hung slack. At that moment, I realized that the old girl was so limber that she had comfortably eased her remarkably flexible hull to accommodate the new tack.

"The final chapter in the *Dorade* story will never be written, for her records will live forever in the hearts of all true sailors. When Franklin Eddy died, he left *Dorade* to the Mystic Seaport Museum for preservation. However, the Mystic Seaport authorities could not finance this project without further endowment for maintenance. Since there was no provision in the will for such funds, *Dorade* was offered for sale. A former Seattle-ite, Tony Lopez, now engaged in his family's California wine business, stepped forward to buy her so that she would remain permanently in the Seattle Yacht Club."

DORADE / KENNETH OLLAR   **SLICING TO WINDWARD**

14/ The 1957 Race Belongs to Maruffa — at Last!

The story of John Graham and his beloved *Maruffa* is woven inextricably into Swiftsure's fabric. Ten long years he had struggled to win outright. In 1957, his dreams came true, ending his apprenticeship as Swiftsure's perennial "Bridesmaid", often first boat home, but never quite saving her time for overall honours.

That all changed at 11:29 a.m. Saturday, June 1, 1957, when the 67 foot yawl swept regally across the finish line to set a new course record, while also becoming the first triple-crown winner in race history, taking the *Swiftsure Trophy; City of Victoria Trophy*; and the newly donated *B.C. Cement Trophy* for AA Class (rating 50 plus).

Although bucking a strong current on both legs of the course, *Maruffa* scored speeds up to 11 knots to come within seconds of the prerace predictions for a 26 hour race, clocking in at 25 hours, 59 minutes, 29 seconds to establish a new course record.

Brisk southwesterlies to 25 knots marked the 9:30 a.m. start on Friday, May 31, sending the 25 boat fleet scudding on starboard tack with at least one reef tucked into their mainsails. As the lead yachts reached Race Passage around 11:30 a.m., they hit currents and slack tide; the lull before the incoming flood which would carry on into Saturday morning. First through the Race, *Maruffa* sliced up to weather against the steady westerly, setting a new outward bound record for the distance between Brotchie Ledge and the *Lightship* of 13 hours and 31 minutes, rounding at 11:01 Saturday evening, before the calm set in. Her efforts were rewarded by cheering from the crews of escort ships *HMCS Fortune* and *James Bay*, who picked up the flying yawl in their searchlights in a brief salute.

At the turn, *Maruffa* held a 40 minute lead on *Diamond Head, Cotton Blossom* and *Sea Fever*, which were closing as the ebb worked against *Maruffa*, struggling back to Tatoosh.

However, it was Graham's superb seamanship and skill during the night which made the difference. Using every facet of his long experience to beat the calms and get his ship close in under the land at Neah Bay, he then worked every puff all the way down the American side to Pillar Point, then headed out across the Strait on a broad reach for Race Rocks.

By 9 a.m. Saturday morning, officials from the *SS Sudbury* spotted *Maruffa* off Sheringham Point, commanding a 30 mile lead over the fleet which had drifted haplessly during the night calms. Playing the back eddies while coasting along under spinnaker, *Maruffa* entered Race Passage just before 10 a.m. Turning the corner into the homestretch and setting her genoa in the 15 knot winds, *Maruffa* left her challengers miles behind, back in the Strait. With the finish line in sight, the crack crew of navigator John Soderberg, and Jack Anderson, Bob Rogers, Walt Little, Fran Le Sourd, Bob Watt, John Allen, John Baillargeon, Barney Jensen, Dick Hooper, Chris Johnson, and Duane Wilson could anticipate the well deserved and long overdue overall win, the finest hour for the remarkable boat and the skipper who never quit.

JOHN GRAHAM / JAMES McVIE

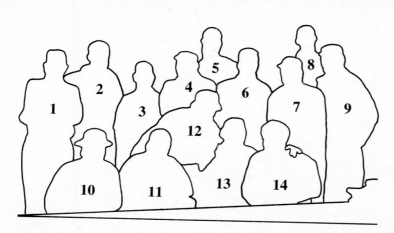

MARUFFA / JAMES McVIE

1 - HUNTER VOGEL, COWICHAN LEADER. 2 - UNIDENTIFIED.
3 - SKIPPER OF ISLAND CHALLENGER. 4 - MAURY GWYNNE, CJVI. 5 - UNIDENTIFIED.
6 - UNIDENTIFIED. 7 - RUTHERFORD HAYES, NEWS PICTORIAL, SEATTLE. 8 - UNIDENTIFIED.
9 - ERIC SCOTT, PHOTOGRAPHER. 10 - MIKE DOYLE, ENGINEER CKDA.
11 - DON McNEIL, R.VIC. SPOTTER. 12 - HUMPHREY GOLBY, "THE VOICE".
13 - UNIDENTIFIED. 14 - JAMES McVIE, PHOTOGRAPHER.

PHOTO TAKEN ABOARD "ISLAND CHALLENGER" 1957-8 BY RUTHERFORD HAYES

15/ *The Maruffa Years*

Maruffa, from her debut in 1947, stamped her personality on Swiftsure. During the middle Fifties, however, she really came into her own. *Maruffa* stole the show, one way or another, no matter who or what the challenge. And her list of laurels grew.

Humphrey Golby comments:

"Certainly one of the outstanding yachts that helped Swiftsure become a recognized international sailing event was John Graham's *Maruffa*. She first came to Swiftsure in 1947, and even in this, her maiden race, she was first boat home. For the next 16 years, she was the public's choice; the photographer's joy; and the true queen of the fleet. Her unparalleled Swiftsure record speaks for itself.

"She was the first boat home in at least six if not seven of her starts. (In the early races, the records kept were very skimpy.) However, since the *City of Victoria Trophy* was presented to PIYA in 1956, *Maruffa* has won it four times. It took John Graham 10 years, from 1947 to 1957, to win the *Swiftsure Trophy*. So many times, *Maruffa* boiled through the race with every rag of sail she could carry, driving for the finish line in an all out last ditch effort to save her time on the fleet. Sometimes, she only lost by a minute or two, and once, only by seconds.

Many times a winner in AA Class, only once in her career did she fail to finish, and that was the race of the great calm in 1958 when 23 yachts finally gave up and powered home.

"*Maruffa* was built in 1936 in the Pendleton Yards in Wescasset, Maine. She was designed by Phil Rhodes and meticulously built to the special order of Henry Babson. Commissioned and sailed on the Great Lakes for three years, she made quite a name for herself in Mackinac and other major events. During the war years, 1943-1946, *Maruffa* was put into storage, and at war's end was sold to John Graham. John recalls that the former owner had two paid hands, and kept them steadily at work on the boat for three years. When Graham saw her, she was gleaming like a concert grand. One look closed the sale. *Maruffa* went to Annapolis for a short time before her proud new owner rounded up a crew to sail her to Seattle.

"In his design, Phil Rhodes had produced a handsome, wholesome boat, beautifully balanced, capable of holding her own on every point of sail. *Maruffa* was at her best in light to medium winds, but even when it blew hard, she could snug down and keep pace. Her real strength was her ability to run, even in the lightest airs. So many times, I have observed *Maruffa* quietly sail away from the fleet on the downwind leg. This great offwind speed once placed her third across the line into Hawaii, a performance that enabled her to beat all but two of the A Class boats, boat for boat, even though she was racing in B Class. In any consideration of *Maruffa's* marvellous Swiftsure years, we have to remember that throughout all those years, she was sailed by John Graham and a crack crew.

"John Graham was a sailing competitor even as a young boy, coming to Victoria in 1919 to sail on the Seattle team against Royal Victoria dinghies. The Seattle-ites used Winslow Kittens, which were much faster than the local boats. John had probably the best sailing teachers that anyone could ask for. He was a member of Ted Geary's *Sir Tom* crew, the famous R boat that dominated the Pacific Coast for so many years. Ted Geary was an acknowledged master of the art of sailing. He picked John to skipper the boat when he was unable to be on board. From R boats to Star boats, John sailed and won. He was a fierce competitor, an intuitive tactician, and he never quit. When Ray Cooke built *Circe* and raced her in 1934 Swiftsure, John Graham was aboard as sailing master. He sailed on *Circe* in all her early Swiftsures. Here again, he had, in Ray Cooke, the best teacher in the business. After World War II, John bought *Maruffa*, starting her Swiftsure saga in 1947.

"Swiftsure records are filled with the exploits of this great yacht. Let me relate two incidents that show just how hard the skipper and crew worked for their laurels. At first light, the escort tug picked up *Maruffa* close in under the land off Neah Bay. She had rounded the Lightship about midnight, and had led the pack on the homeward run. The entrance to the Straits was glassy calm. Boats out in the stream were rolling listlessly without steerageway. John had worked *Maruffa* right inshore where the first morning thermals created the slightest breeze. As the tug followed her, we saw a classic example of how a fantastic skipper can keep even a big boat moving under almost impossible conditions. The wind was shifting back and forth, from the merest offshore zephyr to a few faint puffs from the southwest as the westerly sought to become established. In each of these shifts, from slightly ahead of abeam to dead astern, John had his crew alternate with a light drifter for the offshore puffs, returning to the spinnaker when the westerly caught up. What was happening was simple. When the westerly drove *Maruffa* ahead, she promptly sailed out of the following wind. As quickly as she nosed out of the westerly, she slid forward into the offshore breeze, faint as it might be. For each of these alternating conditions, John had his crew down spinnaker as soon as the westerly quit, and hoist a gossamer drifter to take advantage of the offshore puffs. As we watched, *Maruffa* went through this drill 12 or 15 times. The marvel of it was that John Graham kept *Maruffa* moving while others sat and waited for the morning westerly. When the wind did finally make up, *Maruffa* had gained at least an additional mile on her listless rivals.

"The second incident unfolded right at the finishing line. The late afternoon westerly was unusually fresh in 1955 as *Maruffa* charged through Race Passage with a substantial lead. Skipper Graham had his biggest spinnaker up, and *Maruffa* made a glorious picture as she surged forward at breakneck speed. Just off Work Point, and less than 1,000 yards from the finish, a sudden gust off the land hit *Maruffa*, sending her reeling, but she did not broach. In seconds, she seemed to recover, when suddenly her mast snapped at the upper spreader. The great spinnaker sagged in confusion on the foredeck, while the main hung like a broken wing. Thousands of spectators had gathered to watch her finish. An audible gasp went up as tragedy struck. The committee had timed her nearest rivals through the Race when there was a chance that *Maruffa* would save her time and win it all. Now, these precious minutes ticked away, as *Maruffa's* hopes for the *Swiftsure Trophy* slipped from her grasp once more. Even then, *Maruffa* didn't quit. John swung her round with the mizzen, and sailed her backwards across the line! The *City of Victoria Trophy* for first boat to finish was hers again. And what a finish it was."

Maruffa left the Pacific Northwest to engage in research projects sailing out of Woods Hole Marine Biological Station. For her day and time, *Maruffa* was an outstanding yacht, ahead of her time in design, faultlessly built, and meticulously maintained. She is a living legend. This chapter cannot end without listing *Maruffa's* principal dimensions. She was 67 foot 5½ inches overall, exclusive of the bowsprit. Waterline length 49 foot 7 inches; beam 15 foot 2½ inches with a draft of 8 foot 6 inches.

The *Maruffa* story has a sad postscript. On Sunday, March 4, 1979, she went aground and became a total loss while on a research mission in South New Zealand waters. The tragedy occurred while en route from Dunedin to Stewart Island with a young American crew guiding her.

Skipper Steven Sewell decided to turn back when he met rough seas off the southland coast. During the turning manoeuvre, the main backstay parted. After making temporary repairs he set his course for Tuatuku Bay Lighthouse. However, *Maruffa's* great speed carried her in too close before the order to alter course could be carried out. In the confusion, those vital seconds proved fatal. *Maruffa* drove hard aground. Within minutes she began to break up in the heavy seas. A sad end to a heritage yacht which still had many useful years of service.

In the process of abandoning ship, one of the young crewmen caught his leg between the topsides and the rocks, severing it below the knee in one of the powerful surges. A female crew member lost her thumb, but thankfully no lives were lost.

MODEL OF MARUFFA SHOWING UNDERWATER LINES / H. GOLBY

16/ 1958 — the Great Calm

Five thousand jammed the causeway for the 1958 prerace festivities, which were highlighted by the precision Sunset Ceremony of HMCS *Naden's* highly trained unit, along with the *Naden Band* and a saluting battery.

Humphrey Golby introduced the record 39 entries, ranging in size from 28 feet to 90 feet, along with two visitors, the converted naval vessel SS *Commodore*, representing the 19th century Gold Rush ship, and the local schooner, *Black Dog*.

A last minute navy entry, unheralded and unregistered, was the 32 foot cutter *Foxtrot*, which appeared on Friday morning, set to race. HMCS *Fraser's* wardroom liked the idea of a 40 boat race. And *Foxtrot* was the ship's cutter, an open boat commandeered for the occasion by the *Fraser* men. However, their eight man venture was rejected by the race committee, as *Foxtrot* lacked one safety prerequisite, a self-bailing cockpit.

Prerace projections for a very slow race actualized into a self-fulfilling prophecy, when the committee officially pronounced the slowest race on record. Characterized by very light winds, periods of doldrums and glassy calms, it was an endurance contest for the sailors, who generally put in a tedious night pursuing elusive to non-existent winds all over the Strait. By midnight Monday, only 16 boats had crossed the finish line, with most of the remainder having given up and powered back. So slow was the race that the first boat home, *Diamond Head*, lost and regained her lead 10 times. Skipper Max Wyman estimated they sailed more than double the distance in search of breeze. The earliest casualty, *Adios*, retired at 3 p.m. Saturday, discouraged by the combination of calms and adverse currents.

Because she had ghosted through the fleet during the night, John Graham's *Maruffa* was able to round the Lightship ahead of the pack late Sunday morning. (The only strong winds blew briefly beyond Flattery on Saturday.) It was during the 'Driftsure' conditions on the homeward leg from Neah Bay to Clallam Bay that most abandoned the race, including Mighty *Maruffa* and two-thirds of the AA boats.

In one crucial mini-match, two Kettenberg 38's, *Ono*

and *Panacea*, covered each other over the course. *Ono* managed to nip into Race Passage and work her way to William Head, where she found a puff of wind, while *Panacea* was becalmed. This manoeuvre won *Ono* the race on corrected time, as she finished third, a whisker behind *Kate II*. Victoria's Peter Young, crew when Russ Baker skippered *Buccaneer*, remembers, ''We were trying to buck the ebb by playing the shore around the entrance to Becher Bay. We worked out, having bounced over one rock. We were with *Diamond Head* off Bentinck Island. *Diamond Head* had no steerage way and also bounced off a rock. We finally crossed the line around noon on Monday.''

Meanwhile, on Monday, June 2, the largest and smallest entries were still toughing it out in the Strait. *Oriole* had her usual goal, which was to finish the race. The 28 foot *Mischief* and 33 foot *Blue Wave* had a more tangible prize, the B Class Trophy. However, neither of them claimed it. None of the five B Class entries finished the race.

Besides being almost flat calm, 1958 was also the mildest weather experienced to date on this open sea venture. Press and photographers on the escort tug *Sudbury* worked on deck, even after sundown, in their shirtsleeves. At one point early Saturday morning the chief engineer shut down the engines to make some long needed repairs. He remarked that since no one was going anywhere for the next few hours, he might as well get some jobs done in the engine room.

THE GREAT CALM / JAMES McVIE

PACIFIC SWELL

The Swiftsure story could never have made headlines all over the world if it had not been for the drive and organizational ability of the post-war chairman, Jack Gann. He used every means at his disposal to get the race publicized, but he realized that the big gap in putting together a vital news story of Swiftsure was caused by the lack of any communication from offshore during the actual race.

In answer to his prayers came Harold Elworthy, who offered the services of his company by supplying a tug to cover the race from start to finish. Elworthy was a long time member of the Royal Victoria Yacht Club, which instantly accepted his offer with thanks. Little did the Committee realize the long term magnitude of this offer.

The only strings attached by Elworthy's Island Tug were that the vessel was to be there for the service of the news media: radio, press, and photographers. The first year of coverage was 1957, and Chairman Jack Gann sent out invitations to all local radio stations, newspapers, yachting magazines and professional photographers who were interested in the yachting scene. Notices went to Vancouver and Seattle, Portland, Tacoma, and even down the coast to California. The response was tremendous; all the qualified party had to bring was his equipment and his sleeping bag. Everything else was supplied by Island Tug.

Radio Station CKDA in Victoria was interested in getting some equipment on the tug and doing some reports live from the water. Their engineer, Mike Doyle, was given the job of setting up the transmitter and Humphrey Golby was asked by the club to help him with the broadcasts. "If my memory serves me correctly, the first tug assigned to the job was the *Island Challenger*," Golby says, "and Mike worked against the clock to set up his jury rig. Radio has come a long way in the last 30 years, but in those early days every bit of equipment had to be made up by the engineers. Nothing in the nature of portable sets was available. CKDA was truly pioneering. Mike tried everything he knew to get some sort of reports home from the tug. In that first year, some reports did come through, especially at the start and up to Race Rocks.

"But, once we were through the passage in the Pedder Bay - Sooke area, we ran into massive magnetic interference due to the low grade magnetic iron ore bodies throughout this region. When the tug got further up the Strait and more out in the centre of the channel, we were again able to get signals home. However, all too soon, they were out of range of our set. From then on, we were restricted to the tug's radio telephone. Those early trips were one long problem to try and produce a readable live broadcast right from the scene of the action. In those days the broadcasts and phone calls were relayed into the Committee's plot room right in Eaton's corner window. The results were scrambled, often incomplete and inaccurate, but the Swiftsure Story was being told for the first time, live!

"As each successive year went by, the coverage got steadily better and better, but life on the tug was pretty hectic. We often had at least three radio stations represented, and sometimes four, five or more, plus the various newspaper and news service reporters, who all wanted to use the ship's radio telephone at the same time. Added to our troubles to give each representative a chance to phone, there were hundreds of other tugs, commercial fishing boats and all the other assorted coastal shipping, who wanted, and often insisted, they they were given a free channel. In the late Fifties and early Sixties, there were very few channels allocated, and it was a matter of taking our turn and trying not to hog the airwaves. Blow high or drift aimlessly, the tug crew never tired of trying to help all of the newsmen to get their stories home. Much of the time, individual stories were impossible to transmit, so we had to compromise with getting the latest reports back to the land crew in Eaton's window, and ask them to relay the stories on to the other radio stations and news services.

"During those experimental efforts, Andy Wright, Harry Barnes and I observed, plotted, and broadcast from first light 'til the last faint colours of night had faded in the western sky. Heavy weather, fog, and seasickness took its toll, but the Swiftsure story was being told, and sailors everywhere listened and liked what they heard. As the challenge was thrown out far and wide, each year the entry lists grew and grew. Somewhere in the soul of every sailor lurked the yearning to sail in Swiftsure, to compete with the best, to meet the Strait of Juan de Fuca head on.

"Mushrooming interest in the race brought more and more media people to cover it. By 1961, Harold Elworthy had upped his already tremendous contribution by making the famous *Sudbury I* available for the job.

"The *Sudbury I* came to Swiftsure fresh from her conquests of the open Pacific where she had accomplished a 3,000 mile tow to bring a disabled freighter into Victoria and safety. Among her other triumphs were tows from Japan to the Argentine, and she became a legend wherever seamen met to talk about salvage and towing. The *Sudbury* was basically equipped for salvage operations, but the true source of her fame was her sheer power. Her phenomenal steam power provided the ability to tow anything, anywhere in the world.

"With *Sudbury I* at our disposal, the media crew now numbered 30 bodies. *Life* and *Time* magazines sent photographers. On board were reporters from Nanaimo on Vancouver Island; and from almost every paper in Victoria, Vancouver, Seattle, Portland, Tacoma, and all the way down the coast to San Francisco. The Kodak Company sent research men with new colour film to test. There were still photographers, movie men, newsmen, and yachting publication men; plotters, observers and race officials. The great powerful tug was ideal for our purposes. She provided a stable platform for the photographers. Her steam power was quiet and vibrationless, which made it ideal for radio broadcasting, and there was plenty of room both below and on deck for all concerned.

"The media crew were doubly fortunate in having Harley Blagborne as the *Sudbury I* skipper on at least three occasions. Harley had shared the limelight with the ship on many of her outstanding missions. Deeply attached to his ship, small but stocky with quiet confidence in his every movement, the skipper inspired his crew and ours with his

instant responses and reasoned reaction to any and all problems that came along. He did not give orders. He just let it be known what it was that had to be done, and it was done. The assignment to cover Swiftsure intrigued him, and his interest never flagged. If there were yachts to be found, Harley found them. Nothing was too much trouble. By the time 1960 and 1961 rolled around, the radio reports of yacht positions were being transmitted regularly back to Victoria, Vancouver, Bellingham, and through the news services, on to many outlets in the United States. As the ability of the radio station transmitters improved, more and more of the reports came in live from the tug rather than by use of the ship's radio telephone.

"The day eventually came when *Sudbury I* retired to standby duties while the new twin diesel giant *Sudbury II* took her place. *Sudbury II* was probably one of the best equipped, most powerful salvage tugs afloat, but we missed the quiet hiss of our old favourite steamer.

"Looking back on the years through the late Fifties until the early Seventies, when Island Tug was sold to Seaspan International Ltd., it becomes apparent what a vital part Harold Elworthy's contribution played in the growth of a local yacht race into an internationally recognized race for the world's finest yachts. Island Tug and Barge provided a platform for the media and enabled Swiftsure to blossom into the magnificent spectacle that it now presents. Radio communication is very positive, even for amateur operators, and the race committee has access to continuous sea, air, and land based reports; it is hard to remember the days when nothing was heard of the yachts from the time of the start until the first boat crossed the finish line 36 hours later.

"The story, 'Swell Breakfast' (told elsewhere in this book), is a true page from one of the escort tug's log book, and reflects life as it was as all facets of the news media laboured to report the news of Swiftsure with humour, facts — and a certain undeniable flair.''

SUDBURY I / JAMES McVIE

18/ *1959 — a Year of Firsts*

An international flavour pervaded 1959, when Prince Phillip's Dragon, *Bluebottle*, arrived to race, concluding with the Maple Bay Regatta on Labour Day weekend. Farther afield, John Guzzwell's *Trekka*, built in Victoria, was setting new records in solo circumnavigations.

Swiftsure 1959 got underway at 9:30 a.m. on May 30 with past Commodore F.M. Ohrt, R.Vic firing the gun for a brisk starboard tack start. By noon, the steady 15 knot southwest wind had built to 25, enabling the AA yachts to lead the pack.

The fleet split into its three usual sections: Max Wyman's *Diamond Head* led *Maruffa* and Phil Graham's *Troubadour* on the Canadian shore; Ed Halton's *Cotton Blossom* elected mid-channel, while Lt. Cmdr. Joe Prosser at the helm of HMCS *Oriole* led Ray Cooke's *Circe*, Ned Skinner's *Kate II* and Dick Philbrick's *Sea Fever* across to the southern shore.

During the afternoon, *Maruffa* covered *Diamond Head* closely on a course which found them in mid-channel, level with Flattery, as the winds lightened at sundown, well ahead of the fleet. Five miles behind on the Canadian shore were Ralph Farris' *Hawk*, Harry Cloutier's *Derevo*, and Spencer Clark's *Dahut*. *Cotton Blossom*, *Spirit*, *Troubadour*, *Mary Bower* and *Oriole* worked the southern shore, although *Oriole's* progress was slowed when she made makeshift repairs to a torn mainsail.

During Saturday night the wind died completely, but by dint of hard work, perseverence, and Lady Luck, some yachts rounded the Lightship by mid-morning Sunday. The bulk of the fleet rolled gently to and fro in the area between Neah Bay and Port Renfrew. The Press Tug drifted in with the leaders: *Sudbury's* magnificent steam power plant registering zero revs. As the tug approached Neah Bay, a large yacht was spotted with all sails down, close in under the American shore. Wishing to identify the yacht, the tug headed over and there, to the astonishment of the media and crew, was *Adios*. Dr. Carl Jensen and crew had the midship awning set, deck chairs circling the cockpit, and every man jack with a fishing line. Carl hailed the tug and held up two beautiful coho.

Said Humphrey Golby, ''I will always remember the picture of a happy crew, aboard one of Sparkman Stephens finest yachts, making the best of a calm day — Swiftsure's rarest phenomenon!''

To make the day replete with joy all around, the escort tug was able to negotiate with *Adios* for sadly needed refreshments. The long, hot hours had played havoc with the media's beer stock. In Swiftsure, as in any sport, no beer, no report!

At dusk, as the wind dropped and the tide changed, the continuous ocean swells increased. The outward bound pack met the flood tide head on. *Mary Bower* moved up behind *Maruffa* in mid-Strait, while *Diamond Head* tried tacking toward the Canadian shore. Tidal brakes effectively stalled the becalmed frontrunners, allowing the smaller yachts to ghost up from behind. Under these conditions, the 40 foot sloop *Cotton Blossom* appeared out of nowhere off Tatoosh Island, to round first at 4:05, retreating again to Tatoosh. Another Seattle yacht, *Rebel*, was next to round at 4:40, followed closely by Bob Ross' *Concerto*, *Ono* and *Circe*. Pat Leslie's brand new *Tricia*, *Spirit*, *Mary Bower*, *Sea Fever*, *Buccaneer III*, *Diamond Head*, and *Maruffa* had all rounded by 6:30.

Dawn's haze revealed *Oriole* stalled mid-Straits, while shore-hugging *Cotton Blossom* found the first wisp of morning breeze and popped her chute for the long homeward haul. An hour later, the wind had worked across the Straits to the Canadian shore, where it was picked up by *Rebel*, *Concerto*, *Ono*, and *Tricia*, who paced a steady nine knots while *Mary Bower* slowly worked her way over from mid-Strait. By early afternoon, the wind had again picked up to southwest 20, with *Mary Bower* and *Maruffa* well up and *Rebel* and *Ono* ahead of *Concerto*.

While this little drama unfolded off Sooke, *Cotton Blossom* reached, rail down on her final hitch across the Strait in late afternoon, on a course which beat out *Rebel*, leading the front group into Race Passage.

At this point, *Maruffa* made a last-ditch attempt to salvage the race, hoisting all the sail she could carry, surging past the group at 11 knots.

Cotton Blossom's strategy, however, had established a three mile gap which *Maruffa* couldn't close, despite her 11th hour push. *Mary Bower, Rebel, Ono*, and *Concerto* all finished within 30 minutes, in one of the most exciting stretch battles ever.

Cotton Blossom won the coveted *City of Victoria Trophy: Rebel* beat out *Ono* by 15 minutes, capturing the *Swiftsure Trophy*, while *Tricia*, Pat Leslie's new Lapworth 36, which was to place consistently near the top for the next decade, was third, 15 minutes behind *Ono*.

EATON'S WINDOW, VICTORIA

CARTOON BY BARRON OF VICTORIA PRESS LTD.

WESTWARD HO ROUNDING / KENNETH OLLAR

63

19/ HMCS Oriole — "Never a Bride"

"For God's sake, don't do that. It will take two hours to put her about!"

A classic elephant/mouse situation, it happened during one of those flat spells. There they were, mid-Strait, outward bound. Tail end Charlies in their respective races.

In a situation reminiscent of a Stephen Leacock tale, masterful irony found the Cal 20 *Heather*, the smallest Juan de Fuca yacht, dwarfed by the dimensions of the approaching HMCS *Oriole*. Everyone else had long since disappeared over the horizon. There was just a hint of breeze, barely enough for *Oriole* to overtake.

Mischievously, *Heather* went through the motions of luffing up. Much consternation ensued on the *Oriole*. A forced tack in that situation would have been an unmitigated disaster!

This illustrates *Oriole's* perennial problem: the general lack of strong, steady winds over the course of any given Swiftsure. Even so, Victoria's perennial "Bridesmaid" is the city's sentimental favourite.

The only commissioned sailing yacht in the Canadian Armed Forces, the HMCS *Oriole* links the present plastic era with a more leisured time, when yachts had traditional graceful lines, two masted rigs, and heavy displacement.

Designed along the lines of the "J" boats, then in their heyday, by New York architect George Owen for Royal Canadian Yacht Club's Commodore G.H. Gooderham, she was the fourth *Oriole* in a distinguished family's yacht roster (the visiting Prince of Wales was hosted on board the *Oriole III*.)

In 1921, the templates were all made, and much of the steel plate had been cut for her hull when labour troubles suspended construction at Toronto's Dominion Shipbuilding Company. Eventually, these disputes forced closure of the entire Toronto shipbuilding industry, and the $65,000 contract for *Oriole's* construction was lost for the area. Undaunted by the delays, Gooderham gathered together the existing parts and dispatched them to Boston, for completion by George Lawley and Sons.

However, post World War I rail conditions were chaotic, and the shipment from Toronto was lost for months. The Lawley Corporation finally built the new *Oriole IV* from the blueprints up, escalating Gooderham's total costs to over $100,000, along with attendant frustrations and worries.

The Commodore's new flagship was finally launched in June, 1921, embodying the latest in yacht design specifically for freshwater cruising and racing. Originally, she had a centreboard, which naturally increased her windward capability, while her moderate draft was suited to lake conditions. At first, the *Oriole IV* had no bowsprit, but two marconi masts, with the mainmast 105 feet and mizzen 55 feet.

With this rig, before the days of synthetic fibre, the single halyard put such a strain on the mainsail at its one point of support that the cloth pulled out of the headboard in winds over 20 knots. To correct this problem, the mast was reduced to little over 89 feet, giving an easily handled cut down mainsail. However, this effectively restricted the *Oriole* as a competitive racing yacht, except in a hard and steady breeze, preferably on her quarter.

As a privately owned yacht flying the Royal Canadian Yacht Club burgee, *Oriole's* halcyon existence ended with the Second World War, when she was acquired by the Toronto branch of the Navy League of Canada.

The Royal Canadian Navy leased her from the Navy League for $1 in 1943, officially acquiring her in 1949. Formally commissioned as the HMCS *Oriole* in 1952, she fell heir to all the perks and privileges of an orthodox war vessel. Thus began the second phase of *Oriole's* career: in the service of the Canadian public with the Canadian Armed Forces.

Her first assignment under Royal Canadian Navy control was reserve training vessel for HMCS *York*, where she was used for sea cadet training. In 1949, she left the Great Lakes, sailing up the St. Lawrence just ahead of the winter freeze to Digby, Nova Scotia. There, as tender to HMCS *Cornwallis* under Lieut. Baldwin, the *Oriole* gave ordinary seamen their basic training. In 1950, she was transferred to HMCS *Stadacona* in Halifax, where she was refitted and operational again by 1952, attached to the administrative branch of the seamanship school.

The *Oriole's* east coast escapades included a Halifax-Bermuda Race and surviving sailing through the eye of a hurricane off George's Bank in the summer of 1953 when the crew, including Jim Butterfield (later her Commanding Officer) laboured successfully to save the ship.

In 1954, the navy transferred the HMCS *Oriole* to HMCS *Venture*, the officer training school on the west coast. Lieutenant Commander E.T. (Tubby) Coggins (later the master of HMS *Bounty* replica and *Bluenose II*), was in command from the Maritimes for the trip through the Panama Canal to her new home at Esquimalt, where she arrived on October 3, 1954, escorted up the west coast by the HMCS *Porte de la Reine*.

The *Oriole's* west coast career covers many extended sail training cruises, as well as major yacht races, including the biennial Victoria - Maui Race. While official host ship for the 1978 Captain Cook Bicentennial celebrations, the *Oriole* captured the Cutty Sark Friendship Trophy as overall winner of the 1978 Pacific International Sail Training Race. This climaxed a 2,700 mile match race against Lol Killam's *Greybeard*, from Hawaii to Victoria. Although she once ran the Swiftsure course in 17 hours on a sail training cruise, *Oriole's* Swiftsure exploits have been marked by a series of disasters and mediocre finishes, usually fluctuating between DNF and last boat to finish. (Her best was eighth across the line, in 1976.)

During her first Swiftsure, in 1955, her bowsprit snapped at a critical moment near the Lightship. Sails and gear were recovered, and a forestay jury-rigged, but on the homeward drive, the spinnaker boom parted in three places. Such was her maiden Swiftsure venture.

In 1966, with Lt. Cmdr. James Butterfield at the helm, they were among the first 10 off Pillar Point, "just hurtling along", with gusts hitting 23 knots. The big jenny was scooping badly, and the strain of the water broke the mast at the 50 foot level. All the rigging went soggy. "It was one of the saddest moments of my life," recalls Butterfield. (He helmed *Oriole* in Swiftsure 1965, 1966, and 1967, with four races as crew since then.)

The *Oriole* is not fitted out to cope with light airs sailing. She is large, heavy, and old fashioned. The gear is all very heavy, and the sails are all very heavy. "To hang on in anything more than a zephyr, you have to be all bright and on the bit," relates Butterfield. "True sailors are enormously appreciative of the hard work involved to make the *Oriole* go."

The reason the *Oriole* needs a 32 man crew to race is because all halyards and running backstays are rigged luff on luff with triple purchase blocks. There isn't a winch on board. It's all "Henry Armstrong tackles, pully-hauly." They need roughly four men on the mizzen; six men on the main; and 15 men on the spinnaker and headsails. As many as 18 bodies can be required to sheet in the 2,100 square foot Genoa Jib, while up to 30 can be absorbed in the most difficult manoeuvre: jibing 6,600 square feet of spinnaker with the 38 foot, 125 pound aluminum pole, requiring four men just to lift and put in place.

Oriole's present skipper, Lt. Cmdr. Bill Walker, is dedicated to the welfare of his ship, with a great empathy for his charge. Says Butterfield, "He talks to it like a dinghy."

Walker comments, "She just will not go to windward in very light winds. If it is flat calm and no swell, she'll sail in five or six knots, but increase the swell just slightly so that it is on the bow, then it knocks her down and cuts the speed off so that she just sits there and hobbies up and down, up and down. Then, as the swell increases, she begins to roll and the sails don't fill and she literally will not go. So you just have to accept that. It is a bit of a heartbreak. Everybody's all enthusiastic. So you have to have a wind." (In 1976, they had more wind than they wanted: 35-50 knots, which was hard on both ship and crew.)

They used to sail her with a jib and a jib topsail, and she "wouldn't go to windward worth a darn." So you have to have a genoa. Formerly, all headsails were set from the end of the bowsprit, but Walker cut the second headstay back and set them from the stem head, the way she was designed. So now, she doesn't carry helm, and will go to windward. In the early days, she had an additional 18 tons of ballast, but Walker took the ballast out 12 years ago. (It was the weight of a city bus.)

For Swiftsure, Bill Walker carries two complete crews, who "hotbunk it". (With this size vessel, weight is not a consideration.) "You can't sheet in with 20 men unless you keep them on deck for the entire race. They're utterly exhausted by the time the race is half over; they're cold and wet. Then, they're inefficient and the ship is not well sailed." So there is always one watch on deck. With 22 bunks plus settees, they carry close to 40, watch on watch, with four on and four off. "Insist they're below, stretched out, when they are off watch, so that the crew on deck is relatively fresh in heavy weather," Walker says. "Even so, half of them can be seasick below, so you still have 18 men capable of being on deck."

Perhaps it is this mystique of raw manpower which has caught the public imagination. In any case, the HMCS *Oriole* remains the darling of the fans. Here are her specifications: LOA 102 feet; LWL 63 feet; BEAM 19 feet 4 inches; DISPLACEMENT 75 tons; FREEBOARD 6 feet 8 inches forward, 4 feet 8 inches aft; TOTAL RACING SAIL AREA 11,830 square feet (spinnaker is 6,600 square feet, the size of a city lot 100 x 66 feet); COMMANDING OFFICERS: Lt. Cmdr. T. Coggins, Brian Judd, Lt. Cmdr. MacLean, Lt. Cmdr. Joe Prosser, Lt. Cmdr. Jim Butterfield, Lt. Cmdr. Geoff Hilliard, Lt. Cmdr. Peter Cox, Lt. Cmdr. Al Horner, Cmdr. Roger Sweeney, and Lt. Cmdr. Bill Walker, since August 10, 1973.

20/ *Swell Breakfast*

At sundown, the Island Tug and Barge escort tug, *Island Challenger*, took up station just beyond the Lightship. It had been a long, hot, light wind day, and the yachts were well behind the tug and not expected to round for many hours. The vessel did not anchor, but kept just enough headway on to hold her steady in the current. The helmsman had instructions to keep her head into the long, silky swells.

A perfect evening, the last rays of the sunset caught the tops of the undulating sea. One felt that that day's last message was being carried and re-carried endlessly westward. But all too soon, the sun had gone, and the sky colours faded. For many of the newsmen and photographers aboard, they were out of sight of land for the first time in their lives.

The tug rose and fell in easy rhythm as she rode the long Pacific rollers, as one by one, the photogs and reporters found a spot to roll out their sleeping bags. Word had been left with the skipper to call Humphrey Golby as soon as a yacht was sighted. One last turn around the deck reinforced the scene forever in his mind:

"The endless glistening presence of the great Pacific; the soft night air, and the low throb of the idling diesel, and the intermittent brilliance of the masthead beacon on the Lightship focused the brief moment when I could see her red hull with the name *Swiftsure* standing in white letters 10 feet high along her topsides. Then, it was dark again, and the only sign of life was the twinkling, bobbing lights of the fishing fleet, further out and to the south. I was told that the trawlers drag continuously, day and night.

"Sleep came easily, and it only seemed minutes when I heard the skipper's voice calling me: 'There's a sail heading out toward us. No panic, he's got a mile to a mile and a half to go yet, and there is no wind worth mentioning.' He went back into the wheelhouse and scanned the radar for several minutes. 'Hard to say if she's moving or not, but just to make sure, I'll get the cook up and he can start to make breakfast.'

"Harold Elworthy had detailed his best chef for the escort tug, and the food to this point had been amazingly good. Nothing was too much trouble, and no efforts were spared to please the media visitors. Gradually, the gang rolled out of their bags, and the welcome aromas of breakfast brightened them up in no time. I was in the wheelhouse with the skipper when we observed that suddenly the yacht was nearer than we thought. The tide had pushed her out, and she had found a few cat's paws of breeze. It was 4:30 a.m., and the light was just breaking down the Straits. So far, we could not identify the vessel, except to note that it was one of the smaller entries.

"Half an hour dragged by, with all hands fixed on the first yacht to round. The swells would lift her momentarily into full view, and then she would almost disappear into the valley. Consensus was that it was one of the K38s but which one? In the meantime, the cook had bacon and eggs piled high on the back of the ship's range, along with steaming coffee pots lined up ready for the call to come and get it.

"The skipper had worked the tug to a position just ahead of the Lightship about 250 yards from her. The tug still rode easily in the swells. The idea was to have the yacht pass between us and the marker boat. In this way, we could identify the yacht and get an approximate time of rounding. As the yacht passed the Lightship bow, we identified her as *Ono*. I asked the skipper if he would follow her around to give the photographers a chance to get pictures with the Lightship in the background. No sooner said than done. The tug wheeled from her head to sea position and followed the yachts.

"Now rolling wildly with rollers abeam, the tug made a complete circle around the Lightship. At this moment, all hell broke loose in the galley. The chef, wild eyed, his hat askew, his face beet red and gleaming with sweat, burst into the wheelhouse and yelled at the skipper, 'You call yourself a sailor? Any greenhorn punk deck hand 'ud know better than to take a ship into a beam sea, an' the whole God damn breakfast for 20 men shot to hell on the galley floor! I quit. Geez Christ, I quit!' And he stormed out.

"We were flabbergasted, and made our way down to the galley to view the mess. Scrambled eggs, bacon, bacon grease, coffee, dish water, and assorted pots and dishes slid idly to and fro on the galley floor. The skipper appointed himself a committee of one to go see the cook.

"Meanwhile, crew and guests piled in to clear up the wreckage in the galley, and the skipper, with the aid of a little of the best scotch, got the cook to sign a peace treaty and return to the range. By this time, all hands had a nip with the cook. Soon, breakfast was apace once more.

"The eggs sputtered and the bacon sizzled and the coffee pots again beat out their tattoo of 'Good Morning'. The cook smiled and plied his art; he now knew that yachtsmen weren't too bad a lot, just crazy!

"Back in the wheelhouse, we chatted and waited for yacht number two. Within the hour, she showed on the crest of a big swell. Once again it was action stations: someone to check sail numbers; someone to record approximate time of rounding; and someone to check entries to put a name to a vessel. All was ready, and in the light of the rising sun, we recorded the second boat to round. The photographers

shouted, 'Follow her. Follow her.' By the instinct that besets all sailors to follow a command, he followed the second yacht.

"To say that hell once again broke loose is to understate the case. The chef, bless his heart, was apoplectic. His remarks to the skipper, the crew, and the bloody guests left nothing to be desired. He truly covered all aspects of amateur sailing and amateur captains.

"There was nothing left for us to do but salvage what could be eaten and make fresh coffee. The race went on. The cook survived. And Swiftsure smiled. Swell breakfast!

"A postscript to the story was a remarkable picture of that first yacht, taken by dawn's first light. By chance, the Lightship beacon flashed as the shutter clicked. The image of that ghostly ship in the mysterious glimmer of early dawn with the cutting ray of the beacon will always remain in my library and in my memories of the legends of Swiftsure."

(See inside back cover)

SKIPPER HARLEY BLAGBORNE OF SUDBURY I (LEFT) AND UNIDENTIFIED OBSERVER / SIB DOW

21/ *1960 and Consistent Kate*

Consistent *Kate II* came through in 1960 for overall honours, as *Maruffa* once again led the fleet home.

Very light airs on Saturday, May 28 marked the 9 a.m. start. Even so, the lead group reached Race Passage before 11 a.m., including a Seattle Eight Metre, *Wild Goose*, along with the larger *Thetis, Serada, Hawk*, and *Troubadour*. As the wind freshened before noon, another Eight Metre, *Concerto*, with *Maruffa, Tola, Adios* and *Kate II* made it through. However, in the early afternoon, the combination of no wind and adverse tides persuaded many skippers to prudently drop anchor on the northern shore until more favourable conditions developed.

A whisper of wind at 4 p.m. which grew to 10 knots of breeze aided the leaders: Bob Smith's *We're Here* on the Canadian shore; *Thetis* on the U.S. shore followed by *Kate II* and *Stormy Weather*. As so often happens during the night, the ground swells combined with calm to create a slop, which didn't prevent Otis Lamson's 51 foot sloop *Sea Fever* from ghosting up into striking position for first around the mark at 8:12 a.m., Sunday. Jack Balmer's Eight Metre *Fulmar* came next at 8:30, followed by *Hawk* at 8:40, *Wild Goose* at 8:45, *Diamond Head* at 8:48. Then within the half hour, *Mary Bower, Adios, Concerto, Thetis, Troubadour*, and *Serada* formed a procession, leaving *Maruffa* to round 14th and *Kate II* 21st.

Still patchy, winds hauled to the south, increasing to 15 knots. *Concerto, Troubadour*, and *Mary Bower*, had found a favourable tide on the south shore, while *Thetis* and *Spirit* led the group on the north side.

Meanwhile, David Skinner went his own way, on a reach which would be maintained to the finish line as *Troubadour, Concerto* and *Maruffa* worked their way across the Strait to join him on the northern shore. By the time they reached Race Passage, *Kate II* was hot on the heels of the lead yachts. The winds again lightened around Race Rocks, but *Maruffa* had assumed an unassailable lead to cross the line at 7:18 p.m. as the freighters berthed in the harbour joined in the crowd's general salute. A 26 foot yacht, among the smallest to ever enter Swiftsure, topped BB Class: Hunter Vogel's 26 foot *Aida*.

Today, 20 years later and retired from active competition, *Kate II* symbolizes a whole generation of capable boats rendered obsolete through rating evolution. Like many another hot contender, she evolved under the auspices of the Seaborn/Blanchard team.

In 1946, Seattle Yacht Club's Keith Fisken commissioned the Blanchard yard to build him a 45 foot family racer cruiser. The boat was to incorporate all the speed and sailing ability of *Tola* and *We're Here*, but with more freeboard and accommodation. Fisken had saved teak and mahogany during the war, which was well seasoned by the time she was built, while Ben Seaborn drew up the plans. Built of red cedar planking, copper fastened on oak frames, she was constructed using the latest wedge seam and glue methods. The wedge seam process was only used above the water line, the underbody being very lightly caulked. The integrity of the builders and success of the system together with the quality of materials used, is amply upheld by her racing record, and by the remarkable condition that we find her in today, 33 years after her launching.

When David Skinner bought her in the Fifties, he renamed her *Kate II*. On that day, her new career began, as under the hand of her new skipper, she methodically began to enter SYC events. The basic program was to learn all there was to learn about the boat, make improvements in the rig and trim, and train a steady crew. Most important, Skinner concentrated all his energies on Swiftsure; every addition or modification was done with an eye to winning it. He had his consistent crew. Not sailing champions, but all good friends to whom sailing was a hobby, not a vocation.

By spring of 1955, *Kate II* was ready for her first Swiftsure, and right away, the preparation paid off with a second in A Class, and fourth overall. Not a bad start for a new contender. For the next five years, the crew stuck together, learning from their mistakes, while *Kate II* became known as consistent *Kate*. (One such mistake was the year when, while nearing the mark, Skinner relied on following *Diamond Head*, which had radar. What they didn't know was that the radar wasn't working, so they headed out to sea!) Five time winner in A Class, *Kate II* was fourth in 1956, fifth in 1957, third in 1958, seventh in 1959, and in 1960, she won it all.

Observers considered *Kate II* a practical, seaworthy, sensible yacht with no frills attached. She was always sailed to the limit, but never over the limit. Year after year, *Kate* would establish her position among the leaders by simple good seamanship. Skinner had learned early that nothing is gained, and often, much lost, by over canvassing in a 40 mile westerly. Time and again, *Kate II* sailed into the winner's circle while achieving maximum hull speed under a winged out jib, while her rivals, carrying every stitch they could hoist, carried away spars and spinnakers in repeated broaches.

Skinner thinks that "the longest nine miles in sailing in the Pacific Northwest is the distance between Race Rocks and the finish line." His secret weapon to negotiate that and other obstacles was organization. Every preparation had been made, every equipment change had been tested under "at sea" conditions, every meal prepared in advance, and every man in the seven man crew knew his job. They were divided into two watches; three hours on, and three hours off. If conditions warranted, the watches were cut to two-hours, three men on with the skipper floating on either watch. As with all small craft, it was "all hands on deck" for sail changes in heavy weather. Skinner kept a complete log (in capsule form) of all previous races, making a conscious effort to benefit by previous results.

From 1960 onward, the new glass boats and computerized designs began to assert their superiority. Consistent *Kate's* results slid relentlessly back. Time and IOR had taken its toll, and by 1971, *Kate II* had come full circle, once again a handsome, capable, family cruiser. This honest, well conceived yacht wove a memorable pattern of courses made good, and her memory will long live in the minds of those who sailed her to victory against the best that the Northwest could field.

KATE II / JAMES McVIE

69

Laurent Giles' *Myth of Malham*, the first modern light displacement yacht, made her appearance in 1947. She won the 12th Fastnet Race, while registering two other firsts and one second in 3,000 miles of ocean racing in major events that year. This straight sheered, 37 foot 6 inch radical design departure with a bulb keel and high topsides was the prototype for the yachts of the Fifties and Sixties.

Although Giles drew her lines, *Myth* was designed to the specifications of her owner, Captain J. Illingworth R.N., Commodore of both the Royal Ocean Racing Club and the Royal Naval Sailing Association. Illingworth had won his first ocean race in Singapore in 1928. After the 1946 Sydney - Hobart Race, his thinking was that light displacement yachts do not need overhangs. Further, that this would be achieved not by lopping off each end, but rather, by pulling out the waterline. While in Malta in the 1920s, he had actually constructed one such design: converting a 36 foot naval pinnace by adding outside ballast and a deck and cabin.

Paralleling recovery from the Second World War, new developments in materials and building methods allowed California's trend-setting yacht designers, George Kettenberg and Bill Lapworth, to catch the crest of the new design wave and ride it to spectacular success. Both were leaders in designing boats to take advantage of the existing CCA rules. Essentially, this had to do with how much freeboard could be pushed to windward with a small sail area.

A former International 14 sailor, Lapworth influenced world yacht design by popularizing the light displacement trend on the west coast, taking the sailing dinghy hull and applying it to larger yachts.

In this respect, design had come full circle from the 1896 article in *Rudder* magazine on light displacement, by Perry. The dinghy form for larger boats had been tried and abandoned in 1910 because of structural problems encountered when building in wood.

Lapworth's timing was perfect. The advent of new materials, new glues and construction techniques, especially the use of fibreglass for hulls, made the dinghy form not only feasible, but economically profitable for larger boats.

Cheap California labour (often Mexican) working outside in the natural heat of the warm California sun, catapulted the production yacht into a different order of magnitude, in terms of numbers. They came rolling out in waves. Since hull design had departed from ''wineglass'' shapes, due to the light displacement design, fibreglass molding was far less expensive, since the keel, in the majority of the early models, was a cast iron fin added to the completed hull in a separate operation.

Was it the luck of the draw or coincidence that brought a winning skipper and crew together with a winning design in 1957? Ches Rickard built his first *Winsome* in 1946, a 20 foot gaff rigger. One of Vancouver's top Star helmsmen and Six Metre owner, Rickard was casting about for a boat in which he could comfortably cruise as well as race. From Stan Davies, he heard about the impressive racing results of the Lapworth 36 being built in Costa Mesa by Chapman and Kalayjian.

Very good on any point of sail, the L36 was the first of the modern boats. Later, her big sister the Cal 40 was the evolutionary development produced in response to the urging of L36 owners. Fatter and higher sided than contemporary designs, the L36 tended to be a little trickier to sail, with some tendency to broach if the helmsman wasn't careful. She had a comparatively long keel with the rudder attached to the keel, rather than a separate spade rudder.

At the same time, another airline pilot and Star skipper, Pat Leslie, had the plans and even some of the wood for a Seafair. He was persuaded to abandon this project, joining with Rickard and Bill Moore to build simultaneously the first three L36s in Canada: red-hulled *Tricia*, green-hulled *Winsome III* (all Rickard's boats have had green hulls) and Moore's *Nutmeg*.

Because the plans had been brought out for Lapworth's California builder, Chapman, details had to be worked out with the Americans so that Taylor's Vancouver Boatworks could begin construction. The three bought their materials collectively, with Rickard and Leslie doing much of the building themselves at the boatyard, along with the workmen, even to pouring their own lead keels. (Moore's boat was completely built by Taylor.)

Mahogany strip planked, edge nailed and glued, the boats were built over a jig, with no ribs. The jigs were torn out, leaving the bare hull inside. Then, the ribs were bent in on the inside. Built at home, the masts were glued box section spruce, as were the boom and spinnaker pole. At first, they used English sails; later, all genoas were made by Vancouver's Miller Brothers. In 1958, the three boats were launched together over a two day period. They were in the water and sailing for approximately $9,500 each.

In 1961, *Winsome III* swept every major trophy in her class during the July PIYA Regatta, including the long distance race, to take Outstanding Boat honours once again. However, regular skipper and owner, Ches Rickard, a senior Air Canada pilot, was in Eastern Canada taking a DC8 course.

At the helm during that summer of triumph was crack small boat sailor, Bonar Davis. Sailing his third Swiftsure in an L36, Davis showed the yachting world that Vancouver sailors had depth as well as excellence. Davis had crewed for Pat Leslie in 1959 when *Tricia*, the first L36 to enter Swiftsure, netted a third overall in a 39 boat fleet for her maiden effort. Leslie improved his position to second overall the next year, establishing a "bridesmaid" pattern which was to persist, compiling over the years probably the most consistent overall performance of any Canadian yacht. In that same year, 1960, Davis accompanied Rickard in *Winsome's* Swiftsure debut: 14th overall in a 45 boat fleet. The three back-to-back victories were no accident of fate, however, as Rickard was already one of the most successful racing skippers in British Columbia.

Bonar states, "The thing that really did the job for Ches during those years was that we always kept the boats going at night. Many boats, when it gets dark, don't have the feel for keeping them going in the right direction at maximum speed. I think that's where, if any place, that we've always seemed to be able to do a little better than some. Today, with Brookes and Gatehouse and other equipment, more people can sail their boats faster at night. But I think 25 years ago, without that equipment, it was more difficult."

Being an airline pilot, Rickard was also a crack navigator, although none of his boats had any instrumentation other than a knot meter and a depth sounder, RDF, and hand bearing compass. There weren't many navigational things around 20 years ago. Ches did most of the navigation when he was on board. What usually happened at night was that Rickard would do the navigation and Bonar would sail until they at least knew where the mark was. Then Davis would turn in for some rest while Rickard took the helm.

For Swiftsure racing, carrying six, skipper Rickard set no watches. They just drove her hard, reasoning that Swiftsure was rather like running the mile. There is no time to really rest. While it is not quite a sprint, neither is it a marathon race. The main thing was to keep everybody rested, although the crew never even took sleeping bags along. Davis and Rickard alternated on the helm, giving each a chance to look around and get fresh input, plan strategy, and check wind conditions. When navigating, Rickard didn't keep a plot unless there was a problem like fog or drizzle. He relied instead on RDF to find the way, using the three available stations. They were always very happy to see the Lightship, thus confirming their hard night's work.

Ches Rickard considers that the calibre of sailing is very much better today, with so many good sailors and good boats. Now, with 75 per cent of the entries competitive, he reckons that you have to have good luck and capitalize on your breaks, recovering from the bad ones as quickly as possible. In earlier races, you could write off 80 per cent of the fleet, particularly if it got foggy. Not so today.

Along with Ches and Bonar, regular crew during these years included Victoria's Gordie Inglis and Maple Bay's Vic Palmer, with Bob Lance and Rob Maddison from the mainland.

WINSOME III CREW: GORDIE INGLIS, BONAR DAVIS, CHES RICKARD, RAY DELAPLACE / JAMES McVIE

23/ Double Cross — the 1961 Race
Troubadour and the Suckling Pig!

By 1961, the colourful prerace show set in the Inner Harbour's natural stone amphitheatre was anticipated almost as eagerly as the race itself. Ships dressed in vivid signal flags, Humphrey Golby's Swiftsure Roll Call, the Meistersingers' Sea Chanties from the Black Ball wharf, HMCS Naden Band on the Legislative lawn with their Sunset Ceremony, and Jim McVie's slide show lent overtones of Mardi Gras in miniature, while extra mooring buoys accommodated the record 61 entry fleet.

Prerace pundits were touting the 80 foot ketch *Tatoosh* as a threat to *Maruffa*, which had made Swiftsure her private domain in recent years. *Tatoosh*, a Seaborn design two years in the building, belonged to C.P. Paschall, an *Adios* crew veteran.

Swiftsure 1961 start was delayed, with the time set back to 11 a.m., to give the yachts, especially the smaller craft, the advantage of a minimum tide change. Strong winds to 25 knots prevailed, sending 62 yachts off on the last authentic ''Lightship'' Race. These winds held for most of the afternoon, which gave consistent groupings, rather than boats being strung out like beads on a string all over the Strait.

Soon after the gun, *Maruffa* and *Diamond Head* squared off in a match which lasted for most of the race, with *Adios* joining them at Race Rocks early in the afternoon. By late afternoon, with the winds still holding at 20, *Oriole* led the yachts on the Washington shore: *Courageous, Diamond Head, Coral Reef, Mara, Tatoosh, Gabrielle II, Sea Fever, Dorade, Nautilus IV, Buccaneer,* and *Kate II.*

At 5:30, when the ebb started, *Adios* was off Pillar Point, as *Diamond Head* abandoned the south shore and headed over to the Canadian side, where *Maruffa* held the lead. Two more yachts criss-crossed as *Dorade* veered south and *Oriole* north. As the sun slid low on the horizon around 9 p.m., the breeze died, and *Oriole* wallowed on the Canadian side while *Concerto, Spirit,* and *Circe* held down mid-channel positions as another group turned south to take advantage of the stronger ebb on the U.S. shore. This latter group included *Maruffa, Dorade, Diamond Head* and *Adios*, which joined *Gabrielle II, Dahut, Jester, Mary Bower, Courageous, Tricia, Thetis, Bucaneer III, Hawk, Coral Reef, Winsome III,* and *Kate II.*

As light dawned, a very rare situation arose. Because the winds had shifted from westerly to northeast, the last leg into the ocean for the hitch around the *Lightship* was a spinnaker run rather than a beat. *Diamond Head* rounded first, with *Adios, Sulaire* and *Maruffa* following in quick succession. By 11 a.m., all but two were on the return journey: *Alcion* and *Accomplice.* Still the light, flukey northeast winds held, giving a beat back rather than the usual run. *Adios* still led *Diamond Head* in those early return stages, with *Mary Bower* ahead of *Kate II.* On the American shore, *Troubadour, Sea Fever, Sulaire, Maradea, Gabrielle II* and *Tricia* led the pack, while *Maruffa, Dorade, Spirit* and *Tatoosh* split for the Canadian shore. After lunch, the three divisions were led by *Dorade* and *Maruffa* on the north, *Tatoosh* and *Boundless* mid-Strait, and *Adios* and *Diamond Head* on the south.

Mid-afternoon, *Adios, Diamond Head* and *Troubadour* were still leading on the American shore. *Adios* crossed over to keep an eye on *Maruffa*, but chose to remain in mid-channel. By now, it was late afternoon. The wind was again dying, swinging around once more to the northwest, allowing spinnakers to be carried. Through Race Passage, half the fleet was closely grouped, but rapidly running out of wind against the ebb.

Troubadour, Phil Graham's 65 foot yawl, crossed the finish line shortly after 9:30 p.m., followed four minutes later by *Diamond Head* and *Adios*, which finished within a minute of one another. Big boats parading across the line continued with *Kate II, Mary Bower, Sea Fever, Maruffa,* and *Dorade.*

Of the 1961 race, overall winning skipper Bonar Davis recalls: ''We hadn't done awfully well going out. I remember rounding the Lightship, in around 17th place, at 5 or 6 a.m. On the beat back, we could see boats ahead all making for the American shore. There was no sense in following them, because there's no way we'd beat them doing that. So we headed for the Canadian shore. Got over there and realized that was a mistake. So we went back to the American shore. The boats that had been ahead of us had all gone to the Canadian shore so we thought that was super, and stayed on the American shore. That was really what won the race for us. The west wind filled in, and we were able to reach across and left the boats behind that had been ahead of us, originally on the American shore.''

When the corrected times were finalized, *Winsome III* won over her sister ship *Maradea* by one minute. *Thetis* finished four minutes back, with *Heidi* nine minutes behind. *Jay Jay* made the best finish for a Victoria yacht, with a first in B Class and fifth overall.

1961 was a typical enough Swiftsure: shifting winds on the Saturday, the luck of the draw during the long rolling night, and then the wonder of bright skies and the Sunday morning ride for home as the westerly built up all day long. By late afternoon, gusts were in the 35-40 miles per hour range, rolling over the land from Race Rocks in to the finish.

At this point, *Troubadour* was hell-hoopin' for the line, leading the pack. Everything that could fly was driving her long, slim, metre style hull to the limit. As we rushed along behind her, we wondered how long she could go without broaching. Mizzen staysail and spinnaker still set and the wind creeping more and more abeam with each gust rolling her decks under, her quarter wave was immense. No powered craft ever boasted a nobler entry as she plunged on.

The next moment, a super gust hit, literally driving *Troubadour* under. We could see the crew standing waist deep along the leeward rail, but the helmsman kept her on course as slowly she came up, shaking the water out of her sails like a great angry hen. Moments later, she almost repeated the performance, but the drive to be first boat home sustained all hands. *Troubadour* responded with all the breeding inherent in her traditional design. The finish was now at hand. With wild shouts of victory, *Troubadour* ended her long drought. Skipper Phil Graham and the Royal Vancouver Yacht Club could well be proud. The sails came down and *Troubadour* slipped proudly down the harbour to take up her place of honour at the docks as first to finish.

Then it happened. Decks now cleared, lines coiled down, the stage was set for the hatch to slide back. Out of the depths emerged the ship's Chinese master chef in full gleaming white, his chef's hat at a jaunty angle. There on a shining silver platter reposed a steaming hot suckling pig! Even the apple in its mouth could not conceal the glorious smile.

TROUBADOUR / JAMES McVIE

HER FINEST HOUR

24/ The Scandinavian Imports

Scandinavian boats streamed steadily into British Columbia during the Fifties: Dragons, Six Metres, Spitzgatters, and larger yachts.

In the vanguard of this trend, importing three Swedish yachts was Vancouver consulting engineer P.R. Sandwell, whose business frequently took him to Scandinavia just after World War Two. The first of the series, he obtained through her designer, Knud Reimers: a double-ended Tumlarin called *Annalisa*, which placed third in 1964's Juan de Fuca Race, skippered by Larry Pardey.

Several years later, Sandwell brought out another beauty with a gleaming varnished hull, the *Onna*, which was subsequently raced in three Swiftsures by Victoria's Louis Lindholm.

A different order of magnitude was the graceful *Gabrielle II*, which was to race in 10 consecutive Swiftsures, from 1960 through 1970. Five years on Reimer's drawing board, the 48 foot *Gabrielle* and her sister ship *Sirocco*, were an attempt to copy the famous pre-war *Maid of Malham*, which had deliberately been designed to fit between two ocean racing categories, so that she could qualify for either. It was intended that they should be a one design class, known as the Twelve Ton One Design Class. Built in Stockholm in 1947 for a lesser Swedish nobleman, Reimer later bought *Gabrielle* back from the estate for his own use in 1953.

Sandwell was again a trendsetter in the late Sixties, among the first Western yachtsmen to tackle the international ocean racing circuits.

With his *Gabrielle III*, built in McGruer's yard in 1967, Sandwell competed in the 1969 Admiral's Cup and Fastnet, the Sidney-Hobart, Scandinavian Gotland and Skaw Races, and the Plymouth LaRochelle Race.

However, of all the Scandinavian imports, the Spitzgatters have proved to be the most durable Swiftsure competitors, with *Lotte* still appearing in PHRF sailed by Canadian Forces Sailing Association's Ed Haines.

Very few hull lines flare and flow so pleasingly as the double ended Viking Ship. This classic shape was developed into various sized yachts and widely popularized as a very practical family boat for Baltic conditions by Danish Naval Architect, Aage Utzon (whose son designed the controversial Sydney Australia Concert Hall, which somewhat resembles the billowing sails of a ship.)

Dragon sailor and friend of Utzon's, Jorgen Baess, was instrumental in importing five of the sturdy double ended 38 square metre Spitzgatters in the Fifties. They made quite an impact locally, in the hands of some of the area's most avid sailing families.

First came *Skoal* to Victoria's Max Young, followed by Hunter Vogel's *Aida*; A.B. Sanderson had *Eio*; Peter Coombs, *Doxy*; Vancouver's Reid Townley, *Flirt*; and Jorgen Baess, the *Lotte*.

Most Spitzgatters of the 38 square metre size were pre-war, with the exception of wartime *Lotte*. Professionally constructed, they had oak frames with larch planking. Characterized by a very high aspect ratio ¾ rig, originally with no spreaders, the strong one piece mast was usually fir. Consequently, these 26 footers were fairly beamy and stiff, being well ballasted.

In retrospect, Peter Young considers *Skoal* "one of the most fantastic boats we ever had. An extremely powerful boat. We never used the working jib and seldom reefed the mainsail; just drove her hard and ragged the main."

Among *Aida's* collection of honours were two Lipton Cup wins, in the heyday of the Cowichan, Maple Bay, and PIYA Regatta years which immediately followed World War II.

Aida first tackled the Swiftsure course, having no other alternative, in 1960, placing 32nd overall, and first among the four category B yachts. In 1961, conditions favoured smaller yachts, and *Aida* upped her standing to 14th overall, while sistership *Eio*, skippered by Ned Ashe, placed 17th.

Aida had to be favoured for her only Juan de Fuca race, in 1963, when her competition included four Herreshoff 28s in the eight boat fleet. By this time, Vogel had moved from Victoria to Vancouver, so Vancouver again retained Juan de Fuca honours.

Hunter Vogel built boats, including the first Sparkman-

Stephens designed Lightning in B.C., in 1945. His shop, a large shed located just down the road from the original Maple Bay Yacht Club, was later acquired by the Mainguy Sea Scouts for their hall. There, he turned out a succession of smaller boats, including many Lightnings, and the Sailorettes, each named for a bird of a different colour. They are still raced as a one design fleet and on handicap at CFSA Esquimalt, their original home when it was known as the Royal Canadian Naval Sailing Association (Humphrey Golby was the middleman in this transaction).

EIO / SIB DOW

26 FOOT SPITZGATTER

The Juan de Fuca Race —
"Little SWIFTSURE"

The Swiftsure Committee created the Juan de Fuca Race in 1962, for those CCA category C yachts rating between 19 and 21.9. Run concurrently with the longer race, the "Little Swiftsure" goes half the distance, rounding a mark set in Clallam Bay, west of Port Angeles, on the south shore of Juan de Fuca Strait. This gives the advantage of a long distance race with an outward beat in sight of the larger boats, but avoids the open ocean and the frustrations of the long haul, with perhaps too little or too much wind. Admirably suited to the capabilities of the smaller boats, it allows them to finish within a reasonable time limit (important to the race committee, who also have schedules and deadlines to meet).

Although few probably realized it at the time, the stage was set for a separate shorter course when three B category yachts appeared in 1952. These were the 34 foot Roedde Class sloops from the Royal Vancouver Yacht Club, *Hymac*, *Elusive* and *Tomboy*.

Elusive, first entered Swiftsure in 1949, but failed to finish, managing a fifth overall in 1953's 21 boat fleet, and second overall in 1954. However, the CCA handicapping system, which had acknowledged limitations, was further stretched in 1960, when the 26 foot Spitzgatter *Aida* jousted for position on the same start line as the 90 foot *Oriole*.

But this Little Swiftsure was not merely a scaled down version for yachts of scaled down dimensions. From the start, the Juan de Fuca, flavoured by a different frame of reference than had existed in the Thirties, had its own personality. Leaving the experts and hot shots in their finely tuned racing machines to head for Swiftsure Bank, more than one husband and wife teamed up to race a beloved family cruising boat, often joined by their older teenagers to round out their crew.

While Seattle yachts had dominated the first three decades, partly through sheer volume of numbers, Juan de Fuca's Canadian identity was evident from the beginning. This continued through the transition years of the mid-Sixties, when people with wooden boats or no boats were casting about for updated designs in the new fibreglass medium.

During this period, when Victoria and Vancouver designers and builders vied with one another for a share of the burgeoning production boat market, the Juan de Fuca Race often became a proving ground for a yacht's racing merits. Al Nairne's Calgan Marine in North Vancouver built the Lapworth designed Cal 20, 25, and 28. Victoria's Ray Richards designed the Haida 26. Derek Cove's Gulf Island 29 was produced in Vancouver, as was John Brandlmayr's Spencer 35.

Unlike many who dip into the boat business as a sideline to their main occupation, Brandlmayr's success has endured. The Richmond, B.C. plant building Spencer Boats simultaneously built a reputation for high quality glass and wood workmanship combined with competitive designs in the middle range of yachts.

John Brandlmayr's interest in design started in his Saskatchewan boyhood years, when he designed and built a boat to sail on the river, while also dabbling in gliders and aircraft. After obtaining his mechanical engineering degree, John relocated in Vancouver, where he ran into a friend from Saskatoon, Phil Haltse. Together, they incorporated Spencer Boats in 1952. A sideline to John's engineering profession, the new firm employed his wife Pat, part-time, in various managerial aspects.

At first, the new company put out frame kits for power boats in the 14 to 34 foot range. They sold hundreds. Towards the end of the decade, Spencer Boats diversified into sail, moulding seven Spencer 28 hulls.

The Spencer 35, however, established the firm's reputation. *Coho*, the first of over 30, was built in 1962. This name became a Spencer trademark, and was transferred through three subsequent models, each a stock fibreglass yacht designed by John and produced by Spencer Boats. Other Spencer 35s are Hal Roth's *Whisper*, of ocean cruising fame, and Theo de la Mare's *Tandem II*, first to finish Juan de Fuca 1966.

The inaugural Juan de Fuca Race in 1962 had four entries, all Canadian. Three were from West Vancouver Yacht Club, including the winner, Al Cutler's *Celtic Childe*. The 26 foot sloop was a Fleur Blue Class, built in

Japan. Her two sister ships went to San Francisco, but they never caught on locally. *Celtic Childe* won the first San Juan Trophy. Al Cutler, skipper, had as crew, Tom Eckford, Ted Martin, and Dick Kyle.

Jack Pinch's second place *Panacea* and Dusty Miller's sloop-rigged *Arriba,* which failed to finish, were Herreshoff 28s. This was a family cruising boat from Francis Herreshoff's *Common Sense Yachts,* designed as a ketch, but usually raced as a sloop. Third overall was the stout little Vertue, *Kukri,* from the Royal Victoria Yacht Club.

No one would ever pretend that *Kukri* was agile, or a potential winner. Weighing in at around 13,000 pounds, roughly the same weight as a Lapworth 36, the 25 foot 3 inch Vertue earned British architect Laurent Giles the reputation of one of the world's foremost yacht designers.

Resembling a small Bristol Channel pilot cutter, the Vertue was probably the smallest sailboat which could comfortably cross an ocean. Small wonder that over the years, the Vertue was sought by serious ocean going adventurers for just that purpose. (Eric Hiscocks's *Wanderer III* was designed along those lines.)

To this date, about 160 have been built, roughly half at either of two English shipyards, or Hong Kong's Cheoy Lee. Each one is numbered, and the *Kukri* is #75. Betraying her original British Colonial background, she is named for a Gurka Indian knife. H.L. Lyne acquired her from a gentleman farmer, a retired English army officer, who kept her in the Bewley River. Before arriving at Victoria's Ogden Point as a freighter's deck cargo, *Kukri* had sailed the Mediterranean and near Eastern waters.

In the two races, *Kukri* upheld the best British traditions of a spunky wife accompanying her seagoing husband (pioneered so courageously by Beryl Smeeton and Susan Hiscock). H.L. Lyne's crew on that first race included his wife as cook, and fellow expatriates Tony and Audrey Emery as crew. Though conditions were generally foggy with little wind, the foursome had a lot of fun.

In the 1962 race, confusion came at the Clallam Bay marker, which was very difficult to locate, being only a small dinghy with a light in the middle, says Mrs. Lyne, "uncomfortably close to the shore". (Such was the informality of the day.) By contrast, 1963's marker ship was "lit up like a Christmas tree".

In 1963, it was again a happy ship of transplanted Britishers, with Alex James and Monica Coombs joining the Lynes. Monica went along because her husband Peter was involved in the long race. An experience which stood him in good stead for the Juan de Fuca wins he recorded in 1966 and 1970 in *Doxy II*.

Designed in 1961, the first California 20 entered the Juan de Fuca Race in 1964. Typical of Lapworth's Cal series, with a long (18 foot) waterline and ballasted with 900 pounds of iron fin keel, the boat was beamy, stiff, and tough. World design for smaller yachts was influenced by the California 20 concept.

Prior to that date, no self-respecting architect would have hung a rudder on a stern. Outboard rudders were strictly for cruisers or clunkers. The Cal 20 ushered in a whole new era of short stem racing boats.

The British Columbia market was supplied by North Vancouver's Calgan Marine, and builder Al Nairne's *Heather* placed a respectable mid-fleet in 1964. Cal 20s claim the distinction as the smallest yachts to enter Juan de Fuca.

Cal 20 owners followed the Thunderbird lead, quickly establishing a network of fleets from San Diego to Vancouver to promote strictly controlled one design racing. Touted as the ultimate in an easily handled cruiser racer for a man and wife, the Cal 20 combined the zip and responsiveness of a dinghy with the potential to win races on an overall handicap. In Victoria, highly respected Max Young again sniffed a winning design, and joined the keenly competitive around the buoys racing.

Indeed, George Dufour's *Galenaia* in 1965 launched what surely stands as a husband-wife record. For 13 consecutive races (the last in a Columbia 26), wife Pat accompanied George on 12. Identified by one of the first spinnakers built in full technicolour, (for heavy airs, a yellow fleur de lys on blue, honouring George's Channel Island ancestry and a Tudor Rose for light airs), the Dufours always finished their race, no matter how rough the going had been, proving that a 20 foot boat could take the best, and worst that the Strait could hurl at them.

For Pat Dufour, however, an extra special stamina was required. For her, the race was never over when their yacht crossed the finish line. As waterfront reporter for the Victoria Times, her race weekend finished when she filed a first hand account of the action.

HUMPHREY GOLBY BROADCASTING RACE FROM ISLAND CHALLENGER / SIB DOW

The navy supplied two of Friday evening's 1962 prerace highlights. The *HMCS Oriole's* majestic entry into Victoria Harbor, gliding in with the yards fully manned with cadets who completed their performance by sliding down the backstay, was complemented by the 50 man honour guard at the Sunset Ceremony, which included 40 men in two gun crews.

It was *Winsome III* again in 1962, but this time, Ches Rickard was available to pilot his Lapworth 36 to the *Swiftsure Trophy* for the second consecutive year.

Under an overcast sky, a slow start at 9:30 Saturday morning sent 65 yachts across the line, led by Gary Horder's *Dandelion*, with C.A. Newell's *Heidi* ahead of *Zingara*, *Maruffa*, and *Troubadour*, early leaders on the way to Race Rocks. Almost predictably, *Maruffa* pulled ahead, and by noon was leading *Troubadour*, *Coral Reef*, *Zingara*, *Adios*, *Mary Bower*, *Serada*, *Coho*, *Diamond Head*, and *Courageous*, all mid-Strait or en route to the U.S. shore. Electing the Canadian shore were *Sea Fever*, *Sulaire*, *Velaris*, *Boundless*, *Mara*, *Hawk*, and *Ladero*.

By mid-afternoon, the skies had cleared, and a benevolent sun and 10 knot wind caressed the fleet in its three bunched sections. *We're Here*, *Circe*, *Thetis*, and *Dahut* held to mid-Strait. On the north shore, *Maruffa* preceded *Hawk*, *Oceanus*, *Ladero*, *Sulaire*, *Velaris*, and *Diamond Head*, while *Mara* led on the south shore, followed by *Adios*, *Stormy Weather*, and *Troubadour*.

Then once again, dusk embraced overcast skies, coupled by a light rain which misted the fleet, compounding the problems this year. There was no familiar *Lightship* to zero in on. Instead, a fibreglass buoy topped with a yellow flag and a fixed white light marked the shoal, supplemented by the Coast Guard cutter *Yocono*, stationed as a visual aid and radio beacon.

First around the new on-station marker was *Adios* just before 2 a.m., followed by *Maruffa* at 2:15, then *Courageous*, *Mary Bower*, *Kate II*, and *Diamond Head* in the next hour. Daylight produced very light winds, overcast sky and drizzle with barely enough wind to fill the spinnakers of the returning yachts. By mid-morning, *Maruffa* was

fast closing *Adios*, as they both outran the pack including *Dandelion*, *Velaris*, *Sulaire*, *Mary Bower*, *Sea Fever*, *Kate II*, *Courageous*, and *Diamond Head* along the American shore. The most exciting action was the duel between the two American super-yachts, *Maruffa* and *Adios*, the Graham yawl finally taking the lead at mid-day as the wind increased to 28 knots. The wind still built, gusting to 40 knots, with the inevitable results that spinnakers and other sails began blowing out all across the Strait.

Maruffa and *Adios* continued their match race-within-the-race, with *Maruffa* increasing her lead, to finish first. *Winsome III* drove hard during the stretch run to capture the *Swiftsure Trophy*, edging *Kate II* by three minutes. It had been a great race: titanic battles for the lead in winds to 40 knots, with the final hours featuring an almost endless string of brilliant spinnakers hurtling in from Race Rocks to the finish line. As a fitting tribute to the finale, the *RCAF Golden Hawks* stunt team entertained those among the 30,000 spectators lining the waterfront who could lift their gaze from the colourful yachts to the *Golden Jets* high above the line.

This year marked the first Juan de Fuca Race for the smaller yachts, won by Al Cutler's *Celtic Childe*.

ORIOLE DURING CADET TRAINING EXERCISES / DEPARTMENT OF NATIONAL DEFENCE.

A DIAMOND IN THE SUN / SIB DOW

27/ *1963 — Three for Winsome III*

Again in 1963, carnival atmosphere prevailed on the Friday evening as the mark ship *HMCS Jonquiere* illuminated the Inner Harbour and the square dancing exhibition on the Empress Hotel lawns, setting the stage for the weekend contest.

At the beginning, a windless start combined with a strong flood tide to set many boats away from the line in one of the slowest Swiftsure starts ever recorded, a significant factor which spawned one of the most celebrated protests ever filed in Pacific Northwest yacht racing. The declared winner, *Thetis*, was protested by Lol Killam's *Velaris* during the very early drifting. Although it was over a year before the protest was upheld, ultimately, *Winsome III* emerged victorious to set a Swiftsure record which may never again be equalled: three consecutive back-to-back victories. Corinthian Yacht Club's Boat of the Year, Bob Regan's *Thetis*, relinquished the title in one of Swiftsure's hard luck stories.

It was over three hours before the last of the 67 yachts had cleared the line. *Oriole*, *Tatoosh*, and *Dorade* were among 15 to hook into the bottom to avoid being swept backward. The first group to cross the line included *Ladero*, *Courageous*, *Winsome III*, *Nyon*, *Sulaire*, *Nimbus*, and *Fulmar*. Then the drifting began in earnest. *Kate II* paired with *Thetis*, out in front of *Velaris*, *Jandy* and *Winsome III* while *Nimbus* led *Sulaire* and *Courageous* and *Ladero* spun off on her own.

By dusk, steady winds of 15 gusting to 20 prevailed. The usual split fleet found the Canadian shore leaders *Sulaire*, *Courageous*, and *Kialoa* ahead of *Winsome III*, *Nyon*, *Benora II*, and *Maradea*, although *Kialoa* and *Courageous* later split to the southern shore. As darkness fell, Bill Whipple had worked *Ladero* into a good position for overall win, sailing in company of *Sea Fever*, *Diamond Head*, and *Spirit*.

As dawn broke on Swiftsure Bank, a 20 knot westerly whipped seas to a froth of white caps. *Adios*, first around the mark at 5:30, was followed by *Courageous*, *Sulaire*, *Sea Fever*, *Mai Tai*, *Odusa*, *Spirit*, *Fulmar*, *Thetis*, *Cormorant*, *Winsome III*, and *Diamond Head*. At this point,

the hard luck story of the 1963 race occured: *Ladero*, which had sailed a beautiful race, lost her mast a mile from the mark.

The turbulent seas, however, did not discourage the keen skippers from flying their spinnakers as they charged back down the Strait. By 8:30 *Adios*, *Courageous*, *Sea Fever*, and *Sulaire* were battling for the lead. Three hours later, it was still *Adios*, *Sea Fever*, and *Courageous* ahead of *Oceanus*, *Spirit*, *Diamond Head*, *Fulmar*, *Sulaire*, *Odusa*, *Cormorant*, *Mai Tai*, *Kialoa*, and *Mara*.

The wind strengthened again by mid-afternoon. *Adios* cleared Race Passage at 2:45 as the winds reached 35 knots, which accelarated in short order to gusting 40.

Clocking speeds up to 14 knots, this lead group surged down the home stretch. *Adios* crossed at 3:42:48 followed closely by *Sea Fever* with *Courageous*, *Diamond Head*, *Spirit*, and *Sulaire* in hot pursuit as spinnakers blew out in all directions.

At the height of this action, a rain squall struck. The wind died away, and *Courageous* and *Diamond Head* took another hour to cross the finish line. It took a year to let the dust settle after the *Thetis-Velaris* protest, but eventually *Winsome III* was declared the winner with *Odusa* the runner up.

Eight entries contested the second Juan de Fuca Race, with Hunter Vogel's Spitzgatter *Aida* showing the way. After two shots at the long course, *Aida*, with her tough, experienced crew of Vogels, found the shorter course more to her liking, finishing 45 minutes ahead of her nearest competitor.

Second place went to the original Cove 29, prototype of the Gulf Island 29, West Van Naval Architect Derek Cove's *Maia V*, built by Taylor Boatyard.

Once again, home stretch action in the long race had certainly been "Swift" but the outcome, as always, far from "Sure". As an example proving this rule, consider that fate of *Ladero*. At the start, the glassy calm with just the faintest whiff of a northerly left most of the fleet motionless. But for some obscure reason, *Ladero* picked up a puff and gathered steerage way. In moments she was really sailing in her own narrow finger of wind when not a rival was moving. Hard to believe, but *Ladero* sailed in fair north winds until well after noon, and must have been a full 20 miles ahead of the fleet at her best point.

All went well until she hit the incoming westerly off Tatoosh plus a short, steep sea. The pounding was too much, and her mast crumpled to the deck. *Ladero* was one of the early Bill Buchan boats, her mast an experimental laminate. Other newcomers to Swiftsure were the fibreglass versions of Bill Luder's 33 foot Annapolis hulls and Lol Killam's revitalized *Velaris*.

Eric Zahn's *Odusa* was 1963's "Bridesmaid", placing second overall and first in A Class. The trio of sister ships, *Odusa*, Maple Bay's *Cormorant*, and Seattle's *Mai Tai*, solidified a one-two-three sweep of A Class that year, followed by Bill Buchan's fourth place *Mara*.

These three sloops were among the first hulls moulded identically to the classic 1938 Bill Luders yawl which had served the Naval Academy well as its training vessel. This pre-war design enjoyed a brief resurgence as a production sloop built in Bellingham during the early 1960s. The 44 foot hull, with rather low freeboard, long graceful ends and fantail stern, had a fairly short waterline (33 feet), with ends shaped to facilitate increased sailing length at modest angles of heel. Although *Odusa* placed ninth overall in 1965's 72 boat fleet, she was already outdated, and lapsed into obscurity. Very recently, the hull and deck has been reactivated by a Seattle builder.

Involved in that fateful protest, the yacht *Velaris* was another interesting entry. The Alcock family of the Vancouver firm of Alcock, Downing and Wright, were interested in sailing. Before their retirement after the Second World War, they had sailed and raced several yachts in Vancouver waters. When the firm was sold, they moved to Crofton on Vancouver Island, where they started to build their dream yacht as a retirement project. Vancouver's William Halliday designed her. For 16 years, the father and son worked on *Velaris*. They were supreme craftsmen in wood. Both were artists in the manufacture of all the stainless steel fittings, bolts, screws, turnbuckles, winches, etc. which were individually designed and made with a jeweller's care.

Time was of no consideration, and when *Velaris* was finally launched, a shining example of the boatbuilder's art, she had no mast. The chosen spar had been cut and laid out to season for three years. In the meantime, *Velaris* visited up and down the coast under power. Finally, 18 years after the keel was laid, the beautiful stick with a truly piano finish was stepped, and the hand-made turnbuckles set for the first time. English-made Egyptian cotton sails were fitted, making her a most genteel yacht.

The Alcocks never raced her; as a matter of fact, they barely sailed her at all. She was never sailed hard; always the solid mahogany gleamed, and *Velaris* turned all eyes as she passed. When the father died, the son lost all interest in the boat, putting her up for sale. Lol Killam bought her in 1961.

Within weeks of his purchase, Killam entered *Velaris* in her first ever race, the Entrance Island Race across the Gulf to Nanaimo. He borrowed a spinnaker from *Hawk*, soon finding that *Velaris* was the fastest boat in the Royal Van fleet. Halfway across, the gorgeous but untested mast and rig collapsed in a welter of splinters and stainless steel, and once again, *Velaris* was under power. A new aluminum spar was ordered from England, and a new mast head rig designed. A complete set of dacron sails was fitted, transforming *Velaris*, now 25-years-old, into one of the most modern yachts around.

ODUSA / JAMES McVIE

MAI TAI / JAMES McVIE

Prerace Swiftsure was enlivened when five members of the Lions Club Convention staged an impromptu show with a five piece band in the Empress Hotel Lobby with a jug, washboard, accordion, banjo, and guitar.

The next morning, however, was anything but lively. Even the best laid plans of race committees go astray. Saturday's 9:30 a.m. start was delayed for half an hour while a tug and log boom chugged its leisurely way through the starting area. Absence of a steady breeze was to dog the fleet throughout the weekend, along with rain, fog, and the occasional strong breeze.

Although 71 yachts finally crossed the line, the five knot wind was not quite enough to propel them all as far as Race Rocks before the tide change. A new Seattle K50, *Norwester*, assumed an early lead, chased closely by *Tricia, Velaris, Thunder, Oceanus,* and *Sundance*. *Norwester* led a handful of yachts through the race, while *Thetis, Lenore,* and *Tricia* bypassed Race Passage and elected to sail outside Race Rocks on their course for the south shore.

Calm had descended by 1:30. *Norwester* hung powerless in the current. *Tatoosh* played musical rides, three times clearing the race propelled by the slightest breeze, only to be three times swept back by the more powerful currents. *Tricia* and *Hussy's* decision to go outside the Race paid off, as they were among the pre-midnight leaders off Clallam Bay, along with *Thetis, Jandy,* and *Bandit*.

By mid-afternoon the breeze had freshened, although the Canadian shore remained patchy. In mid-Strait, *Jandy, Tricia, Thetis, Bandit, Stella Maris,* and *Astrocyte* scrambled for position.

Dusk came early in 1964. As the wind died, an eerie stillness crept over the Strait; a great fog bank moved in and blanketed the whole area from Neah Bay to the mark. Visibility was soon down to ¼ mile, and many boats dropped out to begin the all night journey home under power. The slow slogging continued through late Sunday morning as the light, almost non-existent wind and thick fog combined to keep half the fleet still beating out to the mark when *Jandy* rounded first. The turning vessel, HMCS *Oshawa,* reported some clearing and light breeze by noon.

By dinner time Sunday, only five yachts had crossed the line led by *Hussy,* a PCC out of Seattle. One-third of the fleet had retired, including AA stalwarts *Oriole, Adios, Oceanus, Spirit,* and *Tatoosh.*

However, for those yachts that happened to be in the right place at the right time, a strong wind streak allowed a flying spinnaker ride home on Sunday afternoon. Under these conditions the Lapworth 36 again proved the merits of its design, winning the overall trophy for the fourth consecutive year. This time, the prize went to an American yacht, a brand new boat out of Tacoma, Gerry Smith's *Bandit. Bandit* saved her time from *Thetis* by half an hour, which translated to a full hour ahead of *Hussy* on corrected time.

Oceanus, which retired from the race, warrants special mention. She was a 60 foot sloop, conceived by a naval architect as his own idea of a comfortable ocean cruiser/racer. William Garden, well known as a traditionalist, designed stock model boats in the late Forties for Blanchard Boat Yard. Now a resident of Victoria, Garden is the only major naval architect to own and skipper one of his own designs in the Swiftsure.

Innovative for the mid-Fifties, *Oceanus* was a deliberate marriage of a cruiser/racer in the largest possible boat which could comfortably be handled by a man and wife team. As a maximum efficiency yacht, easily driven, with comfortable accommodations performing equally well under power and sail, *Oceanus* was the ultimate in a fast, light hull driven by minimum sail area. A long, narrow double ender (one of Garden's favourite hull forms), the *Oceanus* resembled a big canoe. With 12 foot beam, 6 foot draft, 1,000 square feet of sail area, and 11,000 pounds of iron in the keel, she was both simple and strong, yet could be sailed singlehanded without undue exertion or inconvenience. The one major concession to more efficient powering also precluded optimum racing performance. Her 46 foot waterline was too long to be competitive while rating CCA 47 being outside the optimum measurement of the rule.

In Garden's words: "If you could see anything astern on

the finish line, you had lost the race on corrected time."

However, for stability, she was tops, literally sailing herself. During one passage near Race Rocks, the crew of *Oceanus* was observed in the cockpit sipping tea, while boats in the immediate vicinity were broaching. (Mind you, *Oceanus* was not flying a 'chute' like the others.)

The Juan de Fuca Race was really beginning to catch on with the smaller boats, especially among the Canadian clubs. The 1964 version saw 14 entries on the line, with West Van's *Saraband* carrying the day. R.S. Payne's *Poseidon* from Corinthian was second by a scant three minutes. Corrected times gave *Saraband* the edge by almost 11 minutes. The third of the Gulf Island 29 series, she was skippered by Hump Jones.

OCEANUS / SIB DOW

29/ Ned Ashe — Sailor, Gentleman

Once upon a time, Royal Vancouver Yacht Club Commodore and Lieutenant Governor of the province, Eric Hamber, arrived on the Royal Victoria Yacht Club foreshore looking for the Commodore.

A rather grubby chap who was working on his boat cheerfully volunteered to fetch the Commodore; retreated to the Clubhouse, scrubbed up, donned a suitable jacket, and reappeared in his official capacity as Commodore E.P. Ashe to extend a gracious welcome to His Honour.

Unassuming, a gentleman in every sense of the word, master helmsman Ned Ashe enjoys a stature and universal respect accorded to few men during their lifetime. It is well deserved.

Now Honourary Commodore of the Royal Victoria Yacht Club and still sailing, Ned Ashe's involvement spans almost the entire history of Northwest competition. His long tenure was briefly interrupted twice while he went to war.

Since his arrival in Victoria in 1911 at age 16, Ned has collected trophies in every type and class of boat from nine foot dinghies through the entire range of keelboats.

Until 1964, he skippered other people's yachts in the Swiftsure Race. But the highlight of his 16 Swiftsure and six Juan de Fuca stints was the record breaking 1965 Juan de Fuca run at the helm of his Thunderbird *May D II*. He was 70-years-old at the time.

Of this record race, Ned is quick to praise his "very good crew", all experienced Thunderbird sailors. Foredeck man Geoff Arndt was joined by Dave Anstey and son Chris, among the keenest Victoria T-Bird Fleet #13 racers.

Recalls Ned, "We started that morning in a breeze of about nine miles an hour, which gradually increased. I carried on, straight for Race Passage. The larger boats which started 15 minutes ahead of us tacked for Esquimalt. I got a good break by carrying on for Race Passage and not tacking. We were first through Race Passage ahead of the larger boats which started ahead of us. From there on, we carried right across the Straits and ended up at Pillar Point. Then we were lucky enough to get another lift up along the American shore.

"There again was the second break that we had. We were the first boat around the outer mark. Coming home, we still had a good breeze and were planing at one point in the Straits, the first occasion in which I had planed in the Thunderbird. It was quite a thrill. We made very good time, and we were able to carry the spinnaker."

Again, the little chuckle. "Came time to set the spinnaker. I was a little doubtful at first. Anstey said, 'Ned, I'll buy a new spinnaker if it blows out.' So I said, 'Hoist away!' It got up to about 35 mph and that's when she started planing with the spinnaker.

"We only had one mishap: the downhaul for the spinnaker pole came adrift from the cleat under a heavy swell and the spinnaker pole jacknifed which, of course, allowed the boat to broach. But we were very fortunate coming out, and nothing was broken. The spinnaker wasn't ripped.

"We carried on for the rest of the way and used the spinnaker right through to about five miles of the finish line. The squalls were getting pretty wicked and I was afraid of losing the mast at that time. We took the spinnaker down and finished under a small jib and the main. We had such a good lead that I didn't want to run a chance of losing everything by having the mast go over the side. We were very fortunate in every way to finish when we did and everything held. It took 45 minutes to finish the nine miles between Race Rocks and the breakwater."

Are master helmsmen born, or are they made?

Young Ned hauled his first ropes lassooing cattle on the family ranch in Alberta, becoming adept as a youngster at all aspects of riding, rope handling, and even gun handling. But he was destined to perpetuate the Ashe seagoing tradition of his grandfather Paddy, a Rear Admiral in the Royal Navy, who, as a fourth officer of a sailing vessel, made one of the first surveys of Esquimalt Harbour. Paddy Ashe is commemorated twice on local charts by Ashe's Point and Paddy's Pass. On retirement, he had charge of the Royal Observatory at Quebec City.

Four of Ned's uncles were Royal Navy men, and although his father was not a career sailor, the family relocated to a 200 acre waterfront farm at Albert Head, chosen primarily because it had a good anchorage for the 65 foot yawl immediately acquired to fulfill a cherished dream.

In 1912, Gilbert Percy Ashe became the first Canadian ever to enter the Honolulu Race. This caused a minor local stir, when the yacht club affiliation was wrongly attributed to Royal Van. In 1914, G.P. Ashe became vice-commodore at Royal Victoria Yacht Club, where his son was later to have a long standing association.

Just before the First World War, Ned combined long hours of farming chores with learning the wily ways of the sea. First on his father's yawl, *Natoose* (which had been built for Cully Stinson's Lumber Baron father), and next in his dinghy, *Vera*.

Part of the first one design dinghy class in this area, *Vera* was one of several built up the Gorge waterway by Stephenson. Arthur Crease had the first. Other racing companions included Humphrey Golby.

They raced every weekend on a Saturday afternoon. Ned customarily sailed his tiny craft over from Albert Head to Cadboro Bay, raced, and then sailed back. He took it all in his stride, with characteristic good humour.

Ned even sailed around from Albert Head to compete in regattas at Cowichan Bay. No mother ships then for small boats, although much later, Ned was to tow dinghies and Star Boats to Seattle competition in his *Seatime*.

Sometimes the local racers were joined in Cadboro Bay by the Seattle sailors, including young John Graham in his Kitten Class *Dormouse*.

Such was Ned's basic training for the string of victories he was later to compile in keel boats.

During the First World War, his adeptness with animals gained during ranching days got him assigned to a "mule train", supervising the horses and mules which carried ammunition and supplies to the front line trenches in France. In World War II, he was with a mine sweeping detachment in the Firth of Forth. But he always returned to yachting.

Ned's Swiftsure assignments include a roster of out-standing yachts. Three seemed to be a magic number for him. Three times he went on Ray Cooke's *Circe*, three times on Hubie Wallace's *Buccaneer*, and three times on *Gometra*.

While Ray always had command of his *Circe*, Ned was twice co-skipper for the race, joined on occasions by other Victoria crew, Jim Davies, Andrew Wright, and Humphrey Golby. (On one occasion, *Circe* carried 14 men, of whom two were cooks.)

Of the *Circe*, he recalls, "*Circe* used to have a terrible time in the light stuff with the heavy seas. She'd start hobbyhorsing as it was very difficult for her to tack in the heavy sea without much wind. Especially at the mark, where the smaller boats could just nip around."

One chuckle for Ned when he was sailing the *Gometra* was looking over to see the *Circe* down to a reefed main, her genny trailing in the water with Jim Davies alone on deck at the wheel at 4:30 a.m. All other hands were below, suffering from Mal de Mer.

On crew management, Ned advocates running strict watches and making sure everyone gets a good hot meal Saturday night, before the going gets rough, if it isn't already.

"It's very important, because those races are usually won at night."

It's a matter of seeing that the crew get fed at their proper time and get their rest, so that they're in good shape for the early hours of the morning. If you get heavy weather and they're all tired out or seasick, it makes a terrific difference to the way you finish in the race," Ned says.

"Everybody stays up to see what's happening to the other guy and the consequence is that the whole works get tired at once."

On avoiding seasickness: "If your stomach is empty, you get cold and sleepy and that's fatal. Get some food down early in the game. When you're wet and sick, you lose interest. And if you go below, you get sick. It's a great relief to get around the Lightship and get going back down the Strait. That's the happy time in Swiftsure."

KIALOA / JAMES McVIE

30/ *The Buchan Dynasty — 1965*

A welcome relief from the soggy-wind Swiftsures of the previous few years, Swiftsure 1965 kicked off at 9:30 a.m. and Juan de Fuca at 9:45 a.m. on Saturday, May 29th, favoured by winds between 15 and 20 knots, which held fairly for most of the race. CBC TV weatherman, Bob Fortune, accompanied Dr. Charles Gould on *Astrocyte*, covering Swiftsure for the first of a new outdoors series.

First across the line, *Mai Tai*, was followed closely by *Mistral, Winsome III, Tricia, Ladaro*, and *Kialoa*. The next group included *Spirit, Diamond Head, Helene, Adios, Oriole*, and *Circe*. Within the next hour, as the wind whipped up whitecaps, *Dahut* lost her mast, while *Adios* and *Jandy* experienced rigging problems, with *Jandy* subsequently withdrawing.

By the time the fleet reached Race Rocks, *Diamond Head* held the lead. When the fleet split, *Oriole* was well ahead in the group electing the American shore, chased by *Circe*, and *Gabrielle II*, which would also enter the July TransPac. On the Canadian side, *Diamond Head* led *Spirit*, while *Reality, Fulmar, Odusa* and *Courageous* held mid-channel, with *Norwester, Tricia, Penelakut, Cormorant, Thunder*, and *Kialoa*. *Maradea, Velaris*, and *Mai Tai* grouped closer to the Canadian shore.

By early afternoon the wind had moderated. *Norena of Wight* grounded, but worked herself off the rocks to return to Victoria. *Oriole* and *Diamond Head* elected to tack for opposite shores, with the Navy ketch heading for Canada and the Seattle yawl for the United States. By late afternoon, the committee reported *Oriole* ahead, followed by *Spirit, Reality, Circe, Diamond Head, Tricia, Stormy Weather, Bandit, Odusa, Black Hawk* and *Pelagius*.

As darkness descended, the rain lightened while the wind increased. The C Class yachts in the shorter Juan de Fuca Race, Ned Ashe's *May D II* and the only American boat, *Lucy A*, reached their Clallam Bay marker in record time, rounding at 7:32 and 7:58 Saturday evening.

By 10:30 the lead yachts had advanced to within 10 miles of the Swiftsure turning mark, with westerly winds of 8 to 10 knots, a light swell, and good visibility. Three Eight Metres, Jack Balmar's *Fulmar*, Jack Smith's *Reality*, and

H.M. Ellis' *Pandora of Rhu*, rounded in quick succession shortly after midnight. In the larger two sticker category, *Diamond Head* and *Oriole* were still among the leaders, with *Diamond Head* finally advancing to frontrunner, a position which she held for the remainder of the race.

Progress slowed during the morning calm, with winds freshening again to 15 knots as dawn's fingers fanned into morning.

Meanwhile, 20 knot winds gusting to 25 filled spinnakers as the Swiftsure fleet sped homeward. *Diamond Head* surged along at speeds up to 14 knots, opening up a three mile lead on the pack, to cross the line at 12:49 Sunday.

HMCS Oriole had one of her better races. After leading the fleet for most of Saturday, *Oriole* dropped back during the lightened pre-dawn winds, but still nailed down fourth in AA Class. Overall winner Bill Buchan cracked the winner's circle after almost 20 years of Swiftsure competition. First around the mark, *Fulmar*, corrected to fourth overall while Pat Leslie's *Tricia*, second overall, placed highest of the 10 competing Lapworth 36s.

In the Juan de Fuca Race, one of the most comely family crews to grace either race was the dark haired trio trained by Peter Coombs to handle the family Spitzgatter, *Doxy*. Hailing from South Africa, Peter, Monica, and daughters Gillian and Jacquie had no tradition of giving graduation gifts. Nevertheless, when the question was posed to 17-year-old Gillian, she replied that for her graduation "gift", she would like to go on the Juan de Fuca Race. So the *Doxy* was duly outfitted and equipped to meet the safety standards.

In perhaps the only instance of an "all girl crew" executing an important manoeuvre at the finish line in that tiny, confused corner by the end of the breakwater, 16-year-old Jacquie and Monica responded smartly to helmsman Gillian's order to "jibe the spinnaker".

Fourteen boats entered Juan de Fuca this year. At Royal Victoria Yacht Club, however, they always think of 1965 as the year Ned Ashe set a new course record. His Thunderbird, *May D II*, really flew home on a big flood, pushed by the whistling westerly to cross the line at 2:46:33 on Sunday morning. *Lucy A*, sailed by Bill Gardner, Corinthian Yacht

Club, picked up the second slot, but he was still two full hours behind the flying *May D II*.

As the history of Swiftsure unfolds, 1965 seems to be an excellent place to talk about the rising prowess of Bill Buchan, his family, and the Buchan boats.

The Pacific Northwest racing fraternity remembers Bill Buchan Sr. as a man of great charisma. He grew up on the unforgiving northeast coast of Scotland, earning his livelihood as a young man in Aberdeen's herring processing business. The tough times following the First World War influenced the whole family to pull up stakes and move. Their options were Australia or the Pacific Northwest.

Choosing Seattle, the Buchans followed the trade which they knew: they ran a downtown fish market. Leaving his two younger sisters in charge in the summers, Bill would go to Alaska on the boats.

A cherished dream during these early years was to have his own fishboat. This became a reality in the early 1950s coinciding with the sale of the fish business. He was then about 52, and "retired", which meant, in effect, having the time to do what he pleased. The fishboat, *Heather*, was built, but he sold out his interest to his partner within a short time.

However, Bill Buchan's involvement with pleasure boats starts with his arrival in Seattle, and follows an interesting progression. He first built a 17 footer similar to a Snipe. In it, Bill and his bride Irene cruised to the Hood Canal. When he was almost 40, he moved to a miniature Blanchard Knockabout, a 20 footer with accommodation for cruising Puget Sound. With a 28 foot Ed Monk design, Buchan started racing, enrolling in a class given by the "Y" for instruction.

Buchan first tackled Swiftsure in 1947. *Linda* was a heavy 39 foot sloop without much sail area. Apparently, he had become enamoured of the J Boats, and took a series of photos of Sopwith's *Endeavour* illustrations, transposing them into his conception of a similar yacht, which was the *Linda*, named for his daughter.

Three or four years went into planning the next *Heather*, which was basically a lake sailing boat (in those days, all boats were kept in Lake Washington as there was no mooring in the Sound, which had to be reached by going through the Locks). Resembling a Six Metre with a cabin, and no engine at first, *Heather* immediately started winning, serving notice to the Northwest that Buchan was serious about racing. The 37 footer was very competitive in moderate winds and at her best in light winds. Basically an R boat with greater freeboard and more sail area, she was overcanvassed for that day. Carvel cedar planked with steamed oak ribs, she underwent continual modification, first with more lead, and later with an inboard engine added.

Next came the earliest attempt at building a racing/cruising boat. *Thistle*, also a light weather boat, was built in Bill Jr.'s yard, a very narrow conventional cedar planked 38 footer.

By the early 1960s, the operation had expanded to a yard by Madison Park in downtown Seattle, with Buchan and his son John as partner. By now, they were refining their designs. The Buchan 40, cedar strip planked over bent oak frames, was built over a jig. Longer and beamier than *Thistle*, six or seven were built, including one for Bill Whipple and the first *Mara*, which raced in the early 1960s, placing in the top third of the Swiftsure fleet. Still, the Buchan 40 didn't rate well. So, with characteristic determination, they set about to improve the design.

To achieve this, they took the wooden jig and remodelled it, cutting three feet out of the mid-section to shorten the length and increase the beam, while carrying the same sail area. And so, the formidable Buchan 37 was born. There were only two wooden ones: Bill Sr.'s *Thunder*, and John's *Warrior* (the plug for the glass mould).

This was the first boat that Bill Sr. had designed that had good all-round speed, with excellent characteristics on all points of sailing. It was a year before they had the courage to race *Thunder*. She turned out to be phenomenal, winning PIYA hands down and, as mentioned, going on to take the overall Swiftsure Trophy in 1965.

Altogether, starting with Phil People's *Salute*, there were 45 Buchan 37s, almost all owner-completed. The second *Mara*, named for Bill Jr.'s youngest daughter, had the best Swiftsure record, starting with the overall trophy in 1967.

The following copy of a letter dated June 7, 1962, addressed to William Buchan, reveals how the racing yachts can be diverted by situations beyond their control:
"Dear Bill:

Just a line to say how sorry we were on the tug *Sudbury* to interfere with *Mara* in this year's running of the Swiftsure Classic.

As you know, I am in charge of the tug and direct her activities during the race. After we had passed you to leeward I thought we were in the clear, and I went into the chart room to work on the plot. At that particular moment, someone asked the skipper to stop engines while they got a wind speed reading. Before anyone realized it, you had come up on us and the tug being a big heavy ship just could not get going fast enough to clear you.

Apart from this unfortunate happening, I felt that both your boats were going extremely well, and with a little better break during the night, we could have easily had a Buchan 40 in the win column. Good sailing and good luck."

(signed) Humphrey Golby,
Communications, Swiftsure 1962

MARA / KENNETH OLLAR

LINDA / KENNETH OLLAR

HEATHER / KENNETH OLLAR

Climaxing a dramatic homestretch sprint between two classic yachts, the 1966 one second photo finish exhausted the superlatives of all who witnessed it, and the media who recorded it.

Mary Bower and *Diamond Head* were matched in a gruelling 35 hour endurance contest, where gale force winds whipped up steep 12 foot seas, retiring almost half the 87 entries with blown out sails, rigging failure, sprung planks, and dismastings.

First to retire was *HMCS Oriole*, with a split main, and *Maradea,* whose mast, sail and engine were knocked out. She was towed in by the Coast Guard. In her bid for line honours, *Diamond Head* damaged or lost seven sails, ripping out track and fittings.

Placid prerace ceremonies gave no hint of the Swiftsure which sailors would term the roughest, most exciting of all. "Magnificent 1966 Centennial Swiftsure Fleet, we salute you." The pre-race roll call roster reflected Humphrey Golby's observation that, "Year after year, those who have proved superiority come back, again and again, when the toughest ocean yacht race brings together the finest yachts in the Pacific Northwest," which this year were celebrating 100 years of sailing out of Victoria, echoing the days when "famous sailing ships stood tall".

There was *Circe*, the "true veteran of Swiftsure", and "Gary Horder, long-time competitor, former PIYA secretary and worker and contributor to the sport of sailing", in *Haida*. Prophetic words described the "powerful *Mary Bower*"and"*Diamond Head*, a photogenic yacht, if there ever was one, with a tremendous racing history."

As thousands crowded the waterfront, breakwater, and finish line, *Mary Bower* swept in to snatch first to finish honours by one second from *Diamond Head*. While *Mary's* triumph undoubtedly stole the show, it overshadowed the amazing performance of the 31 foot *Mistral*. In near gale conditions, Bill Baillargeon and his tight knit crew had kept *Mistral* in the thick of it. Early results had given *Terna* the overall win, but subsequent remeasurement awarded the top spot to *Mistal*. This truly remarkable yacht was to win again in 1968. (That year's race write-up tells *Mistral's*

detailed life story.)

The first of the Discovery 32 series appeared in 1966. This 32 foot sloop featured a light displacement hull, fin keel, and sharp bow, design advances for that period. Per Christofferson's *Terna*, the first D32, generated much pre-race interest.

Per claimed that *Terna's* wide beam (just over nine feet) was advantageous when sailing reefed down. Another factor which kept her moving in heavy weather was sailmaker Phil Miller's skill, sewing up a split genoa and spinnaker while the sails were still set and pulling without losing boat speed. Other veterans in *Terna's* crew included Vancouver designer Peter Hatfield, builder Carl Peterson (another avid Star sailor), George Mason, and Ian Kirkland.

In the Juan de Fuca Race, Cal 28 *Doxy II* snuffed first-to-finish *Tandem II's* bid for a double victory by a scant two minutes. Overall winner *Doxy's* crew included two teenagers, Bob Dalgleish and Gillian Coombs, as well as T-Bird skipper Alex James and sailmaker Ron Mack.

From the start, *Doxy II* was one of those lucky boats which won just about every race she entered during her first year. States her owner, "The boat surprised us all." Fortunately, he had insisted that Vancouver's Calgan Marine beef up the rigging, supplying heavier rigging than the specifications called for. Nevertheless, the continual pounding shifted the weight of her full watertanks, shaking the forward berths loose from their attached structure.

During the blow, *Aphrodite*, another Cal 28 from Vancouver, campaigned by Calgan Marine manufacturer Al Nairne and sales manager Geoff Coleman, was dismasted when her backstay parted, weakened by a radio antenna spliced into it.

Most skippers select one other yacht as their own personal trial horse. For *Doxy II*, that pace boat was Theo de la Mare's Spencer 35 *Tandem II*. At one point during the race, Coombs decided to nip in behind Pillar Point to reef and change jibs. *Tandem* came bounding along. Rapid reconsiderations ensued. *Doxy* carried on! Out of such split second decisions are races won.

The Victoria built 26 foot *Haida*, designed by Raymond

Richards as an alternative to the T-Bird and Cal 25 and 28 took third overall. Sales manager for Haida builder Mayhew and Strutt, Don McCowan, was the skipper for this race.

This marked the first year that a Swiftsure or Juan de Fuca Race was won by a light displacement fibreglass yacht, another echo from the general American trend which saw Lapworth designs dominating race results.

However, the star of 1966 was *Mary Bower*, for a performance which has never been eclipsed, its lustre untarnished by passing years.

Mary Bower was built in England in 1939, her lines drawn by Robert Clarke. They were truly handsome. The eye could catch the speed potential in the easy powerful sections, while her beautiful wine glass form delighted those who knew a fine yacht when they saw one: 49 feet overall, in solid teak, 11 foot 4 inch beam and 7 foot 6 inch draft. Because Clarke had designed her for offshore racing, *Mary Bower* was no lightweight: 33,000 pounds, with the mast rising 61 feet above the deck with a surprisingly modern ⅞ rig.

Mary Bower came to the attention of the yachting world when she was first boat home in a cross channel race to France in 1945. It was the resumption of yacht racing after the end of hostilities. For the next five years, *Mary Bower* was sailed hard in the channel and in the various meets around England. Her racing record was good, but she fell on hard times. By 1952, she was sadly neglected, remaining on blocks until Ken McRae of Royal Vancouver Yacht Club bought her, sight unseen, and shipped her to Vancouver by freighter in 1955-56.

It was a pretty sorry looking thoroughbred that was unloaded from the ship, her heavy wooden spars lashed along her deck, her topsides stained and pocked, with bags of Egyptian cotton sails stowed in her forepeak. Ken put her in the shipyard. Within the month, *Mary Bower* had started on the first steps to her new life in Canada.

1957 was her first Swiftsure. Ken had done a yeoman job, repairing, refitting, repainting, and restoring the thousand and one things that had fallen into disrepair. Soon, *Mary Bower* looked pretty much like her old British self. Considering the cotton sails and their age, she sailed a very creditable race. Those on the escort tug remarked that here was a boat that had a certain air of authority about her. From that day on, *Mary Bower* was improved each year, becoming a consistent competitor, both overall and in her class.

1962 was a momentous year for sprightly *Mary*. Traded by Ken McRae on a power boat, she once again sat in her cradle waiting for a new owner and another chapter. The saviour appeared in the form of John Long. After some haggling, John and *Mary* became new partners in quest of further glory. The new skipper continued to update and improved her during the winters of 1963 and 1964, sailing with his old pals, for a spotty performance.

Sensing that this boat had real promise, John Long determined to make the most of it. In the winter of 1964, Peter Hatfield corrected her down-by-the-stern tendency, which was accomplished by radical surgery: 1,400 pounds excised from the after end of her lead keel, replaced with a block of yellow cedar. Then Peter Hatfield and Gerry Palmer combined to design a new masthead rig. A new aluminum spar was ordered from England, and the best of sails and rigging fitted. By this time, some of Royal Van's top young sailors became aware that here was a skipper who was sparing no effort or expense to make *Mary Bower* a fine racing machine.

One by one they joined the crew. First, Alex Harrison, then Doug Race, Steve Tupper (now CYA sailing coach), Dave Miller, and Steve Gill. From 1965 on, John and his stellar crew campaigned *Mary Bower* really hard. The planning, the new masthead rig, and the crack small boat sailors in the crew began to pay off. *Mary Bower* started to win.

By 1966, the big boat fleet marked her as the boat to beat. But all this hard sailing, and the now tremendous foretriangle, had put unbearable stress on *Mary*, and she started to leak badly. Examination showed that the mast step was too small, and that the mast thrust was literally shoving the bottom out. Leaking or not, *Mary Bower* now had a fine modern rig, a brand new interior layout, a new Perkins diesel, and Edson wheel steering. It was no secret that by the spring of 1966, *Mary* was going all out for Swiftsure.

Dick Batey and Humphrey Golby covered the race from start to finish for radio station CJVI, following every mile of the now historic battle between *Mary Bower* and *Diamond Head* for 24 hours. Swiftsure 1966 really belongs to *Mary Bower*, her untiring skipper, and her inspired young crew. They took her across the line on gunfire, dropped to fourth position at Albert Head, then regained the lead with a series of short tacks inshore to be first boat through Race Rocks. The reporters followed her into the Race and watched *Mary's* crew change down to a #2 genny, accomplished in seconds without a hitch or real loss of time or distance. Dave Miller later remarked that they had changed headsails 20 more times on the way to the *Lightship*.

The crew sailed her for everything that was there, but they never overpowered her. As the wind increased to 30 mph with higher gusts, *Mary Bower* was down to working jib and reefed main. *Diamond Head* once again assumed the lead as a tacking duel began up the American shore. As the sea increased, it became obvious that the *Bower* was gradually catching her rival. *Diamond Head*, plunging badly because of her long, fine bow, was having a tough time in the foreshortened waves. On the other hand, this was the typical English Channel conditions that *Mary* had been designed for.

Mary's short overhang and tremendous power took her past *Diamond Head* at Neah Bay where, for the first time, her crew dared to think that the old girl could be first to round. However, as the wind died and the sea moderated, *Diamond Head* once more regained the lead. At Tatoosh, *Mary Bower* picked the best of the night airs, rounding first at 2:10 a.m. At dawn, *Mary* still led the fleet, but if the usual pattern held, it seemed certain that the morning breeze would fill in from offshore, bringing up the stragglers. But 1966 was *Mary's* year. As it turned out, the breeze built as she sailed. The further she sailed down the Strait, the better it got. By mid-morning, *Mary Bower* was firmly in the lead and gaining by the minute.

Meals had been pretty sketchy during the night, so now it was steak breakfast. Even the weak stomachs responded to John Long's culinary efforts. Things were just too good: disaster struck! During the second jibe, a line jammed sending the pole right through the spinnaker. It was down in seconds, replaced by the #1 genny hoisted while the crew feverishly taped the rip. In minutes, the spinnaker was flying again, but the wind was freshening noticeably. Would the tape hold, or would it blow? The answer came suddenly. This time, for good.

The second spinnaker was hoisted. It was now or never for *Mary Bower*. *Diamond Head* now had the wind and was closing the gap. As they came into Race Passage, *Mary* dropped her chute and selected a #3 genny to get through the rip tides and sudden gusts that can set any boat reeling. *Diamond Head* was pouring it on and blew her last spinnaker just as she entered the passage. However, it was a short reprieve. With her great speed, she passed *Mary* again about half way to the finish.

The skipper had kept *Mary Bower* on a course well below the finish while Kotkins held up toward the Esquimalt shore. Another break: the wind lightened inshore. Once again, it was neck and neck! Five hundred yards from the tip of the breakwater, skipper Long hardened up to cut the end of the breakwater close. The fans at the end of the breakwater had a lifetime thrill as the great red and white striped spinnaker billowed over their heads as *Mary* rushed by almost close enough to touch. With only yards to go, *Diamond Head*, with no spinnaker to drive her, was now dead before the wind, while the *Bower* was charging for the line! It was a matter of inches as the gun rang out, with not enough time to reload between. Magnificent *Mary Bower* was the first boat to finish — by one second!

DIAMOND HEAD / JAMES McVIE

HIGH DRAMA AT SEA.

32/ *Hussy Hustles but Mara Wins — 1967*

For another record entry, 92 Swiftsure and 29 Juan de Fuca yachts, 1967 Swiftsure's first lesson was to disregard the weather predictions which forecast cloudy, clearing in the afternoon, and 15 knot winds increasing to 25. The second lesson was patience.

The reality was rain, fog, and prevailing two to five knot winds, except for a brief period Sunday afternoon over a small section of the course, resulting in boats ghosting across the finish line through the darkness of Monday evening and Tuesday morning. Experienced skipper, Bill Buchan Jr. in *Mara*, scored a triple win, rounding the mark first, taking the overall *Swiftsure Trophy* and first in Division 3. In a repeat of his 1964 performance, another Seattle skipper, Robert Page in *Hussy*, was among the leaders soon after the start, maintaining his position into the homestretch, where he assumed the lead and finished first.

In the early stages of the race, most yachts carried their chutes, but found it hard to keep them filled in the light easterly. Early leaders included *Norwester, Anitra, Hussy, Klahanie, Sanguine, Mara, Thunder, Maruffa, Moea, Ta'aroa, Lancer, Mai Tai, Kialoa, Mary Bower* and *Adios*, with *Klahanie, Adios* and *Mary Bower* jockeying for the lead spot. By 1:30, *Adios* was leading second place *Hussy* as a light fog bank wafted out down the Strait. By mid-afternoon, *Adios* still led, with the fleet spread out mid-Strait, with some favouring the Canadian shore slightly.

By this time, the wind had faded to almost zero, while the tide started to flood, the clouds closed in, and fog reduced visibility to eight miles. By late afternoon, *Hussy* had passed *Adios* to assume the lead, with *Mara* closing the gap. Meanwhile, *Diamond Head, Anitra* and *Oriole* put down anchors off Sooke to hold positions against the fading winds. During Saturday night, light winds, fog, and rain prevailed, giving way to Sunday morning's penetrating clammy cold fog. When they left the Strait to head for the mark ship, some boats found a little wind. Many skippers were unable to hear the radio signals, resorting to dead reckoning to locate the ship.

Still very light, the winds had shifted to the northwest, giving a spinnaker run homeward bound. At this point,

Hussy led, followed by *Mara, Moea* and *Crusader*, with the next group including *Norwester, Winsome III, Klahanie, Velaris, Concerto, White Squall, Ariel V, Tricia, Calypso, Vamose, Cormorant, Odusa, Traveuni, Penelakut, Anitra* and *Sea Fever*.

At Sheringham, the leaders picked up freshened winds. From there to the finish line, these boats held winds up to 15 knots, while the rest of the fleet still straggled behind in five knots or less.

Hussy crossed the finish line at 20:25:30, nearly 11 minutes ahead of *Mara* and 23 minutes in front of *Moea*. Corrected times gave *Mara* the overall win, with *Moea* second and *Hussy* third. The long race had caused many yachts whose crew members had shore commitments to withdraw, leaving only 26 of the starters to finish the race by Monday morning.

Seattle's clan Buchan placed three boats in the top seven. Bill Jr., a triple winner in *Mara* (a Buchan 37) took the *Swiftsure Trophy*, the *RCN Trophy* for first boat to round, and the Seattle Yacht Club Trophy for first in Division 3. Brother John's *Warrior* was fifth overall, and Bill Sr.'s *Thunder* seventh overall. As outlined in a previous chapter, the standings surprised no one.

For two decades, the versatile, hard-driving Buchan family has outbuilt, outsailed, and outshone almost every boat in almost every major Pacific Northwest keel boat competition.

Tough and tenacious, Bill Buchan Sr. founded a dynasty of outstanding helmsmen which has now entered its third generation. By the time Bill Jr. was 35, in 1970, he had chalked up a string of laurels which included two World Star Class championships (San Diego 1961 and Sweden 1970), as well as North American Star Titles (the 1955 Mallory Cup and the Charles H. Briggs International Skipper of the Year Trophy, not just once, but twice). In 1978, he won the *Swiftsure Trophy* for the second time, and narrowly missed capturing the World ¾ Ton Championship, sailing against his old Star rival Lowell North, who crewed on the winning yacht.

Younger by five years, Bill's brother John reigned supreme in the Two Ton Class in the late Seventies, with his Perry designed *Heather* (arch-rival John Newton elected the Admiral's Cup series in 1979, shipping *Pachena* to England).

Bill's children inherit their sailing abilities from both sides of the family. Karen Buchan's father, Carl Sahlin, was an active member of the Bellingham Yacht Club, and a later owner of the *Gossip*, which he guided to third overall placing in 1956 Swiftsure. Carl Buchan, who excels in Finns and Lasers, was selected in 1975 — appropriately in Scotland — as a World Youth Champion, and was elected to the U.S. Intercollegiate Hall of Fame in 1977. Mara often crews for her brother and father.

Juan de Fuca racers, meanwhile, enjoyed a good run home in the 1967 race as compensation for the slow outward leg. W. Van's, Gerry Kidd and Bob McColl in Cal 28 *Aphrodite III*, led the fleet across the line. R. Marshall's *Seaquin* (CYC) and Dave Gibberd's *Gypsy G* (W. Van.)

saved their time, dropping *Aphrodite III* to third, in a 24 boat fleet.

A new milestone was passed this year when the Swiftsure committee set the stage for the first official competition under the *Performance Handicap Racing Fleet* rating rules. We dealt at length in an earlier chapter on the PHRF system as applied in this area. Suffice it to say that Tom Wheeler of the Seattle Yacht Club was the driving force behind the acceptance of this system by the committee. In their first time out, PHRF only mustered five entries, but it was a start, and the growth was destined to be phenomenal. It was to be 1969 before the new ratings were accepted into Swiftsure itself.

It is only fitting that Tom Wheeler's hard work in getting PHRF started paid off with the first win under the rule. His *Stormalong II* was first to finish, with Tacoma's *RainBird*, skippered by W.B. Johnson, placing second.

MARA: MANUFACTURING THE FAMOUS BUCHAN 37 / Forty-five of these remarkable boats were built and their records speak for the capabilities of this completely self-designed yacht. The Buchan family worked, and dreamed and sailed against the best, and time and again one of these doughty sailors brought a Buchan boat into the winner's circle. / BILL BUCHAN.

33/ *Mistral Again and Moonglow*

Swiftsure 1968 was a prelude to the second Victoria-Maui Race. Interest focused on the decade's wonder boat, the legendary Cal 40, and Bill Killam's newly launched, locally designed and built Discovery 47, *Porpoise III*.

Bill Neilson's Cal 40, *Moonglow III*, hit Race Passage in second position behind *Mary Bower* at 11 a.m. Saturday (maximum ebb), then crossed to the American shore. Here the light morning westerly shifted to a light sou-easter. Yachts on the U.S. shore were the first to benefit and soon popped their chutes. The winds were fickle and very patchy. Those favouring the American side made progress, but those in midstream stopped in their tracks when the flood set in. *Mary Bower*, *Moonglow III*, *Hussy*, and *Mara* hung onto the lead all afternoon, but farther back, a small yacht was creeping up. It was *Mistral*. Clinging to the shore in the back eddies, she passed 50 boats, and by evening was running in third place. During the night, the lead group stayed pretty much in the same order, with *Mary Bower* rounding first, then *Moonglow*, *Mara*, *Hussy*, and *Porpoise III* in close order.

After rounding, *Moonglow III* made two long tacks, following the breeze to the Canadian side, and by the time she reached Sheringham Point, she was able to set her spinnaker. In an all out sprint to finish first, *Moonglow's* surfing speeds were clocked at over 12 knots. *Mistral*, meanwhile, sailed confidently with her big sisters, while *Porpoise III* closed the gap on the lead boats; first beating into the teeth of the strong easterly before finding the westerly halfway home.

Porpoise picked off a fifth overall, and then went on to prove her potential in the Victoria-Maui Race the next month, finishing first, while retaining first overall corrected time.

Porpoise, and later, *Graybeard*, anchored the upper end of Peter Hatfield's Discovery series, which attracted the cream of Vancouver's Star and Davidson Dinghy skippers, including Ches Rickard and Bonar Davis. Starting with Per Christopherson's D32 *Terna*, which almost won the 1966 race, through Bonar's modified *Hyak*, more than 20 of the 32 footers were produced.

Designer Hatfield's solid training included four years at University, followed by a year-and-a-half (1961-63) with Sparkman and Stephens in New York. There, he worked on hull designs in wood, glass, and aluminum. Before branching out on his own, Hatfield worked at John Bradlmayr's Spencer Boats, and was also associated with Gerry Palmer.

For her time, *Porpoise* was innovative. A fast, easily driven hull with great stability, even though comparatively light for her size, *Porpoise* was one of the first B.C. boats to utilize foam sandwich construction, built in Killam's ICL Engineering Ltd.

Bill Killam, at first a power boat man who, like his brother Lol, literally got his feet wet in sailing competition via the Davidson dinghy frostbite route, had a long association with technical people in the electronics field. In 1968, *Porpoise's* sophisticated navigation equipment was the exception rather than the rule. One example, a wind deflection compass, had only recently been evolved for America's Cup racing. Aided by her electronic helpers, *Porpoise* gained 14 places in two hours, improving her speed by better than two knots in a heavy swell and light winds.

Hunter Vogel brought a new entry to Swiftsure in 1968, the double ended *Lollipop*. Hunter was so enamoured with the double ended concept, after his success in *Aida*, that he engaged Danish designer, Utzon, to draft the lines of the Hunter 30. She was built at Steveston, combining the underwater lines of a good Six Metre with a modern cruiser/racer's accommodation. *Lollipop* came fourth overall behind *Mistral*, *Jolly Olly*, and *Moonglow III*. It was to be her best ranking. The class failed to catch on among the local enthusiasts. Now, as promised in a previous chapter, the fascinating story of *Mistral*.

Mistral is the offshore wind that sweeps the Mediterranean from the south coast of France. It is the 'master-wind' known by all sailors in the Mediterranean, who respect its vagaries and sudden power.

Ben Seaborn's *Mistral* is a 40 year veteran of the Pacific Northwest, a true daughter of Seattle. Her story begins in 1939. Keith Fiskin, manager of the Seattle Cedar Company, had been setting aside the choicest of his red cedar and air drying it in the yard loft, for several seasons. Blanchard Boat Company was commissioned to build a 31 footer to designs by Ben.

Seaborn's design was a melody to the eye with nothing overemphasized: a beautifully proportioned, harmonious hull. Just to see her taking shape was to know that here would be an easily driven craft, yet quite powerful and, above all, responsive. Throughout her long life, several owners, and many name changes, she led a marvellously balanced life. When first launched, she was christened *Romp II*; Fiskin was very happy with her performance, but with his growing family, he found her too small. So, within a year, he sold her to John Warren, who rechristened her *Cirrus II*. With the exception of the war years, he competed actively in PIYA Regattas in the Sound. In 1955-56, *Cirrus II* was sold to Jim McCurdy, who renamed her once again. This time, *Yum Yum*. Throughout all these changes, the boat was not altered in any way. She still had her 7/8 rig with jumper struts and running back stays. Cotton sails were still the order of the day.

In the winter of 1961, Joseph Cebert (Bill) Baillargeon entered the scene. Bill Baillargeon had always cherished a dream of owning the boat he had watched the Blanchards build back in 1939. She was on the next slip to where his father was having a Senior Knockabout built for the family. Young Bill Baillargeon was fascinated with *Romp II*, spending many hours watching as the skilled Blanchard crew pushed her to completion. Even at nine years of age, he saw himself as owner of that particular boat. Then and there, a bond was established that led to a very strange happening many years later.

Baillargeon had served with the U.S. Navy during the war, completing his stint as a Junior Navigation Officer on board a battleship, training that was to stand him in good stead. For several years now, he had been working in Seattle, but still had no boat. Then it happened. As he drove to work one November morning, he sensed that Jim McCurdy had a boat for sale. So strong was the feeling that when he got to the office, he promptly phoned. McCurdy was completely taken aback by the call, because he and his wife had just decided the night before to sell *Yum Yum*. "How the hell did you know about the boat? We haven't spoken to anyone." Baillargeon could only reply weakly, "Someone told me."

Once the contact had been made, a sale was arranged. For the fourth time, Ben Seaborn's beauty changed owners and names. At long last, the boy who dreamed of owning this yacht, now really did own her. Following his family's French heritage, he named her *Mistral*.

During 1962 and 1963, *Mistral* was campaigned locally and at PIYA, with enough success for the new skipper to realize that he had in *Mistral* a real competitor.

Now it was time to update the rig and buy new synthetic sails. The work took place during the winter of 1963. *Mistral* lost her original round spruce mast in favour of a wooden box spar sufficiently strong to carry a masthead rig. The hoist of the main was exactly the same as before, but the boom was shortened, and a permanent backstay fitted. The new sails looked terrible, but *Mistral* was going fast and starting to win in and around Seattle. In 1964, lifelines were installed. She entered the Vashon Island Race, winning her class.

Of those early races, Baillargeon says, "Since we only had the three sails, we were never in doubt as to what sails to fly. We had three choices: main and jenny, reefed main and jenny, or main and spinnaker. As a result, the skipper and crew could put their every ounce of effort into getting the most out of the boat. After Vashon Island, it was Swiftsure or bust.

With the thoroughness that was to become *Mistral's* trademark, Baillargeon set to work with his picked crew in preparation for Swiftsure 1964. The criterion for the crew was very specific. Each man had to be a competent helmsman in his own right, and also familiar with every station on the boat. Each had to be compatible and completely responsive to rigid ship's discipline. The division of jobs, watches, and meals was carefully worked out. The resulting plan was quite unique. Each man took the helm for an hour only. This rule was strictly kept throughout the race. The only exception was that on long downwind runs, their top downwind expert, Bill Booth, sometimes took a double shift.

Each man was required to rest, sleep if possible, for two hours, while taking hot food every four hours. As a result of this routine, *Mistral* never faltered on her racing mission. She always had a fresh, rested, well-fed man on the helm. Since she was often the smallest boat in the fleet, it was absolutely necessary for her to move forward at her best pace throughout the whole 24 hours. That first race in 1964 provided experience and very little else. It was the year of the great calm: 36 yachts finished and 35 gave up. *Mistral* was among the latter. Her second attempt was a truer test of boat and crew. She finished 24th overall and first in B Class.

1966 was to be *Mistral's* year. Now she had the experience, was much better equipped, and meticulously prepared. It was blowing hard from the sou'west, gusting above 40 knots at times, with a breaking short sea set up by the outgoing tide. Most of the fleet made a break for the U.S. side after clearing Race Rocks. Sizing up the situation and realizing that the breaking seas were no place for so small a yacht, the skipper hung in under the Canadian shore, to take advantage of the smoother water, and short tacked all afternoon up the Canadian side. Towards 5 p.m. the wind had moderated somewhat, and had fetched considerably more to the west. Double reefed with a working jib, *Mistral* set out for the other shore. It was a rough ride, but they kept going. With the advantage of the westerly lift, they found themselves among the leaders as they closed the U.S. shore in the vicinity of Neah Bay. It turned out that the lead boats had taken such a beating when they crossed the Strait and subsequently as they hitched up the American coast, that their progress had been slow; every foot was paid for in sheer crew exhaustion. *Mistral* and her crew, under their rigid discipline, were fresh and strong and had no difficulty in holding their position during the night. The run home on Sunday was pure joy. Although the big boys rushed by her on their mad flight to the finish, *Mistral* knew that she had her precious time more than saved and, God willing, would be the first 31 footer to win it all. And she did! To heighten the drama, the committee announced that *Terna* from Royal Van had won. It was not until a few days later when *Terna's* corrected rating was applied that *Mistral* was officially declared to be the winner.

In the 1967 race, *Mistral* again won her class, Division 4, but missed the overall. Then came 1968. The weather was soft and warm. The sea lay smooth in the Strait. The Swiftsure demon lurked not in the squalls and breaking sea, but in the all pervading calms. As usual, *Mistral* sailed to plan. Minimum time wasted. Maximum headway maintained. And careful scrutiny of the lead boat's progress. As the afternoon wore along and the flood tide set in, the skipper decided to get in under the American shore and work any shore breeze that might develop in the late afternoon and evening. They were in so close that *Mistral* actually rounded Clallam Bay marker boat as she went up the shore. Taking advantage of her shoal draft of five feet, Baillargeon tacked when he had to, hoisted spinnaker when

shifts came aft, and stayed within a hundred feet or so of the shore all the way up to Neah Bay. The fleet in mid-Strait lay totally becalmed. Soon, it became obvious that *Mistral* had passed 50 boats and now was running third. Only *Mara* and *Hussy* were still ahead. At Neah Bay, she passed inside *Hussy*, coming to within a few yards of *Mara*, but couldn't pass her. For the next few hours of darkness, hope burned aboard *Mistral* that, improbable as it might seem, she could, with luck, be first boat to round. It was not to be. But she did round with many of the top yachts, running gently among her big sisters who, to say the least, were puzzled by her presence. As the westerly freshened, the bigger yachts drew away to battle for the first boat honours, but *Mistral* swept on, sure in the knowledge that her handicap had placed her, once again, in the winner's circle.

For Ben Seaborn, *Mistral* was a jewel, and he had just reason to be proud of the perky little yacht, one of his stable of winning thoroughbred designs. But to Bill Baillargeon and his crew of Bill Booth, Phil Johnson, and Wayne Stone, the achievement of two Swiftsure wins will burn bright forever in their memories. While *Mistral* can nod for many a year to come at many a friendly mooring, before so small a yacht will match her shining record.

MISTRAL / JAMES McVIE

DOUBLE OVERALL WINNER

In 1969, the largest ocean racing fleet ever assembled in Canada gathered in Victoria's Inner Harbour on Friday evening: 164 boats entered in both Swiftsure and Juan de Fuca. Added to the IOR Swiftsure fleet this year were 12 PHRF boats, the first performance group ever to compete in the offshore event. In this their first outing, James Marta's *Intrepid* from Seattle took first, with *Hansa*, skippered by R. Carlson, Gig Harbor, taking second.

A new high profile powerhouse joined the IOR fleet in the shape of Langdon Hedrick's *Six Pack*. During the evening her crew spread her tremendous 2.2 oz. drifter on the Empress lawn in order to attach telltales. The sheer size of this sail gave fair warning of light weather speed.

From the 9:30 a.m. start on Saturday, May 31st, light northerly and easterly breezes sent the fleet away in a series of multi-hued crescents, as each class fanned out for sailing room with spinnakers in full bloom. From the air, the whole Strait seemed to be covered with floating blossoms; the fair winds held and built up to around 15 knots before dying away at dusk.

Mary Bower took an early lead and only relinquished it twice during the whole race: once when *Six Pack* edged her at the turning vessel, *RCN's Miramichi*, and again when *Diamond Head* nipped her by three minutes at the finish. It was one of the slowest races on record with the first boat crossing at 10 p.m. on Sunday in very light airs. It was late in the afternoon when the stragglers got a break and westerlies to 20 knots set them boiling for home. Even then, boats were finishing all night long and well into Monday morning.

When it was all over, *Diamond Head* had some small revenge for her one second loss to *Mary Bower* in 1966; this time, she led *Mary* across the line by a scant three minutes. On corrected time, *Mary Bower* won the overall, *Swallow*, sailed by Phil Johnson Jr., Seattle Y.C. took second, and *Six Pack*, third. Bonar Davis' *Hyak*, a modified Discovery 32, out of Royal Van nailed down a solid fourth. The inclusion of PHRF classes in both Swiftsure and Juan de Fuca swelled the number of entries to an all time high and gave fair notice that Swiftsure was to become one of the

biggest and best known events on the International yachting scene.

Juan de Fuca winners were West Van's Gordon Hill, whose *Ariki IV* finished first and placed first overall in CCA Division I. Division II was won by Richard Marshall's *Seaquin* (CYC). PHRF winner of the *Anacortes Yacht Club Trophy* was Edmonds Yacht Club's Albert W. Priest in *Telani*.

TAVEUNI / JAMES McVIE

SUNBIRD / JAMES McVIE

35/ SWIFTSURE 1970 and Lol Killam's Graybeard

Yachts become paired, in retrospect, as time blurs statistics: matched duos like *Maruffa* and *Adios* from the Fifties; *Mary Bower* and *Diamond Head* from the Sixties, and the 1970 antagonists, *Endless Summer* and *Graybeard*.

When the America's Cup Challenger, *Dame Pattie*, was purchased by Vancouver's George O'Brien, arriving in Vancouver in April from Australia, the stage was set for the first Swiftsure win by a hot, all out racing machine which had been designed to meet the challenge of match racing at its most competitive.

Hastily converted to meet CCA and PIYA racing requirements, and renamed *Endless Summer*, after the film on globetrotting surf chasers, the 12 Metre acquired a removable self-draining cockpit, chemical toilet, fold-up berths, camp-out galley, and outboard engine with an exceptionally long shaft. Towed from race to race by a runabout tender, she appeared, poised, on the Swiftsure start line, rating 67.8, a full 11 feet less than her newly launched rival, *Graybeard*.

Endless Summer was in luck. The wind patterns, for the first time in 25 years, gave a beat both ways. With her ability to outpoint every other boat on the course, she sliced up to windward, favoured by a light to moderate sou'wester which held all day Saturday, and a moderate southeasterly all day Sunday. Taking an early lead, she outdistanced the fleet, crossing the line around 2 p.m. Sunday, to sweep all four trophies available: first around the mark, first to finish, first overall, and first in Division I.

Placing second, just days after launching, Lol Killam's *Graybeard* announced her potential, while tuning up for the Maui Race. *Graybeard* was second around the mark, second finisher, and second in Division I.

With *Velaris*, Lol Killam learned something. "If you're going to have a boat to race, don't have things that are all beautiful and will annoy you. Build something rough and tough that will meet any abuse of a careless crew member."

He did. *Greybeard* was almost an ugly duckling, compared to her elegant, polished predecessor. In *Velaris*, Lol logged 14 consecutive Swiftsures. Along the way, he was bitten by the Ocean Cruising Bug. In 1965, he and fellow

Royal Van clubmate Jim Innes rounded up three yachts willing to go on the first Victoria-Maui Race. Namely, Killam, Innes, and one other, which happened to be Victorian Ronnie Ramsay's steel hulled Robert Clark designed *Norena of Wight*.

Killam chuckles in the recollection: "It was huge fun. The people in Hawaii didn't know we were coming. They didn't wake up until the week after we got there that there had even been a race. Then, they just went nuts. Started having receptions. Wanted to promote the thing and keep it going."

They did. Out of that experience, Killam discovered that he loved ocean racing more than racing in triangles. In fact, just ocean passages. Even the trip back was just as much fun. The experience that really confirmed it was travelling with *Stormvogel*, just for the ride, from Vancouver to San Francisco, and then being invited to go on the Mexican Race with Brunzeel.

Killam discovered that a man can have a 73 foot boat, if he gets a whole lot of strong young guys to do all the work. He never would have dared if he hadn't had that experience with *Stormvogel*.

And so, the *Graybeard* idea incubated. Lol was now more interested in cruising than racing. But he didn't want a slow cruising boat. All his ideas of speed went into the design. The thought was, "If it goes fast, it can go in some races. If it doesn't, so what?" The new boat had to be comfortable and efficient. "Beauty it just doesn't have. We never even discussed anything like that."

And so, with a scratch pad of his own ideas, Lol Killam approached naval architect Peter Hatfield to "design such a thing." Hatfield went home and made a preliminary drawing which included an overhang at the stern, which all his previous designs had. This was the first thing to go. Killam wanted a transom right down to the water. He got one.

This was hard for an architect to live with: an owner who asked for detailed reasons if any of his ideas would not or could not be implemented. The reverse was not true. Lol admits, "No big architect would have done it." Hatfield was flexible, and the *Graybeard* was a winner.

Peter Hatfield and Lol Killam produced a boat between them unique in its design and ideas. Brother Bill Killam's ICL Engineering firm, which knew all about fibreglass through building tanks and pipes for pulp mills, was eager to build the brainchild. So emerged a three way partnership. Meeting once a week, the designer, owner, and builder would check the progress, while Lol worked 15 to 16 hours a day, keeping abreast of all the details.

Says Killam, ''This type of construction is still unique. I don't think anybody has ever built one of this type since, with all of these square fibreglass pipe stringers, which are tremendously strong. It was 13 months from the time I first talked to Peter until she was launched.'' Which was pretty fast, considering that Hatfield had never before designed a yacht of that magnitude; ICL had never built any, and Killam had never designed or even built a boat.

As he spoke, Lol quietly ignored the calendar behind him on the main saloon wall. It pictured a trading schooner of the last century. The Killams of Yarmouth, Nova Scotia, then led the building and sailing of a fleet which carried Nova Scotia fish to the Caribbean, returning with sugar and related products. One round trip paid for the building of the boat. The rest was gravy. Killams of Yarmouth are still active on the Nova Scotia shorelines.

Graybeard's first Swiftsure found her far from complete. ''The main idea was to give it some little test before going around the world,'' Killam says. ''We didn't have cleats by the winches, for example, and had to tie the lines. Four fellows from the factory were still building it, laying inside covers on the floor, drilling, bolts being put in here and there all through the race. We didn't dare go through Race Passage and have to do any short tacking without any cleats. So we went outside and got trapped, as you would expect, for four hours while the whole fleet disappeared over the horizon.''

One ''bug'' that got ironed out in a hurry was the wind speed indicator which, jammed by a piece of metal, didn't register over 20 knots. The whole clew came out of the #1 genoa, and they figured afterward that it was blowing between 25 and 30 knots.

Even so, *Graybeard* salvaged a solid second out of that maiden race in 1970, overshadowed by *Endless Summer*. Subsequent Swiftsures yielded *Graybeard* her rightful laurels.

Very apty named, befitting an ocean roamer, the name *Graybeard* has special significance. A *Graybeard* is an old wave, which goes around and around the globe, never touching land, building up a terrific weight before it crashes on itself. This is what makes Cape Horn and Cape of Good Hope so rough.

While all the headlines of the 1970 race went to *Endless Summer* and her record breaking performance, and to the brand new wonder boat *Graybeard*, there were 167 other entries.

On the long course, after an unusually trouble-free race because of the generally light weather conditions, the lead yachts crossed the line in this order: *Endless Summer*, 2:20; *Graybeard*, 3:30; *Six Pack*, 6:25; *Crusader*, 6:27; *Adios*, 6:31; *Mara*, 6:35; *Porpoise III*, 6:47; *Gospel*, 6:55; *Diamond Head*, 6:56; *Moea*, 7:07. Corrected times put Bill Buchan's *Mara* in third spot, the Whipple/McClinton *Moea* finished fourth. Swiftsure PHRF with 13 entries gave first place to Dr. Paul McCullough's *Kaiulani*, Bremerton Yacht Club, with Robert Klein's *Dutch Flute*, Tacoma Yacht Club, taking second.

In the Juan de Fuca CCA, a Division II boat took the overall. *Kehloke*, sailed by West Van's D'Arcy McLeish, was first boat home, first in Division II, and first overall. Royal Vic's Peter Coombs' *Doxy II* won Division I. There were 33 entries.

LOL KILLAM / JAMES McVIE

GRAYBEARD / DENIS MASON

Celebrations reached a peak as the 1971 Swiftsure Eve party included a Victoria Days costume parade on the Causeway. Competing yachts, 191 strong, lay gunwale to gunwale, across the whole breadth of the harbour, their crews echoing the gaiety by returning the roll call roster with horns, ships bells, and shouts. The band guard of the Rainbow Royal Sea Cadets performed their Sunset Ceremony on the Legislative lawns, immaculate in tropical whites, and augmented by a field gun crew.

Scudding clouds and westerly squalls sent the fleet off on Saturday morning. A short sea sent the spray flying, causing many an entry to shorten down before reaching Race Passage. The tide was ebbing full bore through the Passage, while the winds were gusting to 45 knots outside. The full ebb with the westerly striving to hold the water back built up a king size tide rip, both inside the narrow pass and beyond. Eight to 10 foot waves leaped at the yachts in frenzied irregular patterns, breaking, cresting, curling, as the boats leaped and pounded in a nerve tingling display.

Something had to go: masts began to crumple knocking out many of Swiftsure's finest with breakages in those few wild minutes. *Sunbird, Six Pack, Warrior, Cubara, Lancer,* and *Norwester* were among the early casualties. Twenty-three yachts were forced out at this point; common problems were rigging failures, ripped sails, broken or damaged masts and booms, plus the sailor's bogeyman — seasickness.

It had been a thrilling start, and the big boats ate it up. *Diamond Head* found a new challenger in Joe Pollack Jr.'s *Min Sette* as they drove out into the lead. *Min Sette* was an all aluminum model built by a group of Boeing Airplane Company engineers. Her masts were especially fabricated to incorporate the internal bracing as utilized in building an airplane wing spar. She was a powerhouse in the heavy going, but she could not hold *Diamond Head*. By dusk the weather system had passed. By the time the leaders were off Neah Bay, the wind had moderated to a gentle evening breeze. During the long beat, *Diamond Head* worked out a lead of about one mile on the competition, with *Pemaquid, Adios,* and *Min Sette* in hot pursuit. *Gospel, Winsome IV,*

Kaos, and *Hyak* had sailed fast all afternoon. They were among the next group, and certainly within striking distance of the leaders.

Air spotters noted *Diamond Head* and *Pemaquid* closest to the mark boat as night fell. During the night, the wind failed completely leaving the yachts rolling aimlessly on the oily sea. The flat calm and heavy swells kept the leaders prisoner all night while the lighter boats well down the Strait managed to keep moving up. When the morning westerly finally filled in, the big boats had lost all the ground gained during the night time Saturday blow. Time had run out for the high handicappers. It became obvious that the smaller yachts would do well in the overall.

When prizes were awarded, Carl Jensen in *Adios* was first boat home; *Pemaquid* first to round the mark; and Tom O'Brien's *Hooligan* overall winner by 15 seconds over Bonar Davis' *Hyak.* Skipper O'Brien credits his win to his navigator, Jack Lidral, a 17 year veteran of Swiftsure.

1971 also marked the first entry of C & C yachts in Swiftsure. Toward the end of the CCA era in the late 1960s, two young naval architects, George Cuthbertson and George Cassian, combined in partnership with three Ontario builders, Bruckmann Manufacturing, Belleville Marine, and Hinterhoeller, with the object of building fast racing yachts which would also be equally comfortable as family cruisers. By 1971, C & C were the fourth largest sailboat builders on the continent, behind Whitaker Corp. (Columbia); Jensen Marine (California "Cal"), and Morgan.

The new corporation's first production boat, the C & C 35, was a comparatively light (as were most latter day CCA boats), yet very stiff six berth cruiser which was also fast. Very fine forward, short ended, with maximum beam aft, this design had a high aspect ratio sail plan. Vancouver's Tony Loach had one of the first 10 boats out of the mould. Christened *Tangent II,* she was still competitive in PHRF a decade later. Per Christofferson's *Terna II* was another C & C 35.

The IOR Juan de Fuca boats found the going to their liking, and for the leaders, the winds held on through the night. West Van's Dave Gibberd (who learned his early sailing in Victoria) brought *Gypsy G* home in 13 hours and 22 minutes to claim line honours and first in Division I. *Gypsy G*, a Spencer 31, was an experimental model used by John Brandlmayr to test trim tabs, etc,, under the name of *Coho*. Gibberd's remarkable time cut nearly four hours off Ned Ashe's 1965 record.

Second in Division I was the Corinthian entry *Cirrus*, skippered by J.W. Golberg, with third going to another Spencer 31, *Skilfish*, Don West, West Van. Gordon Hill led Division II in his Redwing 30 *Ariki*, followed by Don Miller in *High Life*, and Frank Musson's *Meltimi*. PHRF fleet winner in Juan de Fuca was Roger Oldham sailing out of the Canadian Forces Sailing Association in *Te-Pah*.

SUNBIRD / JAMES McVIE

MIN CETTE / JAMES McVIE

37/ *Spinnakers Up! — 1972*

A warm northeast wind provided an added bonus for shoreline spectators: a brilliant spinnaker start, the first in many years. An aerial observer covering those first few miles to Race Rocks had this to say: "It was an unbelievable sight; two great crescents of colour. From high above the fleet the tiny boats with their myriad coloured sails appeared as hundreds of bright blossoms carried by the current on the surface of a great river. Then just as suddenly, when they passed through Race Passage, the coloured lines dispersed, and each tiny dot of colour was on its own. The amazing fantasy of the spinnakers was over. The race was now on in earnest."

Favoured by steady winds and generally smooth seas, the offshore winds never reached more than 20 knots. It was inevitable that Swiftsure 1972 would break records. In this, one of the fastest races in memory, many veteran sailors rounded the markship in daylight for the first time. George O'Brien's *Endless Summer* established her lead within minutes of the gun, coasting to an easy win which knocked an incredible *two* hours and *six* minutes off *Maruffa's* 1957 record time, to finish at 9:24 Sunday morning, just 23 hours, 53 minutes and 32 seconds after the start.

The Twelve Metre, which had been so hastily converted from a racing machine in 1970, by now had added 1,700 pounds, and also traded her earlier longshaft outboard for an 85 hp Perkins diesel. Aussie designer Warwick Hood, who had given her life as *Dame Pattie*, was among an international crew which included Californians and one comely female New Zealander.

In the absence of *Graybeard*, off around the world, Seattle's *Adios* paced *Endless Summer*, and with her great offwind ability, led the Twelve Metre around the mark just before 7 p.m. Thanks to the following wind, yachts remained grouped on the outbound leg. Within half an hour after the two frontrunners rounded, another small cluster made the turn. At this point they were all potential winners on corrected time.

Here, luck rode on the skipper's decisions. Those who chose to go directly to the Canadian shore won out over those who headed south for the U.S. side. The wrong choice made a difference of half a day at the finish line.

For example, two yachts which rounded in the first group went their separate ways, and ended up 79 places apart in the final standings.

A prerace favourite, John Newton's new C & C 39, *Pachena,* in spite of carrying Swiftsure aces Ches Rickard and Pat Leslie, Olympic sailor Steve Tupper, and top foredeck man Doug Race, fell into a hole off Flattery, and by 10 p.m. Saturday had drifted down to Neah Bay, where she still sat at 9 a.m. Sunday morning. Meanwhile, Per Christoffersen's C & C 35 *Terna,* which rounded ninth behind *Pachena,* struck out for the British Columbia shore after observing *Pachena's* plight. Once there, she picked up enough wind to reef her main, finishing at 1:27 p.m. Sunday. Luckless *Pachena* ultimately finished at 5:47 p.m. *Terna* missed first in Division III by abandoning the B.C. coast too soon. Per felt sure that his old rival *Pachena* would be coming down the American side and moved out into mid-stream to cover her. The move cost *Terna* her Division III win, since Steve Crary's *Jubilee,* a Seattle C & C 35, which rounded much later than *Terna,* struck immediately for the Canadian shore and followed the Vancouver Island coast in stronger westerlies, all the way in to the finish. She crossed seven minutes ahead of *Terna* to win her division and place fifth overall.

Final standings on corrected time gave *Endless Summer* a clean sweep; first boat home, first in Division I, and first overall. Corinthian's *Hooligan,* sailed by Lerch & McVittie, was no match for *Endless Summer,* but her very creditable showing gave her a solid second. Next in overall order were C. Bamford's *Checkmate, Adios, Jubilee,* and *Terna.* Division II honours went to Royal Van's *Caroline,* with *Jubilee* taking Division III. *Vancouver Yacht Club Trophy* for Division IV was won by *Hooligan.*

PHRF Division A winner was *Jeunesse II,* Paul Cote's 48 foot Hughes yawl. Jim Smith, University of Washington Sailing Club, skippered *Predicament II,* winning Division B.

The 28 boat Juan de Fuca fleet made fast time with *Ambush,* a Cal 29 from Tacoma, first boat home at 4:06

Sunday. Corrected times gave first overall to *Climax,* Don Smith's Catalina 27 from Port Madison. Steve Merriman's Columbia 26 *Vandal,* Royal Vic, took Division II.

Juan de Fuca PHRF mustered 47 entries, resulting in great racing. *Avenger II,* J. Upward, West Van, won out overall and took first in Division D. Maple Bay's Peter White topped Division C in *White Squall.*

1972 broke many Swiftsure records, including the biggest entry to date, 213 boats. Spinnakers up? You bet. Two hundred and thirteen of 'em!

DIAMOND HEAD / JAMES McVIE

38/ "Driftsure" — 1973

Since her debut in 1970, *Graybeard* had lost two major ocean races to converted America's Cup Twelve Metre yachts. In Swiftsure 1970, she lost to *Endless Summer,* followed in 1972 by the Sidney-Hobart Race which she lost to Ted Turner's *American Eagle,* after a titanic boat for boat, battle across the Tasman sea. However, by 1973's Swiftsure, *Endless Summer's* potential powerhouse had been reduced by modifications to bring her within PIYA specifications: most notably, her mast shortened by 17 feet, a significant factor when it came to drifting in light airs.

An hour after the start, *Graybeard,* outpointing and outpacing *Endless Summer,* went through to weather in the 10 knot westerly, establishing a lead which she never relinquished. Sailing easily and very fast, *Graybeard* rounded the mark vessel on the Bank at 11 p.m. Other lead boats rode the steady westerlies to make the turn just after midnight.

The boats that did well held to the Canadian side on the way out as far as Sooke, before crossing to the American shore. In so doing they had the advantage of 20 knot winds which pushed them well on their way before the tide began to flood at 4 p.m. Those who crossed too soon after clearing Race Passage, encountered much lighter winds and stronger adverse tides on the U.S. side.

After midnight, drifting conditions prevailed, with most of the fleet unable to round until dawn. At first light a gentle southeaster allowed many to fly their chutes out to the mark. They started their homeward course on a beat, until the breeze petered out altogether around noon on Sunday.

This section of the race turned into a classic "Driftsure" as a flukey westerly struggled and failed to become established. When the strong ebb set in against them on Sunday night, many yachts anchored to hold the precious ground they had gained in their day long battle to reach Race Rocks. Many skippers retired due to shore commitments, including *Endless Summer.* The more determined stuck it out, as witnessed by yachts trickling across the finish line as late as Monday noon.

Although *Graybeard's* sweep was the top news story, there were other interesting performances: Seattle's Bill Buchan, competing for the first time in a "non-family" boat, skippered *Bydand,* a brand new one ton Ranger 37, to a convincing win in Division III, and second overall. Division II settled into a contest between John Newton's C & C 39, *Pachena,* and Harvie Davidson's Redline 41 *Wingaway.* John led as far as Sheringham Point where he sailed into a flat spot. Harvie quickly spotted *Pachena's* plight, staying clear of his becalmed rival. He held this advantage to the line, finishing four minutes ahead.

The 30 foot Scampis made their mark, as Vlad Plavsic brought *Orao* across the line seven minutes ahead of *Mistral* to take Division IV. In the Juan de Fuca Race, another Scampi, the new *Malda,* helmed by novice saltwater skipper from landlocked Alberta, Colm Hogan, rounded Clallam Bay far ahead of the fleet, romping home to also claim line honours. Hogan chose to cross the Strait at Sooke. A factor which, by good luck or good management, allowed him to lay the mark while those competitors venturing as far west as Sheringham overstood the mark by as much as five miles. *Malda* was racing in PHRF Division C.

Juan de Fuca IOR Division I went to Vance Bingham's *Ambush,* a Cal 29, from Port Angeles. Division II honours went to Brian Griffin's *Finisterre,* a Ranger 26 from Bellingham. First in PHRF Division D was Royal Vic's Bert Buchanan in Cal 25 *Lairig Ghru.*

Whereas the calms and tides played havoc with the Swiftsure fleet with 63 dropouts, only four abandoned the Juan de Fuca event. For many a skipper, 1973 will go down as a frustrating experience. But in spite of light winds, entries continued to build. Driftsure it was. But 255 yachts gave it their best go.

PACHENA / **JAMES McVIE**

39/ A Foggy Start — 1974

Not a ripple marred the sea at the start line as the record 262 yacht fleet powered back and forth. Then, adding insult to injury, fog descended a scant 10 minutes prior to the 10 minute warning gun. Over the next few hours, this blanket reduced visibility to 100 yards. During a short break in the blanket, IOR started, delayed by an hour and a half, but nevertheless, underway under spinnaker in a gentle southeasterly.

Once again the mist socked in and it took another hour and a half before Swiftsure PHRF and Juan de Fuca started, under handicap of a mere whisper of southeasterly wind.

Chutes set and aided by a strong ebb, the IOR fleet ghosted to Race Rocks, led by a new C & C 43 from Seattle, Charles Schiff's *Epic*. Sliding through Race Passage on the strength of the current, they hit the westerly which was to prevail in varying strengths for the remainder of the weekend. By 3 p.m. the flood had started, catching those yachts which started after noon and had managed to drift on the fading southeaster in a direct line to Race Rocks. There they sat for an hour while the yachts which had gone close inshore picked up the westerly which started along the shoreline.

This group reached Race Rocks to meet the flood and westerly gusting to 25 knots. The best strategy under these conditions was to play the back eddies as close to shore as possible, while allowing for very shifting winds patterns. After an hour of these confused conditions, most boats had cleared the Race, only to face the strong flood for another five hours. At 6 p.m., the stragglers were still fighting to clear Race Passage.

The generally strong, steady westerly blowing over 30 in mid-channel had the tide with it, but blew longer on the American side. During the night, as usually happens, winds lightened with the westerly filling in at 9 a.m. around the mark boat. Under these conditions, it was *Graybeard* first around the mark and across the line, unchallenged in her second sweep of the four available firsts.

Cal yachts were still winning although, by now, relegated to PHRF. Guv Teats' flush deck Cal 40, *White Squall* was first in Division A.

C & C yachts were unbeatable, skimming the three top places off both Division II and Division III. John Newton's C & C 39 *Pachena*, followed by Harvie Davidson's *Wingaway*, Bob Crary's C & C *Midnight Special*, and Brian Wertheimer's sister ship *Biscuit Eater*, both from Seattle, led Division II. In Division III, Greg Oliver's Viking 33 *Distant Drummer* came first, followed by two sister ships, Bill van Leewen's *Labrisa* and Dutchman ace Peter Byrne and Don Speirs' *Beserker*, all brand new within the year.

Because 1974 was also a Maui Race year, Swiftsure also drew entries tuning up for the ocean event, including two of Royal Van's Spencer 53s: Dick Nelson's *Naknek* and F.W. Patterson's *Andante*. John Buchan appeared in *Assault*, placing second in Division I and fifth overall. A very much modified Buchan 37, flat bottomed with fin keel and foam ends, *Assault* was a custom yacht; John designed, built, and later, modified her with radical keel surgery, creating a unique entry in the best Buchan tradition.

Unlike the larger race, 1974 Juan de Fuca never ran out of wind. At 6 a.m., while the Bank was bathed in light airs, these yachts surged home with 25 knots of wind behind them, led by Ray Fiedler's Cal 29 *Gem*, a Seattle boat.

By this time, the level rated "ton" yachts were leaving their mark on the available trophies. Overall IOR winner was Bob Vynne's Ranger 26 *June Bug*, also from Seattle. Meanwhile, *Fred*, skippered by Vancouver's Dr. George Wilkins, won IOR Division II, in the first of what was to become his "even year victories", a string which he extended through 1976 and 1978.

A former Dragon sailor, Wilkins' hobby is building and campaigning level rated yachts. Originally from Perth, Australia, Wilkins' flair extends to the whimsical naming of his boats, *Fred, Fred Jr.,* and *Fred Again* (the initials stand for Flaming Ridiculous Economic Disaster). The first *Fred*, fresh from her Swiftsure triumph, went on to the 1974 World Quarter Tons in Sweden, where it placed 10th out of 56. Manufacturer Don Clark, along with Vancouverites Bill Cote and Doug Race, made up the crew. This *Fred* evolved from a San Juan 24 hull, the hot yacht designed by Canadian small boat sailor Bruce Kirby, one-time Olympic

Finn representative and long-time International 14 racer whose Laser is the most successful dinghy of the decade. In fact, San Juan 24's have been compared to dinghies for their ease of handling.

Wilkins' next boat, *Fred Jr.,* placed 10th in the 1975 Worlds in France, but he bounced back again in 1976 with *Fred Again,* another modified Kirby design which won the IOR overall Juan de Fuca trophy in 1976, prior to competing in the Texas Quarter Ton Worlds in 1977, where he placed seventh overall.

Humphrey Golby comments on the race: "It was about 9 a.m. Sunday when we picked up *Graybeard* from the observation plane. The sun shone and the wind was northeasterly about 12 to 15 miles per hour. *Graybeard,* mid-channel in the vicinity of Sombrio Point, had the Strait to herself. Not another yacht was in sight. As we flew over her, we were privileged to see one of the world's finest ocean racers in action. The tremendous genny, the high aspect main and mizzen were flawless in the morning sun. As this great lone beauty sliced easily through the Strait, she left the clear "V" of her wake for almost a mile astern."

As scratch boat, *Graybeard* had to give over three hours' handicap time to *Pachena* and *Wingaway*. When the corrected times were in, they proved just how effective the IOR ratings are. *Graybeard* was first overall by 32 minutes over *Pachena* and 37 minutes over *Wingaway*, which has to be excellent handicapping for such widely different yachts over the 170 mile distance.

GRAYBEARD & ENDLESS SUMMER / DENIS MASON

The starting area was hazardous as 321 Swiftsure and Juan de Fuca hopefuls plunged in short, choppy seas and erratic, westerly gusts. Protest flags were the order of the day as yachts collided in the strong wind and crowded conditions, with dismastings and broken gear among the casualties. The big Division 1 boats found the early going much to their liking as *Endless Summer, Warrior, Naknek, Scaramouche, Epic,* and *Race Passage* led the way.

The wind held all afternoon, and *Endless Summer,* with a newly restored regulation Twelve Metre mast, and skippered this year by Al Sturgess and a young Royal Van crew, made the most of the long beat, arriving at Tatoosh so far in the lead that she couldn't identify the boats astern. Then the wind died, and a very disappointed crew squeaked around the mark boat just ahead of Bruce Hedrick's 50 foot Brit Chance designed cutter *Warrior.*

Around the Bank, winds were light to negligible through Saturday evening and all day Sunday as the fleet moved slowly homeward. These conditions were made to order for the smaller yachts, with the leaders in Divisions III, IV, and V gradually but surely closing the gap on the front runners. By noon on Sunday, it became apparent that the overall winners would be among these boats.

At 1:28 Monday morning, *Warrior* finally crept over the line to claim the City of Victoria Trophy for first boat home. *Scaramouche,* another capable Seattle yacht, crossed second, skippered by Bob Alexander. Third spot went to John Buchan's new *Heather* (later disqualified for problems at the start). When time allowances were calculated, *Scaramouche* dropped to 27th overall, while *Warrior's* corrected position slid to 55th!

Elusive, J.E. Sprouse's Ranger 29, sailing out of the Portland Club, with a rating of only 21.6 and a time allowance of 7 hours and 33 minutes, had no difficulty saving her time, and won the *Swiftsure Trophy.* She was closely followed (on corrected times) by Mike Pope's *Vatican II,* Ken Pearce's *Pearce Arrow, Super Pickle, Tonic,* and *Bydand.*

One boat which did exceptionally well, foreshadowing an overall victory in the years ahead, was the Ganbare *Pearce Arrow.* She had rounded, boat for boat, fourth behind *Endless Summer, Warrior,* and *Scaramouche,* continuing among the first five yachts all the way home, crossing the line just before 3:30 a.m. to place third overall.

These two top Canadian yachts chose mirror image courses: *Vatican* followed the Canadian shore outward bound, returning on the American side. *Pearce Arrow* crossed to the American shore on the way out, then rock hopped down the Canadian coast on Sunday, finding no winds over five knots from the mark to the finish.

The Juan de Fuca fleet had better luck with the wind. While the Swiftsure fleet wallowed in dead calms off Tatoosh, the breeze held all night between Clallam Bay and Race Rocks. Over half the Juan de Fuca boats had finished by day-break Sunday. One who didn't make it was R. Zell's *Elan,* a 27 foot Morgan, racing out of the Corinthian in IOR Division I. Running under spinnaker with the tide, she ran aground at Race Passage early Sunday morning, remaining there, high and dry and badly holed, until hauled off by a tug the next day. Initially, Portland's PHRF entry *Destiny* was thought to be first boat home when she crossed at 1:49 Sunday.

When results were finalized after the protests were settled, *Destiny* was disqualified. It is interesting to note that Skipper Bill King ignored the usual pattern for the course. He elected to go outside Race Rocks, both on the way out and on the return, making one long hitch from the start line to the U.S. shore; then making only one tack at Pillar Point before rounding Clallam Bay mark at 5:30 Saturday afternoon, about four miles ahead of the next boat.

Blue Fox, a Tacoma Scampi skippered by J. Gonyea, took first boat home honours and first in Division VII (the old Div. II) Tony Hebert's *Double Entry,* Royal Van, C & C 33, took Division VI (the old Div. I). In PHRF *Union Depot,* Tacoma took Division D; Terry Cattell's *Auriga,* West Van, Division E, and perennial favourite, Bill Gardner's *Lucy Alice,* Seattle, copped honours in Division F.

THE PEARCE ARROW / JAMES McVIE

41/ Man Overboard! — Tragic 1976

The double challenge of Swiftsure, followed by the 1976 Victoria-Maui Race, lured two classy denizens of the world's ocean racing circuits, to hold court in Victoria's Inner Harbour, Jim Kilroy's 79 foot maxi-ketch *Kialoa*, and the 62 foot California sloop, *Ragtime*. Both these giants came with well established records of their prowess across the oceans of the world.

Strong southeast winds provided a colourful spinnaker start as the mighty *Kialoa*, at the leeward end of the line, led the parade toward Race Rocks at 9 a.m. on Saturday, May 29. Ninety-one IOR boats were in that first group and, if there is such a thing as a 'who's who' of yachting, many of the great names passed in grand review that morning. As the weather front passed, the wind rapidly hauled around to the west, and the long, familiar beat to Swiftsure began. Steady winds in the mid 30s marked the outbound leg, and by late afternoon, the sea began to build ominously. Around 5 p.m., *Graybeard's* mast crumpled when a main shroud let go. Killam and his crew struggled to try and save the mast by lashing it alongside, but in the end, they had to cut it loose. The turnbuckle that gave way had sailed the equivalent of two trips around the world, through the worst that the Atlantic, the Pacific, and the Tasman seas could throw at her, yet on this fateful day, the erratic seas of Swiftsure laid her low. Meanwhile, gale force winds in the open ocean beyond Tatoosh built up steep seas of 20 to 25 feet.

Kialoa, chased by Bill Niemi's C & C 61, *Joli*, rounded the mark at 9:30 Saturday, with *Ragtime* in hot pursuit. However, as the front runners swept down the Strait, their size contributing to their momentum, the smaller yachts were caught as the wind died away on Sunday and the strong ebb counteracted any potential progress.

Twenty-seven hours after the starting gun, *Kialoa* crossed the finish line at 12:09 p.m. Sunday. Three minutes later, *Ragtime* zipped over, followed by *Joli* at 12:17 and *Weatherly* at 12:44. This race marked the debut of the former America's Cup defender, *Weatherly*, which had recently been bought by Tacoma yachtsmen Lynn Sommers and Alan Buchan (no relation to the Seattle Buchans). In spite of the heroics of the maxi boats, it fell to a much smaller yacht to win the *Swiftsure Trophy* for the best corrected time performance overall: *Ladybug*, a 30 footer designed and built by Seattle's Star Champion Alan Holt. In fact, the first eight places on corrected time were taken by Division IV boats. *Joli* placed 20th, *Ragtime* 30th, and *Kialoa* 39th. *Kialoa* won first boat to round and first boat home. *Joli* topped Division I, *Surprise* Division II, and Greg Oliver's *Distant Drummer* took Division III for Royal Vic.

At midnight on Saturday, over Channel 16 (the high frequency distress channel) came the frantic cry of a woman's voice: "Help. Man overboard. Help need help." Many stations, the Naval escort vessels, and both Coast Guards were monitoring that channel, but no position or identification was given in that first desperate call for help. Further contact was finally established by the U.S. Coast Guard and the position pinpointed: the yacht was identified as *Native Dancer*.

The story of *Native Dancer's* tragedy has been told and retold in the press and the report of the coroner's inquest. Suffice it that this history records the facts and relates them to the subsequent Fastnet disaster. *Native Dancer* was close hauled on port tack close in under the Canadian shore off Bonilla Point and heading for Carmanah. The predicted gale that weekend came through from the south, southwest, 30 to 35 knots, with sea conditions 14 to 16 foot swells. In the shoal water area where *Native Dancer* found herself, the seas were breaking badly, and these great, cresting waves literally swamped her. *Native Dancer* was knocked flat on her beam ends. Her skipper, Wilbur Willard of Seattle, was swept right out of the cockpit by the second of these giant waves.

He was wearing a floater jacket, and the surf carried him 20 or 30 feet from the boat in a matter of seconds. Crewman, Greg Griffif, struggled with the nylon lashings on the life ring, and by the time he cut it loose and finally threw the ring, pole, and floating light towards Willard, they fell short by about 10 feet. No one saw him again. John Tonan was then discovered to be missing. When the next wave struck the helpless yacht, the life raft broke loose and was washed away. Possibly, this saved the lives of the remaining crew as they stayed in the cabin while the boat beached herself.

The yacht was driven relentlessly onto the beach, and as soon as the water was shallow enough, those left on board, Willard's wife Marly, Judy Martin, David Villua, Gordon Aigner, and Greg Griffif scrambled through the surf to safety. To their great relief and surprise, they met Tonan, who, moments before the tragedy, had donned his wet suit for warmth, and thus equipped, he had been able to reach the beach with only minor cuts and bruises.

The whole incident would appear to be one of errors in navigation and a generally casual approach to the very serious weather conditions of that day. The boat was fully equipped with all required safety gear, but the human factor is one that no committee can, or ever will, be able to govern.

This sudden needless tragedy in May of 1976 resulted in the only loss of life in Swiftsure competition. The realization that such a thing could happen added urgency to PIYA and Swiftsure Committee officials in their reconsideration of all entry requirements. Radical new developments in yacht design and the explosive growth of offshore racing fleets made stricter regulations mandatory. The subsequent disaster during the 1979 Fastnet in August, when 15 lives were lost, gave ample reason for all yachting bodies to give serious consideration to the prerequisites and specifications of all boats who claim the right to participate in organized offshore races.

Swiftsure officials who attended the Royal Yachting Association meetings in England were able to report that PIYA regulations here were far more comprehensive than any in existence in Europe. Certainly the latest revisions will stress safety and common sense, but more than that, the message has gone out loud and clear: when a racing skipper takes his boat and his crew offshore in competition he must give every consideration to the fact that when the yacht puts to sea, she is completely on her own.

World authorities on both sides of the Atlantic have re-emphasized the fact that each vessel, its captain, and its crew, are responsible for their own safety.

Unaware of the troubles on the long course, the Juan de Fuca fleet had somewhat unstable but not overpowering winds. Twenty out of 105 entries failed to finish and most of these in the smaller PHRF boats. *Fred Again*, Dr. George Wilkins, Royal Van, captured first overall by 28 minutes from Jan Huiber's *Sea Spell*. Wilkins took first in Division VII and *Sea Spell* settled for first boat home and first in Division VI.

The 69 PHRF entries were divided into Divisions D, E and F and the honours were divided as follows: first overall, *Lara*, Division D, Ken Clark Royal Van; first in Division E, *Courage Plus*, Stan Johnson, Willamette Y.C.; and *Sara*, Glenn McCormick, Quartermaster Sailing Club carried off Division F.

NATIVE DANCER / *DAISY GOODSPEED*

In 1977 for the first time, the PHRF entry overshadowed the IOR yachts 113 to 88. And this year, with moderate conditions and most of the race off the wind, either running or reaching, smaller yachts were able to share a good piece of the action. While the top honours were split by Vlad Plavsic's two tonner *Kanata* and Bob Smith's larger *Warlock,* 13 of the first 17 overall places went to Division IV yachts.

In the early stages against the flooding tide, it paid to reach along the shore and then play the back eddies on the land side through Race Passage, before emerging in mid-Strait to pick up the first fingers of the ebb. Alvin Narod's *Sunbird,* first through the Race ahead of eventual first-to-finish *Warlock,* made good time, but by late afternoon, the wind had died, leaving all to drift for four hours before the westerly filled in along the Canadian shore.

The main contest of the weekend was between *Warlock* and *Kanata.* Plavsic caught the Seattle yacht within minutes of the markship, rounding at 2:02 a.m. with *Warlock* hot on her heels at 2:08. They both elected to return via the Washington State side, with *Warlock* closer inshore, aiming for a tidal advantage.

Although the wind never broke 22 knots over the weekend, the run home was propelled by breezes strong enough to encourage many to break out bloopers to prevent broaching, while the downwind ride was faster mid-Strait or on the Washington shore, which allowed faster time on a close reach in the flooding tide.

While the *Swiftsure Trophy* went to *Kanata,* a tight contest developed for third and fourth overall between the previous year's winner, Alan Holt's *Ladybug,* and PIYA Measurer John Evetts' *Big Sister.* After an undistinguished start, *Big Sister* finally caught *Ladybug* at Race Passage, and emerged with a 100 yard lead on her rival by playing the back eddies at Race Rocks before turning the corner for the final homestretch run to the finish, where Holt managed to maintain the critical lead. Holt and Evetts were closely tailed by Bill Buchan's *Island,* which finished a close fifth overall, and could just as easily have beaten them both to the wire had Holt chosen to luff Evetts.

Kanata, which is St. Lawrence Indian dialect for Canada, ended up with three top honours: *Swiftsure Trophy; Royal Canadian Navy Trophy* for first to round, and first in IOR Division II. A computerized yacht, she was designed as a winner by Plavsic, a professional architect with a solid background in aeronautical design who had never sailed before 1968. Once bitten by the bug, however, Plavsic pursued success with a singleminded determination in both Canada and Europe. He won 33 out of 43 starts with *Orao,* a Scampi which placed third in the 1971 World Half Ton Championships in England, as well as placing first in Swiftsure IOR Division IV in 1973.

When he set out to build the ultimate racing machine, Plavsic incorporated many ideas from boats he competed against around the world, including some of the hottest one tons. After two years of sifting through all available designs, he established the fastest hull lines, sail/area displacement ratios and keel sections by scrutinizing IOR certificates of the world's leading one tonners.

The PHRF fleet, 113 strong, had plenty of competition on the Swiftsure course with Division C boats taking the four top places on corrected time. Doug Fryer's picturesque *African Star* took first in Division C and first overall.

The *Corinthian Yacht Club Trophy* for first in Division A was won by Bill Watkins in *Jubilee;* the *Stormy Weather Trophy* for Division B went to Donald Flynn in *Outward Bound.*

The Juan de Fuca fleet set sail for Clallam Bay with 28 entries in IOR and 96 in PHRF. Generally wind conditions were good. The problem for many entrants was the extreme tidal flow, flooding against them on Saturday afternoon, and bucking the powerful ebb on the way home. However, there were few casualties, and only 12 yachts failed to finish.

Gotchagain, Bob Diehl, Bellingham, topped Division VI IOR, saving his time for the overall. Division V winner was Gus Hodge's *First Morning,* also from Bellingham. First boat home for the *San Juan Trophy* was *Skilfish,* which also won Division D, PHRF. Division E went to Gary Jacobi's *Salty Dream,* Royal Vic, and Division F, R.

AFRICAN STAR / JAMES McVIE

43/ 1978 — the Ultra Lights, the Maxis and the ¾ Tonners

Again, the 1978 running of the Victoria-Maui Race was the drawing card for some of the world's most successful and exotic yachts to enter Swiftsure. Two of yachting's most glamorous and controversial Ultra Light Displacement boats appeared in the form of *Drifter* and *Merlin*. *Drifter,* registered out of Maui's Lahaina Yacht Club, had sailed over to participate in the return race to Maui in July. *Merlin,* the 61 foot streaker, designed and built by Don Lee in California, was chartered for both Swiftsure and Maui Races by Seattle's Doug Fryer, a veteran Swiftsure competitor in *African Star.*

Light displacement was not really new. Francis Herreshoff's *Common Sense of Yacht Design* many years ago championed light boats, but severe limitations were imposed by the available materials. Much of the technology and many of the materials used in today's Ultra Lights have only been available in the last few years.

These ultra-lights perform best in the surfing conditions found in Trans-Pac. Their presence there has forced race officials to introduce heavily weighted ratings against them in order to preserve some semblance of balance in the fleet. Even the Victoria-Maui Race does not provide optimum conditions. Over the years, Swiftsure has been characterized by stretches of rock crawling in back eddies combined with a lot of windward work, some of it in very light conditions. The very nature of a short windward-leeward course works against the big ULDBs. Or does it?

How did they fare in competition with maxi-sloop *Windward Passage* and Lahaina entry *Bravura*? This big boat onslaught skimmed the foam off the elapsed time results. Aided by a 25 knot westerly which filled in after the start, they crumpled the previous course record of 23 hours, 53 minutes set by *Endless Summer* in 1972. No less than six yachts, two of them local, eclipsed it: Fritz Johnson's *Windward Passage* (20 hours 36 minutes 35 seconds) followed by *Drifter* (20:39:52); *Merlin* (20:48:30); Seattle boats *Warrior* and *Outrageous* (22:19:14 and 22:25:37), and *Bravura* (23:05:40).

A mishap marred *Merlin's* performance when the main halyard broke, disappearing into the mast. She continued under headsail until a new halyard could be jury rigged for the main. (*Merlin* went on to clip 2½ days off the 12½ day Maui Race record set by the C & C 61, *Joli*.)

Even so, the best these boats could manage in terms of trophies was the *City of Victoria* for first boat home (*Windward Passage*) and first to round the mark. Exactly half of the six IOR trophies went to Seattle's Buchan brothers, Bill and John, who copped Swiftsure, first in IOR II, and first in IOR IV.

Swiftsure 1978 was unique for yet another reason. The race supplied an informal tune-up opportunity for most of the ¾ tonners which had assembled for the World Championship in early June, for which the two long distance races followed roughly the Juan de Fuca and Swiftsure courses. Some of the ¾ ton yachts elected the Swiftsure and some the Juan de Fuca; and among them, they adroitly secured both overall trophies, as well as setting a short course record.

Overall Swiftsure honours went to *Sachem,* Bill Buchan's Brit Chance designed daggerboarder. Dubbed a "skimming dish", *Sachem* left the one and two tonners in her wake, reaching past them at speeds in excess of nine knots. It was the first time in race history that the overall trophy had been won by a non-keel boat (something the Deed of Gift didn't make allowances for).

Following the Buchan tradition, *Sachem* was built in Bill's garage, a joint effort employing full-time Chris Maas, a young Finn and Laser sailor (who also joined the crew), assisted by Bill. *Sachem's* hull is foam sandwich construction with two layers of cedar veneers epoxied on each side of the foam.

While Buchan trounced the big boats, Royal Van's *Gogama,* owned by Dave Everett, set a new course record for Juan de Fuca IOR classes. After a delayed start which sent the yachts off at noon on Saturday, *Gogama* rounded Clallam Bay marker at 7:15 p.m. in time to scorch back with the current, finishing at 1:30 a.m., covering the 78 miles in a new record of 13 hours, 5 minutes and 30 seconds, over two hours ahead of *Gotchaforgood,* second over the line. For this race, George Wilkins forsook his

"*Freds*" in order to skipper *Gogama* for Everett, and in so doing, extended his streak of "even year" victories to three.

Gogama scored a double "nautical hat trick" with this win. Already top 1978 Northwest ¾ tonner through earlier victories in Seattle's Great Equalizer and the Southern Strait of Georgia Race, the Peterson design stock Chaser boat swept Little Swiftsure with first to finish, overall handicap, and first in IOR Division V.

These ¾ tonners introduced another new wrinkle to Swiftsure: never had so many yachts come from so far away under someone else's steam to compete in Swiftsure. John MacLaurin's *Pendragon*, the eventual 1978 ¾ Ton World Champion, was designed and built in New Zealand. She crossed the Pacific Ocean on a freighter for the U.S. National ¾ Ton qualifying event in San Diego, before being trucked to Seattle, where she was launched for the final leg of her journey to Swiftsure Rendezvous in Victoria.

Three Graham and Schlageter designs were registered in the Great Lakes: Ron Lester and Don Porter's *Chocolate Chips*; David Hall and John Ball's *Discovery I*; and *Lobo*, owned by Ron Wolfson. These three yachts rode the roads fresh from qualifying victories in California. *Chips* and *Discovery I* had earlier crossed the continent overland to compete in San Diego.

The trials of the *Lobo* reached epic proportions in her bid to compete in the Pacific Northwest. Repairs to her rudder kept her from Swiftsure, while an engine breakdown in Seattle almost precluded her appearance in the ¾ ton event.

Over the course of the two events, Swiftsure and ¾ Ton, *Sachem*, *Chocolate Chips*, and *Pendragon* played musical transoms.

Division IV IOR Swiftsure went first, second, and third to *Sachem*, *Chocolate Chips*, and *Pendragon*. (*Chips*, like *Gogama*, came to the May/June competitions with a string of local successes, as well as first place in the qualifying U.S. Nationals.) However, ¾ Ton Worlds reversed the positions.

Pendragon, whose California crew included Lowell North, won the World Title over *Sachem* in a close series decided only in the last long distance race. A daggerboarder built of cold moulded ply on stringers coated with a layer of glass, *Pendragon* was designed exactly to the ¾ ton rule by New Zealander Laurie Davidson. Her light displacement (7,000 pound) hull was calculated to produce superior boatspeed, with weight centred, and a cut out transom which allowed the leading edge of the wave to pick up the buoyant object and push it forward, with little or no water arriving in the cockpit.

After the series, the controversy swirled around the relative merits of the daggerboarders versus the keel boats, and all the permutations and combinations of weight in this "oversized dinghy" competition.

While the spotlight shone on the ¾ ton Regatta and the Maui ULDBs, Swiftsure's orbit spun off a new race. Not at the end, but the beginning. Portland yachts decided to formalize their northward trek, expanding on an existing offshore race from Astoria down to Tilman and back to Gray's Harbour. In this year, they went international, with the intention of bringing up as many boats as possible for Swiftsure. The sponsoring Corinthian Yacht Club, basically a group of keen river sailors, contacted Royal Victoria Yacht Club requesting help with finding finishing facilities. Club Fleet Captain Barry Wright took on the project, and has anchored the committee operations on this end ever since.

This first year, the race from Astoria around Tilman mark and up to Victoria, some 250 miles, excluded boats in the 26 foot range, which were only allowed to race to the first mark and back.

The winds blew up to 55 mph, and the Coast Guard was very upset, predicting dire repercussions from the seven boat fleet. In actual fact, only one crew — the *Nimble* — had any food at all as they didn't dare go below. Flying chutes, they made record time to Flattery, where they sat becalmed for two full days in the slop. First to cross the line on Monday was Jim Christianson's *Aggression*, a Morgan 34T.

Last boat, Bill Nickerson's *Nimble*, a Cascade 42, deserved more than the bottle of champagne awarded to all finishers. *Nimble's* tenacity and resourcefulness probably came from her offshore experience. She has sailed every TransPac Race since 1967. And always in the crew is designer Bob Smith, who was involved in design on the last of the J boats.

On the first leg, on the way to Tilman, *Nimble* ripped her mainsail and broke her tiller. Deciding to carry on, Nickerson radioed back to Portland to his wife, who was waiting at the dock with an old main and baseball bat (they sailed in to pick up the supplies so they wouldn't be disqualified). Quickly, they fashioned the baseball bat into a new tiller and hoisted the new main, and continued the race!

For the next year, 13 boats made the circuit, and were joined by the HMCS *Oriole* with a raw crew of cadets who, in some cases, had their first taste of salt water en route down. Winners again were *Aggression* in IOR and the C & C *Pegasus* in PHRF. (The *Pegasus* crew are all firemen who "leave Portland to burn" over this racing period!)

By 1980, the race had grown to 20 boats. And again, several took off on the Maui Race, *Wizard* for the second time. This year, the smaller yachts were allowed to participate, with the smallest being Bob Smith Jr.'s San Juan 24 *Dream Machine*. The HMCS *Oriole* again sailed down the coast to join the race.

APHRODITE / JAMES McVIE

Early Saturday morning, the sky was overcast with rain threatening. Fitful puffy light winds came from several directions. A record 409 boat entry created 13 divisions: six in IOR and seven in PHRF for the two races. The first start was set for 9 a.m. for IOR Swiftsure. The committee had hopes of sending the fleet off in rapid order, so the smaller boats could be underway before the flood tide reached its maximum against them in Race Passage.

It was not to be; there were just too many boats in the starting area: 76 IOR Swiftsure yachts jammed the line, with many forced over ahead of the gun. The committee issued a general recall. After another 15 minutes, a comparatively clean start had only three yachts recalled. PHRF, with 163 entries, was even worse, taking two starts to get them away. The Juan de Fuca fleet learned from the earlier line log jams; both IOR and PHRF got off with one set of signals.

The smoke had scarcely cleared when the wind started to pipe up and haul around to the west. By the time the leaders were past Albert Head, many reefs were tucked in, while #2 and #3 genoas appeared. In the fresh going, most boats made the passage in one hitch. By the time the fleet started pouring through the Race, gusts were hitting 35. Confused tidal seas and sudden devastating squalls swept the area. Many boats were caught by the suddenness of the onslaught, plunging into almost immediate trouble. Several masts crumpled. In minutes, many of the smaller boats were doing their best to hang in under only a small working jib. Within two hours, over a hundred had given up. During the early afternoon, gusts were recorded up to 50.

During this period, the venerable *Dorade,* reappearing in Swiftsure after a 16 year absence, rammed the *Zubenubai Two,* which sank within a matter of minutes, fortunately, without injuries to either crew. The accident, involving William Hester's Maui racer and the durable Charlie Ross, with a reportedly undermanned former ocean racer, occurred about five miles east of Pillar Point, around 4 p.m. Saturday. *Dorade,* damaged in the collision which punched an 18 inch by three foot hole in *Zubenubai's* bow, limped back to shelter while Jim William's Cal 40 *Blue Marlin*

picked up the eight crew members in the life raft, who didn't even get their feet wet.

These conditions, however, were ideal for *Graybeard* and *Weatherly,* which soon surged into the lead, while Division I and II leaders were making terrific time to windward: *Warrior, Warlock, Wizard, Outrageous, Kotuku, Kanata, Chiron,* and *Discovery.*

The *Pearce Arrow* and *The Distant Drummer* led Division III. Though smaller, they handled beautifully. And as Greg Oliver said later, "*Distant Drummer,* once we got the rig right, settled down to do what she does best, that is, go like hell to windward. We literally sailed away from most of the competition. Our very narrow, high main, tremendous beam, and deep fin really did the job for us."

Weatherly was first around shortly after 9 p.m. with *Graybeard* 20 minutes astern. Excitement now ran high at Victoria race headquarters that a new course record might be set. With any sort of wind at all, the lead boats could be home by 6 in the morning. However, the wind died, as always, during the night. Dawn found *Weatherly* and *Graybeard* running neck and neck off Jordan river. They were about a mile off the Canadian shore, with *Graybeard* holding a slight lead. As the temperature rose, the wind swung back and forth under the land influence. By 6:30 a.m. they were off Beechey Head. *Graybeard* jibed, heading offshore to avoid the stronger currents at the Head. The ploy worked. *Weatherly* stopped in her tracks, eventually following suit.

In the meantime, *Graybeard* slid forward in the tide shadow of Race Rocks, but as she neared the Passage, the current carried her inshore within yards of Betinck Island. She hung there in the back eddy for 15 or 20 minutes until the first breath of the new day's sou' westerly picked her up, once again filling the great spinnaker, allowing her to slip almost effortlessly through the Passage against the rapidly increasing ebb tide. *Weatherly* decided to try it on the outside, but the wind had not yet filled in that far off shore; she was soon locked in a battle with the outgoing tide. For almost an hour, *Weatherly* never moved ahead by as much as a yard. After 20 hours of fierce competitive sailing, *Weatherly* was now running well behind her rival, with little chance to catch *Graybeard* for first boat honours.

Meanwhile, the morning westerly was building. In rapid order, the Division I, II and III boats, leaders in their fleets, entered the Race, presenting a magnificent picture as they swept through under spinnaker in the morning sun. First through after *Graybeard* was *Warrior*, followed by *Outrageous* and *Warlock* running neck and neck. *Outrageous* hung in the back eddy a moment too long and was stopped dead in her tracks by a shoaling rock. *Warlock* waved goodbye and was gone as *Outrageous* pivoted around, retraced her approach, and within two or three minutes swung free and was off once more in hot pursuit. Next came *Wizard, Heather,* and *Kotuku,* followed by the trio of *Kanata, The Distant Drummer,* and *Illusion,* a scant boat's length apart, with their stems cutting the water in photo finish formation.

It was obvious now that *The Distant Drummer* was well ahead of the lead boats on corrected time. Greg Oliver's only real problem was Ken Pearce's *The Pearce Arrow.* He had to give her 14 minute's time. As both boats were clocked through the Pass, *The Pearce Arrow* was less than 10 minutes astern. Halfway home, *The Distant Drummer* had stretched the lead and looked to have things well in hand. But as he entered the harbour, the wind momentarily slackened. *The Pearce Arrow* picked up a freshening westerly, literally flying those last few hundred yards.

Oliver crossed at 36:22:15, with Pearce following at 36:33:14. Corrected times gave *The Pearce Arrow* an elapsed time of 21:43:21 and 21:46:31 for *The Distant Drummer.* The Victoria boat had lost by the scant margin of 3 minutes 10 seconds. However, Oliver could take consolation in the fact that his second place finish was by far the best showing ever by a Victoria yacht.

For the second consecutive year, John Buchan's *Heather* took Division II; *The Pearce Arrow,* Division III, and Dennis Clark's San Juan 30 *Bumper,* Division IV.

The PHRF fleet had 90 finishers from 163 starters. The gear-busting winds, combined with the irregular tidal seas took a heavy toll of this more relaxed racing group during the first four hours. Many PHRF boats are largely family crewed, and not conditioned to pound the family cruiser/racer to windward for long periods in near gale conditions. From its very tentative beginnings, PHRF rating system is a firmly established aspect of competition. This less exacting rating formula makes it possible for any reasonably capable yacht of not too ancient vintage, to compete with her peers within a frame of reference that gives every competitor a chance at the honours.

Royal Victoria's Roland Bremer sailed his rejuvenated, modified Eight Metre *Reality* home first, an honour for the home club, which rarely fields any winners, and a credit to the owner, who recreated *Reality* in cold mould using the old Eight Metre *Reality* hull as the plug at Bent Jesperson's Sidney Yard. Recycling more than just the hull, the Bremers also used most of the original hardware and keel from the original yacht, including 13,000 pounds of lead. After only five hour's tuning, and carrying builder Bent and his son Eric in the crew, *Reality* proved that there can still be life left in a fine old favourite. (*Reality* raced 1960's Swiftsures when Jack Smith owned her.)

Tacoma's *Deliverance,* skippered by G. Palo (CYC), took first overall in PHRF on corrected time.

However, a Swiftsure "first" went largely unheralded and unannounced, overshadowed by the dramas of the larger race. Namely, the first "all girl" entry. Not only entered, but survived — no mean feat in those conditions — to place sixth in PHRF's 38 boat Division G.

What is spicy, expensive, and orange, weighing in at $8 an ounce? *Saffron.* The name fits the boat, declares San Juan 24 skipper, June Cameron. June, who has only been sailing for three years, attributes her cool to a childhood always around water in a rowboat or fishing. But she was never told to be afraid. She feels that this attitude is the key to successful survival in rough racing conditions.

Alternate skipper and dinghy sailor, Meg Hill, took the helm for the whole beat, "smiling the whole time". On the dozen or so times when the boat pounded in the rough going, she offered an apologetic, "Gee, I'm sorry."

The five woman crew, all from Vancouver, included young university grads Karen Renfrew, Michelle James, and Eleanor Frisk. A pre-start gear failure didn't faze them one little bit. When their jib halyard tangled with the electric wiring in the mast, they substituted the spinnaker halyard, sailing with it for the entire race, and hoisting the spinnaker in stops after rounding the mark.

In Juan de Fuca IOR, two of the top three boats came from a nucleus of six 1978 ¾ Ton World's veterans in the 15 entry Division V section. During the first four hours of pounding, the "Little Swiftsure" was a straightforward course through Race Rocks, bearing off to the U.S. shore, a theme which has had little variation over the years.

First to finish, Gerry Duncan's *Hagar,* a Ron Holland design, failed to save her time, placing second overall behind fellow Seattle-ite Tom Huckle's San Juan 30, *Outlaw,* first overall and first in IOR VI. Last year's record setting *Gogama,* with Dr. George Wilkins again at the helm with owner Dave Everett, hung in for third overall and second in IOR V. Overall PHRF winner was Gordon Cash's Scampi *Spinner.*

PORPOISE III / JOHN McVIE

45/ *Fifty Golden Years — 1980*

The Swiftsure Race Committee commemorated the 50th Anniversary with special events. To set the tone, they brought out a special Golden Anniversary information and race instructions brochure, highlighted by beautiful old sepia prints prepared by Jim McVie, which gave every contestant a worthwhile souvenir of the 1930-1980 era: the first Fifty Years.

General Chairman Frank Piddington and his able crew invited many oldtimers to join with contemporary skippers at a special Anniversary Luncheon in the Empress Hotel's Crystal Ballroom. Accordingly, many a Swiftsure veteran made the trip, and many were the reunions of old friends and old rivals. Frank spoke eloquently of the tremendous work done by early committee members long since retired, with special mention of Beau Ohrt and Monty Christopher, who have now crossed the ultimate finish line, and to Jack Gann, who was present at the luncheon. Jim McVie rated a special category for his constant photographic contributions to the Swiftsure record, while Humphrey Golby received a vote of thanks for his many years of broadcasting the Swiftsure story.

The chairman welcomed Frank Lock and Ace Lindsay, crew members aboard *Minerva* and *Westward Ho*, in the 1930 race. He told the gathering that Swiftsure was not the work of any one person, or even of any one committee, however large; but it was the result of co-operation and limitless contributions by many organizations. The Royal Canadian Navy has provided start vessels, turning mark, and escort vessels, communications service, and anything else that was asked of them, from 1947 through these many years. Also thanked were the United States Coast Guard for every assistance that they had given, the Canadian Coast Guard, and the City of Victoria.

The harbour spectacle presented 429 entries, rafted in orderly rows, nearly filling the whole inner basin. Thousands of passersby were awed by a fleet of this size, signal flags flapping, with mounting tension. Tomorrow morning at 9 a.m., the first warning gun would sound and May 24, 1980 would see the start of the renewal of the classic race.

Morning dawned dull and overcast, with a hint of rain. The wind was shifting from almost south to sou-west and back again. By the time the IOR fleet got away, the breeze had settled somewhat, and Divisions I, II & III were off to a clear start, with only one boat recalled. Wink Vogel's *Dream Machine* hit the line on gunfire and led for one brief moment. John Buchan's new 54 foot *Glory* started at the windward end close to Brotchie Ledge while Tacoma's Twelve Metre *Weatherly* elected the leeward start. These two led the pack, running almost neck and neck, with *Glory* holding the windward berth. By the time they had reached Albert Head, *Weatherly* was creeping through *Glory's* lee; by William Head she was clear ahead and surprisingly, now to windward of *Glory*.

The key to *Weatherly's* early lead, which put her round the outer mark at 8:35 p.m., was her ability to windward. She was almost a mile to weather of the fleet when she disappeared into the grey scud off Sooke.

By the time the bulk of the fleet had cleared Race Passage, the wind had freshened to 18 knots, with considerable sea running. Due in part to the slack tidal flow, there was not the disasterous rip that had floored so many of the smaller yachts in 1979. *Weatherly's* remarkable time on the outward beat signalled a complete reversal of weather. Almost as she rounded, the breeze fell away. It was two full hours before another boat could round. For the next 12 hours, the IOR and PHRF Divisions A, B, C, and D lay entrapped in a glassy doldrums, rocking endlessly in the Pacific swells, conditions which denied all contenders any progress. Daylight found more than 100 boats becalmed in the area off Neah Bay and Tatoosh. Some had rounded and were stalled. Others struggled to make those last few miles to the turn. Seasickness prevailed, as the early leaders saw their advantage vanish.

Now it was the luck of the draw, as here and there a yacht picked up enough air to gather steerage. *Warrior* was the first to get away, soon building a lead that would carry her all the way to the finish. Hard on her heels, but still a long way behind, followed *Glory*, *Whistlewing*, *Weatherly*, and still later, *Defiance*. *Pachena* and *Tomahawk* were together on the way back off Neah Bay, with *Pachena* leading. *Tomahawk* went inshore. In retrospect, Newton feels that he should have covered him, but didn't because he's been in there several times before and lost out. *Tomahawk* picked up a breeze to move ahead, while *Pachena* lost out, once again.

By 9 to 10 a.m. the wind had filled in, and the pack was at last on the move. Many had dropped out during the worst of the calms, but those that hung in were rewarded with a typical homeward run with an ever freshening westerly. Hence, the smaller boats with the high handicap allowance were immediately in the picture, with a better than even chance to wind up in the winner's circle.

During the light going Saturday evening, two Victoria yachts found ways to keep moving. *Country Style*, which topped Canadian standings in IOR with a 12th overall, was just beyond Clallam Bay when the wind faded in the late afternoon. Skipper Steve Merriman sailed much freer than several yachts he passed which were pointing 15 degrees higher, including Donnie Martin and *Prophecy*. Luck rode with him just before Neah Bay when a large hole filled in as he approached.

Dr. Hugh Bacon sailed his *Encounter* about a third of the way offshore into the Strait, and proved once again the axiom that the rudiments of boathandling are best learned in dinghies. *Encounter* was able to keep way on because 16-year-old Stephanie, the skipper's daughter, and fellow Royal Vic junior sailor Jeff Eckard, aged 14, applied the techniques learned while racing Lasers to literally inch the 30 footer toward the mark through the windless slop. Bacon's strategy of returning mid-channel with a bias toward the Canadian shore also paid off. *Encounter* topped Class III PHRF, the only Canadian yacht to stem the flood tide of an otherwise American sweep of Swiftsure honours. *Encounter's* crew included Richard Ackrill, Jack Hemphill and Dr. Norman Wales.

Warrior finished in a blazing run of 31 hours, easily outdistancing her nearest rivals *Glory, Whistlewing* and *Weatherly*. Crossing four and one half hours after *Warrior*, Alan Holt's custom half tonner *Ladybug* was assured her second overall win with a time allowance of over seven and one half hours. Dennis Clarke's San Juan 30 *Bumper* corrected to second, with *Warrior* third.

The Juan de Fuca race leaders crossed the finish line in a fast 13½ hours, with Seattle sweeping Class IV IOR. Gerry Duncan's ¾-ton *Hagar* again made her presence known crossing first, but failed to save her time over Tom Hukle's San Juan 30 *Outlaw*, first overall, and Glen Boudon's *SeaBeater*, second. Canadian boats featured in PHRF honours as Peter and Avril Grove's Paceship 32 *Tarka* and Ray Hingley's San Juan 29 *Romada* topped Class V (Division E), while Bob Lefeaux' Cal 27 *Bad News* and Alan Crowe's *Demara* held Class VI (Divisions F and G).

JOHN BOOTH'S UMPKA, FIRST FIBERGLASS T-BIRD / JAMES McVIE

WHITE SQUALL / JAMES McVIE

46/ *The Ongoing Search*

The Swiftsure story is a microcosm of the evolution of the modern racing-cruising yacht. Much has been said, and much more remains to be said, about the craftsmanship that produced the glorious old boats that dominated Swiftsure in years gone by: the subtle beauty of their lines; the exquisite shipwrightness of their cabinetry; their stubborn longevity and the long lasting salty flavour of the memories they have left with us.

The magic of the old words like golly-wobbler, flying jib tops'l, and dolphin striker, have given way to the prosaic wonders of moulded fibreglass, extruded aluminum shapes, strange underwater configurations, mechanical gadgetry to delight the technocrat, and electronic wizardry to outwit even man himself. After returning home from the 1979 Admiral's Cup matches in England, John Newton says, ''It is very hard for top flight, world class sailors, such as the three crews and three capable boats representing Canada in the Admiral's Cup, to realize that we, as participants, and the yachts that were our couriers, were outdated and outclassed even as they were unloaded for the fray. The speed of change is so swift that none but the ruthlessly modern, manned by none but rigorously trained professionals, could muster any kind of show.''

These two straightforward sentences bespeak the state of the sailing sport in the highest competitive circles. But let us stop for a moment and think of those uncounted thousands of enchanted amateurs who take matchless pleasure from the magic that is a wind blown ship. The great surge in interest in the classic sailing yachts, the wooden gems of yesteryear, accompanies the amazing rebirth of a yearning among men to build again ''a wooden boat''. It is as true among sailors who love the sea for its own sake, as it is for the naturalist who loves the mysteries of the forest, that it matters not to either how fast the ultra-light displacements go, or how high the inter-continental jets scream overhead. The peace of mind that lives within a hand-made wooden hull, or the silence and the beauty of light splotched wooden glens, suffices for the average man.

So many times amid these flying years, the older sailor asks, ''Where are the joys we knew within the heart of a boat we built and loved, surging upon a sea of endless wonder?'' Yet as I watched a modern wood craftsman ply his ultra skills, thus creating a cold moulded hull of sweet smelling red cedar, within me I knew that even as the methods change, the art goes ever on. Competition, with its attendant commercialism and professionalism, is bound to grab the spotlight and flex its miracle spars on centre stage, but just as surely, there is a tremendous body of family sailors who can and do rejoice in the boundless rewards of just sailing.

Swiftsure has seen and been a vital part of the impetus of new design, new methods, new materials, and the new point of view brought to the sport by today's affluence which has provided the opportunity to compete with literally no holds barred. Vast sums of money are involved by owners, by designers, and by production yacht builders. A sudden breakthrough in either design, materials, or outstanding performance, can and does revolutionize the industry in a matter of months. The computer designed, technological masterpiece that is the modern racing machine is truly one of the outstanding achievements of modern man.

No one familiar with present leaders in world class competition can fail to be impressed with the performance of these yachts. The guts and stamina of the bigger boats has been amply demonstrated by such events as Whitbread's Round the World race and other trans-ocean competitions. These tests have proven that maxi boats can be driven at unheard of speeds, 24 hours a day, day and night, for weeks on end, by the superhuman efforts of a picked and highly trained crew, and even under such conditions most of the boats have stood up to the test.

The very real problem for offshore race management committees rests with their decisions as to which ultra lights will be certified to sail, and which designs will be denied. The 1979 Fastnet gale in which 15 lives were lost has brought international offshore authorities together as never before, to debate stronger measures to upgrade safety regulations for offshore competition. Righting capability and actual structural specifications are likely to come under active scrutiny. This is a matter where individual sponsoring clubs or groups must set their own regulations. Most competent yachting bodies realize that there can be no set of rules that legislates complete safety. All rulings should bear in mind that the underlying principal of offshore races is that the vessel should be capable of an "open sea venture".

When you translate that simple phrase, "open sea venture", into its true meaning, it becomes a statement by the entering skipper, "that he and his vessel are completely self sufficient and contemplate the completion of the venture without outside assistance." Swiftsures 1979 and 1980 saw over 400 entries in all categories. The possibility of supervision, search and rescue for such a fleet is virtually nonexistent. Under normal conditions, in daylight hours, assistance is both practical and possible, providing the problem is the usual gear or mechanical failure. At night under storm conditions, the chance of assistance reaching a seriously damaged yacht is almost nil. The safety of 400 boats spread out over 200 square miles of storm tossed waters is a responsibility no committee can assume. Each boat must realize from the start that each vessel must be an entity unto itself, assuming complete responsibility for its own safety.

From the inception, Swiftsure authorities have discussed and continually advanced the safety requirements of all entries. Successive committees have voted for, and taken stringent measures to enforce, common sense and good seamanship in the fleet. The flat, out and out speedsters have always objected to regulation, but the Swiftsure record of accidents, with only one fatality in 50 years, speaks volumes for prerace selection and supervision. Since it is a matter of grave concern to yachting bodies all over the world, the Royal Victoria Yacht Club, as the present management in charge of the regulations that govern entries to

Swiftsure, is certainly not alone in its efforts to ensure that common sense and safety are the ultimate factors for their guidance. Swiftsure Lightship Classic General Chairman Frank A.C. Piddington and Race Committee Chairman Sid Bryant attended the crucial meetings in England by the Royal Yachting Association this year, held specifically to consider the 1979 Fastnet problems. Frank was pleased to report that our Swiftsure regulations are measurably ahead of similar requirements presently in force for offshore events in England and the Continent. Members of the Canadian Admiral Cup team are of the opinion that the sudden rush of new materials and ultra design have come about too fast for any consistent, long range, rule changes to be drafted. The general consensus is that results, worldwide, for 1978 and 1979 must be analyzed and assessed very carefully and throughtfully before the IOR Rule can be amended to regulate, but not stifle, the new technology now universally available.

Many thoughtful writers on the yacht racing scene have come to much the same conclusion: the attitude of the young men in top flight planing dinghy competition has somehow been carried forward and applied to the handling and expectations of the performance of racing yachts up to, and even exceeding, 70 feet. The result of this approach has led to the ever increasing demand for lighter craft. Today's top competitors expect to drive their craft at speeds of 20 knots or better. Is such a craft capable of a true "open sea venture" on her own without supervision? Perhaps moderation and a little financial adversity in the world will win the day for safety: perhaps the marine insurance underwriters can and should add their weight to the scantlings, thus facilitating the ongoing seach for a surer platform for the racing sailor.

COHO / **JAMES McVIE**

EPILOGUE

John Graham probably said it best, when he said: "Swiftsure is not a yacht race, it is a sweepstake, but even then, the guys with the most experience usually have the best tickets."

ELIXIR / JAMES McVIE

FRED AGAIN / JAMES McVIE

SWIFTSURE / KENNETH OLLAR

Race Statistics, Appendices, Trophies and Tables

**SWIFTSURE LIGHTSHIP RACE FOR THE SWIFTSURE TROPHY
JULY 5TH, 1930**

YACHT NAME	SKIPPER(S)	CLUB	RATING	COR ELAPSE TIME	POSITION DIVISION	OVERALL
CLARIBEL	RAY COOKE	SYC	R.O.R.C.		1(AA)	1
WESTWARD HO	H.B. JOHNSON	R.VAN			2(AA)	2
CRESSET	DOUG URRY	R.VAN			3(A)	3
MINERVA	HUBIE WALLACE	R.VAN	(Rounded Lightship)			DNF
ANDI LAILEY	ERNEST ROGERS	R.VAN	(Did not round)			DNF
WHITE CLOUD	RAD PRATSCH	TYC	(Did not round)			DNF

Start Cadboro Bay 11 a.m., finish off Victoria Breakwater

1931

YACHT NAME	SKIPPER(S)	CLUB	RATING	COR ELAPSE TIME	POSITION DIVISION	OVERALL
WESTWARD HO	ST. CLAIRE JELLETT	R.VAN	R.O.R.C.		1(AA)	1
MINENA	HARRY BARNES	R.VIC				DNF
CRESSET	DOUG URRY	R.VAN				DNF
MINERVA	HUBIE WALLACE	R.VAN				DNF

Start Saturday, June 27th at 3:00 p.m. and finish off Victoria Breakwater.

1934

YACHT NAME	SKIPPER(S)	CLUB	RATING	COR ELAPSE TIME	POSITION DIVISION	OVERALL
CIRCE	RAY COOKE	SYC	R.O.R.C.		1(AA)	1
WESTWARD HO	ST. CLAIRE JELLETT	R.VAN				DNF
MINENA	HARRY BARNES	R.VIC				DNF
WHITE CLOUD	RAD PRATSCH	TYC				DNF

Start Friday, 13th of July at 8:00 p.m. and finish off Victoria Breakwater

JUNE 28TH, 1947
START 12:30 P.M. BROTCHIE LEDGE

**PACIFIC INTERNATIONAL YACHTING ASSOCIATION
SWIFTSURE LIGHTSHIP RACE FOR THE SWIFTSURE TROPHY**

YACHT NAME	SKIPPER(S)	CLUB	RATING	COR ELAPSE TIME	POSITION CLASS	OVERALL
OWENS CUTTER	CHAS ROSS	CYC	C.C. of A.		1(BB)	1
DORADE	FRANKLIN EDDY	SYC			AA	2
MARUFFA	JOHN GRAHAM	SYC			AA	3
SEAWEED	A. GRATZER	SYC			AA	4
ALOTOLA	CHAS FRISBIE	SYC			AA	5
CIRCE	RAY COOKE	SYC			AA	6
ANGELICA	JOHN LOCKE	SYC			AA	7
SPIRIT II	HAROLD JONES	R.VAN				DNF
GALATEA	DR. JACK STEWART	R.VIC				DNF
THETIS	DR. ERB	BYC				DNF
TAHUNA						DNF
RED JACKET	GEORGE PARSONS	SYC				DNF
NEOGA		SYC	Finished but over time limit			
LINDA	WM. BUCHAN	CYC	Finished but over time limit			
WHITE CLOUD	RAD PRATSCH	TYC	Finished but over time limit			

Official start time 12:30 p.m. off Brotchie ledge, June 28th, 1947

MAY 29TH-30TH, 1948
START PORT TOWNSEND:
FINISH VICTORIA

**PACIFIC INTERNATIONAL YACHTING ASSOCIATION
SWIFTSURE LIGHTSHIP RACE FOR THE JUAN DE FUCA TROPHY**

YACHT NAME	SKIPPER(S)	CLUB	RATING	COR ELAPSE TIME	POSITION DIVISION	OVERALL
NAUTILUS II	HARBINE MUNROE	TYC-SYC	C.C. of A.	43/38/57	1(A)	1
DORADE	FRANKLIN EDDY	SYC		45/54/11	AA	2
MARUFFA	JOHN GRAHAM	SYC		46/23/33	AA	3
RED JACKET	GEORGE PARSONS	SYC	Finished but times not recorded			
SEAWEED	A. GRATZER	SYC	Finished but times not recorded			
ALOTOLA	CHAS FRISBIE	SYC	Finished but times not recorded			
JINKER			Finished but times not recorded			

Records show that three other yachts entered but did not finish

Race started 11 a.m. Saturday, May 29th from Port Townsend, finished Victoria.

PACIFIC INTERNATIONAL YACHTING ASSOCIATION
SWIFTSURE LIGHTSHIP RACE

YACHT NAME	SKIPPER(S)	CLUB	RATING	COR ELAPSE TIME	POSITION CLASS	OVERALL
AVALONTE	A.G. WOODLEY	SYC	C.C. of A.	11/23/35	1(A)	1
GOSSIP	DR. PHIL SMITH	SYC		11/23/42	2(A)	2
CHOLITA	DOLPH ZUBIC	SYC		11/29/31		3
AMORITA	DR. CARL JENSEN	SYC		11/36/02		4
SWIFTSURE I	NORM BLANCHARD	SYC		12/14/27		5
NAUTILUS III	HARBINE MUNROE	SYC/TYC		12/23/14		6
ANGELICA	JOHN LOCKE	SYC		12/30/19		7
ALOTOLA	CHAS FRISBIE	SYC		12/37/07		8
RED JACKET	GEORGE PARSONS	SYC		1/25/12		9
DORADE	FRANKLIN EDDY	SYC		1/26/41		10
CIRCE	RAY COOKE	SYC		1/51/51		11
SWIFTSURE	A. GRATZER	SYC		7/11/03		12
MARUFFA	JOHN GRAHAM	SYC				DSQ
BUCCANEER	HUBIE WALLACE	R.VAN	not reported at finish			
ELUSIVE	W. MURROW	R.VAN	not reported at finish			
UWHILNA	LYFORD					DNF
TAKU	TED ANDERSON					DNF
FELICITY	ROY HOYT					DNF
NIMBUS	CALVERT/ANDERSON					DNF
WINSOME	HERSH DRUXMAN					DNF
SERADA	CHRIS GOODHOPE	SYC				DNF

PACIFIC INTERNATIONAL YACHTING ASSOCIATION
SWIFTSURE LIGHTSHIP RACE FOR THE SWIFTSURE TROPHY
THE SWIFTSURE TROPHY: Winner Overall on Handicap
Won by: Dr. Phil Smith in GOSSIP

YACHT NAME	SKIPPER(S)	CLUB	RATING	COR ELAPSE TIME	POSITION CLASS	OVERALL
GOSSIP	DR. PHIL SMITH	SYC	C.C. of A.	8/19/32	A	1
NAUTILUS III	HARBINE MUNROE	SYC/TYC		8/39/13	A	2
ONO	DR. HERB DAY	SYC		8/41/53	BB	3
ALOTOLA	CHARLES FRISBIE	SYC		9/03/40	AA	4
RED JACKET	GEORGE PARSONS	SYC		10/25/38	AA	5
DORADE	FRANKLIN EDDY	SYC		10/32/29	AA	6
MARUFFA	JOHN GRAHAM	SYC		10/36/48	AA	7
WESTWARD HO	JOHN HELSELL	SYC		11/12/34	AA	8
SERADA	DR. C. GOODHOPE	SYC		12/05/01	A	9
ANGELICA	JOHN LOCKE	SYC		12/44/22	AA	10
CIRCE	RAY COOKE	SYC			AA	DNF
SWIFTSURE	GUS GRATZER	SYC			AA	DNF

First boat to finish ALOTOLA, time 29 hours, 36 minutes, 17 seconds

PACIFIC INTERNATIONAL YACHTING ASSOCIATION
1951 SWIFTSURE LIGHTSHIP CLASSIC
SWIFTSURE TROPHY: Winner Overall on Handicap
Won by: Dr. Carl Jensen in AMORITA

YACHT NAME	SKIPPER(S)	CLUB	RATING	COR ELAPSE TIME	POSITION CLASS	OVERALL
AMORITA	C. JENSEN	SYC	C.C. of A.	23/39/49	A	1
NAUTILUS III	H. MUNROE	TYC		23/45/33	A	2
DORADE	F. EDDY	SYC		25/14/41	AA	3
ALATOLA	C. FRISBIE	SYC		25/39/02	AA	4
BUCCANEER III	H. WALLACE	R.VIC.		26/42/32	A	5
SERADA	C. GOODHOPE	SYC		27/06/46	A	6
MARUFFA	J. GRAHAM	SYC		27/34/03	AA	7
ANGELICA	J.L. LOCKE	SYC		28/02/43	AA	8
CIRCE	RAY COOKE	SYC		29/04/34	AA	9
ONO	H. DAY	SYC			BB	DSQ

PACIFIC INTERNATIONAL YACHTING ASSOCIATION
1952 SWIFTSURE LIGHTSHIP CLASSIC
SWIFTSURE TROPHY: Winner Overall on Handicap
Won by: Herb Day, SYC, in ONO

YACHT NAME	SKIPPER(S)	CLUB	RATING	COR ELAPSE TIME	POSITION CLASS	OVERALL
ONO	H. DAY	SYC	C.C. of A.	26/11/13	BB(1)	1
GOSSIP	P. SMITH	SYC		26/32/34	A(1)	2
DORADE	F. EDDY	SYC		26/45/31	AA(1)	3
MARUFFA	J. GRAHAM	SYC		27/00/57	AA(2)	4
ALOTOLA	C. FRISBIE	CYC		27/08/41	AA(3)	5

YACHT NAME	SKIPPER(S)	CLUB	RATING	COR ELAPSE TIME	POSITION CLASS	OVERALL
RED JACKET	G. PARSONS	SYC		27/26/25	AA(4)	6
WESTWARD HO	J. HELSELL	SYC		27/27/11	AA(5)	7
REBEL	D. SHERWOOD	SYC		27/28/57	BB(2)	8
BUCCANEER	H. WALLACE	R.VIC.		27/45/14	A(2)	9
CIRCE	RAY COOKE	SYC		28/21/35	AA(6)	10
NAUTILUS III	H. MUNROE	TYC		28/22/04	A(3)	11
REVENGE	C.P. PASCHALL	SYC		28/37/14	BB(3)	12
REVERIE	G. TEATS	TYC		29/23/47	BB(4)	13
L'APACHE	H. RICHMOND	SYC		30/03/07	AA(7)	14
TOM BOY II	H.B. BARKES	R.VAN.		30/06/02	B(1)	15
ELUSIVE	W.R. MORROW	R.VAN.		32/00/02	B(2)	16
DRAGOON	W.B. HOLMES	R.VIC.			AA	DNF
HYMAC	S. DAVIES	R.VAN.			B	DNF
WHITE CLOUD	R. PRATSCH	R.VIC.				DNF

PACIFIC INTERNATIONAL YACHTING ASSOCIATION
1953 SWIFTSURE LIGHTSHIP CLASSIC
SWIFTSURE TROPHY: Winner Overall on Handicap
Won by: Charles Ross, SYC, in GOSSIP

FRIDAY, MAY 29TH, 1953

YACHT NAME	SKIPPER(S)	CLUB	RATING	COR ELAPSE TIME	POSITION CLASS	OVERALL
GOSSIP	C. ROSS	SYC	C.C. of A.	22/51/29	A(1)	1
MARUFFA	J. GRAHAM	SYC		25/01/27	AA(1)	2
L'APACHE	M. WYMAN	SYC		25/39/07	AA(2)	3
ADIOS	C. JENSEN	SYC		29/07/00	AA(3)	4
ELUSIVE	W.R. MORROW	R.VAN.		29/23/29	B(1)	5
MARMETTA	E. HAYES	SYC		31/17/38	A(2)	6
BUCCANEER	H. WALLACE	R.VIC.		32/34/56	A(3)	7
RED JACKET	G. PARSONS	SYC		33/29/11	AA(4)	8
ALOTOLA	C. FRISBIE	CYC			AA	DNF
CIRCE	RAY COOKE	SYC			AA	DNF
DAHUT	S. CLARK	SYC			AA	DNF
DRAGOON	W.B. HOLMES	R.VIC.			AA	DNF
GOMETRA	K.G. GLASS	R.VAN.			A	DNF
HYMAC	S. DAVIES	R.VAN.			B	DNF
MON REVE	C. ESHOM	SYC			B	DNF
NAUTILUS III	H. MUNROE	TYC			A	DNF
ONO	H. DAY	SYC			BB	DNF
REBEL	D. SHERWOOD	SYC			BB	DNF
REVERIE	G. TEATS	TYC			BB	DNF
WESTWARD HO	J. HELSELL	SYC			AA	DNF
ZINGARA	E. ZAHN	QCYC			BB	DNF

PACIFIC INTERNATIONAL YACHTING ASSOCIATION
1954 SWIFTSURE LIGHTSHIP CLASSIC
SWIFTSURE TROPHY: Overall Winner on Handicap
Won by: Henry Kotkins, SYC, in TOTEM

MAY 29TH-30TH, 1954

YACHT NAME	SKIPPER(S)	CLUB	RATING	COR ELAPSE TIME	POSITION CLASS	OVERALL
TOTEM	H. KOTKINS	CYC	C.C. of A.	38/39/51	BB(1)	1
ELUSIVE	W.R. MORROW	R.VAN.		39/22/16	B(1)	2
REVERIE	G. TEATS	TYC		39/59/18	BB(2)	3
POLHO III	H. RICHMOND	SYC		40/01/43	A(1)	4
GOMETRA	K.G. ALARS	R.VAN.		40/50/44	A(2)	5
DORADE	J.F. EDDY	SYC		41/06/11	AA(1)	6
ADIOS	C.D. JENSEN	SYC		41/30/15	AA(2)	7
MARUFFA	J. GRAHAM	SYC		41/57/52	AA(3)	8
WESTWARD HO	J.B. HELSELL	SYC		42/26/22	AA(4)	9
RED JACKET	G.H. PARSONS	SYC		44/35/04	AA(5)	10
DRAGOON	W.B. HOLMES	R.VIC.		45/29/11	AA(6)	11
ALOTOLA	C. FRISBIE	SYC			AA	DNF
ARMIDA	K. HOSTETTER	SYC			B	DNF
CIRCE	RAY COOKE	SYC			AA	DNF
JENETA	F.W. URRY	R.VAN.			AA	DNF

PACIFIC INTERNATIONAL YACHTING ASSOCIATION
1955 SWIFTSURE LIGHTSHIP CLASSIC
SWIFTSURE TROPHY: Overall Winner on Handicap
Won by: Dr. Chris Goodhope, CYC, in SERADA

YACHT NAME	SKIPPER(S)	CLUB	RATING	COR ELAPSE TIME	POSITION CLASS	OVERALL
SERADA	C.D. GOODHOPE	CYC	C.C. of A.	23/06/17	A(1)	1
MARUFFA	J. GRAHAM	SYC		23/17/34	AA(1)	2

YACHT NAME	SKIPPER(S)	CLUB	RATING	COR ELAPSE TIME	POSITION CLASS	OVERALL
WESTWARD HO	J. HELSELL	CYC				
KATE II	D.E. SKINNER	SYC		23/20/32	AA(2)	3
ADIOS	C. JENSEN	SYC		23/21/29	A(2)	4
RED JACKET	G. PARSONS	SYC		23/56/01	AA(3)	5
STORMY WEATHER	G. TEATS	TYC		24/52/01	AA(4)	6
DIAMOND HEAD	M. WYMAN	SYC		25/31/33	A(3)	7
DORADE	F. EDDY	SYC		28/17/57	AA(5)	8
POLHO III	H. RICHMOND	SYC		28/35/29	AA(6)	9
TOTEM	H. KOTKINS	CYC		29/05/51	A(4)	10
GOMETRA	E.J. PALMER	R.VAN.		29/52/00	BB(1)	11
ARMIDA	K. HOSTETTER	CYC		32/10/04	A(5)	12
ORIOLE	B. JUDD	RCN		34/15/21	B(1)	13
DRAGOON	W.B. HOLMS	R.VIC.		39/01/13	AA(7)	14
ELUSIVE	W.R. MORROW	R.VAN.			AA	DNF
ESCAPADE	H. JONES	SYC			B	DNF
MISCHIEF	R. SMITH	PYC			BB	DNF
YANKEE CLIPPER	J. KELLY	CYC			B	DNF
					BB	DNF

PACIFIC INTERNATIONAL YACHTING ASSOCIATION
1956 SWIFTSURE LIGHTSHIP CLASSIC
SWIFTSURE TROPHY: Overall Winner on Handicap
Won by: Dr. Carl Jensen, SYC, in ADIOS
CITY OF VICTORIA TROPHY: First Boat to Finish
Won by: John Graham, SYC, in MARUFFA

JUNE 23RD-24TH, 1956

YACHT NAME	SKIPPER(S)	CLUB	RATING	COR ELAPSE TIME	POSITION CLASS	OVERALL
ADIOS	C.D. JENSEN	SYC	C.C. of A.	25/11/53	AA(1)	1
MARUFFA	J. GRAHAM	SYC		25/23/18	AA(2)	2
GOSSIP	C.U. SAHLIN	BYC		26/35/17	A(1)	3
KATE II	D.E. SKINNER	SYC		26/41/54	A(2)	4
ONO	H.W. DAY	SYC		26/54/56	BB(1)	5
TASCO II	T.A. SHORT	SFYC		27/10/28	A(3)	6
DORADE	J.F. EDDY	SYC		27/10/59	AA(3)	7
WESTWARD HO	J.B. HELSELL	CYC		27/21/34	AA(4)	8
GOMETRA	E.J. PALMER	R.VAN.		27/28/28	A(4)	9
KAREN IV	K. HOSTETTER	CYC		27/37/56	BB(2)	10
MARY BOWER	K.J. MCRAE	R.VAN.		27/49/10	A(5)	11
RED JACKET	G.H. PARSONS	SYC		29/18/56	AA(5)	12
SERADA	C.D. GOODHOPE	QCYC		29/25/29	A(6)	13
ZINGARA	E. ZAHN	CYC		38/18/45	BB(3)	14
TOTEM	H.R. KOTKINS	CYC		33/51/11	BB(4)	15
MISCHIEF	R.A. SMITH	PYC		45/31/37	B(1)	16
RAIN BIRD	H.P. MCLAUGHLIN	CYC		47/40/42	B(2)	17
ESCAPADE	H.B. JONES JR.	SYC			BB	DNF
ORIOLE	R.C. MACLEAN	RCN			AA	DNF
NEOGA II	A.E. EDMUNDS	SYC			A	DNF
STORMY WEATHER	G. TEATS	TYC			A	DNF
YANKEE CLIPPER	J. KELLY	CYC			BB	DNF
YANKEE DOODLE	E.W. DEKORNING	PYC			BB	DNF

PACIFIC INTERNATIONAL YACHTING ASSOCIATION
SWIFTSURE LIGHTSHIP CLASSIC
1957 TROPHY WINNERS

SWIFTSURE (C.C. of A.)

SWIFTSURE TROPHY (OVERALL HANDICAP WINNER)	JOHN GRAHAM	SYC	MARUFFA
CITY OF VICTORIA TROPHY (FIRST BOAT TO FINISH)	JOHN GRAHAM	SYC	MARUFFA
B.C. CEMENT COMPANY TROPHY (FIRST IN AA CLASS)	JOHN GRAHAM	SYC	MARUFFA
T. EATON COMPANY TROPHY (FIRST IN A CLASS)	DAVID SKINNER	SYC	KATE II
"BB" CLASS TROPHY (FIRST IN BB CLASS)	A.D. SHERWOOD	SYC	REBEL
"B" CLASS TROPHY (FIRST IN B CLASS)	LEN MURRELL	R.VAN.	TREVEDA

MAY 31ST - JUNE 1ST, 1957

SWIFTSURE (C.C. of A.) 1957 RESULTS

YACHT NAME	SKIPPER(S)	CLUB	RATING	COR ELAPSE TIME	POSITION CLASS	OVERALL
MARUFFA	J. GRAHAM	SYC	C.C. of A.	21/08/25	AA(1)	1
SEA FEVER	R.C. PHILBRICK	SYC		25/38/13	AA(2)	2
REBEL	A.D. SHERWOOD	SYC		25/51/09	BB(1)	3
KAREN IV	K. HOSTETTER	CYC		26/00/26	BB(2)	4

YACHT NAME	SKIPPER(S)	CLUB		COR ELAPSE TIME	POSITION CLASS	OVERALL
KATE II	D.E. SKINNER	SYC		26/01/19	A(1)	5
ZINGARA	E.H. ZAHN	CYC		26/09/25	BB(3)	6
STORMY WEATHER	G. TEATS	TYC		26/36/18	A(2)	7
COTTON BLOSSOM	E.H. HALTON	SYC		26/42/52	AA(3)	8
MARY BOWER	K.J. MCRAE	R.VAN.		26/50/35	A(3)	9
DIAMOND HEAD	M.H. WYMAN	SYC		26/54/44	AA(4)	10
NAUTILUS IV	H. MUNROE	SYC		26/56/20	A(4)	11
ALATOLA	C.J. FRISBIE	CYC		27/13/20	AA(5)	12
AURORA	R.E. DUNHAM	SYC		27/38/01	AA(6)	13
ADIOS	C.D. JENSEN	SYC		27/44/26	AA(7)	14
DORADE	J.F. EDDY	SYC		28/19/04	AA(8)	15
LENORE	W.F. OSTRANDER	SYC		28/30/25	A(5)	16
SERADA	C.D. GOODHOPE	CYC		28/34/07	A(6)	17
ONO	H.W. DAY	SYC		29/09/37	BB(4)	18
TOTEM	H.L. KOTKINS	CYC		29/37/44	BB(5)	19
TREVEDA	L. MURRELL	R.VAN.		29/49/23	B(1)	20
RED JACKET	G.H. PARSONS	SYC		30/25/44	AA(9)	21
GOMETRA	E.J. PALMER	R.VAN.		30/28/08	A(7)	22
DELPHIN	A.W. WAY	R.VAN.		31/24/26	BB(6)	23
SUZY-Q	W.H. ROBINSON	PYC		31/34/55	BB(7)	24
ESCAPADE	H.B. JONES	SYC			BB	DNF

PACIFIC INTERNATIONAL YACHTING ASSOCIATION
SWIFTSURE LIGHTSHIP CLASSIC
1958 TROPHY WINNERS

SWIFTSURE (C.C. of A.)	SWIFTSURE TROPHY (OVERALL HANDICAP WINNER)	HERB W. DAY	SYC	ONO
	CITY OF VICTORIA TROPHY (FIRST BOAT TO FINISH)	MAX WYMAN	SYC	DIAMOND HEAD
	B.C. CEMENT COMPANY TROPHY (FIRST IN AA CLASS)	CHAS FRISBIE	SYC	ALOTOLA
	T. EATON COMPANY TROPHY (FIRST IN A CLASS)	DAVID SKINNER	SYC	KATE II
	"BB" CLASS TROPHY (FIRST IN BB CLASS)	HERB W. DAY	SYC	ONO

SWIFTSURE (C.C. of A.) 1958
RESULTS

MAY 30TH-31ST, 1958

YACHT NAME	SKIPPER(S)	CLUB	RATING	COR ELAPSE TIME	POSITION CLASS	OVERALL
ONO	H.W. DAY	SYC	C.C. of A.	42/16/49	BB(1)	1
PANACEA II	R.J. GIBBONS	SYC		42/48/03	BB(2)	2
KATE II	D.E. SKINNER	SYC		43/32/00	A(1)	3
KAREN IV	K. HOSTETTER	CYC		43/37/04	BB(3)	4
LENORE	W.F. OSTRANDER	SYC		43/37/13	A(2)	5
NAUTILUS IV	H. MUNROE	SYC		43/49/16	A(3)	6
BUCCANEER	R.K. BAKER	W.VAN.		44/04/14	A(4)	7
SERADA	C.D. GOODHOPE	SYC		44/47/00	A(5)	8
ALOTOLA	C.J. FRISBIE	CYC		45/30/43	AA(1)	9
DIAMOND HEAD	M.H. WYMAN	SYC		45/43/29	AA(2)	10
SEA FEVER	O.F. LAMSON JR.	SYC		45/47/16	AA(3)	11
CRESSET	G.M. PALMER	R.VAN.		47/32/28	BB(4)	12
TOTEM	H.L. KOTKINS	CYC		49/14/24	BB(5)	13
GOMETRA	E.J. PALMER	R.VAN.		50/21/38	A(6)	14
WESTWARD HO	J.B. HELSELL	CYC		51/16/08	AA(4)	15
ORIOLE	C.A. PROSSER	RCN		76/16/38	AA(5)	16
ADIOS	C.D. JENSEN	SYC			AA	DNF
CIRCE	RAY COOKE	SYC			AA	DNF
COTTON BLOSSOM	E.H. HALTON	SYC			AA	DNF
JENETTA	D.P. URRY	R.VAN.			AA	DNF
MARUFFA	J. GRAHAM	SYC			AA	DNF
TROUBADOUR	P.D. GRAHAM	R.VAN.			A	DNF
CONCERTO	R.D. ROSS	R.VAN.			A	DNF
DEREVO	H.H. CLOUTIER	R.VIC.			A	DNF
HASTY	D. VERGEER	PYC			A	DNF
MARY BOWER	K.J. MCRAE	R.VAN.			A	DNF
TASCO II	T.R. SHORT	SFYC			BB	DNF
APACE	J. BOWRON	W.VAN.			BB	DNF
DELPHIN	A.W. WAY	R.VAN.			BB	DNF
PINK CLOUD	G. AUSTIN	SYC			BB	DNF
REVERIE	T. CHRISTENSEN	TYC			BB	DNF
SUZY-Q	W.H. ROBINSON	PYC			BB	DNF
YANKEE CLIPPER	J.E. KELLY	CYC				

ZINGARA	E.H. ZAHN	CYC		BB	DNF
BLUE WAVE	C.D. CAMPBELL	W.VAN.		B	DNF
ESCAPEE	H.J. BURNETT	R.VAN.		B	DNF
MISCHIEF	R.A. SMITH	PYC		B	DNF
TREVEDA	L. MURRELL	R.VAN.		B	DNF
WAYFARER II	D.C. DUFF	R.VAN.		B	DNF

PACIFIC INTERNATIONAL YACHTING ASSOCIATION
SWIFTSURE LIGHTSHIP CLASSIC
1959 TROPHY WINNERS

SWIFTSURE (C.C. of A.)

SWIFTSURE TROPHY (OVERALL HANDICAP WINNER)	A.D. SHERWOOD	SYC	REBEL
CITY OF VICTORIA TROPHY (FIRST BOAT TO FINISH)	E.H. HALTON	SYC	COTTON BLOSSOM
B.C. CEMENT CO. TROPHY (FIRST IN AA CLASS)	E.H. HALTON	SYC	COTTON BLOSSOM
T. EATON CO. TROPHY (FIRST IN A CLASS)	K.J. McRAE	R.VAN.	MARY BOWER
SEATTLE YACHT CLUB TROPHY (FIRST IN BB CLASS)	A.D. SHERWOOD	SYC	REBEL
ROYAL VANCOUVER YACHT CLUB TROPHY (FIRST IN B CLASS)	R.L. REGAN	CYC	VAGABOND

MAY 29TH-31ST, 1959

SWIFTSURE (C.C. of A) 1959
RESULTS

YACHT NAME	SKIPPER(S)	CLUB	RATING	COR ELAPSE TIME	POSITION CLASS	OVERALL
REBEL	A.D. SHERWOOD	SYC	C.C. of A.	26/41/34	BB(1)	1
ONO	H.W. DAY	SYC		26/57/06	BB(2)	2
TRICIA	J.P. LESLIE	R.VAN.		27/11/48	BB(3)	3
ZINGARA	R.J. CADRANELL	SYC		27/24/43	BB(4)	4
COTTON BLOSSOM	E.H. HALTON	SYC		28/14/22	AA(1)	5
MARY BOWER	K.J. MCRAE	R.VAN.		28/21/37	A(1)	6
KATE II	D.E. SKINNER	SYC		28/47/20	A(2)	7
PANACEA II	R.J. GIBBONS	SYC		28/49/22	BB(5)	8
STORMY WEATHER	G. TEATS	TYC		28/49/58	A(3)	9
CONCERTO	R.D. ROSS	R.VAN.		28/53/33	AA(2)	10
KAREN IV	K. HOSTETTER	CYC		29/19/52	BB(6)	11
SEA FEVER	R.C. PHILBRICK	SYC		29/23/24	AA(3)	12
NAUTILUS IV	H. MUNROE	SYC		29/41/05	A(4)	13
BUCCANEER III	R.D. BAKER	W.VAN.		29/51/54	A(5)	14
MARUFFA	J. GRAHAM	SYC		30/01/28	AA(4)	15
SPIRIT	N.R. McCARVILL	R.VAN.		30/11/38	AA(5)	16
DIAMOND HEAD	M.H. WYMAN	SYC		30/29/16	AA(6)	17
COURAGEOUS	J.B. HELSELL	CYC		31/00/34	A(6)	18
HAWK	R.K. FARRIS	R.VAN.		31/27/06	A(7)	19
ADIOS	C.D. JENSEN	SYC		31/55/21	AA(7)	20
DELPHIN	E. CHISHOLM	R.VAN.		32/29/34	BB(7)	21
DAHUT	C.S. CLARK	SYC		33/17/43	A(8)	22
TOLA	J.C. CARROCK	SYC		33/46/34	A(9)	23
DEREVO	H.H. CLOUTIER	SYC		34/40/55	A(10)	24
TROUBADOUR	P.D. GRAHAM	R.VAN.		36/39/18	AA(8)	25
CORAL REEF II	A.W. WAY	R.VAN.		37/23/02	A(11)	26
TOTEM	H.L. KOTKINS	CYC		38/37/04	BB(8)	27
VAGABOND	R.L. REGAN	CYC		47/44/45	B(1)	28
ORIOLE	C.A. PROSSER	RCN		57/18/08	AA(9)	29
ADOREE	D. JOHNSON	SYC			BB	DNF
BOUNDLESS	E.H. ZAHN	CYC			BB	DNF
BLUE WAVE	C.D. CAMPBELL	W.VAN.			B	DNF
BUCCANEER V	R.V. KIRKBY	W.VAN.			B	DNF
SERADA	C.D. GOODHOPE	CYC			A	DNF
SWEET THURSDAY	T.T. WHITE	CYC			BB	DNF
CIRCE	RAY COOKE	SYC			AA	DNF
HEIDI	C.A. NEWELL	SYC			BB	DNF
TREVEDA	L. MURRELL	R.VAN.			B	DNF
ESCAPADE	H.B. JONES JR.	SYC			BB	DNF

PACIFIC INTERNATIONAL YACHTING ASSOCIATION
SWIFTSURE LIGHTSHIP CLASSIC
TROPHY WINNERS 1960

SWIFTSURE (C.C. of A.)

SWIFTSURE TROPHY (OVERALL HANDICAP)	DAVID E. SKINNER	SYC	KATE II
CITY OF VICTORIA TROPHY (FIRST BOAT TO FINISH)	J. GRAHAM	SYC	MARUFFA

B.C. CEMENT TROPHY (FIRST IN AA CLASS)	OTIS F. LAMSON	SYC	SEA FEVER
T. EATON TROPHY (FIRST IN A CLASS)	DAVID E. SKINNER	SYC	KATE II
SEATTLE YACHT CLUB TROPHY (FIRST IN BB CLASS)	J.P. LESLIE	R.VAN.	TRICIA
ROYAL VANCOUVER YACHT CLUB TROPHY (FIRST IN B CLASS)	HUNTER VOGEL	R.VIC.	AIDA

28 MAY 1960
RACE STARTED 0900

SWIFTSURE (C.C. of A.) 1960
RESULTS

YACHT NAME	SKIPPER(S)	CLUB	RATING	COR ELAPSE TIME	POSITION CLASS	OVERALL
KATE II	D.E. SKINNER	SYC	C.C. of A.	27/48/25	A(1)	1
TRICIA	J.P. LESLIE	R.VAN.		28/01/44	BB(1)	2
THISTLE	W. BUCHAN	CYC		28/05/51	BB(2)	3
REBEL	D. SHERWOOD	SYC		28/25/57	BB(3)	4
STORMY WEATHER	G. TEATS	TYC		28/43/24	A(2)	5
TOLA	J. CORROCK/J. SCHULZ	SYC		28/44/12	A(3)	6
CONCERTO	R.D. ROSS	R.VAN.		29/02/15	A(4)	7
MARY BOWER	K.J. MCRAE	R.VAN.		29/15/16	A(5)	8
SEA FEVER	O.F. LAMSON	SYC		29/16/55	AA(1)	9
ZINGARA	R.J. CADRANELL	SYC		29/16/55	BB(4)	10
BOUNDLESS	ERIC ZAHN	CYC		29/19/08	BB(5)	11
HAWK	R.K. FARRIS	R.VAN.		29/32/33	A(6)	12
COURAGEOUS	W. & A. HELSELL	CYC		29/46/34	A(7)	13
WINSOME II	C.L. RICKARD	R.VAN.		29/47/34	BB(6)	14
LENORE	W.F. OSTRANDER	SYC		29/56/43	A(8)	15
MARUFFA	J. GRAHAM	SYC		29/56/51	AA(2)	16
WE'RE HERE	C.R. SMITH	SYC		30/06/11	A(9)	17
SERADA	C.D. GOODHOPE	CYC		30/18/05	A(10)	18
ONO	H.W. DAY	SYC		30/21/33	BB(7)	19
TROUBADOUR	P.D. GRAHAM	R.VAN.		30/26/24	AA(3)	20
SPIRIT II	N.R. McCARVILL	R.VAN.		30/59/03	AA(4)	21
DIAMOND HEAD	H. KOTKINS	CYC		31/01/29	AA(5)	22
WILD GOOSE	G.M. OLSEN	SYC		31/24/42	AA(6)	23
FULMAR	L.E. BALMER	R.VAN.		32/04/50	AA(7)	24
ADIOS	C. JENSEN	SYC		32/06/39	AA(8)	25
CIRCE	RAY COOKE	SYC		33/11/07	AA(9)	26
THETIS	R.L. REGAN	CYC		35/59/21	BB(8)	27
DELPHIN	E. CHISHOLM	R.VAN.		36/19/51	BB(9)	28
NAUTILUS IV	H. MUNROE	SYC		36/24/27	A(11)	29
HEIDI	C.A. NEWELL	SYC		36/34/43	BB(10)	30
DAHUT	C.S. CLARK	SYC		37/05/22	A(12)	31
AIDA	H. VOGEL	R.VIC.		45/25/33	B(1)	32
VAGABOND	J.H. ABERLE	CYC		45/25/51	B(2)	33
DANDELION	G. HORDER	CYC		45/39/07	B(3)	34
TREVEDA	L. MURRELL	R.VAN.		45/52/57	B(4)	35
ORIOLE	J. PROSSER	RCN		52/03/57	AA(10)	36
ADOREE	A.D. JOHNSON	SYC			BB	DNF
CONCUBINE	A.B. TEITGE	TYC			BB	DNF
CORAL REEF II	A.W. WAY	R.VAN.			A	DNS
GABRIELLE II	P.R. SANDWELL	R.VAN.			A	DNF
HEATHER VI	J.G. INNES	R.VAN.			BB	DNF
JACUNDA	H. PENZ	KITYC			B	DNF
LALONGA II	R.V. JAMES	R.VIC.			A	DNF
SWEET THURSDAY	T.A. WHITE	CYC			BB	DNF
TOROA	MRS. A.J. REES	R.VAN.			B	DNF

PACIFIC INTERNATIONAL YACHTING ASSOCIATION
SWIFTSURE LIGHTSHIP CLASSIC
1961 TROPHY WINNERS

SWIFTSURE (C.C. of A.)				
	SWIFTSURE TROPHY (OVERALL HANDICAP WINNER)	C.L. RICKARD	R.VAN.	WINSOME III
	CITY OF VICTORIA TROPHY (FIRST BOAT TO FINISH)	P. GRAHAM	R.VAN.	TROUBADOUR
	B.C. CEMENT COMPANY TROPHY (FIRST IN AA CLASS)	R.C. COE	SYC	SEA FEVER
	T. EATON COMPANY TROPHY (FIRST IN A CLASS)	D.E. SKINNER	SYC	KATE II
	SEATTLE YACHT CLUB TROPHY (FIRST IN BB CLASS)	C.L. RICKARD	R.VAN.	WINSOME III
	ROYAL VANCOUVER YACHT CLUB TROPHY (FIRST IN B CLASS)	J.C. REED	R.VIC.	JAY JAY

SWIFTSURE (C.C. of A.) 1961
RESULTS

YACHT NAME	SKIPPER(S)	CLUB	RATING	COR ELAPSE TIME	POSITION CLASS	OVERALL
WINSOME III	C.L. RICKARD	R.VAN.	C.C. of A.	26/20/50	BB(1)	1
MAREDEA	R.G. LUNDY	R.VAN.		26/21/44	BB(2)	2
THETIS	R.L. REGAN	CYC		26/24/41	BB(3)	3
HEIDI	C.A. NEWELL	SYC		26/29/13	BB(4)	4
JAY JAY	J.C. REED	R.VIC.		26/32/24	B(1)	5
INTERLUDE	L.H. MERCILLE	TYC		26/35/43	B(2)	6
TRICIA	J.P. LESLIE	R.VAN.		26/26/11	BB(5)	7
TOTEM	R.L. BROWN JR.	CYC		26/40/53	BB(6)	8
JESTER	S.B. WATTS	R.VAN.		26/48/25	BB(7)	9
KATE II	D.E. SKINNER	SYC		27/00/39	A(1)	10
CIRRUS	R.B. GREGORY	TYC		27/04/38	B(3)	11
MAYA	W. BUCHAN	CYC		27/17/51	A(2)	12
MANDARIN	H.D. CLEVELAND	W.VAN.		27/21/17	B(4)	13
AIDA	H. VOGEL	R.VIC.		27/23/02	B(5)	14
LENORE	W.F. OSTRANDER	SYC		27/30/16	A(3)	15
CONCUBINE	R.B. TEITGE	TYC		27/31/44	BB(8)	16
EIO	A.B. SANDERSON	R.VIC.		27/32/09	B(6)	17
CORAL REEF II	A.W. WAY	R.VAN.		27/35/09	A(4)	18
ZINGARA	R.J. CADRANELL	CYC		27/35/09	BB(9)	18
SEA LARK	G.F. CLARK	W.VAN.		27/37/12	BB(10)	20
HAZEL MAID	R.H. ELLISON	R.VAN.		27/43/49	BB(11)	21
DELPHIN	J.W. CHISHOLM	R.VAN.		27/47/03	BB(12)	22
GABRIELLE II	R.K. BAKER	R.VAN.		27/55/01	A(5)	23
ACCOMPLICE	J. HOOD	CYC		27/56/22	A(6)	24
NAUTILUS IV	H. MUNROE	SYC		28/01/07	A(7)	25
MARY BOWER	K.J. MCRAE	R.VAN.		28/02/13	A(8)	26
SALEE	C.J. FRISBIE	CYC		28/08/47	BB(13)	27
VAGABOND	J.H. ABERLE	CYC		28/11/21	B(7)	28
NYON	D.G. SIMPSON	R.VAN.		28/11/59	BB(14)	29
WINDSONG II	J. RUSSELL	CYC		28/12/07	B(8)	30
UWILA	R.H. TRYTHALL	R.VIC.		28/18/30	B(9)	31
ADOREE	D. JOHNSON	CYC		28/20/22	B(10)	32
STORMY WEATHER	G. TEATS	TYC		28/29/47	A(9)	33
TOROA	MRS. A. REES	R.VAN.		28/30/21	B(11)	34
BLUE WAVE	P.C. RICHARDS	W.VAN.		28/30/48	B(12)	35
MUYA	R.K. LABODA	QCYC		28/35/16	B(13)	36
HAWK	R.K. FARRIS	R.VAN.		28/37/03	A(10)	37
LALONGA II	R.V. JAMES	R.VIC.		28/38/05	A(11)	38
SEA FEVER	R.C. COE	SYC		28/38/42	AA(1)	39
TREVEDA	L. MURRELL	R.VAN.		28/38/46	B(14)	40
WE'RE HERE	C.R. SMITH	SYC		28/39/21	A(12)	41
SULAIRE	T. HALTON JR.	CYC		28/47/13	AA(2)	42
SERADA	C.D. GOODHOPE	CYC		28/49/05	A(13)	43
DAHUT	W.D. HOFIUS	SYC		28/52/34	A(14)	44
VELARIS	L.H. KILLAM	R.VAN.		28/57/26	A(15)	45
COURAGEOUS	R. HELSELL	CYC		28/57/55	A(16)	46
DORADE	J.F. EDDY	SYC		29/07/04	AA(3)	47
ALCION	C.D. CAMPBELL	R.VAN.		29/12/02	A(17)	48
EXCALIBUR	W.D. ALBISTON	SYC		29/12/48	BB(15)	49
ADIOS	C. JENSEN JR.	SYC		29/16/08	AA(4)	50
FULMAR	J.E. BALMER	R.VAN.		29/32/03	A(18)	51
CONCERTO	R.D. ROSS	R.VAN.		29/36/17	A(19)	52
BUCCANEER III	V. GRIMSON	BYC		29/36/43	A(20)	53
TROUBADOUR	P. GRAHAM	R.VAN.		29/41/42	AA(5)	54
SPIRIT	N.R. McCARVILL	R.VAN.		29/47/13	AA(6)	55
CIRCE	RAY COOKE	SYC		29/55/48	AA(7)	56
DIAMOND HEAD	H.L. KOTKINS	CYC		29/56/59	AA(8)	57
MARUFFA	J. GRAHAM	SYC		30/02/31	AA(9)	58
TATOOSH	C.P. PASCHALL	SYC		31/09/09	AA(10)	59
ORIOLE	J. PROSSER	RCN		32/42/38	AA(11)	60
BOUNDLESS	E.H. ZAHN	CYC			BB	DNF
KHORASAN	R.O. SYLVESTER	SYC			B	DNF

PACIFIC INTERNATIONAL YACHTING ASSOCIATION
1962 SWIFTSURE LIGHTSHIP CLASSIC AND JUAN DE FUCA RACE
1962 TROPHY WINNERS

SWIFTSURE (C.C. of A.)	SWIFTSURE TROPHY (OVERALL HANDICAP WINNER)	C.L. RICKARD	R.VAN.	WINSOME III

CITY OF VICTORIA TROPHY (FIRST BOAT TO FINISH)	J. GRAHAM	SYC	MARUFFA
B.C. CEMENT COMPANY TROPHY (FIRST IN AA CLASS)	C. JENSEN, JR.	SYC	ADIOS
T. EATON COMPANY TROPHY (FIRST IN A CLASS)	D.E. SKINNER	SYC	KATE II
SEATTLE YACHT CLUB TROPHY (FIRST IN BB CLASS)	C.L. RICKARD	R.VAN.	WINSOME III
ROYAL VANCOUVER YACHT CLUB TROPHY (FIRST IN B CLASS)	J.H. GALBRAITH	TYC	CIRRUS
JUAN DE FUCA (C.C. of A.) * JUAN DE FUCA TROPHY (OVERALL HANDICAP WINNER C CLASS)	A.G. CUTLER	W.VAN.	CELTIC CHILDE
* SAN JUAN TROPHY (FIRST BOAT TO FINISH C CLASS)	A.G. CUTLER	W.VAN.	CELTIC CHILDE

* 1962 marks first year of Juan de Fuca Race.

SWIFTSURE (C.C. of A.) 1962
RESULTS

26 MAY 1962
RACE STARTED: 0930

YACHT NAME	SKIPPER(S)	CLUB	RATING	COR ELAPSE TIME	POSITION CLASS	OVERALL
WINSOME III	C.L. RICKARD	R.VAN.	C.C. of A.	23/32/14	BB(1)	1
KATE II	D.E. SKINNER	SYC		23/35/04	A(1)	2
THETIS	R.L. REGAN	SYC		23/40/01	BB(2)	3
CIRRUS	J.H. GALBRAITH	TYC		23/41/59	B(1)	4
JESTER	S.B. WATTS	R.VAN.		23/46/55	BB(3)	5
TRICIA	J.P. LESLIE	R.VAN.		23/46/55	BB(3)	5
BOUNDLESS	E.H. ZAHN	CYC		23/49/06	BB(5)	7
ADIOS	C.D. JENSEN	SYC		23/58/29	AA(1)	8
VELARIS	L.J. KILLAM	R.VAN.		24/08/20	A(2)	9
COURAGEOUS	R. HELSELL	CYC		24/18/07	A(3)	10
MARY BOWER	K.J. MCRAE	R.VAN.		24/23/04	A(4)	11
MARUFFA	J. GRAHAM	SYC		24/25/04	AA(2)	12
MARA	W. BUCHAN	CYC		24/37/50	A(5)	13
EXCALIBUR	B. ALBISTON	SYC		24/39/07	BB(6)	14
STORMY WEATHER	G. TEATS	TYC		24/40/09	A(6)	15
SEA FEVER	R.C. PHILBRICK	SYC		24/40/32	AA(3)	16
METEORA	D.L. THOMPSON	SYC		24/56/34	B(2)	17
ZINGARA	R.J. CADRANELL	SYC		24/58/20	BB(7)	18
SULAIRE	R. HAYES	CYC		25/00/17	AA(4)	19
HAWK	R.K. FARRIS	R.VAN.		25/28/09	A(7)	20
OCEANUS	W. GARDNER	CYC		25/49/29	AA(5)	21
DIAMOND HEAD	H.L. KOTKINS	SYC		25/51/44	AA(6)	22
TATOOSH	C.P. PASCHALL	SYC		26/20/48	AA(7)	23
SEA LARK	G.F. CLARK	W.VAN.		26/21/59	BB(8)	24
WE'RE HERE	C. SMITH	SYC		26/25/47	A(8)	25
LONG GONE	J. INNES	R.VAN.		26/29/32	BB(9)	26
WATAUGA	J. FORD	SYC		26/29/44	B(3)	27
LADARO	W.C. WHIPPLE	CYC		26/34/19	A(9)	28
ALCION	C.D. CAMPBELL	R.VAN.		26/42/30	A(10)	29
BARCA DE VELA	A. WESTON	W.VAN.		26/46/46	B(4)	30
SUNDANCE	T.O. MURPHY	TYC		26/46/51	A(1)	31
SERADA	C.D. GOODHOPE	CYC		26/57/15	A(12)	32
COHO	G.M. PALMER	R.VAN.		26/59/38	B(5)	33
CORAL REEF II	A.W. WAY	R.VAN.		27/07/14	A(13)	34
JAY JAY	J.C. REED	R.VIC.		27/20/22	B(6)	35
HEIDI	C.A. NEWELL	SYC		27/23/07	BB(10)	36
CONCUBINE	A.B. TEITGE	TYC		27/29/59	BB(11)	37
PANDORA OF RHU	J.K. SLOAN	R.VAN.		27/46/49	A(14)	38
DAHUT	W.D. HOFIUS	SYC		27/55/05	A(15)	39
DELPHIN	J.W. CHISHOLM	R.VAN.		28/14/30	BB(12)	40
GABRIELLE II	R.K. BAKER	R.VAN.		28/18/05	A(16)	41
MUYA	R.K. LABODA	QCYC		28/22/45	B(7)	42
TROUBADOUR	P. GRAHAM	R.VAN.		28/47/32	AA(8)	43
KHORASAN	R.O. SYLVESTER	SYC		28/52/38	B(8)	44
NYON	D.G. SIMPSON	R.VAN.		28/56/23	BB(13)	45
NAUTILUS IV	V. AUSTIN	CYC		28/00/01	A(17)	46
TOLA	J. CORROCK	SYC		29/10/44	A(18)	47
DANDELION	G. HORDER	CYC		29/33/32	B(9)	48
NORENA OF WIGHT	N.R. RAMSEY	R.VIC.		29/42/52	A(19)	49
MAXYMUM	P. YOUNG	R.VIC.		29/05/42	B(10)	50
MANDARIN	H.G. BAKER	W.VAN.		30/06/57	B(11)	51
WINDSONG II	J. RUSSELL	CYC		30/07/14	B(12)	52
PETRONILLA	W.F. FORREST	PYC		30/21/38	BB(14)	53

CONCERTO	R.D. ROSS	R.VAN.		31/00/14	A(20)	54
TOROA	A.J. REES	R.VAN.		31/50/02	B(13)	55
UWHILNA	T. McKEOWN	QCYC		38/58/06	A(21)	56
ORIOLE	J. PROSSER	RCN		43/15/37	AA(9)	57
CIRCE	RAY COOKE	SYC			AA	DNF
ACCOMPLICE	A.L. SAMBONI	CYC			A	DNF
MAREDEA	B. LUNDY	R.VAN.			BB	DNF
ADOREE	D. JOHNSON	SYC			BB	DNF
TREVEDA	LEN MURRELL	R.VAN.			B	DNF
BLUE WAVE	P.C. RICHARDS	W.VAN.			B	DNF
BARRACOUTA II	J. GRIEVE	MBYC			B	DNF
TAKU	S.J. BECKER				B	DNF

JUAN DE FUCA CLUB (C.C. of A.) 1962
RESULTS

YACHT NAME	SKIPPER(S)	CLUB	RATING	COR ELAPSE TIME	POSITION CLASS	OVERALL
CELTIC CHILDE	A.G. CUTLER	W.VAN.		15/35/35		1
PANACEA	J. PINCH	W.VAN.		17/55/56		2
KUKRI	H.L. LYNE	R.VIC.		19/00/23		3
ARRIBA	A. MILLAR	W.VAN.				DNF

PACIFIC INTERNATIONAL YACHTING ASSOCIATION
SWIFTSURE LIGHTSHIP CLASSIC AND JUAN DE FUCA RACE
1963 TROPHY WINNERS

SWIFTSURE (C.C. of A.)	SWIFTSURE TROPHY (OVERALL HANDICAP WINNER)	CHES RICKARD	R.VAN.	WINSOME III
	CITY OF VICTORIA TROPHY (FIRST BOAT TO FINISH)	CARL JENSEN	SYC	ADIOS
	OCEAN CEMENT TROPHY (FIRST IN AA CLASS)	R. COE	SYC	SEA FEVER
	T. EATON COMPANY TROPHY (FIRST IN A CLASS)	ERIC ZAHN	CYC	ODUSA
	SEATTLE YACHT CLUB TROPHY (FIRST IN BB CLASS)	CHES RICKARD	R.VAN.	WINSOME III
	ROYAL VANCOUVER YACHT CLUB TROPHY (FIRST IN B CLASS)	B. GREGORY	TYC	CIRRUS
JUAN DE FUCA (C.C. of A.)	JUAN DE FUCA TROPHY (OVERALL WINNER)	HUNTER VOGEL	R.VAN.	AIDA
	SAN JUAN TROPHY (FIRST BOAT TO FINISH)	HUNTER VOGEL	R.VAN.	AIDA

NOTE: In the race results for 1963 and subsequent years the column headed "Corrected Elapse Time" indicates the clock time of arrival on Sunday, adjusted for the appropriate time allowance, unless an "M" follows the time, indicating a Monday finish time.

SWIFTSURE (C.C. of A.) 1963
RESULTS

YACHT NAME	SKIPPER(S)	CLUB	RATING	COR ELAPSE TIME	POSITION CLASS	OVERALL
WINSOME III	C.L. RICKARD	R.VAN.	C.C. of A.	09/43/12	BB(1)	1
ODUSA	E.H. ZAHN	CYC		09/49/48	A(1)	2
CIRRUS	R.B. GREGORY	TYC		10/00/53	B(1)	3
CORMORANT	G.T. REEVE	MBYC		10/06/19	A(2)	4
SEA FEVER	R.C. COE	SYC		10/13/14	AA(1)	5
MAI TAI	C. ROSS	CYC		10/20/33	A(3)	6
MARA	W. BUCHAN	CYC		10/21/01	A(4)	7
CONDOR	D. RAMSAY	R.VIC.		10/21/12	B(2)	8
ADIOS	C.D. JENSEN	SYC		10/24/06	AA(2)	9
COURAGEOUS	J.B. HELSELL	CYC		10/29/38	A(5)	10
NYON	D.G. SIMPSON	R.VAN.		10/35/01	BB(2)	11
WATAUGA	J. FORD	SYC		10/36/58	B(3)	12
SULAIRE	K. FRINELL	CYC		10/40/23	A(6)	13
FULMAR	J.E. BALMER	R.VAN.		10/43/42	A(7)	14
LONG GONE	J. INNES	R.VAN.		10/47/30	BB(3)	15
JESTER	S.B. WATTS	R.VAN.		10/48/26	BB(4)	16
BENORA II	R.A. DELAPLACE	R.VAN.		10/50/16	BB(5)	17
STORMY WEATHER	G. TEATS	TYC		10/52/33	BB(6)	18
METEORA	D.L. THOMPSON	SYC		10/52/46	BB(7)	19
VELARIS	L.H. KILLAM	R.VAN.		10/54/06	A(8)	20
MAREDEA	R.G. LUNDY	R.VAN.		10/56/28	BB(8)	21
KIALOA	C.W. BRASIER	TYC		10/58/23	A(9)	22
PANACEA II	R.J. GIBBONS	SYC		11/03/52	BB(9)	23
TRICIA	J.P. LESLIE	R.VAN.		11/04/02	BB(10)	24
ZINGARA	R.J. CADRANELL	SYC		11/04/20	BB(11)	25

YACHT NAME	SKIPPER(S)	CLUB		CLASS	OVERALL
GABRIELLE II	P.R. SANDWELL	R.VAN.	11/05/02	A(10)	26
NIMBUS	H. PALMER	CYC	11/16/56	BB(12)	27
KATE II	D.E. SKINNER	SYC	11/19/31	A(11)	28
CHINOOK	J. KOREN	CYC	11/20/56	B(4)	29
DORADE	J.F. EDDY	SYC	11/31/28	AA(3)	30
SUNDANCE	T.O. MURPHY	TYC	11/44/54	A(12)	31
EXCALIBUR	W.B. ALBISTON	SYC	11/47/19	BB(13)	32
ALCION	C.D. CAMPBELL	R.VAN.	11/48/27	A(13)	33
SERADA	C.D. GOODHOPE	CYC	11/49/18	A(14)	34
SPIRIT	N.R. McCARVILL	R.VAN.	11/51/48	AA(4)	35
LENORE	W.F. OSTRANDER	SYC	11/52/14	BB(14)	36
JANDY	G.A. PRENTICE	SYC	12/07/22	A(15)	37
OCEANUS	W. GARDEN	CYC	12/11/18	AA(5)	38
COHO	J. BRANDLMAYR	R.VAN.	12/12/39	B(5)	39
SEA LARK	C.F. CLARK	W.VAN.	12/30/57	BB(15)	40
DIAMOND HEAD	H.L. KOTKINS	SYC	12/32/13	AA(6)	41
MARY BOWER	J. LONG	R.VAN.	12/39/39	A(16)	42
VIXEN	R.R. WEST	SYC	12/42/21	A(17)	43
PENELAKUT	R.D. ROSS	R.VAN.	12/44/04	A(18)	44
NAUTILUS IV	VAL AUSTIN	CYC	12/52/11	A(19)	45
DAHUT	W.D. HOFIUS	SYC	13/00/32	BB(16)	46
BARRACOUTA II	J. GRIEVE	MBYC	13/23/30	B(6)	47
KHORASAN	R.O. SYLVESTER	SYC	13/27/34	B(7)	48
TROUBADOUR	P. GRAHAM	R.VAN.	13/30/54	AA(7)	49
NORENA OF WIGHT	N.R. RAMSEY	R.VIC.	13/35/52	B(8)	50
TATOOSH	C.P. PASCHALL	SYC	13/49/40	AA(8)	51
LISEN	F.A. TURNA	CYC	13/55/03	B(9)	52
WINDSONG II	J. RUSSELL	CYC	14/07/07	B(10)	53
MUYA	R.K. LABODA	PMYC	14/16/22	B(11)	54
HAZEL MAID	R.H. ELLISON	R.VAN.	14/36/32	B(12)	55
CIRCE	RAY COOKE	SYC	15/11/03	AA(9)	56
ORIOLE	BILL WALKER	RCN	16/59/12	AA(10)	57
UWHILNA	J.A. McKEOWN	QCYC	Finished	A	NR
MAXYMUM	P. YOUNG	R.VIC.	Time Not	B	NR
TAKU	S. BECKER	SYC	Reported	B	NR
HAWK	R.K. FARRIS	R.VAN.		A	DNF
POLARIS	G.W. CAMPBELL	QCYC		BB	DNF
LADARO	W.C. WHIPPLE	CYC		BB	DNF
ONNA	L.F. LINDHOLM	R.VIC.		B	DNF
TREVEDA	L. MURRELL	R.VAN.		B	DNF
JAY JAY	J.C. REED	R.VIC.		B	DNF
THETIS	R.L. REGAN	SYC		BB	DSQ

JUAN DE FUCA CLUB (C.C. of A.) 1963
RESULTS

YACHT NAME	SKIPPER(S)	CLUB	RATING	COR ELAPSE TIME	POSITION CLASS	OVERALL
AIDA	H. VOGEL	R.VAN.	C.C. of A.	04/03/35		1
MAIA V	D.S. COVE	W.VAN.		04/30/38		2
MELODY	D.B. SMITH	W.VAN.		04/34/50		3
KUKRI	H.L. LYNE	R.VIC.		04/47/28		4
DOMINIQUE	R. RAWSON	SYC		05/11/56		5
PANACEA	J. PINCH	W.VAN.		05/24/41		6
H 28	T. WHEELER	SYC		06/10/53		7
ARRIBA	A. MILLAR	W.VAN.		06/19/17		8

PACIFIC INTERNATIONAL YACHTING ASSOCIATION
SWIFTSURE LIGHTSHIP CLASSIC AND JUAN DE FUCA RACE
1964 TROPHY WINNERS

SWIFTSURE (C.C. of A.)	SWIFTSURE TROPHY (OVERALL HANDICAP WINNER)	G.O. SMITH	TYC	BANDIT
	CITY OF VICTORIA (FIRST BOAT TO FINISH)	R.G. PAGE	SYC	HUSSY
	B.C. CEMENT COMPANY TROPHY (FIRST IN AA CLASS)	J.F. EDDY	SYC	DORADE
	T. EATON COMPANY TROPHY (FIRST IN A CLASS)	R.G. PAGE	SYC	HUSSY
	SEATTLE YACHT CLUB TROPHY (FIRST IN BB CLASS)	G.O. SMITH	TYC	BANDIT
	ROYAL VANCOUVER YACHT CLUB TROPHY (FIRST IN B CLASS)	R.A. SPENCER	TYC	ALLEGRO

YACHT NAME	SKIPPER(S)	CLUB	RATING		
JUAN DE FUCA (C.C. of A.)	JUAN DE FUCA TROPHY (OVERALL HANDICAP WINNER)	H. JONES	W.VAN.	SARABAND	
	SAN JUAN TROPHY (FIRST BOAT TO FINISH)	H. JONES	W.VAN.	SARABAND	

SWIFTSURE (C.C. of A.) 1964
RESULTS

YACHT NAME	SKIPPER(S)	CLUB	RATING	COR ELAPSE TIME	POSITION CLASS	OVERALL
BANDIT	G.O. SMITH	TYC	C.C. of A.	09/45/17	BB(1)	1
THETIS	R.L. REGAN	SYC		10/17/07	BB(2)	2
HUSSY	R.G. PAGE	SYC		10/47/38	A(1)	3
JANDY	G.A. PRENTICE	SYC		10/49/16	A(2)	4
TRICIA	J.P. LESLIE	R.VAN.		11/44/55	BB(3)	5
STORMY WEATHER	G. TEATS	TYC		14/27/47	BB(4)	6
MAI TAI	C.R. ROSS	CYC		15/03/44	A(3)	7
ZINGARA	R.J. CADRANELL	SYC		15/07/28	BB(5)	8
FULMAR	J.E. BALMER	R.VAN.		15/40/45	A(4)	9
VELARIS	L.H. KILLAM	R.VAN.		15/45/46	A(5)	10
SANDERLING	A.H. MEAKIN	R.VAN.		17/16/41	BB(6)	11
ASTROCYTE	C.E. GOULD	W.VAN.		18/14/06	A(6)	12
KIALOA	C.W. BRASIER	TYC		18/16/33	A(7)	13
PANDORA OF RHU	J.K. SLOAN	R.VAN.		18/30/11	A(8)	14
WINSOME III	C.L. RICKARD	R.VAN.		18/32/43	BB(7)	15
LONG GONE	J. INNES	R.VAN.		18/48/12	BB(8)	16
VELEDA	J. GRUBBE	R.VAN.		19/03/01	BB(9)	17
DORADE	J.F. EDDY	SYC		19/14/58	AA(1)	18
ALLEGRO	R.A. SPENCER	TYC		20/21/48	B(1)	19
LADARO	W.C. WHIPPLE	CYC		20/32/21	A(9)	20
DIAMOND HEAD	H.L. KOTKINS	SYC		20/33/45	AA(2)	21
COURAGEOUS	J. HELSELL	CYC		20/37/51	A(10)	22
TROUBADOUR	P.D. GRAHAM	R.VAN.		20/39/50	AA(3)	23
KATE II	D.E. SKINNER	SYC		20/41/59	A(11)	24
SEA FEVER	O.F. LAMSON	SYC		20/47/43	AA(4)	25
NORWESTER	B. HOFIUS	SYC		21/12/07	A(12)	26
MAREDEA	A.W. WAY	R.VAN.		21/36/59	BB(10)	27
ALCION	C.D. CAMPBELL	R.VAN.		22/13/46	A(13)	28
LENORE	W.F. OSTRANDER	SYC		23/08/31	A(14)	29
ONNA	L.F. LINDHOLM	R.VIC.		02/14/31M	B(2)	30
WESTERLY	J.M. SEYMOUR	CYC		02/23/40M	B(3)	31
NAUTILUS IV	VAL AUSTIN	CYC		02/59/19M	A(15)	32
CALYPSO	H.B. GARRIGUES	SYC		03/12/37M	BB(11)	33
SUNDANCE	T.O. MURPHY	TYC		04/30/46M	A(16)	34
MARY BOWER	J.H. LONG	R.VAN.		04/49/05M	A(17)	35
CIRRUS	J.H. GALBRAITH	TYC		05/12/07M	B(4)	36
ADIOS	C.F. JENSEN	SYC			AA	DNF
OCEANUS	W. GARDEN	CYC			AA	DNF
ORIOLE	W.D. WALKER	RCN			AA	DNF
SPIRIT	N.R. McCARVILL	R.VAN.			AA	DNF
TATOOSH	C.P. PASCHALL	SYC			AA	DNF
CORMORANT	G.T. REEVE	MEYBYC			A	DNF
DAHUT	A.D. WORTHINGTON	CYC			A	DNF
DIOSA	E. HOPPEN	GHYC			A	DNF
GABRIELLE II	P.R. SANDWELL	R.VAN.			A	DNF
GWENDOLYN II	J. NEWCOMB	CYC			A	DNF
HAWK	R.K. FARRIS	R.VAN.			A	DNF
ODUSA	E. ZAHN	CYC			A	DNF
PENELAKUT	R.D. ROSS	R.VAN.			A	DNF
SERADA	C.D. GOODHOPE	CYC			A	DNF
ACCOMPLICE II	A. SAMBONI	CYC			BB	DNF
EXCALIBUR	W.B. ALBISTON	SYC			BB	DNF
GEO. KITAMIKE	H. DAVIDSON	R.VAN.			BB	DNF
NYON	D.G. SIMPSON	R.VAN.			BB	DNF
PELAGIUS	S.A. BECKER	SYC			BB	DNF
SABRINA	P.R. ANDERSON	EYC			BB	DNF
SERAPIS	A.J. FORSYTHE	R.VAN.			BB	DNF
SONIA	J.W. ROGERS	RCNSA			BB	DNF
THUNDER	W. BUCHAN	CYC			BB	DNF
WE'RE HERE	C.R. SMITH	SYC			BB	DNF
BLACK HAWK	H.H. BOYD	CYC			B	DNF
CHINOOK	J. KOREN	CYC			B	DNF
DANDELION	G. HORDER	CYC			B	DNF

YACHT NAME	SKIPPER(S)	CLUB			CLASS	OVERALL
KHORASAN	R.O. SYLVESTER	SYC			B	DNF
MISTRAL	J.C. BAILLARGEON	SYC			B	DNF
NORENA OF WIGHT	H.R. RAMSEY	R.VIC.			B	DNF
STELLA MARIS V	S.C. HUNTINGFORD	W.VAN.			B	DNF
TREVEDA	L. MURRELL	R.VAN.			B	DNF
ULL II	H.D. PERRY	W.VAN.			B	DNF
VAGABOND	J.H. ABERLE	CYC			B	DNF
WATAUGA	J. FORD	SYC			B	DNF

JUAN DE FUCA (C.C. of A.) 1964
RESULTS

YACHT NAME	SKIPPER(S)	CLUB	RATING	COR ELAPSE TIME	POSITION CLASS	OVERALL
SARABAND	H. JONES	W.VAN.		10/46/18		1
POSEIDON	R.S. PAYNE	CYC		10/55/04		2
ANNALISA	L.F. PARDY	W.VAN.		11/05/27		3
MAY D II	E.P. ASHE	R.VIC.		11/27/47		4
SPINDRIFT	H.R. DURSCH	CYC		11/28/00		5
FLIRT	R. TOWNSLEY	W.VAN.		11/29/18		6
HEATHER	A. NAIRNE	W.VAN.		11/53/35		7
ICHIBAN	T. WHEELER	SYC		12/10/52		8
PANACEA	J. PINCH	W.VAN.		12/17/56		9
HANNA	J. DAMGAARD	R.VIC.		12/38/43		10
MELODY	D.B. SMITH	W.VAN.		12/45/02		11
DOXY	P.R. COOMBS	R.VIC.		13/15/17		12
EIO	A.B. SANDERSON	R.VIC.		13/21/09		13
BLUE MOON	A.J. JAMES	R.VIC.		13/22/39		14

PACIFIC INTERNATIONAL YACHTING ASSOCIATION
SWIFTSURE LIGHTSHIP CLASSIC AND JUAN DE FUCA RACE
1965 TROPHY WINNERS

SWIFTSURE (C.C. of A.)	SWIFTSURE TROPHY (OVERALL HANDICAP WINNER)	W. BUCHAN	CYC	THUNDER
	CITY OF VICTORIA (FIRST BOAT TO FINISH)	H.L. KOTKINS	SYC	DIAMOND HEAD
	B.C. CEMENT COMPANY TROPHY (FIRST IN AA CLASS)	V.R. SCHEUMANN	SYC	HELENE
	T. EATON COMPANY TROPHY (FIRST IN A CLASS)	C.W. BRASIER	TYC	KIALOA
	ROYAL VANCOUVER YACHT CLUB TROPHY (FIRST IN BB CLASS)	WILLIAM BUCHAN	CYC	THUNDER
	SEATTLE YACHT CLUB TROPHY (FIRST IN B CLASS)	J.C. BAILLARGEON	SYC	MISTRAL
JUAN DE FUCA (C.C. of A.)	JUAN DE FUCA TROPHY (OVERALL HANDICAP WINNER)	E.P. ASHE	R.VIC	MAY D II
	SAN JUAN TROPHY (FIRST BOAT TO FINISH)	E.P. ASHE	R.VIC.	MAY D II

SWIFTSURE (C.C. of A.) 1965
RESULTS

YACHT NAME	SKIPPER(S)	CLUB	RATING	COR ELAPSE TIME	POSITION CLASS	OVERALL
THUNDER	W. BUCHAN	CYC	28.9	11/11/25	BB(1)	1
TRICIA	J.P. LESLIE	R.VAN.	28.6	11/29/41	BB(2)	2
KIALOA	C.W. BRASIER	TYC	34.4	11/34/34	A(1)	3
FULMAR	J.E. BALMER	R.VAN.	35.2	11/46/28	A(2)	4
NORWESTER	W.D. HOFIUS/K. BROWN	SYC	35.5	11/52/15	A(3)	5
LADARO	W.C. WHIPPLE	CYC	31.6	11/58/36	A(4)	6
SERADA	C.D. GOODHOPE	CYC	32.1	12/00/15	A(5)	7
WINSOME III	C.L. RICKARD	R.VAN.	28.7	12/01/52	BB(3)	8
ODUSA	E. ZAHN	CYC	31.4	12/05/06	A(6)	9
HELENE	V.R. SCHEUMANN	SYC	39.5	12/17/45	AA(1)	10
BANDIT	G.O. SMITH	TYC	28.5	12/18/07	BB(4)	11
DIAMOND HEAD	H.L. KOTKINS	SYC	49.9	12/19/23	AA(2)	12
PANDORA OF RHU	H.M. ELLIS	R.VAN.	38.6	12/21/04	A(7)	13
MAREDEA	A.W. WAY	R.VAN.	28.8	12/22/45	BB(5)	14
SEA FEVER	R.C. PHILBRICK	SYC	40.3	12/23/34	AA(3)	15
PENELAKUT	R.D. ROSS	R.VAN.	34.1	12/26/02	A(8)	16
COURAGEOUS	J. HELSELL	CYC	36.3	12/33/30	A(9)	17
STORMY WEATHER	G. TEATS	TYC	29.3	12/36/50	BB(6)	18
VELARIS	L.H. KILLAM	R.VAN.	33.2	12/42/24	A(10)	19
REALITY	J.D. SMITH	R.VIC.	37.7	12/45/13	A(11)	20
ALCION	K.J. McRAE	R.VAN.	32.6	12/49/31	A(12)	21
MAI TAI	C.R. ROSS	CYC	31.4	12/51/56	A(13)	22

CORMORANT	G.T. REEVE	MBYC	31.4	12/54/46	A(14)	23
MISTRAL	J.C. BAILLARGEON	SYC	22.7	12/56/37	B(1)	24
JESTER	S.B. WATTS	R.VAN.	28.8	13/06/26	BB(7)	25
LONG GONE	J. INNES	R.VAN.	28.6	13/07/00	BB(8)	26
SALUTE	P. PEOPLES	CYC	29.0	13/08/46	BB(9)	27
WESTERLY	E.V. MOCK	CYC	24.4	13/27/07	B(2)	28
ADELANTE	E.B. McKEE	SYC	23.9	13/37/21	B(3)	29
BLEW BIRD	J.N. ANDERSON	CYC	24.0	13/42/02	B(4)	30
ORIOLE	J. BUTTERFIELD	RCN	64.0	13/42/41	AA(4)	31
SUNDANCE	T.O. MURPHY	TYC	34.1	13/51/13	A(15)	32
HAIDA	G. HORDER	SYC	28.8	13/59/08	BB(10)	33
ALLEGRO	R. SPENCER	TYC	25.2	14/01/36	B(5)	34
CIRCE	J. SEABORN	SYC		14/01/53	AA(5)	35
NYON	D.G. SIMPSON	R.VAN.	28.4	14/04/26	BB(11)	36
VROLIJK	E.H. WALL	SYC	22.8	14/08/27	B(6)	37
CIRRUS	R.B. GREGORY	TYC	24.0	14/08/45	B(7)	38
JOLLY OLLY	V. RUSKIN	R.VAN.	22.1	14/09/44	B(8)	39
ANAHERRA	C.G. MORRISON	W.VAN.	22.1	14/13/51	B(9)	40
GEO. KITAMIKE	H. DAVIDSON	R.VAN.	28.0	14/14/56	BB(12)	41
KHORASAN	R.O. SYLVESTER	SYC	22.8	14/15/05	B(10)	42
SPIRIT	N.R. McCARVILL	R.VAN.	43.4	14/15/36	AA(6)	43
PELAGIUS	S.J. BECKER	SYC	27.7	14/19/40	BB(13)	44
EXCALIBUR	W.B. ALBISTON	SYC	28.6	14/23/24	BB(14)	45
ADIOS	C.D. JENSEN	SYC	46.5	14/24/05	AA(7)	46
GABRIELLE II	P.R. SANDWELL	R.VAN.	35.5	14/29/34	A(16)	47
JEUNESSE	P.T. COTE	R.VAN.	25.1	14/33/18	BB(11)	48
BENORA	P.D. GRAHAM	R.VAN.	28.9	14/33/38	BB(15)	49
BLACK HAWK	H.H. BOYD	CYC	24.6	14/41/09	B(12)	50
SANDERLING	A.H. MEAKIN	R.VAN.	29.1	14/46/45	BB(16)	51
T'SOLO	R.C. DENNY	R.VIC.		14/52/09	B(13)	52
SERAPIS	A.J. FORSYTH	R.VAN.	28.8	14/52/25	BB(17)	53
SYMRA	F.T. HALEY	TYC	33.2	15/02/17	A(17)	54
MUYA	R.K. LABODA	PMYC	24.1	15/08/19	B(14)	55
KATE II	D.E. SKINNER	SYC	32.2	15/08/26	A(18)	56
SABRINA	F.R. ANDERSON	EYC	28.0	15/17/50	BB(18)	57
LENORE	W.F. OSTRANDER	SYC	30.2	15/30/47	A(19)	58
WATAUGA	J. FORD	SYC	23.3	15/36/09	B(15)	59
ACCOMPLICE II	A. SAMBONI	CYC	28.3	15/36/30	BB(19)	60
ASTROCYTE	C.E. GOULD	W.VAN.	37.5	15/40/53	A(20)	61
ONNA	L.F. LINDHOLM	R.VIC.		15/54/26	B(16)	62
MARY BOWER	J.H. LONG	R.VAN.	37.8	15/58/05	A(21)	63
RAINBIRD	W.B. JOHNSON	TYC	23.9	16/14/24	B(17)	64
TREVEDA	L. MURRELL	R.VAN.	24.6	18/04/56	B(18)	65
DELPHINIUS	J.E. BOULDING	NYC	23.5	18/41/36	B(19)	66
TAKU II	J. PHELPS	W.VAN.	29.9		BB	* NR
NORENA OF WIGHT	N.R. RAMSEY	R.VIC.	25.8		B	DNF
KANOA	F. HOLLMAN	CYC	23.7		B	DNF
DAHUT	A.D. WORTHINGTON	CYC	30.1		A	DNF
JANDY	G.A. PRENTICE	SYC	34.4		A	DNF
DIOSA	E. HOPPEN	GHYC	32.2		A	DNF

* NR — Finish not recorded.

JUAN DE FUCA (C.C. of A.) 1965
RESULTS

YACHT NAME	SKIPPER(S)	CLUB	RATING	COR ELAPSE TIME	POSITION CLASS	OVERALL
MAY D II	E.P. ASHE	R.VIC.		23/47/59		1
LUCY A	W.H. GARDNER	CYC		00/52/09		2
SARABAND	H. JONES	W.VAN.		01/29/32		3
MELODY	D.B. SMITH	W.VAN.		01/45/43		4
FLIRT	J. ROOCROFT	W.VAN.		01/54/37		5
ALOHA II	S.J. HUNTINGFORD	W.VAN.		02/01/37		6
MAIA V	D.S. COVE	W.VAN.		02/05/59		7
BLUE MOON	A.J. JAMES	R.VIC.		02/12/04		8
HEATHER	A. NAIRNE	W.VAN.		02/45/30		9
DOXY	P.R. COOMBS	R.VIC.		03/50/04		10
GALENAIA	G.A. DUFOUR	R.VIC.		05/27/40		11
SIKI	T. REPARD	R.VAN.		05/31/05		12
MURRELET	W. VOGEL	R.VIC.		06/12/35		13
HANNA	J. DAMGAARD	R.VIC.		12/39/49		14

SWIFTSURE (C.C. of A.)	SWIFTSURE TROPHY (OVERALL HANDICAP WINNER)	J.C. BAILLARGEON	SYC	MISTRAL
	CITY OF VICTORIA (FIRST BOAT TO FINISH)	J.H. LONG	R.VAN.	MARY BOWER
	OCEAN CEMENT TROPHY (FIRST IN DIVISION I)	R. COE	SYC	SEA FEVER
	T. EATON COMPANY TROPHY (FIRST IN DIVISION II)	E. ZAHN	SYC	ODUSA
	SEATTLE YACHT CLUB TROPHY (FIRST IN DIVISION III)	P.I. CHRISTOFFERSON	W.VAN.	TERNA
	ROYAL VANCOUVER YACHT CLUB TROPHY (FIRST IN DIVISION IV)	J.C. BAILLARGEON	SYC	MISTRAL
JUAN DE FUCA (C.C. of A.)	JUAN DE FUCA TROPHY (OVERALL HANDICAP WINNER)	P.R.A. COOMBS	R.VIC.	DOXY II
	SAN JUAN TROPHY (FIRST BOAT TO FINISH)	T.J. DE LA MARE	R.VIC.	TANDEM

SWIFTSURE (C.C. of A.) 1966
RESULTS

				COR ELAPSE	POSITION	
YACHT	**SKIPPER(S)**	**CLUB**	**RATING**	**TIME**	**CLASS**	**OVERALL**
MISTRAL	J.C. BAILLARGEON	SYC	22.5	16/24/11	1(4)	1
TERNA	P. CHRISTOFFERSON	W.VAN.	26.2	17/08/13	1(3)	2
VROLIJK	E.H. WALL	SYC	23.0	17/09/31	2(4)	3
JOLLY OLLY	V. RUSKIN	R.VAN.	22.1	17/11/12	3(4)	4
LANCER	N. LARABEE	CYC	28.6	17/20/44	2(3)	5
TRICIA	P. LESLIE	R.VAN.	28.6	17/28/44	3(3)	6
ARIEL V	K. LOCHHEAD	R.VAN.	28.0	17/33/57	4(3)	7
CIRRUS	J.H. GALBRAITH	TYC	24.6	17/35/27	4(4)	8
WINSOME III	C. RICKARD	R.VAN.	28.9	17/35/40	5(3)	9
HAIDA	G. HORDER	SYC	28.9	17/42/09	6(3)	10
SANDERLING	A. MEAKIN	R.VAN.	29.2	17/49/08	7(3)	11
ODUSA	E. ZAHN	SYC	31.3	18/00/45	1(2)	12
BANDIT	G. SMITH	TYC	28.9	18/05/43	8(3)	13
DIOSA	E. HOPPEN	GIG HBR.	32.3	18/23/39	2(2)	14
MARY BOWER	J.H. LONG	R.VAN.	37.4	18/24/23	3(2)	15
VELARIS	L. KILLAM	R.VAN.	34.5	18/26/26	4(2)	16
CONCUBINE	F. BUSH	R.VIC.	26.7	18/28/07	9(3)	17
LOLLIPOP	H. VOGEL	R.VAN.	25.3	18/37/24	5(4)	18
CORMORANT	G. REEVE	MBYC	31.2	18/40/23	5(2)	19
NORWESTER	K. BROWNE	SYC	35.9	18/46/51	6(2)	20
SERADA	C. GOODHOPE	CYC	32.9	18/51/40	7(2)	21
KATE II	D. SKINNER	SYC	32.4	18/56/13	8(2)	22
SEA FEVER	R. COE	SYC	41.3	18/56/24	1(1)	23
COURAGEOUS	J. HELSELL	CYC	36.3	18/56/33	9(2)	24
ALLEGRO	R.A. SPENCER	TYC	25.7	18/59/21	6(4)	25
STORMY WEATHER	G. TEATS	TYC	29.7	19/08/20	10(3)	26
MAI TAI	C. ROSS	CYC	30.7	19/17/34	10(2)	27
DIAMOND HEAD	H. KOTKINS	SYC	51.3	19/20/20	2(1)	28
WESTERLY	J.M. SEYMOUR	CYC	24.8	19/34/03	7(4)	29
MARUFFA	J. GRAHAM	SYC	49.6	19/42/19	3(1)	30
GEORGE KITAMIKE	H. DAVIDSON	R.VAN.	28.7	19/46/09	11(3)	31
LONG GONE	J. WEST	R.VAN.	28.6	19/51/59	12(3)	32
SUNDANCE	T. MURPHY	TYC	32.4	20/43/04	11(2)	33
MONDAY						
AVATAR	R. POPPE	CYC	24.8	21/16/35	8(4)	34
VAGABOND	J.E. STEWART	CYC	23.7	23/16/30	9(4)	35
KANOA	F.S. HOLMAN	CYC	24.1	24/43/10	10(4)	36
TEPAH	D.J. LAWSON	R.VIC.	24.0		(4)	DNF
BLACK HAWK	H.H. BOYD	CYC	24.8		(4)	DNF
KIALOA	W. BRAZIER	TYC	34.4		(2)	DNF
T'SOLO	R.C. DENNY	R.VIC.	25.3		(4)	DNF
LENORE	W. OSTRANDER	SYC	30.7		(2)	DNF
DAHUT	A. WORTHINGTON	CYC	30.1		(2)	DNF
SERAPIS	A. FORSYTH	R.VAN.	29.0		(3)	DNF
MAREDEA	W. BURGESS	R.VAN.	28.8		(3)	DNF
SPIRIT	N. McCARVILL	R.VAN.	45.9		(1)	DNF
NORENA OF WIGHT	N.R. RAMSEY	R.VIC.	25.8		(4)	DNF
CIRCE	R. RUSSELL	SYC	47.9		(1)	DNF
GABRIELLE	P. SANDWELL	R.VAN.	36.3		(2)	DNF

PENELAKUT	R. ROSS	R.VAN.	34.1		(2)	DNF
SEANCE	R.L. KYLE	W.VAN.	25.1		(4)	DNF
THUNDER	WM. BUCHAN	CYC	28.9		(3)	DNF
CALYPSO	H. GARRIGUES	SYC	28.7		(3)	DNF
PELAGIUS	C. HALL	SYC	28.3		(3)	DNF
MERMAID	R. TOWNSLEY	W.VAN.	24.6		(4)	DNF
DANDELION	R. BENSON	PMYC	24.1		(4)	DNF
WINDSONG II	R.C. BROWN	CYC	25.3		(4)	DNF
JEUNESSE	P. COTE	R.VAN.	25.2		(4)	DNF
EXCALIBUR	W. ALBISTON	SYC	29.1		(3)	DNF
YONDER PEASANT	G. STEWART	NYC	32.5		(4)	DNF
PANDORA OF RHU	J. KLYMACK	R.VAN.	38.6		(2)	DNF
SABRINA	F. ANDERSON	EUGENE	28.0		(3)	DNF
ORIOLE	J. BUTTERFIELD	RCNSA	63.9		(1)	DNF
ACCOMPLICE II	A. SAMBONI	CYC	28.5		(3)	DNF
BLEW BIRD	J.N. ANDERSON	SYC	24.3		(4)	DNF
MUYA	R.K. LABODA	PMYC	24.1		(4)	DNS
RAIN BIRD	W.B. JOHNSON	TYC	24.2		(4)	DNS
NANTUK	W.M. YOUNG	R.VAN.	23.1		(4)	DNF

JUAN DE FUCA RACE (C.C. of A.) 1966
RESULTS

YACHT NAME	SKIPPER(S)	CLUB	RATING	COR ELAPSE TIME	POSITION CLASS	OVERALL
DOXY II	P.R.A. COOMBS	R.VIC.	21.5	23/26/33		1
TANDEM	T.J. DE LA MARE	R.VIC.	24.2	23/28/22		2
HAIDA	D. McGOWAN	R.VIC.	20.7	0/15/14		3
SCUTUM	G. MERVYN	W.VAN.	18.9	04/18/53		4
KALARA	L. WALTERS	R.VAN.	21.9	05/30/30		5
WHISTLER	S. HALLS	R.VIC.	20.9	5/32/18		6
SAGA	E.P. ASHE	R.VIC.	20.2	5/41/53		7
SURFER	T. REPARD	R.VAN.	20.8	6/59/07		8
MUTINEER II	S. TOY	W.VAN.	21.3	7/19/49		9
ANTARES	J. ALLAN	W.VAN.	21.1	12/49/48		10
GALENAIA	G. DUFOUR	R.VIC.	16.6	13/31/42		11
TREVEDA	L. MURRELL	R.VAN.	25.3	14/31/35		12
SEA URCHIN	H. WHITE	NANAIMO	16.7	16/02/29		13
LUCY A	W. GARDNER	CYC	20.3			DNF
ARIKI II	G. HILL	W.VAN.	18.6			DNF
APHRODITE	A. NAIRNE	W.VAN.	21.8			DNF
BILLABONG	F. RUSSELL	R.VAN.	21.2			DNF
HANNA	J. DAMGAARD	R.VIC.	17.9			DNF
WE THREE	D. ERICKSON	GIG HBR.	20.8			DNS

PACIFIC INTERNATIONAL YACHTING ASSOCIATION
SWIFTSURE LIGHTSHIP CLASSIC AND JUAN DE FUCA RACE
1967 TROPHY WINNERS

SWIFTSURE (C.C. of A.)	SWIFTSURE TROPHY (OVERALL HANDICAP WINNER)	WM. E. BUCHAN JR.	CYC	MARA
	CITY OF VICTORIA (FIRST BOAT TO FINISH)	ROBERT PAGE	SYC	HUSSY
	OCEAN CEMENT TROPHY (FIRST IN DIVISION I)	ROBERT PAGE	SYC	HUSSY
	T. EATON COMPANY TROPHY (FIRST IN DIVISION II)	W.D. HOFIUS/ K.W. BROWNE	SYC	NORWESTER
	SEATTLE YACHT CLUB TROPHY (FIRST IN DIVISION III)	W.E. BUCHAN JR.	CYC	MARA
	ROYAL VANCOUVER YACHT CLUB TROPHY (FIRST IN DIVISION IV)	J.C. BAILLARGEON	SYC	MISTRAL
	ROYAL CANADIAN NAVY TROPHY (FIRST TO ROUND SWIFTSURE MARK)	WM. E. BUCHAN JR.	CYC	MARA
JUAN DE FUCA (C.C. of A.)	JUAN DE FUCA COMMEMORATION TROPHY (FIRST IN DIVISION I)	R. MARSHALL	CYC	SEAQUIN
	ROYAL CANADIAN NAVY TROPHY (FIRST IN DIVISION II)	GLEN MERVYN	W.VAN.	SCUTUM
	SAN JUAN TROPHY (FIRST BOAT TO FINISH)	G. KIDD/ R. McCOLL	W.VAN.	APHRODITE III
JUAN DE FUCA (P.H.R.F.)	PACIFIC HANDICAP RACING FLEET (FIRST BOAT TO FINISH)	W.B. JOHNSON	TYC	RAINBIRD

SWIFTSURE (C.C. of A.) 1967
RESULTS

YACHT	SKIPPER(S)	CLUB	RATING	COR ELAPSE TIME	POSITION CLASS	OVERALL
MARA	WM. E. BUCHAN JR.	CYC	32.7	18/40/32	1(3)	1

MOEA	W.C. WHIPPLE	CYC	32.4	18/49/36	2(3)	2
HUSSY	ROBERT PAGE	SYC	43.4	19/32/47	1(1)	3
NORWESTER	W.D. HOFIUS/K.W. BROWNE	SYC	39.5	21/54/45	1(2)	4
WARRIOR	JOHN BUCHAN	CYC	32.6	21/55/13	3(3)	5
CRUSADER	K.J. McRAE	R.VAN.	44.8	22/04/36	2(1)	6
THUNDER	W. BUCHAN, Sr.	CYC	32.5	22/28/27	4(3)	7
WHITE SQUALL	GOVNOR TEATS, M.D.	TYC	34.7	22/31/48	2(2)	8
WINSOME III	C. RICKARD	R.VAN.	31.6	22/34/36	5(3)	9
VELARIS	LOL KILLAM	R.VAN.	39.0	22/34/50	3(2)	10
KLAHANIE	H.W. WITHINGTON	CYC	31.6	22/35/45	6(3)	11
CONCERTO	ARNOLD BOOTH	R.VAN.	39.5	23/10/40	4(2)	12
ARIEL V	K.Y. LOCHHEAD	R.VAN.	30.6	24/18/03	7(3)	13
MISTRAL	J.C. BAILLARGEON	SYC	24.6	24/48/20	1(4)	14
TERNA	P.T. CHRISTOFFERSEN	W.VAN.	29.1	25/43/18	8(3)	15
TRICIA	PAT LESLIE	R.VAN.	31.4	25/54/44	9(3)	16
CALYPSO	H.B. GARRIGUES	SYC	32.2	25/58/45	10(3)	17
ODUSA	E.H. ZAHN	SYC	34.3	26/11/06	5(2)	18
CORMORANT	GEORGE T. REEVE	MBYC	34.5	26/14/14	6(2)	19
ALCION	C.D. CAMPBELL	R.VAN.	36.6	26/46/17	7(2)	20
PANDORA OF RHU	JOHN KLYMAK	R.VAN.	41.5	27/09/46	8(2)	21
SEA FEVER	OTIS LAMSON	SYC	47.0	27/20/43	3(1)	22
KIALOA	C.W. BRASIER	TYC	36.8	29/59/25	9(2)	23
LA RUINA	R.J. GIBBONS	SYC	35.6	30/05/50	10(2)	24
AVATAR	R.F. POPPE	CYC	26.8	34/50/55	2(4)	25
BLACK HAWK	HERSCHELL BOYD	MBYC	26.9	35/21/50	3(4)	26
WHALE'S TALE	W.M. BLACK	CYC	28.2	35/34/43	4(4)	27
TE-PAH	D.J. LAWSON	R.VIC.	27.0	35/34/44	5(4)	28
KIMJE	J.H. EASTMAN	R.VAN.	27.3	35/47/03	6(4)	29
PENELAKUT	R. ROSS	R.VAN.	37.2	36/03/03	11(2)	30
MARADEA	W.G. BURGESS	R.VAN.	32.1	36/08/00	11(3)	31
HEIDI	ROBT. BENSON	PT. MAD	33.1	36/49/46	12(2)	32
CARITA	BOB BOLLONG	SYC	34.9	36/59/12	13(2)	33
WINDSONG II	R.C. BROWN	CYC	26.9	37/13/20	7(4)	34
ANITRA	R.S. LINT	SYC	54.9	37/42/47	4(1)	35
JOLLY OLLY	V. RUSKIN	R.VAN.	25.2	38/07/42	8(4)	36
SABRINA	F. ANDERSON	EUG.YC.	31.6	39/37/23	12(3)	37
ADIOS	CARL JENSEN JR.	SYC	50.0		(1)	DNF
DIAMOND HEAD	HENRY L. KOTKINS	SYC	54.5		(1)	DNF
MARUFFA	JOHN GRAHAM	SYC	54.6		(1)	DNF
MIR	GEORGE O'BRIEN	R.VAN.	61.9		(1)	DNF
HMCS ORIOLE	JAMES BUTTERFIELD	RCNSA	66.9		(1)	DNF
ALLEGRA	ART WAY	R.VAN.	35.8		(2)	DNF
ALOHA II	G. REYNOLDS	W.VAN.	33.7		(2)	DNF
COURAGEOUS	R.M. HELSELL	SYC	39.0		(2)	DNF
EOS	H.R. DURSCH	ANAC.YC.	32.7		(2)	DNF
FINESSE	R. HUTTON	SYC	36.4		(2)	DNF
GABRIELLE II	P.R. SANDWELL	R.VAN.	40.1		(2)	DNF
HAWK	F.R. (BILL) KILLAM	R.VAN.	39.0		(2)	DNF
LENORE	W.F. OSTRANDER	SYC	35.0		(2)	DNF
MAI TAI	C. ROSS	MBYC	36.0		(2)	DNF
MARY BOWER	J.H. LONG	R.VAN.	40.9		(2)	DNF
MOSHULU	R.O. SYLVESTER	SYC	35.1		(2)	DNF
SERADA	DR. C.D. GOODHOPE	CYC	35.8		(2)	DNF
SUNDANCE	T.O. MURPHY	TYC	35.1		(2)	DNF
TAVEUNI	R.I. THIEME	EYC	38.2		(2)	DNF
VAMOSE	BILL LIEBERMAN	CYC	33.1		(2)	DNF
ACCOMPLICE II	A. SAMBONI	CYC	32.0		(3)	DNF
BANDIT	G.O. SMITH	TYC	32.2		(3)	DNF
BARBAN	K. REID	WVYC	28.7		(3)	DNF
BILLABONG	FRED/K.E. RUSSELL	WVYC	29.6		(3)	DNF
CLOUDRACE	IAN L. HAMILTON	RVYC	29.6		(3)	DNF
CONCUBINE	F.S. BUSH	R.VIC.	29.5		(3)	DNF
JESTER	S.B. WATTS	R.VAN.	32.4		(3)	DNF
KITAMIKE	H. DAVIDSON	R.VAN.	31.2		(3)	DNF
LANCER	N. LARABEE	CYC	31.6		(3)	DNF
LOLLIPOP	H. VOGEL	R.VAN.	28.5		(3)	DNF
MAREDEA	BILL BURGESS	R.VAN.	32.1		(3)	DNF
NAVITA (SEATTLE)	A.A. HEMENWAY	QCYC	34.3		(3)	DNF
NORENA OF WIGHT	N.R. RAMSEY	R.VIC.	29.8		(3)	DNF
NYON	DR. D.G. SIMPSON	R.VAN.	31.2		(3)	DNF
PICNIC	G. INGLIS	R.VIC.	29.2		(3)	DNF

SANDERLING	A.H. MEAKIN	R.VAN.	31.6		(3)	DNF
SANGUINE	D. TAYLOR	TYC	32.2		(3)	DNF
SEA SMOKE	R. HIGGINS	RCNSA	30.5		(3)	DNF
SERAPIS	A.J.B. FORSYTH	R.VAN.	31.4		(3)	DNF
SHIRLEY J	DONALD F. McKAY	TYC	29.8		(3)	DNF
TA'AROA	C.A. MABEE	SYC	32.1		(3)	DNF
ANAHERA	C.G. MORRISON	WVYC	25.3		(4)	DNF
CIRRUS	R.B. GREGORY	TYC	27.0		(4)	DNF
DELPHINIUS	J.E. BOULDING	NYC	24.7		(4)	DNF
FLYING CLOUD	M. LUND	SHILSHOLE BYC	26.7		(4)	DNF
JEUNESSE	P.T. COTE	R.VAN.	27.3		(4)	DNF
MOA	W.O. MIDDLETON	WVYC	26.3		(4)	DNF
MUYA	R.K. LABODA	PMYC	26.6		(4)	DNF
NANTUK	W.M. YOUNG	R.VAN.	26.2		(4)	DNF
QUOMINUS II	P.M. GUNNAR	PYC	26.9		(4)	DNF
SEA FLIGHT	V.E. DAY	SBYC	26.7		(4)	DNF
SWALLOW	P.G. JOHNSON	SYC	27.8		(4)	DNF
THEORY	BILL FIANDER	CYC	27.7		(4)	DNF
VELEDA	J. GRUBBE	R.VAN.	28.5		(4)	DNF
VIKING	J. KORNING	R.VIC.	25.5		(4)	DNF
WESTERLY	J.M. SEYMOUR	CYC	27.4		(4)	DNF

JUAN DE FUCA (C.C. of A.) 1967
RESULTS

				COR ELAPSE	POSITION	
YACHT	SKIPPER(S)	CLUB	RATING	TIME	CLASS	OVERALL
SEAQUIN	R. MARSHALL	CYC	22.4	13/35/17	1(1)	1
GYPSY G	D.S. GIBBERD	WVYC	23.8	13/35/41	2(1)	2
APHRODITE III	G. KIDD/R. McCOLL	WCYV	24.7	13/38/30	3(1)	3
ANTARES II	JOHN A.R. ALLAN	WVYC	22.9	13/44/20	4(1)	4
ARIKI III	GORDON R. HILL	WVYC	22.6	13/48/10	5(1)	5
KEHLOKE	R.F. HARRISON	WVYC	23.3	13/53/46	6(1)	6
SAGA	E.P. ASHE	R.VIC.	23.3	13/58/59	7(1)	7
SURFER	TONY REPARD	R.VAN.	23.2	14/04/30	8(1)	8
LUCY A	WM. H. GARDNER	CYC	22.5	14/06/12	9(1)	9
AQUILA	R. CARERE	R.VIC.	23.5	14/07/36	10(1)	10
DOXY II	P.R.A. COOMBS	R.VIC.	24.0	14/11/14	11(1)	11
WINDSONG IV	J. GRIEVE	WVYC	23.4	14/15/32	12(1)	12
MUTINEER II	D. STANFIELD	WVYC	23.9	14/17/06	13(1)	13
BARCA DA VELA	F.J. PINE/F. HAHN	WVYC	28.1	14/51/15	14(1)	14
SCUTUM	GLEN MERVYN	WVYC	21.1	14/56/03	1(2)	15
MERMAID	DR. REID TOWNSLEY	WVYC	27.9	15/12/06	15(1)	16
WILLIWAW	ROBERT WELLER	AYC	21.0	15/17/52	2(2)	17
HANNA	J.S. DAMGAARD	R.VIC.	18.5	15/56/15	3(2)	18
TREVEDA	L. MURRELL	R.VAN.	26.3	16/17/47	16(1)	19
GALENAIA	G.A. DUFOUR	R.VIC.	18.9	16/23/20	4(2)	20
SPINDRIFT V	JOHN VAN AMSTEL	RCNSA	23.1	18/17/22	17(1)	21
CRESCENDO	DR. C.Y. BROWN	R.VIC.	23.8		(1)	DNF
KHU	R.W. HUME	R.VIC.	24.4		(1)	DNF
HAIDA	D.M. McCOWAN	R.VIC.	24.0		(1)	DNF

JUAN DE FUCA (P.H.R.F.) 1967
RESULTS

				COR ELAPSE	POSITION	
YACHT	SKIPPER(S)	CLUB	RATING	TIME	CLASS	OVERALL
RAIN BIRD	W.B. JOHNSON	TYC	P.H.R.F.	13/31/40		1
TELANI	A.W. PRIEST	EDMONDS YC	P.H.R.F.	13/41/39		2
AFRICAN STAR	D. FRYER	SYC	P.H.R.F.	13/45/55		3
SAND PIPER	C.D. TURNER	POULSBO YC	P.H.R.F.	13/51/24		4
STORMALONG II	TOM WHEELER JR.	SYC	P.H.R.F.			DNF
SKYLARK	J.D. GARDNER	CYC	P.H.R.F.			DNS

PACIFIC INTERNATIONAL YACHTING ASSOCIATION
SWIFTSURE LIGHTSHIP CLASSIC AND JUAN DE FUCA RACE
1968 TROPHY WINNERS

SWIFTSURE (C.C. of A.)	SWIFTSURE TROPHY (OVERALL HANDICAP WINNER)	J.C. BAILLARGEON	SYC	MISTRAL
	CITY OF VICTORIA TROPHY (FIRST BOAT TO FINISH)	DAVID D. NIELSEN	TYC	MOONGLOW III
	OCEAN CEMENT TROPHY (FIRST IN DIVISION I)	H.L. KOTKINS	SYC	DIAMOND HEAD
	T. EATON COMPANY TROPHY (FIRST IN DIVISION II)	DAVID D. NIELSEN	TYC	MOONGLOW III

				COR ELAPSE	POSITION	
					DIVISION	OVERALL

JUAN DE FUCA (C.C. of A.)	SEATTLE YACHT CLUB TROPHY (FIRST IN DIVISION III)	DAN NORTHFIELD JR.CYC			MONIQUE	

<table>
<tr><td>ROYAL VANCOUVER YACHT CLUB TROPHY
(FIRST IN DIVISION IV)</td><td>J.C. BAILLARGEON</td><td>SYC</td><td>MISTRAL</td></tr>
<tr><td>ROYAL CANADIAN NAVY TROPHY
(FIRST TO ROUND SWIFTSURE MARK)</td><td>J.H. LONG</td><td>R.VAN.</td><td>MARY BOWER</td></tr>
</table>

JUAN DE FUCA (C.C. of A.) JUAN DE FUCA COMMEMORATION TROPHY   WALTER HERMANN CYC   LARA
(FIRST IN DIVISION I)

ROYAL CANADIAN NAVY TROPHY   JOHN L. SIEMENS   PAYC   MONT MARÉ
(FIRST IN DIVISION II)

SAN JUAN TROPHY   WALTER HERMANN CYC   LARA
(FIRST BOAT TO FINISH)

JUAN DE FUCA (P.H.R.F.) PACIFIC HANDICAP RACING FLEET   WM. B. JOHNSON   TYC   RAINBIRD
(FIRST)

SWIFTSURE (C.C. of A.) 1968
RESULTS

YACHT	SKIPPER(S)	CLUB	RATING	COR ELAPSE TIME	DIVISION	OVERALL
MISTRAL	J.C. BAILLARGEON	SYC	24.4	11/59/09	1(4)	1
JOLLY OLLY	V. RUSKIN	R.VAN.	24.9	12/21/42	2(4)	2
MOONGLOW III	DAVID D. NIELSEN	TYC	36.3	12/22/10	1(2)	3
LOLLIPOP	HUNTER VOGEL	R.VAN.	26.9	12/39/11	3(4)	4
AVATAR	RICHARD F. POPPE	CYC	26.8	13/00/16	4(4)	5
WHALE'S TALE	W.M. BLACK	CYC	28.2	13/07/21	5(4)	6
ADELANTE	E. BATES McKEE	SYC	26.5	13/08/26	6(4)	7
JEUNESSE	PAUL T. COTÉ	R.VAN.	27.6	13/14/30	7(4)	8
T'SOLO	ROY C. DENNY	R.VIC.	27.6	13/17/10	8(4)	9
MONIQUE	DAN NORTHFIELD JR.	CYC	28.8	13/20/12	1(3)	10
TENDERLY	JOHN B. GAINER	ROSE CITY	27.3	13/20/55	9(4)	11
SATIN DOLL	TOM BUSH	CYC	27.1	13/20/59	10(4)	12
TA'AROA	CHARLES A. MABEE	SYC	32.2	13/24/35	2(3)	13
MOA	WALT. MIDDLETON	WVYC	26.3	13/26/45	11(4)	14
THEORY	BILL FIANDER	CYC	27.7	13/29/51	12(4)	15
SWALLOW	P.G. JOHNSON	SYC	27.8	13/35/51	13(4)	16
DIAMOND HEAD	H.L. KOTKINS	SYC	54.5	13/35/54	1(1)	17
SHIRLEY J	DR. DONALD F. McKAY	TYC	29.8	13/38/53	3(3)	18
TAVEUNI	R.I. THIEME	EVERETT	38.7	13/40/36	2(2)	19
MARY BOWER	JOHN H. LONG	R.VAN.	40.9	13/41/11	3(2)	20
BLACK HAWK	H.H. BOYD, M.D.	CYC	29.0	13/42/14	4(3)	21
TRICIA	PAT LESLIE	R.VAN.	31.5	13/43/31	5(3)	22
TERNA	P. CHRISTOFFERSEN	W.VAN.	29.5	13/44/46	6(3)	23
MARA	WM. E. BUCHAN	CYC	32.8	13/51/11	7(3)	24
WESTERLY	JACK M. SEYMOUR	CYC	27.4	13/51/42	14(4)	25
BARRACOUTA II	DR. GUY SCREECH	R.VIC.	28.6	13/52/59	8(3)	26
NAVITA	A. ARTHUR HEMENWAY	QCYC	34.4	13/54/27	4(2)	27
CONCUBINE	FRANK BUSH	R.VIC.	29.8	14/04/58	9(3)	28
SERADA	DR. C.D. GOODHOPE	CYC	37.0	14/08/25	5(2)	29
KATE II	DAVID E. SKINNER	SYC	34.4	14/10/27	6(2)	30
LANCER	NORMAN LARABEE	CYC	32.1	14/12/38	10(3)	31
MOEA	W.C. WHIPPLE	CYC	32.4	14/13/09	11(3)	32
LOVE AFFAIR	JOHN ALBERTSON	CYC	33.0	14/13/15	7(2)	33
BRIGADOON	DR. CHUCK GUILDNER	EVERETT	32.9	14/13/33	12(3)	34
BENORA	CHES L. RICKARD	R.VAN.	31.5	14/13/43	13(3)	35
VELARIS	LOL KILLAM	R.VAN.	38.6	14/16/02	8(2)	36
KATE	K.L. PARTLOW II	TYC	29.6	14/17/48	14(3)	37
ALLEGRA	ART WAY	R.VAN.	35.8	14/17/52	9(2)	38
SOLQUEST	F.E. RUSSELL	WVYC	29.4	14/19/11	15(3)	39
FINESSE	D. SHERWOOD/R. HUTTON	SYC	36.6	14/19/38	10(2)	40
FLYING CLOUD	DR. JEROME MURPHY	SHILSHOLE	34.2	14/20/10	11(2)	41
CALYPSO	HENRY B. GARRIGUES, M.D.	SYC	32.0	14/20/58	16(3)	42
SERAPIS	A.J.B. FORSYTH	R.VAN.	31.4	14/25/39	17(3)	43
CUBARA	DONALD J. LAWSON	R.VIC.	33.9	14/28/54	12(2)	44
KLAHANIE	FRANK S. HOLMAN	CYC	31.6	14/29/55	18(3)	45
PIPER	CHARLES D. TURNER	CYC	30.1	14/30/42	19(3)	46
BANDIT	GERALD O. SMITH	TYC	32.2	14/31/38	20(3)	47
KIMJE	J.H. EASTMAN	R.VAN.	27.3	14/32/15	15(4)	48
CORMORANT	GEORGE T. REEVE	MEY.B.	34.5	14/32/33	13(2)	49
SCOTCH MIST	ROBERT D. O'BRIEN	ROSE CITY	32.6	14/33/06	21(3)	50
WARRIOR	JOHN F. BUCHAN	CYC	33.0	14/33/13	14(2)	51
GABRIELLE III	P.R. SANDWELL	R.VAN.	39.6	14/34/36	15(2)	52
JESTER	STUART B. WATTS	R.VAN.	32.4	14/35/21	22(3)	53
OLYMPIAN	PETER G. SCHMIDT	CYC	36.7	14/35/50	16(2)	54

YACHT	SKIPPER(S)	CLUB	RATING	COR ELAPSE TIME	POSITION DIVISION	OVERALL
ADIOS	CARL D.F. JENSEN JR.	SYC	50.0	14/36/09	2(1)	55
SANDERLING	ART. MEAKIN	R.VAN.	31.6	14/36/10	23(3)	56
GEORGE KITAMIKE	HAMISH DAVIDSON	R.VAN.	31.2	14/38/26	24(3)	57
TIFFANY	D. ANGUS	R.VIC.	30.8	14/43/40	25(3)	58
HUSSY	DR. ROBERT WIDMANN	SYC	43.4	14/46/24	3(1)	59
WHITE SQUALL	DR. GOVNOR TEATS	TYC	35.5	14/47/13	17(2)	60
SALUTE	P.L. PEOPLES	CYC	33.1	14/47/20	18(2)	61
ANEMOMILOS	ADRIAN VERMEULEN	CYC	37.3	14/47/27	19(2)	62
L'ESPRIT	F.A. DANZ	SYC	33.4	14/49/14	20(2)	63
CRUSADER	KEN. McRAE	R.VAN.	46.3	14/49/42	4(1)	64
ALOHA III	G.B. REYNOLDS	W.VAN.	33.1	14/50/36	21(2)	65
SABRINA	FOSTER ANDERSON	EUGENE	31.6	14/51/59	26(3)	66
KIALOA	C. WM. BRASIER	TYC	36.8	14/57/07	22(2)	67
ODUSA	ERIC ZAHN	SYC	34.3	14/58/56	23(2)	68
HUSH	H. BLAKE	TYC	30.1	15/00/46	27(3)	69
FILEY BRIG	A.B. SANDERSON	R.VIC.	27.7	15/03/14	16(4)	70
SEA FEVER	DR. RICHARD C. PHILBRICK	SYC	47.3	15/07/05	5(1)	71
NORWESTER	K.W. BROWNE/W.D. HOFIUS	SYC	39.5	15/10/06	24(2)	72
POTLATCH	WALTER MEAKES	RCNSA	31.6	15/14/28	28(3)	73
STORMY WEATHER	GEORGE S. SCHUCHART	SYC	33.3	15/18/54	25(2)	74
PENELAKUT	ROBERT D. ROSS	R.VAN.	37.6	15/19/18	26(2)	75
COURAGEOUS	ROBERT H. HELSELL	SYC	39.1	15/21/13	27(2)	76
SUNDANCE	T.O. MURPHY	TYC	35.1	15/28/17	28(2)	77
LA RUINA	R.J. GIBBONS	SYC	35.6	15/37/21	29(2)	78
GABRIELLE II	RALPH HIGGINS	RCNSA	40.1	15/39/28	30(2)	79
ACCOMPLICE II	A.A. SAMBONI	CYC	32.1	16/03/26	29(3)	80
WINDSONG II	R.C. BROWN	CYC	26.9	16/12/22	17(4)	81
MAELSTROM	EARL MILLAR	CYC	34.0	17/29/57	31(2)	82
QUOMINUS II	JUDGE P.M. GUNNAR	PORTLAND	26.9	17/55/05	18(4)	83
MAI TAI	ARTHUR C. WOOD	MEY.B.Y.C.	34.8	18/28/55	32(2)	84
BARBAN	K. REID	W.VAN.	28.7			DNF
NYON	DR. DEREK SIMPSON	R.VAN.	31.2			DNF
ARIEL V	K.Y. LOCHHEAD	R.VAN.	30.6			DNF
HMCS ORIOLE	LCDR. G.S. HILLIARD	RCNSA	66.9			DNF
LENORE	W.F. OSTRANDER	SYC	34.2			DNF
PORPOISE III	P.R. (BILL) KILLAM	R.VAN.	40.8			DSQ

At the time of printing these results, 11:00 a.m. Monday, June 3, the following yacht had not been reported as finished or withdrawn:

CLOUDRACE	I.L. HAMILTON	R.VAN.	29.6			

JUAN DE FUCA (C.C. of A.) 1968
RESULTS

YACHT	SKIPPER(S)	CLUB	RATING	COR ELAPSE TIME	POSITION DIVISION	OVERALL
LARA	W. HERMANN	CYC	26.8	03/56/06	1(1)	1
WINDSONG IV	J. GRIEVE	WVYC	23.4	04/19/25	2(1)	2
SEAQUIN	R. MARSHALL	CYC	22.4	04/35/34	3(1)	3
ARIKI III	G.R. HILL	WVYC	22.6	04/41/19	4(1)	4
KEHLOKE	F. RUSSELL	WVYC	23.3	04/52/34	5(1)	5
AQUILA	R.P. CARERE	R.VIC.	23.9	04/54/08	6(1)	6
SURFER	T. REPARD	R.VAN.	23.3	04/55/30	7(1)	7
HAIDA	D.M. McCOWAN	R.VIC.	23.1	04/58/19	8(1)	8
MONT MARE	J.L. SIEMENS	PT. ANGELES	20.8	04/59/21	1(2)	9
APHRODITE III	R.C. McCOLL	WVYC	24.5	05/03/41	9(1)	10
ANAHERA	C.G. MORRISON	WVYC	24.7	05/04/10	10(1)	11
POW WOW	C.P. BLANSHARD JR.	CYC	23.9	05/14/34	11(1)	12
MELTEMI	FRANK MUSSON	W.VAN.	23.4	05/17/56	12(1)	13
SAGA	J.M. ROOME	MAPLE BAY	23.3	05/21/36	13(1)	14
SENESCHAL	TOM O'BRIEN	SYC	25.9	05/27/09	14(1)	15
HUSTLER	ROBERT R. SMITH	TYC	23.9	05/34/27	15(1)	16
KHU	R.W. HUME	R.VIC.	24.8	05/41/04	16(1)	17
PSYCHO	DR. MICHELE MADDALOSSO	TYC	24.1	05/41/55	17(1)	18
ANTARES II	JOHN A.R. ALLAN	W.VAN.	23.4	05/44/26	18(1)	19
TE-PAH	S.R. OLDHAM	RCNSA	27.0	05/45/28	19(1)	20
CRESCENDO	DR. CHARLES Y. BROWN	R.VIC.	23.8	05/50/50	20(1)	21
SHENANDOAH	JOHN J. CLINCH	CYC	25.4	05/51/15	21(1)	22
HALCYON	PETER D.C. CLARK	R.VIC.	24.0	06/02/21	22(1)	23
SUERTE	WM. H. GARDNER	CYC	25.3	06/25/48	23(1)	24
SANTINIKETAN	TOM WHEELER, JR.	SYC	25.8	06/39/23	24(1)	25
MERMAID	DR. REID TOWNSLEY	WEST VAN	27.8	06/49/42	25(1)	26
COGNAC	B.K. SCHUELLER	EAGLE S.C.	24.9	06/51/36	26(1)	27

YACHT	SKIPPER(S)	CLUB	RATING	COR ELAPSE TIME	POSITION DIVISION	OVERALL
GALENAIA	GEORGE DUFOUR	R.VIC.	18.8	09/33/41	2(2)	28
KATHY	FRANK SHININGER	PT. ANGELES	19.8	09/44/52	3(2)	29
SPINDRIFT V	JOHN VAN ANSTEL	RCNSA	23.3	11/13/32	27(1)	30
KIWI	C.F. TODD	R.VIC.	26.4	11/18/16	28(1)	31
HANNA	JOHN DAMGAARD	R.VIC.	18.5	12/53/23	4(2)	32
BARCA DE VELA	R.K. BAKER	W.VAN.	28.1		(1)	DNF

JUAN DE FUCA (P.H.R.F.) 1968 RESULTS

YACHT	SKIPPER(S)	CLUB	RATING	COR ELAPSE TIME	POSITION DIVISION	OVERALL
RAIN BIRD	WM. B. JOHNSON	TYC	4.7	03/36/01		1
HAIDA	ROBERT E. DAWSON	PT. MADISON	1.5	04/31/22		2
ALMAR	G.R. SMITH	W.VAN.	2.6	04/31/37		3
AFRICAN STAR	DOUG. FRYER	SYC	3.0	04/54/40		4
PIPPA	J. FRASER	W.VAN.	2.5	05/10/47		5
MIA	ROBERT F. SCHOEN	ORCAS IS.	3.0NFS	05/38/20		6
SOLYMAR II	INGMAR LAURINGSON	W.VAN.	2.3	05/56/28		7
EOS	H. ROBT. DURSCH	ANACORTES	1.1	06/04/55		8
JELLY BEAN	CHARLES MacDONALD	ANACORTES	3.2	06/20/39		9
CORDON BLEU	JACK PINCH	W.VAN.	2.0	07/23/42		10
NOR'WESTING	TOM KINCAID	CYC	5.5	08/06/30		11
NIAMH	RAY LYLE	GIG HBR.Y.C.	3.5			DNF
TELANI	AL PRIEST	EDMONDS	8.0NFS			DNF

PACIFIC INTERNATIONAL YACHTING ASSOCIATION
SWIFTSURE LIGHTSHIP CLASSIC AND JUAN DE FUCA RACE
1969 TROPHY WINNERS

SWIFTSURE (C.C. of A.)	SWIFTSURE TROPHY (OVERALL HANDICAP WINNER)	JOHN H. LONG	R.VAN.	MARY BOWER
	CITY OF VICTORIA TROPHY (FIRST YACHT TO FINISH)	HENRY L. KOTKINS	SYC	DIAMOND HEAD
	OCEAN CEMENT TROPHY (FIRST IN DIVISION I)	JOHN H. LONG	R.VAN.	MARY BOWER
	T. EATON COMPANY TROPHY (FIRST IN DIVISION II)	W.C. WHIPPLE	CYC	MOEA
	SEATTLE YACHT CLUB TROPHY (FIRST IN DIVISION III)	BONAR A. DAVIS	R.VAN.	HYAK
	ROYAL VANCOUVER YACHT CLUB TROPHY (FIRST IN DIVISION IV)	P.G. JOHNSON JR.	SYC	SWALLOW
	ROYAL CANADIAN NAVY TROPHY (FIRST TO ROUND SWIFTSURE MARK)	L.C. HEDRICK	R.C.Y.C.	SIX PACK
SWIFTSURE (P.H.R.F.)	(HANDICAP WINNER)	JAMES M. MARTA	SYC	INTREPID
JUAN DE FUCA (C.C. of A.)	JUAN DE FUCA COMMEMORATION TROPHY (FIRST IN DIVISION I)	GORDON HILL	W.VAN.	ARIKI IV
	ROYAL CANADIAN NAVY TROPHY (FIRST IN DIVISION II)	R.S. MARSHALL	CYC	SEAQUIN
	SAN JUAN TROPHY (FIRST YACHT TO FINISH)	GORDON HILL	W.VAN.	ARIKI IV
JUAN DE FUCA (P.H.R.F.)	ANACORTES YACHT CLUB TROPHY (HANDICAP WINNER)	ALBERT W. PRIEST	EYC	TELANI

SWIFTSURE (C.C. of A.) 1969 RESULTS

YACHT	SKIPPER(S)	CLUB	RATING	COR ELAPSE TIME	POSITION DIVISION	OVERALL
MARY BOWER	JOHN H. LONG	R.VAN.	40.9	20/43/24	1(1)	1
SWALLOW	P.G. JOHNSON JR.	SYC	27.8	20/44/23	1(4)	2
SIX PACK	L.C. HEDRICK	RCYC	39.8	20/50/21	2(1)	3
HYAK	BONAR A. DAVIS	R.VAN	30.6	21/08/24	1(3)	4
ARIEL V	K.Y. LOCHHEAD	R.VAN.	30.6	21/18/12	2(3)	5
DIAMOND HEAD	H.L. KOTKINS	SYC	54.5	21/18/29	3(1)	6
TRICIA	PAT LESLIE	R.VAN.	31.5	21/21/30	3(3)	7
MOEA	W.C. WHIPPLE	CYC	32.4	21/32/44	1(2)	8
MARA	WM. E. BUCHAN	CYC	32.8	21/36/49	2(2)	9
CRUSADER	KEN McRAE	R.VAN.	46.3	21/39/54	4(1)	10
COURAGEOUS	ROBT. M. HELSELL	SYC	39.1	21/51/51	5(1)	11
MAELSTROM	EARL L. MILLER	CYC	34.0	21/52/00	3(2)	12
SERADA	DR. C.D. GOODHOPE	CYC	37.4	21/55/01	6(1)	13
ODYSSEY	M.E. AGATHER	SYC	34.9	21/59/47	4(2)	14
WHITE SQUALL	DR. GOVNOR TEATS	TYC	35.4	22/03/10	5(2)	15
SATIN DOLL	TOM BUSH	CYC	25.4	22/05/58	2(4)	16
OLYMPIAN	P.G. SCHMIDT	SYC	36.7	22/15/03	6(2)	17
MISS-CHIFF	CHAS. SCHIFF	CYC	36.6	22/21/24	7(2)	18

NORWESTER	K.W. BROWNE	SYC	39.5	22/32/42	7(1)	19
TERNA	P.T. CHRISTOFFERSEN	WVYC	29.5	22/33/41	4(3)	20
PORPOISE III	BILL KILLAM	R.VAN.	41.2	22/40/44	8(1)	21
SUMMER WINDS	ED PRESCESKY	WVYC	41.0	22/44/19	9(1)	22
GABRIELLE II	RALPH HIGGINS	TUR.HD.SA.	39.8	22/51/17	10(1)	23
TA'AROA	CHAS. A. MABEE	SYC	32.2	22/56/03	8(2)	24
NAUTILUS IV	VAL AUSTIN	CYC	40.0	23/00/47	11(1)	25
FLYING CLOUD	JEROME MURPHY	CYC	34.2	23/10/03	9(2)	26
SERAPIS	A.J.B. FORSYTH	R.VAN.	31.4	23/13/15	5(3)	27
CUBARA	D.J. LAWSON	R.VIC.	33.1	23/14/06	10(2)	28
MOONGLOW III	DAVID D. NIELSEN	TYC	36.1	23/21/30	11(2)	29
LANCER	NORMAN LARABEE	CYC	32.6	23/31/08	12(2)	30
CORMORANT	GEO. T. REEVE	MEY. BAY Y.C.	34.5	23/34/51	13(2)	31
JOLLY OLLY	V. RUSKIN	R.VAN.	24.9	23/35/29	3(4)	32
MINX	JOHN P. LIDRAL	SYC	29.0	23/37/22	6(3)	33
STORMY WEATHER	G.S. SCHUCHART	SYC	34.1	23/41/28	14(2)	34
MAVERICK III	B. COBANLI	R.VAN.	30.0	23/43/10	7(3)	35
RAG DOLL	JOHN BUSH	CYC	25.8	00/00/10	4(4)	36
CARITA	KEN BROSTROM	SYC	34.9	00/06/33	15(2)	37
EHA MAKONI	E. SCHALKA/D. EITEL	EVYC	32.1	00/07/27	8(3)	38
WINSOME III	D.F. FRISBY	R.VAN.	31.6	00/13/37	9(3)	39
KATE II	D.E. SKINNER	SYC	34.9	00/28/38	16(2)	40
GANNET II	J.A.R. ALLAN	WVYC	30.1	00/42/52	10(3)	41
LOLLIPOP	HUNTER VOGEL	R.VAN.	27.5	00/46/26	5(4)	42
NINA	LARRY SHORETT	CYC	26.2	00/49/10	6(4)	43
TEASER	THORDARSON/DUDLEY/HOUTZ	TYC	27.9	00/50/16	7(4)	44
THEORY	BILL FIANDER	CYC	27.7	00/51/19	8(4)	45
SOLQUEST	F.E. RUSSELL	WVYC	29.4	00/59/07	11(3)	46
SEA FEVER	DR. R.C. COE	SYC	47.6	01/25/18	12(1)	47
KATE	DR. K.L. PARTLOW	TYC	29.6	01/28/38	12(3)	48
PIPER	CHAS. D. TURNER	CYC	30.1	01/34/14	13(3)	49
MONIQUE	DAN NORTHFIELD	CYC	29.8	01/34/16	14(3)	50
BLACK HAWK	DR. H.H. BOYD	CYC	29.0	01/35/33	15(3)	51
MAURIAH	JACK ROOCROFT	WVYC	30.3	01/45/37	16(3)	52
KARMA	DR. A.R. HAMMER	CYC	33.8	01/54/54	17(2)	53
SANDERLING	ARTHUR H. MEAKIN	R.VAN.	31.6	01/59/22	17(3)	54
VANDAL	JOE A. McDONALD	SYC	27.3	02/07/34	9(4)	55
KLAHANIE	HANS BEBIE	CYC	31.6	02/09/17	18(3)	56
ANEMAMILOS	A. VERMEULEN	CYC	36.8	02/28/01	13(1)	57
KIMJE	J.H. EASTMAN	R.VAN.	34.9	02/38/16	18(2)	58
LA RUINA	R.J. GIBBONS	SYC	35.6	02/44/06	19(2)	59
MISTRAL	J.C. BAILLARGEON	SYC	24.9	02/53/11	10(4)	60
BANDIT	DAN McDONOUGH	TYC	32.2	03/04/41	20(2)	61
DORAN II	ALVIN J. NAROD	R.VAN.	30.1	03/14/31	19(3)	62
HALCYON	PETER D.C. CLARK	R.VIC.	24.0	03/37/35	11(4)	63
ZINGARA	BOB L. CADRANELL	SYC	33.1	03/56/28	21(2)	64
WHALE'S TALE	WM. M. BLACK	CYC	28.2	04/23/06	12(4)	65
HOOLIGAN	THOS. D. O'BRIEN	SYC	26.9	04/45/59	13(4)	66
WESTERLY	JACK M. SEYMOUR	CYC	27.4	04/51/19	14(4)	67
LARA	DR. W. HERRMANN	CYC	27.4	04/58/41	15(4)	68
BARBAN	K.G. REID	WVYC	29.1	05/22/37	20(3)	69
DOXY II	P.R.A. COOMBS	R.VIC.	24.0	05/28/05	16(4)	70
BENORA II	HARRY HERLILY	R.VAN.	31.5	06/08/50	21(3)	71
EXCALIBUR	W.B. ALBISTON	SYC	32.0	06/18/39	22(3)	72
NAVITA	A.A. HEMENWAY	QCYC	34.3	06/32/24	22(2)	73
GEORGE KITAMIKE	HAMISH DAVIDSON	R.VAN.	33.4	06/38/25	23(2)	74
AVATAR	RICHARD F. POPPE	CYC	26.8	06/45/57	17(4)	75
MUTINEER III	THOS. R. BRAIDWOOD	WVYC	31.8	07/30/07	23(3)	76
SHANNON	DENNIS DONOHUE	CYC	32.5	08/26/19	24(2)	77
MOA	W.O. MIDDLETON	WVYC	26.3	14/22/21	18(4)	78
HMCS ORIOLE	G.S. HILLIARD	RCNSA	66.9	16/21/31	14(1)	79
SHIRLEY J	DR. D.F. McKAY	TYC	29.8		(3)	DNF
MERMAID	DR. B.R. TOWNSLEY	WVYC	28.3		(4)	DNF
TAKU II	JOHN L. PHELPS	WVYC	29.9		(3)	DNF
SABRINA	F.R. ANDERSON	EU.Y.C.	31.6		(3)	DNF
EOS	H. ROBERT DURSCH	AYC	32.7		(2)	DNF
TSUNAMI	CONRAD J. MORAN	CYC	29.9		(3)	DNF
TAVEUNI	ROBT. I. THIEME	EV.Y.C.	38.7		(1)	DNF
NORM	OLAV EKROM	CYC	29.3		(3)	DNF
RIVAL	R.B. GREGORY	TYC	36.6		(2)	DNF
TEMPTATION	BRYAN ARCHER	TYC	36.9		(1)	DNF

YACHT	SKIPPER(S)	CLUB	RATING		DIVISION	OVERALL
HASTY	DUANE VERGEER	PYC	36.2		(2)	DNF
HALCYONE	B. WEHLE	BYC	26.3		(4)	DNF
TIFFANY	D. ANGUS	R.VIC.	30.8		(3)	DNF
BARRACOUTA II	DR. GUY SCREECH	R.VIC.	28.6		(4)	DNF
ZAMBOANGO	F.H. BROWNELL	POULSBO Y.C.	28.2		(4)	DNF
MAI TAI	ARTHUR WOOD	MEY. BAY Y.C.	34.8		(2)	DNF
CONCUBINE	F.S. BUSH	R.VIC.	29.8		(3)	DNF
LOVE AFFAIR	JOHN C. ALBERTSON	CYC	33.0		(2)	DNF
PUFFIN II	HARVEY CARRUTHERS	R.VAN.	32.0		(3)	DNF
YANKEE	CARL DOHERTY	CYC	28.1		(4)	DNS

At the time of printing these results, 12:00 Monday, June 2, the following yachts had not been reported finished or withdrawn:

YACHT	SKIPPER(S)	CLUB	RATING			
JEUNESSE	PAUL T. COTE	R.VAN.	27.6		(4)	
INDAL	ROBT. W. ISAACSON JR.	SYC	32.9		(2)	
HIYU	E.R. HAYNES	CYC	28.0		(4)	
TAHITIAN DOLL	R.C. RALLS	CYC	27.1		(4)	

SWIFTSURE (P.H.R.F.) 1969
RESULTS

YACHT	SKIPPER(S)	CLUB	RATING	COR ELAPSE TIME	POSITION DIVISION	OVERALL
INTREPID	JAMES M. MARTA	SYC	1.9	21/18/15	PHRF	1
HANSA	R.E. CARLSON	GHYC	2.4	23/21/13	PHRF	2
WINDSONG II	R.C. BROWN	CYC	3.8	02/13/45	PHRF	3
ARRIBA	N. McCONAGHY JR.	TYC	3.2	02/32/27	PHRF	4
HAIDA	ROBT. W. DAWSON	PMYC	2.6	02/49/57	PHRF	5
SUNDANCE	THOS. O. MURPHY	TYC	2.9	04/15/58	PHRF	6
AFRICAN STAR	DOUG FRYER	SYC	3.5	07/58/08	PHRF	7
EROICA	N.P. THOMSEN	SILVERGATE Y.C. SAN DIEGO, CALIF.	.9		PHRF	DNF
TACITA	ROBT. F. UTTER	CYC	3.1		PHRF	DNF
KAIULANI	P.S. McCULLOUGH	BREM. Y.C.	2.4		PHRF	DNF
SEMPER FI	P.K. LIVINGSTON	SHILSHOLE BAY Y.C.	2.3		PHRF	DNF

At the time of printing these results, 12:00 Monday, June 2, the following yachts had not been reported finished or withdrawn:

YACHT	SKIPPER(S)	CLUB	RATING			
ACCOMPLICE II	ALDO A. SAMBONI	CYC	3.7		PHRF	

JUAN DE FUCA (C.C. of A.) 1969
RESULTS

YACHT	SKIPPER(S)	CLUB	RATING	COR ELAPSE TIME	POSITION DIVISION	OVERALL
ARIKI IV	GORDON HILL	WVYC	24.2	14/25/33	1(1)	1
SEAQUIN	R.S. MARSHALL	CYC	22.4	14/25/39	1(2)	2
HOLIDAY	D.F. BARR/JOHN FORD	CYC	24.0	14/57/32	2(1)	3
FOXEE	R.G. FOXALL	WVYC	24.7	15/20/09	3(1)	4
KEHLOKE	FRANK H. RUSSELL	WVYC	23.3	15/25/14	2(2)	5
COHO	JOHN BRANDLMAYR	R.VAN.	26.8	15/27/40	4(1)	6
VENTURE	KEN PEARCE	R.VIC.	22.0	15/44/34	3(2)	7
AQUILA	R.P. CARERE	R.VIC.	23.6	15/46/40	4(2)	8
HUSTLER	ROBERT R. SMITH	TYC	23.9	15/49/05	5(2)	9
WALANA	WALLY BRAEDT	TYC	26.1	15/51/42	5(1)	10
APHRODITE III	R.C. McCOLL	WVYC	25.0	15/54/50	6(1)	11
UPEPO	C. PETER WHITE	R.VIC.	26.5	16/11/23	7(1)	12
SHIH YEN	F.T. GARDINER	R.VIC.	22.8	16/15/02	6(2)	13
UNICORN	T.N. VARTY	MAPLE BAY Y.C.	22.6	16/20/54	7(2)	14
POWWOW	BLANCHARD/BURDICK/GOVE	CYC	23.9	17/05/46	8(2)	15
MELTEMI	FRANK MUSSON	WVYC	22.9	17/11/07	9(2)	16
HAPPY HOUR	GREGORY OLIVER	R.VIC.	22.2	17/35/36	10(2)	17
BARCA DE VELA	R.K. BAKER/F.J. PINE	WVYC	28.1	17/35/50	8(1)	18
MELEE	F.D. COVERDALE	R.VIC.	24.0	17/44/23	9(1)	19
GALENAIA	GEO. A. DUFOUR	R.VIC.	18.8	18/00/38	11(2)	20
KATHY	FRANK SHININGER	PAYC	19.8	18/03/36	12(2)	21
EVA II	H. GEO. STRICKER	TUR.HD.S.A.	19.9	18/19/27	13(2)	22
MONT MARE	J.L. SIEMENS	PAYC	20.8	18/23/09	14(2)	23
KAFKA	R. CHRIS. ROBINSON	WVYC	22.8	18/38/46	15(2)	24
PSYCHO	DR. M. MADDALOSSO	TYC	23.4	18/46/17	16(2)	25
PIPPA	JAMES FRASER	WVYC	23.3	18/56/54	17(2)	26
IMPULSE	B. SAUNDERS	R.VIC.	23.2	18/57/22	18(2)	27
SUBEE	A.E. BOHME	WVYC	23.3	18/59/59	19(2)	28
COGNAC	B.K. SCHUELLER	KYC	22.3	19/01/35	20(2)	29
KHU	R.W. HUME	R.VIC.	24.8	19/26/16	10(1)	30
TE-PAH	DR. ROGER OLDHAM	RCNSA	27.0	19/30/01	11(1)	31

YACHT	SKIPPER(S)	CLUB	RATING			
WAWATUSI	L.A. SCHUELLER JR., M.D.	PT.AYC	25.5	19/45/18	12(1)	32
KIWI	C.F. TODD	R.VIC.	26.4	19/46/23	13(1)	33
LE CORDON BLEU	JACK PINCH	WVYC	27.5	19/51/54	14(1)	34
DRAKKAR	F. KRABBE	CYC	22.7		(2)	DNF
SPINDRIFT V	J. VAN AMSTEL	TUR.HD.SA	23.3		(2)	DNF
MUTINEER II	A. JURISSON	GLENMORE Y.C.	24.7		(1)	DNF
SAGA	J. ROOME	MAPLE BAY Y.C.	23.3		(2)	DNF

JUAN DE FUCA (P.H.R.F.) 1969
RESULTS

YACHT	SKIPPER(S)	CLUB	RATING	COR ELAPSE TIME	POSITION DIVISION	OVERALL
TELANI	ALBERT W. PRIEST	ED.Y.C.	8.0NFS	12/55/30	PHRF	1
JELLYBEAN	CHAS. MacDONALD	AYC	4.9	15/44/24	PHRF	2
LUCY ALICE	WM. H. GARDNER	CYC	4.0	17/06/16	PHRF	3
LIZ	TOM WHEELER JR.	SYC	3.9	17/22/00	PHRF	4
MIA	ROBT. F. SCHOEN	ORCAS IS.Y.C.	4.2NFS		PHRF	DNF
OCEAN CAPE	SERGE BECKER	SYC	6.0NFS		PHRF	DNF
SA-HAN	D. FEELEY	PAYC	3.8		PHRF	DNF
KEELA	H.S. HOLMAN	R.VIC.	3.8		PHRF	DNF
FOUR B	EDMOND L. BROWN	CYC	5.4		PHRF	DNS
RAIN BIRD	WM. B. JOHNSON	TYC	4.9		PHRF	DNF

At the time of printing these results, 12:00 Monday, June 2, the following yacht had not been reported finished or withdrawn:

MOONBEAM	S.A. HALBERT	PMYC	3.9		PHRF	DNF

PACIFIC INTERNATIONAL YACHTING ASSOCIATION
SWIFTSURE LIGHTSHIP CLASSIC AND JUAN DE FUCA RACE
1970 TROPHY WINNERS

SWIFTSURE (C.C. of A.)	SWIFTSURE TROPHY (OVERALL HANDICAP WINNER)	GEORGE O'BRIEN	R.VAN.	ENDLESS SUMMER
	CITY OF VICTORIA TROPHY (FIRST YACHT TO FINISH)	GEORGE O'BRIEN	R.VAN.	ENDLESS SUMMER
	OCEAN CEMENT TROPHY (FIRST IN DIVISION I)	GEORGE O'BRIEN	R.VAN.	ENDLESS SUMMER
	T. EATON COMPANY TROPHY (FIRST IN DIVISION II)	W.E. BUCHAN	CYC	MARA
	SEATTLE YACHT CLUB TROPHY (FIRST IN DIVISION III)	R.O. GILBERT	R.VAN.	FIRECRACKER
	ROYAL VANCOUVER YACHT CLUB TROPHY (FIRST IN DIVISION IV)	LARRY SHORETT	CYC	EAGLE
	ROYAL CANADIAN NAVY TROPHY (FIRST TO ROUND SWIFTSURE MARK)	GEORGE O'BRIEN	R.VAN.	ENDLESS SUMMER
SWIFTUSURE (P.H.R.F.)	.... (HANDICAP WINNER)	P.S. McCULLOUGH	BYC	KAIULANI
JUAN DE FUCA (C.C. of A.)	JUAN DE FUCA COMMEMORATION TROPHY (FIRST IN DIVISION I)	PETER R.A. COOMBS	R.VIC.	DOXY II
	ROYAL CANADIAN NAVY TROPHY (FIRST IN DIVISION II)	D'ARCY McLEISH	W.VAN.	KEHLOKE
	SAN JUAN TROPHY (FIRST YACHT TO FINISH)	D'ARCY McLEISH	W.VAN.	KEHLOKE
JUAN DE FUCA (P.H.R.F.)	ANACORTES YACHT CLUB TROPHY (HANDICAP WINNER)	E.C. LAGERQUIST	PYC	WILDISH

SWIFTSURE (C.C. of A.) 1970
RESULTS

YACHT	SKIPPER(S)	CLUB	RATING	COR ELAPSE TIME	POSITION DIVISION	POSITION
ENDLESS SUMMER	GEORGE O'BRIEN	R.VAN.	67.8	14/07/22	1(1)	1
GRAYBEARD	LOL. KILLAM	R.VAN.	78.8	15/37/30	2(1)	2
MARA	WM. E. BUCHAN	CYC	34.1	16/27/28	1(2)	3
MOEA	L. WHIPPLE/DR. L.T. McCLINTON	CYC	32.4	16/40/33	2(2)	4
SIX PACK	BRUCE HEDRICK	ROSE CITY Y.C.	39.8	16/59/57	3(1)	5
GOSPEL	JOHN C. ALBERTSON	CYC	36.1	17/06/01	3(2)	6
FIRECRACKER	R.O. GILBERT	CYC	29.7	17/18/18	1(3)	7
CRUSADER	K.J. MCRAE	R.VAN.	46.3	17/26/50	4(1)	8
PORPOISE III	F.R. KILLAM	R.VAN.	41.9	17/31/43	5(1)	9
ANAHERA	DR. C.G. MORRISON	W.VAN.	34.9	17/35/50	4(2)	10
HYAK	BONAR A. DAVIS	R.VAN.	30.6	17/40/15	2(3)	11
EAGLE	LARRY SHORETT	CYC	27.0	17/42/03	1(4)	12
ADIOS	C. JENSON JR./R. JENSON	SYC	52.9	17/45/37	6(1)	13
HOOLIGAN	TOM O'BRIEN	SYC	26.9	17/46/12	2(4)	14
ARIEL V	K.Y. LOCHHEAD	R.VAN.	30.6	17/57/44	3(3)	15
TRICIA	PAT LESLIE	R.VAN.	31.5	18/10/09	4(3)	16

MARY BOWER	JOHN H. LONG	R.VAN.	40.9	18/12/32	7(1)	17
DIAMOND HEAD	HENRY L. KOTKINS	SYC	54.5	18/14/26	8(1)	18
MOONBIRD	JOHN GRIEVE	W.VAN.	34.5	18/22/02	5(2)	19
OLYMPIAN	PETER G. SCHMIDT	CYC	36.7	18/32/41	6(2)	20
KIMJE	J.H. EASTMAN	R.VAN.	34.9	18/41/59	7(2)	21
THEORY	BILL FIANDER	CYC	27.7	18/42/27	3(4)	22
LANCER	NORMAN LARABEE	CYC	33.9	18/43/33	8(2)	23
SINFUL	ROBT. F. HARRISON	W.VAN.	34.8	18/45/15	9(2)	24
LA RUINA	R.J. GIBBONS	SYC	35.6	18/54/05	10(2)	25
MINX	JOHN P. LIDRAL	SYC	28.5	18/54/33	4(4)	26
KATE II	D.E. SKINNER	SYC	34.9	19/03/30	11(2)	27
ZINGARA	ROBT. L. CADRANELL	SYC	33.1	19/15/50	12(2)	28
CORMORANT	GEORGE T. REEVE	MEY. BAY Y.C.	34.5	19/43/34	13(2)	29
COURAGEOUS	ROBT. M. HELSELL	SYC	39.1	19/52/09	9(1)	30
MYSTAIR	C.H. DAVIDSON	R.VAN.	33.3	20/13/46	14(2)	31
WHITE SQUALL	DR. GOVNOR TEATS	TYC	35.4	20/30/54	15(2)	32
JOLLY OLLY	V. RUSKIN	R.VAN.	24.8	20/32/59	5(4)	33
WINSOME IV	CHES. L. RICKARD	R.VAN.	35.4	20/37/05	16(2)	34
VANDAL	JOE A. McDONALD	SYC	27.3	20/54/34	6(4)	35
CAROLINE	EDGAR KAISER JR.	EAGLE HARBOR	32.9	21/04/31	17(2)	36
JEUNESSE	PAUL T. COTE	R.VAN.	27.6	21/09/59	7(4)	37
MACDUFF	WILLIAM BUCHAN	CYC	33.1	21/10/10	18(2)	38
WHALE'S TALE	WM. M. BLACK	CYC	28.2	21/19/19	8(4)	39
DRUMMER BOY	JOHN DUNFIELD	R.VAN.	29.5	21/33/57	5(3)	40
GRENADIER	A. SAMBONE/J. KLASELL	CYC	36.0	21/38/11	19(2)	41
ANEMOMILOS	ADRAIN VERMEULEN	CYC	36.8	21/58/04	10(1)	42
SATIN DOLL	TOM BUSH	CYC	36.2	22/18/35	20(2)	43
RAPID	IAN A. KIRKLAND	R.VAN.	33.0	22/21/10	21(2)	44
MONIQUE	DAN NORTHFIELD	CYC	29.4	22/23/45	6(3)	45
MOONGLOW III	DAVID D. NIELSEN	TYC	36.1	22/51/13	22(2)	46
INTREPID	JAMES M. MARTA	SYC	36.0	22/55/15	23(2)	47
LOVE AFFAIR	DR. I.W. VARLEY	EV.Y.C.	32.8	22/59/16	24(2)	48
TERNA	P.T. CHRISTOFFERSEN	W.VAN.	29.5	23/07/10	7(3)	49
TSUNAMI	CONRAD J. MORAN	CYC	29.9	23/15/13	8(3)	50
NORWESTER	BROWN/WILLIAMS/FOOTH	SYC	39.5	23/16/27	11(1)	51
CUBARA	D.J. LAWSON	R.VIC.	33.1	23/19/46	25(2)	52
RAG DOLL	JOHN BUSH	CYC	27.2	23/41/34	9(4)	53
SEA FEVER	OTIS F. LAMSON JR.	SYC	47.6	23/45/03	12(1)	54
GABRIELLE II	RALPH HIGGINS	R.VIC.	39.8	23/58/19	13(1)	55
SERAPIS	A.J.B. FORSYTH	R.VAN.	31.4	00/14/18	9(3)	56
NORN	OLAV EKROM	CYC	28.3	00/19/02	10(4)	57
MAURIAH	JACK ROOCROFT	W.VAN.	30.3	00/44/03	10(3)	58
SCOTCH MIST	ROBT. D. O'BRIEN	PORTLAND Y.C.	31.8	00/44/25	11(3)	59
QUEST	ALAN S. RUTHERFORD	CYC	26.1	01/02/39	11(4)	60
GOLDEN TIME	DR. A.L. MASLEY	TYC	29.7	01/05/40	12(3)	61
SWALLOW	PHIL JOHNSON	SYC	27.8	01/07/53	12(4)	62
BANDIT	DAN McDONOUGH	TYC	32.2	01/13/42	26(2)	63
BRIGADOON	D. HILLMAN/F. DANZ	SYC	32.9	01/13/58	27(2)	64
CALYPSO	DR. HENRY GARRIGUES	SYC	33.5	01/18/38	28(2)	65
TEASER	DUDLEY W. HOUTZ, M.D.	TYC	27.9	01/26/05	13(4)	66
AVATAR	RICHARD F. POPPE	CYC	27.0	01/27/27	14(4)	67
EMERAUDE	ROBT. B. CONNOR JR.	CYC	27.4	01/33/10	15(4)	68
FLYING CLOUD	E.W. DEKONING	PORTLAND Y.C.	34.2	01/33/32	29(2)	69
ONRUSH	ROBERT W. BROWN	CYC	28.7	01/36/58	16(4)	70
VAMOSE	W.S. LIEBERMAN	CYC	33.0	01/44/46	30(2)	71
MISTRAL	J.C. BAILLARGEON	SYC	24.9	01/49/25	17(4)	72
LONG GONE	J.G. INNES	R.VAN.	36.1	02/01/30	31(2)	73
HALF MOON	BRIAN DAMMEIER	TYC	30.2	02/08/09	13(3)	74
TAVEUNI	ROBT. I. THIEME	EV.Y.C.	39.6	02/16/00	14(1)	75
NAVITA	A. ARTHUR HEMENWAY	QUEEN CITY	34.3	02/28/02	32(2)	76
SANDERLING	ARTHUR H. MEAKIN	R.VAN.	31.6	02/30/51	14(3)	77
SHANNON	DENNIS M. DONOHUE, M.D.	CYC	32.5	02/40/41	33(2)	78
MAISTRAL	VLADIMIR PLAVSIC	W.VAN.	24.4	02/52/12	18(4)	79
AUKELE	MAX. E. AGATHER	CYC	36.2	03/01/45	34(2)	80
CONCUBINE	FRANK BUSH	R.VIC.	29.8	03/03/19	15(3)	81
WESTERLY	JACK M. SEYMOUR	CYC	27.8	03/06/34	19(4)	82
BARBAN	F.I. HOPKINSON	EAGLE HARBOUR	29.1	03/10/49	16(3)	83
LARA	WALTER HERRMANN	CYC	27.4	03/22/58	20(4)	84
BLACK HAWK	DR. H.H. BOYD	CYC	29.0	03/24/18	17(3)	85
BENORA II	H. HERLIHY	R.VAN.	31.5	03/38/32	18(3)	86
LA VIDA	LOUIS H. MERCILLE	TYC	31.3	03/43/44	19(3)	87
FURIANT	JUDGE DAVID MOFFETT	R.VAN.	31.8	03/49/18	20(3)	88

150

EHA MAKANI	E. SCHALKA/D. EITEL	EV.Y.C.	32.1	03/57/19	21(3)		89
KLAHANIE	HANS BEBIE	CYC	30.4	03/58/15	22(3)		90
HALCYON	DR. S.H.S. PECK	R.VIC.	24.0	04/01/24	21(4)		91
LOLLIPOP	HUNTER VOGEL	R.VAN.	27.5	04/20/02	22(4)		92
MOSHULU	ROBERT O. SYLVESTER	SYC	35.1	04/30/38	35(2)		93
CIRRUS	DR. S. SHEA/B. SUNDGREN	SYC	27.0	05/20/06	23(4)		94
HMCS ORIOLE	LT. CDR. PETER COX	CFSA	66.9	11/35/33	15(1)		95
MISS-CHIEF	CHAS. H. SCHIFF	CYC	41.1		(1)		DNS
BRIDGET II	HAROLD SARGANT	OLYMPIA Y.C.	32.4		(2)		DNF
TIFFANY	D. ANGUS	R.VIC.	30.8		(3)		DNF
THRUST	W.A. BARNARD	CYC	33.9		(2)		DNF
POTLATCH II	WALTER G. MEAKES	CFSA	31.6		(3)		DNF
MUTINEER III	THOMAS BRAIDWOOD	W.VAN.	31.8		(3)		DNF
ZAMBOANGO	FRANK H. BROWNELL	POULSBO Y.C.	28.2		(4)		DNF
NAUTILUS IV	VAL. AUSTIN	CYC	40.0		(1)		DNF
WARRIOR	JOHN BUCHAN	SYC	36.1		(2)		DSQ

SWIFTSURE (P.H.R.F.)

YACHT	SKIPPER(S)	CLUB	RATING	COR ELAPSE TIME	POSITION DIVISION	OVERALL
KAIULANI	DR. P.S. McCULLOUGH	BREMERTON	2.4	20/07/47	PHRF	1
DUTCH FLUTE	ROBERT KLEIN	TYC	2.8	20/46/15	PHRF	2
TOLO TSOLO	E.E. WOODSON	CYC	2.6	21/43/43	PHRF	3
SUNDANCE	THOMAS O. MURPHY	TYC	3.2	21/46/45	PHRF	4
AFRICAN STAR	DOUG. FRYER	SYC	3.4	22/40/38	PHRF	5
KEEWAYDIN II	H. ORMOND MURPHY, M.D.	R.VAN.	2.6	23/10/28	PHRF	6
TRIAD	DR. GUY SCREECH	R.VIC.	2.8	00/27/50	PHRF	7
WINDSONG II	R.C. BROWN	CYC	3.8	00/44/05	PHRF	8
INISFAIL	GARRETT HORDER	CYC	3.6	02/37/41	PHRF	9
AMPHITRITE	CLAYTON RICH	PT. MADISON Y.C.	3.2	03/02/21	PHRF	10
ARRIBA	MARK L. GABRIELSON	ANACORTES	3.4		PHRF	DNF

At the time of printing these results, 12:00 Monday, June 1, the following yachts had not been reported finished or withdrawn:

SEMPER FI	PHILIP LIVINGSTONE	SHILSHOLE		PHRF	
SAUMURE	RALPH BRINE	R.VAN		PHRF	

JUAN DE FUCA (C.C. of A.) 1970
RESULTS

YACHT	SKIPPER(S)	CLUB	RATING	COR ELAPSE TIME	POSITION DIVISION	OVERALL
KEHLOKE	D'ARCY McLEISH	WVYC	23.3	09/17/08	1(2)	1
DRAKKAR	FRED KRABBE/LOU RUTTEN	CYC	22.7	09/32/38	2(2)	2
AQUILA	ROBERT P. CARERE	R.VIC.	23.6	09/41/45	3(2)	3
PUFF	J.D. WOODWARD	R.VIC.	22.7	09/43/18	4(2)	4
UNICORN	GORDON INGLIS	MAPLE BAY Y.C.	22.6	09/46/59	5(2)	5
HUSTLER	ROBERT R. SMITH	TYC	23.9	09/55/44	6(2)	6
DOXY II	PETER R.A. COOMBS	R.VIC.	24.6	10/02/50	1(1)	7
WALANA	WALLY BRAEDT	TYC	26.1	10/04/09	2(1)	8
IMPULSE	B. SAUNDERS	R.VIC.	23.2	10/04/47	7(2)	9
FOXEE	R.G. FOXALL	W.VAN.	25.3	10/09/01	3(1)	10
TAHUYA BEAR	PHILIP HAYES	TYC	26.3	10/19/20	4(1)	11
CIERCO	ROGER L. RUE	TYC	26.2	10/19/30	5(1)	12
MELTEMI	FRANK MUSSON	W.VAN.	22.9	10/32/17	8(2)	13
MUTINEER II	GRAHAM C. ALVEY	CALGARY Y.C.	24.7	10/38/41	6(1)	14
MARY D	DARREL B. DAVIS	PT. ANGELES	24.2	10/54/02	7(1)	15
MOA	WALT. O. MIDDLETON	W.VAN.	26.3	11/05/04	8(1)	16
LIGERO	ARCHIE CAMPBELL	R.VIC.	27.1	11/06/00	9(1)	17
SAGA	J.M. ROOME	MAPLE BAY Y.C.	23.3	11/12/29	9(2)	18
ARIKI IV	G.R. HILL	W.VAN.	23.8	11/15/56	10(2)	19
TE-PAH	DR. ROGER OLDHAM	CFSA	27.0	11/27/30	10(1)	20
PSYCHO	M. MADDALOSSO, M.D.	TYC	22.7	11/29/24	11(2)	21
T'WEATHER	GREGORY S. OLIVER	TURKEY HEAD	23.8	11/46/46	12(2)	22
POWWOW	BLANCHARD/BURDICK/GOVE	CYC	23.9	11/47/40	13(2)	23
MELEE	F.D. COVERDALE	R.VIC.	24.0	12/38/05	11(1)	24
SEAQUIN	R.S. MARSHALL	CYC	22.4	12/40/32	14(2)	25
WAWATUSI	DR. L.A. SCHUELER JR.	PT. ANGELES	25.5	13/20/57	12(1)	26
HAIDA III	DON McCOWAN	R.VIC.	23.1	16/42/24	15(2)	27
SA-HAN	DON FEELEY	PT. ANGELES	23.5	18/43/40	16(2)	28
SHIH YEN	F.T. GARDINER	R.VIC.	22.8		(2)	DSQ
HAPPY HOUR	N. ISHERWOOD	TURKEY HEAD	22.2		(2)	DNF
VENTURE	KEN PEARCE	R.VIC.	22.0		(2)	DNF
KATHY	FRANK SHININGER	PT. ANGELES	19.8		(2)	DNF

JUAN DE FUCA (P.H.R.F.) — 1970
RESULTS

YACHT	SKIPPER(S)	CLUB	RATING	COR ELAPSE TIME	POSITION DIVISION	OVERALL
WILDISH	E.C. LAGERQUIST	PORTLAND Y.C.	3.7	08/20/13	PHRF	1
LUCY ALICE	WM. H. GARDNER	CYC	4.2	08/26/42	PHRF	2
VAYU	DEENE O. ALMVIG	ANACORTES	3.3	08/39/26	PHRF	3
GALENAIA II	GEORGE A. DUFOUR	R.VIC.	3.5	08/57/15	PHRF	4
LAIRIG GRHU	H.E. BUCHANAN	R.VIC.	3.7	09/27/16	PHRF	5
OCEAN CAPE	SERGE BECKER	SYC	5.9	09/36/04	PHRF	6
HAMMERHEAD	T.W. LONEY	R.VIC.	3.2	09/46/35	PHRF	7
SCOTCHMIST	WM. ALLEN SANBORN	CYC	3.6	09/48/38	PHRF	8
JAUNTY	WM. R. NELSON	TYC	3.0	10/01/12	PHRF	9
HIYU	E.R. HAYNES	CYC	3.0	10/02/14	PHRF	10
KAI WAHL	KEN KEITH	CFSA	3.7	10/03/43	PHRF	11
PATRICIA ANN II	KEN McLEAN	R.VAN.	5.0	10/39/31	PHRF	12
DELTA SPIRIT	JOHN C. FOOTE	TSAWWASSEN Y.C.	3.1	10/53/18	PHRF	13
JELLYBEAN	CHAS. H. MacDONALD	ANACORTES	4.2	12/04/16	PHRF	14
TELANI	AL. PRIEST	ED.Y.C.	6.0NF	13/18/49	PHRF	15
SERENE	VIC. GARBIN	CYC	3.2	15/48/45	PHRF	16
H-25	KEITH HARDING	CALGARY Y.C.	3.8	16/27/22	PHRF	17
LIMFJORD	BENT JESPERSEN	TURKEY HEAD	5.2NF	16/50/27	PHRF	18
MOONBEAM	SHERIDAN A. HALBERT	PT. MADISON	3.8		PHRF	DNS

PACIFIC INTERNATIONAL YACHTING ASSOCIATION
SWIFTSURE LIGHTSHIP CLASSIC AND JUAN DE FUCA RACE
1971 TROPHY WINNERS

SWIFTSURE (I.O.R.)	SWIFTSURE TROPHY (OVERALL HANDICAP WINNER)	TOM O'BRIEN	SYC	HOOLIGAN
	CITY OF VICTORIA TROPHY (FIRST YACHT TO FINISH)	DR. C.D.F. JENSEN	SYC	ADIOS
	OCEAN CEMENT TROPHY (FIRST IN DIVISION I)	G.S. SCHUCHART	SYC	PEMAQUID
	T. EATON COMPANY TROPHY (FIRST IN DIVISION II)	P. CHRISTOFFERSEN	W.VAN.	TERNA
	CITY OF SEATTLE TROPHY (FIRST IN DIVISION III)	BONAR A. DAVIS	R.VAN.	HYAK
	ROYAL VANCOUVER YACHT CLUB TROPHY (FIRST IN DIVISION IV)	TOM O'BRIEN	SYC	HOOLIGAN
	ROYAL CANADIAN NAVY TROPHY (FIRST TO ROUND SWIFTSURE MARK)	G.S. SCHUCHART	SYC	PEMAQUID
SWIFTSURE (P.H.R.F.)	.... (HANDICAP WINNER)	R.B. CONNOR JR.	CYC	EMERAUDE
JUAN DE FUCA (I.O.R.)	JUAN DE FUCA COMMEMORATION TROPHY (FIRST IN DIVISION I)	D.S. GIBBERD	W.VAN.	GYPSY G
	ROYAL CANADIAN NAVY TROPHY (FIRST IN DIVISION II)	GORDON R. HILL	W.VAN.	ARIKI V
	SAN JUAN TROPHY (FIRST YACHT TO FINISH)	D.S. GIBBERD	W.VAN.	GYPSY G
JUAN DE FUCA (P.H.R.F.)	ANACORTES YACHT CLUB TROPHY (HANDICAP WINNER)	S.R. OLDHAM	CFSA (Esquimalt)	TE-PAH

SWIFTSURE (I.O.R.) 1971
RESULTS

YACHT	SKIPPER(S)	CLUB	RATING	COR ELAPSE TIME	POSITION DIVISION	OVERALL
HOOLIGAN	TOM O'BRIEN	SYC	24.7	17/16/02	1(4)	1
HYAK	BONAR A. DAVIS	R.VAN.	27.0	17/30/59	1(3)	2
TONIC	DAN BRINK	CYC	22.9	17/32/28	2(4)	3
FIRECRACKER	RICHARD O. GILBERT	CYC	26.6	17/47/54	2(3)	4
TERNA	PER CHRISTOFFERSEN	W.VAN.	29.4	17/48/41	1(2)	5
CHECKMATE	CALVIN BAMFORD, JR.	TYC	26.1	17/57/27	3(3)	6
QUEST	ALAN S. RUTHERFORD	CYC	23.0	17/57/55	3(4)	7
WINSOME IV	CHES. L. RICKARD	R.VAN.	31.2	18/01/47	2(2)	8
GOLDEN TIME	DR. A.L. MASLEY	TYC	26.3	18/04/38	4(3)	9
TANGENT II	ANTONY C. LOACH	W.VAN.	29.2	18/16/35	3(2)	10
MOON GLOW III	DAVID D. NIELSEN	TYC	32.8	18/18/55	4(2)	11
VANDAL	JOE A. McDONALD	SYC	24.3	18/27/34	4(4)	12
SINFUL	ROBERT F. HARRISON	W.VAN.	31.1	18/33/32	5(2)	13
WHALE'S TALE	W.M. BLACK	CYC	25.4	18/36/33	5(4)	14
SIREN	GERALD O. SMITH	TYC	30.3	18/48/22	6(2)	15
EHA MAKANI	DR. E. SCHALKA/EITEL	EYC	28.2	18/49/05	5(3)	16
TEASER	STEFAN THORDARSON	TYC	24.3	18/51/27	6(4)	17
PEMAQUID	GEORGE S. SCHUCHART	SYC	37.1	18/52/42	1(1)	18

Boat	Skipper	Club	Rating	Time	Class	Overall
KAOS	BILL RUDOLPH	CYC	32.3	18/56/37	7(2)	19
ARCTURUS	DR. ALLAN D. TOBE	W.VAN.	28.9	18/56/59	8(2)	20
EAGLE	LARRY SHORETT	CYC	24.3	18/57/54	7(4)	21
CYNOSURE	HOWARD C. ELLIS, JR.	TYC	26.5	18/58/01	6(3)	22
KATE	K.L. PARTLOW	TYC	26.2	19/01/19	7(3)	23
ANAHERA	BRUCE MORRISON	WVYC	31.4	19/14/48	9(2)	24
GEM	RAY FIEDLER	CYC	24.4	19/19/41	8(4)	25
SOLQUIST	FRED E. RUSSELL	WVYC	27.6	19/24/00	8(3)	26
ADIOS	CARL D.F. JENSEN, M.D.	SYC	48.4	19/33/30	2(1)	27
SERAPIS	A.J.B. FORSYTH	R.VAN.	29.3	19/34/34	10(2)	28
CAROLINE	EDGAR F. KAISER, JR.	R.VAN.	30.2	19/43/17	11(2)	29
BLACK HAWK	DR. HERSCHELL BOYD	CYC	27.7	19/43/44	9(3)	30
MISS-CHIFF	CHAS. H. SCHIFF	CYC	35.5	19/43/50	3(1)	31
TYEE	WILLIAM C. WHIPPLE	CYC	41.3	19/45/32	4(1)	32
LOVE AFFAIR	DR. IRVING W. VARLEY	EYC	28.6	19/47/04	10(3)	33
DRUMMER BOY	JOHN DUNFIELD	R.VAN.	26.0	19/50/25	11(3)	34
UHURU	TOM COAD	EYC	32.7	19/51/00	12(2)	35
MOONRAKER	LOUIS F. LINDHOLM	R.VIC.	29.4	19/51/22	13(2)	36
MIN SETTE	JOE POLLACK JR.	RCYC	52.7	19/55/06	5(1)	37
TSUNAMI	CONRAD J. MORAN	CYC	26.8	19/58/30	12(3)	38
BANDIT	DAN McDONOUGH	TYC	29.5	20/04/22	14(2)	39
CAMELOT	ROBERT R. SMITH	TYC	30.8	20/06/25	15(2)	40
AUKELE	M.E. AGATHER	CYC	32.4	20/09/12	16(2)	41
KEEWAYDIN II	H. ORMOND MURPHY	R.VAN.	27.5	20/11/40	13(3)	42
PORPOISE III	BILL KILLAM	R.VAN.	39.6	20/12/00	6(1)	43
SARGASSO II	DON EUDALY	PYC	30.2	20/12/04	17(2)	44
MYSTERE	B.R. TEWKSBURY III	R.VAN.	29.3	20/13/44	18(2)	45
COHO	GRANT BRANDLMAYR	R.VAN.	41.3	20/15/08	7(1)	46
GOSPEL	JOHN C. ALBERTSON	CYC	33.6	20/18/17	8(1)	47
SATIN DOLL	TOM BUSH	CYC	31.2	20/24/04	19(2)	48
CONCUBINE	FRANK S. BUSH	R.VIC.	28.2	20/24/43	14(3)	49
THRUST	WILLIAM A. BARNARD	SYC	31.1	20/26/42	20(2)	50
WHITE SQUALL	DR. GOVNOR TEATS	TYC	32.5	20/41/55	21(2)	51
VAMOSE	W.S. LIEBERMAN	CYC	30.4	20/50/22	22(2)	52
MARY BOWER	JOHN H. LONG	R.VAN.	38.0	20/56/52	9(1)	53
DIAMOND HEAD	HENRY L. KOTKINS	SYC	53.2	20/56/53	10(1)	54
JOLLY OLLY III	V. RUSKIN	R.VAN.	24.0	20/59/34	9(4)	55
MARA	WILLIAM E. BUCHAN	CYC	31.8	21/00/23	23(2)	56
KIMJE	J.H. EASTMAN	R.VAN.	32.3	21/01/41	24(2)	57
HANSA	EDWARD HOPPEN	GIG HBR.	35.2	21/04/27	11(1)	58
GRENADIER	A. SAMBONI/J. KLASSELL	CYC	32.3	21/28/57	25(2)	59
HALF MOON	BRIAN F. DAMMEIER	TYC	27.0	21/32/09	15(3)	60
KATE II	D.E. SKINNER	SYC	32.8	21/43/02	26(2)	61
INISFAIL	GARRETT HORDER	SYC	33.5	21/45/26	12(1)	62
LARA	WALTER HERRMANN, M.D.	CYC	24.2	23/17/33	10(4)	63
HUSTLER	DON McHARGUE	CYC	31.0	23/39/25	27(2)	64
ONRUSH	ROBERT W. BROWN	CYC	26.3	00/01/54	16(3)	65
BARBAN	H. WILKINSON	EAGLE HBR.	27.0	00/15/56	17(3)	66
MUTINEER III	TOM BRAIDWOOD	WVYC	28.3	00/51/20	18(3)	67
MOONBIRD	JOHN GRIEVE	WVYC	31.2	01/31/48	28(2)	68
POTLATCH II	WALLY MEAKES	R.VIC.	28.5	06/12/23	19(3)	69
MACDUFF	WM. BUCHAN, SR.	CYC	32.9		(2)	DNF
SWIFT I	ROGER D. HOFFMAN	EVERETT	27.2		(3)	DNF
LUCY ALICE	WM. H. GARDNER	CYC	23.1		(4)	DNF
SIX PACK	BRUCE HEDRICK	ROSE CITY	36.2		(1)	DNF
MOLLY HOGAN II	DANA RAMSAY	R.VAN.	24.0		(4)	DNF
CUBARA	DONALD J. LAWSON	R.VIC.	29.8		(2)	DNF
LANCER	NORMAN LARABEE	CYC	29.7		(2)	DNF
SUNBIRD	ALVIN J. NAROD	R.VAN.	35.8		(1)	DNF
CIRRUS	STEPHEN F. SHEA/BRUCE SUNDGREN	SYC	24.5		(4)	DNF
SWORD	JESS KRITSIS	CYC	31.8		(2)	DNF
NUBIAN	GEORGE P. CLARKE	W.VAN.	25.2		(4)	DNF
HUCKLEBERRY	KEN REID	W.VAN.	26.4		(3)	DNF
MAURIAH	JACK H. ROOCROFT	W.VAN.	27.4		(3)	DNF
GAMIN	LAWRENCE W. ROBINSON	CYC	30.3		(2)	DNF
CO-MOTION	P.L. PEOPLES	CYC	39.3		(1)	DNF
WARRIOR	JOHN F. BUCHAN	CYC	32.4		(2)	DNF
WESTERLY	JACK M. SEYMOUR	CYC	26.1		(3)	DNF
NORWESTER	JOSEPH L. WILLIAMS	SYC	38.9		(1)	DNF
LA RUINA	R.J. GIBBONS		32.8		(2)	DNF
NORN	OLAV EKROM	CYC	25.4		(4)	DNF

YACHT	SKIPPER(S)	CLUB	RATING		DIVISION	OVERALL
ANDANTE II	ART WAY	R.VAN.	40.4		(1)	DNF
OLYMPIAN	PETER G. SCHMIDT	CYC	32.9		(2)	DNF
DUTCH FLUTE	DR. ROBERT KLEIN	TACOMA	26.3		(3)	DNF

SWIFTSURE (P.H.R.F.) 1971
RESULTS

YACHT	SKIPPER(S)	CLUB	RATING	COR ELAPSE TIME	POSITION DIVISION	OVERALL
EMERAUDE	ROBT. B. CONNOR JR.	CYC	3.0	16/37/27	PHRF	1
THEORY	BILL FIANDER	CYC	2.9	17/02/34	PHRF	2
AFRICAN STAR	DOUG. FRYER	SEATTLE	3.6	17/03/18	PHRF	3
TOLO TSOLO	E.E. WOODSON	CYC	2.3	17/16/11	PHRF	4
SUNDANCE	THOS. O. MURPHY	TACOMA	2.9	17/30/40	PHRF	5
BRIDGET II	HAROLD V. SARGENT	OLYMPIA	2.4	18/06/48	PHRF	6
MOSHULU	ROBT. O. SYLVESTER	SEATTLE	2.1	18/29/06	PHRF	7
MAI TAI	A.C. WOOD	MEYDENBAUER BAY	2.0	18/42/42	PHRF	8
JEUNESSE II	PAUL T. COTE	R.VAN.	1.2	19/56/49	PHRF	9
TAVEUNI	ROBT. I. THIEME	EVERETT	2.1	20/26/51	PHRF	10
SEA-FAX III	MURRAY FARMER	R.VIC.	2.8	21/25/43	PHRF	11
SEREN	DR. D.P. JONES	R.VAN.	3.7	01/00/04	PHRF	12
ARRIBA	M.L. GABRIELSON	ANACORTES	3.7	03/11/44	PHRF	13
SNOW GOOSE II	FRANK JONES	EDMONDS	2.7	03/29/51	PHRF	14
SERENDIPITY III	MAJOR D.M. McLEAN	C.F.S.A. (Chilliwack Sqdn.)	3.4NFS	04/03/30	PHRF	15
MA COEUR	R.J. MILLER	R.VAN.	3.4		PHRF	DNF
SAUMURE	R.H. BRINE	R.VAN.	3.0		PHRF	DNF
SABRE II	JOHN C. REED	R.VIC.	2.6		PHRF	DNF
EOS	H. ROBT. DURSCH	ANACORTES	2.2		PHRF	DNF
ARIES	J. KEVORKIAN	CYC	2.8		PHRF	DNF
SWANHILDE	W.L. MERCIER	SHILSHOLE BAY	2.3		PHRF	DNF
GOMETRA	PETER SKIBBE	R.VAN.	2.2		PHRF	DNF
NAUTILUS IV	VAL AUSTIN	CYC	1.9		PHRF	DNF
BARBARA	WYNN E. KAMPE	CYC	2.0		PHRF	DNF
SANGUINE	DR. H. VAN DOOREN	GIG HRBR.	2.3		PHRF	DNF
SEMPER FI	P.K. LIVINGSTON	SEATTLE	2.8		PHRF	DNF
KIMCHOW	DOUG M. GARDINER	R.VAN.	3.0		PHRF	DNF

At the time of printing these results, 12:25 p.m. Monday, May 31, the following yachts had not been reported finished or withdrawn:

YACHT	SKIPPER(S)	CLUB	RATING		DIVISION	OVERALL
ARIEL V	K.Y. LOCHHEAD	R.VAN.	29.5		(II)	
CALYPSO	DR. H.B. GARRIGUES	SEATTLE	30.6		(II)	
STORMY WEATHER	ROBT. W. ISSACSON JR.	SEATTLE	2.1		PHRF	
BENORA II	THOS. MURRAY	EAGLE HRBR.	2.6		PHRF	

JUAN DE FUCA (I.O.R.) 1971
RESULTS

YACHT	SKIPPER(S)	CLUB	RATING	COR ELAPSE TIME	POSITION DIVISION	OVERALL
GYPSY G	D.S. GIBBERD	W.VAN.	24.7	20/23/00	1(1)	1
CIRRUS	J.W. GOLBERG	CYC	23.7	20/35/39	2(1)	2
ARIKI IV	GORDON R. HILL	W.VAN.	21.5	21/14/57	1(2)	3
SKILFISH	D.R. WEST	W.VAN.	24.7	21/24/02	3(1)	4
MORGAN	DR. GUY SCREECH	R.VIC.	24.1	21/27/27	4(1)	5
AMBUSH	STAN R. KIESZLING	TACOMA	24.6	21/59/25	5(1)	6
BARCA DE VELA	F.J. PINE	W.VAN.	25.1	23/11/12	6(1)	7
APPLE-CHEEKS	DR. M. BELL	R.VAN.	24.6	23/30/22	7(1)	8
HIGH LIFE	DONALD MILLER	CYC	21.0	23/55/34	2(2)	9
DOXY II	P.R.A. COOMBS	R.VIC.	23.1	00/01/04	8(1)	10
MELTEMI	FRANK MUSSON	W.VAN.	20.1	01/37/09	3(2)	11
PSYCHO	DR. M. MADDALOSSO	TACOMA	20.4	02/14/11	4(2)	12
HAIDA III	D. McCOWAN	R.VIC.	20.7	02/28/02	5(2)	13
MAISTRAL	VLADIMIR PLAVSIC	W.VAN.	21.4	02/41/38	6(2)	14
SEAQUIN	R.S. MARSHALL	CYC	21.5	02/49/20	7(2)	15
TOUCHE	DR. D.C. SMITH	PT. MADISON	21.8	02/49/33	8(2)	16
MOA	WALT. O. MIDDLETON	W.VAN.	24.4	02/53/32	9(1)	17
FOXEE	R.G. FOXALL	W.VAN.	22.6	03/02/20	10(1)	18
KEHLOKE	R.H. RUSSELL	W.VAN.	22.6	03/06/07	11)1)	19
RHUBARB	ROBBIE BROWN	W.VAN.	24.0	03/06/19	12(1)	20
APHRODITE	R.C. McCOLL	W.VAN.	24.0	03/21/49	13(1)	21
DELTA SPIRIT	JOHN FOOTE	TSAWWASSEN	21.4	06/57/05	9(2)	22
GALENAIA II	GEO. DUFOUR	R.VIC.	21.0	07/23/38	10(2)	23
WELANNE	R.T. WELDON PINCHIN	EAGLE HRBR.	22.7	07/47/39	14(1)	24
CIERCO	ROGER L. RUE	TACOMA	23.1		(1)	DNF

DRAKKAR	FRED KRABBE/LOU RUTTEN	CYC	20.5		(2)	DNF

At the time of printing these results, 12:15 p.m. Monday, May 31, the following yachts had not been reported finished or withdrawn:

PRESTO	F.W. HAYES	SEATTLE	20.5		(II)
NO-NO	ROBT. McVITTIE	W.VAN.	24.3		(I)
CHIMO III	GEOFF. COLEMAN	W.VAN.	21.5		(II)
MOPPET OF HAMBLE	W.M. DOUTHWAITE	KITSILANO	5.2		PHRF
SKAGA	D.W. GLADMAN	MAPLE BAY	4.1NFS		PHRF
KEELA	H.S. HOLMAN	R.VIC.	3.7		PHRF

JUAN DE FUCA (P.H.R.F.) 1971
RESULTS

YACHT	SKIPPER(S)	CLUB	RATING	COR ELAPSE TIME	POSITION DIVISION	OVERALL
TE-PAH	S.R. OLDHAM	CFSA (Esquimalt)	3.1	19/48/08	PHRF	1
AQUILA	ROBT. CARERE	R.VIC.	3.7	20/02/56	PHRF	2
SIROCCO	JOHN. E. SPROUSE	PORTLAND	3.4	21/35/02	PHRF	3
MELEE	F.D. COVERDALE	R.VIC.	3.8	22/18/19	PHRF	4
HAMMERHEAD	T.W. LONEY	R.VIC.	3.3	22/58/53	PHRF	5
LIGERO	ARCHIE CAMPBELL	R.VIC.	3.6	23/26/43	PHRF	6
PEACHES	DR. T.A. SERR	PT. ANGELES	3.7	23/41/20	PHRF	7
WAWATUSI	LARRY SCHUELER	PT. ANGELES	3.8	00/27/14	PHRF	8
PUFF	J.D. WOODWARD	R.VIC.	3.7	00/40/40	PHRF	9
T'WEATHER	GREG. OLIVER	R.VIC.	3.7	00/46/27	PHRF	10
VANDAL	STEVE MERRIMAN	R.VIC.	3.5	00/48/31	PHRF	11
LIMFJORD	BENT JESPERSEN	TURKEY HEAD	5.2NFS	00/54/33	PHRF	12
SHALOM	GARY O. WATSON	WILLIAMETTE	3.4	11/56/16	PHRF	13
KEEMA	R.E. SCHULKE	CYC	3.8	01/32/08	PHRF	14
SA-HAN	DON FEELEY	PT. ANGELES	3.7	01/41/49	PHRF	15
WILDISH	R.P. PASCHALL	PORTLAND	3.7	01/42/01	PHRF	16
SAGA	JOHN M. ROOME	MAPLE BAY	3.7	01/42/48	PHRF	17
MARY D	DARREL B. DAVIS	PT. ANGELES	3.5	01/55/22	PHRF	18
MUTINEER II	GRAHAM C. ALVEY	CALGARY Y.C.	3.4	02/01/52	PHRF	19
MINT	E.P. ASHE	R.VIC.	3.6	02/02/41	PHRF	20
BANANA	TOM MALLOY	ROSE CITY	3.5	02/05/45	PHRF	21
CHANSON	C. WHITE	MAPLE BAY	3.4	02/11/50	PHRF	22
FAIR LADY II	R.J. WHITFIELD	EAGLE HBR.	3.0	02/30/03	PHRF	23
RAINBIRD	WM. B. JOHNSON	TACOMA	5.2	02/32/27	PHRF	24
RUNNING SHOE	JOHN JARMAN	R.VAN.	4.9	13/00/01	PHRF	25
WINDSONG II	R.C. BROWN	CYC	4.2	13/47/26	PHRF	26
KISMET	R.C. DICKIE	MAPLE BAY	3.5	14/42/18	PHRF	27
KHU	A. JURRISSON	GLENMORE (Calgary)	3.4	14/47/56	PHRF	28
WHIRLWIND	C.E. FOSTER	R.VAN.	3.7		PHRF	DNF
GAY ABANDON	BILL NIEMI JR.	SEATTLE	4.0		PHRF	DNF
LAIRIG GRHU	H.E. BUCHANAN	R.VIC.	3.7		PHRF	DNF
IMPULSE	BRIAN SAUNDERS	R.VIC.	3.7		PHRF	DNF
ANWYLL	J.B. MacDONALD	R.VIC.	3.8		PHRF	DNF
VAYU	DEENE ALMVIG	ANACORTES	3.4		PHRF	DNF
SCOTCHMIST	WM. A. SANBORN	CYC	3.6		PHRF	DNF

PACIFIC INTERNATIONAL YACHTING ASSOCIATION
SWIFTSURE LIGHTSHIP CLASSIC AND JUAN DE FUCA RACE
1972 TROPHY WINNERS

SWIFTSURE (I.O.R.)	SWIFTSURE TROPHY (OVERALL HANDICAP WINNER)	GEORGE O'BRIEN	R.VAN.	ENDLESS SUMMER
	CITY OF VICTORIA TROPHY (FIRST YACHT TO FINISH)	GEORGE O'BRIEN	R.VAN.	ENDLESS SUMMER
	OCEAN CEMENT TROPHY (FIRST IN DIVISION I)	GEORGE O'BRIEN	R.VAN.	ENDLESS SUMMER
	T. EATON COMPANY TROPHY (FIRST IN DIVISION II)	EDGAR F. KAISER	R.VAN.	CAROLINE
	CITY OF SEATTLE TROPHY (FIRST IN DIVISION III)	STEVE CRARY	CYC	JUBILEE
	ROYAL VANCOUVER YACHT CLUB TROPHY (FIRST IN DIVISION IV)	D.W. LERCH/ D.R. McVITTIE	CYC	HOOLIGAN
	ROYAL CANADIAN NAVY TROPHY (FIRST TO ROUND SWIFTSURE MARK)	CARL D.F. JENSEN	SYC	ADIOS
SWIFTSURE (P.H.R.F.)	CORINTHIAN YACHT CLUB TROPHY (FIRST IN DIVISION A)	PAUL T. COTE	R.VAN.	JEUNESSE II
	CAPE FLATTERY TROPHY (FIRST IN DIVISION V)	JAMES SMITH	UWSC	PREDICAMENT II
JUAN DE FUCA (I.O.R.)	ROYAL VICTORIA YACHT CLUB TROPHY (FIRST IN DIVISION I)	DONALD SMITH	PORT MADISON	CLIMAX

	ROYAL CANADIAN NAVY TROPHY (FIRST IN DIVISION II)	STEVE MERRIMAN	R.VIC.	VANDAL		
	SAN JUAN TROPHY (FIRST YACHT TO FINISH)	STAN KIESZLING	TYC	AMBUSH		
JUAN DE FUCA (P.H.R.F.)	ANACORTES YACHT CLUB TROPHY (FIRST IN DIVISION C)	PETER WHITE	MAPLE BAY	WHITE SQUALL		
	. . . . (FIRST IN DIVISION D)	J.F. UPWARD	W.VAN.	AVENGER II		

SWIFTSURE (I.O.R.) 1972
RESULTS

YACHT	SKIPPER(S)	CLUB	RATING	COR ELAPSE TIME	POSITION DIVISION	OVERALL
ENDLESS SUMMER	GEORGE O'BRIEN	R.VAN.	58.3	23/17/18	1(1)	1
HOOLIGAN	D.W. LERCH/D.R. McVITTIE	CORINTHIAN	24.4	24/12/29	1(4)	2
CHECKMATE	C. BAMFORD JR.	TACOMA	25.8	24/38/12	2(4)	3
ADIOS	CARL D.F. JENSEN	SEATTLE	47.6	24/17/54	2(1)	4
JUBILEE	STEVE CRARY	CORINTHIAN	29.2	24/24/01	1(3)	5
TERNA	P. CHRISTOFFERSEN	W.VAN.	29.2	24/31/06	2(3)	6
POW WOW	ED GOVE	SEATTLE	26.8	24/35/26	3(3)	7
CYNOSURE	C.B. ADAMS	TACOMA	26.5	24/36/57	4(3)	8
SAGA	S. RASMUSSEN	R.VAN.	29.5	24/37/57	5(3)	9
SIX PACK	B. HEDRICK	ROSE CITY	35.1	24/44/39	3(1)	10
TANGENT II	TONY LOACH	W.VAN.	29.4	24/45/08	6(3)	11
GEMINI	F.W. BIEKER	PORTLAND	26.3	24/51/09	7(3)	12
CAROLINE	EDGAR F. KAISER JR.	R.VAN.	30.8	24/52/31	1(2)	13
MOONRAKER	L. LINDHOLM	R.VIC.	30.0	24/54/55	2(2)	14
CHEROKEE	WM. M. BLACK	CORINTHIAN	27.3	24/55/23	8(3)	15
OUTRAGEOUS	THEO. A. BURNS	BREMERTON	30.8	24/58/19	3(2)	16
UHURU	GERRY MAURER	EVERETT	32.2	24/59/20	4(2)	17
ANAHERA	DR. C.G. MORRISON	W.VAN.	31.0	25/00/12	5(2)	18
CAMELOT	BOB SMITH	TACOMA	30.8	25/01/06	6(2)	19
PATRIOT	JAMES M. MARTA	SEATTLE	30.9	25/06/26	7(2)	20
HOOLIGAN II	TOM O'BRIEN	SEATTLE	32.0	25/07/15	8(2)	21
WINDWARD	JOHN W. ELLIS	CORINTHIAN	32.7	25/10/19	9(2)	22
OLYMPIAN	P.G. SCHMIDT	SEATTLE	32.3	25/13/06	10(2)	23
GOSPEL	J.C. ALBERTSON	CORINTHIAN	33.4	25/11/53	4(1)	24
TEMPTATION	BRAISIER/BUCHAN/NELSON	TACOMA	40.7	25/18/44	5(1)	25
CO-MOTION	P.L. PEOPLES	CORINTHIAN	40.1	25/31/43	6(1)	26
KAOS	BILL RUDOLPH	CORINTHIAN	32.3	25/32/04	11(2)	27
SATIN DOLL	TOM BUSH	CORINTHIAN	31.6	25/39/05	12(2)	28
CUBARA	D.J. LAWSON	R.VIC.	29.4	25/39/07	9(3)	29
DIAMOND HEAD	HENRY L. KOTKINS	SEATTLE	51.5	25/46/16	7(1)	30
SINFUL	R.F. HARRISON	W.VAN.	31.1	25/49/11	13(2)	31
PANDORA	J. ROBT. HORNER	R.VIC.	39.1	25/50/10	8(1)	32
RAPID	I.A. KIRKLAND	R.VAN.	31.6	25/23/46	14(2)	33
GAMIN	LON ROBINSON	CORINTHIAN	30.8	25/57/03	15(2)	34
HABITAT	P.C.G. RICHARDS	W.VAN.	29.4	25/57/03	10(3)	35
MISS-CHIFF	CHAS. SCHIFF	CORINTHIAN	35.5	26/01/54	9(1)	36
LOVE AFFAIR	IRVING W. VARLEY	EVERETT	28.3	26/05/02	11(3)	37
NORWESTER	KEN BROWNE	SEATTLE	37.6	26/07/22	10(1)	38
NAUTICAL II	WM. F. NIEMI JR.	SEATTLE	32.7	26/09/03	16(2)	39
SWORD	JESS KRITSIS	CORINTHIAN	31.8	26/14/00	17(2)	40
RED DOG	D.M. DONOHUE, M.D.	CORINTHIAN	32.3	26/17/31	18(2)	41
VAMOSE	W.S. LIEBERMAN	CORINTHIAN	30.0	26/20/02	19(2)	42
ORAO	VLADIMIR PLAVSIC	W.VAN.	21.6	26/35/16	3(4)	43
SOLQUIST	F.K.E. RUSSELL	W.VAN.	26.9	26/39/10	12(3)	44
ELIXIR	JOHN GRAHAM	SEATTLE	27.8	26/40/17	13(3)	45
TRIAD	ROBT. T. HOSIE, M.D.	R.VIC.	25.4	26/40/59	5(4)	46
MARY BOWER	DAVE THOMAS	MAPLE BAY	38.0	26/42/23	11(1)	47
HUCKLEBERRY	KEN REID	W.VAN.	26.3	26/48/29	14(3)	48
TAVEUNI	ROBT. I. THIEME	EVERETT	34.2	26/50/22	12(1)	49
EAGLE	LARRY SHORETT	CORINTHIAN	24.1	27/10/14	5(4)	50
RENEGADE	HOWARD D. WITKIN	OLYMPIA	24.0	27/15/54	6(4)	51
MINX	W.C. ANDERSON/J.A. MURRAY	SEATTLE	25.6	27/17/10	7(4)	52
MACDUFF	WM. BUCHAN SR.	CORINTHIAN	32.9	27/18/36	20(2)	53
BONGO	RICK MOELLER	O.C.S.A.	37.3	27/18/55	13(1)	54
TYEE	W.C. WHIPPLE	CORINTHIAN	41.7	27/31/27	14(1)	55
ANNA	G.H. LAURENCE	CORINTHIAN	22.3	27/36/30	8(4)	56
VANDAL	J.A. McDONALD	SEATTLE	23.8	27/37/59	9(4)	57
MORGAN	GUY SCREECH	R.VIC.	24.1	27/43/26	10(4)	58
MAURIAH	JACK ROOCROFT	W.VAN.	26.9	27/46/45	15(3)	59

YACHT	SKIPPER(S)	CLUB	RATING	COR ELAPSE TIME	POSITION DIVISION	OVERALL
ARCTURUS	ALLAN D. TOBE	W.VAN.	29.4	27/48/30	16(3)	60
ALANSA	PHIL TUCKER	CORINTHIAN	24.1	27/51/39	11(4)	61
TEASER	STEFAN THORDARSON	TACOMA	24.5	28/01/08	12(4)	62
VIKING	DAVID HADDLETON	KITSILANO	22.8	28/03/39	13(4)	63
SHALON	GARY O. WATSON	WILLIAMETTE S.C.	21.8	28/03/49	14(4)	64
QUORUM II	D.M. FIELD	CORINTHIAN	25.0	28/10/41	15(4)	65
CLOUDRACE	IAN L. HAMILTON	R.VAN.	26.9	28/15/15	17(3)	66
CIRRUS	TIM ERICKSON	CORINTHIAN	23.8	28/22/41	16(4)	67
BALALAIKI	ROBT. H. HURLOW	CORINTHIAN	25.9	28/24/27	17(4)	68
APHRODITE	R.C. McCOLL	W.VAN.	24.2	28/28/36	18(4)	69
TONIC	DAN BRINK	CORINTHIAN	22.7	28/28/57	19(4)	70
MAMATEEK	C.H. CRONHELM, M.D.	R.VAN.	29.0	28/29/41	18(3)	71
NORN	OLAV EKROM	CORINTHIAN	25.4	28/34/12	20(4)	72
WILDFIRE	S. CHADWICK JR.	CORINTHIAN	26.2	28/38/59	19(3)	73
DRUMMER BOY	J. DUNFIELD	R.VAN.	25.5	28/39/16	21(4)	74
ARROW	JON RUNSTAD	SEATTLE	29.1	28/56/26	20(3)	75
GOLDEN TIME	A.L. MASELEY, M.D.	TACOMA	26.0	28/58/49	21(3)	76
LARA	WALTER HERRMANN	CORINTHIAN	23.7	28/59/01	22(4)	77
SWIFT I	ROGER D. HOFFMAN	EVERETT	26.3	28/59/36	22(3)	78
HYAK	BONAR A. DAVIS	R.VAN.	26.7	29/00/43	23(3)	79
FIRECRACKER	LARRY SCHUELER	PT. ANGELES	25.9	29/01/33	23(4)	80
KINOHI	E. RUFER	KITSILANO	32.9	29/07/52	21(2)	81
KATE	K.L. PARTLOW	TACOMA	26.2	29/12/47	24(3)	82
TA'AROA	OTTO A. DEMUTH	PT. MADISON	28.1	29/15/14	25(3)	83
KEEWAYDIN II	H. ORMOND MURPHY	R.VAN.	27.5	29/26/20	26(3)	84
PACHENA	JOHN NEWTON	W.VAN.	32.5	29/37/40	22(2)	85
RUMOR	CHAS. E. OLSON	EDMONDS	27.6	29/42/52	27(3)	86
WESTERLY	J.M. SEYMOUR	CORINTHIAN	26.1	29/47/48	28(3)	87
LA RUINA	R.J. GIBBONS	SEATTLE	32.1	29/53/00	23(2)	88
PEMAQUID	GEO. S. SCHUCHART	SEATTLE	37.3	29/59/13	15(1)	89
SARGASSO II	DON EUDALY	PORTLAND	30.2	30/24/52	24(2)	90
THE GWEN B	ROBT. F. ROEDEL, M.D.	SEATTLE	22.4	30/37/25	24(4)	91
MYSTIC	TIM WASHBURN	CORINTHIAN	31.6	30/43/30	25(2)	92
GABRIELLE III	J.H. LONG	R.VAN.	35.9	30/46/35	16(1)	93
ALLEGRA	JOHN LOUIE	R.VAN.	33.7	30/54/15	17(1)	94
WEST BY NORTH	W.G. TELLIER	R.VIC.	39.0	31/11/42	18(1)	95
DECEPTION	F.M. JONES	EDMONDS	23.9	31/14/51	25(4)	96
ZAMBOANGO	F.H. BROWNELL	PT. MADISON	25.2	31/29/37	26(4)	97
MISTRAL	J.C. BAILLARGEON	SEATTLE	22.2	33/27/32	27(4)	98
QUEST	ALAN S. RUTHERFORD	CORINTHIAN	22.6	35/59/34	28(4)	99
JOLLY OLLY	V. RUSKIN	R.VAN.	23.6	36/16/09	29(4)	100
NO-NO	BOB McVITTIE	W.VAN.	24.1	36/57/10	30(4)	101
SABRINA	F.R. ANDERSON	EUGENE	28.9	38/35/40	29(3)	102
GRENADIER	A. SAMBONI	CORINTHIAN	32.1		(2)	DNF
WHITE SQUALL	GOVNOR TEATS	TACOMA	31.8		(4)	DNF
ONRUSH	ROBT. W. BROWN	CORINTHIAN	25.8		(4)	DNF
CIRRUS	STEPHEN SHEA/BRUCE SUNDGREN	SEATTLE	24.5		(4)	DNF
TSUNAMI	PAUL PEDERSON/CONRAD MORAN	CORINTHIAN	26.9		(4)	DNF
TEMPTATION	BRYAN ARCHER	TACOMA	33.0		(4)	DNS
BLACK HAWK	HUGH MINOR, M.D.	CORINTHIAN	27.2		(3)	DNS

SWIFTSURE (P.H.R.F.) 1972
RESULTS

YACHT	SKIPPER(S)	CLUB	RATING	COR ELAPSE TIME	POSITION DIVISION	OVERALL
JEUNESSE II	PAUL T. COTE	R.VAN.	1.8	23/46/35	1(A)	1
KAIULANI	DR. P.S. McCULLOUGH	BREMERTON	2.2	23/56/56	2(A)	2
TOLO TSOLO	E.E. WOODSON	CORINTHIAN	2.2	24/19/18	3(A)	3
BRIDGET II	H.V. SARGENT	OLYMPIA	2.1	24/32/05	4(A)	4
PREDICAMENT II	JAMES SMITH	U of W	3.2	25/44/25	1(B)	5
AFRICAN STAR	DOUG FRYER	SEATTLE	3.3	26/16/49	2(B)	6
BANDIT	DAN McDONOUGH	TACOMA	2.4	26/22/24	5(A)	7
MADHATTER	NORMAN SEVERIDE	R.VAN.	3.1	26/31/20	3(B)	8
SALLY FORTH	TOM FRIEDLAND	BELLINGHAM	3.0	26/34/44	4(B)	9
EOS	H. ROBT. DURSCH	ANACORTES	2.2	26/52/44	6(A)	10
HMCS ORIOLE	R.D. BISSELL	C.F.S.A.	2.0	26/56/51	7(A)	11
PEER GYNT	TOM SEAVOY	CORINTHIAN	2.6	27/06/02	8(A)	12
BENORA II	K.E. McLEAN	R.VAN.	2.6	27/07/42	9(A)	13
MOSHULU	ROBT. O. SYLVESTER	SEATTLE	2.0	27/09/42	10(A)	14
NINA DEL MAR	CHAS. J. McCANN	OLYMPIA	3.1	27/22/51	5(B)	15
DUTCH FLUTE	ROBT. KLEIN, M.D.	TACOMA	2.6	27/22/20	11(A)	16

YACHT	SKIPPER(S)	CLUB	RATING	COR ELAPSE TIME	DIVISION	OVERALL
GABRIELLE II	ROBT. W. BUTT	R.VAN.	1.9	27/24/10	12(A)	17
MAI TAI	A.C. WOOD	MEYDENBAUER BAY	2.0	14/22/27	13(A)	18
SUNDANCE	THOS. O. MURPHY	TACOMA	2.7	30/17/10	14(A)	19
HANSA	JOS. B. HEITMAN	GIG HARBOR	2.4	30/28/37	15(A)	20
ESCAPE HATCH	BOB FERRIE	BELLINGHAM	3.8	33/08/16	6(B)	21
SERENDIPITY III	CAPT. R.V. LEWIS	C.F.S.A.	3.1	34/37/16	7(B)	22
DEYDREAM II	W.A. DEY	KITSILANO	3.2	34/59/44	8(B)	23
IRISH ROVER	THOS. F. CORRIGAN, M.D.	EVERETT	3.0	35/21/24	9(B)	24
SNOW GOOSE II	JOHN M. MIDGLEY	EDMONDS	2.8	35/28/08	10(B)	25
RENZANCE	BILL REECE	CORINTHIAN	2.7	35/38/25	16(A)	26
ARRIBA	MARK L. GABRIELSON	ANACORTES	3.5		(B)	DNF
MUTINEER II	G.C. ALVEY	CALGARY	3.4		(B)	DNF
BACARRA	DOUGLAS R. DAY	R.VAN.	2.8		(B)	DNS

JUAN DE FUCA (I.O.R.) 1972 RESULTS

YACHT	SKIPPER(S)	CLUB	RATING	COR ELAPSE TIME	POSITION DIVISION	OVERALL
CLIMAX	DONALD C. SMITH	PT. MAD.	22.1	15/33/48	1(1)	1
AMBUSH	STAN KIESZLING	TACOMA	24.6	15/36/10	2(1)	2
ROZINANTE	ROBERT SPANFELNER	SEATTLE	22.9	15/53/06	3(1)	3
SEAFAX	GREG OLIVER	R.VIC.	23.7	15/56/07	4(1)	4
MOODY	JIM PINE	W.VAN.	23.6	15/58/39	5(1)	5
GEM	RAY FIEDLER	CYC	24.6	16/01/25	6(1)	6
DOXY II	PETER R.A. COOMBS	R.VIC.	22.9	16/15/03	7(1)	7
MATOOSK	KENNETH PEARCE	R.VAN.	23.6	16/27/16	8(1)	8
APPLE-CHEEKS	MICHAE BELL	R.VAN.	23.9	16/33/58	9(1)	9
SHIMNA	H.J. GLASS	R.VAN.	25.2	16/42/16	10(1)	10
FAIR JUDGEMENT	M. DAVID WILDER	EAGLE HBR.	21.8	17/24/06	11(1)	11
VANDAL	STEVE MERRIMAN	R.VIC.	21.3	17/37/30	1(2)	12
WHITE MIST	DORR ANDERSON	SEATTLE	22.8	18/09/19	12(1)	13
SEAQUIN	R.S. MARSHALL	CYC	20.9	18/13/58	2(2)	14
FOXEE	R.G. FOXALL	W.VAN.	22.6	18/21/18	13(1)	15
LA POMME	ROBERT C. KERSHAW	CYC	20.7	19/11/08	3(2)	16
ARRIBA	RONALD HART	TACOMA	19.8	19/35/14	4(2)	17
MELTEMI	FRANK MUSSON	W.VAN.	20.1	20/00/12	5(2)	18
ARIETIAN	T. BISHOP WHEELER	CYC	23.8	20/06/58	14(1)	19
WELANNE R.T.	WELDON PINCHIN	EAGLE HBR.	22.7	20/10/14	15(1)	20
PLEIADES	HEYES PETERSON	PORTLAND	23.6	20/50/24	16(1)	21
UMPKA	JOHN R. BOOTH	R.VIC.	21.6	21/18/24	17(1)	22
GALENAIA II	GEORGE A. DUFOUR SR.	R.VIC.	21.0	21/19/47	6(2)	23
PRESTO	F.W. HAYES	SEATTLE	20.1	21/41/13	7(2)	24
GYPSY G	D.S. GIBBERD	W.VAN.	24.7	21/49/48	18(1)	25
LIGERO	ARCHIE CAMPBELL	TURKEY HEAD	21.2	22/06/35	8(2)	26
LITTLE BEAR	IAN HOPKINSON	KITSILANO	21.7	22/41/31	19(1)	27
MOA	WALT. O. MIDDLETON	W.VAN.	24.4	22/46/17	20(1)	28

JUAN DE FUCA (P.H.R.F.) 1972 RESULTS

YACHT	SKIPPER(S)	CLUB	RATING	COR ELAPSE TIME	POSITION DIVISION	OVERALL
AVENGER II	J.F. UPWARD	W.VAN.	5.2	12/49/36	1(D)	1
WHITE SQUALL	PETER WHITE	MAPLE BAY	3.4	14/28/40	1(C)	2
VALHALA	GORDON VICKERY	TURKEY HEAD	3.2	15/02/24	2(C)	3
VAYU	DEENE ALMVIG	ANACORTES	3.4	15/06/42	3(C)	4
AMPHITRITE II	S.E. WILKINSON	R.VAN.	3.4	15/21/23	4(C)	5
PANACEA II	JOHN M. DAUGHTERS	SEATTLE	3.0	15/21/27	5(C)	6
MARY D	DARREL B. DAVIS	PT. ANGELES	3.5	16/42/52	6(C)	7
TE-PAH	S.R. OLDHAM	CFSA ESQUIMALT	3.1	17/06/50	7(C)	8
LUCY ALICE	WM. H. GARDNER	CYC	4.2	17/10/55	2(D)	9
KEEMA	RUSS SCHULKE	CYC	4.2	17/16/13	3(D)	10
LOON	THOMAS SCHNEIDER	CYC	4.3	17/24/16	4(D)	11
MALEESH	E. STANLEY JONES	R.VIC.	3.2	17/25/05	8(C)	12
SA-HAN	DON FEELEY	PT. ANGELES	3.7	17/38/43	5(D)	13
OLYMPUS	THOMAS MURRAY	EAGLE HBR.	3.8	17/39/55	6(D)	14
LIMELIGHT	WILLIAM LEACH	R.VIC.	4.4	17/55/56	7(D)	15
SKAGA	D.W. GLADMAN	MAPLE BAY	3.7	18/17/23	8(D)	16
LOIS J	FRANK SHININGER	PT. ANGELES	3.3	18/20/49	9(C)	17
FOUR D'S	DWAINE MATCHETTE	OLYMPIA	4.8	18/44/54	9(D)	18
KING'S CRUISER	JOHN C. EVETTS	KITSILANO	3.8	18/56/36	10(D)	19
KEHLOKE	D'ARCY McLEISH	W.VAN.	3.7	18/57/41	11(D)	20
WIND BIRD	WILLIAM B. JOHNSON	TACOMA	5.0	18/58/37	12(D)	21

YO-YO	GEOFFREY GREENHALGH	R.VIC.	3.7	19/01/39	13(D)	22
BEBELLE	L. BOULANGER	CFSA	3.0	19/16/35	10(C)	23
MAGUS	ROB'T. H. LINROTHE	TTP	3.9	19/19/42	14(D)	24
BLUE LIBRAN	F.J. FRASER	EAGLE HBR.	3.7	19/21/42	15(D)	25
MERMAID	DR. REID TOWNSLEY	W.VAN.	3.0	19/31/22	11(C)	26
CONCUBINE	FRANK BUSH	R.VIC.	3.1	19/33/53	12(C)	27
MA COEUR	ROBERT J. MILLER	R.VAN.	3.4	19/38/47	13(C)	28
SAUMURE	RALPH H. BRINE	R.VAN.	3.0	19/51/37	14(C)	29
SAGA	J. ROOME	MAPLE BAY	3.7	20/21/45	16(D)	30
CARINA	J. DAMGAARD	R.VIC.	3.4	20/36/58	15(C)	31
PEACHES	TED. A. SERR	PT. ANGELES	3.7	20/45/52	17(D)	32
KEELA	W.D. GAIR	R.VIC.	3.8	20/50/08	18(D)	33
ZEST	PETER YOUNG	R.VIC.	3.5	20/56/42	16(C)	34
SEA WOLF	PHILIP MEERES	KITSILANO	3.5	20/58/45	17(C)	35
WINDSONG II	R.C. BROWN	CYC	4.2	20/00/01	19(D)	36
MARIJO	DR. HUGH M. BACON	R.VIC.	3.6	21/01/02	18(C)	37
BARRACUTA	J. STACEY	CFSA (Esq.)	3.8	21/20/59	20(D)	38
NEPTUNE	S.H.S. PECK	R.VIC.	3.7	21/24/18	21(D)	39
SIRIS	MICHAEL G. RIDGWAY	ANACORTES	3.2	21/30/01	19(C)	40
ALIDA	A. JURISSON	GLENMORE	3.7	21/49/09	22(D)	41
CHANSON	C. WHITE	MAPLE BAY	3.4	22/01/01	20(C)	42
OLHIYU	M.F. LYNCH	BELLINGHAM	3.5	22/19/34	21(C)	43
GAZELLE II	KIM HUSBAND	R.VAN.	3.0	23/03/14	22(C)	44
VALHALLA	JOHN BLACK	ANACORTES	4.2		(D)	DNF
KAFKA	C. & G. ROBINSON	W.VAN.	3.7		(D)	DNF
LA BRISA	W.C. VAN LEEUWEN	W.VAN.	3.0		(C)	DNF

PACIFIC INTERNATIONAL YACHTING ASSOCIATION
SWIFTSURE LIGHTSHIP CLASSIC AND JUAN DE FUCA RACE
1973 TROPHY WINNERS

SWIFTSURE (I.O.R.)	SWIFTSURE TROPHY (OVERALL HANDICAP WINNER)	LOL KILLAM	R.VAN.Y.C.	GRAYBEARD
	ROYAL CANADIAN NAVY TROPHY (1ST TO ROUND SWIFTSURE MARK)	LOL KILLAM	R.VAN.Y.C.	GRAYBEARD
	CITY OF VICTORIA TROPHY (1ST YACHT TO FINISH)	LOL KILLAM	R.VAN.Y.C.	GRAYBEARD
	OCEAN CEMENT TROPHY (FIRST IN DIV. 1)	LOL KILLAM	R.VAN.Y.C.	GRAYBEARD
	T. EATON COMPANY TROPHY (FIRST IN DIV. 2)	HARVIE DAVIDSON BRIAN LAKE	R.VAN.Y.C.	WINGAWAY
	CITY OF SEATTLE TROPHY (FIRST IN DIV. 3)	WILLIAM BUCHAN	CORINTH.	BYDAND
	ROYAL VANCOUVER YATCH CLUB TROPHY (FIRST IN DIV. 4)	V. PLAVSIC	WEST VAN.	ORAD
SWIFTSURE (P.H.R.F.)	CORINTHIAN YACHT CLUB TROPHY (FIRST IN DIV. A)	Y. TEATS	TACOMA	WHITE SQUALL
	CAPE FLATTERY TROPHY (FIRST IN DIV. B)	ROGER HOFFMAN	EVERETT	SWIFT. 1
JUAN DE FUCA (I.O.R.)	SAN JUAN TROPHY (1ST YACHT TO FINISH)	COLM HOGAN	MAPLE BAY	MALDA
	ROYAL VICTORIA YACHT CLUB TROPHY (FIRST IN DIV. 1)	VANCE BINGHAM	PT. ANGELES	AMBUSH
	ROYAL CANADIAN NAVY TROPHY (FIRST IN DIV. 2)	R.S. MARSHALL	CORINTH.	SEAQUIN
JUAN DE FUCA (P.H.R.F.)	ANACORTES YACHT CLUB TROPHY (FIRST IN DIV. C)	COLM HOGAN	MAPLE BAY	MALDA
	(FIRST IN DIV. D)	H.E. BUCHANAN	R.VIC.Y.C.	LAIRIG GRHU

OFFICIAL START TIME: 09/30/00

SWIFTSURE (I.O.R.) 1973
RESULTS

YACHT NAME	SKIPPER(S)	CLUB	RATING	COR ELAPSE TIME	POSITION DIVISION	OVERALL
GRAYBEARD	LOL KILLAM	R.VAN.Y.C.	69.5	40/37/42	1(1)	1
BYDAND	WILLIAM BUCHAN	CORINTHIAN	28.1	41/44/49	1(3)	2
NAKNEK	R.I. NELSON	R.VAN.Y.C.	40.4	42/14/ 2	2(1)	3
PEMQUID	G.S. SCHUCHART	SEATTLE	36.2	42/39/44	3(1)	4
WINGAWAY	HARVIE DAVIDSON/BRIAN LAKE	R.VAN.Y.C.	30.6	42/42/ 7	1(2)	5
PACHENA	JOHN NEWTON	WEST VAN.	32.3	42/48/38	2(2)	6
PATRIOT II	JAMES MARTA	SEATTLE	33.4	42/51/56	4(1)	7
CAMELOT	ROBERT R. SMITH	TACOMA	30.7	42/57/21	3(2)	8
HOOLIGAN II	TOM O'BRIEN	SEATTLE	31.6	43/ 5/ 1	4(2)	9
ASSAULT	JOHN F. BUCHAN	CORINTHIAN	35.1	43/12/48	5(1)	10
BLUNDERBUSS	H.F. HERLIHY	R.VAN.Y.C.	31.8	43/15/ 5	5(2)	11

SIX PACK	BRUCE HEDRICK	ROSE CITY	35.1	43/34/40	6(1)	12
SALTY TIGER	JOHN ALBERTSON	CORINTHIAN	38.6	43/38/34	7(1)	13
PORPOISE III	BILL KILLAM	R.VAN.Y.C.	37.3	43/59/11	8(1)	14
COHO	GRANT BRANDLMAYR	R.VAN.Y.C.	40.8	44/22/25	9(1)	15
DRUMMER BOY	JOHN DUNFIELD	R.VAN.Y.C.	30.4	45/ 3/32	6(2)	16
MOON GLOW IV	DAVID NIELSEN	TACOMA	32.2	45/ 9/ 5	7(2)	17
EAGLE	LARRY SHORETT	CORINTHIAN	27.6	45/18/ 9	2(3)	18
MIDNIGHT SPECIAL	STEVE CRARY	CORINTHIAN	32.9	45/27/30	8(2)	19
TRINGA	F.T. GARDINER	R.VIC.Y.C.	27.8	45/46/55	3(3)	20
VIKING	FRANK THORP	CORINTHIAN	33.6	45/52/22	10(1)	21
ELIXIR	JOHN GRAHAM	SEATTLE	27.5	45/54/41	4(3)	22
SAGA	SVEN RASMUSSEN	R.VAN.Y.C.	29.4	46/ 4/ 1	5(3)	23
TANGENT II	ANTONY LOACH	WEST VAN.	29.3	46/26/ 9	6(3)	24
SQAIP	PHIL JOHNSON	SEATTLE	31.5	46/46/20	9(2)	25
NORWESTER	D.L. FOOTH	CORINTHIAN	37.6	46/56/24	11(1)	26
TEMPTATION	BILL NELSON	TACOMA	40.2	46/57/27	12(1)	27
MISS-CHIFF	CHAS SCHIFF	CORINTHIAN	35.0	47/ 0/26	13(1)	28
RIVAL	WILLIAM RELLIS/LOUIS MERCILLE	TACOMA	31.7	47/11/16	10(2)	29
PANDORA	ROBERT HORNER	R.VIC.Y.C.	38.7	47/19/42	14(1)	30
SALLY LIGHTFOOT	TOM FRIEDLAND	BELLINGHAM	27.2	47/50/48	7(3)	31
TYEE	W.C. WHIPPLE	CORINTHIAN	41.2	48/19/24	15(1)	32
KAOS	W. RUDOLPH	CORINTHIAN	32.0	48/28/30	11(2)	33
HABITAT	P.C.C. RICHARDS	WEST VAN.	29.3	49/20/ 7	8(3)	34
MAURIAH	JACK ROOCROFT	WEST VAN.	26.1	49/55/58	9(3)	35
WHIM WHAM	WM.M. HANSON	CORINTHIAN	32.7	50/ 7/ 1	12(2)	36
ORAO	V. PLAVSIC	WEST VAN.	21.7	52/ 5/46	1(4)	37
MISTRAL	V. BAILLARGEON	SEATTLE	22.2	52/29/58	2(4)	38
JOLLY OLLY	V. RUSKIN	R.VAN.Y.C.	23.4	52/51/36	3(4)	39
IMPULSE	J. KEVORKIAN	CORINTHIAN	23.2	53/17/ 3	4(4)	40
TONIC	DAN BRINK	CORINTHIAN	22.8	53/25/17	5(4)	41
MINX	WIL ANDERSON/JACK MURRAY	SEATTLE	24.5	53/34/31	(4)	42
JACKOE	ROGER HILLS	PT. TOWNSND	24.1	53/43/ 0	7(4)	43
ALANSA	PHIL TUCKER	CORINTHIAN	23.8	53/58/16	8(4)	44
TEASER	STEF THORDARSON	TACOMA	24.7	54/ 4/29	9(4)	45
WIND LASS	RANDY MUELLER	CORINTHIAN	26.8	54/10/25	10(3)	46
GEMINI	RED W. BIEKER	PORTLAND	26.3	54/10/56	11(3)	47
PRIMO	R.V. DENBY	CORINTHIAN	25.7	54/14/26	10(4)	48
OBSESSION	MILES DIGHTON	R.VIC.Y.C.	27.3	54/17/18	12(3)	49
CHEROKEE	WILLIAM BLACK	CORINTHIAN	27.4	54/23/38	13(3)	50
DAWN YANKEE	HAROLD SARGANT	OLYMPIA	27.5	54/26/25	14(3)	51
PACIFIC DAWN	RICH VEDVICK	CORINTHIAN	27.8	54/27/ 6	15(3)	52
GYPSY G.	D.S. GIBBERD	WEST VAN.	27.5	54/28/23	16(3)	53
ROGUE	HOWARD WITKIN	OLYMPIA	27.5	54/29/ 5	17(3)	54
BANJO	RALPH CLASBY/WINK VOGEL	R.VAN.Y.C.	27.7	54/30/ 8	18(3)	55
AKKA	RALPH MARX	TACOMA	26.8	54/36/ 6	19(3)	56
CHECKMATE	C.D. BANFORD JR.	TACOMA	26.0	54/37/36	20(3)	57
KEEWAYDIN II	H.C. MURPHY	R.VAN.Y.C.	26.8	54/53/ 8	21(3)	58
FIRECRACKER	LARRY SCHUELER	PT. ANGELES	25.9	54/56/53	11(4)	59
KATHY	P.S. BRAZEAU	SEATTLE	28.9	54/59/ 5	22(3)	60
JUBILEE	BILL WATKINS	CORINTHIAN	29.0	55/ 2/ 5	23(3)	61
CHEETAH	BLAINE COMFORT	CORINTHIAN	28.7	55/ 2/49	24(3)	62
VELA	WALTER W. PRUE	CORINTHIAN	26.4	55/10/43	25(3)	63
OUTWARD BOUND	DON FLYNN	SEATTLE	26.7	55/11/54	26(3)	64
VANDAL	JOE McDONALD	SEATTLE	23.8	55/18/45	12(4)	65
LOVE AFFAIR	IRVING VARLEY	EVERETT	28.3	55/18/54	27(3)	66
OUTRAGEOUS	TED BURNS	BREMERTON	30.8	55/29/19	13(2)	67
SEA ROBIN	DR. JOHN KEOGH	WEST VAN.	24.6	55/59/12	13(4)	68
DESIDERATA	TOM GEISNESS	SEATTLE	22.9	56/12/ 7	14(4)	69
TAVEUNI	ROBERT THIEME	EVERETT	34.2	56/14/22	16(1)	70
ADIOS	CARL JENSEN JR.	SEATTLE	47.6		DSQ(1)	DSQ
EMERAUDE	BOB CONNORS	CORINTHIAN	28.3		DSQ(3)	DSQ
QUORUM II	D.M. FIELD	CORINTHIAN	25.2		DSQ(4)	DSQ
LA RUINA	R.J. GIBBONS	SEATTLE	32.1		DSQ(2)	DSQ
GAMIN	LON ROBINSON	CORINTHIAN	31.0		DSQ(2)	DSQ
ALLEGRA	JOHN LOUIE	R.VAN.Y.C.	33.0		DSQ(2)	DSQ
SATIN DOLL	TOM BUSH	CORINTHIAN	31.5		DNF(2)	DNF
UHURU	THCMAS COAD	EVERETT	31.9		DNF(4)	DNF
SABRINA	FOSTER ANDERSON	EUGENE	28.9		DNF(3)	DNF
LARA	DR. W. HERRMANN	CORINTHIAN	24.3		DNF(4)	DNF
ELUSIVE I	JOHN E. SPROUSE	PORTLAND	21.7		DNF(4)	DNF
ZAMBOANGO	F.H. BROWNELL	PT. MADISON	24.7		DNF(4)	DNF

YACHT NAME	SKIPPER(S)	CLUB	RATING		
APHRODITE	R.C. McCOLL	WEST VAN.	23.6	DNF(4)	DNF
MAVERICK III	J.P. & T.L. GUEST	R.VAN.Y.C.	26.4	DNF(3)	DNF
RED DOG	DENNIS DONOHUE	CORINTHIAN	32.3	DNF(2)	DNF
HYAK	BONAR DAVIS	R.VAN.Y.C.	26.9	DNF(3)	DNF
VAMOSE	W.S. LIEBERMAN	CORINTHIAN	30.0	DNF(2)	DNF
THEORY	BILL FIANDER	PT. MADISON	24.7	DNF(4)	DNF
HUCKLEBERRY	KEN REID	WEST VAN.	25.8	DNF(4)	DNF
ANAHERA	DR. C.G. MORRISON	WEST VAN.	30.2	DNF(2)	DNF
SPRAY	ED BAUMUELLER	CORINTHIAN	32.1	DNF(2)	DNF
CHAIKA	DR. R. KNIGHT	R.VAN.Y.C.	35.6	DNF(1)	DNF
ANNA	G.H. LAURENCE	CORINTHIAN	22.3	DNF(4)	DNF
THRUST	W.A. BARNARD	CORINTHIAN	31.1	DNF(2)	DNF
LANCER	NORMAN LARABEE	CORINTHIAN	28.5	DNF(3)	DNF
TERNA	P. CHRISTOFFERSEN	WEST VAN.	29.2	DNF(3)	DNF
MAMTEEK	DR. C. CRONHELM	R.VAN.Y.C.	28.8	DNF(3)	DNF
ARCTURUS	ALLAN TOBE	WEST VAN.	29.1	DNF(3)	DNF
TSUNAMI	CONRAD MORAN	CORINTHIAN	27.3	DNF(3)	DNF
EN PASSANT	HUGH MINOR	EVERETT	27.5	DNF(3)	DNF
BLACK HAWK	H.H. BOYD	CORINTHIAN	26.8	DNF(3)	DNF
MATILDA	JOHN POWELL/W. BURDICK	CORINTHIAN	26.8	DNF(3)	DNF
RAVEN	PETER YOUNG	R.VIC.Y.C.	26.7	DNF(3)	DNF
MOONRAKER	LOUIS LINDHOLM	R.VIC.Y.C.	28.9	DNF(3)	DNF
QUALICUM	C.C. HYATT	R.VAN.Y.C.	25.8	DNF(4)	DNF
PREDICAMENT II	JAMES SMITH	U. OF WASH	25.6	DNF(4)	DNF
SQUALL	TOM ALBERG	CORINTHIAN	26.1	DNF(3)	DNF
FLYING CLOUD	E.W. DEKONING	PORTLAND	29.9	DNF(3)	DNF
ARROW	JON RUNSTAD	SEATTLE	28.9	DNF(3)	DNF
WINDWARD	JOHN ELLIS	CORINTHIAN	33.4	DNF(1)	DNF
DU FRIA	JOHN KLASELL	CORINTHIAN	31.3	DNF(2)	DNF
CO-MOTION	PHIL PEOPLES	CORINTHIAN	38.5	DNF(1)	DNF
NORN	OLAU EKROM	CORINTHIAN	24.9	DNF(4)	DNF
SINFUL	R.F. HARRISON	WEST VAN.	30.3	DNF(2)	DNF
DIAMOND HEAD	HENRY KOTKINS	SEATTLE	51.5	DNF(1)	DNF
JEUNESSE II	PAUL T. COTE	R.VAN.Y.C.	34.3	DNF(1)	DNF
ENDLESS SUMMER	GEORGE O'BRIEN	R.VAN.Y.C.	53.8	DNF(1)	DNF
KISMET	L. BLACKWELL	BELLINGHAM	22.0	DNS(4)	DNS
EHA MAKANI	ELDON SCHALKA	EVERETT	27.8	DNS(3)	DNS

SWIFTSURE (P.H.R.F.) 1973 RESULTS

OFFICIAL START TIME: 09/30/00

YACHT NAME	SKIPPER(S)	CLUB	RATING	COR ELAPSE TIME	POSITION DIVISION	POSITION OVERALL
WHITE SQUALL	Y. TEATS	TACOMA	1.9	42/ 3/ 4	1(A)	1
COTTON BLOSSOM II	DOUGLAS COLE	PORTLAND	2.1	44/27/45	2(A)	2
MOSHULU	R.O. SYLVESTER	SEATTLE	2.1	45/20/21	3(A)	3
BLUEY II	D. FINDLAY	R.VAN.Y.C.	2.0	45/49/25	4(A)	4
SUNDANCE	T.O. MURPHY, MD	TACOMA	1.6	46/38/35	5(A)	5
BANDIT	DAN McDONOUGH	TACOMA	2.4	46/42/31	6(A)	6
SWIFT I	ROGER HOFFMAN	EVERETT	3.1	51/34/57	1(B)	7
ARRIBA	M.L. GABRIELSON	ANACORTES	3.3	51/42/14	2(B)	8
BACARRA	T.W. LONEY	R.VIC.Y.C.	2.7	52/26/25	7(A)	9
AFRICAN STAR	DOUG FRYER	SEATTLE	3.3	53/ 3/28	3(B)	10
NINA DEL MAR	C.J. McCANN	OLYMPIA	3.2	53/16/51	4(B)	11
ESCAPE HATCH	BOB FERRIE	BELLINGHAM	3.8	53/30/14	5(B)	12
PARAPHERNALIA	STANLEY MARCUS	BELLINGHAM	2.3	53/37/27	8(A)	13
RANA	HUGH RHODES	R.VAN.Y.C.	2.1	53/46/12	9(A)	14
KATCHEN	DUMONT STAATZ	TACOMA	2.9	53/47/47	6(B)	15
CALLALOO	JOHN CATLEY	R.VAN.Y.C.	2.9	53/59/40	7(B)	16
INTREPID	JOHN HERBERT	CORINTHIAN	1.9	54/15/14	10(A)	17
TOLO TSOLO	E.E. WOODSON	CORINTHIAN	2.1	54/42/26	11(A)	18
MARIAH	J.L. McGINNIS	CORINTHIAN	2.8	55/ 1/ 3	8(B)	19
HMCS ORIOLE	LCDR. (R) HORNER	CFSA	2.0	56/21/ 7	12(A)	20
ONRUSH	ROBERT BROWN	CORINTHIAN	2.8		DNF(B)	DNF
INISFAIL	GARRETT HORDER	SEATTLE	3.4		DNF(B)	DNF
SNOW GOOSE II	HUGH MCKENZIE	EDMONDS	2.8		DNF(B)	DNF
TRIAD	BOB HOSIE	R.VIC.Y.C.	2.7		DNF(A)	DNF
MUTINEER III	TOM BRAIDWOOD	WEST VAN.	2.7		DNF(A)	DNF
CIRRUS	STEPHEN SHEA	SEATTLE	2.9		DNF(B)	DNF
PENZANCE	BILL REECE	CORINTHIAN	2.7		DNF(A)	DNF
JENETTA	RALPH HIGGINS	R.VIC.Y.C.	1.5		DNF(A)	DNF
LEISURE WORLD	RENE LAROCHE	R.VAN.Y.C.	3.0		DNF(B)	DNF

161

YACHT NAME	SKIPPER(S)	CLUB	RATING			DNF/Position
STELLA MARIS	J.O. CAVBENBERGER	PT. TOWNSND	3.8		DNF(B)	DNF
SERENDIPITY III	CAPT. HEWETT	CFB CHIL.	3.1		DNF(B)	DNF
FURIANT	JUDGE MOFFETT	R.VAN.Y.C.	2.8		DNF(B)	DNF
SEACLUSION	D. MATCHETTE	OLYMPIA	2.5		DNF(B)	DNF
STREGA	JOHN W. WOLD	ANACORTES	3.8		DNF(B)	DNF
QUE BEF	PAUL SCHWEDLER	OLYMPIA	2.9		DNF(B)	DNF
GAZELLE II	J. KIM HUSBAND	R.VAN.Y.C.	3.1		DNF(B)	DNF
ALOTOLA	ALMORE STERN	TACOMA	3.4		DNF(B)	DNF
DUTCH FLUTE	ROBERT KLEIN	TACOMA	2.6		DNF(A)	DNF
MARIAH	R.E. BROWN	SHILSHOLE	2.8		DNF(B)	DNF
HANSA	J.B. HEITMAN	GIG HARBOR	2.4		DNF(A)	DNF
BENORA II	I.F. HAWORTH	R.VAN.Y.C.	2.6		DNF(A)	DNF
WHITE MIST	DORR ANDERSON	SEATTLE	3.1		DNF(B)	DNF
ESCAPE	DR. P. BLATT	PORTLAND	2.9		DNF(B)	DNF
GABRIELLE II	KEN F. DOWNIE	R.VAN.Y.C.	1.9		DNF(A)	DNF
LA BAMBA	ARNE NISKA	PT. TOWNSND	3.7		DNF(B)	DNF

JUAN DE FUCA (I.O.R.) 1973
RESULTS

OFFICIAL START TIME: 09/45/00

YACHT NAME	SKIPPER(S)	CLUB	RATING	COR ELAPSE TIME	POSITION DIVISION	OVERALL
AMBUSH	VANCE BINGHAM	PT. ANGELES	24.5	23/51/14	1(1)	1
VATICAN	MICHAEL POPE	EAGLE HRBR	21.7	26/ 3/51	2(1)	2
SEAQUIN	R.S. MARSHALL	CORINTHIAN	20.9	26/ 5/43	1(2)	3
LIGERO	ARCHIE CAMPBELL	R.VIC.Y.C.	20.6	26/12/28	2(2)	4
PUFF II	JACK WOODWARD	R.VIC.Y.C.	23.9	26/46/ 7	3(1)	5
ALFHIE	BRUCE FRASER	R.VAN.Y.C.	18.0	28/45/ 4	3(2)	6
WINDSHIFT	FREDERICK HAYES	SEATTLE	21.6	29/32/27	4(1)	7
MOODY TOO	JIM PINE	WEST VAN.	23.4	30/14/40	5(1)	8
INFIDEL	ROD WHITFIELD	EAGLE HRBR	22.2	30/24/ 6	6(1)	9
SKILFISH	D.R. WEST	WEST VAN.	24.3	30/26/13	7(1)	10
MOCCASIN II	MIKE STONE	MAPLE BAY	25.0	30/26/29	8(1)	11
MORGAN	GUY SCREECH	R.VIC.Y.C.	24.0	30/43/20	9(1)	12
SHIMNA	J.H. GLASS	R.VAN.Y.C.	24.8	30/59/ 3	10(1)	13
MOA	W.O. MIDDLETON	WEST VAN.	24.6	31/43/23	11(1)	14
VANDAL	STEVE MERRIMAN	R.VIC.Y.C.	20.9	31/57/51	4(2)	15
GEM	RAY FIEDLER	CORINTHIAN	24.5	32/16/10	12(1)	16
JUNE BUG	ROBERT E. VYNNE	SEATTLE	21.5	33/19/20	5(2)	17
C. HAKE	MILES MILLER	CORINTHIAN	23.9	33/20/ 0	13(1)	18
FIDDLER'S GREEN	NOLAN MOSS/WALT LORD	WEST VAN.	21.4	33/52/17	6(2)	19
SURGER	A.H. JOHNSTON	WEST VAN.	22.1	34/35/11	14(1)	20
FREESTYLE	M.J. MULCAHY	3-TREE PT.	21.5	34/35/48	7(2)	21
MARROWSTONE LIGHT II	ROBERT CAIRNS	CORINTHIAN	23.8	35/ 8/54	15(1)	22
CLIMAX	MIKE SMITH/DON SMITH	CORINTHIAN	21.6	35/44/32	16(1)	23
NEPTUNE	SHAUN PECK/JAMES DRYDEN	R.VIC.Y.C.	20.4	35/50/50	8(2)	24
DEPARTURE	GREGORY OLIVER	R.VIC.Y.C.	23.9	36/12/ 1	17(1)	25
WATERMELLON	G. INGLIS	MAPLE BAY	22.6	36/17/26	18(1)	26
CHIMO IV	GEOFF. COLEMAN	WEST VAN.	24.8	36/25/ 4	19(1)	27
LUCY ALICE	WM.H. GARDNER	CORINTHIAN	22.5	36/25/36	20(1)	28
GRETEL II	HEIN DRIEHUYZEN	WEST VAN.	21.7	37/13/53	21(1)	29
KIM	I.C. DUNCANSON	R.VIC.Y.C.	23.0	37/40/12	22(1)	30
GUSTY	D.L. WILLITS	TACOMA	22.7	37/50/ 5	23(1)	31
ARRIBA	RON HART	TACOMA	19.8	37/56/50	9(2)	32
CALIENTE	W.L. WILLIAMSON	EDMONDS	21.7	38/29/35	24(1)	33
UMPKA	JOHN BOOTH	R.VIC.Y.C.	21.1	38/39/52	10(2)	34
WARLOCK	R.H. SCHULER	CORINTHIAN	22.9	38/58/33	25(1)	35
GALENAIA II	GEORGE DUFOUR	R.VIC.Y.C.	20.6	39/10/ 9	11(2)	36
TOPIC	IRVIN O. SMITH	TACOMA	23.7		DSQ(1)	DSQ
FINISTERRE	BRIAN GRIFFIN	BELLINGHAM	21.3		DSQ(2)	DSQ
MIDNIGHT SUN	WALLY BRAEDT	TACOMA	22.6		DNF(1)	DNF
BAREFOOT	JAMES WARD	CORINTHIAN	23.0		DNF(1)	DNF
HULLABALOO	GERALD KIDD	WEST VAN.	21.6		DNS(1)	DNS

JUAN DE FUCA (P.H.R.F.) 1973
RESULTS

OFFICIAL START TIME: 09/45/00

YACHT NAME	SKIPPER(S)	CLUB	RATING	COR ELAPSE TIME	POSITION DIVISION	OVERALL
MALDA	COLM HOGAN	MAPLE BAY	3.0	22/40/18	1(C)	1
LAIRIG GRHU	H.E. BUCHANAN	R.VIC.Y.C.	3.7	28/48/27	1(D)	2
SA-HAN	DON FEELEY	PT. ANGELES	3.8	28/56/47	2(D)	3
FOXEE	R.G. FOXALL	WEST VAN.	3.3	29/12/50	2(C)	4
CALABASH	ROGER GOODALL	R.VAN.Y.C.	3.3	29/16/51	3(C)	5

YACHT NAME	SKIPPER(S)	CLUB	RATING	COR ELAPSE TIME	DIVISION	OVERALL
LOIS J	FRANK SHININGER	PT. ANGELES	3.4	29/23/13	4(C)	6
MAGUS	BOB LINROTHE	3-TREE PT.	3.5	29/28/57	5(C)	7
PEACHES	TED SERR	PT. ANGELES	3.7	29/46/27	3(D)	8
WHITE SQUALL	PETER WHITE	MAPLE BAY	3.4	30/53/26	6(C)	9
SEA SPELL	JAN HUIBERS	R.VIC.Y.C.	3.4	31/17/50	7(C)	10
NEREID	RON EARBER	R.VIC.Y.C.	3.3	33/20/46	8(C)	11
LIMELIGHT	WILLIAM LEACH	R.VIC.Y.C.	4.1	33/31/56	4(D)	12
VALHALLA	GORDON VICKERY	R.VIC.Y.C.	3.2	33/40/ 4	9(C)	13
OLYMPIC MIST	G.W. KALAHAR	PT. ANGELES	3.5	34/45/ 6	10(C)	14
DEYDREAM II	W.G. DEY	NANAIMO	3.8	34/57/44	5(D)	15
MARY D.	DARREL B. DAVIS	PT. ANGELES	3.4	35/23/48	11(C)	16
CAMOSACK	ANTHONY LARSEN	R.VIC.Y.C.	3.6	35/37/48	12(C)	17
CIERCO	ROGER L. RUE	TACOMA	3.0	35/44/ 8	13(C)	18
WIND BIRD	WM. JOHNSON	TACOMA	5.0	35/57/45	6(D)	19
KEHLOKE	FRANK RUSSELL	WEST VAN.	3.7	36/44/20	7(D)	20
PARRIKA	FRANK MUSSON	WEST VAN.	3.4	36/59/ 7	14(C)	21
ERRIGAL	HUGH PORTER	R.VIC.Y.C.	3.9	37/ 8/11	8(D)	22
AKVAVIT	G.W. THORSEN	SOUTH SND	3.1	37/ 8/33	15(C)	23
OLYMPUS	THOMAS MURRAY	EAGLE HRBR	3.8	37/11/10	9(D)	24
TWO-FOR-ONE	R.R. WILSON/J.U. COLEMAN	MAPLE BAY	3.7	37/21/41	10(D)	25
MARIAH	STEVE JAHN	GIG HARBOR	3.4	37/24/28	16(C)	26
KEEMA	RUSS SCHULKE	CORINTHIAN	3.8	37/25/22	11(D)	27
SEA WOLF	PHILIP MEERES	KITSILANO	3.0	37/31/ 9	17(C)	28
SKAGA	DONALD GLADMAN	MAPLE BAY	3.7	37/45/47	12(D)	29
ZAP	DOUGLAS BANKSON	KITSILANO	3.6	37/47/23	18(C)	30
IRISH ROVER	THOMAS CORRIGAN	EVERETT	3.1	37/47/31	19(C)	31
MELKEDAE	D.A. GASSER	CFSA ESQ.	3.4	37/59/14	20(C)	32
MARILYN L.	RONALD CARLSON	PT. ANGELES	3.9	38/12/ 9	13(D)	33
THE SLOOP JOHN B.	BOYD IVENS	TSAWWASSEN	3.7	38/43/54	14(D)	34
RAGE	GERALD SHERM	ANACORTES	3.6	39/25/36	21(C)	35
ODIN	GLENN McCORMICK	QRTRMSTR	5.3	42/ 2/56	15(D)	36
VOL-AU-VENT	NORMAN MARTIN	NANAIMO	3.5		DSQ(C)	DSQ
VIKING	ALAN DICKINSON	R.VIC.Y.C.	3.1		DSQ(C)	DSQ
WINDSONG II	R.C. BROWN	CORINTHIAN	4.2		DSQ(D)	DSQ
ENCHANTRESS	BILL FRANCIS	R.VAN.Y.C.	3.1		DNF(C)	DNF
OLHIYU	MAURICE LYNCH	BELLINGHAM	3.5		DNF(C)	DNF

PACIFIC INTERNATIONAL YACHTING ASSOCIATION
SWIFTSURE LIGHTSHIP CLASSIC AND JUAN DE FUCA RACE
1974 TROPHY WINNERS

SWIFTSURE (I.O.R.)	SWIFTSURE TROPHY (OVERALL HANDICAP WINNER)	LOL KILLAM	R.VAN.Y.C.	GRAYBEARD
	ROYAL CANADIAN NAVY TROPHY (1ST TO ROUND SWIFTSURE MARK)	LOL KILLAM	R.VAN.Y.C.	GRAYBEARD
	CITY OF VICTORIA TROPHY (1ST YACHT TO FINISH)	LOL KILLAM	R.VAN.Y.C.	GRAYBEARD
	OCEAN CEMENT TROPHY (FIRST IN DIV. 1)	LOL KILLAM	R.VAN.Y.C.	GRAYBEARD
	T. EATON COMPANY TROPHY (FIRST IN DIV. 2)	JOHN NEWTON	WEST VAN.	PACHENA
	CITY OF SEATTLE TROPHY (FIRST IN DIV. 3)	GREGORY OLIVER	R.VIC.Y.C.	DISTANT DRUMMER
	ROYAL VANCOUVER YATCH CLUB TROPHY (FIRST IN DIV. 4)	FRED BIEKER, MD.	PORTLAND	GEMINI
SWIFTSURE (P.H.R.F.)	CORINTHIAN YACHT CLUB TROPHY (FIRST IN DIV. A)	G. TEATS, MD.	TACOMA	WHITE SQUALL
	CAPE FLATTERY TROPHY (FIRST IN DIV. B)	R. HOFFMAN, MD.	EVERETT	SWIFT I
JUAN DE FUCA (I.O.R.)	SAN JUAN TROPHY (1ST YACHT TO FINISH)	RAY FIEDLER	CORINTHIAN	GEM
	ROYAL VICTORIA YACHT CLUB TROPHY (FIRST IN DIV. 1)	ROBERT VYNNE	SEATTLE	JUNE BUG
	ROYAL CANADIAN NAVY TROPHY (FIRST IN DIV. 2)	DR. G. WILKINS	R.VAN.Y.C.	FRED
JUAN DE FUCA (P.H.R.F.)	ANACORTES YACHT CLUB TROPHY (FIRST IN DIV. C)	J.M. WEIR	R.VIC.Y.C.	FILEY BRIGG
	.... (FIRST IN DIV. D)	HUGH PORTER	R.VIC.Y.C.	ERRIGAL

MAY 27, 1974
OFFICIAL START TIME: 10/55/00

SWIFTSURE (I.O.R.) — 1974
RESULTS

YACHT NAME	SKIPPER(S)	CLUB	RATING	COR ELAPSE TIME	POSITION DIVISION	OVERALL
GRAYBEARD	LOL KILLAM	R.VAN.Y.C.	69.5	25/ 3/30	1(1)	1
PACHENA	JOHN NEWTON	WEST VAN.	32.1	25/35/26	1(2)	2

WINGAWAY	HARVIE DAVIDSON	R.VAN.Y.C.	31.0	25/40/ 2	2(2)	3
GEMINI	FRED BIEKER, MD.	PORTLAND	26.0	25/42/14	1(4)	4
ASSAULT	JOHN BUCHAN	SEATTLE	33.2	25/47/25	2(1)	5
DISTANT DRUMMER	GREGORY OLIVER	R.VIC.Y.C.	27.5	25/51/55	1(3)	6
LA BRISA	W. VAN LEEUWEN	WEST VAN.	27.5	25/53/40	2(3)	7
HUCKLEBERRY	KEN REID	WEST VAN.	25.9	25/55/26	2(4)	8
NAKNEK	R.I. NELSON	R.VAN.Y.C.	40.5	25/58/33	3(1)	9
ORAO	V. PLAVSIC	WEST VAN.	21.7	25/59/39	3(4)	10
MIDNIGHT SPECIAL	STEVE CRARY	CORINTHIAN	32.6	26/ 0/ 4	3(2)	11
BERSERKER	P. BYRNE/D. SPEIRS	KITSILANO	27.5	26/ 0/ 5	3(3)	12
SALLY LIGHTFOOT	TOM FRIEDLAND	BELLINGHAM	27.5	26/ 0/56	4(3)	13
BISCUIT EATER	B. WERTHEIMER	CORINTHIAN	32.1	26/ 2/12	4(2)	14
COUNTER POINT	K.L. PARTLOW	OLYMPIA	27.6	26/ 4/38	5(3)	15
ROGUE	HOWARD WITKIN	OLYMPIA	27.8	26/ 8/17	6(3)	16
CITATION	LARRY SHORETT	SEATTLE	27.5	26/12/37	7(3)	17
EPIC	CHAS. SCHIFF	CORINTHIAN	38.4	26/14/52	4(1)	18
EN PASSANT	HUGH MINOR	EVERETT	27.5	26/15/27	8(3)	19
SURGER	ALEX JOHNSTON	WEST VAN.	22.8	26/19/21	4(4)	20
OLYMPIAN	PETER SCHMIDT	CORINTHIAN	31.9	26/20/26	5(2)	21
SCARAMOUCHE	R.M. ALEXANDER	SEATTLE	38.6	26/21/56	5(1)	22
MOONRAKER	LOUIS LINDHOLM	R.VIC.Y.C.	29.0	26/22/31	6(2)	23
BRER RABBIT	BOB CONNOR	CORINTHIAN	29.5	26/27/50	7(2)	24
TYEE	WILLIAM WHIPPLE	SEATTLE	41.2	26/31/ 8	6(1)	25
SALTY TIGER	J. ALBERTSON	SEATTLE	38.8	26/31/25	7(1)	26
TANGENT II	ANTONY LOACH	WEST VAN.	29.3	26/32/58	8(2)	27
SINE MORA	DONALD HILLMAN	SEATTLE	27.8	26/33/33	9(3)	28
SURPRISE	GERRY MAURER	SEATTLE	29.9	26/34/ 2	9(2)	29
GHOST RIDER	TOM GEISNESS	SEATTLE	24.9	26/35/46	5(4)	30
CO HO	G. BRANDLMAYR	R.VAN.Y.C.	40.8	26/36/36	8(1)	31
OUTWARD BOUND	DON FLYNN	SEATTLE	26.7	26/38/28	10(3)	32
DEFIANCE	RON HART	TACOMA	31.7	26/39/36	10(2)	33
AKKA	RALPH MARX	GIG HARBOR	26.8	26/42/27	11(3)	34
APHRODITE	R.C. McCOLL	WEST VAN.	27.5	26/44/50	12(3)	35
FIREBRAND	RUSSELL NEWMAN	SEATTLE	30.8	26/48/24	11(2)	36
HOOLIGAN II	TOM O'BRIEN	SEATTLE	31.6	26/53/ 2	12(2)	37
PACIFIC DAWN	RICH VEDVICK	CORINTHIAN	27.8	26/54/20	13(3)	38
TONIC	DAN BRINK	CORINTHIAN	22.9	26/55/44	6(4)	39
LOVE AFFAIR	IRVING VARLEY	EVERETT	28.3	26/57/ 6	14(3)	40
RACE PASSAGE	DR. McCULLOUGH	BREMERTON	34.8	27/ 1/ 5	9(1)	41
JOLLY OLLY III	V.W. RUSKIN	R.VAN.Y.C.	23.4	27/ 1/43	7(4)	42
BANJO	DICK VOGEL/WINK VOGEL	R.VAN.Y.C.	27.5	27/ 3/ 9	15(3)	43
STAR	DAVID MEERES	KITSILANO	30.0	27/ 7/35	13(2)	44
OUTRAGEOUS	TED BURNS	BREMERTON	30.1	27/ 9/30	14(2)	45
NERITA	BOB UTTER/BILL BRUCH	CORINTHIAN	31.6	27/ 9/45	15(2)	46
MADRUGADOR	JAMES STENGEL	SEATTLE	31.4	27/10/51	16(2)	47
BEDLAM II	DOUGLAS DAY	R.VAN.Y.C.	31.1	27/11/ 9	17(2)	48
WHIM-WHAM	BILL HANSON	CORINTHIAN	33.2	27/13/10	10(1)	49
KAOS	BILL RUDOLPH	CORINTHIAN	31.8	27/18/45	18(2)	50
CAMELOT	BOB SMITH	TACOMA	30.4	27/18/55	19(2)	51
VIVA	D. BLAKEMORE	CORINTHIAN	31.6	27/22/15	20(2)	52
VELA	T.M. THOMSEN	CORINTHIAN	26.8	27/23/39	16(3)	53
DIAMOND HEAD	HENRY KOTKINS	SEATTLE	51.5	27/25/30	11(1)	54
NAMBA	A.J.B. FORSYTH	R.VAN.Y.C.	33.3	27/26/37	12(1)	55
MEG	BOB HOSIE	R.VIC.Y.C.	27.5	27/45/37	17(3)	56
STRIDER	KEITH JOHNSON	CORINTHIAN	26.8	27/46/34	18(3)	57
DAMN YANKEE	HAROLD SARGENT	OLYMPIA	27.5	27/49/37	19(3)	58
JEUNESSE II	PAUL COTE	R.VAN.Y.C.	33.8	27/50/18	13(1)	59
SIRUS II	DR. J. EADON	ANACORTES	27.6	27/53/58	20(3)	60
JUBILEE	BILL WATKINS	CORINTHIAN	29.0	27/55/10	21(2)	61
PEMAQUID	G. SCHUCHART	SEATTLE	36.2	27/58/25	14(1)	62
TSUNAMI	PAUL PEDERSON/CONRAD MORAN	CORINTHIAN	27.3	28/ 0/ 9	21(3)	63
SEA RAY	JOHN LONG	R.VAN.Y.C.	37.8	28/ 2/35	15(1)	64
CHEROKEE	W.M. BLACK	CORINTHIAN	27.5	28/ 2/37	22(3)	65
DRUMMER BOY	JOHN DUNFIELD	R.VAN.Y.C.	30.4	28/ 9/23	22(2)	66
OBSESSION	MILES DIGHTON	R.VIC.Y.C.	27.0	28/10/43	23(3)	67
ARCTURUS	ALLAN D. TOBE	WEST VAN.	33.7	28/12/56	16(1)	68
GAMIN	LON ROBINSON	CORINTHIAN	31.0	28/19/48	23(2)	69
RED DOG	DENNIS DONOHUE	CORINTHIAN	32.0	28/33/10	24(2)	70
SQAIP	PHIL JOHNSON	SEATTLE	31.5	28/33/26	25(2)	71
FIRECRACKER	LARRY SCHUELER	PT. ANGELES	25.9	28/42/26	8(4)	72
MYFANWY	H. TURPIN, MD.	BAHIA CAL.	23.6	28/47/32	9(4)	73

YACHT NAME	SKIPPER(S)	CLUB	RATING	COR ELAPSE TIME	POSITION DIVISION	OVERALL
PRIMO	BOB DENBY/GEORGE LOWE	CORINTHIAN	25.7	28/48/38	10(4)	74
ELUSIVE I	JOHN SPROUSE	PORTLAND	21.7	28/57/19	11(4)	75
HEADSTRONG	PETER BUSH	R.VIC.Y.C.	21.6	29/ 2/18	12(4)	76
SOLENT WAVE 3	JOHN HORTON	R.N.S.A.	21.7	29/ 8/41	13(4)	77
ANNA	DR. LAWRENCE	CORINTHIAN	22.3	29/19/ 8	14(4)	78
TRINGA	F.T. GARDINER	R.VIC.Y.C.	27.5	29/21/37	24(3)	79
ELISHEBA	MILES MILLER	CORINTHIAN	28.3	29/23/15	25(3)	80
NORN	OLAV EKROM	CORINTHIAN	24.9	29/25/56	15(4)	81
PANDORA	J.R. HORNER	R.VIC.Y.C.	38.7	29/40/13	17(1)	82
JACKAROE	ROGER HILLS	PT. TOWNSND	24.1	29/41/28	16(4)	83
IMPULSE	J. KEVORKIAN	CORINTHIAN	23.2	29/47/16	17(4)	84
VANDAL	JOE McDONALD	SEATTLE	23.4	29/54/ 4	18(4)	85
ARROW	LEE JOHNSON	EVERETT	28.9	30/ 8/15	26(3)	86
WHITE MIST	DORR ANDERSON	SEATTLE	22.4	30/ 8/22	19(4)	87
SPECTRE	J. CAHILL, MD.	SEATTLE	31.6	30/23/38	26(2)	88
TILLICUM	HOWARD RICKETTS	CORINTHIAN	25.8	30/32/28	20(4)	89
ELIXIR	P. MICKELSEN	CORINTHIAN	28.4	30/34/32	27(3)	90
BORDERLORD	BISHOP WHEELER	CORINTHIAN	28.0	30/37/31	28(3)	91
FLIRTATION	JACK TUTTLE	CORINTHIAN	27.5	30/40/ 3	29(3)	92
SCOTCH MIST II	WILLIAM SANBORN	CORINTHIAN	24.5	30/44/ 1	21(4)	93
FRIENDSHIP	TOM GIDLUND/EVAN SCHWAB	CORINTHIAN	27.2	30/44/32	30(3)	94
MAURIAH	J. ROOCROFT	WEST VAN.	26.1	30/45/15	22(4)	95
SQUALL	CAM HALL/TOM ALBERG	SEATTLE	26.1	30/50/49	23(4)	96
SUNFLOWER	M.B. MADENWALD	ANACORTES	27.0	30/59/11	31(3)	97
ELAN	RONALD ZELL	CORINTHIAN	23.4	31/ 1/ 0	24(4)	98
RANA	H.W. RHODES	R.VAN.Y.C.	28.5	31/ 4/55	32(3)	99
QUEST	ALAN RUTHERFORD	CORINTHIAN	32.4	32/ 3/31	27(2)	100
MAVERICK III	TERRY GUEST	R.VAN.Y.C.	26.4	32/46/18	25(4)	101
NATIVE DANCER	WILBUR WILLARD	SHILESHOLE	25.2	33/ 5/ 6	26(4)	102
SEAWYF	R.O. DARBY	C.F.S.A.	25.4	35/ 7/26	27(4)	103
FREJA	WELDON PINCHIN	EAGLE HARB	23.0		DNF(4)	DNF
SABRINA	FOSTER ANDERSON	EUGENE	28.9		DNF(3)	DNF
ON TIME	M. SCHLOSSER	CORINTHIAN	25.8		DNF(4)	DNF
GYPSY G.	DAVE GIBBERD	WEST VAN.	27.5		DNF(3)	DNF
WARRIOR	BRUCE HEDRICK	ROSE CITY	47.5		DNF(1)	DNF
CHAIKA	DR. R. KNIGHT	R.VAN.Y.C.	35.6		DNF(1)	DNF
MIN SETTE	JOE POLLOCK, JR.	ROSE CITY	52.0		DNF(1)	DNF
ARIES	ROBERT STREET	SEATTLE	34.8		DNF(1)	DNF

MAY 27, 1974
OFFICIAL START TIME: 12/30/00

SWIFTSURE (P.H.R.F.) 1974
RESULTS

YACHT NAME	SKIPPER(S)	CLUB	RATING	COR ELAPSE TIME	POSITION DIVISION	OVERALL
WHITE SQUALL	G. TEATS, MD.	TACOMA	1.9	24/49/ 3	1(A)	1
STARWAGON	R.O. GILBERT	CORINTHIAN	2.3	24/56/47	2(A)	2
WINDWARD MARK	VIC PALMER	MAPLE BAY	1.9	25/18/27	3(A)	3
SAGA	SVEN RASMUSSEN	R.VAN.Y.C.	2.1	25/27/24	4(A)	4
TERNA	P. CHRISTOFFERSEN	WEST VAN.	1.9	25/48/35	5(A)	5
SWIFT I	R. HOFFMAN, MD.	EVERETT	3.2	26/21/17	1(B)	6
LANCER	NORM. LARABEE	CORINTHIAN	2.3	26/28/18	6(A)	7
RAPID	K. KIRKLAND	R.VAN.Y.C.	2.0	26/30/40	7(A)	8
MOONGLOW III	RON MOBLO	GIG HARBOR	1.8	26/35/33	8(A)	9
AKVAVIT	G.W. THORSEN	S. SOUND	3.0	26/50/52	2(B)	10
TEMPTATION	BRYAN ARCHER	TACOMA	1.8	27/13/10	9(A)	11
TOLO TSOLO	ED WOODSON	CORINTHIAN	2.4	27/24/55	10(A)	12
BANDIT	DAN McDONOUGH	TACOMA	2.6	27/29/22	11(A)	13
CHECKMATE	C. BAMFORD JR.	TACOMA	2.6	27/31/ 5	12(A)	14
SUNDANCE	THOMAS MURPHY	TACOMA	1.7	27/39/45	13(A)	15
DUTCH FLUTE	R. KLEIN, MD.	TACOMA	2.6	27/45/24	14(A)	16
MALTESE FALCON	RUSS SCHULKE	CORINTHIAN	2.3	27/54/25	15(A)	17
FROSTBITE	ROBERT FROST	SHILSHOLE	2.2	27/57/ 8	16(A)	18
KATCHEN	D. STAATZ, MD.	TACOMA	2.6	27/57/15	17(A)	19
BARBARA	WYNN KAMPE	CORINTHIAN	2.1	28/ 2/31	18(A)	20
MY REVERIE	DR. PEERLESS	R.VAN.Y.C.	2.3	28/14/17	19(A)	21
LA RUINA	R.J. GIBBONS	SEATTLE	2.0	28/30/ 7	20(A)	22
MARIAH	RAMON BROWN	SHILSHOLE	2.7	28/31/49	21(A)	23
TAVEUNI	R.I. THIEME	EVERETT	2.2	28/34/40	22(A)	24
MOSHULU	R.O. SYLVESTER	SEATTLE	2.1	28/39/19	23(A)	25
AFRICAN STAR	DOUG FRYER	SEATTLE	3.6	28/41/48	3(B)	26
RIVAL	WILLIAM KELLIS	TACOMA	1.8	28/55/25	24(A)	27
SEACLUSION	D. MATCHETTE	OLYMPIA	2.4	29/ 1/21	25(A)	28
NINA DEL MAR	CHARLES McCANN	OLYMPIA	3.2	29/ 3/ 9	4(B)	29

YACHT NAME	SKIPPER(S)	CLUB	RATING	COR ELAPSE TIME	POSITION DIVISION	OVERALL
EVANGELINE	CHARLES OLSON	EDMONDS	1.9	29/ 7/34	26(A)	30
HUSSY	NORMAN KREBILL	BELLINGHAM	1.7	29/16/52	27(A)	31
MONTE CARLO	CECIL DION	KITSILANO	2.6	29/27/38	28(A)	32
ESCAPE HATCH	BOB FERRIE	BELLINGHAM	3.5	30/24/53	5(B)	33
TATOOSH	DR. PATTERSON	CORINTHIAN	2.1	30/56/15	29(A)	34
MUYA	RUSSELL LABODA	PT. MADISON	3.5	31/11/58	6(B)	35
SERVUS	GEORGE STRICKER	R.VIC.Y.C.	2.6	31/39/50	30(A)	36
CALLALOO	JOHN CATLEY	R.VAN.Y.C.	2.7	32/ 0/58	31(A)	37
WITCH OF HAMPTON	DAVID WILDER	EAGLE HARB	2.7		DNF(A)	DNF
ESCAPE	DR. P. BLATT	PORTLAND	3.0		DNF(B)	DNF
ARRIBA	M. GABRIELSON	ANACORTES	3.4		DNF(B)	DNF
TIFFANY	J.P. ANGUS	R.VIC.Y.C.	2.8		DNF(B)	DNF
PLEIADES	LANGE	CORINTHIAN	2.9		DNF(B)	DNF
CANADA GREY	JOHN ROWAND	R.VIC.Y.C.	2.9		DNF(B)	DNF
BLACK HAWK	H.H. BOYD, MD.	CORINTHIAN	2.9		DNF(B)	DNF
LA BAMBA	ARNE NISKA	PT. TOWNSND	3.8		DNF(B)	DNF

MAY 27, 1974
OFFICIAL START TIME: 12/45/00

JUAN DE FUCA (I.O.R.) 1974
RESULTS

YACHT NAME	SKIPPER(S)	CLUB	RATING	COR ELAPSE TIME	POSITION DIVISION	OVERALL
JUNE BUG	ROBERT VYNNE	SEATTLE	21.6	16/23/ 6	1(1)	1
PANACHE	DICK DUGGAN	WEST VAN.	21.7	16/25/58	2(1)	2
CALIENTE	W. WILLIAMSON	EDMONDS	21.7	16/32/38	3(1)	3
GEM	RAY FIEDLER	CORINTHIAN	24.5	16/42/17	4(1)	4
FRED	DR. G. WILKINS	R.VAN.Y.C.	18.0	16/54/44	1(2)	5
SHIMNA	J.H. GLASS	R.VAN.Y.C.	24.8	17/ 1/46	5(1)	6
CLIMAX	MIKE SMITH/DON SMITH	CORINTHIAN	21.6	17/11/30	6(1)	7
BAREFOOT	JIM WARD	CORINTHIAN	23.0	17/32/17	7(1)	8
PUFF II	J.D. WOODWARD	R.VIC.Y.C.	23.9	17/38/32	8(1)	9
BLUE FOX	JOHN GONYEA	TACOMA	21.9	17/58/17	9(1)	10
GRETEL II	H. DRIEHUYZEN	WEST VAN.	23.0	18/ 1/32	10(1)	11
EL CID	BOB BERST	SEATTLE	21.5	18/ 1/40	11(1)	12
STREAKER	RICHARD PRATT	CORINTHIAN	21.6	18/ 6/ 1	12(1)	13
SEA SPELL	JAN HUIBERS	R.VIC.Y.C.	21.2	18/12/18	2(2)	14
VANDALL II	STEVE MERRIMAN	R.VIC.Y.C.	23.5	18/16/38	13(1)	15
AVALANCHE	ROBERT KERSHAW	CORINTHIAN	24.3	18/17/46	14(1)	16
MOCCASIN II	MIKE STONE	MAPLE BAY	23.6	18/21/ 8	15(1)	17
WATERMELON	G. INGLIS	CANOE BAY	22.6	18/31/33	16(1)	18
HORNET	TOM HUKLE	CORINTHIAN	18.3	18/32/28	3(2)	19
LORELEI II	JOE ROSINSKI	BELLINGHAM	24.3	18/37/54	17(1)	20
SMALL WORLD	GENE SIBOLD	OLYMPIA	24.3	18/47/25	18(1)	21
SEA ROBIN	DR. J. KEOGH	WEST VAN.	24.6	18/56/ 9	19(1)	22
AMBUSH	VANCE BINGHAM	PT. ANGELES	24.5	19/16/45	20(1)	23
ILLUSIVE	JACK FOSTER	R.VIC.Y.C.	18.0	19/34/ 0	4(2)	24
VALHALLA	GORDON VICKERY	R.VIC.Y.C.	21.8	19/37/ 8	21(1)	25
RISQUE	JON A. POKELA/ILSE L. POKELA	TACOMA	18.4	19/38/27	5(2)	26
WINDSHIFT	F.W. HAYES	SEATTLE	21.6	19/42/32	22(1)	27
PAPRIKA	FRANK MUSSON	WEST VAN.	21.8	19/55/10	23(1)	28
WARLOCK	ROLAND SCHULER	CORINTHIAN	22.9	20/ 8/ 4	24(1)	29
TARQUIN III	G. JOHNSTONE	R.VIC.Y.C.	21.0	20/11/34	6(2)	30
MOODY TOO	F.J. PINE	WEST VAN.	23.4	20/17/57	25(1)	31
YEHL	THOMAS LINDER	ANACORTES	23.4	20/24/ 2	26(1)	32
DEPARTURE	DR. G. SCREECH	R.VIC.Y.C.	23.9	20/26/25	27(1)	33
SKILFISH	D.R. WEST	WEST VAN.	24.3	20/31/12	28(1)	34
CIRRUS	TIM ERICKSON	CORINTHIAN	23.7	20/34/ 9	29(1)	35
VATICAN	MICHAEL POPE	EAGLE HARB	21.7	20/36/54	30(1)	36
UMPKA	JOHN BOOTH	R.VIC.Y.C.	21.1	20/37/42	7(2)	37
SEAQUIN	R. MARSHALL	CORINTHIAN	20.9	20/40/57	8(2)	38
GALENAIA II	GEORGE DUFOUR	R.VIC.Y.C.	20.6	20/41/59	9(2)	39
LUCY ALICE	WM. GARDNER	CORINTHIAN	22.5	20/53/51	31(1)	40
DIFFERENT DRUMMER	BRIAN GRIFFIN	BELLINGHAM	24.5	21/28/41	32(1)	41
WEDDERBURN CASTLE	TOBEY WILKINS	CORINTHIAN	17.9	21/55/56	10(2)	42
KISMET	STEFAN CLARKE	TACOMA	22.4	22/47/42	33(1)	43
SIAN	G. HOWELL-JONES	R.VIC.Y.C.	17.7		DNF(2)	DNF
TOPIC	IRV SMITH	TACOMA	23.6		DNF(1)	DNF
MARIAH	MELTON/PETERSEN & BIEHL	CORINTHIAN	21.6		DNF(1)	DNF
KIM	IAN DUNCANSON	R.VIC.Y.C.	23.0		DNF(1)	DNF
HULLABALOO	GERALD KIDD	WEST VAN.	21.6		DNF(1)	DNF
RUTHLESS	J. KLOSTERMAN	WILLAMETTE	18.2		DNF(2)	DNF
NEPTUNE	JAMES DRYDEN	R.VIC.Y.C.	20.4		DNF(2)	DNF
INFIDEL	MIKE WHITFIELD	EAGLE HARB	22.3		DNF(1)	DNF

166

BALLARD STATION	CHUCK BOUFFIOU	GIG HARBOR	18.0		DNF(2)	DNF
ARIEL II	ERIC DOWELL	R.VIC.Y.C.	24.0		DNF(1)	DNF
GARDEN TOOLS II	GARY BYSTEDT	CORINTHIAN	18.0		DNF(2)	DNF
LADY T	D.A. MARTIN	R.VAN.Y.C.	21.7		DNF(1)	DNF
ALFIE	BRUCE FRASER	R.VAN.Y.C.	18.0		DNS(2)	DNS

MAY 27, 1974
OFFICIAL START TIME: 12/45/00

JUAN DE FUCA (P.H.R.F.) 1974
RESULTS

YACHT NAME	SKIPPER(S)	CLUB	RATING	COR ELAPSE TIME	POSITION DIVISION	OVERALL
FILEY BRIGG	J.M. WEIR	R.VIC.Y.C.	3.2	17/18/43	1(C)	1
GAZELLE II	KIM HUSBAND	R.VAN.Y.C.	3.0	17/27/14	2(C)	2
VIKING	ALAN DICKINSON	CANOE BAY	3.2	17/47/55	3(C)	3
WHITE SQUALL	PETER WHITE	CANOE BAY	3.3	19/ 7/32	4(C)	4
FOXEE	RON FOXALL	WEST VAN.	3.4	19/15/14	5(C)	5
AVENGER II	A.S. BARKER	WEST VAN.	3.1	19/24/54	6(C)	6
PEREGRINE	BOB ROWLETTE	R.N.S.A.	3.3	19/27/13	7(C)	7
THISTLEDOWN	DON FEELEY	PT. ANGELES	3.4	19/29/40	8(C)	8
ERRIGAL	HUGH PORTER	R.VIC.Y.C.	3.8	19/36/33	1(D)	9
SHOW GIRL	DONALD DOBIE	CANOE BAY	3.1	19/40/12	9(C)	10
MOA	WALT MIDDLETON	WEST VAN.	3.0	19/56/27	10(C)	11
TIARA III	WILL JENSEN	CANOE BAY	3.0	19/58/ 2	11(C)	12
MAGUS	BOB LINROTHE	3 TREE PT.	3.4	20/ 1/52	12(C)	13
AURIGA	TERRY CATTELL	WEST VAN.	3.4	20/ 8/34	13(C)	14
CALABASH	ROGER GOODALL	R.VAN.Y.C.	3.4	20/11/21	14(C)	15
SIRIUS	D.K. WATERFALL	MAPLE BAY	3.3	20/12/42	15(C)	16
LA MARQUISE II	J.P. LE DALLIC	C.F.S.A.	3.2	20/13/58	16(C)	17
LOON	J.T. SCHNEIDER	CORINTHIAN	3.7	20/25/40	2(D)	18
MICKEY	HAL PUDDY	PT. ANGELES	3.2	20/31/38	17(C)	19
MALDA	COLM HOGAN	CANOE BAY	3.0	20/34/ 4	18(C)	20
SWEET PEE	DEAN ANDERSON	S. SOUND	2.8	20/36/43	19(C)	21
QUEST	ROBERT EICHLER	SEATTLE	4.5	20/50/15	3(D)	22
MORAG	DICK JENKINS	R.VAN.Y.C.	2.8	20/53/ 3	20(C)	23
MITHRIL	DR. R. HILL	R.VAN.Y.C.	2.9	21/ 3/49	21(C)	24
UNICORN II	M. WELLAND	R.VAN.Y.C.	2.9	21/18/26	22(C)	25
WINDMILL	McLEOD/KILLEEN	TSAWWASSEN	3.2	21/25/13	23(C)	26
WIND BIRD	WM. JOHNSON	TACOMA	3.6	21/35/24	24(C)	27
KEHLOKE	FRANK RUSSELL	WEST VAN.	3.5	21/36/59	25(C)	28
LOIS-J	F. SHININGER	PT. ANGELES	3.3	22/ 8/58	26(C)	29
ISIS	W.J. ELLIS	R.VIC.Y.C.	3.3	22/11/17	27(C)	30
ELACKA	J.K. MARTIN	R.VIC.Y.C.	4.0	22/39/39	4(D)	31
MARILYN L.	RON CARLSON	PT. ANGELES	3.8	23/11/23	5(D)	32
HUSTLER	JACK PATTERSON	TURKEY HD	3.6	23/26/43	28(C)	33
THE SLOOP JOHN B.	BOYD IVENS	TSAWWASSEN	3.7	23/40/57	6(D)	34
CAPRICE	MAJ. H. GARDNER	C.F.S.A.	4.0		DNF(D)	DNF
WINDSONG II	R.C. BROWN	CORINTHIAN	4.0		DNF(D)	DNF
SHONI	DONALD GLADMAN	R.N.S.A.	3.7		DNF(D)	DNF
HELSA	G. CARLSTROM	S. SOUND	3.2		DNF(C)	DNF
OLYMPIC MIST	MIKE KALAHAR	PT. ANGELES	3.4		DNF(C)	DNF
GREENLING	MERVYN OLSON	R.VAN.Y.C.	3.1		DNF(C)	DNF
BUFFLEHEAD II	KENNETH MARTIN	R.VAN.Y.C.	3.1		DNF(C)	DNF
MARY D.	DARREL DAVIS	PT. ANGELES	3.6		DNF(C)	DNF
CHO-CHO SAN	DAVID CHRISTIAN	CANOE BAY	3.1		DNF(C)	DNF
GEORGIA GIRL	BILL MARTIN	CANOE COVE	3.7		DNF(D)	DNF
PEACHES	TED SERR	PT. ANGELES	3.7		DNF(D)	DNF
SWEET AFTON	THOMAS MURRAY	EAGLE HARB	3.8		DNF(D)	DNF
BACARRA	T.W. LONEY	R.VIC.Y.C.	2.8		DNF(C)	DNF
ZEST	PETER YOUNG	R.VIC.Y.C.	3.4		DNS(C)	DNS
TE-PAH	ROGER OLDHAM	C.F.S.A.	3.1		DNS(C)	DNS
TYCHE	ALEX FOLEY	R.VAN.Y.C.	3.6		DNS(C)	DNS

PACIFIC INTERNATIONAL YACHTING ASSOCIATION
SWIFTSURE LIGHTSHIP CLASSIC AND JUAN DE FUCA RACE
1975 TROPHY WINNERS

SWIFTSURE (I.O.R.)	SWIFTSURE TROPHY (OVERALL HANDICAP WINNER)	J.E. SPROUSE	PORTLAND	ELUSIVE I
	CITY OF VICTORIA TROPHY (FIRST YACHT TO FINISH)	B. HEDRICK	SEATTLE	WARRIOR
	ROYAL CANADIAN NAVY TROPHY (FIRST TO ROUND SWIFTSURE MARK)	A.T. STURGESS	R.VAN.	ENDLESS SUMMER
	OCEAN CEMENT TROPHY (FIRST IN DIVISION 1)	R.M. ALEXANDER	SEATTLE	SCARAMOUCHE

T. EATON COMPANY TROPHY (FIRST IN DIVISION 2)	B. CONNOR	CORINTHIAN	BRER RABBIT
.... (FIRST IN DIVISION 3)	K. PEARCE	R.VAN.	THE PEARCE ARROW
CITY OF SEATTLE TROPHY (FIRST IN DIVISION 4)	D. FLYNN	SEATTLE	OUTWARD BOUND
ROYAL VANCOUVER YACHT CLUB TROPHY (FIRST IN DIVISION 5)	J.E. SPROUSE	PORTLAND	ELUSIVE I

SWIFTSURE (P.H.R.F.)

CORINTHIAN YACHT CLUB TROPHY (FIRST IN DIVISION A)	P. CHRISTOFFERSEN	W.VAN.	TERNA
.... (FIRST IN DIVISION B)	D. McDONOUGH	TACOMA	BANDIT
CAPE FLATTERY TROPHY (FIRST IN DIVISION C)	J. SMITH	EDMONDS	PREDICAMENT

JUAN DE FUCA (I.O.R.)

SAN JUAN TROPHY (FIRST YACHT TO FINISH)	J.D. GONYEA	TACOMA	BLUE FOX
ROYAL VICTORIA YACHT CLUB TROPHY (FIRST IN DIVISION 1)	G.A. LIEBERT	R.VAN.	DOUBLE ENTRY
ROYAL CANADIAN NAVY TROPHY (FIRST IN DIVISION 2)	J.D. GONYEA	TACOMA	BLUE FOX

JUAN DE FUCA (P.H.R.F.)

ANACORTES YACHT CLUB TROPHY (FIRST IN DIVISION D)	R.L. RUE	TACOMA	UNION DEPOT
.... (FIRST IN DIVISION E)	T. CATTELL	W.VAN.	AURIGA
.... (FIRST IN DIVISION F)	W.H. GARDNER	CORINTHIAN	LUCY ALICE

SWIFTSURE (I.O.R.) 1975
RESULTS

OFFICIAL START TIME: 9/10/00

YACHT	SKIPPER(S)	CLUB	RATING	COR ELAPSE TIME	POSITION DIVISION	OVERALL
ELUSIVE I	J.E. SPROUSE	PORTLAND	21.6	35/43/55	1(5)	1
VATICAN II	M. POPE	EAGLE HBR.	24.8	36/07/30	2(5)	2
THE PEARCE ARROW	K. PEARCE	R.VAN.	27.5	36/16/01	1(3)	3
SUPER PICKLE	R. MOELLER	PORTLAND	22.5	36/21/29	3(5)	4
TONIC	D. BRINK	CORINTHIAN	22.9	36/25/09	4(5)	5
BYDAND	W. BUCHAN	CORINTHIAN	28.1	36/27/30	2(3)	6
SEA ROBIN	S. CAMPBELL	R.VIC.	24.5	36/56/03	5(5)	7
BETELGEUSE	T. GUEST	R.VAN.	27.5	36/59/41	3(3)	8
RENEGADE	S.P. SMITH	S. SOUND	24.0	37/01/58	6(5)	9
OUTWARD BOUND	D. FLYNN	SEATTLE	26.7	37/03/01	1(4)	10
NAHMA	K. MAXWELL	CORINTHIAN	24.8	37/05/13	7(5)	11
TRUMPETER OF JERICHO	J.H. LONG	R.VAN.	28.9	37/16/01	4(3)	12
MARY D II	D.B. DAVIS	PT. ANGELES	24.7	37/21/33	8(5)	13
DISTANT DRUMMER	G. OLIVER	R.VIC.	27.5	37/21/46	5(3)	14
ELISHEBA	M. MILLER	CORINTHIAN	28.0	37/24/21	6(3)	15
PRIMO	R.V. DENBY/G.A. LOWE	COR/MAD	25.7	37/29/03	2(4)	16
ON TIME	N.L. SCHLOSSER	CORINTHIAN	25.8	37/29/50	3(4)	17
GEMINI	F.W. BIEKER	PORTLAND	25.4	37/34/01	4(4)	18
COUNTERPOINT	K.L. PARTLOW II	OLYMPIA	27.6	37/34/54	7(3)	19
FIRECRACKER	L. SCHUELER	PT. ANGELES	25.9	37/37/03	5(4)	20
BRER RABBIT	B. CONNOR	CORINTHIAN	29.9	37/43/30	1(2)	21
JADAH	P. TUCKER	CORINTHIAN	24.5	37/44/13	9(5)	22
NON SEQUITUR II	J. WESTON JR./D.J. KERMAN	EDMONDS	27.1	37/46/34	6(4)	23
DAMN YANKEE	H. SARGENT	OLYMPIA	27.5	37/46/44	8(3)	24
AKKA	R. NARY	TACOMA	26.8	37/47/46	7(4)	25
DELIVERANCE	G. PALO	GIG HARBOUR	27.5	37/48/21	9(3)	26
SCARAMOUCHE	R.M. ALEXANDER	SEATTLE	38.6	37/51/49	1(1)	27
SALLY LIGHTFOOT	T. FRIEDLAND	BELLINGHAM	27.8	37/54/39	10(3)	28
LADY T	D. MARTIN	R.VAN.	27.5	37/58/14	11(3)	29
JOLLY OLLY IV	V. RUSKIN	R.VAN.	27.5	38/03/39	12(3)	30
HABITAT	P.C.G. RICHARDS	W.VAN.	28.4	38/04/05	13(3)	31
WINGAWAY	H. DAVIDSON/B. LAKE	R.VAN.	31.2	38/04/07	2(2)	32
MEG	B. HOSIE	R.VIC.	27.5	38/04/41	14(3)	33
CITATION	L. SHORETT	SEATTLE	27.5	38/07/41	15(3)	34
LA BRISA	W. VAN LEEUWEN	W.VAN.	27.5	38/07/41	16(3)	35
GOODBYE	T.W. LONEY	R.VIC.	27.5	38/07/51	17(3)	36
TRINGA	F.T. GARDINER	R.VIC.	27.5	38/08/01	18(3)	37
SEA TIGER	A.J. LEES	KITSILANO	27.5	38/08/41	19(3)	38
SUNFLOWER	M.B. MADENWALD	ANACORTES	27.0	38/09/55	8(4)	39
AMERICAN FLYER	J. ALBERTSON	SEATTLE	31.6	38/10/11	3(2)	40
TSUNAMI	C.J. MORAN	CORINTHIAN	27.3	38/11/04	20(3)	41
OUTRAGEOUS	T.A. BURNS, M.D.	BREMERTON	30.5	38/12/12	4(2)	42
PACIFIC DAWN	R. VEDVICK	CORINTHIAN	27.5	38/13/19	21(3)	43

VICTORIA'S INNER HARBOUR / JAMES McVIE

LEAVING HARBOUR / JAMES McVIE

GLORY / PACIFIC YACHTING

GRAYBEARD / DENIS MASON

NIGHT RUNNER / PACIFIC YACHTING

SACHEM / JAMES McVIE

MONTY CHRISTOPHER, JACK GANN,
HUMPHREY GOLBY / SIB DOW

MARA / JAMES McVIE

REPORTERS ON TUG / SIB DOW

THE DISTANT DRUMMER / JAMES McVIE

DIAMOND HEAD / JAMES McVIE

WINSOME III / JAMES McVIE

THE ONE SECOND FINISH / SIB DOW

ADIOS / JAMES McVIE

FRED AGAIN / TOM LEUTWILER (DAEDELUS PHOTOGRAPHY) >

U.S. COAST GUARD / SIB DOW

CANADIAN COAST GUARD / SIB DOW

NED ASHE / PORTRAIT BY DOROTHY OXBOROUGH

TOMAHAWK / PACIFIC YACHTING

AIRBORNE (TARTAN 30) / DENIS MASON

WEATHERLY / JAMES McVIE

KIALOA / JAMES McVIE

YACHT	SKIPPER(S)	CLUB	RATING	COR ELAPSE TIME	POSITION DIVISION	OVERALL
SERVUS	G. STRICKER	R. VIC.	25.8	38/16/59	9(4)	44
ELIXIR	J. GRAHAM	SEATTLE	27.5	38/23/06	22(3)	45
NERITA	B. UTTER/G. BRUCH	CORINTHIAN	32.0	38/25/36	5(2)	46
ROGUE	L. FOX	CORINTHIAN	27.8	38/26/09	23(3)	47
STRIDER	K.R. JOHNSON	CORINTHIAN	26.6	38/28/10	10(4)	48
ARROW	C. GILKEY/A. ARMSTRONG	EVERETT	28.9	38/36/01	24(3)	49
GOOD NEWS	E.W. DE KONING	PORTLAND	30.1	38/37/10	6(2)	50
KANATA	V. PLAVSIC	W. VAN.	32.0	38/37/51	7(2)	51
NIGHT HAWK	E. ODISHAW	KITSILANO	29.1	38/37/52	8(2)	52
IMPULSE	J. KEVORKIAN	CORINTHIAN	23.2	38/38/29	10(5)	53
SURPRISE	G. MAURER	SEATTLE	29.6	38/42/10	9(2)	54
WARRIOR	B. HEDRICK	SEATTLE	47.5	38/43/05	2(1)	55
NAKNEK	R.I. NELSON	R. VAN.	40.5	38/43/50	3(1)	56
SEALION	N.C. MARTIN	NANAIMO	27.5	38/46/46	25(3)	57
LUCIFER	A. NELSON	NANAIMO	32.6	39/20/58	10(2)	58
GOLD RUSH	N.H. RUSSELL	SHILSHOLE	32.0	39/22/06	11(2)	59
DEFIANCE	R. HART	TACOMA	31.7	39/25/06	12(2)	60
MOONGLOW IV	D.D. NIELSEN	TACOMA	32.2	39/25/13	13(2)	61
HUCKLEBERRY	K. REID	W. VAN.	25.9	39/30/03	11(4)	62
PEMAQUID	G.S. SCHUCHART	SEATTLE	36.2	39/30/36	4(1)	63
NAMBA	A.J.B. FORSYTH	R. VAN.	33.0	39/33/03	5(1)	64
CYNOSURE	P.S. HAYES	TACOMA	26.4	39/34/42	12(4)	65
ADIOS	DR. C. JENSEN	SEATTLE	42.2	39/50/57	6(1)	66
VANDAL	J.A. McDONALD	SEATTLE	23.4	39/54/00	11(5)	67
WHIM-WHAM	B. HANSON	CORINTHIAN	33.2	39/58/23	7(1)	68
ANDANTE II	F.W. PATTERSON	R. VAN.	40.2	40/01/21	8(1)	69
PACHENA	J. NEWTON	W. VAN.	32.1	40/05/48	14(2)	70
EPIC	C. SCHIFF	CORINTHIAN	38.4	40/06/23	9(1)	71
SURGER	A.H. JOHNSTON	W. VAN.	23.5	40/22/15	12(5)	72
RED DOG	D. DONOHUE, M.D.	CORINTHIAN	32.0	40/44/11	15(2)	73
ELECTRA	H. DEMBART	CORINTHIAN	24.3	41/01/57	13(5)	74
OBSESSION	R.D. McBRIDE	R. VIC.	27.0	41/14/15	13(4)	75
MIDNIGHT SPECIAL	S. CRARY	CORINTHIAN	32.6	41/24/13	16(2)	76
ENDLESS SUMMER	A.T. STURGESS	R. VAN.	57.7	41/26/45	10(1)	77
MISTRESS II	T.W. VARLEY, M.D.	EVERETT	32.9	41/30/13	17(2)	78
FLIRTATION	J.K. TUTTLE	CORINTHIAN	27.5	41/32/59	26(3)	79
DUDE	J. CRANE	CORINTHIAN	21.7	43/ 6/15	14(5)	80
THUNDER III	W.T.H. CLARK	R. VIC.	25.0	44/15/59	14(4)	81
NATIVE DANCER	W. WILLARD	SHILESHOLE	25.2		(4)	DSQ
SEA RAY	S. REIDI	SQUAMISH	38.6		(1)	DSQ
RACE PASSAGE	DR. P. McCULLOUGH	BREMERTON	34.6		(1)	DSQ
BON VIVANT	J.C. FACER, M.D.	EVERETT	28.0		(3)	DSQ
HEATHER	J. BUCHAN	CORINTHIAN	32.0		(2)	DSQ
NAUTILUS	DR. L. NEVLER	CORINTHIAN	28.2		(3)	DNF
RUNAWAY	R.P. McCULLOUGH	CORINTHIAN	27.0		(4)	DNF
APHRODITE	R.C. McCOLL	W. VAN.	27.5		(3)	DNF
GHOST RIDER	T. GEISNESS	SEATTLE	24.9		(5)	DNF
CHAIKA	DR. R. KNIGHT	R. VAN.	35.8		(1)	DNF
FRIENDSHIP	T. GIDLUND/E. SCHWAB	CORINTHIAN	27.2		(4)	DNF
AMERICAN EXPRESS	H.T. STANLEY	PORTLAND	24.8		(5)	DNF
ARCTURUS	A.D. TOBE	W. VAN.	33.7		(1)	DNF
DRUMMER BOY	J. DUNFIELD	R. VAN.	30.4		(2)	DNF
SCAMPI	E.S. WATERMAN	R. VAN.	21.9		(5)	DNF
DIAMOND HEAD	H.L. KOTKINS	SEATTLE	51.8		(1)	DNF
COHO	G. BRANDLMAYR	R. VAN.	40.7		(1)	DNF
THEORY	M. FIANDER	CORINTHIAN	24.7		(5)	DNF
SUNBIRD	E.J. NAROD	R. VAN.	44.4		(1)	DNF
BEDLAM II	D. DAY/J. DAY	R. VAN.	31.2		(2)	DNS
WHITE MIST	D. ANDERSON	SEATTLE	22.4		(5)	DNS
SOLENT WAVE 3	J.M. HORTON	R.N.S.A.	21.7		(5)	DNS

SWIFTSURE (P.H.R.F.) 1975 RESULTS

OFFICIAL START TIME: 09/25/00

YACHT	SKIPPER(S)	CLUB	RATING	COR ELAPSE TIME	POSITION DIVISION	OVERALL
PREDICAMENT	J. SMITH	EDMONDS	2.7	36/58/56	1(C)	1
TERNA	P. CHRISTOFFERSEN	W. VAN.	2.1	37/05/29	1(A)	2
SAGA	S. RASMUSSEN	R. VAN.	2.1	37/07/49	2(A)	3
JUBILEE	B. WATKINS	SEATTLE	2.1	37/15/54	3(A)	4
BANDIT	D. McDONOUGH	TACOMA	2.6	37/16/48	1(B)	5
RAPTURE	P. JUTTE	CORINTHIAN	2.5	37/18/50	2(B)	6

FOREIGN AFFAIR	W. BLACK	CORINTHIAN	2.4	37/29/57	3(B)	7
GAMIN	L. ROBINSON	SEATTLE	2.0	37/32/26	4(A)	8
BARBARA	W.E. KAMPE	CORINTHIAN	2.3	37/46/19	4(B)	9
LANCER	N. LARABEE	CORINTHIAN	2.4	37/48/57	5(B)	10
PIZAZZ	B. NELSON	CORINTHIAN	2.4	37/56/12	6(B)	11
FROSTBITE	R.B. FROST	SHILSHOLE	2.2	38/01/22	7(B)	12
MERIDIAN PASSAGE	M. WILKINSON	R.VAN.	2.0	38/12/37	5(A)	13
WINDWARD MARK	V. PALMER	MAPLE BAY	1.9	38/21/15	6(A)	14
SQAIP	P. JOHNSON	SEATTLE	2.0	38/21/16	7(A)	15
TANGENT II	T. LOACH	W.VAN.	2.1	38/23/10	8(A)	16
FIREBRAND	R.W. NEWMAN	SEATTLE	2.0	38/26/26	9(A)	17
TAVEUNI	R.I. THIEME	EVERETT	2.1	38/34/57	10(A)	18
RIVAL	W.R. KELLIS	TACOMA	1.8	38/35/50	11(A)	19
AMIEO	D. THOMAS	CANOE BAY	2.0	38/36/11	12(A)	20
WIND CHILD	S. ALTMYEX	OLYMPIA	3.0	38/37/04	2(C)	21
OLYMPIAN	P.G. SCHMIDT	SEATTLE	2.8	38/41/26	13(A)	22
MAURIAH	J.H. ROOCROFT	W.VAN.	2.7	38/44/11	3(C)	23
HOOLIGAN II	T.D. O'BRIEN	SEATTLE	1.8	38/48/25	14(A)	24
SCHLINGEL	M.A. TREIT	ANACORTES	2.4	38/51/27	8(B)	25
CIRRUS	T. ERICKSON	CORINTHIAN	2.8	38/52/28	4(C)	26
TEMPTATION	B. ARCHER	TACOMA	1.8	38/56/05	15(A)	27
MOONGLOW III	R. MOBLO	CORINTHIAN	1.8	38/56/51	16(A)	28
SPECTRE	J.L. CAHILL, M.D.	SEATTLE	1.8	38/59/20	17(A)	29
ASTROLOGER	G.T. ELLIOTT	TACOMA	2.6	39/18/18	9(B)	30
SUNDANCE	T.O. MURPHY	TACOMA	1.7	39/20/28	18(A)	31
GABRIELLE	K.F. DOWNIE	R.VAN.	2.6	39/26/23	10(B)	32
VELA	W. PRUE/T. THOMSEN	CORINTHIAN	2.3	39/27/58	11(B)	33
IONA	W.R. McCABE	PORTLAND	3.1	39/28/07	5(C)	34
MOSHULU	R.O. SYLVESTER	SEATTLE	2.1	39/31/11	19(A)	35
SISSEROU	DR. J.H. KEOGH	W.VAN.	2.0	39/49/41	20(A)	36
BANJO	W. VOGEL/D. VOGEL	R.VAN.	2.2	39/56/27	12(B)	37
SHAZAAM	D. MYERS	CORINTHIAN	2.8	39/59/38	6(C)	38
MUTINEER IV	T. BRAIDWOOD	W.VAN.	1.7	40/03/14	21(A)	39
BENORA III	M. HERLIHY	R.VAN.	1.7	40/05/53	22(A)	40
SKY ONE HUNDRED	F. HILL	W.VAN.	2.7	40/09/06	7(C)	41
MOON DAY	C. BAMFORD	TACOMA	1.8	40/30/40	23(A)	42
ZUBEN'UBI II	W.F. HESTER	CORINTHIAN	2.0	40/51/06	24(A)	43
MALTESE FALCON	R. SCHULKE	CORINTHIAN	2.4	40/52/07	13(B)	44
KATCHEN	D. STAATZ, M.D.	TACOMA	2.7	40/55/11	8(C)	45
RUNNING SHOE	J. JARMAN	R.VAN.	3.0	41/24/22	9(C)	46
DOMINIQUE	W. FAHNING	CANOE BAY	2.2	41/29/42	14(B)	47
SEACLUSION	D. MATCHETTE	OLYMPIA	2.5	41/38/52	15(B)	48
AFRICAN STAR	D. FRYER	SEATTLE	3.6	42/14/06	10(C)	49
ARRIBA	M. GABRIELSON	ANACORTES	3.4	42/20/55	11(C)	50
ESCAPE HATCH	B. FERRIE	BELLINGHAM	3.5	42/21/48	12(C)	51
MADRUGADOR	J.F. STENGEL	SEATTLE	1.8	42/28/28	25(A)	52
TANYA BLUE	E.H. BECKER	OREGON CGR	3.5	42/30/08	13(C)	53
PETER COTTONSAIL	V. LAWRENCE	ROSE CITY	2.8	42/50/36	14(C)	54
TILLICUM	H.J. RICKETTS	CORINTHIAN	2.8	42/50/53	15(C)	55
NINA DEL MAR	C.J. McCANN	OLYMPIA	3.2	43/29/30	16(C)	56
RANA	H. RHODES	R.VAN.	2.2	44/18/47	16(B)	57
HERMES	W.K. HERRMANN	PORTLAND	2.3	45/40/44	17(B)	58
QUEST	A.S. RUTHERFORD	SEATTLE	1.9		(A)	DNF
TRUMPETER	L. BLACKWELL	BELLINGHAM	2.6		(B)	DNF
SIKINI	C.L. JUSTICE	R.N.S.A.	1.9		(A)	DNF
SUNDOWNER IV	R. HIGGINS	R.VIC.	2.7		(C)	DNF
STARWAGON	R.O. GILBERT	SEATTLE	2.3		(B)	DNF
EN PASSANT	H. MINOR	EVERETT	2.3		(B)	DNF
AKVAVIT	G.W. THORSEN	S. SOUND	2.9		(C)	DNF
CHEVALIER	C. WHITE	MAPLE BAY	2.0		(A)	DNF
SPRAY	E. BAUMUELLER	CORINTHIAN	1.9		(A)	DNF
ANDIAMO	R.P. CARERE	R.VIC.	2.5		(B)	DNF
MIRAGE	F.M. JONES	EDMONDS	2.7		(C)	DNF
KAOS	B. RUDOLPH	CORINTHIAN	1.7		(A)	DNF
TREK	G. JAMES	GIG HARBOUR	2.6		(B)	DNF
CHEROKEE	M. MULCAHY/F. RAY	3 TREE PT.	2.3		(B)	DNF
WINDSONG	R.G. BARNHART	BELLINGHAM	2.1		(A)	DNF
EXODUS	R.B. ROBERTS	CORINTHIAN	2.8		(C)	DNF
LADY JANE	D. McKAY	TACOMA	3.5		(C)	DNF
MARY POWELL	W.P. LAWSON	W.VAN.	2.1		(A)	DNF
BACARRA II	J. BELL	C.F.S.A.	2.9		(C)	DNF

YACHT	SKIPPER(S)	CLUB	RATING	DIVISION	OVERALL
SNOWBIRD	P. KARLSEN	W.VAN.	2.1	(A)	DNF
SWIFT I	R.D. HOFFMAN, M.D.	EVERETT	3.1	(C)	DNF
TOLO TSOLO	E.E. WOODSON	ANACORTES	2.5	(B)	DNF
TATUA	H. PALMER/F.A. DANZ	SEATTLE	1.8	(A)	DNF
RAVEN	L. OSTENSOE	R.VIC.	2.5	(B)	DNF
STAR	D. MEERES	KITSILANO	1.8	(A)	DNF
VIVA	D.M. BLAKEMORE	CORINTHIAN	1.8	(A)	DNF
DUTCH FLUTE	R. KLEIN, M.D.	TACOMA	2.6	(B)	DNF
HUSSY	N. KREBILL	BELLINGHAM	1.8	(A)	DNF
CORMORANT	H.H. BOYD, M.D.	CORINTHIAN	2.1	(A)	DNF
LA RUINA	R.J. GIBBONS	SEATTLE	2.0	(A)	DNF
MAMATEEK	DR. C. CRONHELM	R.VAN.	2.2	(B)	DNF
SKOOKUM	B.W. BROCKWAY	CORINTHIAN	2.2	(B)	DNF
THOMASINE	J.H. COOK		3.0	(C)	DNF
ORANGO-TANG	N.S. ELLIOTT	KITSILANO	1.9	(A)	DNF
PABET	J. GOURLEY	R.VAN.	2.0	(A)	DNS
WHITE SQUALL	G. TEATS, M.D.	TACOMA	1.9	(A)	DNS
HANSA	J.B. HEITMAN	GIG HARBOUR	2.3	(B)	DNS
PLEIADES	LANG & ASSOC.	CORINTHIAN	2.5	(B)	DNS
POWDER SNOW	D.C. SELMAN	R.VAN.	1.9	(A)	DNS

OFFICIAL START TIME: 10/00/00

JUAN DE FUCA (I.O.R.) 1975
RESULTS

YACHT	SKIPPER(S)	CLUB	RATING	COR ELAPSE TIME	POSITION DIVISION	OVERALL
BLUE FOX	J.D. GONYEA	TACOMA	21.9	12/07/56	1(2)	1
FORTUNE COOKIE FACT.	B. STEPHENS	CORINTHIAN	18.0	12/14/35	2(2)	2
FUTURE SHOCK	C. BOUFFIOU	CORINTHIAN	21.8	12/19/38	3(2)	3
STREAKER	R. PRATT	CORINTHIAN	21.6	12/49/13	4(2)	4
DOUBLE ENTRY	O.A. LIEBERT	R.VAN.	24.7	12/49/58	1(1)	5
VANDAL II	S. MERRIMAN	R.VIC.	23.5	12/52/17	2(1)	6
DIFFERENT DRUMMER	B.L. GRIFFIN	BELLINGHAM	24.3	12/53/18	3(1)	7
GEM	R. FIEDLER	CORINTHIAN	24.5	12/55/35	4(1)	8
SMALL WORLD	G.W. SIBOLD	S. SOUND	24.3	13/04/30	5(1)	9
CAYAMBE	G. BYSTEDT	CORINTHIAN	22.0	13/10/53	5(2)	10
PUFF II	J. WOODWARD	R.VIC.	23.9	13/12/01	6(1)	11
FIREBIRD	G.L. BURK	OLYMPIA	22.1	13/15/35	7(1)	12
GRETEL II	H. DRIEHUYZEN	W.VAN.	22.8	13/16/56	8(1)	13
PAX	F. RHODES	R.VIC.	24.9	13/19/37	9(1)	14
PROFESSOR	J.E. MATTHEWS	R.VIC.	17.8	13/20/51	6(2)	15
LORELEI II	J. ROSINSKI	BELLINGHAM	24.3	13/29/20	10(1)	16
JUNE BUG	R.E. VYNNE	SEATTLE	21.6	13/32/28	7(2)	17
AVALANCHE	R.C. KERSHAW	CORINTHIAN	24.3	13/44/35	11(1)	18
QUORUM	D.M. FIELD	CORINTHIAN	24.5	13/46/27	12(1)	19
PUSILLANIMOUS	D.B. JONES/G. WATSON	SEATTLE	17.9	13/51/20	8(2)	20
AMBUSH	V.F. BINGHAM	PT. ANGELES	24.5	14/00/38	13(1)	21
GOTCHA	B. DIEHL	BELLINGHAM	18.0	14/06/21	9(2)	22
SEA SPELL	J. HUIBERS	R.VIC.	21.3	14/09/40	10(2)	23
PANACHE	D. DUGGAN	W.VAN.	21.7	14/12/22	11(2)	24
TARQUIN III	G. JOHNSTONE	R.VIC.	21.0	14/13/40	12(2)	25
SNOWBIRD	DR. K. MONDLOCH	SINCLAIR	23.0	14/13/58	14(1)	26
DEPARTURE	J. MILLER	R.VIC.	23.9	14/16/35	15(1)	27
WINDSHIFT	F.W. HAYES	SEATTLE	21.7	14/20/18	13(2)	28
NORN	O. EKROM	CORINTHIAN	24.8	14/28/20	16(1)	29
CIRRUS	T. TATE	ROSE CITY	21.6	14/32/43	14(2)	30
JACKAROE	R.L. HILLS	PT. TWNSND.	24.1	14/32/46	17(1)	31
GO-O-O-O	P. BYRNE	KITSILANO	18.0	14/45/01	15(2)	32
FIRST MORNING	G. HODGE	BELLINGHAM	21.7	14/59/13	16(2)	33
IGNITOR	M.C. MARSHEL	CORINTHIAN	21.7	15/10/44	17(2)	34
KIM	I.C. DUNCANSON	R.VIC.	23.0	15/38/23	18(1)	35
SUNDANCE	R. SCHULER	CORINTHIAN	21.4	15/49/51	18(2)	36
PAPRIKA	F. MUSSON	W.VAN.	21.7	15/58/43	19(2)	37
SEAQUIN	R.S. MARSHALL	CORINTHIAN	20.9	16/26/49	20(2)	38
INFIDEL	R.J. WHITFIELD	EAGLE HARB.	22.5	16/49/04	19(1)	39
UMPKA	J.R. BOOTH	R.VIC.	21.1	19/15/20	21(2)	40
GALENAIA II	G.A. DUFOUR	R.VIC.	20.6	22/45/44	22(2)	41
VOLARE	J. CICERI	R.VIC.	21.4	24/22/18	23(2)	42
SMUGGLER	C.F. LANZINGER	CORINTHIAN	18.0		(2)	DSQ
SOLICITOR	G.A. MEBS	R.VIC.	24.5		(1)	DSQ
ELAN	R. ZELL	CORINTHIAN	23.4		(1)	DNF
TOPIC	I. SMITH	TACOMA	23.6		(1)	DNF

YACHT	SKIPPER(S)	CLUB	RATING		
CALIENTE	M. SMITH/D. SMITH	CORINTHIAN	21.9	(2)	DNF
LOWENSLO	D. CLARK	SEATTLE	17.9	(2)	DNF
CONSULTATION	D. ANDERSON	S. SOUND	24.4	(1)	DNF
GALEB	G.Z. CESAREC	CANOE BAY	18.1	(2)	DNF
KWIN KWIN WHIUKA	P.K. RENTIERS/C.H. DAVIDSON	R.VAN.	24.5	(1)	DNF

JUAN DE FUCA (P.H.R.F.) 1975 RESULTS

OFFICIAL START TIME: 10/00/00

YACHT	SKIPPER(S)	CLUB	RATING	COR ELAPSE TIME	POSITION DIVISION	POSITION OVERALL
LUCY ALICE	W.H. GARDNER	CORINTHIAN	3.7	12/32/39	1(F)	1
UNION DEPOT	R.L. RUE	TACOMA	3.0	12/38/12	1(D)	2
TIARA III	W. JENSEN	CANOE BAY	3.0	12/57/20	2(D)	3
SASSAFRAS	J. WILKE	CORINTHIAN	3.1	13/01/03	3(D)	4
ENCOUNTER	R. ANDREWS/H.M. BACON	R.VIC.	2.8	13/08/44	4(D)	5
MORAG	R.F. JENKINS	R.VAN.	2.9	13/25/19	5(D)	6
JOLLY OLLY III	R. COCKBURN	TURKEY HD.	2.8	13/31/43	6(D)	7
AURIGA	T. CATTELL	W.VAN.	3.4	13/35/58	1(E)	8
CELERITY	J. SPENCER	KITSILANO	2.9	13/39/51	7(D)	9
WANIGAN	J. OREM	BELLINGHAM	2.8	13/40/59	8(D)	10
HUSTLER	J. PATTERSON	CANOE BAY	3.6	13/43/57	2(F)	11
THUMPER	B. FOWLER	ANACORTES	2.8	13/44/05	9(D)	12
MALDA	C. HOGAN	CANOE BAY	2.9	13/45/48	10(D)	13
THISTLEDOWN	D. FEELEY	PT. ANGELES	3.1	13/52/05	11(D)	14
DENT DE LION	G.E. MOHLER	PT. ANGELES	2.8	13/54/44	12(D)	15
CALLALOO	J. CATLEY	R.VAN.	2.9	13/54/49	13(D)	16
BRANDY	R. YORK	CORINTHIAN	2.8	13/59/24	14(D)	17
DYNASTY II	J.F. FAIRLEY	W.VAN.	2.9	14/05/16	15(D)	18
BUFFLEHEAD II	K.R. MARTIN	R.VAN.	3.2	14/06/35	2(E)	19
SIRIUS	D.K. WATERFALL	MAPLE BAY	3.3	14/12/55	3(E)	20
GEORGIA GIRL	W. MARTIN	CANOE COVE	3.7	14/26/46	3(F)	21
TENUVIEL	T. WIGGIN	TACOMA	3.3	14/31/17	4(E)	22
FILEY BRIGG	J.M. WEIR	R.VIC.	3.2	14/34/40	5(E)	23
AVENGER II	A.S. BARKER	W.VAN.	3.1	14/35/30	16(D)	24
SLY FOX	J.B. FOSTER	R.VIC.	3.1	14/51/25	17(D)	25
SKILFISH	D.R. WEST	W.VAN.	2.9	15/01/58	18(D)	26
OBSESSION	DR. M.L. HENRY	TACOMA	2.9	15/08/30	19(D)	27
PANIC	C.D. WHIDDEN	PT. ANGELES	3.0	15/33/54	20(D)	28
FRED JR.	DR. G. WILKINS	R.VAN.	3.1	15/42/16	21(D)	29
KISMET	S.A. CLARKE	TACOMA	3.2	16/39/37	6(E)	30
FREEWHEELER	R.L. SOURS, JR.	CORINTHIAN	3.0	16/47/27	22(D)	31
WHITE SQUALL	P. WHITE	CANOE BAY	3.3	17/21/11	7(E)	32
RISQUE	J.A. POKELA	TACOMA	3.6	18/36/45	4(F)	33
NORTH STAR	T.C. McAFEE	CORINTHIAN	3.3	18/58/36	8(E)	34
LA MARQUISE II	J.P. LE DALLIC	C.F.S.A.	3.2	19/25/15	9(E)	35
EL CID	R.A. BEAST	SEATTLE	3.1	19/41/53	23(D)	36
LAIRIG	H.E. BUCHANAN	R.VIC.	3.6	20/46/35	5(F)	37
PEACHES	DR. T. SERR	PT. ANGELES	3.7	21/10/17	6(F)	38
MORNING LIGHT	T.L. GRAINGER	3 TREE PT.	3.2	21/17/33	10(E)	39
WHIPPET	C.E. OLSON	EDMONDS	3.1	21/43/57	24(D)	40
ISIS	J. ELLIS	R.VIC.	3.3	22/05/21	11(E)	41
LIMFJORD	B. JESPERSEN	CANOE BAY	4.0	22/16/48	7(F)	42
R.T. WELLAINE	E.R.J. RAMSAY	TURKEY HD.	3.8	22/39/31	8(F)	43
NIKE	B. KING	MAPLE BAY	3.6	22/45/46	9(F)	44
KRISTEDA	J.P. GAEDKE	PT. MADISON	3.4	23/01/23	12(E)	45
NOOSA	R.VAN DEN DRIESSCHE	TURKEY HD.	3.3	23/04/14	13(E)	46
TWO-FOR-ONE	J.V. COLEMAN	MAPLE BAY	3.3	23/07/45	14(E)	47
ELACKA	J.K. MARTIN	R.VIC.	4.0	23/24/34	10(F)	48
CALABASH	R. GOODALL	R.VAN.	3.2	23/25/27	15(E)	49
THE SLOOP JOHN B	J.B. IVENS	TSAWWASSEN	3.7	23/29/09	11(F)	50
CAPRICE	H.R. GARDNER	C.F.S.A.	4.0	23/36/26	12(F)	51
TINKERBELLE	L.W. RIGGS	PT. ANGELES	3.8	23/35/25	13(F)	52
FREJA	W. PINCHIN	W.VAN.	3.4	24/10/25	16(E)	53
QUEST	R.M. EICHLER	SEATTLE	4.0	37/15/51	14(F)	54
STREGA	D. BRINK	CORINTHIAN	3.4		(E)	DSQ
DESTINY	W.J. KING	PORTLAND	2.8		(D)	DSQ
LABAMBA	A. NISKA	PT. TWNSHND.	3.8		(F)	DSQ
PEREGRINE	R.D. ROWLETTE	C.F.S.A.	3.3		(E)	DSQ
SURABAYA	R. WILCOX	W.VAN.	3.0		(D)	DNF
WINDSONG II	R.C. BROWN	CORINTHIAN	4.0		(F)	DNF
WHALES TALE	G. COLE	CORINTHIAN	3.0		(D)	DNF

MARILYN L	R. CARLSON	PT. ANGELES	3.8		(F)	DNF
CAMBRIA	H.C. CHARLESWORTH	R.VIC.	3.3		(E)	DNF
ENCHANTRESS	B. FRANCIS	R.VAN.	2.9		(D)	DNF
NEPTUNE	J. DRYDEN	R.VIC.	3.4		(E)	DNF
VIKING	A. DICKINSON	CANOE BAY	3.2		(E)	DNF
SUNBURST	R. LINKLETTER	PT. ANGELES	2.9		(D)	DNF
ARLIS II	L. HILLS	CORINTHIAN	3.3		(E)	DNF
HELSA	G. CARLSTROM	S. SOUND	3.1		(D)	DNF
LOON	T. SCHNEIDER	CORINTHIAN	3.7		(F)	DNS

PACIFIC INTERNATIONAL YACHTING ASSOCIATION
SWIFTSURE LIGHTSHIP CLASSIC AND JUAN DE FUCA RACE
1976 TROPHY WINNERS

RESULTS AT: WEDNESDAY, JUNE 16, 1976

SWIFTSURE (I.O.R.)

SWIFTSURE TROPHY (OVERALL HANDICAP WINNER)	ALAN HOLT	CORINTHIAN	LADYBUG
ROYAL CANADIAN NAVY TROPHY (1ST YACHT TO ROUND SWIFTSURE MARK)	JOHN B. KILROY	SEATTLE	KIALOA
CITY OF VICTORIA TROPHY (1ST YACHT TO FINISH)	JOHN B. KILROY	SEATTLE	KIALOA
OCEAN CEMENT TROPHY (FIRST IN DIVISION 1)	WILLIAM NIENI J.	SEATTLE	JOLI
T. EATON TROPHY (FIRST IN DIVISION 2)	GERRY MAURER	SEATTLE	SURPRISE
CITY OF SEATTLE TROPHY (FIRST IN DIVISION 3)	GREGORY OLIVER	R.VIC.Y.C.	DISTANT DRUMMER
ROYAL VANCOUVER YACHT CLUB TROPHY (FIRST IN DIVISION 4)	ALAN HOLT	CORINTHIAN	LADYBUG

SWIFTSURE (P.H.R.F.)

CORINTHIAN YACHT CLUB TROPHY (FIRST IN DIVISION A)	S. RASMUSSEN	R.VAN.Y.C.	SAGA
STORMY WEATHER TROPHY (FIRST IN DIVISION B)	T.B. WHEELER	CORINTHIAN	BORDERLORD
CAPE FLATTERY TROPHY (FIRST IN DIVISION C)	JACK VOLL	PT MADISON	AFRICAN STAR

JUAN DE FUCA (I.O.R.)

SAN JUAN TROPHY (FIRST YACHT TO FINISH)	JAN HUIBERS	R.VIC.Y.C.	SEA SPELL
ROYAL VICTORIA YACHT CLUB TROPHY (FIRST IN DIVISION 6)	JAN HUIBERS	R.VIC.Y.C.	SEA SPELL
ROYAL CANADIAN NAVY TROPHY (FIRST IN DIVISION 7)	G. S. WILKINS	R.VAN.Y.C.	FRED AGAIN

JUAN DE FUCA (P.H.R.F.)

ANACORTES YACHT CLUB TROPHY (FIRST IN DIVISION D)	KEN CLARK	R.VAN.Y.C.	LARA
(FIRST IN DIVISION E)	STAN JOHNSON	WILLAMETTE	COURAGE PLUS
(FIRST IN DIVISION F)	GLEN McCORMICK	QTRMSTR	SARA

SWIFTSURE YACHTING CLASSIC 1976
FINAL RESULTS

The attached results reflect the outcome of the protest hearings held on June 12, 1976, and the time allowances made by the Race Committee to Yachts that were involved in search and rescue activities.

The following criteria were used as the basis for determining equitable time allowances:

(a) That the report or request for time allowance must be made immediately on finishing.

(b) That it is mandatory for a yacht to respond to a call for help and to go to the aid of a yacht in distress.

(c) That a yacht shall not be penalized for responding to a call for help and, conversely, a yacht shall not gain undue competitive advantage from any time allowance granted.

The method adopted in the current situation for determining the allowances was to assign the best of the following:

(A) A calculated finish time based on the position of the yacht on rounding Swiftsure mark.

(B) A calculated finish time based on the time the yacht rounded Swiftsure mark plus the average time taken by a sampling of similarly rated yachts to sail from Swiftsure mark to the finish.

(C) The actual finish time of the yacht.

		(A)	(B)	(C)
350	ANNIE CADBY	18-09-11	18-12-14	**17-10-01**
9933	SINFUL	**16-56-40**	17-22-04	18-48-48
19579	SOCKEYE	19-12-00	**18-27-31**	19-39-08
29430	PREDICAMENT	16-56-43	**16-48-41**	17-17-41
29604	FLIRTATION	18-30-15	**18-14-21**	18-30-15
29650	FROSTBITE	**17-54-07**	18-07-14	19-10-13
39602	CYGNET	16-40-44	**16-19-55**	16-54-05
39966	LADY BUG	**17-19-18**	19-59-14	17-22-57
49020	SHUR LAY	18-49-00	**18-08-41**	19-37-15
49100	LEPSOYA	**16-54-15**	17-18-32	17-18-36

In addition to the above, the yachts EXODUS and P'ZAZZ also responded to search and rescue requirements but failed to file a report in reasonable time on finishing.

The committee appreciates the search efforts that were made under extremely severe conditions and wishes to commend all yachts that responded to the call for help. It is hoped that all competitors will appreciate the difficulty facing the committee in making a fair compensation.

F.A.C. Piddington, Chairman, Swiftsure Committee,

16 JUNE 1976
OFFICIAL START TIME: 9/10/0

SWIFTSURE (I.O.R.) 1976
RESULTS

YACHT NAME	SKIPPER(S)	CLUB	RATING	COR ELAPSE TIME	POSITION DIVISION	OVERALL
LADYBUG	ALAN HOLT	CORINTHIAN	21.70	24/39/19	1(4)	1
SCAMPI	E.S. WATERMAN	R.VAN.Y.C.	22.40A	25/15/ 3	2(4)	2
JADAH	PHIL TUCKER	CORINTHIAN	24.50	25/43/ 9	3(4)	3
AMERICAN EXPRESS	H. STANLEY JR.	PORTLAND	23.40A	25/45/ 9	4(4)	4

GHOST RIDER	RICK MOELLER	PORTLAND	24.50	25/57/47	5(4)	5
CANDIDE	PHILLIP BRAZEAU	SEATTLE	24.50	26/ 2/26	6(4)	6
TAPOCKETA	ROBERT NEWELL	BELLINGHAM	24.50	26/ 2/49	7(4)	7
AKKA	RALPH MARX	TACOMA	25.80A	26/ 4/38	8(4)	8
DISTANT DRUMMER	GREGORY OLIVER	R.VIC.Y.C.	27.30A	26/ 8/ 1	1(3)	9
NAHMA	KEN MAXWELL	CORINTHIAN	24.50	26/10/39	9(4)	10
COUNTRY STYLE	STEVE MERRIMAN	R.VIC.Y.C.	27.50	26/16/ 4	2(3)	11
SALLY LIGHTFOOT	TOM FRIENDLAND	BELLINGHAM	27.80A	26/16/47	3(3)	12
SHRIKE	CHUCK CROFT	WEST VAN	27.50	26/16/58	4(3)	13
MUSTARD SEED	HERMAN/GRIMES/SCIMELA	EDMONDS	27.50	26/17/30	5(3)	14
GRETEL II	HEIN DRIEHUYZEN	WEST VAN	27.50	26/21/44	6(3)	15
ULTIMATUM	A.L. FOLEY	R.VAN.Y.C.	27.80A	26/22/52	7(3)	16
HUCKLEBERRY	KEN REID	WEST VAN	25.70A	26/22/55	10(4)	17
ERRIGAL	HUGH PORTER	R.VIC.Y.C.	26.80	26/23/26	11(4)	18
TSUNAKI	C.J. MORAN/R.D. MOULTON	CORINTHIAN	26.30A	26/23/57	8(3)	19
JOLI	WILLIAM NIEMI J.	SEATTLE	54.90A	26/24/ 5	1(1)	20
WOTAN	BILL BURDICK	CORINTHIAN	27.80	26/24/16	9(3)	21
CYGNET	D. WAYNE SMYTH	OLYMPIA	28.70	26/25/15	10(3)	22
GOODBYE	T.W. LONEY	R.VIC.Y.C.	27.30A	26/25/16	11(3)	23
JOLLY OLLY IV	VERN RUSKIN	R.VAN.Y.C.	27.50	26/36/36	12(3)	24
BETELGEUSE	TERRY GUEST	R.VAN.Y.C.	27.50	26/38/57	13(3)	25
WEATHERLY	LYNN SOMMERS/ALAN BUCHAN	TACOMA	53.30A	26/43/37	2(1)	26
LEPSOYA	JON RUNSTAD/MARDA RUNSTAD	SEATTLE	27.90	26/44/31	14(3)	27
ROGUE	LEWIS FOX	CORINTHIAN	27.50A	26/46/ 6	15(3)	28
SEA ROBIN	ARCHIE CAMPBELL	R.VIC.Y.C.	24.40A	26/46/29	12(4)	29
RAGTIME	W. WHITE, MD/W. PASQUINI	LONG BEACH	62.20A	26/46/53	3(1)	30
MOODY TOO	JIM PINE	WEST VAN	26.60	26/49/52	13(4)	31
TRUMPETER OF JERICHO	J.H. LONG	R.VAN.Y.C.	28.90	26/50/45	16(3)	32
TRINGA	FRED GARDINER	R.VIC.Y.C.	27.30A	26/51/11	17(3)	33
SURPRISE	GERRY MAURER	SEATTLE	29.60	26/53/49	1(2)	34
SCARAMOUCHE	R.M. ALEXANDER	SEATTLE	36.80A	26/54/22	4(1)	35
MARY D II	DARREL DAVIS	PT. ANGELES	24.60	26/55/38	14(4)	36
THE PEARCE ARROW	KEN PEARCE	R.VAN.Y.C.	27.50	26/57/12	18(3)	37
STRIDER	KEITH JOHNSON	CORINTHIAN	25.70A	26/58/50	15(4)	38
KIALOA	JOHN B. KILROY	SEATTLE	67.40	27/ 0/41	5(1)	39
DIRIGO	JACK TAYLOR	CORINTHIAN	27.50	27/ 2/23	19(3)	40
TRANQUIL PASSAGE	LEN VAN EGMOND	KITSILANO	29.80A	27/ 3/16	2(2)	41
BORU	DONALD BYRNE	R.VAN.Y.C.	27.50	27/ 3/59	20(3)	42
GOOD NEWS	E.W. DE KONING	PORTLAND	29.30A	27/13/50	3(2)	43
SNAKEYES	A.S. WILSON	SEATTLE	29.90	27/14/14	4(2)	44
SUNBIRD	ALVIN NAROD	R.VAN.Y.C.	42.70A	27/16/36	6(1)	45
GOGAMA	DAVID EVERETT	R.VAN.Y.C.	31.70A	27/16/52	5(2)	46
THUNDER	W.J. KING	PORTLAND	27.50	27/18/41	21(3)	47
MYFANWY	G.D. JONES	R.N.S.A.	23.00A	27/20/19	16(4)	48
DORLES	WILLIS KLUDT	THREE TREE	28.20	27/20/24	22(3)	49
HABITAT	P.C.G. RICHARDS	WEST VAN	28.10	27/23/19	23(3)	50
DEFIANCE	RON HART	TACOMA	31.60A	27/23/52	6(2)	51
HEATHER	JOHN BUCHAN	SEATTLE	32.00	27/27/33	7(2)	52
KANATA	V. PLAVSIC	WEST VAN	32.00	27/28/23	8(2)	53
TERNA III	P. CHRISTOFFERSEN	WEST VAN	32.00A	27/31/17	9(2)	54
LUCIFER	AL NELSON	R.VIC. Y.C.	31.60A	27/31/20	10(2)	55
ELIXIR	JOHN GRAHAM	SEATTLE	27.40A	27/32/35	24(3)	56
PACHENA	JOHN NEWTON	WEST VAN	32.20	27/35/58	11(2)	57
AMERICAN FLYER	FRED W. BIEKER	PORTLAND	31.80	27/37/15	12(2)	58
IMPATIENCE	J.E. TRENHOLME/J. DAVIES	R.VIC.Y.C.	24.60	27/44/ 8	17(4)	59
NAMBA	A.J.B. FORSYTH	R.VAN.Y.C.	32.60A	27/44/12	7(1)	60
FIRECRACKER	L. SCHUELER, JR.	PT. ANGELES	25.10A	27/46/ 1	18(4)	61
NERITA	BOB UTTER	CORINTHIAN	31.90A	27/53/58	13(2)	62
RACE PASSAGE	PAUL McCULLOUGH	BREMERTON	34.30A	27/54/ 1	8(1)	63
GOLD RUSH	NATHAN RUSSELL	SHILSHOLE	30.60A	27/56/36	14(2)	64
BONNIE	EARL L. MILLER	PT. MADISON	39.90	28/ 0/ 8	9(1)	65
MISTRESS II	I.W. VARLEY, MD	EVERETT	32.60	28/ 1/ 9	15(2)	66
SERVUS	H.G. STRICKER	R.VIC.Y.C.	25.00A	28/ 9/ 4	19(4)	67
TAVEUNI	R.I. THIEME	EVERETT	32.10A	28/11/36	10(1)	68
NAKNEK	RICHARD NELSON	R.VAN.Y.C.	38.60A	28/23/17	11(1)	69
COHO	G. BRANDLMAYR	R.VAN.Y.C.	38.90A	28/26/ 5	12(1)	70
ANNIE CADBY	LOUIS LINDHOLM	R.VIC. V.C.	33.90	28/35/30	13(1)	71
ANDANTE II	FRED PATTERSON	R.VAN.Y.C.	37.80A	28/36/24	14(1)	72
EPIC	C. SCHIFF	CORINTHIAN	37.90A	28/37/44	15(1)	73
ASSAULT	PRICE/ROBERT STOKES	THREE TREE	33.50	28/47/41	16(1)	74
NIGHTHAWK	EDWARD ODISHAW	KITSILANO	28.20A	28/49/ 6	16(2)	75

YACHT NAME	SKIPPER(S)	CLUB	RATING	COR ELAPSE TIME	POSITION DIVISION	OVERALL
SATURDAY'S CHILD	C. BRAIN	CORINTHIAN	39.40	29/34/49	17(1)	76
DIAMOND HEAD	H.L. KOTKINS	SEATTLE	47.90A	30/ 6/27	18(1)	77
GRAYBEARD	LOL KILLAM	R.VAN.Y.C.	65.60A	DNF	DNF(1)	DNF
MEG	BOB HOSIE, MD	R.VIC.Y.C.	27.30A	DNF	DNF(3)	DNF
WHITE MIST	DORR ANDERSON	SEATTLE	22.40	DNF	DNF(4)	DNF
VATICAN II	MIKE POPE	KITSILANO	24.50	DNF	DNF(4)	DNF
NATIVE DANCER	WILBUR WILLARD	SHILSHOLE	24.70A	DNF	DNF(4)	DNF
DAMN YANKEE	HAROLD SARGENT	OLYMPIA	27.40A	DNF	DNF(3)	DNF
RUNAWAY	R. McCULLOUGH	CORINTHIAN	27.00A	DNF	DNF(4)	DNF
SHAZAM	RANDY MUELLER	CORINTHIAN	27.70A	DNF	DNF(3)	DNF
BRER RABBIT	MIKE LUND	CORINTHIAN	29.90	DNF	DNF(2)	DNF
ELECTRA	BEN DEMBART	CORINTHIAN	24.50	DNF	DNF(4)	DNF
TZORES	TIM ERICKSON	CORINTHIAN	24.50	DNF	DNF(4)	DNF
PROSPECTOR	TOM GEISNESS/LARRY SHORETT	SEATTLE	27.50	DNF	DNF(3)	DNF
SUNRISE	THOMAS HAYES	SEATTLE	21.70	DNF	DNF(4)	DNF
OUTRAGEOUS	TED BURNS, MD	BREMERTON	30.00	DNS	DNS(2)	DNS

16 JUNE 1976
OFFICIAL START TIME: 9/25/0

SWIFTSURE (P.H.R.F.) 1976
RESULTS

YACHT NAME	SKIPPER(S)	CLUB	RATING	COR ELAPSE TIME	POSITION DIVISION	OVERALL
AFRICAN STAR	JACK VOLL	PT. MADISON	3.55	24/52/ 9	1(C)	1
PREDICAMENT II	JAMES SMITH	EDMONDS	2.75	25/ 9/ 8	2(C)	2
RENEGADE	SHERWOOD SMITH	S. SOUND	2.90	25/38/28	3(C)	3
SHAMROCK	GLENN BYRD	S. SOUND	2.90	25/44/32	4(C)	4
PRIMO	ROBERT DENBY/GEORGE LOWE	CORINTHIAN	2.75	26/ 5/ 4	5(C)	5
BORDERLORD	T.B. WHEELER	CORINTHIAN	2.25	26/12/46	1(B)	6
SURGER	KEN E. WRIGHT	KITSILANO	2.60	26/14/48	2(B)	7
NINA DEL MAR	C.J. McCANN	OLYMPIA	3.20	26/15/14	6(C)	8
STARWAGON	R.O. GILBERT	SEATTLE	2.30	26/16/25	3(B)	9
HMCS ORIOLE	LCDR WALKER	C.F.S.A.	2.50	26/16/44	4(B)	10
SCHLINGEL	MICHAEL TREIT	EDMONDS	2.40	26/16/46	5(B)	11
JOLLY ROGER III	ROGER WHEELER	CORINTHIAN	2.45	26/20/59	6(B)	12
FRIENDSHIP	TOM GIDLUND/EVAN SCHWAB	CORINTHIAN	2.50	26/21/ 0	7(B)	13
SMALL WORLD II	GENE W. SIBOLD	S. SOUND	2.30	26/21/ 7	8(B)	14
GAMIN	LON ROBINSON	SEATTLE	2.20	26/23/ 3	9(B)	15
SAGA	S. RASMUSSEN	R.VAN.Y.C.	2.10	26/23/34	1(A)	16
ELISHEBA	MILES MILLER	CORINTHIAN	2.25	26/25/51	10(B)	17
P'ZAZZ	BILL NELSON	CORINTHIAN	2.40	26/26/45	11(B)	18
SHUR LAY	V. McCULLOUGH	CORINTHIAN	2.75	26/29/ 8	7(C)	19
TANGENT II	ANTHONY LOACH	WEST VAN	2.10	26/29/54	2(A)	20
EN PASSANT	HUGH MINOR	EVERETT	2.25	26/30/38	12(B)	21
CITATION	DAVE ROCKETT	LAHAINA	2.30	26/31/26	13(B)	22
CHEROKEE	MIKE MULCAHY/FRED RAY	THREE TREE	2.20	26/37/56	14(B)	23
SINFUL	R.F. HARRISON	WEST VAN	2.15	26/38/51	3(A)	24
OUTWARD BOUND	DONALD A. FLYNN	SEATTLE	2.40	26/39/34	15(B)	25
LIZA-K	K.L. PARTLOW II	OLYMPIA	2.40	26/39/48	16(B)	26
SOCKEYE	PETER KEATE	R.VAN.Y.C.	2.80	26/41/10	8(C)	27
NAUTILUS	L. NEVLER, MD	CORINTHIAN	2.30	26/43/23	17(B)	28
LANCER	NORMAN LARABEE	CORINTHIAN	2.40	26/46/18	18(B)	29
LA RUINA	R.J. GIBBONS	SEATTLE	2.10	26/49/11	4(A)	30
ORANGO-TANG	NORMAN ELLIOTT	KITSILANO	2.10	26/50/41	5(A)	31
IMPOSSIBLE	JAMES WHITTAKER	CORINTHIAN	3.70	26/51/42	9(C)	32
HAFA ADAI	A. VERMAREN	TACOMA	2.70	26/53/28	10(C)	33
MOTHER NATURE	WED JOHNSTON/BOB PERRY	SEATTLE	2.30	26/54/11	19(B)	34
BARBARA	WYNN E. KAMPE	CORINTHIAN	2.05	26/54/13	6(A)	35
DOMINIQUE	WILLI FAHNING	CANOE BAY	2.20	26/57/37	20(B)	36
RAG MAN	DAN McKINNON	EVERETT	1.80	27/ 4/ 4	7(A)	37
SPECTRE	JOHN CAHILL, MD	SEATTLE	1.85	27/ 6/10	8(A)	38
WHITE SQUALL	G. TEATS, MD	TACOMA	1.85	27/ 6/29	9(A)	39
LA BRISA	W. VAN LEEUWEN	WEST VAN	2.20	27/ 8/11	21(B)	40
WILLOW WIND	HARVARD PALMER/FREDRIC DANZ	SEATTLE	1.95	27/11/18	10(A)	41
GYPSY DANCER	JAMES VOGT	CORINTHIAN	2.85	27/11/48	11(C)	42
MOONGLOW III	RON MOBLO	CORINTHIAN	1.80	27/12/13	11(A)	43
THUNDER III	W.T.H. CLARK	R.VIC.Y.C.	2.70	27/12/31	12(C)	44
PABET	JOHN GOURLEY	R.VAN.Y.C.	2.05	27/14/44	12(A)	45
RAIN DROP	J. GAINER	CORINTHIAN	2.00	27/15/37	13(A)	46
OLYMPIAN	P.G. SCHMIDT	SEATTLE	1.85	27/17/11	14(A)	47
MALTESE FALCON	RUSS SCHULKE	CORINTHIAN	2.40	27/17/36	22(B)	48
AIR AFFAIR	C.H. DAVIDSON/P.K. RENTIERS	R.VAN.Y.C.	1.80	27/17/55	15(A)	49
EROS	S.L. FETTERS	SEATTLE	1.80	27/19/52	16(A)	50
SUNFLOWER	M.B. MADENWALD	ANACORTES	2.40	27/20/18	23(B)	51

183

FROSTBITE	ROBERT B. FROST	CORINTHIAN	2.25	27/22/40	24(B)	52
BALALAIKA	ROBERT HURLOW	CORINTHIAN	2.70	27/23/ 1	13(C)	53
POWDER SNOW	DONALD SELMAN	R.VAN.Y.C.	2.00	27/25/24	17(A)	54
OUTRAGEOUS	JOHN HARDIMAN	CORINTHIAN	1.80	27/26/31	18(A)	55
RUNNING SHOE	JOHN JARMAN	R.VAN.Y.C.	2.85	27/26/43	14(C)	56
FIREBRAND	RUSSELL NEWMAN	SEATTLE	1.95	27/26/57	19(A)	57
RASCAL	DENNIS THORNTON	CORINTHIAN	2.40	27/28/10	25(B)	58
VADEMECUM	STEFAN CLARKE	TACOMA	2.50	27/29/50	26(B)	59
TARTAN	DAN INNES/RON ROSENBERGER	ANACORTES	2.40	27/30/54	27(B)	60
SIKINI	C.L. JUSTICE	R.N.S.A.	2.40	27/32/51	28(B)	61
CUBARA	KENT LINDSEY	PENTICTON	2.25	27/33/ 8	29(B)	62
ASTROLOGER	GUY T. ELLIOTT	TACOMA	2.65	27/33/23	30(B)	63
RAPTURE	PAT JUTTE/T.J. GILLESPIE	CORINTHIAN	2.45	27/33/43	31(B)	64
YANKEE GIRL	JOE McDONALD	SEATTLE	1.80	27/35/58	20(A)	65
PEGASUS	JOHN G. BECKER	ORG. CORIN	2.90	27/36/42	15(C)	66
CHIMO V	IAN L. DROST	R.N.S.A.	1.90	27/37/12	21(A)	67
WINDWARD MARK	VIC PALMER	MAPLE BAY	1.90	27/41/52	22(A)	68
FLIRTATION	JACK TUTTLE	CORINTHIAN	2.35	27/45/11	32(B)	69
CALLALOO	JOHN CATLEY	R.VAN.Y.C.	2.90	27/45/33	16(C)	70
STAR	DAVE MEERES	KITSILANO	1.80	27/46/23	23(A)	71
ARROW	ART ARMSTRONG	EVERETT	2.10	27/47/ 8	24(A)	72
DISCOVERY	JOHN DUNFIELD	R.VAN.Y.C.	1.05	27/48/ 0	25(A)	73
JEUNESSE II	PAUL T. COTE	R.VAN.Y.C.	1.80	27/48/26	26(A)	74
ARCTURUS	ALLAN D. TOBE	WEST VAN	1.60	27/51/ 5	27(A)	75
BANDIT	DAN McDONOUGH	TACOMA	2.65	27/56/ 3	33(B)	76
CYNOSURE	PHILIP HAYES	TACOMA	2.40	28/ 2/ 6	34(B)	77
ARIES	ROBERT STREET	SEATTLE	1.65	28/ 2/ 9	28(A)	78
MUTINEER IV	T.R. BRAIDWOOD	WEST VAN	1.70	28/ 3/26	29(A)	79
RAVEN	TOM LINDER	ANACORTES	2.30	28/ 7/ 4	35(B)	80
SPINSTER	JULIAN DEWELL	EVERETT	2.30	28/10/ 6	36(B)	81
CELEBRATION	NEIL B. KELLY	CORINTHIAN	2.30	28/10/23	37(B)	82
CIRRUS	ALAN FORSYTHE	QUATERMSTR	2.90	28/14/45	17(C)	83
WHIM-WHAM	BILL HANSON	CORINTHIAN	1.60	28/17/ 9	30(A)	84
MOONBIRD	JACK SNOWBALL	WEST VAN	2.15	28/19/27	31(A)	85
SEALION	NORMAN MARTIN	NANAIMO	2.20	28/26/29	38(B)	86
VELA	MR. THOMPSEN/MR. PRUE	CORINTHIAN	2.40	28/42/35	39(B)	87
FAEM	LEE McGUIRE	R.VAN.Y.C.	2.10	28/45/32	32(A)	88
ELUSIVE	STEPHEN SHEA	SEATTLE	1.50	29/ 6/30	33(A)	89
EXODUS	RICHARD ROBERTS	CORINTHIAN	2.90	29/34/30	18(C)	90
RAMPART	DON DOBIE	R.VIC.Y.C.	1.70	29/44/ 4	34(A)	91
IONA	WILLIAM McCABE	PORTLAND	3.10	30/56/ 2	19(C)	92
TOLO TSOLO	E.E. WOODSON	ANACORTES	2.45	35/ 9/49	40(B)	93
GALENAIA II	GEORGE DUFOUR	R.VIC.Y.C.	3.45	35/48/19	20(C)	94
TILLICUM	HOWARD RICKETTS	CORINTHIAN	2.85	DNS	DNS(C)	DNS
VIVA	D. BLAKEMORE	CORINTHIAN	1.85	DNF	DNF(A)	DNF
ESCAPE HATCH	BOB FERRIE	BELLINGHAM	3.50	DNF	DNF(C)	DNF
SEAWYF	R.O. DARBY	C.F.S.A.	3.10	DNF	DNF(C)	DNF
CORMORANT	H.H. BOYD, MD	CORINTHIAN	2.10	DSQ	DSQ(A)	DSQ
FURIANT	HON. JUDGE DAVID MOFFETT	R.VAN.Y.C.	3.40	DNF	DNF(C)	DNF
HANSA	J.B. HEITMAN	GIG HARBOR	2.35	DNF	DNF(B)	DNF
MOSHULU	R.O. SYLVESTER	SEATTLE	2.20	DNF	DNF(B)	DNF
TEMPTATION	BRYAN ARCHER	TACOMA	1.75	DNF	DNF(A)	DNF
SEACLUSION	D. MATCHETTE	OLYMPIA	2.50	DNF	DNF(B)	DNF
DYNASTY 2	JOHN FAIRLEY	WEST VAN	2.95	DNF	DNF(C)	DNF
BENORA III	HARRY HERLILBY	R.VAN.Y.C.	1.75	DNF	DNF(A)	DNF
THOMASINE	J.H. COOK	R.VIC.Y.C.	3.00	DNF	DNF(C)	DNF
KATCHEN	D. STAATZ, MD	TACOMA	2.70	DNF	DNF(C)	DNF
ANDIAMO	ROBERT CARERE	R.VIC.Y.C.	2.45	DNF	DNF(B)	DNF
JUBILEE	BILL WATKINS	SEATTLE	2.10	DNF	DNF(A)	DNF
EMERAUDE	STEVE ALTMYER	OLYMPIA	2.15	DNF	DNF(A)	DNF
TANQUERAY	LARRY EMERY	S. SOUND	2.40	DNF	DNF(B)	DNF
WARLORD	JOHN GONYEA	TACOMA	2.00	DNF	DNF(A)	DNF
WINDSONG II	ROGER BARNHART	BELLINGHAM	2.20	DNF	DNF(B)	DNF
THE HUMMER	J.C. SCOTT, MD	SEATTLE	2.50	DNF	DNF(B)	DNF
COURTESAN	GORDON MILLS	R.C.Y.C.	2.45	DNF	DNF(B)	DNF
HOTSPUR	JOHN CLAYTON	R.VAN.Y.C.	2.20	DSQ	DSQ(B)	DSQ
COUNTESS III	PETER JEFFERSON	R.VAN.Y.C.	1.70	DNF	DNF(A)	DNF
OLYMPUS II	TOM MURRAY	EAGLE HRBR	2.30	DNF	DNF(B)	DNF
MAYA	M.M. LE POOLE	R.VAN.Y.C.	3.60	DNF	DNF(C)	DNF
SEA RANGER 2	H. TRONCZEK	TIDDLYCOVE	2.45	DNF	DNF(B)	DNF
SUPER PICKLE	JAN ABBOTT	O.C.S.A.	3.00	DNF	DNF(C)	DNF

YACHT NAME	SKIPPER(S)	CLUB	RATING			
PAPS CHOICE	GENE H. WALTER	PORTLAND	2.55	DNF	DNF(B)	DNF
PETER COTTONSAIL	VERNE LAWRENCE	CORINTHIAN	2.90	DNF	DNF(C)	DNF
DELIVERANCE	GEORGE PALO	CORINTHIAN	2.20	DNF	DNF(B)	DNF
SEAWARD SIDE	DONALD T. SMITH	ROSE CITY	2.40	DNF	DNF(B)	DNF
RAJAH	RUDY E. JOYCE	THREE TREE	2.30	DNF	DNF(B)	DNF
SNOWBIRD	DR. MONDLOCH	SINCLAIR	2.90	DNF	DNF(C)	DNF
RHIANNON	BOB SMITH	PORTLAND	2.95	DNF	DNF(C)	DNF

16 JUNE 1976
OFFICIAL START TIME: 9/40/0

JUAN DE FUCA (I.O.R.) 1976
RESULTS

YACHT NAME	SKIPPER(S)	CLUB	RATING	COR ELAPSE TIME	POSITION DIVISION	OVERALL
FRED AGAIN	G.S. WILKINS	R.VAN.Y.C.	18.00	16/ 2/45	1(7)	1
SEA SPELL	JAN HUIBERS	R.VIC.Y.C.	22.90A	16/30/10	1(6)	2
GOTCHAGAIN	BOB DIEHL	BELLINGHAM	21.60	16/39/51	2(7)	3
CLIMAX	MIKE SMITH/DON SMITH	CORINTHIAN	21.70	17/ 4/33	3(7)	4
DOUBLE ENTRY	E.A. LIEBERT	R.VAN.Y.C.	24.50	17/ 6/38	2(6)	5
CUSTARD PIE	DICK PURDIE	R.VAN.Y.C.	21.70	17/ 8/59	4(7)	6
KAZOO	PHIL MAGRUDER	BELLINGHAM	21.70	17/11/ 9	5(7)	7
SPANISH FLY	TERRY RODGERS	EAGLE HARB	21.50	17/12/51	6(7)	8
GUS	DR. W. HERRMANN	SEATTLE	21.20	17/14/29	7(7)	9
CAYAMBE	GARY BYSTEDT	CORINTHIAN	21.70	17/20/46	8(7)	10
RISQUE	JON POKELA	TACOMA	20.80	17/23/12	9(7)	11
TEGARRI	GLENN BLUE	CORINTHIAN	21.70	17/26/56	10(7)	12
SUDS	DAN BARTMEL	CORINTHIAN	21.70	17/31/11	11(7)	13
PUFF II	JACK WOODWARD	R.VIC.Y.C.	23.30A	17/31/28	3(6)	14
LORELEI II	JOE ROSINSKI	BELLINGHAM	23.60A	17/35/40	4(6)	15
PAX	FRANK RHODES	R.VIC.Y.C.	24.20A	17/43/ 5	5(6)	16
MALEKA	MAXWELL KING	BELLINGHAM	24.50	17/48/51	6(6)	17
PATCHWORK QUILT	J. DRYDEN, MD	R.VIC.Y.C.	24.00	18/ 9/14	7(6)	18
QUORUM	D. MURRAY FIELD	CORINTHIAN	24.50	18/44/ 7	8(6)	19
OUTLAW	THOMAS C. HUKLE	CORINTHIAN	21.70	18/44/26	12(7)	20
CHINOOK	SPANFELNER/GINDROZ/GRAINGER	THREE TREE	21.70	19/14/19	13(7)	21
FUTURE SHOCK	CHUCK BOUFFIOU	CORINTHIAN	21.70	19/28/29	14(7)	22
UMPKA	JOHN R. BOOTH	R.VIC.Y.C.	21.60	19/33/ 5	15(7)	23
DIFFERENT DRUMMER	BRIAN GRIFFIN	BELLINGHAM	23.70A	19/46/48	9(6)	24
PANACEA	DAUGHTERS/HENDERSON	SEATTLE	24.90	20/20/20	10(6)	25
TARQUIN III	G. JOHNSTONE	R.VIC.Y.C.	20.30A	21/45/44	16(7)	26
RADIO	BILL ZERVIS	CORINTHIAN	21.20	22/30/42	17(7)	27
GALEB	GEORGE CESAREC	R.VIC.Y.C.	17.90A	22/41/46	18(7)	28
FIREBIRD	GARY L. BURK	OLYMPIA	22.10	23/ 0/35	11(6)	29
VULCAN	FRED KRABBE	SAN JUAN	18.00	23/17/24	19(7)	30
FRED	FINN NIELSEN	MAPLE BAY	18.00	23/48/50	20(7)	31
O'GABHAIN	JOHN GAVIN	CORINTHIAN	18.00	25/12/34	21(7)	32
FIRST MORNING	GUS HODGE	BELLINGHAM	21.60A	DNF	DNF(7)	DNF
KIM	IAN DUNCANSON	R.VIC.Y.C.	22.90A	DNF	DNF(6)	DNF
TUFTED PUFFIN	AL WHITNEY	KITSILANO	17.80A	DSQ	DSQ(7)	DSQ
STREAKER	MARVIN A. WAYNE	BELLINGHAM	21.50	DSQ	DSQ(7)	DSQ

16 JUNE 1976
OFFICIAL START TIME: 9/40/0

JUAN DE FUCA (P.H.R.F.) 1976
RESULTS

YACHT NAME	SKIPPER(S)	CLUB	RATING	COR ELAPSE TIME	POSITION DIVISION	OVERALL
LARA	KEN CLARK	R.VAN.Y.C.	2.80	16/56/35	1(D)	1
AMBUSH	VANCE BINGHAM	PT. ANGELES	2.80	17/40/ 4	2(D)	2
PANTHER POINT	PAUL SCHOUW	EAGLE HARB.	2.80	17/45/ 8	3(D)	3
UNION DEPOT	ROGER L. RUE	TACOMA	3.05	17/46/ 7	4(D)	4
DENT DE LION	GEORGE MOHLER	PT. ANGELES	2.85	17/52/22	5(D)	5
RHUBARB	ROBBIE BROWN	WEST VAN	2.90	18/ 3/22	6(D)	6
IMAGE RESPONSE	ROGER PALMER	EDMONDS	2.90	18/ 6/17	7(D)	7
TONIC	DAN BRINK	CORINTHIAN	2.85	18/19/ 7	8(D)	8
WANIGAN	JOE OREM	BELLINGHAM	2.90	18/52/41	9(D)	9
CAL-LORRI	CAM THOMSON	CANDO BAY	3.10	19/10/41	10(D)	10
COURAGE PLUS	STAN JOHNSON	WILLAMETTE	3.30	19/11/40	1(E)	11
PRESTO	TOM WHITE	BELLINGHAM	2.90	19/35/ 6	11(D)	12
ENCOUNTER	R. ANDREWS	R.VIC.Y.C.	2.80	19/36/31	12(D)	13
WHITE SQUALL	PETER WHITE	CANOE BAY	3.30	19/42/33	2(E)	14
TIARA III	WILL JENSEN	CANOE BAY	2.90	19/57/54	13(D)	15
WINDSHIFT	FREDERICK HAYES	SEATTLE	2.95	20/ 5/14	14(D)	16
MIRAGE	F.M. JONES	EDMONDS	2.85	20/11/45	15(D)	17
PANIC	CHARLES WHIDDEN	PT. ANGELES	2.90	20/12/11	16(D)	18
JOLLY OLLY III	RICK COCKBURN	SEMIAHMOO	2.85	21/ 0/55	17(D)	19

ARLIS II	LARRY HILLS	SEATTLE	3.25	22/25/12	3(E)	20
IRIDES	DONALD PARKER	CANOE BAY	3.20	22/30/41	4(E)	21
SARA	GLENN McCORMICK	QTRMSTR.	5.15	22/40/46	1(F)	22
GEORGIA GIRL	BILL MARTIN	CANOE BAY	3.60	22/46/ 3	2(F)	23
AEOLUS	PETE McDOUGAL	TACOMA	3.00	23/ 4/12	18(D)	24
FILEY BRIGG	MIKE WEIR	R.VIC.Y.C.	3.25	23/ 7/53	5(E)	25
SEAQUIN	R. MARSHALL	CORINTHIAN	3.90	23/36/18	3(F)	26
LIMFJORD	BENT JESPERSEN	CANOE BAY	4.00	23/50/34	4(F)	27
TYCHE	HUNTLY GORDON	R.VAN.Y.C.	3.40	23/51/20	6(E)	28
MARILYN L	RON CARLSON	PT. ANGELES	3.75	23/56/24	5(F)	29
NOOSA	R. VAN DEN DRIESSCHE	R.VIC.Y.C.	3.30	24/ 4/37	7(E)	30
CAPRICE	H.R. GARDNER	C.F.S.A.	4.00	24/ 5/34	6(F)	31
SALTY DREAM	GARY JACOBI	R.VIC.Y.C.	3.30	24/13/36	8(E)	32
MASSILIA II	E.E. READSHAW	R.VIC.Y.C.	3.45	24/18/11	9(E)	33
LOON	T. SCHNEIDER	CORINTHIAN	3.70	24/19/32	7(F)	34
SUNBURST	R.G. LINKLETTER	PT. ANGELES	2.90	24/22/49	19(D)	35
MORAR	I.M.A. GRANT	WEST VAN	3.80	24/24/36	8(F)	36
SIRIUS	KEITH WATERFALL	MAPLE BAY	3.30	24/27/ 1	10(E)	37
SUMMERSALT	RICK BALDWIN	CANOE BAY	3.30	24/28/20	11(E)	38
WHIPPET	CHARLES OLSON	EDMONDS	3.10	24/32/34	20(D)	39
IOLAIRE	ALEX ORR	EAGLE HARB.	3.00	24/34/22	21(D)	40
AURIGA	TERRY CATTELL	WEST VAN	3.35	24/40/14	12(E)	41
SKYE	ROD McBRIDE	R.VIC.Y.C.	3.30	24/40/15	13(E)	42
THISTLEDOWN	DON FEELEY	PT. ANGELES	3.05	24/43/59	22(D)	43
SPIRIT	GARY MORRIS	TACOMA	3.30	24/44/20	14(E)	44
BUFFLEHEAD II	K.R. MARTIN	R.VAN.Y.C.	3.20	24/44/29	15(E)	45
PAPRIKA	FRANK MUSSON	WEST VAN	2.95	24/44/52	23(D)	46
DEPARTURE	JACK MILLER	R.VIC.Y.C.	2.85	24/47/ 0	24(D)	47
PAX	K.I. McRAE	R.VAN.Y.C.	2.95	24/47/ 2	25(D)	48
SOMETHING	JACK PATTERSON	CANOE BAY	3.15	24/56/13	26(D)	49
VOLARE	JOHN CICERI	R.VIC.Y.C.	3.20	25/ 0/22	16(E)	50
OBSESSION	MEL HENRY	TACOMA	2.90	25/ 3/36	27(D)	51
BEAUJOLAIS	GILES SHEPHERD	EVERETT	3.00	25/25/52	28(D)	52
THE SLOOP JOHN B.	J. BOYD IVENS	TSAWWASSEN	3.70	26/43/51	9(F)	53
GWAIHIR	DOUGLAS BOND	C.F.S.A.	4.55	DNF	DNF(F)	DNF
TINKERBELLE	DR. L. RIGGS	PT. ANGELES	3.80	DNF	DNF(F)	DNF
SKILFISH	D.R. WEST	WEST VAN	2.95	DNF	DNF(D)	DNF
VIKING	ALAN DICKINSON	CANOE BAY	3.25	DNF	DNF(E)	DNF
AVENGER II	A.S. BARKER	WEST VAN	3.10	DNF	DNF(D)	DNF
LUCY ALICE	W.H. GARDNER	CORINTHIAN	3.65	DNF	DNF(F)	DNF
FINISTERRE	J. PETER ROGERS	R.VAN.Y.C.	3.70	DNF	DNF(F)	DNF
MORAG	DICK JENKINS	R.VAN.Y.C.	2.90	DNF	DNF(D)	DNF
SANA	J.K. MARTIN	CANOE BAY	3.10	DNF	DNF(D)	DNF
SUNSHINE	GORD MARTMAN	CANOE BAY	3.10	DSQ	DSQ(D)	DSQ
EL CID	ROBERT BERST	SEATTLE	3.20	DNF	DNF(E)	DNF
GUPPY	GREG KNIGHT	SEMICHMOO	3.30	DNS	DNS(E)	DNS
THUMPER	BOB FOWLER	ANACORTES	2.80	DNF	DNF(D)	DNF
FREESTYLE	TIM C. McAFEE	CORINTHIAN	2.95	DSQ	DSQ(D)	DSQ
SKOOKUM	GERALD PARKER	TACOMA	2.80	DNF	DNF(D)	DNF
FARTHER OUT	JOHN SPROUSE	PORTLAND	3.30	DNF	DNF(E)	DNF

PACIFIC INTERNATIONAL YACHTING ASSOCIATION
SWIFTSURE LIGHTSHIP CLASSIC AND JUAN DE FUCA RACE
1977 TROPHY WINNERS

SWIFTSURE (I.O.R.)	SWIFTSURE TROPHY (OVERALL HANDICAP WINNER)	V. PLAVSIC	W.VAN.	KANATA
	CITY OF VICTORIA TROPHY (FIRST YACHT TO FINISH)	BOB SMITH	TACOMA	WARLOCK
	ROYAL CANADIAN NAVY TROPHY (FIRST YACHT TO ROUND SWIFTSURE MARK)	V. PLAVSIC	W.VAN.	KANATA
	OCEAN CEMENT TROPHY (FIRST IN DIVISION 1)	BOB SMITH	TACOMA	WARLOCK
	T. EATON TROPHY (FIRST IN DIVISION 2)	V. PLAVSIC	W.VAN.	KANATA
	CITY OF SEATTLE TROPHY (FIRST IN DIVISION 3)	TOM FRIEDLAND	BELLINGHAM	SALLY LIGHTFOOT
	ROYAL VANCOUVER YACHT CLUB TROPHY (FIRST IN DIVISION 4)	JOHN EVETTS	KITSILANO	BIG SISTER
SWIFTSURE (P.H.R.F.)	CORINTHIAN YACHT CLUB TROPHY (FIRST IN DIVISION A)	BILL WATKINS	SEATTLE	JUBILEE
	STORMY WEATHER TROPHY (FIRST IN DIVISION B)	DONALD A. FLYNN	SEATTLE	OUTWARD BOUND

	CAPE FLATTERY TROPHY (FIRST IN DIVISION C)	DOUG FRYER	SEATTLE	AFRICAN STAR
JUAN DE FUCA (I.O.R.)	SAN JUAN TROPHY (FIRST YACHT TO FINISH)	D.R. WEST	W.VAN.	SKILFISH
	ROYAL VICTORIA YACHT CLUB TROPHY (FIRST IN DIVISION 5)	GUS HODGE	BELLINGHAM	FIRST MORNING
	ROYAL CANADIAN NAVY TROPHY (FIRST IN DIVISION 6)	BOB DIEHL	BELLINGHAM	GOTCHAGAIN
JUAN DE FUCA (P.H.R.F.)	ANACORTES YACHT CLUB TROPHY (FIRST IN DIVISION D)	D.R. WEST	W.VAN.	SKILFISH
	.... (FIRST IN DIVISION E)	GARY JACOBI	R.VIC.	SALTY DREAM
	.... (FIRST IN DIVISION F)	R. MARSHALL	CORINTHIAN	SEAQUIN

SWIFTSURE (I.O.R.) 1977
RESULTS

OFFICIAL START TIME: 9/10/0

YACHT NAME	SKIPPER(S)	CLUB	RATING	COR ELAPSE TIME	POSITION DIVISION	OVERALL
KANATA	V. PLAVSIC	W.VAN.	31.90	25/44/09	1(2)	1
WARLOCK	BOB SMITH	TACOMA	35.60A	25/58/03	1(1)	2
BIG SISTER	JOHN EVETTS	KITSILANO	21.70	26/04/36	1(4)	3
LADYBUG	ALAN HOLT	SEATTLE	21.70	26/05/04	2(4)	4
I'SLAND	BILL BUCHAN/DAN BARR	CORINTHIAN	21.70	26/05/23	3(4)	5
NIGHT MOVES	WHIPPLE/EGLIT	CORINTHIAN	21.70	26/06/38	4(4)	6
OUTLAW	THOMAS C. HUKLE	CORINTHIAN	21.70	26/26/09	5(4)	7
SUPER APPLE	ROBERT KERSHAW	SEATTLE	21.70	26/33/47	6(4)	8
SALLY LIGHTFOOT	TOM FRIEDLAND	BELLINGHAM	27.20A	26/51/53	1(3)	9
SCRAMBLER	MICHAEL BOOKEY	SEATTLE	21.70	26/54/05	7(4)	10
BAREFOOT II	JIM WARD	CORINTHIAN	24.50	26/59/01	8(4)	11
FLAUNT	ROBERT HAMILTON	TACOMA	21.70A	27/02/27	9(4)	12
PROSPECTOR	TOM GEISNESS/LARRY SHORETT	SEATTLE	27.40	27/14/01	2(3)	13
JADAH	PHIL TUCKER	CORINTHIAN	24.40A	27/15/24	10(4)	14
ANOMALY	WILLIAM ELMER	S. SOUND SS	27.00A	27/26/20	11(4)	15
TZORES	TIM ERICKSON	CORINTHIAN	24.40	27/41/08	12(4)	16
GOLDEN EAGLE	RICHARD ROBERTS	CORINTHIAN	24.50	27/44/20	13(4)	17
TOPKAPI	BOB KITCHEN	W.VAN.	28.20	27/46/25	3(3)	18
SHRIKE	CHUCK CROFT	W.VAN.	27.50	27/55/12	4(3)	19
SUNDANCE	DR. K. OVERBY	TACOMA	21.60	27/56/09	14(4)	20
WOTAN	BILL BURDICK	SEATTLE	27.30A	27/56/27	5(3)	21
TRUMPETER OF JERICHO	J.H. LONG	R.VAN.	29.10	28/03/13	2(2)	22
LEPSOYA	JON RUNSTAD	SEATTLE	27.90A	28/04/01	6(3)	23
DIRIGO	JACK TAYLOR	CORINTHIAN	27.10A	28/09/05	7(3)	24
THE GOOD, BAD & UGLY	ALEX FOLEY	R.VAN.	27.80A	28/09/18	8(3)	25
COUNTRY STYLE	STEVE MERRIMAN	R.VIC.	27.50	28/09/56	9(3)	26
THE DISTANT DRUMMER	GREGORY OLIVER	R.VIC.	27.50	28/15/59	10(3)	27
SHAZAM	RANDY MUELLER	CORINTHIAN	27.10A	28/23/17	11(3)	28
PROPHECY	JOHN JARMAN	R.VAN.	27.50	28/23/33	12(3)	29
GHOST RIDER	RICK MOELLER	PORTLAND	24.50	28/29/58	15(4)	30
ELECTRA	BEN DEMBART	CORINTHIAN	24.50	28/30/02	16(4)	31
WARRIOR	LANGDON HEDRICK	SEATTLE	45.20A	28/30/25	2(1)	32
FLAMENCA	JOHN MICHAEL	CORINTHIAN	24.60A	28/31/31	17(4)	33
MOODY TOO	JIM PINE	W.VAN.	26.60	28/32/20	18(4)	34
TAPOCKETA	ROBERT NEWELL	BELLINGHAM	24.50	28/33/02	19(4)	35
WARLORD	JOHN GONYEA	TACOMA	26.90A	28/33/51	13(3)	36
ELIXIR	JOHN GRAHAM	SEATTLE	27.20A	28/39/44	14(3)	37
SURPRISE	GERRY MAURER	SEATTLE	29.40	28/40/16	3(2)	38
SINE MORA	DONALD HILLMAN	SEATTLE	27.10A	28/46/53	15(3)	39
ARROW	ELDON SCHALKA	EVERETT	28.10A	28/47/47	16(3)	40
AMERICAN FLYER	FRED W. BIEKER	PORTLAND	31.10A	28/48/47	4(2)	41
HEATHER	JOHN BUCHAN	SEATTLE	31.90	28/55/33	5(2)	42
BRER RABBIT	ROBERT CONNOR	CORINTHIAN	30.00	28/55/33	6(2)	43
PACHENA	JOHN NEWTON	W.VAN.	32.00	28/56/59	7(2)	44
BORU	DONALD BYRNE	R.VAN.	27.50	28/57/50	17(3)	45
BEDLAM II	DOUGLAS DAY	R.VAN.	30.10A	28/59/04	8(2)	46
GOLD RUSH	NATHAN RUSSELL	SHILSHOLE	30.60A	29/00/19	9(2)	47
DEFIANCE	RON HART	TACOMA	31.20A	29/02/24	10(2)	48
INDIGO	R.F. HARRISON	W.VAN.	31.00A	29/03/56	11(2)	49
MISTRESS II	T.W. VARLEY, M.D.	EVERETT	31.60A	29/09/58	12(2)	50
THE PHOENICIAN	C. SCHILBACH, M.D.	PORTLAND	33.40	29/10/30	3(1)	51
MARY D II	DARREL DAVIS	PT. ANGELES	24.60	29/10/45	20(4)	52
BARBARIAN	DR. V. BRYAN	POULSBO	27.50A	29/11/17	18(3)	53
HABITAT	P.C.G. RICHARDS	W.VAN.	28.10	29/13/33	19(3)	54

YACHT NAME	SKIPPER(S)	CLUB	RATING	COR ELAPSE TIME	DIVISION	OVERALL
JOLLY OLLY IV	VERN RUSKIN	R.VAN.	27.50	29/15/01	20(3)	55
IRISH ROSE	D. DONOHUE, M.D.	CORINTHIAN	32.30A	29/15/30	13(2)	56
RAMROD	VERNE LAWRENCE	CORINTHIAN	27.10A	29/16/55	21(3)	57
TERNA III	P. CHRISTOFFERSEN	W.VAN.	31.40A	29/17/42	14(2)	58
GRETEL II	HEIN DRIEHUYZEN	W.VAN.	27.50	29/20/16	22(3)	59
SEA ROBIN	ARCHIE CAMPBELL	R.VIC.	23.90A	29/21/31	21(4)	60
FIRECRACKER	LARRY SCHUELER	PT. ANGELES	25.10A	29/30/29	22(4)	61
NIGHTHAWK	EDWARD ODISHAW	KITSILANO	28.20A	29/34/06	15(2)	62
ANNIE CADBY	LOUIS LINDHOLM	R.VIC.	33.20A	29/34/56	4(1)	63
JEZEBEL	B.W. BROCKWAY	SEATTLE	27.00A	29/35/00	23(4)	64
EPIC	C. SCHIFF	CORINTHIAN	37.50A	29/38/54	5(1)	65
TSUNAMI	C.J. MORAN	CORINTHIAN	26.30A	29/43/09	23(3)	66
MIDNIGHT SPECIAL	V. McCULLOUGH	CORINTHIAN	31.30A	29/43/33	16(2)	67
OVERKILL	ERRY BUCHOLZ	CORINTHIAN	27.10A	29/44/08	24(3)	68
OUTRAGEOUS	TED BURNS, M.D.	BREMERTON	41.00	29/47/11	6(1)	69
DISCOVERY	JOHN DUNFIELD	R.VAN.	39.70A	29/55/01	7(1)	70
IMPROBABLE	LEN SCHWAB	CORINTHIAN	36.60A	29/56/28	8(1)	71
NERITA	BOB UTTER	CORINTHIAN	31.00A	29/57/22	17(2)	72
NAKNEK	RICHARD NELSON	R.VAN.	38.60A	29/59/23	9(1)	73
BONNIE	EARL L. MILLER	PT. MADISON	40.00	30/01/45	10(1)	74
RACE PASSAGE	PAUL McCULLOUGH	BREMERTON	33.60A	30/12/44	11(1)	75
AKKA	RALPH MARX	TACOMA	25.90A	30/21/52	24(4)	76
SUNBIRD	ALVIN NAROD	R.VAN.	42.70A	30/24/18	12(1)	77
MUSTARD SEED	HERMAN/GRIMES/SMITH	EDMONDS	27.50	30/32/11	25(3)	78
ULTIMATUM	J.L. WILLIAMS	R.VAN.	27.00A	30/35/25	25(4)	79
SATURDAY'S CHILD	C. BRAIN	SEATTLE	39.40	30/42/59	13(1)	80
WEATHERLY	LYNN SOMMERS/ALAN BUCHAN	TACOMA	51.70A	31/15/23	14(1)	81
DIAMOND HEAD	H.L. KOTKINS	SEATTLE	47.20A	31/41/19	15(1)	82
ASSAULT	J.W. CHILTON	THREE TREE	33.00A	31/52/34	16(1)	83
OUTRAGEOUS	JOHN HARDIMAN	CORINTHIAN	27.00A	33/56/32	26(4)	84
ERRIGAL	HUGH PORTER	R.VIC.	27.30		(3)	DNF
CYGNET	D. WAYNE SMITH	OLYMPIA	28.90		(3)	DSQ
SUNRISE	THOMAS HAYES	SEATTLE	21.70		(4)	DNF

SWIFTSURE (P.H.R.F.) 1977 RESULTS

OFFICIAL START TIME: 9/25/0

YACHT NAME	SKIPPER(S)	CLUB	RATING	COR ELAPSE TIME	POSITION DIVISION	POSITION OVERALL
AFRICAN STAR	DOUG FRYER	SEATTLE	3.55	26/25/19	1(C)	1
THEORY	MURRAY FIANDER	CORINTHIAN	3.10	26/52/42	2(C)	2
CONSULTATION	DEAN ANDERSON	S. SOUND. SS	2.95	27/32/24	3(C)	3
BANJO MUSIC	GEORGE LOWE	MADISON	2.90	27/38/03	4(C)	4
OUTWARD BOUND	DONALD A. FLYNN	SEATTLE	2.40	27/50/46	1(B)	5
NAUTILUS	L. NEVLER, M.D.	CORINTHIAN	2.30	27/51/43	2(B)	6
SMALL WORLD II	GENE W. SIBOLD	S. SOUND	2.30	27/52/22	3(B)	7
JUBILEE	BILL WATKINS	SEATTLE	2.15	27/53/47	1(A)	8
CUSTARD PIE	DICK PURDIE	R.VAN.	2.60	27/56/27	4(B)	9
CHEROKEE	MIKE MULCAHY/FRED RAY	THREE TREE	2.30	27/58/06	5(B)	10
HOTSPUR	JOHN CLAYTON	R.VAN.	2.20	27/58/31	6(B)	11
ELISHEBA	MILES MILLER	CORINTHIAN	2.30	28/01/52	7(B)	12
SAVAGE	LARRY HILLS	SEATTLE	2.20	28/05/21	8(B)	13
TOLO TSOLO	E.B. WOODSON	ANACORTES	2.45	28/07/03	9(B)	14
JACKAROE	R.L. HILLS	TOWNSEND	2.85	28/08/11	5(C)	15
RENEGADE	SHERWOOD SMITH	OLYMPIA	2.85	28/09/35	6(C)	16
CIRRUS	ALAN FORSYTHE/CHUCK GREEN	QUATERMSTR.	2.90	28/11/52	7(C)	17
FLIRTATION	JACK TUTTLE	CORINTHIAN	2.35	28/14/35	10(B)	18
SAGA	S. RASMUSSEN	R.VAN.	2.10	28/14/39	2(A)	19
JOLLY ROGER III	ROGER WHEELER	CORINTHIAN	2.45	28/14/54	11(B)	20
DELIVERANCE	GEORGE PALO	CORINTHIAN	2.20	28/17/01	12(B)	21
ASTARTE	ALAN HOFFMAN	CORINTHIAN	2.65	28/21/57	13(B)	22
GAMIN	LON ROBINSON	SEATTLE	2.20	28/29/10	14(B)	23
CANDYMAN	GUY BOCKUS/HOWARD FREY	PT. MADISON	2.85	28/29/14	8(C)	24
FEDERALIST	JAMES MARTA	SEATTLE	1.75	28/29/22	3(A)	25
WHITE MIST	DORR ANDERSON	SEATTLE	3.00	28/29/57	9(C)	26
MELTEMI	FRANK MUSSON	W.VAN.	2.10	28/33/14	4(A)	27
COHO II	G. BRANDLMAYR	R.VAN.	1.60	28/38/31	5(A)	28
HINA	DARYL DELMOTTE	R.VAN.	2.90	28/40/13	10(C)	29
EN PASSANT	HUGH MINOR	EVERETT	2.30	28/40/30	15(B)	30
SERVUS	H.G. STRICKER	R.VIC.	2.60	28/41/51	16(B)	31
RAINDROP	J. GAINER	CORINTHIAN	2.00	28/41/54	6(A)	32
SUNFLOWER	M.B. MADENWALD	ANACORTES	2.40	28/44/20	17(B)	33

CORMORANT	H.H. BOYD, M.D.	CORINTHIAN	2.10	28/44/34	7(A)	34
ENJOY	KARL LINDGREN	THREE TREE	3.10	28/44/51	11(C)	35
SOCKEYE	PETER KEATE	R.VAN.	2.80	28/45/21	12(C)	36
GYPSY DANCER	JAMES VOGT	CORINTHIAN	2.85	28/46/02	13(C)	37
TREK	GREG JAMES	CORINTHIAN	2.40	28/46/37	18(B)	38
RASCAL	DENNIS THORNTON	CORINTHIAN	2.40	28/48/03	19(B)	39
EMMA	H. HARTWIG	R.VIC.	2.20	28/50/54	20(B)	40
MEG	BOB HOSIE	R.VIC.	2.20	28/51/35	21(B)	41
BARBARA	WYNN E. KAMPE	CORINTHIAN	2.10	28/54/06	8(A)	42
FRIENDSHIP	W.F. GRIFFITH/P.J. FREDERICK	CORINTHIAN	2.50	28/56/22	22(B)	43
PEGASUS	JOHN G. BECKER	CORINTHIAN	2.85	28/56/45	14(C)	44
FAEM	LEE McGUIRE ET AL	R.VAN.	2.15	28/57/56	9(A)	45
RHIANNON	BUSH ALBISTON	SEATTLE	2.00	29/00/29	10(A)	46
MOON DAY	CAL BAMFORD, JR.	TACOMA	1.85	29/02/20	11(A)	47
SPECTRE	JOHN CAHILL, M.D.	SEATTLE	1.85	29/02/31	12(A)	48
SHELCA	ERIC DOWELL	R.VIC.	2.10	29/03/05	13(A)	49
SEALION	NORMAN MARTIN	NANAIMO	2.20	29/03/26	23(B)	50
ADIOS	PHILIP BLATT	PORTLAND	2.70	29/05/36	15(C)	51
HOOLIGAN II	TOM O'BRIEN	SEATTLE	1.85	29/05/57	14(A)	52
PANDEMONIUM	PETER O'REILLY	OLYMPIA	2.95	29/06/43	16(C)	53
TAVEUNI	R.I. THIEME	EVERETT	2.10	29/06/55	15(A)	54
DOMINIQUE	WILLI FAHNING	CANOE BAY	2.20	29/08/44	24(B)	55
BLUE LEAF	T.W. BERKEN	OLYMPIA	2.20	29/11/20	25(B)	56
REALITY	ROLAND BRENER	T.H.S.A.	1.85	29/12/05	16(A)	57
HARRIER	CHARLES OLSON	EDMONDS	2.30	29/12/13	26(B)	58
MALTESE FALCON	RUSS SCHULKE	CORINTHIAN	2.45	29/12/24	27(B)	59
MOSHULU	R.O. SYLVESTER	SEATTLE	2.20	29/12/28	28(B)	60
MUTINEER IV	T.R. BRAIDWOOD	W.VAN.	1.70	29/14/52	17(A)	61
SKARRIETT	R.E. WILSON	THREE TREE	1.95	29/16/19	18(A)	62
BILLIKEN	BILL AIKEN	CORINTHIAN	2.50	29/16/20	29(B)	63
MERIDIAN PASSAGE	BRUCE J. MELI	TSAWASSEN	2.10	29/17/59	19(A)	64
TANGENT II	ANTHONY LOACH	W.VAN.	2.10	29/20/43	20(A)	65
FIREBRAND	R.W. NEWMAN	SEATTLE	1.95	29/22/29	21(A)	66
WINDLESS II	CHESS RICKARD	TIDDLY COVE	1.80	29/26/45	22(A)	67
BENORA III	HARRY HERLIHY	R.VAN.	2.05	29/27/13	23(A)	68
SPINSTER	JULIAN DEWELL	EVERETT	2.30	29/30/02	30(B)	69
SUPER PICKLE	JAN ABBOTT	PORTLAND	2.95	29/33/10	17(C)	70
BLUE MARLIN	M. SCHLOSSER/GENE BAKER	CORINTHIAN	1.85	29/34/02	24(A)	71
DORLES	WILLIS KLUDT	THREE TREE	1.85	29/37/06	25(A)	72
SALTY TIGER	JOHN HERBERT	CORINTHIAN	1.50	29/37/29	26(A)	73
SWALLOW II	PHIL JOHNSON	SEATTLE	1.85	29/37/32	27(A)	74
BLACK WATCH	BILL NELSON	CORINTHIAN	1.55	29/38/58	28(A)	75
MOON RIVER III	JAMES MARVIN	CORINTHIAN	2.90	29/40/56	18(C)	76
YANKEE GIRL	JOE McDONALD	SEATTLE	1.80	29/42/30	29(A)	77
DOUBLE TIME	JOHN LEONARD	ANACORTES	2.40	29/46/58	31(B)	78
WINDSONG II	ROGER BARNHART	BELLINGHAM	2.20	29/47/03	32(B)	79
COUNTESS III	PETER JEFFERSON	R.VAN.	1.60	30/05/02	30(A)	80
WHITE SQUALL	G. TEATS, M.D.	TACOMA	1.85	30/05/43	31(A)	81
ARCTURUS	KEITH MacDONALD	W.VAN.	1.60	30/10/19	32(A)	82
SARDIFF	SID BURGESS	W.VAN.	1.90	30/11/27	33(A)	83
OVERDRAFT TOO	G.M. HESELDIN	R.VAN.	1.80	30/17/21	34(A)	84
WHIM-WHAM	BILL HANSON	CORINTHIAN	1.60	30/24/42	35(A)	85
VIVA	D. BLAKEMORE	CORINTHIAN	1.85	30/34/17	36(A)	86
ELUSIVE	STEPHEN SHEA	SEATTLE	1.50	30/34/47	37(A)	87
ASTROLOGER	GUY T. ELLIOTT	TACOMA	2.70	30/45/50	19(C)	88
ARTEMIS II	R.M. BOYD	R.VAN.	2.95	33/09/49	20(C)	89
LISA K	K. PARTLOW	OLYMPIA	2.40	33/27/39	33(B)	90
RAMPART	DON DOBIE	R.VIC.	1.70	35/02/43	38(A)	91
WILLOW WIND	HARVARD PALMER/FREDRIC DANZ	SEATTLE	1.85	38/29/17	39(A)	92
RASPUTIN	BRIAN HEYES	R.N.S.A.	3.05	43/32/26	21(C)	93
CELEBRATION	NEIL B. KELLY	CORINTHIAN	2.35	44/10/45	34(B)	94
DISCOVERY	JAN DIEPENHEIM	CORINTHIAN	2.60		(B)	DNF
TANGERINE	GEOFFREY CRAGG	R.VAN.	2.35		(B)	DNF
HMCS ORIOLE	LCDR. WALKER	C.F.S.A.	2.50		(B)	DNF
SUNDANCE	THOMAS MURPHY	TACOMA	1.75		(A)	DNF
GOMETRA	DAVID MILLIS	R.N.S.A.	2.35		(B)	DNF
ESCAPE HATCH	BOB FERRIE	BELLINGHAM	3.50		(C)	DNF
LA RUINA	R.J. GIBBONS	SEATTLE	2.10		(A)	DNS
THE BEBELLE	R.J. MORRISON	MAPLE BAY	3.40		(C)	DNF
MONTE CARLO	CECIL DION	KITSILANO	2.50		(B)	DSQ
DUTCH FLUTE	R. KLEIN, M.D.	TACOMA	2.65		(B)	DNS

YACHT NAME	SKIPPER(S)	CLUB	RATING		POSITION	
KATCHEN	D. STAATZ, M.D.	TACOMA	2.70		(C)	DNF
STRIDER	KEITH JOHNSON	CORINTHIAN	2.50		(B)	DNF
SPRAY	EB BAUMUELLER	CORINTHIAN	2.05		(A)	DNF
STARWAGON	R.O. GILBERT	SEATTLE	2.30		(B)	DNF
CHEETA	THOM LANE	QTRMSTR.	2.25		(B)	DNS
ZUBEN'UBI II	WILLIAM HESTER	CORINTHIAN	2.20		(B)	DNF
FLO	ROBERT WHEELER	CYC	2.95		(C)	DNF
VALIANT LADY	EARL LASHER	SEATTLE	2.80		(C)	DNF
SASSY	STEFAN CLARKE	TACOMA	2.55		(B)	DNF

SWIFTSURE 1977 FINAL RESULTS

The attached results include:
  A. Corrections to errors in finishing times and identification.
  B. Disqualifications resulting from protests.
  C. A 45 minute time allowance given to the yacht CONSULTATION which went to the aid of a boat in distress.
We hope that you enjoyed Swiftsure and are planning to enter again next year.

F.A.C. Piddington

JUAN DE FUCA (I.O.R.) 1977 RESULTS

OFFICIAL START TIME: 9/40/0

YACHT NAME	SKIPPER(S)	CLUB	RATING	COR ELAPSE TIME	POSITION DIVISION	OVERALL
GOTCHAGAIN	BOB DIEHL	BELLINGHAM	21.70	13/19/51	1(6)	1
FIRST MORNING	GUS HODGE	BELLINGHAM	21.60A	13/28/56	1(5)	2
SEA BEATER	GLEN BOUDON	CORINTHIAN	21.70	13/37/38	2(6)	3
DIFFERENT DRUMMER	BRIAN GRIFFIN	BELLINGHAM	23.70A	13/51/11	2(5)	4
CLIMAX	MIKE SMITH/DON SMITH	CORINTHIAN	21.70	14/21/43	3(6)	5
STREAKER	MARVIN A. WAYNE	BELLINGHAM	21.50	15/40/05	4(6)	6
SPANISH FLY	TERRY RODGERS	EAGLE HARB.	21.70	15/44/09	5(6)	7
NORN III	OLAV EKROM	CORINTHIAN	24.80	16/25/33	3(5)	8
IMPATIENCE	J.E. TRENHOLME	R.VIC.	24.50	16/29/19	4(5)	9
QUORUM	DAVID M. FIELD	CORINTHIAN	24.50	16/31/37	5(5)	10
MARIONETTE	BOB SPANFELNER	SEATTLE	24.50	16/44/11	6(5)	11
GOGAMA	GEORGE WILKINS	R.VAN.	24.50	16/55/54	7(5)	12
KIM	IAN DUNCANSON	R.VIC.	22.50A	16/59/52	8(5)	13
GALEB	GEORGE CESAREC	R.VIC.	21.80	17/08/18	6(6)	14
ROO	JOHN POWELL	SEATTLE	21.70	17/09/18	7(6)	15
MALEKA	MAXWELL KING	BELLINGHAM	24.50	17/21/22	9(5)	16
FRED	FINN NIELSEN	MAPLE BAY	17.70	17/46/13	8(6)	17
LORELEI II	JOE ROSINSKI	BELLINGHAM	23.60A	17/47/39	10(5)	18
SKIN TIGHT	STAN JOHNSON	WILLAMETTE	18.00	17/47/51	9(6)	19
VULCAN	FRED KRABBE	SAN JUAN	18.00	17/50/31	10(6)	20
LADY T	DON MARTIN	R.VAN.	18.80	18/25/48	11(6)	21
FARTHER OUT	JOHN SPROUSE	PORTLAND	17.90A	18/45/09	12(6)	22
UKRAINIAN MAGIC	DICK TUDAN	R.N.S.A.	21.90	19/02/38	13(6)	23
THE PROFESSOR	FRANK VAN DAM	R.VIC.	17.60A	19/30/22	14(6)	24
IMPOSITION	W.A. SHELDON	S.SOUND SS	24.50	19/48/59	11(5)	25
DOUBLE ENTRY	E.A. LIEBERT	R.VAN.	24.50		(5)	DNS
FRED AGAIN	BILL COTE	R.VAN.	18.00		(6)	DNF
CHINOOK	THOMAS GRAINGER	THREE TREE	21.60		(6)	DNF

JUAN DE FUCA (P.H.R.F.) 1977 RESULTS

OFFICIAL START TIME: 9/40/0

YACHT NAME	SKIPPER(S)	CLUB	RATING	COR ELAPSE TIME	POSITION DIVISION	OVERALL
SEAQUIN	R. MARSHALL	CORINTHIAN	3.90	12/20/48	1(F)	1
LIMFJORD	BENT JESPERSEN	CANOE BAY	4.00	12/28/41	2(F)	2
SALTY DREAM	GARY JACOBI	R.VIC.	3.30	12/45/48	1(E)	3
SKILFISH	D.R. WEST	W.VAN.	2.95	12/55/17	1(D)	4
BRIGADOON	VIC BISHOP	W.VAN.	3.00	12/55/19	2(D)	5
TUFTED PUFFIN	AL WHITNEY	KITSILANO	3.35	13/01/17	2(E)	6
LA MARQUISE II	J.P. LE DALLIC	C.F.S.A.	3.25	13/21/56	3(E)	7
SPIRIT	GARY MORRIS	TACOMA	3.25	13/22/36	4(E)	8
TRIAD	RONALD RAY	TACOMA	2.90	13/29/58	3(D)	9
PATCHWORK QUILT	J. DRYDEN, M.D.	R.VIC.	2.80	13/32/35	4(D)	10
CALCULATED RISQUE	BOB STEPHENS	CORINTHIAN	3.30	13/35/16	5(E)	11
BUFFLEHEAD II	K.R. MARTIN	R.VAN.	3.20	13/36/53	6(E)	12
WINDSHIFT	FREDERICK HAYES	SEATTLE	2.95	13/39/47	5(D)	13
LOON	T. SCHNEIDER	CORINTHIAN	3.70	13/43/29	3(F)	14
TERRAPIN	GARY BOWDEN	CORINTHIAN	3.05	13/45/38	6(D)	15
SOMETHING	JACK PATTERSON	CANOE BAY	3.15	13/47/19	7(D)	16
BEAUJOLAIS	GILES SHEPHERD	EVERETT	2.90	14/03/35	8(D)	17

YANKEE DOODLE	C.D. WHIDDON	P.A.Y.C.	2.95	14/07/35	9(D)	18
PUFF II	JACK WOODWARD	R.VIC.	2.90	15/12/31	10(D)	19
ENCOUNTER	DR. HUGH BACON	R.VIC.	2.80	15/17/20	11(D)	20
SEA SPELL	JAN HUIBERS	R.VIC.	2.90	16/11/44	12(D)	21
DECEPTION	MARTIN HAINES	BELLINGHAM	2.95	16/19/05	13(D)	22
CAL-LORRI	CAM THOMSON	CANOE BAY	3.10	16/28/22	14(D)	23
MIRAGE	VANCE BINGHAM	PT. ANGELES	2.80	16/29/37	15(D)	24
MARILYN L	RON CARLSON	PT. ANGELES	3.75	16/35/27	4(F)	25
WATERMELLON	PETER WHITE	CANOE BAY	2.90	16/42/27	16(D)	26
SUMMERSALT	RICK BALDWIN	CANOE BAY	3.30	16/48/38	7(E)	27
BANDIT	BOB JORGENSON/MO JORGENSON	BELLINGHAM	3.30	16/49/32	8(E)	28
TANTIVY	RAY MARTIN	W.VAN.	2.95	16/50/27	17(D)	29
THALASSIC	CHUCK VIELE	CORINTHIAN	3.05	17/06/36	18(D)	30
FILEY BRIGG	MIKE WEIR	R.VIC.	3.30	17/06/44	9(E)	31
THISTLEDOWN	DON FEELEY	PT. ANGELES	3.05	17/09/14	19(D)	32
MORAG	DICK JENKINS	R.VAN.	3.00	17/09/17	20(D)	33
MITHRIL	ROB HILL	R.VAN.	2.95	17/14/47	21(D)	34
DYNASTY II	JOHN FAIRLEY	W.VAN.	2.95	17/16/21	22(D)	35
DESTINY	J. CHRISTENSEN	CORINTHIAN	2.85	17/16/33	23(D)	36
IRIDES	DONALD PARKER	CANOE BAY	3.20	17/17/49	10(E)	37
OBSESSION	MEL HENRY	TACOMA	2.90	17/26/13	24(D)	38
IMPULSE	J. KEVORKIAN	CORINTHIAN	3.10	17/27/57	25(D)	39
THOMASINE	J.H. COOK	R.VIC.	3.00	17/33/35	26(D)	40
DENT DE LION	GEORGE MOHLER	PT. ANGELES	2.85	17/40/23	27(D)	41
VIKING	ALAN DICKINSON	CANOE BAY	3.15	17/40/48	28(D)	42
SLY FOX	JACK FOSTER	R.VIC.	3.25	17/51/23	11(E)	43
MOCCASIN II	GEOFFREY NEILY	MAPLE BAY	2.90	17/52/40	29(D)	44
PIPE DREAM	R. ABENDROTH	SEATTLE	4.15	18/22/15	5(F)	45
HAIMHAUSEN	SIEGFRIED BREDL	CORINTHIAN	4.10	18/25/24	6(F)	46
THE SLOOP JOHN B.	J. BOYD IVENS	TSAWWASSEN	3.70	18/29/19	7(F)	47
LIBRE	BOB DEAN	R.VIC.	3.65	18/30/24	8(F)	48
MAPLE SUGAR	WAITE BROOKS	R.VIC.	3.65	18/35/19	9(F)	49
GEORGIA GIRL	BILL MARTIN	CANOE BAY	3.70	18/36/19	10(F)	50
ROMADA	ROY HINGLEY	CANOE BAY	3.50	18/44/26	11(F)	51
ILLUSIVE	E. BRUCE JOHNSON	R.VIC.	3.50	18/44/54	12(F)	52
MASSILIA II	E.E. READSHAW	R.VIC.	3.45	18/48/13	12(E)	53
SUNSHINE	GERRY PORTER	R.VIC.	3.40	18/49/18	13(E)	54
DEMARA	ALAN CROWE	TIDDLY COVE	3.50	18/52/44	13(F)	55
YELLOW JACKET	RICHARD SMITH	P.A.Y.C.	3.40	18/53/53	14(E)	56
HALCYON	P.D.C. CLARK	R.VIC.	3.75	18/55/59	14(F)	57
SANTOSA	KEN DANCHUK	TACOMA	3.30	18/57/52	15(E)	58
NOOSA	R. VAN DEN DRIESSCHE	R.VIC.	3.30	18/59/34	16(E)	59
SIRIUS	K. WATERFALL	MAPLE BAY	3.30	19/01/47	17(E)	60
VOLARE	JOHN CICERI	R.VIC.	3.30	19/01/47	18(E)	61
BAGHEERA II	ANDY COPELAND/LIZA COPELAND	R.VAN.	3.30	19/08/47	19(E)	62
GUPPY	GREG KNIGHT	SEMIAHMOO	3.35	19/12/41	20(E)	63
SANA	J.K. MARTIN	CANOE BAY	3.10	19/12/59	30(D)	64
COLD MILK	DEAN ERICKSON/STEVE ERICKSON	EDMONDS	3.10	19/16/34	31(D)	65
STIMULATOR	MIKE KERNAN SUND	CORINTHIAN	3.05	19/16/46	32(D)	66
UNION DEPOT	ROGER L. RUE	TACOMA	3.05	19/17/54	33(D)	67
BAREFOOT	DONALD RUSSELL	CORINTHIAN	3.00	19/20/32	34(D)	68
RAVEN	C.F.G. CRISP	R.VIC.	3.00	19/20/32	35(D)	69
CANTAMAR II	RUSS LUMSDEN	R.VAN.	2.95	19/25/27	36(D)	70
PRESTO	TOM WHITE	BELLINGHAM	2.95	19/25/27	37(D)	71
KEHLOKE	JOHN KINE/JANET KINE	R.VAN.	2.95	19/26/29	38(D)	72
RESOLUTE 2	BOB DEUTSCHER	TACOMA	2.85	19/30/53	39(D)	73
JOLLY OLLY III	RICK COCKBURN	SEMIAHMOO	2.85	19/30/53	40(D)	74
DEPARTURE	JACK MILLER	R.VIC.	2.85	19/33/01	41(D)	75
UMPKA	JOHN R. BOOTH	R.VIC.	3.40	19/34/22	21(E)	76
VANDAL II	JIM MacFARLANE	MAPLE BAY	2.90	19/36/45	42(D)	77
IMAGE RESPONSE	ROGER PALMER	EDMONDS	2.80	19/36/48	43(D)	78
SKOOKUM	GERALD PARKER	TACOMA	2.80	19/44/15	44(D)	79
LUCY ALICE	W.H. GARDNER	CORINTHIAN	3.65	19/55/30	15(F)	80
RHIANNON	MIKE WARD	PORTLAND	3.20	20/47/29	22(E)	81
WINDY WENDY TWO	DR. A. SHEARER	R.VAN.	3.00	20/49/55	45(D)	82
TOLUCA	T.A. KRIEGER	R.VIC.	3.40	20/56/17	23(E)	83
JESSICA	CLINT CURRIE	KITSILANO	3.70	21/02/43	16(F)	84
SUNSHINE	GORD MARTMAN	CANOE BAY	3.10	21/44/48	46(D)	85
CAPRICE	H.R. GARDNER	C.F.S.A.	4.00	21/47/58	17(F)	86
CHINOOK	D.J. BURKE	MAPLE BAY	4.10	22/59/19	18(F)	87
WINDIGO	E.W. DEKONIG/P. DEKONIG	PORTLAND	3.30		(E)	DSQ

TRITON	ERIC WICHERTS	R.VIC.	3.55		(F)	DSQ
AVENGER II	A.S. BARKER	W.VAN.	3.10		(D)	DSQ
LITTLE WITCH	DAVID WILDER	EAGLE HAR.	3.40		(E)	DNS
ELEN TARI	R.L.D. WRIGHT	R.VIC.	3.45		(E)	DSQ
GEMINI	J. VAN OMMEN	BELLINGHAM	3.00		(D)	DSQ
BANDIDO	R.G. FOXALL	W.VAN.	2.95		(D)	DNF
AJAX	GERRY STORCH	RNSA	3.20		(E)	DNS
RAINBOW CHASER	LON RIGGS	PT. ANGELES	3.20		(E)	DSQ

PACIFIC INTERNATIONAL YACHTING ASSOCIATION
SWIFTSURE LIGHTSHIP CLASSIC AND JUAN DE FUCA RACE
1978 TROPHY WINNERS

RESULTS AT: AUGUST 21, 1978 Final results following protest hearings and error corrections.

SWIFTSURE (I.O.R.)	SWIFTSURE TROPHY (OVERALL HANDICAP WINNER)	BILL BUCHAN	CORINTHIAN	SACHEM
	CITY OF VICTORIA TROPHY (1ST YACHT TO FINISH)	FRITZ JOHNSON	N.Y.Y.C.	WINDWARD PASSAGE
	OCEAN CEMENT TROPHY (FIRST IN DIVISION 1)	TED BURNS, MD	BREMERTON	OUTRAGEOUS
	T. EATON TROPHY (FIRST IN DIVISION 2)	JOHN BUCHAN	SEATTLE	HEATHER
	CITY OF SEATTLE TROPHY (FIRST IN DIVISION 3)	TOM GEISNESS LARRY SHORETT	SEATTLE	PROSPECTOR
	ROYAL VANCOUVER YACHT CLUB TROPHY (FIRST IN DIVISION 4)	BILL BUCHAN	CORINTHIAN	SACHEM
SWIFTSURE (P.H.R.F.)	.... (OVERALL HANDICAP WINNER)	M. FIANDER WAYNE WHITE	CORINTHIAN	APPARITION
	ROYAL CANADIAN NAVY TROPHY (1ST YACHT TO FINISH)	G. ANDERSON	SEATTLE	BACCARAI
	CORINTHIAN YACHT CLUB TROPHY (FIRST IN DIVISION A)	FRANK MUSSON	WEST VAN	MELTEMI
	STORMY WEATHER TROPHY (FIRST IN DIVISION B)	DR. R. BARNHART	BELLINGHAM	WINDSONG II
	CAPE FLATTERY TROPHY (FIRST IN DIVISION C)	M. FIANDER WAYNE WHITE	CORINTHIAN	APPARITION
JUAN DE FUCA (I.O.R.)	.... (OVERALL HANDICAP WINNER)	DR. G. WILKINS	R.VAN.Y.C.	GOGAMA
	SAN JUAN TROPHY (1ST YACHT TO FINISH)	DR. G. WILKINS	R.VAN.Y.C.	GOGAMA
	ROYAL VICTORIA YACHT CLUB TROPHY (FIRST IN DIVISION 5)	DR. G. WILKINS	R.VAN.Y.C.	GOGAMA
	ROYAL CANADIAN NAVY TROPHY (FIRST IN DIVISION 6)	SCOTT RUSH	CYC	FOULWEATHER BLUFF
JUAN DE FUCA (P.H.R.F.)	PORT ANGELES YACHT CLUB TROPHY (OVERALL HANDICAP WINNER)	DON CLARK	SEATTLE	PIECE O'CAKE
	.... (1ST YACHT TO FINISH)	DON CLARK	SEATTLE	PIECE O'CAKE
	ANACORTES YACHT CLUB TROPHY (FIRST IN DIVISION D)	DON CLARK	SEATTLE	PIECE O'CAKE
	.... (FIRST IN DIVISION E)	BOB LEFEAUX	TIDDLYCOVE	BAD NEWS
	.... (FIRST IN DIVISION F)	RON CARLSON	PT ANGELES	MARILYN L

SWIFTSURE (I.O.R.) 1978 RESULTS

OFFICIAL START TIME: 11/40/00

YACHT NAME	SKIPPER(S)	CLUB	RATING	COR ELAPSE TIME	POSITION DIVISION	OVERALL
SACHEM	BILL BUCHAN	CORINTHIAN	24.50	20/ 7/27	1(4)	1
OUTRAGEOUS	TED BURNS, MD	BREMERTON	41.00	20/12/ 1	1(1)	2
WARRIOR	LANGDON HEDRICK	SEATTLE	42.70A	20/18/10	2(1)	3
WINDWARD PASSAGE	FRITZ JOHNSON	N.Y.Y.C.	65.70A	20/21/57	3(1)	4
BRAVURA	IRVING LOUBE	LAHAINA	38.40	20/29/40	4(1)	5
DRIFTER	RON HART/DICK WARREN	LAHAINA	71.80	20/46/ 0	5(1)	6
MERLIN	DOUG FRYER	SEATTLE	71.00	20/51/55	6(1)	7
SCARAMOUCHE	BOB ALEXANDER	SEATTLE	34.70A	21/10/ 7	7(1)	8
HEATHER	JOHN BUCHAN	SEATTLE	31.90	21/11/58	1(2)	9
PROSPECTOR	TOM GEISNESS/LARRY SHORETT	SEATTLE	27.40	21/46/35	1(3)	10
SHRIKE	CHUCK CROFT	WEST VAN	27.50	21/52/17	2(3)	11
MISTRESS II	I.W. VARLEY, MD	EVERETT	30.30A	21/52/26	2(2)	12
CHOCOLATE CHIP	RON LESTER/DON PORTER	MICH. CITY	24.50	21/52/27	2(4)	13
EPIC	C. SCHIFF	CORINTHIAN	36.00A	21/55/48	8(1)	14
ENDURANCE	HUGH MINOR	EVERETT	30.80A	21/58/50	3(2)	15
PENDRAGON	J.C. MACLAURIN	CALIFORNIA	24.50	22/ 6/51	3(4)	16
NAKNEK	RICHARD NELSON	R.VAN.Y.C.	38.60A	22/13/50	9(1)	17

PURSUIT	WILLIAM ENGLE	SEATTLE	30.20A	22/19/26	10(1)	18
DISCOVERY	JOHN DUNFIELD	R.VAN.Y.C.	37.90A	22/32/ 8	11(1)	19
MUSTARD SEED	DOVE HERMAN/SPUD GRIMES	EDMONDS	27.50	22/37/29	3(3)	20
LADYBUG	ALAN HOLT	SEATTLE	21.70	22/40/49	4(4)	21
SUNRISE	THOMAS HAYES	SEATTLE	21.70	22/48/21	5(4)	22
NITE MOVES	VERNER EGLIT	CORINTHIAN	21.70	22/51/35	6(4)	23
SALLY LIGHTFOOT	TOM FRIEDLAND	BELLINGHAM	26.10A	22/52/52	4(3)	24
AMERICAN FLYER	FRED W. BIEKER	PORTLAND	29.90A	22/53/34	4(2)	25
INDIGO	R.F. HARRISON	WEST VAN	29.80A	22/59/36	5(2)	26
THE DISTANT DRUMMER	GREGORY OLIVER	R.VIC.Y.C.	27.50	23/ 3/14	5(3)	27
PAGEANT	STUART ARCHER	TACOMA	30.50A	23/ 4/42	6(2)	28
LEVEL CROSSING	ALEX FOLEY	R.VAN.Y.C.	27.50	23/ 7/23	6(3)	29
TAPOCKETA	ROBERT NEWELL	BELLINGHAM	24.50	23/11/43	7(4)	30
AGGRESSION	J. CHRISTENSEN	CORINTHIAN	25.80A	23/15/43	7(3)	31
MIDNIGHT SPECIAL	V. McCULLOUGH	SYC	30.40A	23/23/ 6	7(2)	32
COHO II	JOHN H. LONG	R.VAN.Y.C.	36.10	23/32/32	12(1)	33
TZORES	MIKE KERNAN	CYC	24.00A	23/35/ 9	8(4)	34
ALLIANCE	T. GIDLUND/E. SCHWAB	CORINTHIAN	27.80	23/40/41	8(3)	35
SPITFIRE	H.E. MCBRAYER	CEDAR PT.	27.80	23/44/46	9(3)	36
ANOMALY	WILLIAM ELMER	CORINTHIAN	26.60A	23/45/39	10(3)	37
BIG SISTER	JOHN EVETTS	VANC.ROWNG	21.60	23/46/58	9(4)	38
SAVAGE SPIRIT	R.G. LINKLETTER/GEORGE OAKES	PT. ANGELES	27.50	24/ 2/30	11(3)	39
TERNA III	P. CHRISTOFFERSEN	WEST VAN	30.10A	24/ 3/23	8(2)	40
ULTIMATUM	J.L. WILLIAMS	R.VAN.Y.C.	26.60A	24/ 5/54	12(3)	41
COUNTESS III	PETER JEFFERSON	R.VAN.Y.C.	29.50A	24/ 6/ 6	9(2)	42
JEZEBEL	CHUCK BROCKWAY	SEATTLE	26.60A	24/ 9/48	13(3)	43
WOTAN	BILL BURDICK	SEATTLE	26.40A	24/10/25	14(3)	44
SIRIS II	GEORGE KING/MR OAKLAND	SEATTLE	26.70A	24/17/22	15(3)	45
SINE MORA	DONALD HILLMAN	SEATTLE	26.30A	24/18/25	16)3)	46
NERITA	MICHAEL STORIE	CORINTHIAN	30.10A	24/20/51	10(2)	47
PANGAEA	M.B. MADENWALD	ANACORTES	30.20	24/30/17	11(2)	48
HYPERTENSION	ROGER PALMER	EDMONDS	26.60	24/31/12	10(4)	49
WHITEBIRD	ALEX BOOME	R.VAN.Y.C.	26.50	24/31/16	11(4)	50
RAINDROP	J. GAINER	CORINTHIAN	27.60A	24/31/19	12(2)	51
DISCOVERY I	DAVID HALL/JOHN BALL	G. TRAVERSE	24.50	24/33/28	12(4)	52
TOPKAPI	BOB KITCHEN	WEST VAN	28.20	24/37/27	17(3)	53
ERRIGAL	HUGH PORTER	R.VIC.Y.C.	27.30	24/38/50	18(3)	54
BETELGEUSE	TERRY GUEST	R.VAN.Y.C.	27.50	24/40/ 6	19(3)	55
PARADOX	JOHN MCGOWEN	TACOMA	27.50	24/48/31	20(3)	56
WARLOCK	BOB SMITH	TACOMA	34.20A	24/58/38	13(1)	57
WINDWARD	CECIL J. DION	WEST VAN	26.60	25/ 3/40	13(4)	58
OUTRAGEOUS	JOHN HARDIMAN	CYC PORTLD	27.68A	25/ 4/54	21(3)	59
BORU	DONALD BYRNE	R.VAN.Y.C.	27.50	25/ 4/59	22(3)	60
BAGHEERA	ANDY COPELAND	R.VAN.Y.C.	24.20	25/14/57	14(4)	61
THE PHOENICIAN	C SCHILBACH, MD	PORTLAND	33.40	25/24/56	14(1)	62
DIAMOND HEAD	H.L. KUTKINS	SEATTLE	43.50A	25/34/18	15(1)	63
ELIXIR	JOHN GRAHAM	SEATTLE	25.70A	25/36/55	23(3)	64
HARPOON	WILLIAM BRASIER	TACOMA	32.50A	25/38/13	16(1)	65
HABITAT	P.C.G. RICHARDS	WEST VAN	27.70A	25/39/57	24(3)	66
BARBARIAN	DR. V. BRYAN	POULSBO	26.70A	25/53/41	25(3)	67
WINGAWAY I	GERRY KIDD	W.V.Y.C.	28.20A	25/54/21	13(2)	68
SUNSET	TERRY BUCHOLZ/ED BLACKBURN	CORINTHIAN	32.00A	25/55/38	17(1)	69
SATURDAY'S CHILD	C. BRAIN	SEATTLE	38.90	26/ 0/50	18(1)	70
NIMBLE	WM.A. NICKERSON	PORTLAND	31.30A	26/ 3/40	19(1)	71
ABRAXAS II	D.C. SELMAN	R.VAN.Y.C.	30.30A	26/23/23	14(2)	72
SURPRISE	GERRY MAURER	SEATTLE	28.50A	26/27/20	15(2)	73
SHAZAM	RANDY MUELLER	CORINTHIAN	26.30A	26/27/34	26(3)	74
NIGHTHAWK	EDWARD ODISHAW	KITSILANO	26.60A	30/ 5/50	16(2)	75
IMPROBABLE	LEONARD SCHWAB	CORINTHIAN	35.10	DNF	DNF(1)	DNF
WARLORD	JOHN D. BARLINE	TACOMA	25.80A	DNF	DNF(3)	DNF
PACHENA	JOHN NEWTON	WEST VAN	32.00	DNF	DNF(2)	DNF
GOLD RUSH	NATHAN RUSSELL	SHILSHOLE	29.40A	DSQ	DSQ(2)	DSQ
BRER RABBIT	JOHN ALBERTSON/M. RUNSTAD	CORINTHIAN	29.10A	DNF	DNF(2)	DNF
THUNDER	WM.J. KING	PORTLAND	30.20A	DNF	DNF(2)	DNF
SPEARHEAD	V. PLAVSIC	WEST VAN	24.50	DNF	DNF(4)	DNF
GOLDEN EAGLE	RICHARD ROBERTS	CORINTHIAN	24.50	DNF	DNF(4)	DNF
IRISH ROSE	D. DONOHUE, MD	CORINTHIAN	32.00	DNF	DNF(2)	DNF
WIZARD	EDWIN DE KONING	PORTLAND	32.00	DNF	DNF(2)	DNF
JO	TOM WHITE	BELLINGHAM	24.50	DNF	DNF(4)	DNF

OFFICIAL START TIME: 12/10/00

YACHT NAME	SKIPPER(S)	CLUB	RATING	COR ELAPSE TIME	POSITION DIVISION	POSITION OVERALL
APPARITION	M. FIANDER/WAYNE WHITE	CORINTHIAN	2.90	22/47/37	1(C)	1
PANDEMONIUM	PETER O'REILLY	OLYMPIA	2.95	23/ 3/31	2(C)	2
CANDYMAN	GUY BOCKUS/DAWN BOCKUS	PT MADISON	2.95	23/ 4/ 8	3(C)	3
MELTEMI	FRANK MUSSON	WEST VAN	2.10	23/23/49	1(A)	4
FLO	ROBERT WHEELER	SYC	2.95	23/24/31	4(C)	5
CONSULTATION	DEAN ANDERSON	OLYMPIA	2.80	23/28/ 4	5(C)	6
WINDSONG II	DR. R. BARNHART	BELLINGHAM	2.50	23/33/17	1(B)	7
MOLLY SQUASH	ANDY ROITLER	SEATTLE	2.55	23/39/51	2(B)	8
TANGENT II	ANTHONY LOACH	WEST VAN	2.10	23/45/45	2(A)	9
FROSTBITE	R.B. FROST	SHILSHOLE	2.30	23/53/57	3(B)	10
SMALL WORLD II	GENE W. SIBOLD	OLYMPIA	2.30	23/54/29	4(B)	11
MATILDA	J.C. ERICKSON	S. SOUND	2.45	23/54/54	5(B)	12
TSUNAMI	C.J. MORAN	CORINTHIAN	2.35	23/57/56	6(B)	13
NAHMA	K. MAXWELL	CORINTHIAN	2.55	23/59/34	7(B)	14
ASTARTE	ALAN HOFFMAN	CORINTHIAN	2.55	24/ 0/39	8(B)	15
ZUBEN'UBI II	WILLIAM HESTER	CORINTHIAN	2.20	24/ 3/ 9	9(B)	16
CHEROKEE	MIKE MULCAHY/H. HANSON	THREE TREE	2.30	24/ 3/40	10(B)	17
COUNTERPOINT	TIM CLARK	CORINTHIAN	2.35	24/ 5/34	11(B)	18
GAMIN	LUN ROBINSON	SEATTLE	2.20	24/ 6/27	12(B)	19
STRIDER	KEITH JOHNSON	CORINTHIAN	2.45	24/ 7/25	13(B)	20
RASCAL	DENNIS THORNTON	CORINTHIAN	2.30	24/ 8/10	14(B)	21
OVERDRAFT TOO	G.M. HESELDIN	R.VAN.Y.C.	1.80	24/ 8/21	3(A)	22
MAGNUM	R.E. AXFORD	R.VAN.Y.C.	2.40	24/ 9/18	15(B)	23
ROWDY LADY II	ARTHUR HAUGE	PORTLAND	2.30	24/20/28	16(B)	24
ELISHEBA	MILES MILLER	CYC-SEATTLE	2.15	24/22/11	4(A)	25
SAVAGE	LARRY HILLS	SEATTLE	2.20	24/23/42	17(B)	26
TRINGA	FRED GARDINER	R.VIC.Y.C.	2.20	24/25/34	18(B)	27
SCRIMSHANDER	JACK MILLER/HUGH LAMONT	CANOE BAY	2.30	24/25/46	19(B)	28
DELIVERANCE	GEORGE PALO	CORINTHIAN	2.20	24/28/45	20(B)	29
MENEHUNE	DONALD WILSON	CANOE BAY	2.15	24/29/28	5(A)	30
OLYMPIAN	PETER G. SCHMIDT	SEATTLE	1.85	24/30/ 4	6(A)	31
MOSHULU	R.O. SYLVESTER	SEATTLE	2.20	24/32/15	21(B)	32
REALITY	ROLAND BRENER	T.H.S.A.	1.85	24/32/23	7(A)	33
GOODBYE	T.W. LONEY	R.VIC.Y.C.	2.20	24/33/55	22(B)	34
ALBERTA BOUND	P.J. ROGERS	KITSILANO	2.40	24/35/ 5	23(B)	35
SUNDANCE	KRISTAN OVERBY	T.C.Y.C.	2.95	24/35/36	6(C)	36
BACCARAT	G. ANDERSON	SEATTLE	1.35	24/36/ 2	8(A)	37
ARROW	PAUL ELVSTROM	SEATTLE	1.90	24/39/15	9(A)	38
MUTINEER IV	T.R. BRAIDWOOD	WEST VAN	1.90	24/39/17	10(A)	39
SHANNON	R.G. RAYMANT	WEST VAN	2.70	24/42/36	7(C)	40
NORTHERLY	WILLIAM CHUBB	SEATTLE	1.90	24/44/ 5	11(A)	41
MADRUGADOR	E. ANDERSON	SEATTLE	1.85	24/47/40	12(A)	42
PEGASUS	JOHN G. BECKER/EUGENE BECKER	CORINTHIAN	2.80	24/50/ 8	8(C)	43
EROS	STUART FETTERS	SEATTLE	1.80	24/50/36	13(A)	44
WHITE SQUALL	G. TEATS, MD	TACOMA	1.85	24/53/15	14(A)	45
FIREBRAND	R.W. NEWMAN	SEATTLE	1.95	24/56/15	15(A)	46
SYDEILSUMA	K. DAVIDSON/R. KANIA	EAGLE HAR	1.75	24/56/42	16(A)	47
NOMAD	BILL LIEBERMAN	CORINTHIAN	2.25	24/57/59	24(B)	48
THALASSIC	CHUCK VIELE	CORINTHIAN	2.15	24/58/43	17(A)	49
HOOLIGAN II	TOM O'BRIEN	SEATTLE	1.85	24/58/51	18(A)	50
AVENGER II	A.S. BARKER	WEST VAN	3.10	24/58/51	9(C)	51
SQAIP	CONOR W. BOYD	CORINTHIAN	2.15	24/59/56	19(A)	52
MOON DAY	J. HEALY/DAVID NEFF	CORINTHIAN	1.85	25/ 2/12	20(A)	53
COLUMBINE	TOM LINDER	ANACORTES	1.90	25/ 2/26	21(A)	54
FAEM	D. GILLILAND	R.VAN.Y.C.	2.15	25/ 6/13	22(A)	55
TONIC	DAN BRINK	CORINTHIAN	2.90	25/11/ 6	10(C)	56
TARTUFFE	JAMES E. DEPOE	PT. MADISON	2.80	25/13/13	11(C)	57
YANKEE GIRL	JOE MCDONALD	SEATTLE	1.80	25/14/27	23(A)	58
SAGA	S. RASMUSSEN	R.VAN.Y.C.	2.10	25/26/11	24(A)	59
DOUBLE TIME	JOHN LEONARD	ANACORTES	2.40	25/31/26	25(B)	60
SUNDANCE	THOMAS MURPHY	TACOMA	1.75	25/31/36	25(A)	61
MAHRI II	RON MACKENZIE	R.VAN.Y.C.	2.05	25/34/27	26(A)	62
RHIANNON	BUSH ALBISTON	SEATTLE	2.00	25/36/24	27(A)	63
SNOOSE	CHARLES OLSON	EDMONDS	2.20	25/39/55	26(B)	64
HOTSPUR	J.T. CLAYTON	R.VAN.Y.C.	2.20	25/40/57	27(B)	65
CALLALOO	JOHN CATLEY	R.VAN.Y.C.	2.90	25/41/1	12(C)	66
SCHLINGEL	MICHAEL TREIT	CORINTHIAN	2.40	25/42/57	28(B)	67

Boat	Skipper	Club	Rating			
BENORA	HARRY HERLIHY	R.VAN.Y.C.	2.05	25/47/44	28(A)	68
ESCAPE HATCH	BOB FERRIE	BELLINGHAM	3.50	25/52/ 7	13(C)	69
ATLANTEAN	DENNY COVERDALE	SL TAVERN	2.15	25/52/27	29(A)	70
SPECTRE	JOHN CAHILL, MD	SEATTLE	1.85	25/53/ 7	30(A)	71
RAMPART	J.A. ROSS	MAPLE BAY	1.60	25/53/52	31(A)	72
RAVEN	BRIAN JOHNSON	SEATTLE	1.90	25/59/48	32(A)	73
BEAUJOLAIS	GILES SHEPHERD	EVERETT	2.80	26/ 0/13	14(C)	74
SWALLOW II	PHIL JOHNSON	SEATTLE	1.85	26/ 1/ 3	33(A)	75
LUCKY LADY	FRED L. KRABBE	SAN JUAN	2.75	26/ 6/42	15(C)	76
ELUSIVE	STEPHEN SHEA	SEATTLE	1.55	26/ 7/ 7	34(A)	77
TERNA	R.J. DE ROOS/L. HARTNEY	R.VAN.Y.C.	2.10	26/ 8/37	35(A)	78
GOLDEN APPLE	ROBERT KERSHAW	SEATTLE	1.70	26/10 1	36(A)	79
KOTUKU*	DR. R. MATHEWSON	T.H.S.A.	2.10	26/12/17	37(A)	80
EMMA	H. HARTWIG	R.VIC.Y.C.	2.20	26/13/43	29(B)	81
NAUTILUS	L. NEVLER, MD	CYC	2.30	26/14/44	30(B)	82
JOLLY ROGER III	ROGER WHEELER	CORINTHIAN	2.45	216/18/16	31(B)	83
DEUCE COUPE	GEORGE LOWE	PT MADISON	1.85	26/18/57	38(A)	84
SARDIFF	SID BURGESS	WEST VAN	1.80	26/20/15	39(A)	85
LORD JIM	DON STABBERT	SEATTLE	1.85	26/28/44	40(A)	86
SEALION	NORMAN MARTIN	NANAIMO	2.20	26/33/29	32(B)	87
CRYSTALSHIP	JOHN E. SPROUSE	PORTLAND	1.80	26/41/48	41(A)	88
DORLES	WILLIS KLUDT	THREE TREE	1.90	26/43/59	42(A)	89
TIN MAN	NED FLOHR	SEATTLE	3.70	26/51/44	16(C)	90
WINDLESS II	CHESS RICKARD/T. REICHGELD	TIDDLY CVE	1.80	26/55/23	43(A)	91
FINAL SOLUTION	COLIN SHINN	R.N.S.A.	1.80	26/57/25	44(A)	92
TOLO TSOLO	E.E. WOODSON	ANACORTES	2.45	26/59/53	33(B)	93
ANGELA K	JESS KRITSIS	CORINTHIAN	2.10	27/ 1/54	45(A)	94
KATCHEN	D. STAATZ, MD	TACOMA	2.70	27/21/19	17(C)	95
TRINORCA	LARS PEDERSEN	R.VAN.Y.C.	2.95	27/35/57	18(C)	96
RIVAL	JANGARD/KELLIS	TACOMA	1.85	27/39/15	46(A)	97
VIVA	D. BLAKEMORE	CORINTHIAN	1.85	28/ 0/16	47(A)	98
ODIN	ALAN HARTE	R.N.S.A.	3.15	28/ 6/ 1	19(C)	99
RASPUTIN	BRIAN HEYES	R.N.S.A.	3.05	28/27/ 4	20(C)	100
TOOTH & NAIL	RON MARTIN	TIDDLYCOVE	2.90	28/39/56	21(C)	101
HOME MAID	ASHLEY DERMER	R.N.S.A.	2.50	28/48/ 7	34(B)	102
KEEMA	R.D. TUCKER	BELLINGHAM	2.50	28/49/23	35(B)	103
TARUN	PETER HENDRIE	R.VAN.Y.C.	2.50	29/ 1/57	36(B)	104
HWYLIO	LARRY ROBERTS	ROSE CITY	2.95	31/19/ 4	22(C)	105
SHAMAN	DR.G. MIDDLETON	CORINTHIAN	1.85	DNF	DNF(A)	DNF
SKARRIETT	R.E. WILSON	THREE TREE	1.95	DSQ	DSQ(A)	DSQ
KISMET	M.J. CARLSON	EVERETT	1.90	DNS	DNS(A)	DNS
MUTINEER	KEN BOSMA	GLENMORE	2.85	DNF	DNF(C)	DNF
GOMETRA	DAVID MILLIS	R.N.S.A.	2.35	DNF	DNF(B)	DNF
SEA DANCE	J.P. LEDALLIC	C.F.S.A.	1.60	DNF	DNF(A)	DNF
CIRRUS	ALAN FORSYTHE	QUATERMSTR	2.90	DNF	DNF(C)	DNF
BIGBIRD	ALLAN LAIRD	R.VAN.Y.C.	1.80	DSQ	DSQ(A)	DSQ
LANCER	NORMAN LARABEE	CORINTHIAN	2.40	DNF	DNF(B)	DNF
ARROW	DON RIPLEY/CAROL RIPLEY	THREE TREE	1.95	DNF	DNF(A)	DNF
BARBARA	WYNN E. KAMPE	CORINTHIAN	2.10	DNF	DNF(A)	DNF
SERVUS	H.G. STRICKER	R.VIC.Y.C.	2.70	DNF	DNF(C)	DNF
MEG	BOB HOSIE	R.VIC.Y.C.	2.20	DNS	DNS(B)	DNS
MALTESE FALCON	ROSS SCHULKE	SYC	2.40	DNS	DNS(B)	DNS
DU FRIA	JOHN A. KLASELL	SHILSHOLE	2.25	DNF	DNF(B)	DNF
ORANGO-TANG	NORMAN ELLIOTT	R.VAN.Y.C.	2.10	DNF	DNF(A)	DNF
WHITE MIST	DORR ANDERSON	SEATTLE	3.10	DNF	DNF(C)	DNF
BAREFOOT 2	JIM WARD	CORINTHIAN	2.55	DNF	DNF(B)	DNF
STARWAGON	R.O. GILBERT	SEATTLE	2.30	DSQ	DSQ(B)	DSQ
JACKAROE	R.L. HILLS	TOWNSEND	2.90	DNF	DNF(C	DNF
BLACK WATCH	BILL NELSON/HARRY WINGARD	CORINTHIAN	1.55	DNF	DNF(A)	DNF
UKRAINIAN MAGIC	DICK TUDAN	CORINTHIAN	2.50	DNF	DNF(B)	DNF
MARANDA	R.D. HUGHES	R.N.S.A.	2.35	DNF	DNF(B)	DNF
EDELWEISS II	PAUL WAGNER	R.VAN.Y.C.	2.20	DNF	DNF(B)	DNF
VANSCAP	LLOYD ANDERSON	PENTICTON	3.30	DNF	DNF(C)	DNF
ANYLOVE	D. MARSHALL	CORINTHIAN	2.45	DNS	DNS(B)	DNS
SPINSTER	JULIAN DEWELL	EVERETT	2.30	DNF	DNF(B)	DNF
LIZA K	K. PARTLOW II	OLYMPIA	2.40	DNF	DNF(B)	DNF
PRO TANTO	WILLIAM STANGE	U OF WASH	2.95	DNF	DNF(C)	DNF
LIBERTY BELL	D. MATCHETTE	OLYMPIA	1.80	DNF	DNF(A)	DNF
GOLDEN GIRL	FREDERICK HALL	PORTLAND	2.50	DNS	DNS(B)	DNS
JEANOYCE	THOS. A. CLARK	LAHAINA	2.50	DNF	DNF(B)	DNF
DECEPTION	ROBERT CAIRNS/JOHNSON, LEAP	SEATTLE	2.20	DNF	DNF(B)	DNF

YACHT NAME	SKIPPER(S)	CLUB	RATING	COR ELAPSE TIME	POSITION DIVISION	OVERALL
DREAMBOAT ANNIE	MIKE WARD	CYC, PORTLD	2.40	DNF	DNF(B)	DNF

JUAN DE FUCA (I.O.R.) 1978
RESULTS

YACHT NAME	SKIPPER(S)	CLUB	RATING	COR ELAPSE TIME	POSITION DIVISION	OVERALL
GOGAMA	DR. G. WILKINS	R.VAN.Y.C.	24.50	9/38/ 6	1(5)	1
FOULWEATHER BLUFF	SCOTT RUSH	CORINTHIAN	21.50	11/15/ 0	1(6)	2
SEA BEATER	BLEN BOUDON	CYC	21.70	11/21/31	2(6)	3
SCRAMBLER	MICHAEL B.OKEY/ROBIN BOOKEY	SEATTLE	21.70	11/43/38	3(6)	4
GOTCHAFERGOOD	BOB DIEHL	BELLINGHAM	24.50	11/57/12	2(5)	5
SACRE BLEU	BRIAN GRIFFIN	BELLINGHAM	24.50	12/ 0/55	3(5)	6
FLAUNT	ROBERT HAMILTON	TACOMA	21.70A	12/18/31	4(6)	7
NORN III	OLAV EKROM/SCOTT NORTON	CORINTHIAN	24.50	12/34/ 6	4(5)	8
POISSON SOLUBLE	R HORSLEY	CORINTHIAN	24.50	12/35/ 9	5(5)	9
GALEB	GEORGE CESAREC	R.VIC.Y.C.	21.80	12/44/16	5(6)	10
CLIMAX	MIKE SMITH/DON SMITH	CORINTHIAN	21.70	13/ 5/54	6(6)	11
PEREGRINE	M.L. HAINES	BELLINGHAM	24.50	13/ 8/17	6(5)	12
DENIZEN	R.E. KREYBIG	CORINTHIAN	24.50	13/ 8/19	7(5)	13
TENACIOUS	JOE DREM	BELLINGHAM	24.50	13/10/36	8(5)	14
ADVERSARY	TIM MALEDY/HOLLY MALEDY	R.VAN.Y.C.	21.70	13/37/24	7(6)	15
BRIDGET	H.V. SARGENT	OLYMPIA	21.70	13/45/50	8(6)	16
SCAMPI	TED WATERMAN	R.V.Y.C.	21.80A	14/17/27	9(5)	17
DREAM MACHINE	ROBERT C. SMITH	PORTLAND	17.70A	14/23/18	9(6)	18
THE PROFESSOR	JACK MATTHEWS	R.VIC.Y.C.	17.00A	14/35/ 7	10(6)	19
QUORUM	DAVID M. FIELD	CORINTHIAN	24.20A	14/51/54	10(5)	20
MIDNIGHT MADNESS	MIKE WHITE	CORINTHIAN	24.40	14/58/39	11(5)	21
MARY D II	DARREL DAVIS	PT. ANGELES	24.60	15/ 5/42	12(5)	22
BROOM HILDA	CHARLES WILSON	PT. ANGELES	21.50	15/16/ 0	11(6)	23
EAGLE	GUS HOUGE	BELLINGHAM	24.40	15/24/42	13(5)	24
SOCKEYE	LARRY SALKIELD	SEATTLE	24.40	15/38/ 7	14(5)	25
NEW INFIDEL	ROD WHITFIELD	EAGLE HARB	24.50	DNF	DNF(5)	DNF
RIOTOUS ASSEMBLY	FINN NIELSEN	MAPLE BAY	24.50	DNF	DNF(5)	DNF
PUSILLANIMOUS	R.G. ALEXANDER	CORINTHIAN	17.30A	DSQ	DSQ(6)	DSQ
OUTLAW	THOMAS C. HUKLE	SYC	21.70	DNF	DNF(6)	DNF
COOKIE MONSTER	MARVIN WAYNE	BELLINGHAM	21.70	DNF	DNF(6)	DNF
RED ONION	SCOTT SCHOCK	NEWPORT	18.40	DNF	DNF(6)	DNF

JUAN DE FUCA (P.H.R.F.) 1978
RESULTS

YACHT NAME	SKIPPER(S)	CLUB	RATING	COR ELAPSE TIME	POSITION DIVISION	OVERALL
PIECE O'CAKE	DON CLARK	SEATTLE	2.85	12/30/27	1(D)	1
BAD NEWS	BOB LEFEAUX	TIDDLYCOVE	3.10	12/37/16	1(E)	2
PANTHER POINT	PAUL SCHOUW	EAGLE HARB	2.80	12/42/48	2(D)	3
BAREFOOT*	DONALD RUSSELL	CORINTHIAN	3.00	13/02/30	3(D)	4
IMPULSE	J. KEVORKIAN	CORINTHIAN	3.10	13/45/22	2(E)	5
THOMASINE	J.H. COOK	R.VIC.Y.C.	3.00	13/45/48	3(D)	6
GEM	RAY FIEDLER	CORINTHIAN	2.75	14/14/29	4(D)	7
MIRAGE	VANCE BINGHAM	PT. ANGELES	2.60	14/26/13	5(D)	8
BANDIDO	R.G. FOXALL	WEST VAN	2.95	14/41/27	6(D)	9
GAZELLE II	J. MASON	R.VAN.Y.C.	3.00	14/42/24	7(D)	10
PATCHWORK QUILT	J. DRYDEN, MD	R.VIC.Y.C.	2.90	14/44/59	8(D)	11
RISQUE	JON A. POKELA	TACOMA	3.05	14/46/ 7	3(E)	12
MARILYN L	RON CARLSON	PT. ANGELES	3.75	14/48/28	1(F)	13
WILLY WILLY	JIM CHILTON	THREE PT.	2.90	14/49/17	9(D)	14
SWEET CHEEKS	CHUCK CROCKER	CORINTHIAN	2.70	14/50/33	10(D)	15
CAL-LORRI	CAM THOMSON	CANOE BAY	3.10	14/51/ 7	4(E)	16
ENCOUNTER	DR. HUGH BACON	R.VIC.Y.C.	2.75	14/53/53	11(D)	17
MOCCASIN II	GEOFF NEILY	MAPLE BAY	2.90	14/54/ 3	12(D)	18
SKILFISH	D.R. WEST	WEST VAN	2.95	14/54/40	13(D)	19
SPINNER	GORDON CASH	CORINTHIAN	2.85	14/54/49	14(D)	20
RAGDOLL	BARRY FOLLMAN	THREE TREE	2.80	14/55/ 7	15(D)	21
TRIAD	RONALD RAY	TACOMA	2.90	14/55/24	16(D)	22
IMPOSITION	W.A. SHELDON	OLYMPIA	2.60	14/59/24	17(D)	23
MOE-TIVATOR	D.E. MOE	PT. ANGELES	2.75	15/ 1/14	18(D)	24
DROP OUT	JIM LAVALLE	TACOMA	3.20	15/ 2/25	5(E)	25
AILSA CRAIG	J.W. CRAIG	R.VIC.Y.C.	2.90	15/ 3/28	19(D)	26
ILLUSIVE	E.B. JOHNSON	R.VIC.Y.C.	3.50	15/ 4/30	2(F)	27
DEMARA	ALAN CROWE	TIDDLY CVE	3.50	15/ 6/42	3(F)	28
MASSILIA II	E.E. READSHAW	R.VIC.Y.C.	3.50	15/ 9/41	4(F)	29
IRRAWADDY	RON SAUNDERS	R.VIC.Y.C.	3.50	15/14/ 7	5(F)	30

LOTTE	ED HAINES	CFSA	4.10	15/14/34	6(F)	31
PENNYWEIGHT	CHARLES WEBBER	CORINTHIAN	2.95	15/15/23	20(D)	32
CANTAMAR II	RUSS LUMSDEN	R.VAN.Y.C.	2.95	15/19/17	21(D)	33
GEMINI	J. VAN OMMEN	ANACORTES	3.00	15/19/17	22(D)	34
UMPKA	JOHN R. BOOTH	R.VIC.Y.C.	3.30	15/21/49	6(E)	35
JACKAL	JERRY CORNELL	PT. ANGELES	2.85	15/23/ 1	23(D)	36
TOLUCA	T.A. KRIEGER	R.VIC.Y.C.	3.30	15/24/24	7(E)	37
LOON	T. SCHNEIDER	CORINTHIAN	3.70	15/24/35	7(F)	38
THISTLEDOWN	DON FEELEY	PT. ANGELES	3.05	15/25/40	8(E)	39
LORELEI II	JOE ROSINSKI	BELLINGHAM	2.75	15/27/23	24(D)	40
VANDAL II	JIM MACFARLANE	MAPLE BAY	2.90	15/29/ 7	25(D)	41
HARMONY	BARRY WILTON	R.VIC.Y.C.	3.40	15/29/21	9(E)	42
VOLARE	JOHN CICERI	R.VIC.Y.C.	3.30	15/32/17	10(E)	43
SLY FOX	JACK FOSTER	R.VIC.Y.C.	3.25	15/32/58	11(E)	44
TEGARRI	TIM C. MCAFEE	CYC	2.70	15/34/32	26(D)	45
PONEMAH	M.D. DALE	TIDDLYCOVE	3.30	15/35/40	12(E)	46
LUCY ALICE	W.H. GARDNER	LYC	3.65	15/35/55	8(F)	47
THE MOCKINGBIRD	JIM A. HARRIS	BROWNSVILL	2.80	15/37/24	27(D)	48
SUNSHINE	GERRY PORTER	T.H.S.A.	3.30	15/37/32	13(E)	49
ALTROLOGER	GUY T. ELLIOTT	TACOMA	2.80	15/38/ 3	28(D)	50
UNION DEPOT	ROGER L. RUE	TACOMA	3.05	15/38/50	14(E)	51
SPIRIT	GARY MORRIS	TACOMA	3.25	15/39/26	15(E)	52
SOCKEYE	PETER KEATE	R.VAN.Y.C.	2.80	15/41/ 8	29(D)	53
SAFFRON	JUNE CAMERON/SVEN DONALDSON	TIDDLYCOVE	3.50	15/43/53	9(F)	54
ARATAI	JAMES ROBINSON	R.VIC.Y.C.	3.50	15/44/ 4	10(F)	55
YELLOW JACKET	RICHARD SMITH	P.A.Y.C.	3.60	15/45/16	11(F)	56
NASTY JACK	DAVID BRINK	CORINTHIAN	2.95	15/45/48	30(D)	57
LOUP DE MER	GORDON/SULLIVAN	NANAIMO	3.15	15/46/23	16(E)	58
TARQUIN IV	G. JOHNSTONE	R.VIC.Y.C.	3.10	15/47/30	17(E)	59
SHIMNA	W.H. BRADBROOK	T.C.Y.C.	2.80	15/47/33	31(D)	60
ELEN TARI	LESLIE WRIGHT	R.VIC.Y.C.	3.45	15/48/ 1	18(E)	61
RESOLUTE 2	BOB DEUTSCHER	TACOMA	2.90	15/49/47	32(D)	62
FIREFLY	WILLIAM WEAVER	CORINTHIAN	2.90	15/51/ 8	33(D)	63
RAVEN	C.F.G. CRISP	R.VIC.Y.C.	3.00	15/51/42	34(D)	64
ERIKEIR	JOHN MADSEN	MAPLE BAY	3.45	15/51/48	19(E)	65
ODIN	LARRY PETERSON/RON WILMOTH	S. SOUND	3.00	15/55/40	35(D)	66
TANTIVY II	RAY MARTIN	W.VAN.Y.C.	2.95	15/55/48	36(D)	67
WINDIGO	BOB ANKERSMIT	SLOOPTAVRN	3.30	15/56/26	20(E)	68
RAINBOW CHASER	LON RIGGS	PT. ANGELES	3.20	15/56/56	21(E)	69
MAPLE SUGAR	WAITE BROOKS	R.VIC.Y.C.	3.65	15/57/22	12(F)	70
WINDSHIFT	FREDERICK HAYES	SEATTLE	3.05	15/59/17	22(E)	71
OBSESSION	MEL HENRY	TACOMA	2.90	16/ 0/19	37(D)	72
SANA	J.K. MARTIN	CANOE BAY	3.20	16/ 0/21	23(E)	73
HINA	DARYL DELMOTTE	R.VAN.Y.C.	2.80	16/ 0/44	38(D)	74
VAHEVALA	KEN BROWN	CANOE BAY	3.60	16/ 1/22	13(F)	75
WINDY WENDY TWO	DR. A. SHEARER	R.VAN.Y.C.	3.00	16/ 2/15	39(D)	76
CALCULATED RISQUE	BOB STEPHENS	CYC SEATTLE	3.40	16/ 5/ 5	24(E)	77
ACHILLES	W.J. WILLIAMS	R.VIC.Y.C.	3.50	16/ 6/ 9	14(F)	78
MO'BETTAH	DAVE SHARPE/CHUCK PEPKA	SEATTLE	2.70	16/ 6/16	40(D)	79
DORADO	STAN JOPLIN	R.N.S.A.	3.05	16/ 6/33	25(E)	80
SEA RANGER	DAVID WILDER/HARRY FRONCZEK	WEST VAN	3.50	16/12/21	15(F)	81
ZEPHYRUS	DAVID SKINNER	ANACORTES	3.40	16/12/37	26(E)	82
TERRAPIN	GARY BOWDEN	CORINTHIAN	3.05	16/19/35	27(E)	83
LEESOME	J. PATTERSON	CANOE BAY	3.20	16/19/44	28(E)	84
CIRCE	DAVID LISTER	THSA-VICT	3.45	16/19/46	29(E)	85
DARK STAR	ROBERT A. GEBO	CORINTHIAN	2.95	16/26/52	41(D)	86
TOYBOX	GORDON COOPER	CANOE BAY	3.30	16/40/13	30(E)	87
LIMFJORD	BENT JESPERSEN	CANOE BAY	4.00	16/44/29	16(F)	88
SALTY DREAM	GARY JACOBI	R.VIC.Y.C.	3.30	16/44/50	31(E)	89
SCHOCK WAVE	MIKE FALCONER	R.VAN.Y.C.	3.70	16/56/12	17(F)	90
PUFFIN	F.J. POMEROY	CORINTHIAN	3.05	17/54/33	32(E)	91
HAIMHAUSEN	SIEDFRIED BREDL	CORINTHIAN	3.75	DSQ	DSQ(F)	DSQ
STANDFAST	BRUCE MATTHEWS	R.VAN.Y.C.	2.90	DNF	DNF(D)	DNF
TILLICUM	H.J. RICKETTS	CORINTHIAN	3.05	DNF	DNF(E)	DNF
PIPE DREAM	R. ABENDROTH	SEATTLE	4.15	DNF	DNF(F)	DNF
TRITON	E. WICHERTS	R.VIC.Y.C.	3.55	DNF	DNF(F)	DNF
GEORGIA GIRL	W. MARTIN	C.B.S.C.	3.60	DSQ	DSQ(F)	DSQ
SQUARE 1	DAVID ADAMS	R.VIC.Y.C.	3.30	DSQ	DSQ(E)	DSQ
MORAG	DICK JENKINS	R.VAN.Y.C.	2.95	DNF	DNF(D)	DNF
THE SLOOP JOHN B.	J. BOYD IVENS	TSAWWASSEN	3.70	DNF	DNF(F)	DNF
PEACHES	TED SERR	PT. ANGELES	3.70	DNS	DNS(F)	DNS

SUMMERSALT	RICK BALDWIN	CANOE BAY	3.30		DNF	DNF(E)	DNF
TUMBO	LARRY STRAITH	TURKEY HD	3.90		DNF	DNF(F)	DNF
CAPRICE	H.R. GARDNER	C.F.S.A.	4.00		DNF	DNF(F)	DNF
LIBRE	BOB DEAN	R.VIC.Y.C.	3.55		DNS	DNS(F)	DNS
ROMADA	ROY HINGLEY	R.VIC.Y.C.	3.50		DNF	DNF(F)	DNF
BEOWULF	RON JEWULA	TURKEY HD	3.30		DNF	DNF(E)	DNF
METAXA	DAVID COOK	CANOE BAY	4.60		DNF	DNF(F)	DNF
SWEETNESS	CARMEN PASCOE	C.F.S.A.	3.40		DNF	DNF(E)	DNF
BAREFOOT	DONALD RUSSELL	CORINTHIAN	3.00		DNF	DNF(D)	DNF
MEERSCHAUM	RUSSELL COHN	CORINTHIAN	2.85		DSQ	DSQ(D)	DSQ
CALLIPYGIA	BILL BUSH	CORINTHIAN	3.10		DNF	DNF(E)	DNF
BANJO MUSIC	ARMAND MARION	CORINTHIAN	2.90		DNF	DNF(D)	DNF
DEBORAH ANN	PETER ROGERS	R.VAN.Y.C.	4.00		DNF	DNF(F)	DNF
SILVER CLOUD	G. BEVERIDGE	WEST VAN	3.40		DNS	DNS(E)	DNS
DESPERADO	DOUGLAS J. COOK	CORINTHIAN	3.20		DNF	DNF(E)	DNF
FROGBONE	TODD OVERBY	CORINTHIAN	3.35		DSQ	DSQ(E)	DSQ

RE: JUAN DE FUCA YACHT RACE, 1978

Please accept my apologies for the error in the Juan de Fuca race results which you refer to in your letter of September 6.

On checking our records we can confirm that your yacht BAREFOOT finished at 05:29:18. The (DNF) notation in all of our lists is the result of confusing your vessel with BAREFOOT II, entered in Swiftsure, and which is correctly marked 'DNF'. Regretably, this same error was repeated in all of our checks.

The finishing time of 05:29:18 produces a corrected elapsed time of 13:02:30 and places BAREFOOT in 3rd position in Division D and 4th overall.

It is unfortunate that you did not point out the error on receipt of the preliminary results list. At this time, prizes are being produced and distributed and under these circumstances we do not think we can print a new list and change the prizes now being issued.

To make amends, we are arranging for an additional third prize for Juan de Fuca PHRF Division D to be awarded to BAREFOOT. This will, of course, result in two yachts holding prizes engraved for third place.

A copy of this letter will be sent to all Juan de Fuca PHRF prize winners so that they may know of this action.

I trust that our solution to the problem created by our error will be satisfactory to you and that we may look forward to seeing BAREFOOT entered again next year.

Your truly,
F.A.C. Piddington,
Swiftsure Committee Chairman

PACIFIC INTERNATIONAL YACHTING ASSOCIATION
SWIFTSURE LIGHTSHIP CLASSIC AND JUAN DE FUCA RACE
1979 TROPHY WINNERS

RESULTS AT: JUNE 22, 1979

SWIFTSURE (I.O.R.)	SWIFTSURE TROPHY (OVERALL HANDICAP WINNER)	KEN PEARCE	R.VAN.	THE PEARCE ARROW
	CITY OF VICTORIA TROPHY (1ST YACHT TO FINISH)	L. KILLAM	R.VAN.	GRAYBEARD
	OCEAN CEMENT TROPHY (FIRST IN DIVISION 1)	E.W. DE KONING	PORTLAND	WIZARD
	T. EATON TROPHY (FIRST IN DIVISION 2)	JOHN F. BUCHAN	SEATTLE	HEATHER
	CITY OF SEATTLE TROPHY (FIRST IN DIVISION 3)	KEN PEARCE	R.VAN.	THE PEARCE ARROW
	ROYAL VANCOUVER YACHT CLUB TROPHY (FIRST IN DIVISION 4)	D. CLARK	SEATTLE	BUMPER
SWIFTSURE (P.H.R.F.)	PACIFIC RIM TROPHY (OVERALL HANDICAP WINNER)	G. PALO	CYC (TAC)	DELIVERANCE
	ROYAL CANADIAN NAVY TROPHY (1ST YACHT TO FINISH)	ROLAND BRENER	R.VIC.	REALITY
	.... (FIRST IN DIVISION A)	BOB HARRISON	WEST VAN.	INDIGO
	CORINTHIAN YACHT CLUB TROPHY (FIRST IN DIVISION B)	G. COLE	CYC (SEA)	THUNDER CHICKEN
	STORMY WEATHER TROPHY (FIRST IN DIVISION C)	G. PALO	CYC (TAC)	DELIVERANCE
	CAPE FLATTERY TROPHY (FIRST IN DIVISION D)	STEFAN CLARKE RAMON ESCURE	TACOMA	SASSY
JUAN DE FUCA (I.O.R.)	.... (OVERALL HANDICAP WINNER)	THOMAS HULKE	SEATTLE	OUTLAW
	SAN JUAN TROPHY (1ST YACHT TO FINISH)	G. DUNCAN W. RUDOLPH	SEATTLE	HAGAR
	ROYAL VICTORIA YACHT CLUB TROPHY (FIRST IN DIVISION 5)	G. DUNCAN W. RUDOLPH	SEATTLE	HAGAR
	ROYAL CANADIAN NAVY TROPHY (FIRST IN DIVISION 6)	THOMAS HULKE	SEATTLE	OUTLAW
JUAN DE FUCA (P.H.R.F.)	PORT ANGELES YACHT CLUB TROPHY (OVERALL HANDICAP WINNER)	V.F. BINGHAM	PT. ANGELES	MIRAGE
	.... (1ST YACHT TO FINISH)	V.F. BINGHAM	PT. ANGELES	MIRAGE
	ANACORTES YACHT CLUB TROPHY (FIRST IN DIVISION E)	V.F. BINGHAM	PT. ANGELES	MIRAGE
	.... (FIRST IN DIVISION F)	D. BRINK	CYC (SEA)	TONIC
	.... (FIRST IN DIVISION G)	J.A. ROBINSON	R.VIC.	ARATAI

SWIFTSURE (I.O.R.) 1979
RESULTS

YACHT NAME	SKIPPER(S)	CLUB	RATING	COR ELAPSE TIME	POSITION DIVISION	OVERALL
THE PEARCE ARROW	KEN PEARCE	R.VAN.	26.90	21/43/21	1(3)	1
THE DISTANT DRUMMER	G. OLIVER	R.VIC.	27.60	21/46/31	2(3)	2
HEATHER	JOHN F. BUCHAN	SEATTLE	31.50	22/ 2/35	1(2)	3
WIZARD	E.W. DE KONING	PORTLAND	32.40	22/ 6/50	1(1)	4
ILLUSION	NICK ORR	CYC (SEA)	29.90	22/20/59	2(2)	5
KOTUKU	ROSS MATHEWSON	THSA	33.00	22/30/ 9	2(1)	6
KANATA	V. PLAVSIC	WEST VAN	31.20	22/42/21	3(2)	7
WARLOCK	C. BAMFORD JR	TACOMA	34.40	23/ 7/32	3(1)	8
CHIRON	BRYAN ARCHER	TACOMA	36.50	23/15/33	4(1)	9
DISCOVERY	JOHN DUNFIELD	R.VAN.	37.80	23/55/14	5(1)	10
WARRIOR	L. BRUCE HEDRIC	SEATTLE	44.50	23/57/13	6(1)	11
BONNIE	E. MILLER	PT. MADISON	40.20	24/19/38	7(1)	12
GRAYBEARD	L. KILLAM	R.VAN.	67.90	24/33/36	8(1)	13
WEATHERLY	LYNN SOMMERS/ALAN G. BUCHAN	TACOMA	50.60	24/42/34	9(1)	14
BUMPER	D. CLARK	SEATTLE	21.70	25/38/34	1(4)	15
PROSPECTOR	L. SHORETT	SEATTLE	27.30	25/39/ 5	3(3)	16
COUNTRY STYLE	STEVE MERRIMAN	R.VIC.	27.40	25/47/50	4(3)	17
COLETTE	G. HESS	CYC (SEA)	27.20	25/48/52	5(3)	18
ENDURANCE	H. MINOR	EVERETT	30.40	25/50/ 3	4(2)	19
RHAPSODY	J. SMITH	EDMONDS	24.60	25/51/29	2(4)	20
PARADOX	JOHN McGOWEN	TACOMA	27.00	25/52/37	6(3)	21
MUSTARD SEED	D.J. HERMAN	EDMONDS	27.50	26/ 0/22	7(3)	22
SALLY LIGHTFOOT	T. FRIEDLAND	BELLINGHAM	26.20	26/10/55	8(3)	23
WOTAN	BILL BURDICK	SEATTLE	26.40	26/13/55	9(3)	24
WHITEBIRD	ALEX BOOME	R.VAN.	25.90	26/17/33	10(3)	25
JADAH IV	P. TUCKER	CYC (SEA)	31.30	26/18/45	5(2)	26
LADYBUG	A. HOLT	SEATTLE	21.60	26/20/ 6	3(4)	27
PROPHECY	J. JARMAN	R.VAN.	27.00	26/23/ 2	11(3)	28
ANOMALY	W. ELMER	CYC (SEA)	26.30	26/24/ 2	12(3)	29
KNIGHTMARE	G. KNIGHT	VAN.ROWING	27.30	26/32/21	13(3)	30
PANGAEA	MAC MADENWALD	ANACORTES	30.20	26/36/48	6(2)	31
PHOENIX	S. CRARY	LAHAINA	31.20	26/49/27	7(2)	32
HABITAT	PCG RICHARDS	W.V.Y.C.	27.40	26/56/59	14(3)	33
ALLIANCE	T. GIDLUND/E. SCHWAB	SEATTLE	27.80	27/ 9/44	15(3)	34
LAERTES	PETER A CROWE	VAN.ROWING	22.80	27/18/42	4(4)	35
M.M. CRUMBAKER	GERALD PARKER	TACOMA	28.90	27/19/ 3	8(2)	36
FANNY	GREG STEVENSON	CYC (SEA)	24.50	27/21/43	5(4)	37
KELEA	D. DELMOTTE	R.VAN.	25.10	27/22/ 6	16(3)	38
MOODY TOO	J. PINE	W.VAN.	26.10	27/27/ 7	17(3)	39
MIDNIGHT SPECIAL	V. McCULLOUGH	SEATTLE	30.40	27/27/42	9(2)	40
STARGAZER	B. HEADDEN	BALBOA	24.30	27/32/36	6(4)	41
COUNTESS III	P. JEFFERSON	R.VAN.	29.70	27/34/32	10(2)	42
SAVAGE SPIRIT	G. OAKES	PT. ANGELES	27.10	27/41/ 2	18(3)	43
OUTRAGEOUS	J.B. HARDIMAN	CYC (POR)	27.70	27/43/50	19(3)	44
FLAMENCA	JOHN MICHAEL	CYC (SEA)	24.00	27/48/47	7(4)	45
AGGRESSION	J.W. CHRISTENSEN	PORTLAND	26.60	27/51/ 3	20(3)	46
HYPERTENSION	ROGER PALMER	EDMONDS	26.70	28/ 2/58	21(3)	47
SCHUSS	M. KERNAN/L. SUND	CYC (SEA)	24.10	29/ 0/10	8(4)	48
TAPOCKETA	ROBERT NEWELL	BELLINGHAM	24.30	29/ 2/ 4	9(4)	49
TOPKAPI	R.B. KITCHEN	W.VAN.	27.70	29/10/51	22(3)	50
MARY D II	D.B. DAVIS	PT. ANGELES	24.20	29/14/ 3	10(4)	51
BARBARIAN	VINCENT BRYAN	POULSBO	26.80	29/14/16	23(3)	52
ANNIE CADBY	LOUIS LINDHOLM	R.VIC.	32.50	29/30/12	10(1)	53
MIDNIGHT MADNESS	M. WHITE	CYC (POR)	24.50	29/32/21	11(4)	54
THUNDER	WM. J. KING	PORTLAND	30.40	29/40/50	11(2)	55
AKKA	R. MARX	TACOMA	25.00	29/45/38	24(3)	56
SHAZAM	R. MUELLER	CYC (SEA)	26.20	29/57/ 1	25(3)	57
WINDWARD	J. CICERI	R.VIC.	26.30	30/ 6/44	26(3)	58
ASSAULT	FRED ROSWOLD	3 TREE PT.	32.70	30/13/56	11(1)	59
RAIN DROP	J. GAINER	CYC (POR)	28.70	30/45/22	12(2)	60
GOLDEN EAGLE	R.B. ROBERTS	CYC (SEA)	24.20	31/19/14	12(4)	61
FIREWATER	R. MOELLER	PORTLAND	24.30	DNF	DNF(4)	DNF
DIAMOND HEAD	HENRY L. KOTKINS	SEATTLE	46.00	DNF	DNF(1)	DNF
DORADE	C. ROSS	SEATTLE	35.20	DSQ	DSQ(1)	DSQ
NAKNEK	R.I. NELSON	R.VAN.	37.30	DNF	DNF(1)	DNF
BROTHER GOOSE	BOB SEVENICH	EVERETT	24.00	DNF	DNF(4)	DNF
DAMN YANKEE	GLENN M. BYRD	OLYMPIA	26.20	DNF	DNF(3)	DNF

SINE MORA	D.E. HILLMAN	SEATTLE	26.30	DNF	DNF(3)	DNF
NERITA	BILL BRUCH	CYC (SEA)	30.02	DNF	DNF(2)	DNF
GOLD RUSH	N.H. RUSSELL	SHILSHOLE	29.60	DNF	DNF(2)	DNF
MILKSHAKE	B. LEAVENS/P. LEAVENS	CYC (SEA)	21.60	DNF	DNF(4)	DNF
JEZEBEL	S. BROCKWAY	CYC (SEA)	26.30	DNF	DNF(3)	DNF
SUNRISE	THOMAS HAYES	SEATTLE	21.60	DNF	DNF(4)	DNF
OUTRAGEOUS	T. BURNS	BREMERTON	42.80	DSQ	DSQ(1)	DSQ
THE PHOENICIAN	C. SCHILBACH	PORTLAND	33.40	DNF	DNF(1)	DNF
ESCARGOT	SAM SCIMECA	SEATTLE	26.20	DSQ	DSQ(3)	DSQ

SWIFTSURE (P.H.R.F.) 1979 RESULTS

OFFICIAL START TIME: 10/00/00

YACHT TIME	SKIPPER(S)	CLUB	RATING	COR ELAPSE TIME	POSITION DIVISION	OVERALL
DELIVERANCE	G. PALO	CYC (TAC)	2.20	25/32/20	1(C)	1
GAMIN	L. ROBINSON	SEATTLE	2.25	25/51/18	2(C)	2
THUNDER CHICKEN	G. COLE	CYC (SEA)	2.00	25/52/57	1(B)	3
SMALL WORLD II	G.W. SIBOLD	OLYMPIA	2.30	25/55/11	3(C)	4
HOOLIGAN II	TOM O'BRIEN	SEATTLE	1.85	25/56/38	2(B)	5
SURPRISE	G. MAURER	SEATTLE	1.95	25/58/49	3(B)	6
TANGENT II	ANTONY C. LOACH	WEST VAN.	2.00	26/ 6/ 0	4(B)	7
POISSON SOLUBLE	R. HORSLEY	CYC (SEA)	2.40	26/26/52	4(C)	8
INDIGO	BOB HARRISON	W.VAN.	1.65	26/30/52	1(A)	9
TERNA III	CHRISTOFFERSEN	W.VAN.	1.65	26/35/26	2(A)	10
BLACK WATCH	B. NELSON	CYC (TAC)	1.55	26/38/41	3(A)	11
REALITY	ROLAND BRENER	R.VIC.	1.50	26/39/48	4(A)	12
ARROW	C. NEU	SEATTLE	2.00	26/39/53	5(B)	13
COHO II	PETE HANSON	SEATTLE	1.60	26/41/22	5(A)	14
MOONGLOW IV	D.D. NIELSEN	TACOMA	1.65	26/49/14	6(A)	15
SASSY	STEFAN CLARKE/RAMON ESCURE	TACOMA	2.50	26/54/18	1(D)	16
MILLTOWN	P COTE SR./B. COTE	R.VAN.	1.40	26/55/52	7(A)	17
SYDEILSUMA	K. DAVIDSON	KITSILANO	1.75	26/58/55	8(A)	18
OLYMPIAN	P.G. SCHMIDT	SEATTLE	1.85	27/ 1/28	6(B)	19
DORLES	WILLIS KLUDT	3 TR. POINT	2.00	27/ 4/21	7(B)	20
OVERDRAFT TOO	G.M. HESELDIN	R.VAN.	1.80	27/ 9/ 8	9(A)	21
BIGBIRD	ALLAN LAIRD	R.VAN.	1.80	27/20/10	10(A)	22
MORNING STAR	M.B. DUFFY	CYC (SEA)	2.45	27/24/ 2	5(C)	23
SEALION	N.C. MARTIN	NANAIMO	2.20	27/26/10	6(C)	24
NATURAL HIGH	R.M. RANKIN	CYC (SEA)	2.00	27/31/49	8(B)	25
SANTANA	B. PEDERSEN	SEATTLE	1.80	27/33/26	11(A)	26
SPINSTER	J. DEWELL	EVERETT	2.30	27/35/50	7(C)	27
L.L.L.R.	D.B. JONES	SEATTLE	2.00	27/47/58	9(B)	28
SATURDAY'S CHILD	C. BRAIN	SEATTLE	1.30	27/55/55	12(A)	29
EPIC	C. SCHIFF	CYC (SEA)	1.25	28/11/ 0	13(A)	30
THALASSIC	C. VIELE	CYC (SEA)	2.00	28/16/55	10(B)	31
APPARITION	M. FIANDER/W. WHITE	CYC (SEA)	2.70	28/18/ 8	2(D)	32
MELTEMI	FRANK MUSSON	WEST VAN.	2.00	28/23/58	11(B)	33
JOLLY ROGER III	R. WHEELER	CYC (SEA)	2.45	28/24/15	8(C)	34
WHANGAREI	RICK SWANSON	CYC (SEA)	1.70	28/27/10	14(A)	35
NAHMA	K. MAXWELL	CYC (SEA)	2.55	28/28/ 2	3(D)	36
BELUGA	D. FLYNN	SEATTLE	2.30	28/30/ 7	9(C)	37
PEGASUS	J. BECKER	CYC (POR)	2.70	28/35/29	4(D)	38
SHINGEBISS	L.P. BAILEY	CYC (SEA)	2.45	28/38/10	10(C)	39
WINDSONG II	ROGER BARNHARDT	BELLINGHAM	2.50	28/38/12	5(D)	40
CONSULTATION	D. ANDERSON/G. NORTON	OLYMPIA	2.90	28/38/38	6(D)	41
WHITE SQUALL	G. TEATS	TACOMA	1.85	28/39/ 5	12(B)	42
SCAMPI	TED WATERMAN	R.VAN.	2.60	28/42/34	7(D)	43
HARPOON	W. BRASIER	TACOMA	1.30	28/43/42	15(A)	44
AIRBORNE	E.W. HARRISON	TIDDLY COV.	3.10	28/45/22	8(D)	45
PETER COTTON SAIL	O. SNOER	CYC (SEA)	2.90	28/45/26	9(D)	46
TREK	G. JAMES	CYC (TAC)	2.40	28/52/55	11(C)	47
MUYA	RUSSELL LABODA	PT. MADISON	3.80	28/55/ 9	10(D)	48
FEDERALIST	JAMES M. MARTA	SEATTLE YC	1.75	28/57/42	16(A)	49
PANDEMONIUM	P. O'REILLY	OLYMPIA	2.95	28/58/26	11(D)	50
ODIN	LARRY PETERSON	SSSS	2.90	29/ 4/59	12(D)	51
BARBARA	W.E. KAMPE	CYC (SEA)	2.00	29/ 8/21	13(B)	52
SWALLOW II	P. JOHNSON	SEATTLE	2.00	29/13/30	14(B)	53
RICKY NELSON	EARL LASHER	SEATTLE	2.30	29/15/23	12(C)	54
CHEROKEE	M. MULCAHY/H. HANSON	3 TREE PT.	2.30	29/24/18	13(C)	55
JURA	K. SCHIBLI	R.VIC.	2.40	29/26/ 0	14(C)	56
LIZA-K	K. PARTLOW	OLYMPIA	2.40	29/27/ 8	15(C)	57
VENTURE	E.M. SCHALKA	EVERETT	1.85	29/29/32	15(B)	58

HMCS ORIOLE	LCDR W.D. WALKER	CFSA	2.50	29/30/57	13(D)	59
CHOISEUL	P. DANIELS	R.VAN.	1.80	29/31/41	17(A)	60
LORD JIM	D. STABBERT/S. STABBERT	SEATTLE	1.85	29/32/39	16(B)	61
CALLALOO	J.A. CATLEY	R.VAN.	2.90	29/38/26	14(D)	62
ROWDY LADY II	A.L. HAUGE	PORTLAND	2.30	29/40/32	16(C)	63
WINDLESS II	R.W. WICKSTROM	CANOE BAY	1.80	29/42/53	18(A)	64
THE PRETENDER	G. McGLASHAN	TIDDLYCOVE	1.70	29/43/47	19(A)	65
ALBERTA BOUND	ROBERT E. NOWACK	VAN. ROW C.	2.40	29/47/36	17(C)	66
GOLDEN GIRL	FREDERICK HALL	PORTLAND	2.50	29/51/27	15(D)	67
FAEM	D.M. GILLILAND	R.VAN.	2.05	29/57/29	17(B)	68
STIXSTOBER	D.L. VAUGHAN	W.VAN.	2.50	29/58/ 5	16(D)	69
MEG	B. HOSIE	R.VIC.	2.20	29/59/ 0	18(C)	70
SCHLINGEL	M.A. TREIT	CYC (SEA)	2.40	29/59/25	19(C)	71
MENEHUNE	DONALD WILSON	CANOE BAY	2.15	29/59/36	18(B)	72
PACEMAKER	J.A. MAZZARELLA	CYC (SEA)	2.30	30/ 3/29	20(C)	73
MADRUGADOR	W. ANDERSON	SEATTLE	1.85	30/ 5/23	19(B)	74
CARTHAGINIAN	W.M. HANSON	CYC (SEA)	1.15	30/ 8/ 4	20(A)	75
RHIANNON	BUSH ALBISTON	SEATTLE	2.00	30/ 9/18	20(B)	76
VIVA	D.M. BLAKEMORE	CYC (SEA)	1.85	30/25/54	21(B)	77
SALTY TIGER	T. OSBORN	3 TR. PT.	1.30	30/32/32	21(A)	78
PAP'S CHOICE	GENE WALTER	PORTLAND	2.45	30/36/19	21(C)	79
MOLLY SQUASH	A. ROTTLER	SEATTLE	2.55	30/41/29	17(D)	80
CELOX II	E. ZELLMER	SLOOP TAV.	1.90	30/44/53	22(B)	81
ORCA	FRANK THOMPSON	R.VAN.	2.20	30/45/39	22(C)	82
WIND WARRIOR	D.L. WILLITS	TACOMA	2.50	30/46/33	18(D)	83
VIRGINIA DARE	B. ADAM	SEATTLE	1.80	31/ 5/20	22(A)	84
SHOGUN	D. BEER	EAGLE HAR.	2.30	31/14/29	23(C)	85
CHEETAH	P. CLARKE	QTR. MASTER	2.25	31/26/25	24(C)	86
BORU	B. GRIERSON	R.VAN.	1.80	31/27/20	23(A)	87
SIKINI	P.J. TORDOFF	RNSA	2.40	34/11/32	25(C)	88
AGAPE	P. MURRAY	CLEVELAND	2.80	DNF	DNF(D)	DNF
EAGLE	GLENN MARQUARDT	CYC (SEA)	2.00	DNF	DNF(B)	DNF
PRISM	B. McPAKE	CYC (SEA)	2.00	DNF	DNF(B)	DNF
BLUE WING	C.T. TURNER	QTR. MASTER	2.00	DNS	DNS(B)	DNS
AKAMAI	G. CAVIN	CYC (SEA)	2.60	DNF	DNF(D)	DNF
SHAMAN	DAVID L. DINGMAN	CYC (SEA)	1.85	DNF	DNF(B)	DNF
SKARRIETT	R.E. WILSON	3 TR. PT.	1.95	DNF	DNF(B)	DNF
MUKLUKS	H. BUCKLEY	BELLINGHAM	1.75	DNF	DNF(A)	DNF
DEUCE COUPE	G. LOWE	PT. MADISON	1.85	DNF	DNF(B)	DNF
SANNU SANNU	GLENN WAKEFIELD	R.VIC.	3.40	DNF	DNF(D)	DNF
GITAND	JAMES E. DEPUE	PT. MADISON	2.55	DNF	DNF(D)	DNF
KISMET	CARLSON/GUILDNER	EVERETT	1.90	DNF	DNF(B)	DNF
SUNDANCE	T.D. MURPHY	TACOMA	1.85	DNF	DNF(B)	DNF
BLUE MARLIN	JIM WILLIAMS	CYC (SEA)	1.85	DNF	DNF(B)	DNF
MISTRESS II	W.I. VARLEY	EVERETT	1.65	DNF	DNF(A)	DNF
CRESSET	J. HUTCHINSON	R.VAN.	3.05	DNF	DNF(D)	DNF
GOMETRA	D.A. MILLIS	RNSA	2.35	DNF	DNF(C)	DNF
ESCAPE HATCH	B. FERRIE	BELLINGHAM	3.50	DNS	DNS(D)	DNS
NORDLYS	BRUCE SAMPSON	MAPLE BAY	2.90	DNS	DNS(D)	DNS
CORMORANT	H.H. BOYD	CYC (SEA)	2.05	DNF	DNF(B)	DNF
WINGAWAY	D.S. BRYNELSEN	VAN ROWING	1.80	DNF	DNF(A)	DNF
TSUNAMI	C.J. MORAN	CYC (SEA)	2.35	DNF	DNF(C)	DNF
LEGEND	C. STEWARD	SEATTLE	1.85	DNF	DNF(B)	DNF
TOLO TSOLO	E.E. WOODSON	ANACORTES	2.45	DNF	DNF(C)	DNF
SCRIMSHANDER	JACK MILLER	R.VIC.	2.20	DNF	DNF(C)	DNF
TRINGA	FRED GARDINER	R.VIC.	2.20	DNF	DNF(C)	DNF
SHELCA	ERIC DOWELL	R.VIC.	2.10	DNF	DNF(B)	DNF
WINDWARD MARK	V. PALMER	MAPLE BAY	2.35	DNF	DNF(C)	DNF
MADELEINE	JIM MORRIS	CANOE BAY	2.20	DNF	DNF(C)	DNF
MAHRI II	R. McKENZIE	R.VAN.	2.10	DNF	DNF(B)	DNF
KATCHEN	D. STAAT	TACOMA	2.75	DNF	DNF(D)	DNF
STRIDER	KEITH JOHNSON	CYC (SEA)	2.45	DNF	DNF(C)	DNF
MUTINEER IV	T.R. BRAIDWOOD	W.VAN.	1.70	DNF	DNF(A)	DNF
MAGNUM	R.E. AXFORD/BRIAN WOOD	R.VAN.	2.35	DNF	DNF(C)	DNF
SURTSEY	B. McKEE	SEATTLE	1.60	DNF	DNF(A)	DNF
MAIN BRACE	L. MOFFORD	R.VIC.	2.20	DNF	DNF(C)	DNF
ENCOUNTER	DR. H. BACON	R.VIC.	2.75	DNF	DNF(D)	DNF
RAVEN	COLIN F.G. CRISP	R.VIC.	3.00	DNF	DNF(D)	DNF
RAMPART	J. ROSS	MAPLE BAY	1.70	DNF	DNF(A)	DNF
STARWAGON	N.C. BAILEY	SHILSHOLE	2.30	DNF	DNF(C)	DNF
FINESSE	DR. R. SMITH	R.VIC.	2.00	DNF	DNF(B)	DNF

RAZZMATTAZZ	KEN BROWN	R.VIC.	2.50	DNF	DNF(D)	DNF
ROSY	ROBERT FARRELL	CANOE BAY	3.80	DNF	DNF(D)	DNF
COUNTERPOINT	TIM CLARK	CYC (SEA)	2.35	DNF	DNF(C)	DNF
YANKEE GIRL	J.A. McDONALD	SEATTLE	1.80	DNS	DNS(A)	DNS
BEAUTIFUL NOISE	F. SHRIVER/M. SHRIVER	3 TR. PT.	2.40	DNF	DNF(C)	DNF
LEIKO	G.M. SAKATA	KITSILANO	2.00	DNF	DNF(B)	DNF
ELISHEBA	M. MILLER	CYC (SEA)	2.00	DNF	DNF(B)	DNF
RASPUTIN	A.B. HEYES	RNSA	3.05	DNF	DNF(D)	DNF
TRINORCA	L. PEDERSEN	R.VAN.	2.95	DNF	DNF(D)	DNF
ODIN	ALAN HARTE	RNSA	3.15	DNF	DNF(D)	DNF
FINAL SOLUTION	C.D. SHINN	RNSA	1.80	DNF	DNF(A)	DNF
'KSAN	BONAR A DAVIS	R.VAN.	1.70	DNF	DNF(A)	DNF
ZUBEN'UBI II	W.F. HESTER	CYC (SEA)	2.20	DNF	DNF(C)	DNF
RIOTOUS ASSEMBLY	FINN NIELSEN	MAPLE BAY	1.70	DNF	DNF(A)	DNF
EDELWEISS II	P. WAGNER	R.VAN.	2.35	DNF	DNF(C)	DNF
COFFEE POT	MIKE GANSKE	TIDDLY CVE	2.10	DNF	DNF(B)	DNF
MAYA	M.M. LE POOLE	RVYC	2.15	DNF	DNF(B)	DNF
NYON III	DEREK G. SIMPSON	R.VAN.	2.75	DNF	DNF(D)	DNF
NAUTILUS	L. NEVLER	CYC (SEA)	2.30	DNF	DNF(C)	DNF
ANYLOVE	D. MARSHALL	CYC (SEA)	2.55	DNF	DNF(D)	DNF
SOLEDAD	JERRY NORMAN	PORTLAND	1.90	DNF	DNF(B)	DNF
SASSAFRAS	J. WILKE	CYC (SEA)	2.50	DNF	DNF(D)	DNF
CANDYMAN	H. FREY/G. BOCKUS	PT. MADISON	2.85	DNF	DNF(D)	DNF
FLO	ROBERT WHEELER/JAN WHEELER	SEATTLE	2.95	DNF	DNF(D)	DNF
A BIENTOT	G.R. KACZOR	SEATTLE	3.00	DNF	DNF(D)	DNF
BILLIKEN	B. AIKEN	SHILSHOLE	2.40	DNF	DNF(C)	DNF
SAVAGE	L. HILLS	SEATTLE	2.20	DNF	DNF(C)	DNF
ANGELA K.	JES KRITSIS	CYC (SEA)	2.10	DNF	DNF(B)	DNF
PRO TANTO	BOB STANGE	CYC (SEA)	3.00	DNF	DNF(D)	DNF
MARIA	T.M. WEBSTER	TACOMA	2.55	DNF	DNF(D)	DNF
NOMAD	BILL LIEBERMAN	CYC (SEA)	2.25	DNF	DNF(C)	DNF
TIN MAN	NED FLOHR	SEATTLE	3.70	DNF	DNF(D)	DNF
DECEPTION	R.A. CAIRNS	SEATTLE	2.15	DNF	DNF(B)	DNF
NOSTRADAMUS	JOHN CORNELL	S. SOUND	2.20	DSQ	DSQ(C)	DSQ
KATE	C.E. OLSON	EDMONDS	2.60	DNF	DNF(D)	DNF

SWIFTSURE YACHTING CLASSIC 1979

The enclosed Swiftsure and Juan de Fuca results include changes made to correct errors, reflect the results of protests, and the following time allowances for yachts which whent to the aid of another yacht in distress.

19959	MOODY TOO	7 MINUTES	SWIFTSURE FOR DIV. 3
29456	CHEROKEE	10 MINUTES	SWIFTSURE PHRF DIV. C
7732	VIVA	30 MINUTES	SWIFTSURE PHRF DIV. B
39530	MIRAGE	25 MINUTES	JUAN DE FUCA PHRF DIV. E

JUAN DE FUCA (I.O.R.) 1979
RESULTS

OFFICIAL START TIME: 10/15/00

YACHT NAME	SKIPPER(S)	CLUB	RATING	COR ELAPSE TIME	POSITION DIVISION	OVERALL
OUTLAW	THOMAS HULKE	SEATTLE	21.50	11/46/ 6	1(6)	1
HAGAR	G. DUNCAN/W. RUDOLPH	SEATTLE	24.40	11/51/40	1(5)	2
GOGAMA	GEORGE WILKINS/DAVE EVERETT	R.VAN.	24.50	12/14/53	2(5)	3
SEA BEATER	G.D. BOUDIN	CYC (SEA)	21.50	12/16/32	2(6)	4
EAGLE	G. HODGE	BELLINGHAM	24.40	12/29/59	3(5)	5
SACRE BLEU	BRIAN L. GRIFFIN	BELLINGHAM	24.50	12/37/21	4(5)	6
BAGHEERA	A. COPELAND/L. COPELAND	R.VAN.	24.20	12/44/36	5(5)	7
TENACIOUS	J. OREM	BELLINGHAM	24.50	12/49/49	6(5)	8
FLAUNT	B. HAMILTON/N. McCONAGHY	TACOMA	21.40	13/ 4/ 4	3(6)	9
CHAOS	MARVIN A. WAYNE	BELLINGHAM	24.20	13/ 9/55	7(5)	10
SOCKEYE	L. SALKIELD	SEATTLE	24.40	13/31/ 3	8(5)	11
MAXIMUS	MAXWELL KING	BELLINGHAM	24.50	13/36/25	9(5)	12
GOTCHAFERGOOD	BOB DIEHL	BELLINGHAM	24.50	13/36/37	10(5)	13
SPEARHEAD	DAVID SPEIRS	KITSILANO	24.70	13/39/21	11(5)	14
JO	T. WHITE	BELLINGHAM	24.50	13/53/57	12(5)	15
IMPATIENCE	TED TRENHOLME	R.VIC.	24.50	14/23/20	13(5)	16
STERLING SHAMROCK	JIM BROWN/LYNNE BROWN	R.VAN.	21.40	DNF	DNF(6)	DNF
FIRST MORNING	S. STANLEY	OAK HARBOR	21.20	DNF	DNF(6)	DNF
LUCY ALICE	W.H. GARDNER	CYC (SEA)	21.20	DNF	DNF(6)	DNF
ADVERSARY	TIM MALEDY/HOLLY MALEDY	R.VAN.	21.50	DNF	DNF(6)	DNF
CLOCKWORK ROCKETSHIP	E.A. LIEBERT	R.VAN.	24.60	DNF	DNF(5)	DNF
PEN DRAGON	DARYL GRIMSON/SHERL GRIMSON	R.VAN.	21.30	DNF	DNF(6)	DNF
SUDS	JAMES FULTON	CYC (SEA)	21.20	DNF	DNF(6)	DNF
AIRPOWER	DAVE CAMPBELL	CYC (SEA)	21.50	DNF	DNF(6)	DNF
SCRAMBLER	R. BOOKEY/M. BOOKEY	SEATTLE	21.50	DNF	DNF(6)	DNF
FLYER	P.A. NYENHUIS	EVERETT	21.70	DNF	DNF(6)	DNF

ERIKEIR	JOHN MADSEN	MAPLE BAY	3.45	20/51/45	16(G)	66
CIRCE	DAVID I. LISTER	CBSC	3.45	20/56/34	17(G)	67
UNION DEPOT	ROGER L. RUE	TACOMA	3.10	20/59/40	26(F)	68
FROYA	ERIC QUALLEY	MAPLE BAY	4.40	21/ 0/16	18(G)	69
IO	LESLIE WRIGHT	R.VIC.	3.45	21/ 2/48	19(G)	70
VANDAL II	J.N. MacFARLANE	MAPLE BAY	2.90	21/10/24	26(E)	71
GEORGIA GIRL	BILL MARTEN	CANOE BAY	3.60	21/10/24	20(G)	72
HWYLIO	L. ROBERTS	ROSE CITY	2.95	21/14/11	27(F)	73
FROGBONE	T. OVERBY	CYC (TAC)	3.35	21/24/26	28(F)	74
ALAKAZAM	DR. P. BERGMAN	ANACORTES	3.15	21/26/10	29(F)	75
DRIFTER	RON STEWART	MAPLE BAY	3.00	21/39/16	30(F)	76
MAPLE SUGAR	W. BROOKS	R.VIC.	3.75	21/43/ 5	21(G)	77
MURPH'S LAW	S. McCOY	3 TR. PT.	3.30	22/14/38	31(F)	78
NIAMH II	S.P. SLINN	W.VAN.	2.80	22/14/42	27(E)	79
DARK STAR	ROBERT A. GEBO	CYC (SEA)	2.95	22/23/56	32(F)	80
PUFFIN	F. POMEROY	CYC (SEA)	3.05	22/28/26	33(F)	81
BRASS TACKS	P.G. COURTNEY	EAGLE HRBR.	2.90	DNF	DNF(E)	DNF
HAIMHAUSEN	S. BREDL	CYC (POR)	4.10	DNS	DNS(G)	DNS
PIPE DREAM	R.D. ABENDROTH	SEATTLE	4.15	DNF	DNF(G)	DNF
TRITON	ERIC WICHERTS	R.VIC.	3.55	DNF	DNF(G)	DNF
BEBELLE	BRYAN SHAW	R.VIC.	2.80	DNF	DNF(E)	DNF
FILEY BRIGG	J.M. WEIR	R.VIC.	3.30	DNF	DNF(F)	DNF
MELKEDAE	J.K. BUCHANAN	TURKEY HD	3.40	DNF	DNF(G)	DNF
AIRBORNE	MAJOR JD HARRIS	C.F.S.A.	3.60	DNF	DNF(G)	DNF
LOON	J.T. SCHNEIDER	CYC (SEA)	3.70	DNF	DNF(G)	DNF
AQUILA	BRENT WESTON	R.VIC.	3.70	DNF	DNF(G)	DNF
MOCCASIN II	G.T. NEILY	MAPLE BAY	2.90	DNF	DNF(E)	DNF
PUFF II	JACK WOODWARD	R.VIC.	2.90	DSQ	DSQ(E)	DSQ
AVENGER II	A.S. BARKER	WEST VAN.	3.10	DNS	DNS(F)	DNS
AURIGA	G. GUEST	CANOE BAY	3.40	DNF	DNF(G)	DNF
SQUARE I	DAVID ADAMS	R.VIC.	3.30	DNF	DNF(F)	DNF
LA-MARQUISE II	JEAN PIERRE/LE DALLIC	CFSA	3.25	DNF	DNF(F)	DNF
THE PROFESSOR	J.H.L. JENSEN	R.VIC.	3.45	DNF	DNF(F)	DNF
DUTCH FLUTE	R. KLEIN	TACOMA	2.70	DNS	DNS(E)	DNS
BAD NEWS	BOB LEFEAUX	TIDDLEY CV	3.10	DNF	DNF(F)	DNF
PEACHES	T. SERR	PT. ANGELES	3.70	DNF	DNF(G)	DNF
MARILYN L	R. CARLSON	PT. ANGELES	3.75	DNF	DNF(G)	DNF
GAVIA	REG SKARET	THSA	3.40	DNF	DNF(G)	DNF
SHAZBOTZ	D. HORN	EDMONDS	3.30	DNF	DNF(F)	DNF
TOYBOX	GORDON COOPER	R.VIC.	3.30	DNF	DNF(F)	DNF
RUSH	GRANT WATSON	R.VIC.	2.75	DNF	DNF(F)	DNF
SKYBIRD	S. WALFORD	SCHOONER	4.00	DNF	DNF(G)	DNF
DESTINY	W.E. OLSON	CYC (POR)	2.80	DNF	DNF(E)	DNF
MAAKEN	STEVE C. NELSEN	BRWNSVILLE	2.70	DNF	DNF(E)	DNF
RESOLUTE 2	B. DEUTSCHER	TACOMA	2.70	DNS	DNS(E)	DNS
BEAUJOLAIS	GILES SHEPHERD	EVERETT	2.70	DNS	DNS(E)	DNS
RAGDOLL	B.J. FOLLMAN	3 TR. PT.	2.80	DNF	DNF(E)	DNF
BANDIT	S.H. HILLER	BELLINGHAM	3.30	DNF	DNF(F)	DNF
BANJO MUSIC	ARMAND MARION	CYC (SEA)	2.90	DNF	DNF(E)	DNF
DEMARA	A. CROWE	TIDDLYCOVE	3.50	DNF	DNF(G)	DNF
KWEISHA	J.E. SNOBALL	W.VAN.	3.20	DNF	DNF(F)	DNF
DORADO	S. JOPLIN	RNSA	3.05	DNF	DNF(F)	DNF
AFTERNOON DELIGHT	G.H. THRELFALL	R.VAN.	3.30	DNF	DNF(F)	DNF
SINE	R.S. HOSSACK	TIDDLY CV.	3.60	DNS	DNS(G)	DNS
QUORUM	D.M. FIELD/F.E. COLE	CYC (SEA)	2.60	DNF	DNF(G)	DNF
HI OCTANE	MIKE FALCONER	R.VAN.	2.85	DNF	DNF(E)	DNF
IMPOSITION	W.A. SHELDON	SOUTHSOUND	2.60	DNF	DNF(E)	DNF
DROP OUT	J.F. LAVELLE	CYC (TAC)	3.20	DNF	DNF(F)	DNF
SUPER APPLE	M. COLLINS	SEA EXPL.	2.60	DNF	DNF(F)	DNF
RISQUE	J.A. POKELA	TACOMA	3.05	DNF	DNF(F)	DNF
TERRAPIN	G. BOWDEN/M. BOUFFION	CYC (SEA)	3.05	DNF	DNF(F)	DNF
SWEET THING	J.B. COLLINS	PT. ANGELES	3.50	DNF	DNF(G)	DNF
WESTVIKING	J. GAEDKE	PT. MADISON	3.00	DNF	DNF(F)	DNF
ORCA	S. LEONARD	SEATTLE	3.25	DNF	DNF(F)	DNF
WHISTLER	D.H. PEDERSEN	CYC (SEA)	2.60	DNF	DNF(E)	DNF
RAINBOW CHASER	L. RIGGS	PT. ANGELES	3.20	DNF	DNF(F)	DNF
YELLOW JACKET	RICHARD SMITH	PT. ANGELES	3.60	DNF	DNF(G)	DNF
COOKIE MONSTER	CHARLES WHIDDEN	PT. ANGELES	2.60	DNF	DNF(E)	DNF
BREAKAWAY	D.L. HARRINGTON	OAK HAR.	2.85	DNF	DNF(E)	DNF
MOE-TAVATOR	DAVID E. MOE	PT. ANGELES	2.85	DNS	DNS(E)	DNS
SOUNDS OF SILENCE	M. VEITH	SHILSHOLE	3.10	DNF	DNF(F)	DNF

| DENIZEN | R.E. KREYBIG | CYC (SEA) | 24.40 | | DNF | DNF(5) | DNF |

JUAN DE FUCA (P.H.R.F.) 1979
RESULTS

YACHT TIME	SKIPPER(S)	CLUB	RATING	COR ELAPSE TIME	POSITION DIVISION	OVERALL
MIRAGE	V.F. BINGHAM	PT. ANGELES	2.60	13/24/ 5	1(E)	1
SPINNER	G. CASH	CYC (SEA)	2.70	13/34/ 5	2(E)	2
ARATAI	J.A. ROBINSON	R.VIC.	3.50	13/54/46	1(G)	3
TONIC	D. BRINK	CYC (SEA)	2.95	14/13/20	1(F)	4
SEA SPELL	J. HUIBERS	R.VIC.	2.90	14/15/ 5	3(E)	5
LUCKY LADY	FRED KRABBE	SAN JUAN	2.85	14/16/46	4(E)	6
IRRAWADDY	RON SAUNDERS	R.VIC.	3.50	14/18/47	2(G)	7 TIE
SCALLYWAG*	D. HADDLETON	V. ROWING		14/21/13	2(G)	7 SEE NOTE 1
AILSA CRAIG	J.W. CRAIG	R.VIC.	2.90	14/19/42	5(E)	8
SJ28	S. RUSH	CYC (SEA)	2.85	14/20/46	6(E)	9
PANTHER POINT	P. SCHOUW	EAGLE HAR.	2.80	14/22/32	7(E)	10
LIBRE	R. DEAN	R.VIC.	3.55	14/23/39	3(G)	11
MONTE CARLO	G. LAMBERT	VAN. ROWING	2.70	14/23/50	8(E)	12
GAZELLE II	GEORGE MASON	R.VAN.	3.00	14/28/37	2(F)	13
SUNDANCE	K.K. OVERBY	CYC (TAC)	2.85	14/28/44	9(E)	14
SILVER SPRAY	B. KELLY	WVYC	2.70	14/29/54	10(E)	15
WINDSHIFT	F.W. HAYES	SEATTLE	3.05	14/31/19	3(F)	16
SHIMNA	W.H. BRADBROOKE	TCYC	2.80	14/39/54	11(E)	17
HINA	HEINZ J. THIEL	R.VAN.	2.80	14/41/59	12(E)	18
GALEB	GEORGE CESAREC	R.VIC.	2.60	14/42/54	13(E)	19
ACHATES	S. DONALDSON	TIDDLYCOVE	2.90	14/43/27	14(E)	20
GHOSTRIDER	J. FROHNMAYER/WM BARBER	PORTLAND	2.60	14/43/56	15(E)	21
CAYENNE	KENNETH BRIGGS	SEATTLE	2.90	14/46/12	16(E)	22
PATCHWORK QUILT	JAMES DRYDEN	R.VIC.	2.90	14/48/11	17(E)	23
3RD ESCAPE	L.T. SALLOUM/VIC. BLEWETT	KELOWNA	3.15	14/49/51	4(F)	24
WILLY WILLY	J.W. CHILTON	3 TREE PT.	2.95	14/50/10	5(F)	25
TARKA	PETER GROVE	R.VAN.	2.65	14/52/17	18(E)	26
IMPULSE	J. KEVORKIAN	CYC (SEA)	3.10	14/53/19	6(F)	27
MADHATTER	N. SEVERIDE	R.VAN.	3.00	14/57/32	7(F)	28
NASTY JACK	DAVID BRINK	CYC (SEA)	2.95	15/ 0/ 8	8(F)	29
CHICANERY	J. SEVERS	CYC (POR)	2.60	15/ 6/55	19(E)	30
PONEMAH	M. DALE	TIDDLYCOVE	3.30	15/ 8/ 2	9(F)	31
GONZO	J. CRANE	CYC (POR)	2.80	15/13/23	20(E)	32
CHANTILLY	DAVID G. FREWIN	WEST VAN.	2.80	15/18/49	21(E)	33
BANDIDO	R.G. FOXALL	W.V.Y.C.	2.95	15/19/ 4	10(F)	34
SKILFISH	D.R. WEST	W.VAN.	2.95	15/21/44	11(F)	35
TRIAD	RONALD RAY	TACOMA	2.90	15/30/39	22(E)	36
LEESOME	J. PATTERSON	CANOE BAY	3.20	15/56/32	12(F)	37
MORAG	D. JENKINS	R.VAN.	2.95	15/58/10	13(F)	38
TILLICUM	H.J. RICKETTS	CYC (SEA)	3.05	16/ 8/57	14(F)	39
SEEKER	MURRAY FARMER	R.VIC.	2.85	16/12/22	23(E)	40
MASSILIA II	EE READSHAW	R.VIC.	3.50	16/23/30	4(G)	41
BEOWULF	R. JEWULA	TURKEY HD.	3.30	16/33/33	15(F)	42
DIRK	D. HEUKELOM	W.VAN.	3.40	16/34/43	5(G)	43
SAFFRON	JUNE CAMERON	TIDDLYCOVE	3.50	16/38/35	6(G)	44
WARM WIND	K.W. McCARTY	CYC (SEA)	3.05	16/39/31	16(F)	45
BAREFOOT	DONALD RUSSELL	CYC (SEA)	3.00	16/50/56	17(F)	46
FIREFLY	B. WEAVER	CYC (SEA)	2.90	17/ 9/30	24(F)	47
NOOSA	VAN DEN DRIESCH	R.VIC.	3.30	17/20/59	18(F)	48
TARQUIN IV	G. JOHNSTONE	R.VIC.	3.00	17/22/23	19(F)	49
THOMASINE	J.H. COOK	R.VIC.	3.00	17/23/46	20(F)	50
AUDACE	R.N. HAUGEN	CYC (SEA)	3.05	17/25/ 1	21(F)	51
OLYMPIC MIST	MICHAEL KALAHAR	PT. ANGELES	3.50	17/53/25	7(G)	52
SUFI	H.E. BUCHANAN	CANOE BAY	2.80	18/ 1/24	25(E)	53
FLYING HIGH	H.J. TIMMEMAN	TIDDLYCOVE	3.50	18/16/ 3	8(G)	54
MENOS	M.B. BALDERSTON	R.VIC.	3.85	18/19/43	9(G)	55
THISTLEDOWN	D. FEELEY	P. ANGELES	3.05	18/54/26	22(F)	56
WINGS	B. KLAVER	R.VIC.	3.60	18/58/26	10(G)	57
SALTY DREAM	G. JACOBI	R.VIC.	3.30	18/59/ 6	23(F)	58
VELOCITAS	C.C. VANEE	EAGLE HAR.	3.40	19/49/56	11(G)	59
HARMONY	B. WILTON	R.VIC.	3.40	20/ 8/40	12(G)	60
LOTTE	ED HAINES	CFSA	4.10	20/19/ 0	13(G)	61
ILLUSIVE	BRUCE JOHNSON	R.VIC.	3.50	20/24/16	14(G)	62
GEMINI	J.D. VAN OMMEN	ANACORTES	3.00	20/28/ 7	24(F)	63
SEAQUIN	R.S. MARSHALL	CYC (SEA)	3.90	20/30/22	15(G)	64
ARTEMIS II	R. BOYD	R.VAN.	2.95	20/38/22	25(F)	65

CHARON	JOHN EASTHAM/ERIC PETERSEN	SEATTLE	2.75		DNF	DNF(E)	DNF
DAZZLER	BILL VAUX	ANACORTES	2.70		DNF	DNF(E)	DNF
NEPENTHE	B. JOHNSON	3 TR. PT.	3.25		DNF	DNF(F)	DNF
SHOOTING STAR	M.V. SCHMIDT	SEATTLE	3.20		DNF	DNF(F)	DNF
KEEMA	J. SEZNICK	CYC (SEA)	2.70		DNF	DNF(E)	DNF

SWIFTSURE & JUAN DE FUCA YACHT RACES 1979

Thank you for sending me a copy of your letter of 16 July, 79. At that time I was out of the country on holiday and unfortunately did not see your original letter. Upon investigation I found that the letter was indeed received at the Yacht Club and in my absence was promptly attended to by the Race Committee Chairman, Sid Bryant.

I understand that Sid Bryant phoned your home and passed a message in which he apologized for the date entry error that placed your yacht one day way from the actual finishing time and also that an order had been given for a prize in your name for second place in Division C. (This prize will be delivered shortly by mail.)

Because prizes have been produced and issued against the original list and because we do not think it is reasonable to withdraw any prize, there will be two holders of second prize for Division G.

I sincerely hope that this arrangement is satisfactory to you and ask that you please accept our apologies for unfortunate series of errors that have cause this situation.

Yours truly,
F.A.C. Piddington
Swiftsure Chairman

PACIFIC INTERNATIONAL YACHTING ASSOCIATION
SWIFTSURE LIGHTSHIP CLASSIC AND JUAN DE FUCA RACE
1980 TROPHY WINNERS

SWIFTSURE (I.O.R.) CLASS I	SWIFTSURE TROPHY (OVERALL HANDICAP WINNER)	LADYBUG	SEATTLE	A. HOLT
	CITY OF VICTORIA TROPHY (FIRST YACHT TO FINISH)	WARRIOR	SEATTLE	L. BRUCE HEDRIC
	OCEAN CEMENT TROPHY (DIVISION 1)	WARRIOR	SEATTLE	L. BRUCE HEDRIC
	T. EATON TROPHY (DIVISION 2)	TOMAHAWK	BALBOA	J.E. ARENS
	CITY OF SEATTLE TROPHY (DIVISION 3)	WOTAN	SEATTLE	WM. BURDICK
	ROYAL VAN. YACHT CLUB TROPHY (DIVISION 4)	LADYBUG	SEATTLE	A. HOLT
SWIFTSURE (P.H.R.F.) CLASS II	PACIFIC RIM TROPHY (OVERALL HANDICAP WINNER)	DELICATE BALANCE	SEATTLE	DR. R. GUNSOLUS
	ROYAL CANADIAN NAVY TROPHY (FIRST YACHT TO FINISH)	JAZZ	ANACORTES	D. SKINNER
	(DIVISION A)	JAZZ	ANACORTES	D. SKINNER
	CORINTHIAN YACHT CLUB TROPHY (DIVISION B)	DELICATE BALANCE	SEATTLE	DR. R. GUNSOLUS
SWIFTSURE (P.H.R.F.) CLASS III	(OVERALL HANDICAP WINNER)	ENCOUNTER	R.VIC..	DR. H. BACON
	(FIRST YACHT TO FINISH)	BANKSHOT	EVERETT	A. HEINIG
	STORMY WEATHER TROPHY (DIVISION C)	BANKSHOT	EVERETT	A. HEINIG
	CAPE FLATTERY TROPHY (DIVISION D)	ENCOUNTER	R.VIC.	DR. H. BACON
JUAN DE FUCA (I.O.R.) CLASS IV	(OVERALL HANDICAP WINNER)	OUTLAW	SEATTLE	T. HUKLE
	SAN JUAN TROPHY (FIRST YACHT TO FINISH)	HAGAR	SEATTLE	G. DUNCAN
	ROYAL VIC. YACHT CLUB TROPHY (DIVISION 5)	HAGAR	SEATTLE	G. DUNCAN
JUAN DE FUCA (P.H.R.F.) CLASS V	ROYAL CANADIAN NAVY TROPHY (DIVISION 6)	OUTLAW	SEATTLE	T. HUKLE
	(FIRST YACHT TO FINISH)	TARKA	R.VAN.	P. GROVE/A. GROVE
	ANACORTES YACHT CLUB TROPHY (DIVISION E)	ROMADA	R.VIC.	R. HINGLEY
JUAN DE FUCA (P.H.R.F.) CLASS VI	PORT ANGELES YACHT CLUB TROPHY (OVERALL HANDICAP WINNER)	BAD NEWS	TIDDLY CVE	R. LEFEAUX
	(FIRST YACHT TO FINISH)	BAD NEWS	TIDDLY CVE	R. LEFEAUX
	(DIVISION F)	BAD NEWS	TIDDLY CVE	R. LEFEAUX
	(DIVISION G)	DEMARA	TIDDLY CVE	A. CROWE

SWIFTSURE (CLASS I) — 1980
RESULTS

OFFICIAL START TIME: 9/10/00

YACHT NAME	SKIPPER(S)	CLUB	RATING	COR ELAPSE TIME	POSITION DIVISION	OVERALL
LADYBUG	ALAN HOLT	SEATTLE	21.50	27/46/01	1(4)	1
BUMPER	D. CLARK	SEATTLE	21.50	27/52/36	2(4)	2
WARRIOR	BRUCE HEDRIC	SEATTLE	42.90	29/00/52	1(1)	3
RHAPSODY	JIM SMITH/SCOTT SMITH	EDMONDS	24.50	29/03/45	3(4)	4
ALERT	EUSTACE VYNNE JR.	FRIDAY HRB	24.40	29/06/16	4(4)	5

TOMAHAWK	JOHN ARENS	BALBOA	31.80	29/06/57	1(2)	6
WOTAN	BILL BURDICK	SEATTLE	25.80	29/17/34	1(3)	7
HYPERTENSION	ROGER PALMER	CORINTHIAN	26.70	29/22/09	2(3)	8
DEFIANCE	RON HART	TACOMA	35.20	29/27/11	2(1)	9
PROSPECTOR	LARRY SHORETT	SEATTLE	26.80	29/27/15	3(3)	10
STARGAZER	BILL HEDDEN	SEATTLE	24.30	29/27/46	5(4)	11
COUNTRY STYLE	STEVE MERRIMAN	R.VIC.	26.80	29/32/26	4(3)	12
AKKA	RALPH MARX	TACOMA	24.10	29/33/03	6(4)	13
ANOMALY	BILL ELMER	CORINTHIAN	25.60	29/35/49	5(3)	14
EX-SACHEM	R. ALEXANDER	SEATTLE	25.20	29/37/24	6(3)	15
WHISPER	DORR ANDERSON/JEFF ABRAMS	SEATTLE	24.80	29/38/43	7(4)	16
MOONDANCE	R. BUFFAN/P. DENNIS	R.VIC.	26.80	29/38/49	7(3)	17
MUSTARD SEED	CHRIS OTOROWSKI/DOUG HERMAN	PANHANDLE	27.50	29/39/51	8(3)	18
PACHENA	JOHN NEWTON	WEST VAN	31.20	29/42/38	2(2)	19
LAERTES	PETER CROWE	VAN ROWING	21.90	29/42/41	8(4)	20
AGGRESSION	J. CHRISTENSEN	PORTLAND	25.90	29/42/45	9(3)	21
KELEA	D. DELMOTTE	R.VAN.	24.90	29/45/25	9(4)	22
WHANGAREI	DON MAYER/JIM KNUTSON	CORINTHIAN	29.30	29/47/50	3(2)	23
TOPKAPI	ROBERT KITCHEN	WEST VAN	27.40	29/50/03	10(3)	24
JEZEBEL	STEPHEN BROCKWAY	CORINTHIAN	25.60	29/53/08	11(3)	25
KNIGHTMARE	G. KNIGHT	VAN ROWING	26.90	29/54/14	12(3)	26
ALLIANCE	TOM GIDLUND/EVAN SCHWAB	SEATTLE	27.80	29/56/01	13(3)	27
DREAM MACHINE	WINK VOGEL	R.VAN.	32.80	30/00/04	3(1)	28
PROPHECY	J. JARMAN	R.VAN.	26.60	30/02/42	14(3)	29
PHOENIX	STEVE CRARY	LAHAINA	30.60	30/05/10	4(2)	30
PARADOX	GEORGE McGOWEN	TACOMA	26.60	30/06/42	15(3)	31
TONIC	DAN BRINK	CORINTHIAN	27.50	30/08/51	16(3)	32
SCHUSS	MIKE KERNAN/L. SUND	CORINTHIAN	23.70	30/09/16	10(4)	33
OVERDRAFT TOO	MILES HESILDIN/LEN RUSSELL	R.VAN.	27.80	30/12/18	17(3)	34
FANNY	G. STEVENSON	CORINTHIAN	24.50	30/12/59	11(4)	35
WHISTLEWING	G. ANDERSON	SEATTLE	41.30	30/13/22	4(1)	36
TAPOCKETA	ROBERT NEWELL	BELLINGHAM	24.00	30/15/19	12(4)	37
INNAMORATA	CLIFFORD LANZING	CORINTHIAN	32.00	30/15/59	5(1)	38
OUTRAGEOUS	JOHN HARDIMAN	CORINTHIAN	27.10	30/15/59	18(3)	39
SURTSEY	B. McKEE	SEATTLE	35.20	30/18/38	6(1)	40
ESCARGOT	S. SCIMECA	SEATTLE	26.00	30/19/59	19(3)	41
IRISH ROSE	DENNIS DONOHUE	CORINTHIAN	32.10	30/20/48	7(1)	42
INDOMITABLE	JOHN LONG	R.VAN.	34.30	30/21/51	8(1)	43
JADAH IV	PHIL TUCKER	CORINTHIAN	31.30	30/23/03	5(2)	44
ANNIE CADBY	LOUIS LINDHOLM	R.VIC.	31.60	30/23/40	6(2)	45
KANATA	V. PLAVSIC	WEST VAN.	31.00	30/23/41	7(2)	46
VIRGINIA DARE	B. ADAM	SEATTLE	27.50	30/25/29	20(3)	47
ALBERTA BOUND II	BOB NOWACK	R.VAN.	31.90	30/26/25	8(2)	48
RACE PASSAGE	DR. P. McCULOUGH	BREMERTON	35.40	30/27/23	9(1)	49
PASSAGES	RICHARD BELL	CORINTHIAN	31.90	30/27/47	9(2)	50
BORU	BILL GRIERSON	R.VAN.	26.70	30/28/27	21(3)	51
SINE MORA	D. HILLMAN	SEATTLE	25.70	30/29/24	22(3)	52
A BIENTOT	ROBERT KACZOR	SEATTLE	27.90	30/31/57	23(3)	53
GLORY	JOHN BUCHAN	SEATTLE	44.10	30/33/56	10(1)	54
MILLENNIUM FALCON	ALAN DAVIS	CORINTHIAN	32.00	30/34/18	11(1)	55
NERITA	BILL BRUCH	CORINTHIAN	29.60	30/39/21	10(2)	56
SCARAMOUCHE	KATE ALEXANDER	SEATTLE	34.00	30/39/23	12(1)	57
DORLES	WILLIS KLUDT	3 TREE PT.	26.90	30/39/54	24(3)	58
HEATHER	FRED ROSWOLD	EXP. POST	31.20	30/41/15	11(2)	59
BROTHER GOOSE	BOB SEVENICH	EVERETT	30.60	30/45/40	12(2)	60
IMPOSSIBLE	JIM WITTAKER	CORINTHIAN	35.30	30/45/40	13(1)	61
SABRA	MILES MILLER	SEATTLE	32.00	30/46/38	14(1)	62
WEATHERLY	LYNN SOMMERS/ALAN BUCHAN	TACOMA	45.80	30/46/52	15(1)	63
CHIRON	B. ARCHER	TACOMA	36.40	30/51/52	16(1)	64
WARLOCK	CALVIN BAMFORD	TACOMA	33.40	30/54/38	17(1)	65
LEPSOYA	JOHN RUNSTAD	SEATTLE	35.20	30/56/23	18(1)	66
GOLDEN EAGLE	RICHARD ROBERTS	CORINTHIAN	24.00	30/56/32	13(4)	67
THE DISTANT DRUMMER	GREG OLIVER	R.VIC.	27.40	30/57/14	25(3)	68
DISCOVERY	JOHN DUNFIELD	R.VAN.	37.10	30/57/46	19(1)	69
WIZARD	NEIL KELLY	CORINTHIAN	32.40	31/00/26	20(1)	70
PANGAEA	M. MADENWALD	ANACORTES	30.20	31/01/22	13(2)	71
QUINTET	FRED DIEKER	PORTLAND	34.80	31/05/58	21(1)	72
WINDWARD	JOHN CICERI	R.VIC.	26.00	31/12/48	26(3)	73
NAKNEK	RICHARD NELSON	R.VAN.	36.40	31/26/25	22(1)	74
BOHEMIA	ROBERT HELSELL	SEATTLE	29.80	31/44/38	14(2)	75
NIMBLE	WM. NICKERSON	PORTLAND	30.90	32/19/58	15(2)	76

YACHT NAME	SKIPPER(S)	CLUB	RATING	COR ELAPSE TIME	POSITION DIVISION	OVERALL
GRAYBEARD	L. KILLAM	R.VAN.	65.50	33/02/56	23(1)	77
WARLORD	JOHN GONYEA	TACOMA	25.40	DNF	DNF(3)	DNF
KOTUKU	R. MATHEWSON	R.VIC.	32.10	DNF	DNF(1)	DNF
HARPOON	WILLIAM BRASIER	TACOMA	32.20	DNF	DNF(1)	DNF
DIAMOND HEAD	HENRY KOTKINS	SEATTLE	41.40	DNF	DNF(1)	DNF
THURSDAY NIGHT	LAWRENCE WEISS	ROSE CITY	21.80	DNF	DNF(4)	DNF
TRIUMPH	JIM NAPOLITANO	CORINTHIAN	25.80	DSQ	DSQ(3)	DSQ
ILLUSION	NICK ORR	CORINTHIAN	29.90	DNS	DNS(2)	DNS
MOODY TOO	JIM PINE	WEST VAN.	25.80	DNS	DNS(3)	DNS
WHITEBIRD	ALEX BOOME	R.VAN.	25.60	DNS	DNS(3)	DNS
BRIGADOON	VIC BISHOP	WEST VAN.	26.90	DNS	DNS(3)	DNS

1. The attached results reflect changes made as a result of protests, the correction of errors, and the application of special time allowances for yachts that went to the aid of a ''yacht in distress''.
2. Yachts given special time allowances were: MORNING STAR   —   3 minutes
   HAWK WING   —   20 minutes
3. A protest made by the yacht JAZZ with respect to her P.H.R.F. rating remains unresolved at the time of printing these results. The outcome may alter the overall handicap winner of CLASS II.

SWIFTSURE (CLASS II) 1980
RESULTS

OFFICIAL START TIME: 09/20/00

YACHT NAME	SKIPPER(S)	CLUB	RATING	COR ELAPSE TIME	POSITION DIVISION	OVERALL
DELICATE BALANCE	DR. ROY GUNSOLUS	SEATTLE	2.00	29/45/23	1(B)	1
JAZZ	DAVID SKINNER	ANACORTES	1.60	29/53/28	1(A)	2
NATURAL HIGH	ROBERT RANKIN	CORINTHIAN	2.00	29/57/19	2(B)	3
DELIVERANCE	GEORGE PALO	CORINTHIAN	2.10	29/57/55	3(B)	4
SOUTHPAW	STEVE KINSEY	TSWWASSEN	2.10	30/01/17	4(B)	5
FLYING MACHINE	CHARLES WALSH	CORINTHIAN	2.00	30/05/03	5(B)	6
ADASTRA	KEES FRANSBERGEN	WEST VAN.	2.00	30/10/56	6(B)	7
SURPRISE	G. MAURER	SEATTLE	1.95	30/13/27	7(B)	8
PRISM	BOB McPAKE	SEATTLE	2.00	30/14/50	8(B)	9
LEIKO II	DR. G. SAKATA	TIDDLY CVE.	1.60	30/27/40	2(A)	10
NORSTRADAMUS	DR. JOHN CORNELL	CORINTHIAN	2.10	30/28/20	9(B)	11
HOOLIGAN II	TOM O'BRIEN	SEATTLE	1.85	30/29/37	10(B)	12
NAMBA	A.J.B. FORSYTH	R.VAN.	1.60	30/32/45	3(A)	13
BARBARA	WYNN KAMPE	CORINTHIAN	2.00	30/32/50	11(B)	14
MOONGLOW IV	DAVID NEILSEN	TACOMA	1.60	30/32/55	4(A)	15
RAIN DROP	J. GAINER	ROSE CITY	2.00	30/35/16	12(B)	16
ABRAXAS II	PETER KEATE	R.VAN.	1.65	30/38/15	5(A)	17
COUNTESS III	PETER JEFFERSON	R.VAN.	1.90	30/38/21	13(B)	18
ZUBEN´UBI IV	WILLIAM HESTER	CORINTHIAN	2.00	30/38/43	14(B)	19
SKARRIETT	BOB WILSON	3 TREE PT.	1.95	30/39/44	15(B)	20
MADRUGADOR	DOUGLAS STEWART	CORINTHIAN	1.85	30/40/06	16(B)	21
FAEM	RONALD ARMSTRONG	R.VAN.	2.05	30/41/26	17(B)	22
M.M. CRUMBAKER	GERALD PARKER	TACOMA	1.90	30/46/44	18(B)	23
SYDEILSUMA	S. BULFORD/DAVIDSON/CHICON	KITSILANO	1.75	30/50/30	6(A)	24
TRINGA	F. GARDINER	R.VIC.	2.10	30/50/41	19(B)	25
CASSIOPEIA	CARL NEU JR.	SEATTLE	1.80	30/51/27	7(A)	26
WHITE SQUALL	DR. G. TEATS	TACOMA	1.85	30/52/26	20(B)	27
SHAMAN	DR. D. DINGMAN	CORINTHIAN	1.85	30/52/29	21(B)	28
CHOISEUL	PAUL DANIELS	R.VAN.	1.80	30/53/58	8(A)	29
THALASSIC	CHUCK VIELE	CORINTHIAN	2.05	30/55/19	22(B)	30
SCRIMSHANDER	JACK MILLER	R.VIC.	2.10	30/57/09	23(B)	31
WINGAWAY	D. BRYNELSEN	VAN ROWING	1.80	30/57/26	9(A)	32
MEG	BOB HOSIE	R.VIC.	2.10	30/57/39	24(B)	33
BAGHEERA	ANDY COPELAND	R.VAN.	1.85	30/59/15	25(B)	34
INDIGO	BOB HARRISON	WEST VAN.	1.65	30/59/17	10(A)	35
SEALION	N. MARTIN	NANAIMO	2.10	30/59/29	26(B)	36
BOBBY FOSTER	G. LOWE	PT. MADISON	1.85	31/00/18	27(B)	37
CIRCE	BOB BARTLESON/TOM GEISNESS	SEATTLE	1.75	31/02/45	11(A)	38
MILLTOWN	BILL KOTE/PAUL KOTE SR.&JR.	R.VAN.	1.40	31/03/00	12(A)	39
VIVA	DAVID BLAKEMORE	CORINTHIAN	1.85	31/03/07	28(B)	40
MENEHUNE	D. WILSON	CANOE BAY	2.10	31/03/28	29(B)	41
COHO II	PETE HANSON	SEATTLE	1.60	31/04/03	13(A)	42
EPIC	CHAS SCHIFF	CORINTHIAN	1.25	31/07/42	14(A)	43
SWALLOW II	PHIL JOHNSON	SEATTLE	1.85	31/07/50	30(B)	44
BLUE MARLIN	JIM WILLIAMS	CORINTHIAN	1.85	31/08/12	31(B)	45
SPECTRE	J. CAHILL	SEATTLE	1.85	31/08/28	32(B)	46
BLACK WATCH	BILL NELSON	CORINTHIAN	1.55	31/10/11	15(A)	47
BIG JUAN	RONALD RAY	TACOMA	2.15	31/11/08	33(B)	48
SNAKE	LEE KEARNEY	CORINTHIAN	1.85	31/14/18	34(B)	49

YACHT NAME	SKIPPER(S)	CLUB	RATING	COR ELAPSE TIME	POSITION DIVISION	OVERALL
MIDNIGHT SPECIAL	VERN McCULLOUGH	SEATTLE	1.55	31/15/25	16(A)	50
WINDLESS II	RONALD WICKSTROM	CANOE BAY	1.80	31/16/51	17(A)	51
OUTRIDER	GERRY KIDD	WEST VAN	1.70	31/17/20	18(A)	52
PACIFIC GOLD	LAWRENCE LAMBERT	CANOE BAY	1.80	31/17/56	19(A)	53
MADELEINE	JIM MORRIS	CANOE BAY	2.10	31/18/23	35(B)	54
TANGENT II	ANTHONY LOACH	WEST VAN	2.00	31/22/12	36(B)	55
ERRIGAL	HUGH PORTER	R.VIC.	1.95	31/27/45	37(B)	56
K-SEA	C. NIEWERTH	EAGLE HRBR	1.90	31/30/21	38(B)	57
QUICKSILVER	JOHN RILEY	SEATTLE	1.30	31/32/20	20(A)	58
SAVAGE SPIRIT	GEORGE OAKES	PT. ANGELES	1.75	31/32/31	21(A)	59
MISTRESS III	T. VARLEY	EVERETT	1.65	31/33/40	22(A)	60
SATURDAY'S CHILD	C. BRAIN	SEATTLE	1.30	31/33/42	23(A)	61
MELTEMI	FRANK MUSSON	WEST VAN	2.00	31/34/53	39(B)	62
SKEAN DHUB	DR. WM. DUNCAN	CORINTHIAN	2.00	31/36/11	40(B)	63
LEGEND	CHARLES STEWARD	SEATTLE	1.85	31/37/05	41(B)	64
PIETARSAARI	ROGER BARNES	CORINTHIAN	1.55	31/37/09	24(A)	65
ARROW	DON RIPLEY	3 TREE PT.	1.85	31/37/32	42(B)	66
HIGH ROLLER IV	LYLE KERR	VAN ROWING	2.00	31/37/35	43(B)	67
HAWK WING	LARRY ULM	CORINTHIAN	1.70	31/40/13	25(A)	68
RAMPART	JACK ROSS	COMOX	1.70	31/41/15	26(A)	69
SIRENA	DONALD RUSSELL	CORINTHIAN	2.00	31/41/25	44(B)	70
NIGHT RUNNER	DOUG FRYER	SEATTLE	1.10	31/41/38	27(A)	71
WENDIGO	BRAD NEWELL	PT. LUDLOW	1.90	31/48/15	45(B)	72
MERINO	PHILIP HAYES	TACOMA	1.50	31/48/49	28(A)	73
RHIANNON	BUSH ALBISTON	SEATTLE	2.00	31/51/30	46(B)	74
DRAMBUIE	RICHARD KOCH	BROWNSVILL	2.00	31/51/59	47(B)	75
CARTHAGINIAN	WILLIAM HANSON	CORINTHIAN	1.25	31/52/05	29(A)	76
PRIORITY	SHERWOOD SMITH	OLYMPIA	2.00	31/53/30	48(B)	77
RED SHIFT	JACK WILSON	CORINTHIAN	2.00	31/55/09	49(B)	78
THUNDER	WILLIAM KING	PORTLAND	1.50	31/59/59	30(A)	79
ADVERSARY	DUANE VERGEER	PORTLAND	1.55	32/13/17	31(A)	80
NIMBUS	DAVID SELLER	R.VAN.	2.05	32/18/59	50(B)	81
YANKEE GIRL	J. McDONALD	SEATTLE	1.80	32/25/43	32(A)	82
RAMROD	STEVE McCOY	3 TREE PT.	1.90	32/25/45	51(B)	83
JESTER	ROBERT HURLOW	CORINTHIAN	1.75	32/45/54	33(A)	84
NIMPKISH II	G. SALMON	DEEP COVE	1.45	33/16/36	34(A)	85
HUSTLER	MARTIN YAPP	SLOOP TRVN	1.95	35/01/29	52(B)	86
CORMORANT	DR. H. BOYD	CORINTHIAN	2.05	35/08/31	53(B)	87
CHAMPAGNE CHARLIE	T. TAYLOR	LONG BEACH	2.00	38/12/47	54(B)	88
KISMET	M. CARLSON	EVERETT	1.85	DNF	DNF(B)	DNF
KSAN	BONAR DAVIS	R.VAN.	1.70	DNF	DNF(A)	DNF
COFFEE POT	DOUGLAS WARDROP	TIDDLY CVE	2.10	DNF	DNF(B)	DNF
BITTERSWEET	GERALD SMITH	TACOMA	1.70	DNF	DNF(A)	DNF
SUNDANCE	THOMAS MURPHY	TACOMA	1.85	DNF	DNF(B)	DNF
AMITA	GRANT WATSON/M. MUENCH	R.VIC.	2.00	DNF	DNF(B)	DNF
BLUE ODYSSEY	JAMES PARTLON	TURKEY HD	1.70	DNF	DNF(A)	DNF
MAHRI II	RON MacKENZIE	R.VAN.	2.10	DNF	DNF(B)	DNF
VOLCANO	TOLLY ALLEN	CORINTHIAN	2.10	DNF	DNF(B)	DNF
MADE IN JAPAN	MARK HAUGAN	CORINTHIAN		DNS	DNS(A)	DNS
LLLR	ELLIOTT JONES	SEATTLE	2.00	DNS	DNS(B)	DNS
JEUNESS II	P. COTE	R.VAN.	1.80	DNS	DNS(A)	DNS
HOTSPUR	JOHN CLAYTON	R.VAN.	2.00	DNS	DNS(B)	DNS

SWIFTSURE (CLASS III) 1980 RESULTS

OFFICIAL START TIME: 09/30/00

YACHT NAME	SKIPPER(S)	CLUB	RATING	COR ELAPSE TIME	POSITION DIVISION	OVERALL
ENCOUNTER	DR. HUGH BACON	R.VIC.	2.75	29/30/23	1(D)	1
WINDSONG II	ROGER BARNHART	BELLINGHAM	2.50	29/48/22	2(D)	2
SASSY	S. CLARKE	TACOMA	2.50	29/53/11	3(D)	3
CONSULTATION	D. ANDERSON/G. NORTON	OLYMPIA	2.80	30/03/58	4(D)	4
BANKSHOT	ALAN HEINIG	EVERETT	2.30	30/08/43	1(C)	5
MORNING STAR	M. DUFFY	CORINTHIAN	2.35	30/13/22	2(C)	6
TEKA	JAN HUIBERS	R.VIC.	2.35	30/14/06	3(C)	7
COUNTERPOINT	TIM CLARK	CORINTHIAN	2.25	30/17/06	4(C)	8
SMALL WORLD II	GENE SIBOLD	OLYMPIA	2.25	30/25/20	5(C)	9
GAMIN	LON ROBINSON	SEATTLE	2.25	30/30/22	6(C)	10
JURA	KASPAR SCHIBLI	R.VIC.	2.40	30/45/31	7(C)	11
ORCA	DR. F. THOMPSON	R.VAN.	2.20	30/47/32	8(C)	12
CHEETAH	PETER CLARKE	QUARTRMSTR	2.20	30/53/35	9(C)	13
TSUNAMI	CONRAD MORAN	CORINTHIAN	2.35	31/05/01	10(C)	14
ROWDY LADY II	ART HAUGE	PORTLAND	2.20	31/07/46	11(C)	15

YACHT NAME	SKIPPER(S)	CLUB	RATING		DIVISION	OVERALL
EDELWEISS II	P. WAGNER	R.VAN.	2.35	31/15/14	12(C)	16
SHOGUN	DICK BEER	EAGLE HRBR	2.20	31/15/21	13(C)	17
MERIJANO	JOHN GYAPJAS	TSWWASSEN	2.70	31/15/29	5(D)	18
MARY D. II	DARREL DAVIS	PT. ANGELES	2.35	31/16/24	14(C)	19
IMAGE RESPONSE	MARK FREY/HOWARD FREY	PT. MADISON	2.75	31/19/06	6(D)	20
DECEIVER	H. RAMEY	CANOE BAY	2.90	31/33/32	7(D)	21
SPINSTER	JULIAN DEWELL	EVERETT	2.30	31/34/01	15(C)	22
FLETCHER	MIKE EUDALY	ROSE CITY	2.40	31/47/08	16(C)	23
JOLLY ROGER III	ROGER WHEELER	CORINTHIAN	2.35	31/54/09	17(C)	24
NAUTILUS	DR. L. NEVLER	CORINTHIAN	2.30	31/57/52	18(C)	25
POISSON SOLUBLE	R. HORSLEY	CORINTHIAN	2.40	32/04/21	19(C)	26
DULCINEA	R. SPANFELNER/D. & M. SMITH	SEATTLE	2.30	32/04/45	20(C)	27
MORAG	DICK JENKINS	R.VAN.	2.95	32/12/35	8(D)	28
GITAND	JAMES DEPUE	PT. MADISON	2.55	32/21/32	9(D)	29
JACKAROE	ROGER HILLS	PT. TOWNSEND	2.75	32/25/27	10(D)	30
ANDANTE	IAN HOPKINSON	DEEP COVE	2.70	32/39/28	11(D)	31
GUS	BERT LUNDGAARD	PT. MADISON	2.90	32/52/30	12(D)	32
POUDRE D'OR	BUDDY HULSCHER	VAN ROWING	2.80	32/56/22	13(D)	33
PRO TANTO	BOB STANGE	CORINTHIAN	2.95	32/57/31	14(D)	34
FAT CAT	TOM OSBORN	3 TREE PT.	2.55	33/01/12	15(D)	35
MOLLY SQUASH	ANDY ROTTLER	SEATTLE	2.45	33/01/57	21(C)	36
FOREIGN AFFAIR	WILLIAM BLACK	CORINTHIAN	2.30	33/06/05	22(C)	37
BEAUTIFUL NOISE	FRANK SHRIVER	3 TREE PT.	2.35	33/19/01	23(C)	38
SUNSHINE	JIM PASSAGE	SEATTLE	2.35	33/19/43	24(C)	39
MOODY BLUES	DAVID STIER	CORINTHIAN	2.25	33/27/30	25(C)	40
FROSTBITE	ROBERT FROST	SHILSHOLE	2.30	33/30/35	26(C)	41
GOMETRA	D. MILLIS	R.C.N.S.A.	2.35	33/37/41	27(C)	42
PACIFIC LADY II	KEN WILSON	CANOE BAY	2.30	33/37/49	28(C)	43
SQUAW DUCK	DARRELL WILLITS	TACOMA	2.30	33/53/15	29(C)	44
CALLALOU	JOHN CATLEY	R.VAN.	2.95	33/59/44	16(D)	45
RASPUTIN	BRIAN HEYES	R.C.N.S.A.	3.05	36/12/12	17(D)	46
JASMINE	DONALD GLOCKNER	CORINTHIAN	2.45	DNF	DNF(C)	DNF
HINA	KEN CROSS	DEEP COVE	2.80	DNF	DNF(D)	DNF
ODIN	ALAN HARTE	R.C.N.S.A.	3.15	DNF	DNF(D)	DNF
MAHANA TAMARI'I	RON GROFF	GIG HARBOR	3.50	DNF	DNF(D)	DNF
SHINGEBISS	L. BAILEY	CORINTHIAN	2.35	DNF	DNF(C)	DNF
JUBILEE	B. NEIL BLACK	SHILSHOLE	2.60	DNF	DNF(D)	DNF
WARM WIND	KENNETH McCARTY	CORINTHIAN	3.05	DNF	DNF(D)	DNF
ELUSIVE	JOHN ASMUNDSON	BELLINGHAM	2.20	DNF	DNF(C)	DNF
CLOUSEAU	MICHAEL STAINSBY	3 TREE PT.	2.45	DNF	DNF(C)	DNF
BILLIKEN	BILL AIKEN	SHILSHOLE	2.40	DNF	DNF(C)	DNF
GOLDEN GIRL	FREDERICK HALL	PORTLAND	2.50	DNF	DNF(D)	DNF
TIN MAN	NED FLOHR	SEATTLE	3.70	DNF	DNF(D)	DNF
SURGER	KEN WRIGHT	VAN ROWING	2.95	DNF	DNF(D)	DNF
HMCS ORIOLE	C.D.R. W.M. WALKER	C.F.S.A.	2.50	DNF	DNF(D)	DNF
HALCYON PASSAGE	DR. PETER CLARK	R.VIC.	2.40	DNF	DNF(C)	DNF
SHANNON	BOB RAYMANT	WEST VAN	2.80	DNF	DNF(D)	DNF
AKAMAI	GREG CAVIN	CORINTHIAN	2.60	DNF	DNF(D)	DNF
SUNDANCE KID	DOUG SOLOMON	VAN ROWING	2.80	DNF	DNF (D)	DNF
STARWAGON	N.C. BAILEY	SHILSHOLE	2.20	DNF	DNF(C)	DNF
STRIDER	KEITH JOHNSON	SEATTLE	2.35	DNF	DNF(C)	DNF
PASSING CLOUD	JACK STACEY	C.F.S.A.	3.20	DNF	DNF(D)	DNF
THE SHINING	KARL ROLLINS	EVERETT	2.20	DNF	DNF(C)	DNF
CIRRUS	ALAN FORSYTHE	QUARTRMSTR.	2.90	DNF	DNF(D)	DNF
SANNU SANNU	G. WAKEFIELD	R.VIC.	3.25	DNF	DNF(D)	DNF
CHEROKEE	MIKE MULCAHY	3 TREE PT.	2.20	DNF	DNF(C)	DNF
ESCAPE HATCH	BOB FERRIE	BELLINGHAM	3.50	DNF	DNF(D)	DNF
EASY TOO	DR. WALTER SCHUMA	CORINTHIAN	2.70	DSQ	DSQ(D)	DSQ
MAGNUM	BOB AXFORD	R.VAN.	2.35	DNS	DNS(C)	DNS
TOLO TSOLO	ED WOODSON	ANACORTES	2.45	DNS	DNS(C)	DNS
MAYA	M LEPOULE	R.VAN.	2.25	DNS	DNS(C)	DNS
DRAKE	CHAS KENNEDY	VAN ROWING	2.40	DNS	DNS(C)	DNS
PANDEMONIUM	PETER O'REILLY	OLYMPIA	2.85	DNS	DNS(D)	DNS

OFFICIAL START TIME: 09/40/00

JUAN DE FUCA (CLASS IV) 1980 RESULTS

YACHT NAME	SKIPPER(S)	CLUB	RATING	COR ELAPSE TIME	POSITION DIVISION	OVERALL
OUTLAW	THOMAS HUKLE	SEATTLE	21.30	09/52/38	1(6)	1
SEA BEATER	GLEN BOUDON	CORINTHIAN	21.30	09/56/45	2(6)	2
HAGAR	G. DUNCAN	SEATTLE	24.50	09/57/34	1(5)	3
SWEET CHEEKS	JACK SINTON/SANDY SINTON	CORINTHIAN	21.30	10/03/48	3(6)	4

YACHT NAME	SKIPPER(S)	CLUB	RATING	COR ELAPSE TIME	POSITION DIVISION	OVERALL
SLY	R. MOELLER	CORINTHIAN	23.70	10/14/57	2(5)	5
GOTCHAFERGOOD	BOB DIEHL	BELLINGHAM	24.50	10/16/44	3(5)	6
SITKA	H. MALEDY/T. MALEDY	R.VAN.	24.40	10/25/01	4(5)	7
SOCKEYE	LARRY SALKIELD	SEATTLE	24.40	10/27/30	5(5)	8
EVADER	WALTER CLAYTON/MIKE MILBURN	SLOOP TVRN.	21.50	10/28/57	4(6)	9
EAGLE	G. HODGE	BELLINGHAM	24.40	10/30/56	6(5)	10
SNOOSE	CHARLES OLSON	EDMONDS	24.60	10/31/34	7(5)	11
MEZUZA	BOB BECK	NANAIMO	22.50	10/31/54	8(5)	12
DENIZEN	R. KREYBIG	CORINTHIAN	24.40	10/34/44	9(5)	13
CLOCKWORK ROCKETSHIP	E. LIEBERT	R.VAN.	24.60	10/36/21	10(5)	14
SACRE BLEU	B. GRIFFIN	BELLINGHAM	24.50	10/38/25	11(5)	15
MIDNIGHT MADNESS	MIKE WHITE	CORINTHIAN	24.40	10/39/16	12(5)	16
COHO	GRANT BRANDLMAYR	R.VAN.	24.90	10/40/07	13(5)	17
JO	TOM WHITE	BELLINGHAM	24.50	10/40/24	14(5)	18
SPARTAN	RON DEFIEUX	EAGLE HRBR.	24.10	10/40/59	15(5)	19
MAXIMUS	MAXWELL KING	BELLINGHAM	24.50	10/43/43	16(5)	20
CHAOS	MARVIN WAYNE	BELLINGHAM	23.80	10/55/12	17(5)	21
GREEN WITCH	WILLIAM HESTON	EDMONDS	24.40	10/56/32	18(5)	22
RAZZMATTAZZ	KEN BROWN	R.VIC.	21.70	10/56/33	5(6)	23
GHOSTRIDER	WILLIAM BARBER/JIM FROHNMAYER	PORTLAND	23.60	11/02/02	19(5)	24
SPANISH FLYER	GORD HENDERSON	R.VAN.	21.10	11/04/17	6(6)	25
SAKURA	TAL GODDING	CORINTHIAN	23.60	11/05/55	20(5)	26
FRED	FINN NIELSEN	MAPLE BAY	16.80	11/13/48	7(6)	27
TENACIOUS	JOE OREM	BELLINGHAM	24.50	11/20/40	21(5)	28
ARGO	BRUCE HAULMAN	QUARTRMSTR.	21.20	11/33/25	8(6)	29
AIRPOWER	DAVE CAMPBELL	CORINTHIAN	21.50	11/37/43	9(6)	30
HORTENCE	DENNIS MAXWELL	R.VAN.	21.90	11/40/49	10(6)	31
PENDRAGON	DARYL GRIMSON	R.VAN.	21.10	12/01/41	11(6)	32
FIRST MORNING	M. STANLEY	OAK HARBOR	20.30	12/06/06	12(6)	33
ALEGRA	CARL FREDRICKSON	QUARTRMSTR.	21.20	12/08/24	13(6)	34
THE MAID	J. MADDOX	OLYMPIA	21.20	12/17/13	14(6)	35
STERLING SHAMROCK	KEN MARTIN	R.VIC.	21.80	12/45/49	15(6)	36

JUAN DE FUCA (CLASS V) 1980 RESULTS

OFFICIAL START TIME: 09/50/00

YACHT NAME	SKIPPER(S)	CLUB	RATING	COR ELAPSE TIME	POSITION DIVISION	OVERALL
ROMADA	ROY HINGLEY	R.VIC.	2.85	10/55/55	1(E)	1
TARKA	PETER GROVE/AVRIL GROVE	R.VAN.	2.65	10/58/17	2(E)	2
DISCRETION	JAN OLSEN	R.VIC.	2.80	11/00/16	3(E)	3
PUFF II	J. WOODWARD	R.VIC.	2.90	11/10/23	4(E)	4
MIRAGE	VANCE BINGHAM	PT. ANGELES	2.55	11/11/25	5(E)	5
CHINOOK	T. GRAINGER/K. GINDROZ	3 TREE PT.	2.75	11/14/30	6(E)	6
QUORUM	D. FIELD	CORINTHIAN	2.50	11/15/12	7(E)	7
SUNDANCE	K. OVERBY	CORINTHIAN	2.85	11/15/19	8(E)	8
GALEB	GEORGE CESAREC	R.VIC.	2.60	11/17/00	9(E)	9
NAUTICAL DREAMER	BILL MAXWELL	PORTLAND	2.50	11/18/48	10(E)	10
MONTE CARLO	GLEN LAMBERT	VAN ROWING	2.70	11/21/28	11(E)	11
IMPOSITION	W. SHELDON	S. SOUND	2.60	11/22/57	12(E)	12
SPINNER	GORDON CASH	CORINTHIAN	2.70	11/37/27	13(E)	13
NIJINSKY	DAVID HENDRY	R.VAN.	2.80	11/48/26	14(E)	14
TIFFANY	JIM ALLEN	R.VIC.	2.80	12/10/10	15(E)	15
SEAHAWK	RICK JENNESS/JOHN MILLS	CORINTHIAN	2.60	12/34/08	16(E)	16
FIREFLY	BILL WEAVER	CORINTHIAN	2.90	12/43/41	17(E)	17
LUCKY LADY	FRED KRABBE	FRIDAY HRB.	2.85	12/47/07	18(E)	18
AILSA CRAIG	BILL CRAIG	R.VIC.	2.90	12/48/11	19(E)	19
KYDAKA	DON LOFGREN	CORINTHIAN	2.90	13/00/05	20(E)	20
KATCHEN	DR. D. STAATZ	TACOMA	2.75	13/04/26	21(E)	21
JACKAL	JERRY CORNELL	PT. ANGELES	2.75	13/05/14	22(E)	22
RENAISSANCE	GREG RAVEAUX/JIM POMAJEVICH	SYSCO	2.80	13/09/35	23(E)	23
COOKIE MONSTER	CHARLES WHIDDEN	PT. ANGELES	2.60	13/13/44	24(E)	24
MOETAVATOR	DAVID MOE	PT. ANGELES	2.85	13/14/05	25(E)	25
DENOLI	LARRY GORMAN	BROWNSVILL	2.80	13/19/11	26(E)	26
DAZZLER	BILL VAUX	ANACORTES	2.80	13/22/44	27(E)	27
LITTLE LIZA-K	K. PARTLOW	OLYMPIA	2.80	13/22/55	28(E)	28
MOCCASIN II	GEOFF NEILY	MAPLE BAY	2.90	13/28/11	29(E)	29
SHIMMA	HOWARD BRADBROOK	TIDDLY CVE.	2.80	13/29/02	30(E)	30
ACHATES	SVEN DONALDSON	TIDDLY CVE.	2.70	13/29/23	31(E)	31
CAYENNE	KEN BRIGGS	SEATTLE	2.90	13/29/29	32(E)	32
IOLAIRE	ALEX ORR	EAGLE HRBR.	2.90	13/31/12	33(E)	33
SKEDADDLE	G. BEVERIDGE	WEST VAN	2.70	13/31/25	34(E)	34
ALAKAZAM	PAUL BERGMAN	ANACORTES	2.85	13/32/51	35(E)	35

YACHT NAME	SKIPPER(S)	CLUB	RATING	COR ELAPSE TIME	POSITION DIVISION	OVERALL
BRASS TACKS	PETER COURTNEY	EAGLE HRBR.	2.70	13/33/01	36(E)	36
COLD MILK	DAVID PECK	CORINTHIAN	2.80	13/41/41	37(E)	37
TOOTH & NAIL	RON MARTIN	VAN ROWING	2.90	13/43/01	38(E)	38
BYTE	ALAN KELLY	R.VIC.	2.55	13/44/23	39(E)	39
MILKSHAKE	BILL LEAVENS	CORINTHIAN	2.75	13/52/23	40(E)	40
SUPER APPLE	GORDON BRYAN	SEA EXPLOY	2.60	13/53/39	41(E)	41
PATCHWORK QUILT	JAMES DRYDEN	R.VIC.	2.90	14/04/26	42(E)	42
FREE SPIRIT	JAMES WADDLE	CORINTHIAN	2.80	14/10/35	43(E)	43
FLEETWOOD	JACK OMMEN	ANACORTES	2.80	14/48/44	44(E)	44
BREEZE	JAMES LORENZ JR.	TACOMA	2.90	14/52/50	45(E)	45
CHARON	JOHN EASTHAM	SEATTLE	2.75	15/43/48	46(E)	46
TEMERAIRE	R.VAN DEN DRIESS	R.VIC.	2.85	15/53/09	47(E)	47
WILDFIRE	JUDY McCOY/TERRY OSWALD	3 TREE PT.	2.50	16/36/22	48(E)	48
SAM I. AM	FRANK PARSONS	R.VAN.	2.80	DNF	DNF(E)	DNF
LANCER	NORMAN LARABEE	SHILSHOLE	2.50	DNS	DNS(E)	DNS
NIAMH II	STEVE SLINN	WEST VAN.	2.80	DNS	DNS(E)	DNS
FOULWEATHER BLUFF	CAROL RUSH	CORINTHIAN	2.70	DNS	DNS(E)	DNS

JUAN DE FUCA (CLASS VI) 1980
RESULTS

OFFICIAL START TIME: 10/00/00

YACHT NAME	SKIPPER(S)	CLUB	RATING	COR ELAPSE TIME	POSITION DIVISION	OVERALL
BAD NEWS	BOB LEFEAUX	TIDDLY CVE.	3.00	11/38/35	1(F)	1
SKILFISH	D. WEST	WEST VAN.	2.95	11/57/29	2(F)	2
DEMARA	ALAN CROWE	TIDDLY CVE.	3.50	12/18/01	1(G)	3
GAZELLE II	J. MASON	R.VAN.	2.95	12/20/25	3(F)	4
MIDNIGHT SUN	WALLY BRAEDT	TACOMA	3.20	12/20/43	4(F)	5
BEOWULF	RON JEWULA	R.VIC.	3.30	12/24/00	5(F)	6
SKYE	FRED PYE	R.VIC.	3.30	12/26/53	6(F)	7
IMPULSE	J. KEVORKIAN	CORINTHIAN	3.10	12/27/38	7(F)	8
AUDACE	RICHARD HAUGEN	CORINTHIAN	3.05	12/29/14	8(F)	9
TILLICUM	HOWARD RICKETTS	CORINTHIAN	3.05	12/30/23	9(F)	10
SCALLYWAG	DAVID HADDLETON	VAN ROWING	2.95	12/30/32	10(F)	11
VANDAL II	J.N. MacFARLANE	MAPLE BAY	2.95	12/31/00	11(F)	12
MALA	BOB WALSH	WEST VAN	3.00	12/31/09	12(F)	13
UNION JACK	MARK LINROTHE/BOE FLETCHER	CORINTHIAN	3.25	12/36/03	13(F)	14
TEASER	PETER STANLEY	TACOMA	2.95	12/39/21	14(F)	15
RAVEN	COLIN CRISP	R.VIC.	3.00	12/46/09	15(F)	16
WINDSHIFT	FREDERICK HAYES	SEATTLE	3.05	12/46/33	16(F)	17
OLYMPIC MIST	GORDON KALAHAR	PT. ANGELES	3.40	12/47/57	2(G)	18
WINDQUEST	JACK BAZHAW	BELLINGHAM	2.95	12/49/19	17(F)	19
ARATAI	J. ROBINSON	R.VIC.	3.50	12/54/14	3(G)	20
WINDIGO	B. ANKERSMIT	FRIDAY HRB.	3.30	13/00/39	18(F)	21
FIRST EDITION	L. McGRUER/E. McGRUER	R.VAN.	2.95	13/20/38	19(F)	22
WINGS	BRUCE KLAVER	R.VIC.	3.60	13/20/58	4(G)	23
DROP OUT	JIMMIE LAVELLE	CORINTHIAN	3.20	13/30/31	20(F)	24
OPO	B. SYROID	R.VIC.	3.30	13/39/17	21(F)	25
LIBRE	R. DEAN	R.VIC.	3.55	13/42/41	5(G)	26
PONEMAH	MIKE DALE	TIDDLY CVE.	3.30	13/46/39	22(F)	27
CAL-LORRI	C. THOMSON	CANOE BAY	3.05	14/19/27	23(F)	28
DORADO	S. JOPLIN	VAN ROWING	3.05	14/21/23	24(F)	29
BANJO MUSIC	ARMAND MARION	CORINTHIAN	2.95	14/26/25	25(F)	30
TOYBOX	G. COOPER	R.VIC.	3.30	14/26/26	26(F)	31
MALUHIA	RICHARD HAZELTON	3 TREE PT.	3.00	14/27/09	27(F)	32
UNION DEPOT	R. RUE	CORINTHIAN	3.10	14/32/03	28(F)	33
IRRAWADDY	RONALD SAUNDERS	R.VIC.	3.50	14/32/42	6(G)	34
BEBELLE	H.B. SHAW	R.VIC.	3.00	14/36/07	29(F)	35
HARMONY	B. WILTON	R.VIC.	3.40	14/41/33	7(G)	36
DARK STAR	ROBERT GEBO	CORINTHIAN	3.15	14/43/35	30(F)	37
LEESOME	J.D. PATTERSON	CANOE BAY	3.20	14/44/30	31(F)	38
SALTY DREAM	G. JACOBI	R.VIC.	3.30	14/54/40	32(F)	39
MUMBLES II	TREVOR JENKINS	TIDDLY CVE.	3.20	15/00/03	33(F)	40
FLYING HIGH	JOHN TIMMERMAN	TIDDLEY CVE.	3.50	15/01/30	8(G)	41
KACHINA	HOWARD KELLY	TIDDLY CVE.	3.30	15/20/19	34(F)	42
SWEETTHING	JOE COLLINS	PT. ANGELES	3.50	15/27/41	9(G)	43
MASSILIA II	E. READSHAW	R.VIC.	3.50	15/28/23	10(G)	44
RAINBOW CHASER	DR. LON RIGGS	PT. ANGELES	3.20	15/33/26	35(F)	45
PUFFIN	FLETCHER POMEROY	CORINTHIAN	3.05	15/34/12	36(F)	46
LUCY ALICE	WILLIAM GARDNER	CORINTHIAN	3.65	15/40/05	11(G)	47
THE GOOD LIFE	G. BAILLARGEON	PORTLAND	3.70	15/45/06	12(G)	48
AQUILA	BRENT WESTON	R.VIC.	3.55	15/45/16	13(G)	49
KWEISHA	JACK SNOWBALL	WEST VAN	3.20	15/47/00	37(F)	50

MARILYN L	RON CARLSON	PT. ANGELES	3.65	15/48/06	14(G)	51
MENOS	M. BALDERSTON	R.VIC.	3.75	15/51/03	15(G)	52
SHOT-PUTT	THOMAS SCHACHT	3 TREE PT.	3.10	15/55/07	38(F)	53
BLUE COLLARS	DONALD McNEES JR.	BELLINGHAM	3.20	16/12/07	39(F)	54
MAELSTROM	BERT MOFFITT	CORINTHIAN	3.20	16/12/49	40(F)	55
DREAM MACHINE	R. SMITH	PORTLAND	3.40	16/14/47	16(G)	56
SHAZBOTZ	DALE HORN/SUE MARSHEL	EDMONDS	3.30	16/22/30	41(F)	57
MAGICIAN	TOM BURLINGTON	TIDDLY CVE.	3.50	16/52/53	17(G)	58
AURIGA	G. GUEST	CANOE BAY	3.40	17/00/09	18(G)	59
IMPATIENCE	JOHN ULMAN	CORINTHIAN	2.95	17/19/28	42(F)	60
HAIDA III	G. SCHRADER	R.VIC.	3.80	17/44/32	19(G)	61
YELLOW JACKET	RICHARD SMITH	PT. ANGELES	3.60	17/44/49	20(G)	62
DRACONIAN	C. MOLSBERRY	CANOE COVE	3.50	17/47/11	21(G)	63
MERRY	TREVOR HAYWARD	R.VIC.	3.60	17/49/47	22(G)	64
WINTER FOX	JERRY CEIS	SLP. TAVRN.	3.85	18/12/15	23(G)	65
FROGBONE	TOD OVERBY	CORINTHIAN	3.35	18/21/59	43(F)	66
LOTTE	ED HAINES	C.F.S.A.	4.10	18/23/19	24(G)	67
TRITON	ERIC WICHERTS	R.VIC.	3.55	18/26/46	25(G)	68
DREAM WEAVER	D. PATTERSON	R.VAN.	3.30	18/45/09	44(F)	69
FROYA	ERIC QUALLEY	MAPLE BAY	4.40	19/56/15	26(G)	70
MAPLE SUGAR	WAITE BROOKS	R.VIC.	3.75	DNF	DNF(G)	DNF
KITSUNE	HOWARD KING	ANACORTES	5.00	DNF	DNF(G)	DNF
TARQUIN IV	G. JOHNSTONE	R.VIC.	3.00	DNF	DNF(F)	DNF
THE PROFESSOR	PIERRE LAVALLEE	R.VIC.	3.45	DNS	DNS(G)	DNS
GRAY GOOSE	GUY ESSMEIER	CORINTHIAN	3.40	DNS	DNS(G)	DNS

DIVISION OF CLASSES AS OF 1980

SWIFTSURE

Class 1 (I.O.R.) International Code Numeral 1

Division 1	32.0 and above
Division 2	28.0 to 31.9
Division 3	25.0 to 27.9
Division 4	21.6 to 24.9

Class II (P.H.R.F.) International Code Numeral 2

Division A	0.0 to 1.80
Division B	1.81 to 2.19

Class III (P.H.R.F.) International Code Numeral 3

Division C	2.20 to 2.49
Division D	2.50 to 3.89

JUAN DE FUCA

Class IV (I.O.R.) International Code Numeral 4

Division 5	22.1 to 24.9
Division 6	16.0 to 22.0

Class V (P.H.R.F.) International Code Numeral 5

Division E	2.50 to 2.90

Class VI (P.H.R.F.) International Code Numeral 6

Division F	2.91 to 3.39
Division G	3.40 to 5.0

The Race Committee reserves the right to adjust the number of divisions or the rating limits for each division after all entry forms have been received (10 days prior to the race).

The changes in yacht design, rating formulas, and number of entries have necessitated many new classes and divisions over the years. The race has grown rapidly in complexity and numbers, so that, in 1980 we find six classes, encompassing thirteen divisions.

Note: For details of Classes and Divisions as used in any given year see complete tables of results as shown on the official lists that follow.

TROPHY LIST AS OF 1980

SWIFTSURE CLASS I [I.O.R.]

Overall Handicap Winner	Swiftsure Trophy	1930
First Yacht to Finish	City of Victoria Trophy	1956
Division 1	Ocean Cement Trophy	1957
Division 2	T. Eaton Trophy	1957
Division 3	City of Seattle Trophy	1959
Division 4	Royal Vancouver Yacht Club Trophy	1959

SWIFTSURE CLASS II [P.H.R.F.]

Overall Handicap Winner	Pacific Rim Trophy	1979
First yacht to finish	Royal Canadian Navy Trophy	1978
*Division A		
*Division B	Corinthian Yacht Club Trophy	1972

SWIFTSURE CLASS III [P.H.R.F.]

Overall Handicap Winner		
First to finish		
*Division C	Stormy Weather Trophy	1976
*Division D	Cape Flattery Trophy	1972

JUAN DE FUCA CLASS IV

Overall Handicap Winner		
First Yacht to Finish	San Juan Trophy	1962
Division 5	Royal Victoria Yacht Club Trophy	1972
Division 6	Royal Canadian Navy Trophy	1970

JUAN DE FUCA CLASS V [P.H.R.F.]

First to finish		
*Division E	Anacortes Yacht Club Trophy	1969

JUAN DE FUCA CLASS VI [P.H.R.F.]

Overall Handicap Winner	Port Angeles Yacht Club Trophy	1979
First to finish		
*Division F		
*Division G		

NOTE: After the jammed starts in the 1979 race, the Race Committee set separate starting times this year, 1980, for the PHRF groups as follows: —
(The basis for decision was to divide the starts into lots of approx. 100 boats.)

*Class II PHRF, Divs. "A" & "B" one gun
*Class III PHRF, Divs. "C" & "D" one gun
*Class V PHRF Div. "E" Separate gun
*Class VI PHRF Divs. "F" & "G" one gun

Since yachts with different starting times cannot fairly compete with one another, the ruling has, in effect, set up two independent races for PHRF over the Swiftsure course and two PHRF races over the Juan de Fuca course. With todays entry list approaching 450 yachts, the Committee had to decide between divided starts or restricting the number of entries. At the time of writing entries will be allowed to expand.

Overall winners on handicap — 1930-1980

SWIFTSURE LIGHTSHIP CLASSIC

YEAR	RATING FORMULA USED	ENTRIES	CLASS/ DIV	YACHT NAME	SKIPPER(S)	CLUB	LOA/RIG	DESIGNER
1930	RORC	6	1(AA)	CLARIBEL	RAY COOKE	SYC	42' STAYSAIL SCHOONER	WINSLOW
1931		4	1(AA)	WESTWARD HO	B.L. JOHNSON/H.S. JELLETT	R.VAN.	54' YAWL	EDSON SCHOCK
1934		4	1(AA)	CIRCE	RAY COOKE	SYC	63' CUTTER	BEN SEABORN
1947	CC of A	15	1(BB)	OWENS CUTTER	CHAS ROSS	CYC	40' SLOOP	OWENS YACHT CO.
1948		10	1(A)	NAUTILUS II	HARBINE MUNROE	SYC/TYC	45' SLOOP	BEN SEABORN
1949		20	1(A)	AVALONTE	A.G. WOODLEY	SYC	42' SLOOP	BEN SEABORN
1950		12	1(A)	GOSSIP	DR. PHIL SMITH	SYC	46'4'' PCC SLOOP	G.W. KETTENBERG
1951		13	1(AA)	AMORITA	DR. CARL JENSEN	SYC	CALIFORNIA 32 SLOOP	NICK POTTER
1952		19	1(BB)	ONO	DR. HERBERT DAY	SYC	K 38	G.W. KETTENBERG
1953		21	1(A)	GOSSIP	DR. PHIL SMITH	SYC	46'4'' PCC SLOOP	G.W. KETTENBERG
1954		15	1(BB)	TOTEM	HENRY KOTKINS/CHAS ROSS	CYC	K 38	G.W. KETTENBERG
1955		19	1(A)	SERADA	DR. CHRIS GOODHOPE	CYC	42' YAWL	SPARKMAN-STEPHENS
1956		23	1(AA)	ADIOS	DR. CARL JENSEN	SYC	59' YAWL	SPARKMAN-STEPHENS
1957		24	1(AA)	MARUFFA	JOHN GRAHAM	SYC	67' YAWL	PHIL RHODES
1958		39	1(BB)	ONO	DR. HERB DAY	SYC	K 38	G.W. KETTENBERG
1959		36	1(BB)	REBEL	DOUG SHERWOOD	SYC	K 38 SLOOP	G.W. KETTENBERG
1960		44	1(A)	KATE II	DAVID SKINNER	SYC	45' SLOOP	BEN SEABORN
1961		62	1(BB)	WINSOME III	CHES RICKARD	R.VAN	L 36 SLOOP	WM. LAPWORTH
1962		60	1(BB)	WINSOME III	CHES RICKARD	R.VAN	L 36 SLOOP	WM. LAPWORTH
1963		69	1(BB)	WINSOME III	CHES RICKARD	R.VAN	L 36 SLOOP	WM. LAPWORTH
1964		71	1(BB)	BANDIT	GERRY O. SMITH	TYC	L 36 SLOOP	WM. LAPWORTH
1965		73	1(BB)	THUNDER	BILL BUCHAN	CYC	36' SLOOP	WM. BUCHAN
1966		67	1 DIV 4	MISTRAL	J.C. BAILLARGEON	SYC	31'5'' SLOOP	BEN SEABORN
1967		89	1(3)	MARA	BILL BUCHAN	CYC	36' SLOOP	WM. BUCHAN
1968		91	1(4)	MISTRAL	J.C. BAILLARGEON	SYC	31'5'' SLOOP	BEN SEABORN
1969		103	1(1)	MARY BOWER	JOHN LONG	R.VAN	49' CUTTER	ROBT. CLARK
1970		105	1(1)	ENDLESS SUMMER	GEORGE O'BRIEN	R.VAN	12 METRE	WARWICK HOOD
1971	IOR	94	1(4)	HOOLIGAN	TOM O'BRIEN	SYC	CAL 2-30	WM. LAPWORTH
1972		109	1(1)	ENDLESS SUMMER	GEORGE O'BRIEN	R.VAN	12 METRE	WARWICK HOOD
1973		119	1(1)	GRAYBEARD	LOL KILLAM	R.VAN	73' KETCH	PETER HATFIELD
1974		111	1(1)	GRAYBEARD	LOL KILLAM	R.VAN	73' KETCH	PETER HATFIELD
1975		103	1(5)	ELUSIVE	J.E. SPROUSE	PYC	ERICSON 29	BRUCE KING
1976		91	1(4)	LADY BUG	ALAN HOLT	CYC	HOLT 30	ALAN HOLT
1977		87	1(2)	KANATA	VLAD PLAVSIC	W.VAN	CTM. 40.95 SLOOP	VLAD PLAVSIC
1978		86	1(4)	SACHEM	BILL BUCHAN JR.	CYC	¾ TONNER	BRIT CHANCE
1979		76	1(3)	PEARCE ARROW	KEN PEARCE	R.VAN	GANBARE 35	DOUG PETERSON
1980		87	1(4)	LADY BUG	ALAN HOLT	CYC	HOLT 30	ALAN HOLT

Alan Holt and his Ladybug have made Swiftsure history. This custom designed and built 30 footer out of Seattle has to her credit: an overall win in 1976 — a 4th overall in 1977 and capped her career with another sparkling win in Swiftsure's Golden Anniversary 1980 race. Ladybug, under the gifted hand of her owner, skipper, designer and navigator, has made her indellible mark in the record books. Alan Holt with his Ladybug has joined Bill Baillargeon's Mistral in capturing two overall Swiftsures and proving to the world that a well sailed small yacht is hard to beat.

Congratulations!

LADYBUG / JAMES McVIE

**LIGHTSHIP
PRESS LTD.**